Central Bank Strategy, Credibility, and Independence

Central Bank Strategy, Credibility, and Independence: Theory and Evidence

Alex Cukierman

The MIT Press
Cambridge, Massachusetts
London, England

This book was set in Times Roman by Asco Trade Typesetting Ltd., Hong Kong and was printed and bound in the United States of America.

Library of Congress Cataloging-in-Publication Data

Cukierman, Alex.
    Central bank strategy, credibility, and independence: theory and
evidence / Alex Cukierman.
        p.   cm.
    Includes bibliographical references and index.
    ISBN 0-262-03198-1
    1. Inflation (Finance)—Econometric models. 2. Monetary policy—Econometric
models. 3. Banks and banking, Central—Econometric models. I. Title.
HG229.C82   1992
332.1'1—dc20   92-16775
                                                                    CIP

To Tali, Dani, and Ofri

Contents

Preface

The last decade has witnessed the emergence of the "new political economy" which, like its older counterpart, combines the study of economic and political behavior. Historically investigations of economic and of political phenomena were inseparable. But with the formalization of economic analysis, from the mid-1930s on, the economic discipline narrowed its area of investigation to pure economic behavior, taking political objectives and their influence on economic policy as exogenous. This somewhat artificial compartmentalization proved beneficial in that it enabled economists to develop a whole range of new and powerful methods of analysis. Some of these methods were occasionally applied to the study of public policymaking. Since the beginning of the 1980s this trend accelerated, producing a remarkable revival in the joint study of economic and political processes and of their effect on the choice of public policy.

The feature that distinguishes the new political economy from its older counterpart is mostly the methodology. In both instances economic and political behavior are studied jointly, and the two-way interaction between them is put at center stage. But the new political economy utilizes modern tools and concepts from economic theory, game theory, and econometrics and merges them with recent insights from political science. To date these developments have produced a deeper understanding of the interaction between the economic and political behavior of individuals, on the one hand, and the choice of economic policy, on the other. Some of the main themes of this literature are that distributional considerations, institutions, and asymmetric information play an important role in the choice of public policy.

This book summarizes and extends the insights from the new political economy literature in the area of monetary policy. I have tried to make it broadly based in terms of both coverage and audience. As a consequence the book contains both theory and evidence as well as simple and advanced materials, which are grouped into different chapters. A modular guide to the book by levels of difficulty appears at the end of the introductory chapter. There are obvious risks in putting both elementary and advanced materials into one volume. My feeling is that the benefits associated with such a unified framework that presents elementary materials and later integrates them with advanced materials more than outweigh the cost.

Monetary policy is usually, though not exclusively, made by central banks. There are normally various and often conflicting demands by government and other sectors from monetary policy and the central bank. As a consequence the degree of independence of the bank and other institutional details affect policy choices. There is a lot of cross-country variation in the institutions of monetary policy and in the degree of central bank independence. Here too I have tried to take a broad view by documenting and analyzing a wide sample of both developed and developing countries on a unified basis.

Most contemporary economists agree that monetary policy has important real effects only when it is unanticipated. This implies that the type, magnitude, and persistence of the private information available to policymakers affects their ability to stabilize the economy, the degree of activism, and various macroeconomic variables. Despite the variety of ways in which private information interacts with the economy and policy outcomes, a small number of general principles emerge. They are discussed informally in chapter 8.

An important objective of the book is to bridge some of the gap between theory and practice. My hope is that it will convince both practical policymakers and academics that the methods of economic analysis, when appropriately adapted, can contribute a lot to our understanding of the interactions between monetary policy and the economy without sacrificing rigor. The formal models in the book make it possible to systematically discuss a wide range of issues such as what are the political determinants of seigniorage, how is monetary policy affected by the degree of time preference of policymakers, how will an eventual monetary union in Europe affect the commitment to price stability, and why do some central banks smooth interest rates?

Some of the material appearing in chapters 3, 4, 9, 10, 14, and 16 has been adapted from articles that originally appeared in the *American Economic Review*, *Econometrica*, the *Journal of Monetary Economics*, the *Federal Reserve Bank of St. Louis Review*, and in a volume on monetary policy and uncertainty edited by M. J. M. Neumann and published by Nomos Verlagsgesellschaft. I am grateful to the editors and publishers of these journals and books for their permission to use this material. Some of the empirical chapters draw on a joint working paper with Steven Webb and Bilin Neyapti.

While working on the book I benefited from the feedback of many colleagues. Three anonymous reviewers read several drafts of the book at various stages of completion. Their suggestions, particularly those made in the early stages, influenced the general structure of the book as well as some chapters. Larry Ball, Michael Bruno, Ben Eden, David Gilat, Nissan Liviatan, Henri Pagès, and Guido Tabellini made very useful suggestions. I would also like to thank George Alogoskoufis, James Alt, Matthew Canzoneri, Alessandra Casella, Carl Christ, Behzad Diba, June Flanders, Haim Fershtman, Thomas Havrilesky, William Keech, Leonardo Leiderman, Allan Meltzer, Maurice Obstfeld, and Terry Vaughn.

In trying to assess the actual policy objectives and the actual degree of independence of various central banks, I was helped by discussions and in some cases by the systematic cooperation of many individuals. The help of Walter Wasserfallen in obtaining qualified answers to a questionnaire on central bank independence from various central banks was particularly instrumental. So was the cooperation of economists and other officers from the central banks who participated in this effort. Ann Johannessen from the Central Banking Department at the IMF greatly facilitated the collection of legal information. I had helpful discussions with Tomas Baliño, Ed-Gardo Baradiaran, Paul Beckerman, Mario Blejer, Max Corden, Andrew Crockett, Patrick Downes, Herman-Josef Dudler, Robert Effros, John Flemming, Valeriano Garcia, Charles Goodhart, D. Hiss, Sergio Pereiro Leite, Alfredo Leone, Akiva Offenbacher, Robert Raymond, Klaus Richel, Helmut Schlesinger, Wolfgang Schill, Meir Sokoler, Marc-Olivier Strauss-Kahn, V. Sundararajan, Mark Swinburne, Richard Webb, Eduardo Wiesner, and Paul Volcker.

Partial financial support was provided by the David Horowitz Institute Project on Central Bank Policies[1] and by the Foerder Institute for Economic Research, both at Tel-Aviv University. Stella Padeh at Tel-Aviv University and Claudia Stoy at Princeton University provided excellent typing support.

---

1. This project was sponsored by the Bundesbank, the Bank of England, the Bank of Italy, the Bank of Israel, the Bank for International Settlements, and the Bank of the Netherlands.

Central Bank Strategy, Credibility, and Independence

1 Introduction

Traditional economic analysis takes the behavior of policymakers, in particular the behavior of monetary policymakers, as exogenous. Currently most, if not all, economists agree with the view that inflation is a monetary phenomenon, in the sense that there would be no inflation in the long run without sustained increases in the money supply. This leads to the obvious policy statement that long-run price stability can be achieved by limiting the rate of monetary growth to the long-run real rate of growth of the economy. Despite this wide spread consensus monetary authorities of most countries usually allow monetary expansion in excess of the rate of real output growth. As a consequence rates of inflation in most countries and periods are positive.[1] Since inflation is widely believed to be "bad," this outcome is, to say the least, surprising.

This book attempts to uncover and analyze the reasons for positive inflation and positive rates of monetary expansion. It focuses on the motives and constraints of the monetary policymaking authorities, which are often (though not exclusively) central banks. The fundamental theme is that the money supply, and therefore inflation, are not exogenous. The behavior of these variables is a consequence of strategic and informational interactions between monetary policymakers and individuals or institutions within the private sector. This point of view makes it possible to identify some of the institutional, political, and other features of a country that are more or less conducive to inflationary environments. Factors such as the ability to precommit policy, the rate of time preference of policymakers, the precision of their control over the price level, and the degree of political instability as reflected in frequent changes in emphasis on alternative objectives are identified as some of the fundamental determinants of the distributions of inflation and of monetary growth.

A basic objective of the book is to bridge some of the existing gap between theory and practice in the area of monetary policy and institutions. At the theoretical level this is done by recognizing that policy reacts to the economy, that it is driven by political and distributional considerations, and by applying modern analytical techniques from economic and game theories to the analysis of those issues. At the empirical and applied levels this is done by presenting new evidence on central bank independence and on political instability for a broad sample of countries and then using it to evaluate the effects of independence and of political instability on policy outcomes.

Practitioners and observers of monetary policy often regard theoretic analysis, and game-theoretic analysis in particular, as too abstract to be useful for understanding reality. They focus instead on institutions and other idiosyncracies like personalities and regulations. This book is based on the view that these two areas of investigation are complements rather than substitutes. Simple game theory provides a natural framework for effectively organizing institutional information so as to understand the two-way interactions between monetary policy and the private economy. Factors such as the structure of information, the degree of central bank independence, the precision of control over the money supply, and the stability of the political system are all examples of institutional elements whose effect on policy outcomes can be discussed more effectively and precisely by blending institutional information with simple game-theoretic concepts. The book does not presuppose any previous knowledge of game theory. Models that are deemed useful for the analysis of the policy issue under consideration are developed from basic principles within the context of that particular issue.

The main focus of the book is positivistic. The central question posed is: How do central banks or, more generally, monetary policymakers behave? The book draws on and utilizes the recent literature on dynamic inconsistency and monetary policy games. Part of this literature is based on the hypothesis that monetary policymakers act as social planners. In the interest of comprehensiveness, this hypothesis is discussed briefly and evaluated. But in reality monetary policy is influenced by various political considerations in which redistributional objectives play an important role. There is a growing body of literature that suggests that even the Federal Reserve, with its high degree of statutory independence, is not immune to political pressures (Mayer 1990). Hence a political approach to monetary policymaking provides a more realistic positive framework for understanding the formation of monetary policies. Most of the book relies therefore on the paradigm that the objective function (or functions) of policymakers is generated by political-redistributional considerations.

Recognition of the interactive-endogenous nature of monetary policy sheds new light on old and discredited notions about inflation. There is an old literature that attributes inflation to the existence of unions. Bronfenbrenner and Holzman (1963) survey and correctly criticize this literature on the ground that union power can cause a *high price level* but cannot, on its own, produce a *rising price level*. However, as shown in chapter 3, when the central bank is concerned about employment, the existence of unions that maintain the real wage above its market-clearing level may create a dynamic inconsistency problem that leads to a permanent inflationary bias.

Governments or central banks inflate in order to achieve a whole range of objectives such as high employment, financing of the government budget, stability of the financial system, and the attainment of balance-of-payments objectives. When policy is discretionary, the attempt of policymakers to use monetary policy to achieve such objectives often produces excessively high inflation rates without achieving these objectives. These prisoner's dilemma aspects of monetary policy generally arise whether policymakers have or do not have private information. But it is easier to illustrate them in the absence of private information. Part I discusses the interaction between policy and the private economy under perfect information in the presence of alternative motives for monetary expansion.

Most economists agree that only unanticipated monetary policy has real effects. Since there is little doubt that changes in monetary policy have temporary real effects on the economy, it is important to also understand the interaction between policy and the economy when policymakers possess an information advantage about variables that influence their policy decisions. Policymakers may possess a temporary information advantage about their own forecasts, constraints, objectives, and commitment ability. In addition the central bank is normally better positioned to evaluate changes in its independence from political authorities than the general public. Because of its central role in enabling monetary policy to have real effects, private information constitutes a basic cornerstone of the discussion in part II, in most of part III, and in the first chapter of part IV. Private information is also essential for a realistic view of periodic changes in the credibility of policymakers.

Whenever policymakers become more concerned about price stability than they previously were, the credibility of monetary policy becomes a prime determinant of the output costs of disinflation. The book discusses and evaluates various measures of credibility under perfect and asymmetric information. With perfect information a given policy is either fully credible or not credible at all, depending on whether it is dynamically consistent.[2] However, in the presence of asymmetric information the public is not perfectly informed about the objectives of policymakers and therefore about the subset of policies that are dynamically consistent.

Under those circumstances credibility becomes a continuous variable that is inversely related to the absolute value of the difference between the plans of policymakers and what the public believes about those plans. Several chapters investigate some of the fundamental determinants of credibility under asymmetric information and identify factors that influence the output and employment costs of disinflation.

The recent literature on monetary policy games has drawn an important distinction between discretionary policy and precommitments. Chapter 3 uses this distinction in order to derive the well-known result that the rate of inflation is excessively high under discretion and perfect information. There is little doubt that in most countries and periods, policy is discretionary. This observation, in conjunction with the analysis of chapter 3, might lead one to conclude that there is little to restrain policymakers from inflating at excessively high rates under discretion. But the discussion in part II suggests that in the presence of asymmetric information the temptation to inflate, when policy is discretionary, is attenuated by the fact that current inflation and monetary growth affect the public's future inflationary expectations. In fact, if the central bank weighs the future and the present equally and if there is sufficient persistence in its objectives, the inflationary bias vanishes even in a discretionary regime. In less extreme cases it moderates the temptation to inflate. Thus reputational considerations moderate the inflationary bias of policy in discretionary regimes.

The book highlights the central role of inflationary expectations and of the way they are formed for the conduct of monetary policy. In particular it stresses that the fundamental trade-off between achieving a better value for objectives today or tomorrow is due to the fact that current policy decisions alter future inflationary expectations by providing noisy but meaningful new information to the public. Private information is thus an essential ingredient of this trade-off. Without it individuals would have nothing to learn from current actions about future policies, making it unnecessary for policymakers to consider the impact of their current actions on future expectations.

A substantial part of the recent literature has modeled "reputation" by using trigger strategies from supergames to model the process of expectations formation by the public. For the sake of completeness this approach is reviewed in chapter 11. But the main approach to expectations formation adopted in the book is based on the view that individuals are constantly learning about the shifting objectives of policymakers. This process of learning, of which policymakers are aware, makes them sensitive to reputational considerations. As a consequence changes in their reputations occur as a by-product of learning by the public rather than through an exogenously specified "punishment" strategy.

Economists and policymakers do not always agree about the desirable level of policy activism. The discussion of policymaking under discretion and asymmetric information identifies factors that influence the level of activism under discretion, thus providing a positive theory of activism. Some central banks have an inclination for secrecy. Such a tendency has been documented for the Federal Reserve by Goodfriend (1986). A chapter in part II discusses two, not mutually exclusive, reasons for this phenomenon. One is based on a symbiotic relationship between the central bank as a bureaucracy and the politically motivated legislative branch of government. This explanation seems to be largely specific to the United States. The other is based on the observation that some ambiguity about the emphasis it puts on alternative objectives enables the monetary authority to choose the timing of surprises and therefore of the direction and magnitude of its effect on unemployment and output. In a world with changing objectives, such ability is valuable. This mechanism is not restricted to a particular institutional structure.

Institutions such as the legal framework within which policy operates are important determinants of policy outcomes. In particular the independence of central banks from their respective political authorities can influence the degree of policy activism and the distribution of inflation. Part IV presents alternative measures of central bank independence for a sample of up to seventy countries. These measures draw on three types of sources. One is based on the legal independence of the central bank, the second on the turnover rate of central bank governors, and the third on responses by central bankers to a questionnaire on central bank independence. Practitioners in the area of monetary policy and informed observers generally believe that a higher level of central bank independence is conducive to more price stability. This and related hypotheses are tested in part IV. An interesting finding is that legal independence is a significant determinant of inflation in developed countries. But in less developed countries inflation is more strongly related to the turnover rate of central bank governors. Both measures are combined in order to produce a single inflation-based ranking of central banks by their independence in both groups of countries.

The first chapter in part IV develops theoretical implications concerning central bank independence, on the one hand, and the mean level of inflation and its variability, on the other. This chapter serves as a framework for some of the empirical tests in subsequent chapters. The various rankings of central banks show that there are substantial differences in independence across banks. The last chapter of part IV contains a discussion of structural and other factors that are likely to induce such differences.

The book is composed of four parts. The first part is devoted to situations of perfect information. In addition to dynamic inconsistency problems caused by policymakers' attempts to attain various real objectives, this part features two explanations for interest rate smoothing by central banks and an analysis of the consequences of monetary unification in Europe. Chapter 4 on the revenue motive also contains two sections dealing with the effects of political instability and economic structure on seigniorage and one section that presents tests of those implications. An intuitive introduction and summary of the main ideas in part I appears in chapter 2.

Part II develops the fundamental private information framework used in many chapters of the book. The basic notion is that due to changes in the relative strength of various pressure groups or in the degree of central bank independence, the relative emphasis of monetary policy on economic activity versus price stability changes continually but gradually over time. These changes are the private information of policymakers, and the public learns about them gradually but optimally by observing past inflation rates. Gradual learning is optimal because the public cannot perfectly distinguish between persistent changes in the emphasis of policy and transitory monetary control errors.

An important characteristic of this framework is that although it learns continually, the public is almost always imperfectly informed about current and future policy objectives. The reason is that by the time the public recognizes past changes in objectives, new changes take place. This continuous process of rational but sluggish learning in which the emphasis of policy (or the policymakers' "type") continually changes appears to be more realistic than models with fixed policymaker types. It is therefore the main vehicle used to model the simultaneous determination of nominal contracts and of monetary policy.[3] Chapter 9 develops this framework when policymakers have a minimal information advantage, and chapter 10 extends it to the case in which they have an extended information advantage. These chapters are used to characterize concepts such as credibility, activism, and the speed of learning as well as their determinants. A mostly intuitive discussion of alternative notions of credibility and reputation appears in chapter 11. Motives for ambiguity and secrecy in monetary policy are discussed in chapter 12.

Part III contains five chapters dealing with additional aspects of imperfect information. The first three are within the same methodological mold as the discussion of part II in the sense that either the objectives or the economic forecasts of policymakers are private information and they change continually over time. Chapter 13 considers the case of private forecasts of money demand by the central bank as in Canzoneri (1985). As in part II the public learns gradually about changes in policy objectives. But now learning is imperfect because the public cannot disentangle persistent changes in the emphasis of policy from money demand forecast errors by the central bank. Chapter 14 considers the impact of mandatory but noisy announcements of monetary targets on inflation, credibility, and other issues.

Most existing literature on stabilization policy when policymakers behave strategically abstracts from the stabilization of shocks to the natural level of employment by assuming that the monetary authority offsets shocks that emanate only from the financial sector (Canzoneri 1985; Flood and Isard 1989; Oh and Garfinkel 1990). A recent exception is Lohmann (1992) which, following Fischer (1977), conceives of stabilization policy in terms of an attempt to offset shocks to natural employment. But this framework abstracts from learning. Chapter 15 introduces learning by the public about the future stance of monetary policy into a similar framework by recognizing that policymakers may have private forecasts about the permanence of shocks to the natural level of employment. The private information here concerns the changing constraints facing policymakers rather than their objectives. Such a framework seems particularly appropriate in developing countries in which the monetary authority usually has better information about aggregate trends than most of the general public. For countries such as the United States in which the quality of information available to private forecasters is high, the framework of this chapter can be reinterpreted in terms of changing objectives. An important implication of either interpretation is that inflationary bursts should be more persistent under discretion than under rules. This implication is supported by recent empirical evidence reported in Alogoskoufis (1991). One section in chapter 15 explores other mechanisms, such as overlapping nominal contracts and backward-looking wage indexation, which also contribute to the persistence of inflation.

Chapter 16 discusses policymaking behavior when the public is uncertain about the commitment ability of the central bank. The chapter also discusses private information about policy objectives when these objectives are fixed over time (as in Vickers 1986) and compares policy outcomes in this case with outcomes when private information concerns the commitment ability of the monetary authority. Chapter 17 presents the Alesina-Sachs (1988) partisanship theory of monetary policy. There is no private information in this framework, but there is uncertainty about electoral outcomes. Since different parties have different policy preference, this framework implies that there are monetary surprises following elections. As fiscal policy, economic circumstances, and the mood of the public change not only around election periods, there may be politically motivated changes in the emphasis of policy within the term of the same administration. Havrilesky (1987) argues that some or those shifts are due to an attempt of monetary policy to offset of mask the adverse consequences of redistributive fiscal policies. Chapter 17 also discusses and evaluates this hypothesis. In particular the chapter stresses that the tendency of policymakers to use monetary policy for quick reactions to developments that they had not anticipated is due to its flexibility in comparison to fiscal policy and to the fact that its real effects are temporary. These characteristics of monetary policy make it an ideal short-run shock absorber in a world in which politicians are uncertain about the permanence of shifts in the mood of the public or about the permanence of economic shocks.

For the convenience of readers who are interested in the main concepts and results, but not in technical details, chapter 8 presents a general overview of models of monetary policy under private information. The chapter reviews and explains the main ideas in parts II and III (except for chapter 17) and in chapter 18 in an intuitive manner. Being self-contained, the chapter can be read alone. But it can also be used as an introduction to the more specific chapters that it reviews.

The last part of the book is devoted to the issue of central bank independence. Central bank independence can be viewed as one way of committing monetary policy to focus mainly on the objective of price stability. Various degrees of independence lead to various levels of commitment. Chapter 18 provides a theoretical framework for some of the subsequent chapters, all of which are either empirical or descriptive. Alternative measures of central bank independence are presented in chapter 19. They are related to inflation in chapter 20. Chapter 21 combines some of these measures in order to produce an overall inflation-based index of independence. Chapter 22 presents empirical evidence on the hypothesis (developed in chapter 18) that the strong positive cross-country association between the mean and the variance of inflation is due to their common link to central bank independence. This chapter also reports tests of the effectiveness of legal limitations on lending in checking the expansion of central bank credit to the public sector. Structural reasons for cross-country differences in central bank independence are discussed in chapter 23.

A Modular Guide for Reading and Teaching the Book

In the interest of comprehensiveness the book includes both simple and advanced materials. But to make it usable by readers with different shades of interest in alternative aspects of monetary policy and with different levels of technical skills, the book is structured modularly. Most chapters fall into three clearly defined levels of difficulty or "modules": a basic module, an intermediate module, and an advanced module. The basic module is issue oriented and presupposes little previous technical or other background. This module is suitable for junior or senior undergraduates and for practitioners in the area of monetary policy who are looking for a nontechnical but authoritative treatment of recent theoretical and empirical developments in the political economy of monetary policy. Although simple from an analytical point of view, some of those chapters (like the more empirically oriented ones) may be of interest for more advanced readers as well, since they contain novel material.

The intermediate module is suitable for advanced undergraduate and graduate students of monetary policy, as well as for policy-oriented monetary economists with some background in formal thinking. It contains fully worked out, but somewhat simplified (usually by means of particular informational assumptions), versions of many of the basic models in the book. Individuals with prior knowledge in monetary policy games can probably go directly to the theoretical chapters in this module.

The advanced module contains fuller versions of some of the models in the intermediate module and a number of extensions and reinterpretations of the more basic models. The chapters in this module make a further step toward realism at the cost of more expositional complexity. They are suitable for graduate students of monetary policy and researchers in this area. Unlike most of the chapters in the previous module, most of the chapters here build on more basic corresponding chapters in the intermediate module. The classification of chapters into the three modules follows.

The Basic Module

This module includes

1. The general introduction (chapter 1), the overview of models of monetary policy under perfect information (chapter 2), and the overview of models of monetary policy under private information (chapter 8). These three chapters introduce and summarize most of the material in the first three parts of the book. Reading them and skimming one or two empirical chapters in part IV (like chapter 19 or 20) will give the quick reader a good idea of what this book is about.

2. Chapter 11 on alternative notions of credibility and reputation and chapter 17 on political parties and monetary policy.

3. All the empirical chapters in part IV except chapter 22. These include chapters 19, 20, 21, and 23.

Intermediate Module

This module includes

1. All the chapters on motives for monetary expansion under perfect information. Chapter 3 on the employment motive, chapter 4 on the revenue motive, chapter 5 on the balance-of-payments motive, and chapter 7 on the financial stability motive and the theory of optimal seigniorage.

2. Chapter 6 on the consequences of European monetary unification.

3. A basic sequence of models of monetary policy with private information. Chapter 9 on continually changing objectives with a minimal information advantage, chapter 12 on the politically optimal level of ambiguity (which builds on chapter 9), chapter 13 on private information about money demand with continually changing objectives, and chapter 16 on fixed policymaker types where the type is conceived in terms of the ability to commit or in terms of policy preferences.

Advanced Module

This module includes

1. Chapter 10 which extends chapter 9 to the case of an extended information advantage, chapter 14 which extends chapter 10 to allow for the effect of mandatory monetary targets, and chapter 18 that uses the framework of chapter 10 to derive implications of differing levels of central bank independence.

2. Chapter 15 on the persistence of inflation under discretion. This chapter allows endogenous countercyclical monetary policy by endowing policymakers with private forecasts about the persistence of natural employment.

3. Chapter 22 which tests empirically the common link of the mean and the variance of inflation to central bank independence. In terms of technical difficulty this chapter could have been grouped in the intermediate or even the basic module. It is grouped here only because it includes tests of an implication that is developed in chapter 18, which in turn belongs to the advanced module.

An attempt has been made, when possible, to use the same symbol for similar concepts in different chapters and under different informational structures. For example, the symbol A, which represents the fixed relative preference of policymakers for high employment versus price stability under perfect information (chapters 3 and 6), also represents the mean value of the same concept under changing objectives and private information in other parts of the book.

I MOTIVES FOR MONETARY EXPANSION UNDER PERFECT INFORMATION

2 Overview of Part I

2.1 Introduction

The chapters in this part deal with various motives of policymakers for monetary expansion under perfect information. These are the employment motive (chapter 3), the revenue motive (chapter 4), the balance-of-payments motive (chapter 5), and the financial stability motive (chapter 7). In addition the strategic framework of chapter 3 is used as a building block to investigate likely changes in policy outcomes due to replacement of the current European Monetary System by an eventual full monetary union. This is done in chapter 6.

A unifying theme of many of these chapters is that when policy is discretionary, the rate of inflation is excessively high because of dynamic inconsistency problems. Dynamic inconsistency occurs when the best policy planned currently for some future period is no longer the best when that period arrives. Section 2.2 contains an informal introduction on dynamic inconsistency and its interaction with the various motives for monetary expansion. A basic lesson from this discussion is that the extent of wage push is itself endogenous. In particular it reflects what individuals know about the central bank's tendency to accommodate prices, labor costs, and budgetary deficits.

Central bankers seem to be aware of their limited ability to resist such accommodative pressures. For example, in a recent lecture on the role of central bank independence, the Deputy Director General of the Bank of Italy, Antonio Fazio, said:

> In a large and complex economic system the level of prices is strongly affected by other variables and circumstances, first of all fiscal policy and labor costs. In such cases the reliance solely on monetary policy to achieve monetary stability can be extremely costly in terms of other economic objectives. (Fazio 1991, p. 135)

This statement is obviously true and realistic. But it ignores the effect of what the public and the political authorities know about the accommodative tendencies of the central bank on the behavior of wages, prices, and the fiscal deficit. Many chapters in this book are devoted to explicit consideration of the simultaneous interaction of the effect stressed by Fazio with the one he ignores. In particular, chapters 3, 5, and 6 highlight the fact that the degree of preoccupation of a central bank with economic activity is an important determinant of long-run inflation and of "wage stickiness."

Extraction of revenue for the government budget through seigniorage has several aspects in addition to dynamic inconsistency. Chapter 4 highlights two of these: political instability and the sectoral composition of the economy. Many central banks tend to smooth interest rates. Chapter 7 offers two positive explanations for this behavior and compares them. One is based on the central bank concern for financial stability. The other on optimal taxation considerations over time as well as across regular taxes and seigniorage.

This overview chapter summarizes the main ideas in part I in an informal manner. It is meant to serve a double purpose: first, as a broad introduction to the positive analysis of monetary policy for readers who want to get a feel for the main ideas in this new area without bothering with the details of particular models and, second, as an introduction to the more specific chapters in part I. Section 2.2 reviews various motives for monetary expansion and the effects of dynamic inconsistency. Section 2.3 reviews two explanations for the tendency of some central banks to smooth interest rates. Section 2.4 describes intuitively the effects of political instability and the sectoral composition of the economy on seigniorage. Section 2.5 sketches out a framework for the systematic comparison of policy outcomes in an adjustable pegs system with outcomes in a monetary union.

2.2   Why Do Governments Inflate?—Alternative Aspects of Dynamic Inconsistency

The world rate of inflation as well as that of most countries is positive on average (see table 4.1 for the average rate of inflation in seventy-nine countries). Since sustained inflation is possible only if the money supply also increases in a sustained manner, persistent inflation would not have been possible if policymakers had not allowed or tolerated the persistent expansion of national money supplies. To explain this phenomenon, it therefore is necessary to understand the motives and constraints of monetary policymakers, which usually are central banks with varying degrees of autonomy from the executive and legislative branches of government. Since there may be differences of emphasis on alternative policy objectives between central banks and political authorities, the actual course of policy usually represents a compromise between alternative views. This part of the book takes this compromise as exogenous by postulating a given objective function for policymakers and by treating the central bank, government, or policymakers in general as if they were one entity with the same objective function.[1]

Government normally inflates in order to achieve real objectives. The most widely discussed motives for monetary expansion are high employment and financing of the deficit in the government budget. We refer to them as the employment and the revenue motives, respectively. Other motives are financial stability and, usually for fixed peg countries, avoidance of excessive deficits in the balance of payments. Chapters 3 and 4 discuss the employment and the revenue motives for monetary expansion, and chapters 5 and 7 discuss the mercantilistic and the financial stability motives. A common thread in all these chapters is that in trying to achieve one or more of these objectives, government and the general public are drawn into a prisoner's dilemma that leads to positive and excessively high rates of inflation. This section describes intuitively the mechanisms leading to this result for various alternative motives for monetary expansion and brings out the unifying principles that underly them.

The prisoner's dilemma aspects of monetary policy are best illustrated by means of the employment motive. It is based on three key relationships. First, the economy is one in which deviations of employment from its natural level are positively related to unanticipated inflation. This is due to the existence of nominal wage contracts in conjunction with a real wage which (due to unions or minimum wage legislation) is normally above the market-clearing real wage rate. As a consequence the demand for labor is the binding constraint on employment, so bursts of inflation that were not anticipated at contracting time reduce the real wage rate and temporarily increase employment. Second, policymakers have an objective function that gives a positive weight to stimulation of employment even beyond the natural rate and a negative weight to inflation.[2] Finally, the public knows the objectives of policymakers and understands their mode of behavior. Employers and workers bargain over nominal wages at the beginning of each contracting period and set a nominal wage rate for the period. Since they aim at a certain *real* wage, the contract *nominal* wage becomes a function of the rate of inflation that they expect for the contract period. In the absence of inflationary surprises this will also be the *actual* real wage rate. The corresponding demand for labor determines natural employment. During the period government chooses a rate of monetary expansion, and therefore a rate of inflation that maximizes its objectives. In doing that, it takes the contract nominal wage (and consequently the beginning periods' inflationary expectations) as given. The "best" rate of inflation is determined so as to minimize the combined costs of inflation and of low employment. Since the marginal costs of each of these two "bads" are increasing, the minimizing rate of inflation is positive.

Let us now go back to employers and workers at contracting time. Since they know government's objective function, they can deduce in advance what is the rate of inflation that will be produced by government once they settle on a given nominal wage. They therefore adjust the contract nominal wage so as to achieve the real wage they are aiming at. As a consequence, when government inflates, they obtain exactly the real wage rate that they had aimed at, in the first place, and employment remains at its natural level. Thus government's attempt to push employment above its natural level does not succeed, but this (known) attempt leads to an equilibrium with positive inflation.

A zero rate of inflation could have been achieved if *prior* to the signing of nominal contracts government would have *credibly* committed itself to a zero rate of inflation. Since the commitment is credible, nominal contracts are settled on the assumption that inflation will be zero and for the same reason actual inflation is also zero. Thus employment is still at the natural level, but inflation is zero. The upshot is that when government has the *discretion* to pick inflation after the settlement of contracts, an excessively high positive inflation arises. However, the presence of pre-commitments eliminates this bias. This fact constitutes a basic argument in favor of *fixed rules* and against *discretion*.

The inflationary bias of monetary policy in the presence of employment objectives is due to what has been labeled by Kydland and Prescott (1977) as "dynamic inconsistency." Dynamic inconsistency arises when the best plan currently made for some future period by one of the players in a dynamic game is no longer optimal from his or her point of view when that period arrives. In the example above the best rate of inflation for policymakers prior to the determination of nominal contracts is zero. But once contracts have been hammered out, policymakers take them as given, and the best rate of inflation becomes positive.

A similar phenomenon arises in the presence of the revenue motive for monetary expansion. The amount of real purchasing power that government can extract from the public by printing money (known as *seigniorage*) depends on the rate of monetary expansion chosen by government and on the quantity of money held by the public. The higher are either of these quantities the larger the amount of seigniorage. The public chooses the amount of money balances on the basis of expected inflation. If it expects a higher inflation, it holds less real money balances, and thus the amount of seigniorage extracted, for a given rate of monetary expansion, is lower. Suppose that government objectives are positively related to the amount of seigniorage revenues and negatively related to monetary inflation. In each period the public decides how much money balances to hold, and then government chooses the rate of inflation. Prior to the choice of nominal balances for the period, government takes into consideration the negative effect that higher inflation has on seigniorage revenues through the effect that higher inflationary expectations have on the amount of nominal balances held by the public. This partially deters government from inflating. But after individuals have chosen the amounts of money balances to be held, government takes the public's nominal balances as given, and the deterring effect ceases to operate. Hence, under discretion, government ends up inflating at a rate that is higher than the rate it would have inflated at if it could commit to some rate of inflation prior to the choice of money balances by the public.

This seigniorage-motivated dynamic inconsistency of monetary policy is one explanation for the fact that, during some hyperinflations, policymakers could have increased seigniorage revenues by committing to lower rates of inflation than those that actually occurred. In this view, since the public correctly perceived their inability to precommit, it reduced its money balances below those it would have held in the presence of such an ability. This reduced money balances so much that even the higher rates of monetary expansion chosen by policymakers could not restore seigniorage revenues to their magnitude in the presence of commitments.

Although the analogy between the employment and the revenue-motivated dynamic inconsistencies of monetary policy is strong, there is also a difference between the two cases. In the first case government does not affect employment at all, whereas in the second it succeeds in obtaining some seigniorage. In the second case the suboptimality of discretionary policy arises from the fact that the same amount of seigniorage revenues could have been extracted at a lower rate of inflation if government could have credibly committed to this rate.

A third instance of a suboptimally high rate of inflation because of dynamic inconsistency arises in the presence of balance-of-payments objectives. Such objectives may arise because of a desire to have a sufficient level of foreign exchange reserves in a system with a fixed peg or due to a mercantilistic philosophy. Consider a small open economy with a fixed but adjustable peg that takes world prices as given. Suppose government dislikes deficits in the balance of payments and also dislikes inflation. As in the case of the employment motive, the labor market is characterized by a natural real wage that is above market clearing and by nominal wage contracts. After these contracts have been concluded, government can either devalue or maintain the fixed peg. If it chooses to devalue, government incurs a cost, since domestic prices and inflation go up. But there is also a benefit for government's objectives. By raising the domestic price level, a devaluation reduces the real wage rate, increases employment and output, and leaves more resources for exports or for the production of import substitutes. This reduces the balance-of-payments deficit or increases its surplus. Supposing that the balance of payments is initially in a state of deficit, government has an incentive to devalue and to tolerate some inflation in order to reduce the balance-of-payments deficit. Government chooses this rate, taking nominal contracts as given so as to minimize the combined costs of inflation and of deficits in the balance of payments.

Let us now step back to contracting time in the labor market. Since they aim at a certain real wage rate during the contract period, unions and employers choose the contract nominal wage rate on the basis of the rate of devaluation that they expect for the period of the contract. Knowing government's objective functions, they can calculate precisely what will be this rate and use this knowledge to set nominal wages so as to neutralize any possible effects of devaluations on the real wage rate. As a consequence, although government devalues after contracts have been signed, the real wage and output remain at their natural levels, and there is no effect on the deficit in the balance of payments. Again, government's discretionary attempt at devaluing only produces a devaluation bias with no real effects. Once more the source of the bias is dynamic inconsistency. Prior to the signing of wage contracts the "best" rate of devaluation for the contract period is zero, but after that point it becomes positive, leading to suboptimally high rates of inflation and of devaluation. In the presence of precommitments, the balance of payments would have remained the same, but inflation and the rate of devaluation would have been zero, yielding a better value for governmental objectives.

The underlying source of dynamic inconsistency can be traced in all cases to some basic conflict between policymakers and some groups within the private sector. In the case of the employment and the balance-of-payments motives, the conflict concerns the real wage. Because of its employment and/or balance-of-payments objectives, government prefers a real wage that is lower than the one desired by unions or by constituencies that support minimum wage legislation.[3] In the case of seigniorage, the conflict concerns the distribution of resources between the private and the public sector. Government tries to obtain more resources by inflating at a higher rate, and the public partially resists this attempt by reducing money balances.

The relative preference of policymakers for achieving alternative objectives and the stance of fiscal policy affect the magnitude of the inflationary bias. For example, the higher the relative concern of policymakers for employment, the higher will be the inflationary bias. Similarly the higher the deficit in government's budget and therefore in the balance of payments, the higher will be the rate of devaluation under discretion. Details appear in the respective chapters (3 and 5). The incentive to inflate is also higher, the larger the outstanding amount of nominally denominated government debt. Details appear in section 4.4 of chapter 4.

For expositional simplicity the effect of each of the motives for monetary expansion is analyzed separately. In practice monetary expansion may be motivated by the desire to simultaneously achieve several real objectives. In addition the weights attributed to different policy objectives differ in general across countries. It is likely that in developed countries with well-functioning capital markets, the employment motive dominates monetary policy. But in countries with thin capital markets and relatively inefficient tax systems, the need to resort to inflationary finance of budgetary deficits is a prime motive for inflation. This is more likely to be the case in developing countries or in developed countries that experience particularly unstable circumstances such as external or internal armed conflicts.

Those tentative generalizations are supported by several observations. First, many recent hyperinflations have occurred in developing countries with thin capital markets (Bruno et al. 1988). When hyperinflations occurred in developed economies, it was usually during or after wars or acute internal conflicts. Second, the *tax-smoothing hypothesis*, which posits that inflation is driven by optimal public finance considerations, is not supported by the data in most developed economies (Grilli, Masciandaro, and Tabellini 1991). Third, the acceleration of inflation to very high rates triggers mechanisms that increase the importance of the revenue motive in comparison to the employment motive. By temporarily reducing tax revenues (the so-called Olivera-Tanzi effect), an inflationary acceleration increases government's dependence on seigniorage. By shortening and compressing the duration of nominal contracts, it also steepens the short-run Phillips trade-off, making it less advantageous to inflate in order to achieve employment objectives. Finally, countries in which seigniorage is an important source of government revenues are usually developing economies (see table 4.1).

2.3 Why Do Central Banks Smooth Interest Rates?

There is evidence that central banks in a number of developed countries partially smooth movements in interest rates. For example, after the establishment of the Federal Reserve in 1914, violent spikes in interest rates during financial panics virtually disappeared (Donaldson 1989). There are at least two explanations for this behavior. One is that it arises from the concern of the central bank for the stability of the financial system (Cukierman 1990). The other is that it is a by-product of government's attempt to optimally allocate the burden of government's finances across various taxes, including seigniorage, as well as over time (Mankiw 1987; Mankiw and Miron 1990). We refer to these two hypotheses as the *financial stability motive* and the *optimal seigniorage theory*, respectively.

The financial stability hypothesis relies on the notion that to reduce the likelihood of financial collapse, the central bank is willing to compromise on the objective of price stability, particularly when the stability of the financial system seems to be threatened. In economies with developed financial markets various intermediaries normally commit to loan contracts that stretch over longer periods than the term for which deposits are committed to them. This makes them vulnerable to surprise increases in market rates, since in the short run such increases affect their cost of funds more quickly than their revenues from loans. When such increases materialize, the central bank injects liquidity into the economy in order to reduce the resulting threat to the stability of the financial system. This moderates temporarily the increase in interest rates. Conversely, when market rates unexpectedly go down, the profits and stability of banks and other intermediaries go up. At such times the central bank mops up some of the liquidity previously injected into the economy because it is also concerned with price stability. These reactions of the central bank to both upward and downward movements in interest rates dampen the fluctuations of these rates.

The optimal seigniorage theory states that monetary policy is dominated by optimal public finance considerations in which the revenue motive plays a central role. Revenues from seigniorage entail, like any other tax, deadweight losses. Hence, in this view, monetary policy is conducted so as to minimize the discounted present value of deadweight losses from regular taxes and seigniorage subject to the constraint that a certain (fluctuating) level of public expenditures is financed. Provided that the marginal social costs of both regular taxes and seigniorage are increasing, this hypothesis implies that seigniorage, and therefore inflation, should be positively related to the relative size of regular taxes.[4] In the long run nominal interest rates and inflation are positively related because of the inflation premium in nominal rates. Hence the optimal seigniorage theory implies that nominal rates should be positively related to the relative size of government and of regular taxes.

More important from the perspective of interest rate smoothing, the optimal seigniorage theory implies that the marginal costs of seigniorage should be equated across periods. Since the opportunity cost of holding money is the nominal interest rate, the intertemporal aspect of the theory implies that fluctuations in nominal rates will be ironed out. This provides an alternative explanation for interest rate smoothing. Both explanations are presented and contrasted in chapter 7.

It is interesting to note that a financial stability motive on the part of central banks produces an inflationary bias similar to the biases produced by the motives for monetary expansion that were discussed in the previous section. This bias is related to the fact that debitory rates normally respond to changes more slowly than creditory rates in conjunction with the central bank's concern for the financial stability of banks and other financial intermediaries.

2.4   Seigniorage, Political Instability, and the Structure of the Economy

There generally are substantial and persistent cross-country differences in the relative importance of seigniorage as a source of government revenue.

A basic determinant of the degree of reliance on seigniorage is the efficiency of the tax system. Sections 4.5 and 4.6 of chapter 4 present a political theory of the determinants of this efficiency and through it of seigniorage. Section 4.7 of the same chapter presents supporting empirical evidence on seigniorage, political instability, and the structure of the economy.

The basic idea is that the efficiency of the tax system, and therefore seigniorage, are affected by the sectoral composition of the economy and by political instability and polarization. For example, agricultural sectors are harder to tax than the mining and manufacturing sectors, and it is relatively easy to tax foreign trade. In addition the efficiency of the tax system is also affected by the degree of political instability and polarization. An inefficient tax system (i.e., one that facilitates tax evasion and imposes high tax collection costs) acts as a constraint on the revenue-collecting ability of government. This constraint may be welcome by those who disagree with the goals pursued by the current government. In particular previous governments (or legislative majorities) may deliberately choose to maintain an inefficient tax system so as to constrain the behavior of future governments (or majorities) with which they might disagree. Of course this is more likely to happen in countries with more unstable and polarized political systems.

2.5 Adjustable Pegs as a Partial Commitment Device and European Monetary Unification

The recent acceleration in the process of European economic and monetary integration raised the far-reaching possibility that the European Economic Community (EEC) will eventually have a single currency managed by one monetary authority. Under the current monetary system (known as the European Monetary System, EMS) the EEC countries maintain fixed pegs among their respective currencies. But each country reserves the right to adjust its peg under exceptional circumstances. Thus the EMS functions as a partial commitment device. The reason is that countries deciding to go through a realignment incur a political cost. As a consequence pegs are adjusted only under sufficiently extreme circumstances.

Peg adjustments reflect basic policy differences and conflicts across countries within the community. Such conflicts exist irrespectively of whether each country manages its own currency or whether there is one central bank for the entire community. But their resolution differs between the two regimes. Chapter 6 compares policy outcomes in an adjustable peg system such as the current EMS with policy outcomes in a monetary union under the presumption that policy decisions in the latter case will reflect the will of a (possibly weighted) majority. The basic presumption is that (as is the case under the EMS) there will be a limited commitment to price stability also in a monetary union. But policy outcomes under the two regimes differ first because divergent monetary policies are not possible in a monetary union, and second because the commitment to price stability is abandoned under different circumstances.

Chapter 6 compares the probability that a single country in the EMS will adjust its peg with the probability that a monetary union will abandon the commitment to price stability. The comparison is done under the presumption that the distributions of real shocks affecting the countries in the union is the same in the two cases. The chapter shows that even if the probability that a single country in an adjustable pegs system goes through a realignment is relatively small, the probability that at least one country in such a system adjusts its peg may be substantial. The implications of this result for the desirability of having a "stage two," as proposed in the Delors Report, are discussed and evaluated.[5] The chapter also compares average inflation in the community under an adjustable peg system and under a monetary union. In general average inflation may be higher or lower under a monetary union. But, if the (common across systems) political cost of reneging on price stability is sufficiently high, average inflation is lower in a monetary union.

3 The Employment Motive for Monetary Expansion

3.1 Introduction

Conventional wisdom in macroeconomics implies that employment and output can be influenced by unanticipated inflation and therefore by unanticipated monetary growth. This can result from either the existence of Fischer (1977)-Taylor (1980) long-term contracts or a Lucas (1973) type short-run Phillips curve. To the extent that monetary policymakers find the natural level of employment too low, they may be tempted to create monetary surprises in order to push employment above its natural level even at the cost of some inflation.

The recent literature provides several explanations for the dissatisfaction of policymakers with the existing natural level of employment. One approach views policymakers as benevolent social planners who conduct monetary policy so as to maximize a single well-defined social welfare function (Barro and Gordon 1983b). In this view the natural level of employment is too low because of distortionary taxes on labor. Such taxes, by driving a wedge between the cost of labor to employers and the (net) wage rate received by workers, drive employment below its socially optimal level. As a consequence socially minded policymakers are motivated to produce some inflation in order to move employment closer to its socially optimal level. Another approach views monetary policymakers as being at least partially responsive to political pressures arising from distributional considerations. In this view policymakers' preferences for a level of employment above the natural rate is due to the fact that a sufficiently important part of each of their constituencies is adversely affected by a low level of employment (Woolley 1984). In this approach the importance assigned to preventing inflation relative to stimulating the economy depends on the relative influence on the central bank of the pro-stimulation and anti-inflation advocates within government and the private sector.

Obviously the two approaches are not mutually exclusive. The central bank may be interested in both price stability and in maintaining employment above the natural level because it is concerned with social welfare and also because it partially responds to political pressures. In either case the concern of the central bank for high employment produces an inflationary bias and does not lead to any gains in employment.[1] Since this fundamental result arises independently of whether central bank objectives reflect those of a social planner or those of a politically sensitive bureaucracy, it is illustrated initially in a framework that does not take a position on the more fundamental determinants of central bank objectives. The relative merits of the two approaches are discussed in section 3.7.

3.2   The Inflationary Bias of Monetary Policy—A Basic Model

Consider a central bank that is concerned with both price stability and high employment. More precisely, let the objective of the bank be to maximize

$$-\left[\frac{A}{2}(N^* - N)^2 + \frac{\pi^2}{2}\right], \qquad N^* - N \geq 0, \tag{3.1}$$

where N and N^* are the actual and the desired levels of employment, π is the rate of inflation, and A is a positive parameter that reflects the relative concern of the central bank for high employment and price stability. The higher the A, the stronger is the relative concern of monetary policymakers for maintaining employment near its desired level N^*. This formulation is consistent with both a social welfare and a political interpretation of central bank objectives.

The notion that, due to the existence of long-term contracts or because of a Lucas-type confusion between aggregate nominal and real relative shocks, the deviation of employment from its natural level is positively related to unanticipated inflation is captured by equation (3.2):

$$N - N_n = \alpha(\pi - \pi^e), \qquad \alpha > 0. \tag{3.2}$$

Here N_n is the natural level of employment[2] and π and π^e are actual and expected inflation, respectively. Abstracting from real shocks, growth, and changes in velocity, the rate of inflation is equal to the rate of monetary growth m.[3] Hence inflationary expectations are equal to expected money growth m^e, and the short-run Phillips relation in (3.2) can be restated as

$$N - N_n = \alpha(m - m^e). \tag{3.2a}$$

Substituting the Phillips relation in (3.2a) into equation (3.1), the objective of the central bank becomes

$$\max_{m} - \left\{\frac{A}{2}(N^* - N_n - \alpha(m - m^e))^2 + \frac{m^2}{2}\right\}, \tag{3.3}$$

where due to the existence of distortionary taxes on labor, political considerations, or other reasons, $N^* > N_n$. The central bank chooses m taking inflationary expectations m^e as given. The first-order condition for the maximization problem in equation (3.3) implies that

$$m = \frac{\alpha A}{1 + \alpha^2 A}(N^* - N_n) + \frac{\alpha^2 A}{1 + \alpha^2 A} m^e \equiv \phi(m^e). \qquad (3.4)$$

Since desired employment is larger than natural employment, the central bank picks a positive rate of monetary growth even when expected inflation is zero ($\pi^e = m^e = 0$).

We turn next to the formation of expectations. There is no uncertainty of any kind. In particular the public is perfectly informed about the objectives of the central bank. It can therefore calculate, using equation (3.4), what is the rate of monetary growth picked by the central bank at each level of expectations m^e. Any expectation that does not reproduce itself through equation (3.4) is not rational from the public's point of view, since it implies that the public believes inflation will be m^e despite the fact that it knows that with such an expectation the central bank's best response is a rate of monetary growth that differs from m^e. Hence under certainty a rational expectations equilibrium implies that

$$m^e = m. \qquad (3.5)$$

Combining (3.5) and (3.4), we obtain the equilibrium rate of monetary expansion:

$$m = A\alpha(N^* - N_n). \qquad (3.6)$$

Since desired employment N^* is larger than the natural rate N_n the equilibrium rate of monetary expansion is positive.

Figure 3.1 illustrates the equilibrium. The positively sloped lines labeled $P(m^e = m_i)$ in panel a of the figure depict short-run Phillips trade-offs for alternative values of the expected rate of monetary expansion. Policymakers' indifference contours are plotted in panel a of the figure. The ideal point from their perspective is zero inflation ($m = 0$) and employment at N^*. Indifference contours that are farther away from this ideal point represent successively worse values for policymakers' objectives. Given expectations and therefore a particular short-run Phillips curve, the central bank picks the point that corresponds to the indifference contour that is nearest to the ideal point ($N^*, 0$). This occurs at a tangency point of the short-run trade-off curve and of the indifference map. When expected monetary expansion is zero, the tangency is at point B and the rate

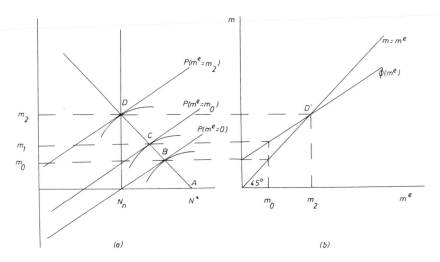

Figure 3.1
The inflationary bias of monetary policy

of monetary expansion chosen is m_0, which is positive. Had individuals expected this rate, the short-run trade-off curve would have been $P(m^e = m_0)$, and the rate of inflation chosen would have been m_1, which is larger than m_0. The locus of tangency points is the reaction function of the central bank. It shows the rate of monetary expansion chosen at each level of expectations. This reaction function is the curve labeled $\phi(m^e)$ in panel b of figure 3.1. Equation (3.4) implies that the slope of this curve is smaller than one. Since $N^* - N_n > 0$ (the optimal employment level being larger than the natural level), it cuts the vertical axis at a positive value. Hence $\phi(m^e)$ intersects the 45-degree line, along which actual and expected rates of monetary expansion are equal, at one and only one point labeled D'.

Of all the tangency points in panel a, there is only one for which the action taken by the central bank validates the public's expected rate of monetary expansion. This occurs at point D in panel a and correspondingly at point D' in panel b of the figure. Panel b emphasizes why any expected rate of monetary expansion other than m_2 is not a rational expectations equilibrium. When, for example, beliefs are at m_0, the reaction function in panel b implies that the choice of monetary expansion by the central bank is m_1, which is different from m_0. Since the public knows the policymakers' reaction function, it cannot rationally entertain the view that monetary expansion will be m_0, knowing that such an expectation induces the central bank to pick a different rate of monetary expansion. The only possible equilibrium is therefore at m_2 where actual and expected rates of monetary expansion coincide and policymakers' actions are determined by their reaction function.

Since actual and expected inflations are equal, the central bank has no effect on employment, which remains at its natural level. But the rate of inflation is positive. Given the central bank's objective function in equation (3.1), this outcome is obviously dominated by one in which employment is still at the natural rate, but both actual and expected inflations are zero. Hence prior to the determination of expectations the policymakers' best strategy is to pick a zero rate of inflation. However, once expectations have been set, policymakers take them as given. As a result their incentives change, and they are motivated to pick a positive rate of inflation. Panel a of figure 3.1 suggests that the incentive to inflate is present independently of whether the public believes that monetary growth will be zero or positive. Thus as long as expectations have been set at a nonnegative value,[4] the choice of a positive rate of monetary expansion is a *dominant strategy* for the central bank. The public, being aware in advance of this change in the structure of incentives, anticipates that the rate of inflation will be m_2, since this is the only rate that, if expected, induces policymakers to reproduce it.

The upshot is that when (no matter for what reason) the level of employment desired by the central bank is higher than the natural level, monetary policy has an inflationary bias. This bias is directly traceable to the fact that monetary policy is chosen after expectations and actions based on these expectations have been determined. This is one of the best-known examples of dynamic inconsistency.[5] Recall from chapter 2 that dynamic inconsistency arises when the plan currently made for some future period by one of the players in a dynamic game is no longer optimal from that player's point of view when that period arrives.[6] In the present simple context there is dynamic inconsistency because the best choice of monetary growth for a period is different before and after expectations have been set. For concreteness, suppose that expectations for the period are set at the beginning of each period. Then prior to the setting of expectations the best choice for the period's inflation is zero. But once within the period, the best choice involves a positive rate of monetary expansion.

The equilibrium described here is sometimes referred to as "discretion-ary" because policymakers retain the discretion to alter monetary policy at any moment in time. Prior to the setting of expectations, policymakers may try to claim that they are contemplating a zero rate of inflation for the period. However, the public will ignore such claims, since it knows that, no matter what they say, policymakers have an incentive to inflate at a positive rate once expectations have been set.

Before concluding this section, it is useful to comment on the features of the discretionary solution in equation (3.6). The greater the relative concern of policymakers for employment (the higher A) and the greater the short-run effect of unanticipated money on output (the larger α), the larger is the equilibrium rate of monetary expansion. Thus, other things remaining the same, a greater concern by the central bank for employment induces a higher rate of inflation despite the fact that the higher inflation has no effect on employment. In addition, for given A and α, the inflationary bias is larger, the larger the discrepancy between the natural and the desired levels of employment (the larger $N^* - N_n$). Note also that the equilibrium occurs in the range of N for which $N^* - N$ is strictly positive so the restriction in equation (3.1) is satisfied.

3.3   Commitment as a Device to Eliminate the Inflationary Bias

The fact that the discretionary equilibrium results in a suboptimally high inflationary bias leads to the following natural question: How can the institutional framework within which monetary policy operates be reformed so as to eliminate the bias? One answer is that the central bank should irrevocably commit its policy for the period prior to the setting of expectations. Under this institutional setup pronouncements made by the central bank about future policy are fully believed since the public knows that the bank is committed to fulfill the announced policy. As a result any announcement of policy is credible. By giving up the discretion to alter policy after expectations have been set, the bank gains the ability to affect expectations by simply announcing its intentions.

In contrast to the discretionary regime, policymakers now take into consideration that any choice of monetary growth has an immediate and full impact on expected monetary growth. As a consequence, with a commitment, the policymakers' decision problem from equation (3.3) becomes

$$\max_{m} -\left[\frac{A}{2}(N^* - N_n)^2 + \frac{m^2}{2}\right].$$ (3.3a)

The solution to this problem is obviously $m = 0$. Hence the presence of credible commitments eliminates the inflationary bias of the central bank. Equation (3.7) gives the values of central bank objectives attained under discretion and commitments[7]

Discretion $-\frac{A}{2}(1 + A\alpha^2)(N^* - N_n)^2$ (3.7a)

Commitment $-\frac{A}{2}(N^* - N_n)^2.$ (3.7b)

Hence the ability to commit enhances the objectives of policymakers by $[(A\alpha)^2/2](N - N_n)^2$.

3.4   A Multiperiod Extension

As pointed out by Barro and Gordon (1983b), under discretion the inflationary bias of monetary policy carries over to the case in which the central bank cares about the future as well as about the present. This can be illustrated by generalizing the objective function of the central bank as shown in equation (3.8):

$$-\sum_{i=0}^{\infty} \beta^i \left[\frac{A}{2}(N^* - N_i)^2 + \frac{\pi_i^2}{2}\right], \qquad 0 < \beta \le 1,$$ (3.8)

where β is the discount factor applied by policymakers to future values of their objectives. Using equation (3.2) and $\pi_i = m_i$ in equation (3.8), the objective of policymakers can be restated as[8]

$$\max_{\{m_i, i=0,1,2,...\}} -\sum_{i=0}^{\infty} \beta^i \left\{\frac{A}{2}[N^* - N_n - \alpha(m_i - m_i^e)]^2 + \frac{m_i^2}{2}\right\}.$$ (3.8a)

Suppose that inflationary expectations are set at the beginning of each period for the period. Just before the setting of expectations for period 0, the best rate of monetary expansion for that period under discretion is zero, as are the rates planned for all future periods. However, once the expectation m_0^e has been set, policymakers reoptimize taking it as given. Since there is nothing that links the periods, it is possible to consider the objective function for period 0 in isolation. Being equivalent to the one-period problem under discretion, this leads to the discretionary solution given by equation (3.6) for period 0's monetary growth. As for the remaining periods $(1, 2, \ldots)$ since, as of period 0, the expectations for those periods have not been set, the best choice of monetary growth for those periods is still zero. However, once the expectation for period 1 is set, policymakers take it as given and reoptimize. Again, this leads to the discretionary solution in equation (3.6) for period 1. Since this argument generalizes to any period, equation (3.6) gives the equilibrium choice of inflation under discretion for all periods. The upshot is that for policy-makers who are concerned about employment, discretion produces an inflationary bias in both multiperiod and single-period settings.

3.5   A Critical Look at the Economic Structure Underlying the Inflationary Bias Result

The inflationary bias result discussed in the previous sections arises because policymakers have an incentive to try to surprise the public in order to stimulate employment. There are currently two, not necessarily competing, views about the way unanticipated money affects output. One is the Lucas (1972, 1973) aggregate-relative confusion. The other is the nominal contracts approach associated with Fischer (1977) and Taylor (1980). Either one of these economic mechanisms seems to be able to support the inflationary bias result. However, closer consideration suggests that the matter is more involved.

Strictly speaking, unanticipated monetary shocks affect employment in Lucas's framework because individuals in the economy do not distinguish immediately between aggregate nominal shocks and real relative shocks. Essentially this mechanism works because the public is temporarily uncertain about the magnitude of the aggregate nominal shocks that affect the economy. When individuals are fully informed about the magnitude of current nominal shocks, those shocks have no effect on employment (Cukierman 1984, ch. 3). In terms of the model of the previous subsections, this implies that the trade-off coefficient α is zero and that (from equation 3.6) there is no inflationary bias. Hence, a model of the type presented in section 3.2 in which the public has perfect information about the rate of monetary growth chosen by the central bank will not produce an inflationary bias if money affects output only because of the aggregate-relative confusion. There are two ways out of this difficulty. One is to incorporate this confusion explicitly into the model and then to investigate whether such a consistently specified model reproduces the inflationary bias result. The other possibility is to retain the simplicity of the perfect foresight model presented above and to rely on a nominal wage contract approach to deliver the effects of money on employment. This track is explored in the remainder of this section and in the following one.

Consider first a competitive labor market in which the nominal wage W for the period is contracted at the beginning of the period. Let w_n be the real wage rate that clears the labor market, and let P^e be the price level expected for the period at its beginning. Then the contract nominal wage rate W_c is determined so as to attain the real wage rate w_n. That is,

$$W_c = w_n P^e \equiv w_n P_{-1}(1 + \pi^e), \tag{3.9}$$

where P_{-1} is the price level in the previous period and π^e is the rate of inflation expected to occur between the previous and the current period at the beginning of the current period. For the model of section 3.2, π^e can be replaced by m^e so that equation (3.9) becomes

$$W_c = w_n P_{-1}(1 + m^e). \tag{3.10}$$

Thus the rate of monetary expansion expected at the beginning of the period becomes embodied in the wage contract for the period. The actual real wage during the period is, for the model of section 3.2,

$$w \equiv \frac{W_c}{P} = w_n \frac{1 + m^e}{1 + m}. \tag{3.11}$$

A critical ingredient responsible for the inflationary bias result is the notion that due to the existence of distortionary labor taxes, the natural level of employment N_n is lower than the desired rate N^*. If, as in Barro and Gordon (1983b), the policymakers' objective function is taken to be a social welfare function, then N^* would correspond to the employment arising in a competitive equilibrium of the labor market in the absence of distortionary taxes.

The top panel of figure 3.2 clarifies the relationship between N_n and N^* in the context of the labor market. The curve labeled D is the demand for labor. The curves labeled S_n and S are the supplies of labor with and without distortionary labor taxes, respectively. The intersection of D and of S_n determines the natural level of employment and correspondingly the

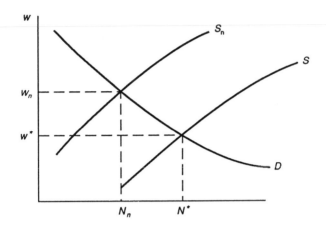

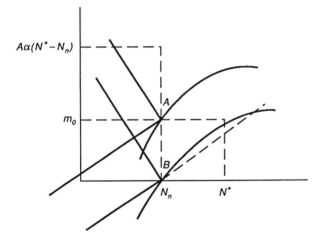

Figure 3.2
Disappearance of the inflationary bias results in the presence of the short-end rule (nominal contracts framework)

natural (gross) real wage w_n. The intersection of D and S determines the socially optimal level of employment N^* (which would obtain in the absence of labor taxes) and the corresponding real wage w^*. In the absence of monetary disturbances individuals in the labor market aim at obtaining (and paying) the real wage w_n and also achieve it. Employment is therefore at the natural rate N_n. Since this level of employment is lower than the desired rate N^*, monetary policymakers have an incentive to alter the real wage after W_c has been set in order to increase employment beyond N_n.

However, it is not clear that this necessarily translates into an inflationary bias. It does if, for any deviation of the actual wage from the market-clearing wage w_n, employment is determined along the demand curve. But whereas such behavior is reasonable for the range of w above w_n in which labor is in excess supply, it is less plausible in the range $\{w < w_n\}$ in which labor is in excess demand. Since in this range the binding constraint is the supply of labor, it is more plausible that employment is determined along the supply curve S_n. In other words, whenever the actual real wage deviates temporarily from its market-clearing value, employment is determined by the short side of the market—the so-called short-end rule. It is almost obvious that in this case policymakers have no reason to choose a rate of monetary expansion that is higher than the one that was expected when the nominal wage contract was set. The reason is that by raising m above m^e, they not only increase inflation but also decrease employment, since in the range $\{w < w_n\}$ disequilibrium employment is governed by the labor supply curve.

As a matter of fact in the presence of the short-end rule the best response of policymakers, given the public's expectation, is to validate this expectation by making the actual rate of monetary expansion equal to its expectation. This result is illustrated in the bottom panel of figure 3.2 which displays two short-run trade-off curves, one for $m^e = 0$ and the other for $m^e = m_0$. Due to the operation of the short-end rule all the short-run trade-off curves change slopes along the vertical line originating at N_n. The switch point occurs at the rate of monetary expansion that corresponds to the given public's expectation. Hence the range of employment above N_n is not accessible to policymakers. Given a trade-off curve, the policymakers' objectives are maximized at the point on the curve for which their isoobjective curve is nearest to the ideal point of zero inflation and employment at N^*. It can be seen from the bottom panel of figure 3.2 that when $m^e = m_0$, this point is A, which implies an actual rate of monetary expansion of m_0. Similarly, when $m^e = 0$, the best response occurs at point B, which corresponds to an actual rate of monetary expansion of zero. The upshot is that as long as $m^e \leq A\alpha(N^* - N_n)$, any rate of monetary expansion is a self-fulfilling equilibrium.[9]

In all those equilibria employment is at the natural level. Hence the best one from policymakers' point of view is the one for which both actual and expected inflation are zero. All equilibria except this one can be eliminated by appealing to a refinement similar to the Cho and Kreps (1987) intuitive criterion. The policymaker could address the public in the following manner: "I am going to choose a zero rate of monetary expansion. You should believe that I will do that since, if you do, it is in my best ex-post interest to maintain the money supply constant." In view of policymakers' reaction function under the short-end rule, this statement is credible. Hence it is rational for the public to believe it.[10]

The upshot is that unless we make the strong assumption that in disequilibrium employment is always demand determined, the presence of distortionary taxes and nominal contracts does not, by itself, induce an inflationary bias on the part of policymakers. Does this result imply that we should abandon the notion that monetary policy has an employment-motivated inflation bias? I believe not. It does, however, suggest the need for better foundations for this result. This is the topic of the next section.

3.6   Alternative Foundations for the Employment-Motivated Inflation Bias[11]

The discussion in the previous section implies that a competitive equilibrium view of the labor market does not deliver an inflationary bias even in the presence of distortionary labor taxes and nominal contracts. However, if, due to the existence of unions, the real wage rate is higher than its competitive counterpart, an inflationary bias is likely to reappear. This is demonstrated first for the case in which all the economy is unionized and subsequently for the case in which the labor market also contains a competitive segment. The first case is represented in panel a of figure 3.3 which, for now, should be interpreted as encompassing the entire labor market. Since the union has market power, it sets the contract nominal wage, given its expectation, so as to get the real wage $\hat{w}_u$. At this wage rate the demand for labor is the binding constraint. It would appear therefore that the central bank could stimulate employment by producing a decrease in the real wage rate. This is the case in turn only if the union allows its members

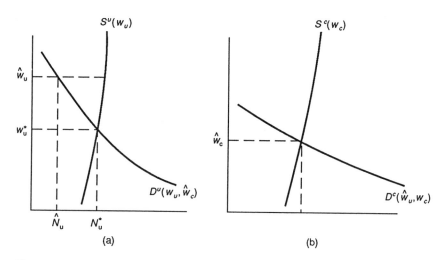

Figure 3.3
The structure of the labor market and the inflationary bias of monetary policy: the no-intervention equilibrium

to supply labor ex-post according to their individual supply curves rather than through a centralized arrangement. The following discussion demonstrates that this is indeed the case provided the union is concerned about the welfare of its members.

A precondition for ex-ante maintenance of the real wage at $\hat{w}_u$ by the union is that it effectively controls the labor supply of its members at $\hat{N}_u$ as long as the real wage rate they receive is $\hat{w}_u$. But if, due to policymakers' actions, the real wage decreases below $\hat{w}_u$, there is no more point for the union's leadership, if it cares about the welfare of its members, to hold employment at $\hat{N}_u$. Holding employment down to $\hat{N}_u$ will not restore the real wage rate to $\hat{w}_u$, since the nominal wage has been preagreed with the employers and they stick to their part of the agreement by paying it. Since the lower real wage rate is due to the action of a third party, the union leadership cannot claim breach of agreement on the part of employers. It therefore takes the lower real wage as given and, being concerned about the welfare of its members, lets them do what is best for them given this real wage. But the best level of employment for each individual at a given wage rate is given by his or her supply curve. Hence, given that the real wage rate has decreased not because of breach of contract by employers, the best ex-post strategy for the union is to let its members supply their labor along the $S^u(w_u)$ supply curve (see panel a of figure 3.3). As long as $w_u > w_u^*$, this implies that employment is demand determined, for in this range demand constitutes the short end of the market. Since the central bank knows that this will be the ex-post response of union members, it is tempted to use monetary policy in order to boost employment up toward N_u^* and the inflationary bias reappears.

In most countries, including the United States, the labor market is composed of unionized as well as of competitive segments. It is therefore important to determine under what circumstances the existence of a partially unionized labor market will induce an inflationary bias on the part of an employment-concerned central bank. The following discussion clarifies this issue.

Consider a labor market composed of a unionized and of a competitive segment. Suppose that as is the case in most western economies, the nominal wage rate in the unionized sector is preset through nominal contracting. Let the real wage rate in the competitive segment adjust continually so as to clear this segment of the labor market.[12] The union aims at achieving the real wage $\hat{w}_u$. Panels a and b of figure 3.3 describe the no-intervention equilibrium in the unionized and nonunionized segments of the labor market. The contract nominal wage rate in the unionized sector is determined as in section 3.5. Given what it expects about the rate of inflation between the time it contracts and the time the contract applies to, the union sets the contract nominal wage so as to attain the real wage $\hat{w}_u$. Once the nominal wage is set, the central bank can erode the real wage rate and push employment in the unionized sector toward N_u^*. But the decrease in real union wages triggers changes in the demand for labor in the competitive segment. To the extent that union and nonunion labor are substitutes in production, a decrease in the price of one type of labor decreases the demand for the other type. More precisely, let $D^u(w_u, w_c)$ and $D^c(w_u, w_c)$ be the demand functions for union and nonunion labor, respectively. Let D_j^i, $i, j = u, c$, be the partial derivative of demand in the ith segment of the labor market with respect to the jth real wage. The hypothesis of substitutability between the two kinds of labor and the negativity of own price effects can be formulated as

$$D_u^c > 0, \quad D_c^u > 0, \tag{3.12a}$$

$$D_u^u < 0, \quad D_c^c < 0. \tag{3.12b}$$

In the absence of intervention equations (3.13) below determine the employment levels in the two sectors and the real wage rate in the competitive segment of the labor market for a given value of the real wage rate $\hat{w}_u$ chosen by the union

$$\hat{N}_u = D^u(\hat{w}_u, \hat{w}_c), \tag{3.13a}$$

$$\hat{N}_c = D^c(\hat{w}_u, \hat{w}_c) = S^c(\hat{w}_c). \tag{3.13b}$$

Here N_u and N_c are the employment levels in the unionized and competitive segments of the labor market and $S^c(w_c)$ is labor supply in the competitive segment. The function $S^u(w_u)$ represents labor supply in the unionized segment when the union members act as wage takers and make their labor supply decisions individually rather than collectively.

Consider now what would happen if, after the conclusion of nominal contracts, the central bank manages to surprise the union and to decrease its real wage below $\hat{w}_u$. Since there is continual clearing in the competitive segment of the labor market, the nominal wage rate in this market always adjusts so as to clear this segment. But the change in w_u induces a shift in the demand for labor in the competitive segment of the labor market. As a result the equilibrium real wage in that segment changes—which induces an additional feedback on the equilibrium of the unionized segment.

To determine the effect of a decrease in w_u on total employment, we perform a comparative statics experiment with respect to w_u. The resulting expression is

$$\frac{dN}{dw_u} \equiv \frac{dN_u}{dw_u} + \frac{dN_c}{dw_u} = \frac{1}{S_c^c - D_c^c}[(D_u^u + D_u^c)S_c^c - (D_u^u D_c^c - D_c^u D_u^c)]. \tag{3.14}$$

A decrease in w_u stimulates total employment provided that the term in brackets on the right-hand side of (3.14) is negative. Given equations (3.12), jointly sufficient conditions for this to be the case are $D_u^u + D_u^c < 0$ and $D_u^u D_c^c - D_c^u D_u^c > 0$. Even if $D_u^u + D_u^c \geq 0$, the expression in equation (3.14) will be negative provided that S_c^c is small.[13] The economic content of those conditions is that employment is a decreasing function of the real wage rate if own effects dominate cross effects in labor demands or if the supply of labor in the competitive segment of the labor market is relatively irresponsive to the real wage rate, or if both conditions hold. We will henceforth assume that at least one of those conditions holds so that the central bank is able to stimulate total employment by decreasing the real wage rate.

Indeed under these conditions the employment-motivated inflationary bias of monetary policy reappears.

If the competitive segment of the labor market is also characterized by contracts, there is an additional effect over and above those discussed above. When the price level rises, the real wage decreases below its market-clearing level, and employment becomes constrained by supply. Hence there is a decrease in employment in the competitive segment of the labor market. However, if the supply curve is relatively inelastic, this effect is small and may still be dominated by the expansionary effects of inflation in the unionized sector of the labor market. Recall that in this sector the slope of labor demand determines the extent of expansion in employment. Hence, if the demand for labor in the unionized sector is sufficiently more elastic than the supply of labor to the competitive segment of the labor market, surprise inflation stimulates total employment and the inflationary bias of policy remains.

Minimum wage legislation is also likely to induce an inflationary policy bias provided that it is legislated in nominal terms, which is usually the case. Such legislation is binding only in those parts of the labor market in which the market-clearing wage is lower than the minimum wage. The inflationary bias of policy can be derived by reinterpreting panel a of figure 3.3 as that part of the labor market in which the minimum-wage legislation is binding and panel b of the figure as the rest of the labor market. In this case $\hat{w}_u$ should be reinterpreted as the real wage that would emerge in the first segment of the labor market in the absence of inflation. The inflationary bias result then follows by noting the complete analogy between this case and the case in which the labor market is partially unionized.

There is an old literature that attributes inflation to the existence of unions (a survey appears in Bronfenbrenner and Holzman 1963, sec. 3). This literature has correctly been criticized on the grounds that unions may bring about a high price level, but there is no reason to believe that they cause a rising price level. This section implies that when the interaction between the central bank and the labor market is taken into consideration, the notion that inflation will be higher in the presence of union power is not totally off the mark. However, that literature did not provide an explanation for the central bank's tendency to inflate in the presence of unions. The analysis in this section provides the missing link.

3.7 The Social Welfare versus the Political Approach to Central Bank Behavior

The recent literature on monetary policy games has given two competing interpretations to the objective function of monetary policymakers in equation (3.1). One part of the literature regards this function as a social welfare function and the central bank as a benevolent social planner (Kydland and Prescott 1977; Barro and Gordon 1983a, 1983b; Backus and Driffill 1983b; Rogoff 1985; and to some extent Canzoneri 1985). The other part views the central bank as a mediator between different interest groups that try to push monetary policy in various, not necessarily consistent, directions. In this view the objective function in equation (3.1) reflects a distributionally motivated political compromise reached through the central bank between the advocates of employment stimulation and the advocates of price stability (Weintraub 1978; Burns 1979; Kane 1980, 1982; Beck 1982; Wooley 1984; Hetzel 1985; Cukierman and Meltzer 1986a; Cukierman 1986; Havrilesky 1987; Willet 1988; Mayer 1990). The coefficient A then reflects the relative political clout of the two groups (Cukierman and Meltzer 1986a; Cukierman 1986).

The rationale for the social welfare approach to the modeling of central bank objectives rests on the notion that due to distortionary taxes or union power, or both, employment is lower than its socially optimal level and on the social costs of inflation. The negative effect of inflation on social welfare results from the familiar loss of consumer surplus that inflation produces through the decrease in the public's real money balances.

The social welfare approach seems best suited to describe how a central bank should behave when all individuals in the economy are identical. However, it is a relatively weak paradigm for explaining the actual policies chosen by central bankers. In most countries central banks are highly dependent on the government in general and the treasury or ministry of finance in particular.[14] As a result the policies implemented by central bankers in those countries are not independent from the general political process in which distributional considerations hold the center stage. The impact of these considerations on the choice of policy varies with the bank's independence level. The higher the level of independence given to the bank by law, the smaller will be the impact of distributional and other political considerations on monetary policy. But even the Fed with its high degree of statutory independence is not totally divorced from the general political process. There is evidence that the Fed responds to the wishes of the president (Beck 1982; Havrilesky 1987; Alesina and Sachs 1988) and sets policy so as not to alienate Congress to which it is legally accountable (Kane 1980, 1982; Hetzel 1989). Former Chairman of the Board of Governors Arthur Burns shares the view that the Fed is not immune to political influences. He believes that the Fed can work to achieve price stability only if the policy does not adversely affect production and employment and does not irritate Congress. In Burns' words, the role of the Fed is to continue "probing the limits of its freedom to undernourish ... inflation" (Burns 1979, p. 16).

The social welfare approach to central bank behavior also raises a number of conceptual problems, the first two of which relate to the notion that distortionary labor taxes necessarily induce an inflationary bias on the part of a socially minded central bank.[15] First, this notion relies only on the distortionary effect of taxes on the allocation of time between labor and leisure, neglecting the utility from the public good that is financed by these taxes. Since individuals take the level of the public good provided by government as being independent from their individual labor-leisure decisions, while the central bank takes into consideration that this level depends on total tax collections—which depend in turn on total employment—there is also an externality.

If the socially optimal level of the public good is higher than the amount that can be financed through the taxes collected in the absence of central bank intervention, the bank has an incentive to increase total tax collections. Whether this implies that it has an incentive to increase or decrease employment depends on the tax structure and the elasticity of labor demand. In the latter case the tax distortion and the public good externality have conflicting effects on the socially optimal level of employment in relation to its general equilibrium level in the absence of central bank intervention. Cukierman and Drazen (1987) show, within a nominal contracts framework, that if the demand for labor is sufficiently inelastic, the last effect dominates, producing an incentive to decrease employment via unanticipated deflation. Furthermore the range of cases in which the central bank turns out not to have an inflationary bias is by no means negligible.[16]

Second, if the level of employment is too low because of distortionary taxes, a full analysis of the behavior of policymakers should be able to determine simultaneously both inflation and other taxes, taking into consideration the tax revenues from inflation. When this is done, the socially optimal rate of inflation is no longer zero. Such an analysis, with separate fiscal and monetary authorities, appears in Alesina and Tabellini (1987).

Because of these problems and its better descriptive realism, the political approach to central bank behavior is adopted as the ruling paradigm in the remainder of the book. An additional advantage of this approach will become apparent when (as is the case in parts II and III) there is more than one possible type of central banker, and the public does not know, at least initially, what is the type currently in office. The social welfare function interpretation of policymakers' objectives does not fit very well with the notion that there is more than one type of policymaker. One possibility might be that there are several potential social welfare functions that characterize the economy. If that is the case, however, it seems peculiar that the relevant one is known only to policymakers. Indeed, this possibility seems untenable. By contrast, potential differences in emphasis on alternative objectives fit quite well with the political approach in which the emphasis on alternative objectives is in a constant state of flux. They also fit quite naturally with the notion that the public may not be fully informed about the current attitudes of the central bank toward inflation and economic activity.

4 The Revenue Motive for Monetary Expansion

4.1 Introduction

To this point we have abstracted from the fact that monetary expansion is a means of financing government expenditures. The ability of government to borrow from the central bank is often restricted by various institutional devices. But there are substantial cross-country variations in the extent to which the government is allowed to borrow from the central bank (CB). In countries such as Germany and the United States there are strict limitations on government borrowing from the CB, and they are well adhered to. Hence the importance of the revenue motive in such countries is small relative to the employment motive. However, in many other countries the government is entitled to borrow directly from the central bank and utilizes this privilege to finance a nonnegligible fraction of its budget. In particular, countries with relatively narrow capital markets whose governments cannot issue substantial amounts of debt tend to rely more heavily on seigniorage to finance budgetary deficits. In some cases even countries with relatively strict legal limitations on government borrowing at the CB rely substantially on such borrowings due to poor compliance with the law. Detailed information about legal limitations on borrowing at the CB in seventy countries appears in chapter 19, section 19.2. The extent of adherence to the law is discussed in chapter 22, section 22.3.

Seigniorage revenues are defined as the amount of real resources bought by the government by means of new base money injections. Denoting by M and P the stock of base money and the price level, respectively, seigniorage revenues are given by

$$S \equiv \frac{\dot{M}}{P} = \frac{\dot{M}}{M}\frac{M}{P} = \mu L(\pi^e), \tag{4.1}$$

where μ is the rate of monetary growth, $L(\cdot)$ is the demand for real base money balances, π^e is the expected rate of inflation, and $\dot{M}$ denotes the time derivative of M. The last equality in equation (4.1) follows from the money market equilibrium condition. By analogy to public finance, μ is usually referred to as the tax rate and $L(\cdot)$ as the tax base.

Table 4.1 presents evidence on average seigniorage and inflation for seventy-nine countries during the period 1971–82. Seigniorage is measured in terms of the increase in base money as a percentage of total government revenues inclusive of the increase in base money. Inflation is defined as the rate of change in the consumer price index. The table shows that the extent

Table 4.1
Seigniorage and inflation: Average 1971–82 (percentages)

Country	Seigniorage	Inflation	Country	Seigniorage	Inflation
Australia	3.0	10.4	Malaysia	7.3	6.2
Austria	2.7	6.2	Mauritania	3.0	0.1
Belgium	1.8	7.5	Mauritius	10.6	14.6
Bolivia	21.6	30.3	Mexico	23.9	21.2
Botswana	3.6	11.4	Morocco	7.3	9.0
Brazil	17.7	47.4	Netherlands	1.1	7.1
Burma	15.2	9.9	New Zealand	1.6	13.0
Burundi	6.4	12.1	Nicaragua	8.8	16.8
Cameroon	5.1	10.8	Niger	9.4	12.2
Canada	3.0	8.6	Nigeria	7.2	15.5
Central African Republic	20.0	10.5	Norway	2.1	9.0
Chad	9.5	10.1	Oman	4.4	9.3
Chile	17.5	147.6	Pakistan	12.8	12.0
Colombia	17.1	22.0	Papua, New Guinea	0.4	8.6
Congo, People's Republic	4.6	9.7	Paraguay	15.4	12.8
Cote d'Ivoire	1.1	11.5	Peru	20.7	38.2
Denmark	0.7	10.0	Philippines	6.7	14.3
Dominican Republic	6.7	10.0	Portugal	16.6	18.8
Ecuador	14.4	13.2	Rwanda	10.3	12.5
El Salvador	11.4	11.2	South Africa	2.8	11.3

Ethiopia	9.6	9.0	Sierra Leone	9.5	13.7
Finland	1.6	11.2	Singapore	8.8	6.6
France	2.1	10.1	Somalia	15.4	18.8
Gabon	3.6	12.0	Spain	9.1	14.9
West Germany	2.5	5.2	Sri Lanka	7.1	9.8
Ghana	28.0	47.8	Sudan	16.9	18.7
Greece	14.6	15.8	Sweden	2.2	9.4
Honduras	5.8	8.3	Tanzania	9.3	16.4
India	13.1	8.4	Thailand	7.9	9.8
Indonesia	9.0	16.7	Togo	10.3	11.1
Iran	12.9	14.3	Trinidad and Tobago	4.2	13.0
Ireland	5.8	14.5	Tunisia	4.9	6.9
Italy	12.4	14.7	Turkey	15.3	33.6
Jamaica	4.7	17.0	Uganda	24.8	34.3
Japan	8.3	8.2	United Kingdom	1.7	13.2
Jordan	20.9	10.7	United States	2.3	7.9
Kenya	4.5	12.7	Venezuela	5.7	9.2
Kuwait	2.6	8.9	Zaire	15.5	42.8
Lesotho	2.4	0.1	Zambia	2.6	11.5
			Zimbabwe	4.0	8.3

Source: Cukierman, Edwards, and Tabellini (1992).
Note: Seigniorage is defined as the increase in base money as a percentage of total government revenues, including the increase in base money.

to which countries use money creation to finance their expenditures varies widely, with some countries relying on seigniorage to cover over 25 percent of their revenues. The table also points to a very wide range of inflationary experiences.

There are at least three approaches to the determinants of seigniorage revenues. One views seigniorage as one among several taxes and derives its magnitude from considerations of efficient taxation that are designed to minimize total tax distortions. This approach is discussed briefly in section 7.5 of chapter 7. After a brief review of the Laffer-type trade-off between the seigniorage tax rate and its tax base, this chapter focuses on dynamic inconsistency aspects of seigniorage and public debt and on the effect of political instability on seigniorage. Section 4.2 describes the Cagan (1956)-Bailey (1956) well-known trade-off between the seigniorage tax rate and tax base and notes the puzzling fact that in a number of cases the rate of monetary expansion was higher than the rate that maximizes steady state seigniorage revenues. An explanation for this fact which relies on dynamic inconsistency is presented in section 4.3. This section also shows that precommitment of policy eliminates the puzzling behavior mentioned above. The additional inflationary temptations that are due to the existence of nominal debt are discussed in section 4.4.

The next three sections take up the relationship between political instability and the structure of the economy, on the one hand, and the tendency to rely on seigniorage as a source of government revenue, on the other.[1] Section 4.5 presents a simple model in which seigniorage depends, through the efficiency of the tax system, on political instability and polarization and on structural features of the economy. The existence of polarization and political instability induce governments to devise tax systems that are not always as efficient as feasible in view of the structure of the economy. This aspect of the theory and its implications for seigniorage are discussed in section 4.6. Empirical evidence is presented in section 4.7. This is followed by concluding remarks.

4.2 The Cagan-Bailey Analysis and the Seemingly Irrational Behavior of High-Inflation Governments

It is well known that past a sufficiently high rate of inflation further increases in the rate of monetary expansion decrease seigniorage revenues at least in the steady state. This is due to the fact that a permanent rise in the tax rate, once understood, raises inflationary expectations. At sufficiently high rates of inflation the increase in inflationary expectations reduces the tax base $L(\cdot)$ by more than the increase in μ. As a consequence seigniorage revenues drop. It is obviously important to know in particular instances at what point seigniorage revenues stop going up with further accelerations in the rate of monetary growth and start going down. An answer to this question for eight episodes of hyperinflation in Europe was given in Cagan's (1956) classic study of hyperinflation for steady state situations. The steady state is characterized by the condition that actual and expected inflation are equal. The money market equilibrium condition implies that in the absence of real growth, actual inflation is equal to the rate of monetary growth. Hence in a no-growth steady state

$$\pi^e = \pi = \mu. \tag{4.2}$$

We combine (4.2) and (4.1) so that steady state seigniorage revenues may be expressed as

$$S = \mu L(\mu). \tag{4.1a}$$

Maximal steady state seigniorage revenues are achieved when the rate of monetary expansion is set at the level for which the elasticity of real money demand with respect to its argument is equal to unity in absolute value.

Cagan posited a semilogarithmic money demand function of the form

$$L(\pi^e) = \exp(-\alpha\pi^e) \tag{4.3}$$

and estimated the coefficient α for each of the countries in his sample. Noting that $-\alpha\pi^e$ is the elasticity of money demand with respect to expected inflation and using equation (4.3) in equation (4.1a), steady state seigniorage revenues are maximized when

$$\alpha\mu = 1 \quad \text{or} \quad \mu = \frac{1}{\alpha}. \tag{4.4}$$

Cagan's money demand function implies that seigniorage revenues initially rise with monetary expansion, reach a maximum at $\mu = 1/\alpha$, and then gradually decrease. Figure 4.1 illustrates the relationship between steady state seigniorage and monetary expansion.

Cagan's estimates of α imply that in most of the hyperinflations he examined the rates of monetary expansion actually observed were higher than $1/\alpha$, implying that governments could increase their seigniorage re-

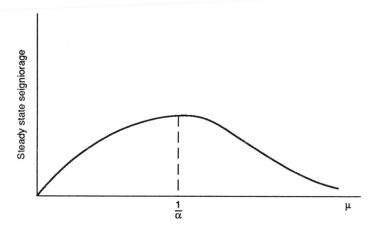

Figure 4.1
Steady state seigniorage as a function of monetary expansion for a semilogarithmic demand
for money

venues by lowering their rates of monetary expansion but failed to do so.
Later studies by Sargent (1977) and Christiano (1987), which came up with
revised estimates of α for some of the countries in Cagan's sample, do not
alter this basic conclusion. The tendency of governments to inflate at rates
beyond $1/\alpha$ has also appeared in some recent high-inflation episodes in
Israel and in some Latin American countries.[2]

This behavior of central bankers or of the governmental authorities that
forced them to increase the money supply at such high rates does not seem
rational. By slowing down the rate of monetary expansion, they could have
decreased inflation and increased seigniorage revenues. Yet they failed to
do so. One explanation for this phenomenon relies on a combination of
rational, but lagging, inflationary expectations with policymakers who
have a strong degree of positive time preference. Since expectations are
lagging, policymakers have the ability to temporarily raise seigniorage
revenues even if such policy eventually reduces those revenues. Since they
have a strong time preference, policymakers also have the incentive to
engage on such a course of action. Cukierman (1988b) contains an explanation along those lines and an extensive documentation of the view that
there were substantial lags in the adjustment of inflationary expectations
during the post–World War I German hyperinflation. This point of view
implies that once expectations have adjusted, there is no more point in
continuing to inflate at hyperinflationary rates. At that point the au-

thorities decide to stabilize. The fact (documented in tables 1 and 2 of Cukierman 1988b) that during most of the German hyperinflation sei-gniorage revenues rose with the rate of monetary expansion also supports this point of view.

However, there is also an additional explanation for inflation at rates above $1/\alpha$ in figure 4.1 that does not rely on imperfect information. It is based instead on a dynamic inconsistency of monetary policy in the context of the revenue motive. This type of dynamic inconsistency was first analyzed by Calvo (1978) and later on by Barro (1983). It is taken up in the next section.

4.3 A Seigniorage-Related Dynamic Inconsistency of Monetary Policy under Discretion and the Effect of Precommitments

Consider a government whose objectives are positively related to the amount of seigniorage revenues it gets and negatively related to both actual and expected inflation. Equation (4.5) presents a formalization of such an objective function

$$\delta S - \phi(\pi, \pi^e), \qquad \delta > 0, \ \phi_\pi > 0, \ \phi_\pi e > 0. \tag{4.5}$$

The use of the term "government" rather than "central bank" is deliberate since, when the extraction of seigniorage is the main motive for inflation, decisions about the money supply are normally dominated by the executive branch of government rather than by the central bank. To reflect this tendency, we use the term "policymakers" or "government" to denote the institution that makes decisions about the supply of base money.

The postulated negative effect of π^e on government's objectives is due, among other things, to the fact that with higher inflationary expectations there is a welfare cost associated with decreased money holdings by the public. This is the familiar "shoe leather" cost of perfectly anticipated inflation. The negative effect of actual inflation proxies, among other things, for the loss of regular tax revenues triggered by higher inflation in the absence of base structure indexing[3] as well as for other undesired redistributions. δ is a parameter that measures the relative importance attributed by government to seigniorage revenues and to the costs of inflation. Substituting equation (4.1) into equation (4.5) government's objective function becomes

$$\delta \mu L(\pi^e) - \phi(\pi, \pi^e). \tag{4.5a}$$

The dynamic inconsistency of monetary policy arises because the incentives of government to inflate change before and after the public has chosen the level of real money balances. Before the public commits itself to a given level of real balances, government takes into consideration the downward effect that a higher rate of inflation has on real money balances and therefore on the tax base. But, after this choice has been made, government takes the level of real money balances as given and reoptimizes. To make this effect more precise, suppose that expectations, and therefore real money balances, are chosen at the beginning of the period for the period. Subsequently, during the period, government picks μ taking expectations π^e as given. Since $L(\pi^e)$ is given, the money market equilibrium condition implies that $\mu = \pi$.[4] Hence government's problem after expectations have been set is

$$\max_{\mu} \delta\mu L(\pi^e) - \phi(\mu, \pi^e), \tag{4.5b}$$

with corresponding first-order condition

$$\delta L(\pi^e) - \phi_\pi(\mu, \pi^e) = 0. \tag{4.6}$$

This equation provides an implicit solution for μ as a function of π^e which is government's ex-post reaction function. When it sets the expected rate of inflation at the beginning of the period, the public knows that after it commits to a certain level of real balances, money growth and inflation will be determined by equation (4.6). Since there is no uncertainty, any expectation that does not induce government to pick $\mu = \pi = \pi^e$ is not rational. Hence in a rational expectations equilibrium this equality must hold. Combining it with government's reaction function in equation (4.6) and rearranging, we obtain

$$\eta = \frac{L'(\mu)}{L(\mu)}\mu = \frac{\delta}{\phi_\pi(\mu, \mu)}\mu L'(\mu), \tag{4.7}$$

where the left-hand side is the elasticity η of money demand with respect to expected inflation and $L'(\cdot)$ is the derivative of real money demand with respect to its argument. Examination of this equation reveals that if $\delta/\phi_\pi(\cdot)$ is sufficiently large, government will choose to operate in a range of inflation in which the elasticity η is larger than one in absolute value. This implies that if government values seigniorage revenues a lot in comparison to its marginal valuation of the costs of inflation, rates of monetary expansion and of inflation may be in a range in which steady state seigniorage revenue could be increased by lowering the rate of monetary expansion.

An example may help clarify this result. Suppose that money demand assumes the semilogarithmic form in equation (4.3) and that the function $\phi(\cdot)$ takes the particular form

$$\phi(\pi, \pi^e) = \exp(\gamma_1 \pi + \gamma_2 \pi^e). \tag{4.8}$$

In this case the equilibrium level of monetary expansion is (from equation 4.7)

$$\mu = \frac{\ln[\delta/\gamma_1]}{\alpha + \gamma_1 + \gamma_2}. \tag{4.9}$$

Recall from figure 4.1 that any rate of monetary growth above $1/\alpha$ is inefficient from government's point of view since inflation can be brought down and seigniorage revenues increased by decreasing the rate of money growth to $1/\alpha$. It is easily seen from equation (4.9) that government may choose to operate in this range if δ/γ_1 is sufficiently large.

Why does government operate in this range despite its obvious inefficiency in terms of its own objectives? The answer is that in the absence of commitments government follows the best course once expectations have been set, and knowing that, the public expects such behavior in advance and picks its money balances in accordance. The inability to commit monetary policy prior to the choice of real balances induces an inefficient equilibrium in terms of government's own objectives. Thus in the absence of commitments the dynamic inconsistency of monetary policy provides a way to understand the fact that during some hyperinflations rates of monetary growth penetrated and stayed substantially above the rate $1/\alpha$ in figure 4.1. Such inefficient outcomes indicate that at the time the inflating governments had a very high valuation of seigniorage relative to their aversion to the costs of inflation.

The inefficient equilibrium occurs because during the period government optimizes for a given real money demand. However, prior to the choice of money demand by the public, government takes the effect of its action on expectations and money demand into consideration. If government can commit its action for the period already at this stage, it will never choose to operate in the inefficient range. The following discussion establishes this result.

In the presence of commitments government announces the rate of inflation for the period prior to the choice of money balances by the public and actually delivers this rate during the period. Since government's ability to commit is common knowledge, the announcement is credible. It therefore affects the choice of real money balances by the public so that government's decision problem in (4.5) now becomes[5]

$$\max_{\mu} \ [\delta\mu L(\mu) - \phi(\mu, \mu)]. \tag{4.10}$$

The crucial difference between this expression and the one obtained in the absence of a commitment is that now government possesses the ability to influence the public's expectations. Essentially by giving away its discretion to change policy within the period government gains an additional ex-ante policy instrument. The first-order condition necessary for the maximization of (4.10) is

$$\delta \frac{\partial}{\partial\mu} [\mu L(\mu)] = \phi_{\pi} + \phi_{\pi} e. \tag{4.11}$$

Since the right-hand side of (4.11) is positive (by equation 4.5), it follows that

$$\frac{\partial}{\partial\mu} [\mu L(\mu)] > 0.$$

That is, in the presence of a credible commitment, the rate of monetary growth chosen by government is always in the efficient range. Hence an advance commitment by government resolves the dynamic inconsistency associated with the revenue motive under discretion.

4.4 Nominal Debt and Dynamic Inconsistency

The presence of nominal debt whose real value can be reduced by unanticipated inflation reinforces the incentive of government to inflate under discretion. But, in the presence of credible commitments, the existence of debt does not alter the behavior of government. This section derives and explicates the intuitive bases for those results.

Suppose that prior to the formation of expectations, government desires to issue a quantity of bonds whose real value is b. Suppose further that the real rate of interest at which the public is willing to hold those bonds is r.

Hence, if the rate of inflation that is expected for the period is π^e, the nominal rate demanded by the public is

$$n(\pi^e) = r + \pi^e. \tag{4.12}$$

The revenue part of government's objective function in equation (4.5) is respecified so as to recognize that govermnent has now additional expenses in the form of nominal interest payments on the debt but also an additional nominal asset whose real value can be reduced by inflating. This is the content of equation (4.13):

$$\delta\{S + [\pi - n(\pi^e)]b\} - \phi(\pi, \pi^e). \tag{4.13}$$

Under discretion the real demand for money is taken as predetermined by policymakers. Hence, as was the case in the previous section, $\mu = \pi$ and the within-period maximization problem of the government can be formulated as

$$\max_{\mu} G \equiv \max_{\mu} \{\delta[\mu L(\pi^e) + (\mu - n(\pi^e))b] - \phi(\mu, \mu^e)\}. \tag{4.13a}$$

Within the period government takes the nominal interest rate as predetermined. Hence the first-order condition for the maximization problem in (4.13a) is

$$G_\mu \equiv \delta[L(\pi^e) + b] - \phi_\pi(\mu, \pi^e) = 0. \tag{4.14}$$

Since $\mu = \pi$ and since in equilibrium the public correctly anticipates the rate of inflation in advance,

$$\pi^e = \mu. \tag{4.15}$$

Combining (4.14) and (4.15), we obtain

$$\delta[L(\mu) + b] - \phi_\pi(\mu, \mu) = 0, \tag{4.14a}$$

which impicitly determines μ as a function of b. Then performing a comparative statics experiment with respect to b on equation (4.14a), we obtain

$$\frac{d\mu}{db} = -\frac{\delta}{G_{\mu\mu}},$$

which is positive since $G_{\mu\mu}$ is negative by the second-order condition for maximization of the problem in (4.13a). Hence, at least locally, a larger debt induces government to inflate at higher rates under discretion. The intuitive reason is that the presence of a larger debt increases the effectiveness of inflation as a revenue-raising device for government. It therefore pays policymakers to inflate at a higher rate.

We turn next to the case in which government is able to precommit to a given rate of inflation before the public decides on the quantity of money and of bonds to be carried into the period. Prior to those decisions government announces a rate of inflation π^a. Since it is credibly precommited, government is believed and

$$\pi^e = \pi^a. \tag{4.16}$$

Those expectations determine the real quantity of money to be carried into the period at $L(\pi^a)$ and the nominal interest rate for the period at $n = r + \pi^a$. Since real money demand within the period is predetermined, the money market equilibrium condition implies that government must expand the money supply at the rate π^a in order to deliver on its promise that inflation will be π^a. Hence

$$\mu = \pi^a. \tag{4.17}$$

Equations (4.16) and (4.17) imply that

$$L(\pi^e) = L(\pi^a) = L(\mu) \quad \text{and} \quad n(\pi^e) = n(\pi^a) = r + \mu. \tag{4.18}$$

Hence government's problem in the presence of precommitments is, using (4.18) in (4.13),

$$\max_{\mu} \{\delta[\mu L(\mu) - rb] - \phi(\mu, \mu)\}. \tag{4.19}$$

Since the choice of μ has no effect on the real rate r, this problem is equivalent to problem (4.10) in the previous section whose solution does not depend on the quantity of bonds outstanding.

The final conclusion is that in the presence of credible commitments, the outstanding quantity of bonds has no effect on the propensity of government to inflate. The intuitive reason is that when it has to commit in advance to a certain rate of inflation, government takes into consideration that any inflation-induced decrease in the value of the debt is fully compensated by an appropriate increase in the nominal rate of interest. Hence there is no net revenue gain from decreases in the value of the debt at the margin. By contrast, when government retains the discretion to choose monetary growth within the period, the size of the debt affects its choice of monetary growth since it optimizes taking the nominal interest rate as given.

4.5 Seigniorage, Political Instability, and the Structure of the Economy

We saw in the introduction to this chapter that there are substantial and persistent cross-country differences in the relative importance of seigniorage as a source of government revenue. This raises a natural question about the origin of these differences. How can we explain, for example, that during the period 1971–82 seigniorage constituted over 21 percent of government revenues including seigniorage in Bolivia, about 11 percent in El Salvador, and less than 2 percent in the Netherlands?

A fundamental determinant of the degree of reliance on seigniorage is the efficiency of the tax system. The larger the costs associated with the collection of taxes, the stronger is the incentive of policymakers to use seigniorage as a source of government revenue. This basic, but obvious, observation leads to a further question about the factors that determine the efficiency of the tax system. A traditional answer is that the efficiency of tax systems is determined by structural and institutional factors. The sectoral composition of GNP, the general level of development of the economy, and the degree of urbanization are examples of such structural features. Agricultural sectors are hard to tax due to relatively high collection costs. In the mining and manufacturing sectors these costs are relatively small. It is also relatively easy to collect taxes on foreign trade, since the taxes can be administered at relatively little cost at the points of entry and exit from the country. Hence we should expect countries with large agricultural sectors to have relatively inefficient tax systems and countries with large mining, manufacturing, and foreign trade sectors to possess more efficient tax systems. A high level of urbanization and of economic development also makes it more likely that it is easier to collect taxes.[6]

The efficiency of the tax system is also affected by the degree of political instability and polarization. An inefficient tax system (i.e., one that facilitates tax evasion and imposes high tax collection costs) acts as a constraint on the revenue-collecting ability of the government. This constraint may be welcome by those who disagree with the goals pursued by the current government. In particular previous governments (or legislative majorities) may deliberately choose to maintain an inefficient tax system so as to constrain the behavior of future governments (or majorities) with which they might disagree. Of course this is more likely to happen in countries with more unstable and polarized political systems.

The structuralist and political explanations for the efficiency of tax systems in conjunction with the view that reliance on seigniorage is heavier in countries with less efficient tax structures lead to the following empirically testable implication: After controlling for the structure of the economy and its stage of development, more unstable and polarized countries collect a larger fraction of their revenues by means of seigniorage compared to stabler and more homogeneous societies. This idea is modeled more precisely in the remainder of this section. The implications of the model are developed in the following section, and empirical evidence is presented in section 4.7.

For simplicity the model features only the effects of political factors on the efficiency of the tax structure, and through it on seigniorage.[7] Its central feature is a distinction between fiscal policy and tax reforms. A fiscal policy is the choice of tax rates and the level and composition of government spending. A tax reform is the broad design of a tax system that determines the available tax bases and the technology for collecting taxes. Even though in practice it may be difficult to decide where to draw the line, this distinction has important implications at the conceptual level. A tax reform that changes the tax system will typically take time and resources, since it requires investment in the acquisition of information and in infrastructure as well as a possibly lengthy legislative process. A fiscal policy, on the other hand, can be implemented more swiftly. Thus, at any given moment in time, the existing tax system acts as a constraint on the fiscal policy of the current government. This suggests that tax reforms are also determined by strategic considerations: A tax system is designed by taking into account how it will constrain, and therefore partially precommit, the fiscal policies of future governments. The main idea is that, other things the same, if there is political instability and political polarization, these strategic considerations may induce the current government to leave to its successors a tax system that is not as efficient as is feasible in view of the structure of the economy.

The economy consists of a private and a public sector. The public sector utilizes its revenue to produce two different public goods. Individuals derive utility from private consumption and from both types of public goods. But there are two groups of individuals that differ in their relative preference for the two public goods. The budget constraints of the government and of the private sector are given, respectively, by

$$g_t + f_t \leq \tau_t(1 - \theta_{t-1}) + s_t, \tag{4.20}$$

$$c_t \leq 1 - \tau_t - s_t - \delta(\tau_t) - \gamma(s_t). \tag{4.21}$$

Subscripts denote time periods. Each individual is endowed with one unit of output in each period. g_t and f_t are the two different public goods in per capita terms, and c_t is private consumption, also per capita. The government collects from each individual an amount s_t in the form of seigniorage and an amount τ_t of tax revenue. The main difference between taxes and seigniorage is that a fraction θ_{t-1} of the tax revenue is wasted due to tax collection costs, whereas seigniorage carries no administrative costs. Both taxes and seigniorage impose deadweight losses on the private sector, equal to $\delta(\tau_t)$ and $\gamma(s_t)$, respectively. These distortions increase at an increasing rate. Thus $\delta'(\cdot) > 0$, $\delta''(\cdot) > 0$, $\gamma'(\cdot) > 0$, and $\gamma''(\cdot) > 0$.

In equation (4.20) θ_{t-1} is a rough measure of the efficiency of the tax system. A lower value of θ implies a more efficient tax system. Thus in this model a tax reform amounts to a choice of θ, whereas a fiscal policy is a choice of g, f, τ, and s. To capture the greater inertia in reforming the tax system than in changing fiscal policy, we assume that θ, but not the other policy variables, must be chosen one period in advance. Thus θ_{t-1} is chosen at time $t - 1$, but it exerts an influence on tax collection costs only at time t (see equation 4.20).

There are two possible policymaker types L and R who randomly alternate in office. The policymaker of type i, $i = L, R$ maximizes

$$W_t^i = E_t \left\{ \sum_{k=0}^{\infty} \beta^k [U(c_{t+k}) + H^i(g_{t+k}, f_{t+k})] \right\}, \qquad 1 > \beta > 0, \tag{4.22}$$

where $E_t(\cdot)$ denotes the expectation operator, $U(\cdot)$ is a concave and twice continuously differentiable utility function, and $H^i(\cdot)$ is defined as follows: If $i = L$,

$$H^L(g, f) = \frac{1}{\alpha(1 - \alpha)} \min[\alpha g, (1 - \alpha)f], \qquad 1 > \alpha > 0, \tag{4.23}$$

and if $i = R$, then $H^R(\cdot)$ is defined as in (4.23), but with α replaced by $(1 - \alpha)$. Thus these two policymaker types differ only in the desired composition of the public good. For simplicity their disagreement is parameterized by α. When $\alpha = 1/2$, the two policymaker types have identical objectives. The more distant is α from $1/2$, the more they disagree. By construction, the overall weight given to private versus public consumption does not depend on α. These two policymaker types can be viewed as representing different constituencies. The policymaker who assigns a larger weight to public good g is committed to serve the interest of individuals who derive relatively more utility from this good. The other policymaker is committed to represent the interest of individuals who obtain more utility from public good f.

The political system is described as a Markov process with transition probabilities π and $(1 - \pi)$. The government in office at time t has a fixed probability $(1 - \pi)$ of being reappointed next period. With probability π, it loses office, and the other policymaker type is appointed. For simplicity the link between individual voters and the probability of retaining or gaining office is not modeled explicitly.[8]

In this model, then, the political system has two important features: its instability, represented by the probability of losing office π, and the degree of polarization between the alternating governments, represented by the disagreement parameter α. As we will see in the next section, these two features determine (along with structural features) the equilibrium efficiency of the tax system.

We turn next to a characterization of the equilibrium choice of τ_t, s_t, g_t, and f_t for a given value of θ_{t-1}. The choice of θ is studied in the next section. Since, in each period, θ is predetermined by the decision of the previous government, the equilibrium values of τ, s, g, and f as a function of θ are found by solving the static problem of maximizing $[U(c) + H^i(g,f)]$ subject to (4.20) and (4.21). Time subscripts are omitted when superfluous. We only describe the equilibrium when type L is in office. For concreteness we assume that $\alpha > 1/2$. By symmetry the opposite case of R in office is obtained by replacing g with f. Party L always chooses the proportion of the two public goods so that

$$f^L = \frac{\alpha}{1 - \alpha} g^L, \qquad\qquad (4.24)$$

where the L superscripts remind us that party L is in office. Any other choice of this proportion would be a waste in view of party L's objective function in equation (4.23). It follows that total public expenditures by government L can be written

$$x^L \equiv f^L + g^L = \frac{g^L}{1 - \alpha}. \tag{4.25}$$

Equations (4.24) and (4.25) imply that

$$H^L(g, f) = \frac{1}{\alpha(1 - \alpha)} \min[\alpha(1 - \alpha)x, (1 - \alpha)\alpha x] = x \tag{4.26}$$

and

$$g^L = (1 - \alpha)x^L, \quad f^L = \alpha x^L. \tag{4.27}$$

In view of equation (4.26) the optimization problem of government L is

$$\max[U(c) + x]. \tag{4.28}$$

However, x is equal to total tax collections $(1 - \theta)\tau + s$, and since individuals do not waste resources, consumption c is equal to disposable income which is given by $1 - \tau - s - \delta(\tau) - \gamma(s)$. Hence the problem in equation (4.28) can be reformulated as

$$\max_{\tau, s} \{U[1 - \tau - s - \delta(\tau) - \tau(s)] + (1 - \theta)\tau + s\}. \tag{4.28a}$$

After some transformations, the first-order conditions for this problem are given by[9]

$$1 = U'(c)[1 + \gamma'(s)], \tag{4.29a}$$

$$1 + \gamma'(s) = \frac{1 + \delta'(\tau)}{1 - \theta}. \tag{4.29b}$$

Equation (4.29a) compares the marginal utility of public and private consumption. In the presence of distortionary taxes at an optimum the marginal utility of public consumption (unity) exceeds the marginal utility of private consumption. Equation (4.29b) is the Ramsey rule: It equates at the margin the distortions associated with the last dollar collected from each source of revenue. The two first-order conditions in equations (4.29) determine τ and s. Given these values, consumption is determined from the definition of disposable income in equation (4.21). Total public expenditures are determined from the government budget constraint

$$g^L + f^L = x^L = (1 - \theta)\tau + s. \tag{4.30}$$

Since the first-order conditions in equations (4.29) do not depend on the type of government in office, neither do τ and s. It follows (from equation 4.30) that total public expenditures and private consumption are the same under either type of government. The only difference between them concerns the allocation of the same level of public expenditures between the two public goods. Replacing α with $(1 - \alpha)$ in equation (4.28), we obtain

$$g^R = \alpha x, \quad f^R = (1 - \alpha)x, \tag{4.31}$$

where x is the (common across types of governments) equilibrium level of public expenditures.

Equations (4.21), (4.29), and (4.30) implicitly determine the equilibrium values of consumption, public spending, taxes, and seigniorage as functions of the efficiency of the tax system θ;

$$c^* = C(\theta), \quad x^* = X(\theta), \quad S^* = S(\theta), \quad \tau^* = T(\theta). \tag{4.32}$$

The effect of θ on those variables can be obtained by applying the implicit function theorem. Details appear in appendix A at the end of this chapter. Results are summarized in the following proposition:

PROPOSITION 4.1   Let a prime denote a partial derivative. Then

$$X'(\theta) < 0, \quad S'(\theta) > 0, \quad C'(\theta) > 0, \quad T'(\theta) < 0.$$

Thus, as suggested by intuition, a more inefficient tax system discourages public spending and forces the government to rely more on seigniorage and less on regular taxes as a source of revenue. Also a more inefficient tax system raises private consumption.[10] Proposition 4.1 plays an important role in the determination of the equilibrium value of θ. This is the topic of the next section.

4.6   Determination of the Efficiency of the Tax System and Its Effect on Seigniorage

We now turn to the question of how the efficiency of the tax system is determined in equilibrium. Since, by assumption, θ has to be set one period in advance and there is no cost in changing it, it is sufficient to look one period ahead in order to characterize the infinite horizon equilibrium. With probability $1 - \pi$, tomorrow type L is reappointed in office. In this case, by (4.22) and (4.26), his utility is

$$U(C(\theta_t)) + X(\theta_t),$$ (4.33)

where $X(\theta_t)$ is total public spending.[11] With probability π, type R is appointed tomorrow. By symmetry, $g^R = f^L$ and $f^R = g^L$. Hence, by (4.23) and (4.27), and given $\alpha > 1/2$, type L utility if out of office is

$$U(C(\theta_t)) + \frac{1-\alpha}{\alpha} X(\theta_t), \qquad \frac{1-\alpha}{\alpha} < 1.$$ (4.34)

Thus θ_t is chosen so as to maximize the following expected utility function (because of the symmetry of the model, this is also the utility function of type R when in office):

$$(1 - \pi_t)[U(C(\theta_t)) + X(\theta_t)] + \pi_t[U(C(\theta_t)) + \frac{1-\alpha}{\alpha} X(\theta_t)]$$

$$= U(C(\theta_t)) + \beta(\pi, \alpha) X(\theta_t),$$ (4.35)

where

$$0 \le \beta(\pi, \alpha) = (1 - \pi) + \frac{\pi(1 - \alpha)}{\alpha} \le 1.$$

The equilibrium value of θ satisfies the first-order condition

$$G(\theta, \pi, \alpha) \equiv U'(C(\theta))C'(\theta) + \beta(\pi, \alpha)X'(\theta) \le 0,$$ (4.36)

which holds with equality if $\theta > 0$. Time subscripts are omitted from now on since all periods are alike. The first term on the left-hand side of (4.36) is the marginal gain of raising the inefficiency of the tax system. Since $C'(\theta) > 0$, this gain takes the form of higher private consumption. The second term is the expected marginal cost of a more inefficient tax system that takes the form of reduced public consumption (recall that $X'(\theta) < 0$).

According to equation (4.36) the magnitude of this expected marginal cost depends on $\beta(\alpha, \pi)$. The following facts about $\beta(\cdot)$ are worth noting:

$$\beta_\pi(\pi, \alpha) < 0, \quad \beta_\alpha(\pi, \alpha) < 0, \quad \lim_{\substack{\alpha \to 1 \\ \pi \to 1}} \beta(\pi, \alpha) = 0,$$ (4.37)

where a subscript denotes a partial derivative. Thus (1) the more unstable and (2) the more polarized the political system, the lower the expected marginal cost of having an inefficient tax system. In the limit this marginal cost tends to zero as the political system becomes extremely unstable and polarized.

By equations (4.36) and (4.37), the equilibrium efficiency of the tax system $\theta*$ is a function of the stability and polarization of the tax system; $\theta* = \Theta(\pi, \alpha)$. The following proposition, whose proof appears in appendix B to this chapter, summarizes the effects of instability and polarization on the efficiency of the tax system:

PROPOSITION 4.2

1. In the absence of either instability or polarization, the tax system is as efficient as feasible; that is, $\Theta(0, \alpha) = \Theta(\pi, \frac{1}{2}) = 0$.

2. There exists a pair $\pi_0 < 1$ and $\alpha_0 < 1$ such that $\Theta(\pi, \alpha) > 0$ for any $\pi > \pi_0, \alpha > \alpha_0$.

3. If $\theta* > 0$, then $\Theta_\pi(\cdot) > 0$ and $\Theta_\alpha(\cdot) > 0$.

This proposition summarizes the central theoretical result of this section. If the current government is certain of being reappointed, or if there is no polarization, then it always brings about the most efficient tax system. However, with a sufficient degree of political instability or polarization, a more inefficient system may be preferred. More generally, the lower the probability is that the current government will remain in office and the greater the polarization, the more inefficient is the tax system left as a legacy to future governments. This happens for a purely strategic reason, and even though it is costless (by assumption) to improve the efficiency of next period's tax system; a more inefficient tax collection apparatus discourages future governments from collecting taxes and spending them on goods that are not valued by the incumbent policymakers. The equilibrium value of θ is chosen so as to equate the expected marginal benefit of constraining future governments to the marginal cost caused by inefficient taxation. When π decreases, the marginal cost of an inefficient tax system rises because the current government is more likely to be reappointed. This marginal cost also rises when α approaches 1/2, since with little polarization there is not much difference between the policies of the two governments. In both cases $\theta*$ decreases. Combining propositions 1 and 2 yields the following central empirical implication:

PROPOSITION 4.3   Countries with more unstable and polarized political systems rely more heavily on seigniorage as a source of revenue than more stable and homogeneous societies.

For simplicity the formal model has focused on the effect of political instability on the efficiency of the tax structure without explicitly modeling structurally caused cross-country differences in the efficiency of the tax system. The model can be extended to allow for such differences by postulating that there is a cost $\lambda h(1 - \theta)$ in terms of private consumption to maintain efficiency level $1 - \theta$. The effect of different sectoral structures and levels of development on the efficiency of the tax system is then captured through cross-country variations in the (positive) parameter λ. The larger the λ, the less conducive is the economic structure to the maintenance of an efficient tax system. Provided that $h(\cdot)$ is increasing at an increasing rate and subject to an additional mild restriction, propositions 4.1 through 4.3 hold also in the more general case. Moreover it can be shown that, other things the same, a higher λ leads to the choice of a less efficient tax structure (a higher θ) and therefore to a higher equilibrium level of seigniorage.

In the extended model, then, seigniorage is positively related to political instability and polarization and to structural factors that make it more costly to maintain an efficient tax system.[12] Empirical evidence regarding these implications is presented in the next section.

4.7 Evidence on Seigniorage, Economic Structure, and Political Instability

To test the implications of the theory developed in the previous two sections, seigniorage has to be related to structural factors that affect the efficiency of the tax system and to measures of political instability. This is done in two steps. First, the cross-country variability in seigniorage from table 4.1 is related only to structural and developmental economic variables. Then measures of political variables are added to the regressions and their additional contribution is evaluated.

In the first stage seigniorage is related to three categories of independent variables:

1. *The sectoral composition of gross domestic product, to account for differences in administering tax collection across sectors.* We expect the agricultural sector to be the hardest to tax and thus to have a positive coefficient in the regressions. The mining and manufacturing sectors are generally regarded as the easiest to tax and are thus expected to have a negative coefficient. The ratio of foreign trade to GNP is also included, since in many developing countries imports and exports are a cheap tax base; hence its coefficient is expected to be negative.

2. *Two measures of economic development, namely, GDP per capita and a dummy variable taking a value of* 1 *for the industrialized countries and* 0 *otherwise.* We expect both variables to have a negative coefficient, since the technology for enforcing tax collection is likely to be less efficient in less developed countries.

3. *A measure of urbanization.* Since tax collection costs are likely to be smaller in urban areas than in rural areas, we expect a negative coefficient. Most variables in the regressions are averaged over the period 1971–82. An exception is the measure of urbanization which is an average of two years, 1965 and 1985. The dependent variable seigniorage is defined (as in table 4.1) as the ratio of the increase in base money to total government revenues inclusive of seigniorage during the period 1971–82.

The results are reported in table 4.2 for alternative specifications of the regressions. The first three columns refer to all the countries in the sample. The last two columns refer to developing countries only. Most of the coefficients have the expected sign. One exception is the share of manufacturing and mining, which is positive, in column 5. Its coefficient is, however, insignificant. A second exception refers to the coefficient of urbanization, which is always positive and significant. There are two possible ways of interpreting this result. First, a higher degree of urbanization may result in an increase in "underground" economic activities, encouraging the use of the inflation tax. Alternatively, it is possible to interpret this result as providing preliminary evidence in favor of a political explanation of seigniorage differentials. As noted by political scientists, political awareness and political conflicts are likely to be more prominent in urban areas than in rural societies.

In column 3 of table 4.2 two dummies that group countries into continents are added. The Latin American dummy is positive and significant at the 5 percent level. This suggests that noneconomic variables play a role in explaining cross-country inflation differentials.

To implement the second stage, a measure of political instability, defined as the probability of a government change as perceived by the current government, is needed. This probability is unobservable. Cukierman, Edwards, and Tabellini (1992) construct a measure of political instability from the data of Charles L. Taylor and David A. Jodice (1983). These data contain yearly observations on regular and irregular (i.e., coups) government transfers, unsuccessful coup attempts, executive adjustments, and other political events. The measure of political instability is constructed by

Table 4.2
Seigniorage and structural variables

Explanatory variables	Seigniorage in all countries[a]			Seigniorage in developing countries only[b]	
	(1)	(2)	(3)	(4)	(5)
Intercept	0.0558 (0.0404)	0.1185** (0.0194)	0.0343 (0.0312)	0.0156 (0.0316)	−0.0167 (0.0696)
Agriculture	0.0014* (0.0006)	—	0.0017** (0.0006)	0.0020** (0.0006)	0.0024* (0.0011)
Mining and manufacturing	—	$-0.50E-4$ $(0.68E-3)$	—	—	0.0007 (0.0013)
Foreign trade	−0.0514** (0.0184)	−0.0626** (0.0184)	−0.0418* (0.0192)	−0.0546* (0.0190)	−0.0512* (0.0203)
GDP per capita	$-0.58E-5*$ $(0.25E-5)$	$-0.72E-5*$ $(0.30E-5)$	$-0.57E-5*$ $(0.25E-5)$	$-0.40E-5$ $(0.25E-5)$	$-0.55E-5$ $(0.39E-5)$
Urbanization	0.0014* (0.0004)	0.0010** (0.0004)	0.0011* (0.0004)	0.0022** (0.0004)	0.0023** (0.0005)
Industrialized	−0.0467* (0.0190)	−0.0511* (0.0203)			
Asia	—	—	0.0293 (0.0183)	—	—
Latin America	—	—	0.0430* (0.0210)	—	—
$\bar{R}^2$	0.333	0.281	0.357	0.369	0.360
Standard error of regression	0.054	0.056	0.053	0.052	0.052

Note: The dependent variable is seigniorage. Numbers in parentheses are standard errors. The method of estimation is ordinary least squares. An asterisk denotes significance at the 5 percent confidence level; two asterisks at the 1 percent level.
a. The number of countries observed was seventy-nine.
b. The number of developing countries was fifty-eight.

estimating a yearly probit model on time series data or on pooled time series and cross-country data over the period 1948–82. The dependent variable takes a value of 0 for the years in which there is no government change (regular or irregular) and a value of 1 otherwise. The explanatory variables in the probit model fall into three broad classes: economic variables designed to measure the recent economic performance of the government, political variables accounting for significant political events that may signal the imminence of a crisis, and structural variables accounting for institutional differences and country-specific factors that do not change or change only slowly over time. These structural variables consist of three dummy variables that group countries, according to their political institutions into (1) democracies, (2) democracies in which the election date is determined by the constitution, and (3) democracies ruled by a single majoritarian party. Even though these three groups are too broad to account for the variety of existing political institutions, at least they discriminate between very different constitutional environments. All these variables are defined in appendix C to this chapter.

Table 4.3 reports the results of the probit regression when all countries are pooled and a country-specific dummy is included. Most variables have the expected sign, even though only some are significant. In particular government change is made more likely by unusual inflation in the previous year and by unusually low growth of private consumption over the current and previous two years. Moreover riots, political repressions, adjustments in the composition of the executive, and unsuccessful attempts to change the government all signal the imminence of a political crisis. Two of the institutional dummies are significant. Democracies have more frequent government changes than nondemocratic regimes, and coalition governments or minority governments are less stable than majoritarian governments. Several of the country-specific dummies (not reported in the table) are also significant, indicating that there are additional factors contributing to instability of the political system that are not fully captured by the explanatory variables. These estimates are very robust to changes in the model specification.

Using the pooled time series, cross-country, and country-specific probit regressions, two alternative estimated frequencies of government change in each country during the period 1971–82 are computed. They are obtained by averaging the estimated probabilities of government change from each of the probit regressions over that time period. These two estimated fre-

Table 4.3
Probit estimates of the probability of government change, 1948–82

Explanatory variables	Dependent variable: Government change		
	Current	Lagged once	Lagged twice
Government change	—	−0.0793 (0.0822)	−0.0315 (0.0774)
Inflation	—	0.0020 (0.0012)	−0.0030 (0.0023)
Consumption growth	−0.3894 (0.2652)	—	—
Riots	0.0052 (0.0040)	−0.0016 (0.0040)	0.0060 (0.0037)
Repressions	0.0047** (0.0018)	−0.0013 (0.0009)	0.0019 (0.0013)
Executive adjustment	0.0828** (0.0242)	0.0493* (0.0234)	−0.0182 (0.0226)
Attempts	0.3995** (0.0670)	−0.0138 (0.0358)	0.0232 (0.0357)
Years	−0.0004 (0.0113)	—	—
GDP per capita	0.13E − 4 (0.23E − 4)	—	—
Democracy	0.6195** (0.2010)	—	—
Election	−0.2436 (0.2259)	—	—
Majority	−0.3291* (0.1341)	—	—

Note: Standard errors are in parentheses. An asterisk denotes significance at the 5 percent level; two asterisks at the 1 percent level. The country-specific dummies have been omitted from the table but included in the regression. Out of a total of 1,992 observations there are 1,399 observations for which the "government change" dummy is zero and 593 observations for which it is 1. If a country became independent after 1948, only the years since independence have been included.

quencies of government change provide two alternative measures of political instability. They are labeled P and PS, respectively. A third measure of political instability is the actual frequency F of government change. These three measures of political instability are highly correlated with each other. They are also correlated with other measures, estimated from alternative specifications of the probit model.

The next step is to estimate an equation whose general form is

$$s_i = \alpha + \beta z_i + \gamma p_i + u_i, \tag{4.38}$$

Table 4.4
Seigniorage and political variables

Explanatory variables	Seigniorage in all countries					Seigniorage in developing countries
	(1)	(2)	(3)	(4)	(5)	(6)
Intercept	0.0071 (0.0294)	0.0898** (0.0189)	-0.0015 (0.0301)	0.0158 (0.0290)	0.0340 (0.0281)	-0.0201 (0.0319)
Agriculture	0.0016** (0.0006)	—	0.0018* (0.0006)	0.0013* (0.0006)	0.0012* (0.0006)	0.0021* (0.0005)
Mining and manufacturing	—	-0.0007 (0.0168)	—	—	—	—
Foreign trade	-0.0430* (0.0166)	-0.0511 (0.0169)	-0.0350* (0.0177)	-0.0415* (0.0162)	-0.0474** (0.0166)	-0.0431* (0.0182)
GDP per capita	-0.52E - 5* (0.22E - 5)	-0.53E - 5* (0.27E - 5)	-0.46E - 5* (0.23E - 5)	-0.52E - 5* (0.22E - 5)	-0.51E - 5* (0.22E - 5)	-0.44E - 5 (0.24E - 5)
Urbanization	0.0013** (0.0004)	0.0008* (0.0003)	0.0011* (0.0004)	0.0013** (0.0004)	0.0015** (0.0004)	0.0019** (0.0004)
Industrialization	-0.0746** (0.0182)	-0.0844* (0.0218)	—	-0.0694** (0.0180)	-0.0767** (0.0201)	—
Asia	—	—	0.0036 (0.0180)	—	—	—
Latin America	—	—	0.0268 (0.0196)	—	—	—
P	0.1840** (0.0421)	0.1849** (0.0456)	0.1759** (0.0458)	0.1468** (0.0449)	—	0.1583** (0.0539)
RF[a]	—	—	—	—	0.0540** (0.0200)	—
Coups[b]	—	—	—	0.1326* (0.0623)	0.1865** (0.0593)	—

$\bar{R}^2$	0.461	0.407	0.461	0.486	0.464	0.448
Standard error of regression	0.048	0.051	0.048	0.047	0.048	0.049
ρ^d	0.1923 (0.0895)	0.2460 (0.0289)	0.2192 (0.0523)	0.1632 (0.1508)	0.1216 (0.2857)	0.2704 (0.0401)

Note: The dependent variable is seigniorage. Number of observations is seventy-nine. All observations are yearly averages, over the period 1971–82. P is the estimated frequency of government change obtained from table 4.3 for the 1971–82 period. An asterisk denotes significance at the 5 percent confidence level; two asterisks at the 1 percent level.

a. RF is the actual frequency of regular government transfers in 1971–82.

b. Coups is the average actual frequency of coups (over 1971–82).

c. Standard errors of coefficients are in parentheses. The numbers inside the parentheses below the ρ estimate give the significance probability of the estimate under the null: $\rho = 0$.

d. ρ is the Spearman rank correlation coefficient between the estimated residuals and the index of totalitarianism (averaged over 1971–82).

where the subscript refers to country i, s_i denotes the level of seigniorage as a fraction of total government revenues (including seigniorage), z_i is a vector of variables measuring the economic structure of country i, p_i is a vector of political variables designed to capture the degree of instability and of polarization of the political system, and u_i is an error term. We are interested in the sign of the estimated vector of coefficients γ.

Table 4.4 reports the estimates of equation (4.38) on the cross-country data. In the first three columns the measure of political instability (P) estimated in table 4.3 is added to seigniorage regressions. This variable is positive and has a highly significant estimated coefficient in every regression. It remains so even after including dummy variables that group countries into continents. Compared with table 4.2, the estimated coefficients of these dummies drop significantly, and the $\bar{R}^2$'s improve considerably. The same results emerge if we replace P with the other two measures of political instability discussed in the previous subsections, or if we estimate the equation on developing countries only (column 6).[13] These results then provide clear support for the view that after controlling for structural variables, countries with a more unstable political system rely more heavily on seigniorage as a source of revenue.

The model in sections 4.5 and 4.6 suggests that the degree to which countries rely on seigniorage depends not only on political instability but also on political polarization. A problem with this proposition at the empirical level is that it is not easy to find indices of polarization. To tackle this issue, a number of proxies for polarization are considered. Note first that the variable P which appears as a regressor in table 4.4 does not discriminate between regular government changes and those originated by coups. This distinction, however, may be important as an indicator of polarization: A government change taking the form of a coup is likely to be a much more radical change than one occurring through regular democratic procedures. Hence, according to the theory, seigniorage should be positively related to the expected frequency of coups, even after controlling for other measures of instability. This prediction is borne out by the regression analysis. In column 4 of table 4.4 the actual frequency of coups is included among the explanatory variables. Its estimated coefficient is positive and highly significant. In equation (5) in table 4.4 the idea that the frequency of coups captures polarization is refined further. This equation includes as separate variables the actual frequency of regular government changes RF in 1971–82 and the actual frequency of coups. Both variables have a positive and significant estimated coefficient. But the estimated coefficient of coups is much larger than that of regular government changes, which is consistent with the view that in addition to instability the frequency of coups also proxies for polarization. This provides preliminary evidence that both instability and polarization positively affect the reliance on seigniorage.

Democracies are more likely to be viable in societies with a higher degree of internal cohesiveness (Usher 1981). Thus democracies are likely to have lower levels of polarization than totalitarian regimes. Consequently the theory suggests that, controlling for political instability, seigniorage should be larger in more totalitarian countries. To test this conjecture, the coups variable in column 4 of table 4.4 is replaced by a dummy taking a value of 1 in democratic regimes and 0 otherwise. Its estimated coefficient (not reported in the table) is negative and highly significant; it remains negative (even though it becomes barely significant) if the coups variable is also included. In addition to this dummy variable, a ranking of totalitarianism compiled by Freedom House (higher numbers corresponding to more totalitarian regimes) is used. This index of totalitarianism is qualitative, and it does not make much sense to include it in the regressions as an explanatory variable.[14] To overcome this difficulty, the Spearman rank correlation coefficient between this index of totalitarianism and the estimated residuals of each of the equations in table 4.4 is calculated. This coefficient, denoted by ρ at the bottom of table 4.4, is always positive but almost never significant.[15]

Finally, as noted above, the positive and significant estimated coefficient of urbanization can also be regarded as an indication that seigniorage is higher in more polarized countries. As remarked by several political scientists, political conflicts are generally more intense and disruptive in urban areas than in rural societies.[16]

A possible objection to the results presented in table 4.4 is that they could be due to reverse causality. Governments that create excessive inflation lose popular support and are more likely to be thrown out of office. Hence inflation can lead to political instability rather than the other way around. But this seems unlikely. Political stability also reflects other, permanent or slowly changing, features of a political system. Political institutions, culture, tradition, underlying conflicts, cleavage of the population in organized groups, extent of political participation and involvement of the citizens, are all semipermanent features of a country that affect its political stability. However, the problem deserves careful scrutiny. Indeed the probit estimates of table 4.4 indicate that previous inflation, although not significant, reduces the probability of reappointment.

To cope with this problem, equation (4.38) is reestimated by means of instrumental variables. The economic variables are used as instruments for themselves. As an instrument for political instability the expected frequency of government change in the previous decade—estimated by truncating the probit regressions of table 4.4 in 1970 and computing the expected frequency in the decade 1960–70—is used. This variable is highly positively correlated with the estimated frequency for the period 1971–82, used in table 4.4, confirming that political instability is a semipermanent feature of a country. The results from the instrumental variable estimation (not reported) confirm those of table 4.4. Further details and additional tests for robustness appear in Cukierman, Edwards, and Tabellini (1992).

The upshot is that the data are strongly consistent with the predictions of the theory: More unstable countries collect a larger fraction of their revenue in the form of seigniorage. Moreover the evidence is not inconsistent with the view that political polarization also induces more reliance on seigniorage. In addition the results imply that the quantitative impact of political instability on seigniorage is large by comparison to the other explanatory variables. This can be seen more sharply by computing the standardized estimates of the coefficients. For example, in equation (1) of table 4.4 the following standardized estimates are obtained: agriculture, 0.415; foreign trade, -0.206; GDP per capita, -0.287; urbanization, 0.466; industrialization dummy, -0.571; political instability, 0.593.

4.8   Concluding Remarks

For methodological reasons the employment and the revenue motives for monetary expansion have been analyzed separately. In practice both of them can affect monetary policy. It is likely, however, that the narrower the capital market of a country is and the less effective the limitations on government borrowing from the CB, the more important is the revenue motive in determining the rate of monetary expansion. Narrower capital markets limit the ability of government to borrow from the public and increase its reliance on seigniorage. In addition countries with narrow capital markets are less likely to have independent central banks (see section 23.4 of chapter 23). This further weakens the resistance of such countries to inflation.

Hyperinflations, or very high inflations, usually occur when the main motive for inflation is the revenue motive. Such situations normally develop when the CB is not very independent or when, for structural or strategic reasons, it is hard to collect taxes. The employment motive alone does not normally lead to hyperinflations. The reason is that at very high rates of inflation nominal contracts become so short and condensed that the short-run trade-off all but disappears. More precisely α in equation (3.2) tends to zero and the incentive to inflate because of employment considerations vanishes (m in equation 3.4 becomes zero). On the other hand, even at hyperinflationary rates it is still possible to obtain some revenues for the government budget by inflating.[17] Hence the revenue motive does not vanish during hyperinflations. As a matter of fact its importance as a motive for monetary expansion rises relative to that of the employment motive.

Bursts of (revenue-motive-induced) high inflation tend to be self-aggravating for some time because of the Olivera-Tanzi effect.[18] When inflation accelerates, the lags in tax collection lead to a reduction in the real value of tax revenues. This temporarily increases the temptation to inflate in order to recoup the missing revenues and raises the rate of monetary expansion. In addition high inflation tends to erode the independence of the central bank (see section 20.7 of chapter 20). This diminishes further the effectiveness of anti-inflationary institutions.

During the stabilization of high, but not excessively high inflations, both the employment and the revenue motive may be operative. In such situations it is important to identify the main motive for inflation. If the main motive is seigniorage, fiscal solvency may be sufficient to make a stabilization program credible. But, if the main motive relates to maintenance of high economic activity, demonstration of fiscal responsibility alone may not suffice to establish credibility. Further discussion of this issue appears in Cukierman and Liviatan (1992).

For simplicity the discussion in section 4.4 does not distinguish between internal and external debt. When the external debt is in foreign currency, only the part of the debt that is in domestic currency is subject to the temptation to inflate it away, and the matter ends at that. But the distinction between foreign and domestic debt becomes more interesting when both types of debt are denominated in terms of domestic currency, enabling policymakers to inflate away both types of debt. Although an inflationary burst reduces both types of debt by the same amount, domestic policymakers' incentives to inflate differ between the two debt types. The reason is that a reduction in the real value of internal debt involves a redistribution between domestic residents and the domestic government. A reduction in the real value of external debt, on the other hand, involves a redistribution between the entire domestic economy and the rest of the world. It is therefore likely that the tendency of domestic policymakers to inflate away the debt differs between the two types of debt. This difference in incentives to inflate is particularly important when, as is currently the case in the United States, the external debt is nonnegligible. Bohn (1991) investigates these issues in the context of the recent increase in the U.S. foreign debt.

There is also a literature that considers debt as a device used by current governments or majorities to limit the ability of future governments to spend and tax (Persson and Svensson 1988, 1989; Alesina and Tabellini 1990; and Tabellini and Alesina 1990). This literature implicitly assumes that reputational considerations are sufficiently strong to deter policymakers from inflating part of the debt away. This assumption is likely to be more realistic in countries with wide financial markets in which partial reneging on the debt by government is rather costly, since it shuts off government from borrowing relatively large amounts at reasonable rates. By contrast, when government faces narrow markets to start with, the forgone borrowing opportunities due to reneging on the debt are smaller and the assumption that debt functions as a commitment device is less realistic. A summary view of debt as a commitment device appears in Persson and Tabellini (1990).

The empirical evidence in section 4.7 linking seigniorage to political instability could be due to reasons other than those discussed in section 4.6. Political instability, for instance, could reflect a collective decision process that is temporarily blocked. Seigniorage would then reflect the inability to reach any policy decision, rather than being due to costs of enforcing and administering tax collections. Alesina and Drazen (1991) study a theoretical model with this property. But their model implies that after the identity of the weaker party in the struggle over shares is revealed, the use of seigniorage should subside. It therefore seems that their framework is more appropriate for explaining temporary bursts of seigniorage, whereas the framework in sections 4.5 and 4.6 is better suited for explaining persistent cross-country differences in seigniorage of the type illustrated by the data in table 4.1. Aizenman (1989) and Sanguinetti (1990) propose other explanations of why countries rely on seigniorage, emphasizing the importance of decentralized decision making in the policy formation process. Edwards and Tabellini (1991) test the model of sections 4.5 and 4.6 against the "weak" government approach to seigniorage and find more support for the first approach.

Appendix A: Proof of Proposition 4.1

Rearranging the first-order conditions in equations (4.29) and using the budget constraint in (4.21), we obtain two functions that implicitly define $s^* = S(\theta)$ and $\tau^* = T(\theta)$:

$$F(\tau, s, \theta) \equiv -[1 + \delta'(\tau)] + (1 - \theta)[1 + \gamma'(s)] = 0,$$

$$H(\tau, s, \theta) \equiv 1 - [1 + \gamma'(s)] U'[1 - \tau - s - \delta(\tau) - \gamma(s)].$$

$$(4A.1)$$

Let F_x and H_x be the partial derivative of $F(\cdot)$ and $H(\cdot)$ with respect to x. Then, by the implicit function theorem,

$$S'(\theta) = -\frac{1}{\Delta}[F_\tau H_\theta - H_\tau F_\theta],$$

$$T'(\theta) = -\frac{1}{\Delta}[H_s F_\theta - H_\theta F_s],$$

$$(4A.2)$$

where

$$\Delta \equiv -\delta''[(1 + \gamma')^2 u'' - \gamma'' U'] - U(1 + \gamma')(1 + \delta')(1 - \theta)\gamma'' U''.$$

Since δ'' and γ'' are positive and U'' is negative, Δ is positive. Calculating the partial derivatives on the right-hand sides of equations (4A.2), we obtain

$$S'(\theta) = -\frac{1}{\Delta}(1 + \gamma')^2(1 + \delta')U'' > 0, \qquad\qquad (4A.3a)$$

$$T'(\theta) = \frac{1}{\Delta}(1 + \gamma')(-\gamma'' U' + (1 + \gamma')^2 U'') < 0. \qquad (4A.3b)$$

The signs of these expressions follow by inspection and by using the facts that $\Delta > 0$, $\gamma'' > 0$, and, by the concavity of the utility from private consumption, $U'' < 0$.

Differentiating equation (4.30) totally with respect to θ, we have

$$X'(\theta) = -\tau + (1 - \theta)T'(\theta) + S'(\theta). \tag{4A.4}$$

Then, inserting equations (4A.3) into (4A.4), we obtain

$$X'(\theta) = \frac{1}{\Delta}\{\tau\delta''[(1 + \gamma')^2 U'' - \gamma''U'] + \tau(1 - \theta)(1 + \delta')(1 + \gamma')\delta''U''$$

$$- (1 - \theta)(1 + \gamma')\gamma''U'\}. \tag{4A.5}$$

Inspection of equation (4A.5) in conjunction with the applicable sign restrictions reveals that $X'(\theta)$ is negative. Specializing the budget constraint in equation (4.21) to an equality, differentiating it totally with respect to θ, using (4A.3), and rearranging yields

$$C'(\theta) = \frac{\gamma''}{\Delta}(1 + \delta')(1 + \gamma')U' > 0. \tag{4A.6}$$

□

Appendix B: Proof of Proposition 4.2

When $\pi = 0$ or $\alpha = 1/2$, $\beta(\cdot) = 1$ and equation (4.36) reduces to

$$U(C(\theta))C'(\theta) + X'(\theta) \leq 0. \tag{4A.7}$$

Using (4A.5) and (4A.6) in (4A.7), we reduce this last expression to

$$\frac{\tau}{\Delta}\{\delta''[(1 + \gamma')^2 U'' - \gamma''U'] + (1 - \theta)\gamma''(1 + \delta')(1 + \gamma')U''\}, \tag{4A.7a}$$

which is unambiguously negative for all values of θ and in particular for $\theta = 0$. It follows that when $\pi = 0$ or $\alpha = 1/2$, the equilibrium value of θ is zero. This establishes part 1 of the proposition.

To demonstrate part 2, we note that when $\pi = \alpha = 1$, $\beta(\cdot) = 0$, so $G(\cdot)$ in equation (4.36) is positive for any value of θ and in particular for $\theta = 0$. It follows that for $\pi = \alpha = 1$, the equilibrium value of θ is positive. By (4.37), $\beta(\cdot)$ is a decreasing function of both π and α, so $G(\cdot)$ is lower for the same θ when π and α are smaller than 1. By continuity of $G(\cdot)$ there exist values of π and α that are strictly smaller than one for which $G(\cdot)$ is still positive for the same θ. Denote these values by π_0 and α_0. Since $\beta(\cdot)$ is a decreasing function of both α and π, it follows a fortiori that for any $\pi \geq \pi_0$

and $\alpha \geq \alpha_0$, $G(\cdot)$ is positive at a positive value of θ. It follows that the equilibrium value of θ for any $\pi \geq \pi_0$, $\alpha \geq \alpha_0$, is positive. This establishes part 2.

When $\theta^* > 0$, the first-order condition in equation (4.36) holds as an equality. Applying to it the implicit function theorem, we obtain

$$\Theta_\pi(\cdot) = -\frac{X'(\theta)}{G_\theta(\cdot)}\beta_\pi(\cdot), \tag{4A.8a}$$

$$\Theta_\alpha(\cdot) = -\frac{X'(\theta)}{G_\theta(\cdot)}\beta_\alpha(\cdot). \tag{4A.8b}$$

By proposition (4.1), $X'(\theta) < 0$. $G_\theta(\cdot)$ is negative by the second-order condition for a maximum of equation (4.35), and from (4.37), $\beta_\pi(\cdot)$ and $\beta_\alpha(\cdot)$ are negative. Hence $\Theta_\pi(\cdot)$ and $\Theta_\alpha(\cdot)$ are positive. This establishes part 3 of the proposition. $\square$

Appendix C: Definitions of the Variables in Table 4.3

The variables inflation, consumption growth, protests, riots, and repressions are all in deviations from their country-specific means.

1. *Government change.* Government change $\equiv$ dummy variable taking a value of 1 for the years in which there is either a coup or a regular government transfer and a value of 0 otherwise (source: Taylor-Jodice 1983).

2. *Economic performance.* Inflation $\equiv$ annual rate of growth of GDP deflator (source: constructed from Summers-Heston 1988). Economic growth $\equiv$ cumulative rate of growth of private consumption in the current and previous two years (source: Summers-Heston 1988).

3. *Political events.* Riots $\equiv$ violent riots (source: Taylor-Jodice 1983). Repressions $\equiv$ political executions and government-imposed sanctions (source: Taylor-Jodice 1983). Executive adjustments $\equiv$ changes in the composition of the executive not resulting in government transfers (source: Taylor-Jodice 1983). Attempts $\equiv$ unsuccessful attempts to change the government, taking the form of unsuccessful coups and unsuccessful government transfers (source: Taylor-Jodice 1983). Years $\equiv$ years from previous government change.

4. *Structural variables.* GDP per capita ≡ constant 1975 U.S. $ (source: Summers-Heston 1988). Democracy ≡ dummy variable taking a value of 1 for democracies and 0 otherwise (source: Banks and Overstreet, various volumes). Elections ≡ dummy variable taking a value of 1 if the election date is determined by the constitution and 0 otherwise (source: Banks and Overstreet, various volumes). Majority ≡ dummy variable taking a value of 1 for presidential systems, or for parliamentary governments supported by a single majority party, and 0 otherwise (source: Banks and Overstreet, various volumes).

5 The Mercantilistic or Balance-of-Payments Motive for Monetary Expansion

5.1 Introduction

Policymakers of countries with persistent deficits in the current account of the balance of payments might be tempted to reduce such deficits by devaluing the currency. This policy is effective if it also results in a real devaluation of the currency. However, the central bank, or whoever else decides on monetary policy, directly controls only the nominal rate of exchange. The real rate of exchange is also affected by the actions of individuals in the private sector and the makers of fiscal policy.

A nominal devaluation may reduce a balance-of-payments deficit or increase a surplus in it through several channels. First, in the presence of nominal wage contracts and unions that set the real wage above its market-clearing level, a nominal devaluation—by reducing the real wage rate—stimulates employment and output.[1] This increases the amount of resources available for exports or for import substitutes and decreases the current account deficit. The increase in output also increases income and therefore domestic consumption. The effect of this change is to increase the current account deficit. However, if the marginal propensity to consume is smaller than one, the first effect dominates, and the combined effect of the nominal devaluation is still to reduce the current account deficit. Second, a nominal devaluation also reduces the public's consumption by reducing the real value of nominally denominated government obligations held by the public.[2] This decrease in domestic absorption also contributes to reduction of the current account deficit.

There are a number of episodes in which governments or central banks of countries with current account deficits devalued, causing an upward bulge in the rate of inflation, without any apparent improvement in the balance of payments. This phenomenon, although not restricted to such countries, seems to be more prevalent in countries with high degrees of unionization. A dramatic example is Israel during 1984 and early 1985, just prior to the successful July 1985 stabilization program. Most of the Israeli labor force is unionized under a general umbrella organization known as the "Histadruth." During the second half of 1984, the government and the Histadruth reached an agreement known as a "package deal," one component of which was the temporary freezing of nominal wages. In return the government promised to refrain from raising taxes and reducing subsidies for the period of the deal. Although freezing the exchange rate was not part of the deal, there was an understanding that the rate of exchange would not be actively used as an instrument of external balance. But in late 1984, due to increasing concern over the growing current account deficit, government devalued. This led to an acceleration in the rate of inflation without much effect on the current account deficit. There were subsequent attempts to reduce inflation through package deals. But the labor union demanded such high nominal wage increases, in return for its willingness to agree to additional freezes, that government was forced to devalue just to prevent a deterioration in the balance of payments. There ensued a spiral of broken package deals, devaluations, and nominal wage increases with no apparent improvement in the balance of payments. This process came to an end with the successful June 1985 stabilization.[3]

This chapter shows that dynamic inconsistency problems similar to those presented in previous chapters explain why nominal devaluations do not improve the current account's position and only cause inflation. The basic idea is that under discretion the public knows in advance that policymakers are willing to tolerate devaluations and inflation in order to improve the balance of payments. Since policymakers are not bound by any commitments, individuals know that once nominal wage and financial assets contracts have been concluded, government and the central bank will have an incentive to devalue. They therefore ask and obtain higher nominal wage rates and interest rates. After the conclusion of those contracts, government indeed devalues at the expected rate. However, relative to a situation with no expectations and no devaluation, such action has no effect on the current account, since the prior actions of the public have neutralized such an effect.

5.2   A Simple Game between the Central Bank and a Union in the Presence of a Balance-of-Payments Motive

Consider a small open economy with one good that is traded internationally. All workers in the economy are unionized in one labor union that sets the nominal wage rate for each period at the beginning of the period.[4] At the same time individuals also choose the nominal amounts of money balances and of government bonds to be carried into the period. To focus on the strategic interaction between policymakers and the union with minimum complications, we assume that purchasing power parity holds. That is,

$$P = eP^*, \tag{5.1}$$

where P and P^* are the domestic and the foreign price levels, respectively, and e is the nominal exchange rate (measured as the number of units of domestic currency per unit of foreign currency). Since the foreign price level is taken as given, it is normalized, without loss of generality to one. Hence

$$P = e, \qquad\qquad (5.1a)$$

so the choice of exchange rate by policymakers fully determines the domestic price level.[5]

Abstracting from domestic investments the current account balance is

$$B = Y - C(\cdot) - G, \qquad\qquad (5.2)$$

where Y is domestic output, $C(\cdot)$ is the consumption function, and G is government consumption.

The policymakers' objective is to minimize the combined costs, from their point of view, of deviations of B from a target level B^* and of inflation. This is stated

$$\max V \equiv \max - \left[\frac{a}{2}(B - B^*)^2 + \frac{1}{2}\pi^2 \right], \qquad B - B^* \le 0, \qquad (5.3)$$

where π is the rate of inflation. For $B^* = 0$, equation (5.3) states that policymakers incur political costs from deficits in the current account but are indifferent between alternative levels of surpluses in the current account. When B^* is strictly positive, equation (5.3) states that the policymakers' preferred position for the current account is a surplus and that any downward deviation from it is costly. But once the desired surplus is reached, policymakers are indifferent between alternative higher values of the surplus. Such a mercantilistic bias may reflect the relative weight given by government to the interests of exporters. The coefficient a reflects the relative concern of policymakers for the balance of payments versus price stability. The larger the a, the more concerned are policymakers with the current account of the balance of payments.

Governments of small open economies with persistent current account deficits are usually concerned about those deficits because of the risk that foreign exchange reserves or foreign loans will not suffice in the future to finance basic productive imports such as raw materials and machine tools. Their concern for the current state of the balance of payments derives therefore from a more basic concern for the economy's ability to import basic productive inputs in an undisturbed manner over the entire future. The concern for the current state of the balance of payments, which is built into the objective function in equation (5.3), is a proxy for those longer-term considerations. Like many other shortcuts it does not fully reflect the dynamics of the problem. But it does preserve enough structure to bring out in a simple manner forces that would be present also in a fully blown dynamic formulation.

Although it normally implements exchange rate policy, the central bank does not decide on it alone. In most countries decisions about exchange rate policy are made by the political authorities like the treasury in consultation with the central bank. Although, for briefness, we refer sometimes to equation (5.3) as the "objective function of the central bank," it should be remembered that this function usually represents inputs from various governmental agencies besides the central bank.

Output is produced by means of an aggregate production function,

$$Y = F(N) \tag{5.4}$$

whose only variable factor of production is labor N. The marginal productivity of labor is positive and decreasing in the quantity of labor, $F_N > 0$ and $F_{NN} < 0$. Demand for labor is competitive, so the quantity of labor demanded is determined by the condition

$$F_N(N) = w \equiv \frac{W}{P} = \frac{W}{e}, \tag{5.5}$$

where w and W are the real and the nominal wage rates, respectively, and the last equality follows from equation (5.1a).

The labor union's objective function is positively related to the real wage and to employment.[6] We assume that in the absence of active policy by the central bank the optimal real wage demanded and obtained by the union is higher than its market-clearing counterpart. Hence the natural level of employment is below its market-clearing level, and the demand for labor is on the short side of the market in this range. Consequently, if the central bank succeeds in reducing the real wage below the real wage imposed by the union, employment and output increase along the demand for labor function. This function is determined implicitly by equation (5.5) and is given by

$$N^d = D(w), \qquad D_w < 0, \tag{5.6}$$

where D_w denotes the partial derivative of D with respect to w and is negative, since $F_{NN} < 0$.

Let w_n be the real wage that maximizes the union's objective function. At the beginning of the period the union sets the contract nominal wage W so as to achieve the real wage w_n, taking into consideration the exchange rate e^e which it expects for the period. Hence

$$W = w_n e^e. \tag{5.7}$$

The explicit form of the consumption function is

$$C(\cdot) = c(Y - T) + d\frac{S}{P}, \qquad 0 < c < 1, d > 0, \tag{5.8}$$

where T are total taxes and S is the nominal amount of government debt carried into the period by the public. The first term represents the effect of disposable income on consumption, and the second term represents the effect of financial wealth on consumption. The debt pays a nominal interest n that is determined at the beginning of the period. The nominal quantity of bonds is chosen by the public at the beginning of the period. The demand for bonds is

$$S^d = s(n - \pi^e)P_{-1} = s(n - \pi^e)e_{-1}, \tag{5.9}$$

where s is the real demand for bonds at the beginning of the period, π^e is the expected rate of inflation, and P_{-1} is the price level at the beginning of the period. This price level is identical to the price level at the end of the previous period and is therefore denoted P_{-1}. The second equality in equation (5.9) follows from equation (5.1a). Let S be the nominal value of outstanding government bonds at the beginning of the period. Beginning-of-period equilibrium in the bond market implies that

$$S = s[n(\pi^e) - \pi^e]e_{-1}. \tag{5.9a}$$

Equation (5.9a) states that given expectation π^e and the outstanding nominal value of bonds, the nominal rate of interest adjusts so as to clear the bond market.

Since employment is determined by labor demand, a decrease in the real wage rate causes an increase in employment and output. More precisely, using equation (5.6) in equation (5.4), we obtain

$$Y = F\left[D\left(\frac{W}{e}\right)\right] = f\left(\frac{W}{e}\right), \tag{5.10}$$

where the derivative $f'(\cdot)$ of output with respect to the real wage rate is negative. Since W has been precommitted by a contract, the central bank can affect employment and output by appropriate choice of the exchange rate e.

During the period the central bank takes the nominal wage in (5.7), the nominal interest rate, and expected inflation as given and picks the rate of exchange so as to maximize the objective function in equation (5.3). Using (5.9a) in (5.8) and the resulting expression in (5.2), and using the latter expression in equation (5.3), the maximization problem of the central bank can be rewritten as

$$\max_{e} - \left[\frac{a}{2} \left\{ (1 - c) f\left(\frac{W}{e}\right) - d \frac{s[n(\pi^e) - \pi^e] e_{-1}}{e} [1 + n(\pi^e)] \right. \right.$$

$$\left. \left. + cT - G - B^* \right\}^2 + \frac{1}{2}\left(\frac{e}{e_{-1}} - 1\right)^2 \right], \tag{5.11}$$

where use has been made of the fact that $\pi = e/e_{-1} - 1$ and where $\pi^e \equiv e^e/e - 1$. The term $1 + n(\pi^e)$ that multiplies $s(\cdot)$ reflects the fact that nominal interest payments on bonds accrue during the period.

After rearrangement, the first-order condition corresponding to the problem in equation (5.11) yields

$$\pi(1 + \pi) = a(B - B^*) \left[(1 - c)\frac{W}{e}f'\left(\frac{W}{e}\right) - ds[n(\pi^e) - \pi^e]\frac{1 + n(\pi^e)}{1 + \pi} \right]. \tag{5.12}$$

Since $f'(\cdot) < 0$ and $s(\cdot) \geq 0$, the last term in large brackets on the right-hand side of equation (5.12) is negative. If the actual position of the balance of payments B is lower than the desired level B^*, the entire expression on the right-hand side of equation (5.12) is positive, and the rate of devaluation π is positive too. If, for example, $B^* = 0$ so that policymakers are concerned about the balance of payments only when there is a deficit in the current account, the central bank will devalue whenever there is such a deficit. More generally, if policymakers have a mercantilistic bias so that $B^* > 0$, the central bank will have a devaluation bias, and consequently an inflationary bias, whenever the current account surplus falls short of B^*.[7]

Equation (5.12) implicitly determines the rate of exchange chosen by the central bank as a function of W, n, e_{-1}, T, and G. The union and other members of the public know the reaction function of policymakers in equation (5.12). Since there is no uncertainty of any kind, they can calculate

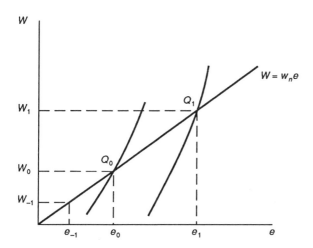

Figure 5.1
Equilibrium in the game between the union and the central bank

in advance what will be the choice of exchange rate by the central bank without any error. As a consequence

$$e^e = e \quad \text{and} \quad \pi^e = \pi, \tag{5.13}$$

and the reaction function of the union can be reformulated as

$$W = w_n e. \tag{5.7a}$$

The reaction functions of the union and of the central bank (equations 5.7a and 5.12, respectively) are plotted in figure 5.1. The union chooses W as a function of e and, given n, e_{-1}, T, and G, the central bank chooses e as a function of W. Equilibrium occurs when both players are on their reaction functions. This occurs at point Q_0 with corresponding equilibrium values W_0 and e_0 for the nominal wage rate and the exchange rate.

Since the union correctly perceives the exchange rate that will be chosen by the central bank during the period, it sets W exactly at the level necessary to obtain the real wage w_n. As a result the devaluation has no effect on employment, and therefore no effect on the balance of payments through the output channel. By setting the nominal wage at W_0, the union ensures that even when the central bank retains the discretion to subsequently alter the exchange rate, the real wage remains at w_n. The reason is that at the nominal wage W_0, the best choice of exchange rate for the central bank is such that W_0/e_0 equals the real wage desired by the union.

How about the real wealth channel? Does the central bank succeed in improving the balance-of-payments position by reducing the real value of government debt and consumption? To answer this question, note that equation (5.13) implies that the ex-ante and the ex-post real rates of interest are equal. Denoting by r_n this common value and noting that, to a first approximation, $n - \pi = (1 + n)/(1 + \pi) - 1$, we find that the real value of bonds outstanding is

$$(1 + r_n)s(r_n). \tag{5.14}$$

Hence the real value of government bonds is independent of the rate of devaluation. In particular it is the same whether the rate of exchange is fixed or whether there is a devaluation. The reason for this invariance is that the public correctly expects the rate of inflation π and demands an appropriate premium in order to continue to hold the real quantity of bonds outstanding at the beginning of the period. This is attained by an upward adjustment in the nominal rate whose magnitude is such that the resulting real rate is exactly at the level necessary to entice the public to willingly hold the outstanding real quantity of government bonds.

To summarize, in the presence of current account deficits and concern about those deficits, discretionary policy induces a devaluation bias. The devaluation produces, as in the case of the employment motive, a sub-optimally high rate of inflation. The reason is that by committing to a stable exchange rate prior to the formation of nominal contracts, policy-makers could have achieved a zero rate of inflation without any deterioration in the current account balance. In the absence of precommitments the central bank has to devalue at the rate expected by the public just in order to maintain the current account at its original position. The reason is that the union and individuals demand and receive upward adjustments in the nominal wage rate and in the nominal rate of interest that are based on the presumption that the central bank will devalue at rate π. Given the high values of those predetermined nominal variables, the rate of devaluation picked by the central bank during the period only serves to maintain the current account at its original position.

5.3   Factors Affecting the Size of the Devaluation Bias

In view of the preceding discussion the equilibrium rate of devaluation (denoted π_0) is using (5.13) in (5.12),

$$\pi_0(1 + \pi_0) = a(B - B^*)[(1 - c)w_n f'(w_n) - d(1 + r_n)s(r_n)],$$

$$B - B^* < 0, \qquad (5.12a)$$

where in equilibrium the current account balance is

$$B = (1 - c)f(w_n) - d(1 + r_n)s(r_n) + cT - G. \qquad (5.15)$$

Examination of those equations confirms that the current account balance is independent of the nominal rate of exchange and that the equilibrium rate of devaluation is positive provided that the configuration of real variables that affect B is such that the current account balance is smaller than B^*. Note in particular that a larger government budget (G), a smaller level of taxes (T), a higher natural real wage (w_n), and a higher real government debt (s) all contribute to increase the current account deficit. Equation (5.12a) implies that, other things being the same, the larger the $B^* - B$, the larger is the equilibrium rate of devaluation. Hence a larger G, a smaller T, or both, induce higher rates of devaluation and of inflation.

Thus a link is created between the size of the budget deficit and inflation. However, this relation arises through the strategic interaction among the union, the public, and the central bank when the latter is concerned about the balance of payment, and this concern is common knowledge. By raising the current account deficit, a higher budgetary deficit increases the discretionary rate of devaluation chosen by the central bank after the wage contract has been concluded and positions in government bonds taken. Since the union and the public recognize the increased incentive to devalue, they demand and obtain a higher nominal wage and a higher nominal interest rate. As a consequence the central bank has to devalue at a higher rate just in order to maintain the balance of payments at its natural position. Thus an increased, publicly known, incentive to devalue on the part of the central bank leads to a higher rate of devaluation with no effect on the balance of payments. In terms of figure 5.1, an increase in the budgetary deficit shifts the reaction function of the central bank to the right and the equilibrium point from Q_0 to Q_1. Correspondingly the rate of devaluation and the rate of nominal wage inflation rise from $e_0/e_{-1} - 1$ to $e_1/e_{-1} - 1$, respectively.

Equations (5.12a) and (5.15) also imply that the larger the debt inherited from the beginning of the period, the higher will be the equilibrium rate of devaluation. This happens for two reasons. A larger debt increases domestic consumption and the balance-of-payments deficit, raising the central bank's incentive to devalue. In addition the higher the government debt, the more effective is a devaluation in reducing the current account deficit at the margin. This also raises the discretionary rate of devaluation. The intuition underlying the second effect is that a marginal increase in the rate of devaluation reduces the public's wealth more as the debt becomes larger. This triggers, at the margin, a larger decrease in consumption and therefore a larger improvement in the current account balance. If the real quantity of bonds held by the public is an increasing function of the real rate r, the preceding analysis also implies that the equilibrium rate of devaluation is higher the larger r_n.

Finally, subject to a mild restriction on the production function,[8] the higher the real wage w_n desired by the union, the higher will be the equilibrium rate of devaluation. Because of the current account deficit, the real wage preferred by the central bank is lower than the natural rate w_n set by the union. The higher the w_n, the larger will be this difference and the current account deficit. As a consequence the discretionary rate of devaluation is larger. Part of the inflationary bias arises because of the basic conflict between the union and the central bank about the appropriate level of the real wage rate. The more intense this conflict, as measured by the discrepancy between the two wage rates, the stronger will be the policymakers' incentive to inflate. Since this is public knowledge, the equilibrium rate of inflation is therefore larger.

5.4   Precommitments versus Discretion

The discretionary equilibrium described above is obviously suboptimal in terms of policymakers' objectives; the same current account position could have been achieved with a zero rate of inflation. As a matter of fact, prior to the conclusion of wage contracts and of individual portfolio choices, the central bank has an incentive to abstain from trying to improve the balance of payments by devaluating and to announce that the rate of exchange will remain constant. But once wage contracts have been struck and positions in government bonds taken, policymakers have an incentive to devalue independently of whether the union and the public believe it or not. Thus, when $B - B^* \leq 0$, devaluing at a positive rate is a dominant strategy. In the presence of credible precommitments the announcement will be believed and carried out. But in the absence of a precommitment, policymakers will always find a devaluation to be worthwhile ex-post, and the discretionary, subgame perfect equilibrium will arise.

Do these results imply that there is no effective way to correct a current account imbalance? The answer is no. But they do imply that other means like fiscal policy should be used for this task, leaving the nominal rate of exchange and the underlying monetary policy free to ensure price stability.

5.5 Applicability of the Model

The model of this chapter is particularly suitable for small open economies with a high degree of unionization like Israel, Greece, Austria, and the Scandinavian countries. We have seen at the beginning of this chapter how discretionary attempts to improve the balance of payments by Israeli policymakers after the conclusion of package deals in 1984 resulted in substantial inflationary accelerations with little or no effect on the balance of payments. The successful July 1985 comprehensive inflation stabilization that followed worked as a precommitment device. The government credibly precommitted to abstain from using the nominal exchange rate as an instrument of external balance and tackled the current account imbalance by a deep cut in the budgetary deficit. In return the general labor union agreed to a temporary wage freeze and to a suspension of wage indexation.[9] The credibility of the entire program and of government's commitment not to devalue was greatly enhanced by the personal and forceful involvement of the prime minister in the arduous negotiations that paved the way for the stabilization program. Thus the Israeli stabilization program can be viewed as a switch from a discretionary regime in which government can alter the exchange rate at any time to a regime in which it commits to maintain the exchange rate fixed for a certain length of time.[10] Greece, with its persistent postwar current account deficits and relatively high degree of unionization, is another example of a case in which discretionary devaluations designed to reduce the deficit resulted in persistent inflation.

Policymakers of highly open economies with persistent current account deficits and widespread unionization normally have a strong incentive to devalue. But this does not imply that all countries with such features will have a balance-of-payments-induced inflationary bias. Austria, for example, despite having all those characteristics, enjoys a high degree of price stability. The reason is that it pegs its currency to the German mark and adjusts its monetary policy so as to maintain this peg. Since this policy has been consistently followed for many years, it is widely known and believed by unions and the public. This keeps nominal wages and interest rates low, making it unnecessary to devalue just in order to keep the current account at its natural level. Austrian policymakers have in effect credibly pre-committed to peg their currency to the mark and to subjugate their monetary policy to this rule.

The current account motive is normally not in evidence in countries with large current account surpluses like West Germany and Japan. However, periodic episodes of exogenously caused deficits in the West German current account balance are consistent with the view that German policy-makers are sensitive to such deficits and may even dislike states in which current account surpluses are too low. In terms of the model this means that German policymakers can be characterized by a nonnegative and perhaps strictly positive B^*. The fact that they allowed inflation to acceler-ate during the second oil shock, when the current account surplus was severely reduced and even turned into a deficit, is consistent with this view.

The model in this chapter focused on two channels through which devaluations improve the current account. One operates through an ex-pansion in employment and output. The other operates by reducing the real value of monetary assets held by the public and, with it, domestic absorption. The relative potency of those effects may differ widely across countries depending on the particular institutional structure of each coun-try. In Israel, for example, the incentive to devalue in order to reduce the real value of government debt is rather limited since a large fraction of the debt is indexed. At the other extreme, in countries like Germany in which there is virtually no indexation the wealth-induced effects of a devaluation may by substantial. A dramatic example is the virtual obliteration of the large German national debt during the first half of the post–World War I hyperinflation.[11]

5.6   Extensions and Qualifications

The formal analysis in this chapter is based on a number of abstractions. One is that all the labor force is unionized. This abstraction can be easily generalized to the case in which there is only partial unionization along the lines of chapter 3. If the conditions in section 3.6 are satisfied, there is still a negative relationship between the real wage and employment and therefore an incentive for policymakers concerned about the balance of payments to devalue. However, the temptation to devalue is probably smaller, the nearer real wages are to their competitive market-clearing levels.

By assuming that there is only one good, the model abstracted from the existence of a third channel through which a nominal devaluation can improve the current account balance. This channel is the relative price effect which, following a devaluation, makes foreign goods more expensive in relation to domestic goods, decreasing imports, and increasing exports. A precise characterization of this additional effect would require distinguishing between different types of goods such as foreign and domestic or traded and nontraded goods. An analysis along these lines appears in Agenor (1991). But even without fully modeling this additional relative price effect, it is clear that its existence increases the incentive of mercantilistically minded policymakers to devalue. Since individuals also anticipate a larger devaluation bias, nominal wages, prices, and interest rates are all appropriately higher. It is therefore likely that had the relative price effect been incorporated explicitly, inflation would have been higher in equilibrium but the current account would still remain at its natural level.

The model also abstracted from the existence of narrowly defined money which does not pay interest. In the presence of such money, devaluations trigger a tax on real money balances. This tends to improve the current account by reducing domestic absorption, so a devaluation does bring about some change in the current account balance. However, this effect is likely to be small particularly if, due to high inflationary expectations, real money balances held by the public are small.

Finally, use of the exchange rate as an anchor for stable prices works in the long run only if the money stock is adjusted so as to support the exchange rate peg. A drawback of using the exchange rate as a nominal anchor is that it may tempt policymakers to tolerate the development of substantial divergences between the actual supply of money and the supply necessary to sustain the exchange rate at its predetermined peg over the long run.

6 Comparison of Policy Outcomes under a System of Adjustable Pegs with Outcomes under a Commonly Managed Currency System and Its Consequences for European Monetary Unification

6.1 Introduction

This chapter is motivated by recent attempts to accelerate the process of monetary integration within the EEC (European Economic Community) during the end of the 1980s and the beginning of the 1990s. Since the end of the 1970s most EEC countries have strived to maintain, within the framework of the European Monetary System (EMS), fixed parities among their respective currencies. The EMS handles the inflationary temptations described in previous chapters by making it costly for policymakers in individual EEC countries to change parities. This cost checks the temptation to inflate as long as the potential benefits from monetary expansion to an individual government are smaller than the political and other perceived costs of parity adjustments. But when country-specific shocks make the potential benefits larger than this cost, monetary policy in the concerned country deviates from the community norm, and sooner or later a parity change follows. Hence the current EMS is an adjustable pegs system in which the commitment to maintain the peg is limited. When shocks fall within certain bounds, policymakers stick to the fixed exchange rate commitment.[1] However, they revert to discretion at the level of the individual country when shocks fall outside these bounds.

The recent acceleration in the process of economic and monetary integration in the EEC raises the far-reaching possibility that the Community may eventually have a single currency managed by one central monetary authority. Following the Single Act, the European council appointed in mid-1988 a commission headed by Jacques Delors which was entrusted with the task of proposing concrete stages leading toward economic and monetary integration. The commission submitted its report in 1989. The report proposes to achieve full monetary union in three stages. During the first two stages all obstacles to financial integration would be removed, and coordination of monetary policies would be intensified. However, each central bank would continue to manage the national currency separately. According to article 52 of the Delors Report, in stage one "realignments of exchange rates would still be possible," but an effort would be made to use other adjustment mechanisms. A similar fixed parities system with separately managed currencies is envisaged for stage two as well except that in this stage exchange rate realignments would be made only under "exceptional circumstances" (article 57). The final stage would irrevocably lock exchange rates, transfer monetary management to a single European Central Bank and eventually replace all national currencies with a single Community currency.

This chapter compares policy outcomes under a commonly managed currency system (CMCS) of the type envisaged for stage three of the Delors Report with policy outcomes under a system of adjustable pegs (AP) such as the current EMS or the system envisaged for stage two of the Delors Report. The chapter's presumption is that a system of partial commitments of monetary policy will be in place also in the CMCS and that it will be implemented similarly by imposing a cost on the political authorities in case they renege on the commitment. Hence the commitment to price stability (which may take the form of a fixed peg in one case and that of a quantitative monetary target in the other) will be broken under some circumstances. Nevertheless, policy outcomes under the two systems differ for two reasons. First, because divergent monetary policies are not possible with a centrally managed currency and, second, because the commitment to price stability is abandoned under different sets of circumstances in the two systems.

The basic question that is posed and answered in this chapter is the following: For the same distribution of real shocks, how do policy outcomes differ between the AP system and the CMCS? The answer to such a question is important for two reasons. First, it may give an indication about likely differences in policy outcomes between the current EMS and an eventual European Central Bank. Second, stage two of the Delors Report is also an AP system. The comparison in this chapter thus gives an indication about likely differences in policy outcomes between the second stage and the last stage of the Delors Report. The chapter also uses this comparison in order to evaluate the wisdom of having a stage two.

A main result of the chapter is that a single country under a system of adjustable pegs is more likely to renege on the commitment to price stability than the central bank of a commonly managed currency. This result is essentially a consequence of the fact that under a commonly managed central bank whose board of directors makes decisions by majority rule, the decision to renege requires the approval of several member countries. The approval is given only if the realization of shocks is such that a sufficient number of members finds it profitable to renege. But such a realization of shocks is less likely than a realization that makes it profitable for at least one country to renege under an AP system. Basic policy conflicts are not eliminated by the creation of a commonly managed currency. But their resolution differs under the two systems. The chapter also shows that in general joining a CMCS can either raise or lower a country's average inflation rate. But if the political cost for reneging on the commitment to price stability under both systems is sufficiently large, average inflation under a CMCS is likely to be lower than in an AP system.

The analysis in the chapter is somewhat limited but precise. Despite its limitations, which are discussed more fully in the conclusion to this chapter, I believe it provides a useful benchmark for the systematic comparison of AP systems with CMCS.

6.2   Policy Outcomes under an Adjustable Peg System

The analysis is conducted within the framework of the employment motive. There are n countries, each with its own policymaking authoritites. In each case policymakers face a domestic union that maintains the real wage at a level that makes domestic employment lower than the level desired by policymakers. The typical objective function is given by equation (3.1), and the structure of the economy is given by a short-run Phillips relation as in equation (3.2). As in chapter 3 the union moves first and picks the nominal wage based on its expectations π^e. Then policymakers choose actual inflation π, taking π^e as given. The analysis of chapter 3 implies that under these circumstances the rate of inflation chosen by policymakers under discretion is

$$\pi_d = A\alpha s, \tag{6.1}$$

where $s \equiv N^* - N_n$ is the difference between the level of employment preferred by policymakers and the natural level of employment. Suppose that due to various real shocks, s fluctuates randomly over time but is always positive. Policymakers precommit to a zero rate of inflation by adhering to a monetary policy that maintains a fixed parity with a country that has a zero rate of inflation. There is a fixed political cost c of breaking this commitment. As long as the gains from breaking the commitment are smaller than the advantages from reneging on it, the commitment is maintained. But in the opposite case policymakers break the commitment.[2]

Whether national policymakers renege and change the peg or maintain it depends on the realization of the shock and on what the domestic union believes about monetary policy. The remainder of this section characterizes the ranges of s for which policymakers maintain and renege on their precommitments.

Substituting (3.2) into (3.1), we obtain the policymakers' objectives as a function of their action π, the union's expectation π^e, and the shock s:

$$W(\pi, \pi^e, s) \equiv -\left\{\frac{A}{2}[s - \alpha(\pi - \pi^e)]^2 + \frac{\pi^2}{2}\right\}. \tag{6.2}$$

For simplicity, we abstract from faulty perceptions (and therefore from a possible stabilizing role for monetary policy) by assuming that both policymakers and the union learn about the realization of the shock s as soon as it occurs. Within each period the timing of events is as follows: First, the shock s occurs and is observed by everybody. Second, based on its expectation of the subsequent action by policymakers, a nominal wage contract is agreed upon. Finally, government decides whether to keep or to renege on its commitment.[3]

Since expectations are rational and the cost of reneging c is common knowledge, the union can always "enter into the shoes" of policymakers and calculate when it will pay policymakers to renege, given the union's contract, and when it will not. Hence in equilibrium the union always forecasts correctly the subsequent action of policymakers. Two conditions are of particular interest in characterizing the possible equilibria. One is that when the union anticipates that the commitment will be kept, it pays government to honor the commitment. The other is that when the union expects government to renege, it indeed pays government to renege. Both conditions are implied by the rationality of expectations and are given in equations (6.3a) and (6.3b), respectively:

Peg is maintained when

$$W[\pi_d(0, s), 0, s] - W(0, 0, s) < c, \tag{6.3a}$$

or peg is adjusted when

$$W[\pi_d(\pi_d, s), \pi_d, s] - W(0, \pi_d, s) > c, \tag{6.3b}$$

where $\pi_d(\pi^e, s)$ is the discretionary rate of inflation chosen by policymakers when the union expects this rate to be π^e and the divergence between the natural and the desired levels of employment is s. Given the values of π^e and of s, the discretionary action $\pi_d(\pi^e, s)$ is, from equation (3.4) in chapter 3,

$$\pi_d(\pi^e, s) = \frac{\alpha A}{1 + \alpha^2 A}(s + \alpha\pi^e). \tag{6.4}$$

Using (6.4) in equations (6.3), and rearranging, we find that the conditions for maintaining the peg and for adjusting it (in rational expectations equilibria) are, respectively,

$$s^2 < \frac{2c}{(\alpha A)^2}(1 + \alpha^2 A) \equiv S_H^2, \tag{6.5a}$$

$$s^2 > \frac{2c}{(\alpha A)^2}\frac{1}{1 + \alpha^2 A} \equiv S_L^2. \tag{6.5b}$$

Since $\alpha^2 A$ is positive S_H^2 is larger than S_L^2. Hence, if s falls in the open range (S_L, S_H), both reneging as well as maintenance of the fixed peg qualify as possible self-fulfilling equilibria. However, since the status quo involves a fixed peg, it seems reasonable to assume that when both types of equilibria are possible, the fixed peg one will prevail. In addition, whenever either type of equilibrium can arise, it is possible to eliminate the discretionary one by appealing to the Cho-Kreps (1987) intuitive criterion. Whenever s falls in the multiple equilibrium range, the government can approach the union prior to settlement of the wage contract and argue as follows: I am going to maintain the fixed peg as promised. You should believe me and settle on a wage contract that is based on this premise, for if you do, I have (as you can verify) no incentive to adjust the peg.[4] In view of those arguments the remainder of the discussion is based on the presumption that whenever $S_L < s < S_H$, the commitment to a fixed peg is honored and the union knows that. I further assume that when indifferent between maintaining and reneging on the fixed parity, the government sticks to its precommitment and maintains the peg. Hence[5] precommitment to peg is honored if

$$s \le S_H; \tag{6.6a}$$

precommitment to peg is broken if

$$s > S_H. \tag{6.6b}$$

Basically, when the divergence between actual and desired employment(s) becomes larger than the threshold S_H, the benefits to government from stimulating employment become large enough to justify the costs of a devaluation taking as given that the union anticipates such behavior. For reasons elaborated upon in chapter 3, this outcome arises despite the fact that the divergence between actual and desired employment stays at s in the resulting equilibrium.[6] Faced with a forward-looking and intelligent union and adverse shocks, government has to devalue just to prevent this divergence from getting any bigger.

6.3 Policy Outcomes under a Commonly Managed Currency System

Consider now a commonly managed currency system in which the commitment to price stability is abandoned only if there is a majority on the board of the common central bank for such action. Suppose further that all countries in the system are represented on the board and that each representative votes for or against reneging on the commitment, taking only the objectives of his or her own government into consideration. The commitment to price stability is the status quo, and it is abandoned only if there is a (possibly weighted) majority in favor of discretion. To maintain comparability with the previous case, I assume that the costs of reneging at the individual country level are the same as under the AP system. Another way of stating this assumption is that the communitywide costs of reneging on price stability under a CMCS are equal to the sum of the individual country costs under an AP system. This seems to be a reasonable description of the possible modus operandi of a European System of Central Banks (ESCB) in stage three of the union as conceived in article 60 of the Delors Report. With differences in the parameters α, A, and c across countries, the discretionary rates of inflation of different countries generally differ. For simplicity, I abstract from those differences by assuming that those parameters are identical across countries. Under those circumstances the discretionary rate of inflation preferred by the policymaker of a country that sustained a shock s and whose union contracts for nominal wages on the basis of expectation π^e is given by equation (6.4).

Even with identical parameters, the discretionary rates of inflation preferred by the different governments differ since the realizations of the shocks s differ across countries. Despite this conflict of interest, the actual and the expected rates of inflation are uniform across countries in a CMCS. The reason is that whether the decision is to stick to or to abandon the commitment to price stability, it binds all countries in the community. Since unions in the individual countries are aware of this fact, their inflationary expectations converge. This brings about uniformity in nominal wage settlements throughout the community in comparison to an AP system.

It is likely that when a European central bank eventually comes into being, the voting powers of representatives from different countries at the bank's board will not necessarily be shared equally. To reflect this possibility, we assume that decisions about whether to renege or not and about the (uniform) discretionary rate to be chosen in the first case are made by weighted majority. In particular let

$$1 > \lambda_i > 0 \tag{6.7a}$$

be the proportion of votes allocated to country i. Obviously

$$\sum_{i \in N} \lambda_i = 1, \tag{6.7b}$$

where N is the set of countries in the CMCS. If there is a country that has more than half of the votes it makes all the decisions alone and the problem becomes trivial. We therefore assume that there is no country on the board of the common central bank that is decisive alone:

ASSUMPTION 1 $\lambda_x \equiv \max_{i \in N} \lambda_i < 1/2$.

Since the realizations of s differ across countries, equation (6.4) implies that given the common value of π^e and given a majority decision to abandon the commitment to price stability, there will be disagreements about the discretionary rate of monetary growth to follow. In particular, if i and j are two countries in the community such that $s_i > s_j$, policymakers in country i will desire a larger discretionary rate than policymakers in country j.

Let $\underline{s} = (s_1, s_2, \ldots, s_n)$ be the current realization of shocks in the n countries. Suppose, without loss of generality, that

$$s_1 \leq s_2 \leq \cdots \leq s_n. \tag{6.8}$$

The country at the weighted median of this distribution is a country with index m such that[7]

$$\sum_{i=1}^{m-1} \lambda_i < \frac{1}{2} \quad \text{and} \quad \sum_{i=1}^{m} \lambda_i \geq \frac{1}{2} \tag{6.9}$$

Equation (6.4) implies that the discretionary rates preferred by different countries have the same ranking as the realizations of the shocks s_i. We assume that if the board of the CMCS decides to renege, the precise discretionary rate chosen is the one most preferred by the country at the median of the distribution of the shocks in equation (6.8). This is stated precisely in assumption 2:

ASSUMPTION 2 (Decisiveness of the Median over the Discretionary Rate) If the majority within the commonly managed central bank is for abandoning the commitment to price stability, the precise rate of inflation that is chosen coincides with the discretionary rate preferred by country m.

Country s_m (meaning "the policymakers of the country that sustained the shock s_m") votes for maintaining the commitment to price stability when $\pi^e = 0$ if

$$W(\pi_d(0, s_m), 0, s_m) - W(0, 0, s_m) < c. \tag{6.10}$$

If we combine equations (6.4) and (6.10) and rearrange them, this condition is equivalent to

$$s_m < s_H. \tag{6.10a}$$

Condition (6.10) (or its alternate form in equation 6.10a) states that country s_m votes for maintaining the commitment (when unions throughout the community believe the commitment will be honored) provided that the benefit from the switch to the discretionary rate $\pi_d(0, s_m)$ is smaller than its political cost c. By assumption 2 in case the central bank council decides to renege, $\pi_d(0, s_m)$ will be the discretionary rate chosen. Hence country $i \neq m$ votes against reneging if

$$W(\pi_d(0, s_m), 0, s_i) - W(0, 0, s_i) < c, \tag{6.11}$$

which is equivalent to the condition

$$2(1 + \alpha A)s_i s_m - (1 + \alpha^2 A)s_m^2 < \frac{2c}{(\alpha A)^2}(1 + \alpha A)^2. \tag{6.11a}$$

Condition (6.10a) implies that condition (6.11a) is satisfied for all countries with $s_i \leq s_m$. Hence, when the country at the median of the discretionary rates opposes reneging, given $\pi^e = 0$, there is a majority against reneging at the central bank council and the expectation $\pi^e = 0$ is self-fulfilling. This leads to the following proposition:

PROPOSITION 6.1   When the median country m is decisive over the discretionary rate, and unions expect the common central bank to honor its commitment, this expectation is self-fulfilling if country m is better off when the commitment is honored. This is the case in turn if condition (6.10a) is satisfied.

Similar considerations, which are elaborated in appendix A to this chapter, lead to the following proposition:

PROPOSITION 6.2   Provided the median country m is decisive over the discretionary rate, and unions expect the common central bank to renege on its commitment, this expectation is self-fulfilling if country m is better off when the CMCS reneges on its commitment. This is the case in turn when

$$s_m > S_L. \tag{6.12}$$

Given the natural order of shocks in equation (6.8), the median in this case is defined as the value of m such that

$$\sum_{i=m+1}^{n} \lambda_i < \frac{1}{2} \quad \text{and} \quad \sum_{i=m}^{n} \geq \frac{1}{2}. \tag{6.9a}$$

We now sum countries in a decreasing order of shock realizations since reneging occurs only if there is a sufficient number of countries with high realizations of shocks.

Since $S_H > S_L$, there are both self-fulfilling reneging and nonreneging equilibria when $S_H > s_m > S_L$. However, the reneging equilibria in this range can be eliminated by appealing again to the Cho-Kreps (1987) intuitive criterion. The central bank council can argue that if unions believe the commitment will be maintained there indeed will be a majority at the council to maintain it.[8] I also assume that when country m is indifferent between honoring and not honoring the commitment (for $\pi^e = 0$), the status quo prevails. This leads to the following proposition:

PROPOSITION 6.3   When the median country m is decisive over the discretionary rate, the community central bank maintains its commitment if $s_m \leq S_H$ and reneges on it if $s_m > S_H$.

6.4   Comparison of the Probability of Reneging under a CMCS with This Probability under an AP System

Let R_p and R_c be, respectively, the event that at least one country in the community reneges on its commitment under an AP system and the event that the CMCS reneges on its commitment. In view of equations (6.6) and proposition 6.3, the precise definition of those events is

$$R_p \equiv \{s > S_H \text{ for at least one country}\}, \tag{6.13a}$$

$$R_c \equiv \{s_m > S_H\}. \tag{6.13b}$$

Since s_m is the weighted median of s across countries, the event R_c is also equivalent to the event that $s_i > S_H$ for at least half of the eligible votes in the council of the common central bank. Assumption 1 implies that this is equivalent to the event that $s_i > S_H$ for at least two countries. R_p is obviously a proper subset of this event, and therefore of R_c, since the realization of R_c always implies that R_p realizes, but the reverse is not always true. Hence the probability that at least one country in an AP system reneges is larger than the probability that the central bank of a CMCS reneges. This leads to the following proposition:

PROPOSITION 6.4   Under an AP system, and provided that assumption 1 is satisfied, the probability that at least one country will renege on its commitment and follow policies that necessitate an adjustment of the peg is larger than the probability that a CMCS will renege.

Note that this result is obtained even under the conservative assumption that the degree of independence of the central bank in a CMCS is the same as the degree of independence of each individual central bank from its national fiscal authority under the current AP system. It is likely, however, that the centralization of monetary authority within one European central bank will make this bank more independent than its national counterparts for most countries in the community. Central banks are normally thought to be relatively more concerned about price stability than fiscal authorities. In terms of the model this implies that A is effectively lower in a CMCS than in an AP system.[9] It is demonstrated in appendix B to this chapter that when A is lower, S_H is higher, making the probability of broken commitments under a CMCS even lower.

Proposition 6.4 can be viewed as the major result of this chapter. Since it is based on an inclusion argument and does not rely on particular features of the distribution of shocks, it has a fairly wide applicability. But the characteristics of the distribution of shocks obviously affects the likelihood that a CMCS will renege on the commitment to price stability. In particular the likelihood that there will be a majority for reneging on the central bank council is larger when there is a positive cross-country correlation between the shocks than when the shocks are statistically independent. The likelihood of reneging under statistically independent shocks is in turn larger than this likelihood when the shocks are negatively correlated across countries. Proposition 6.5 summarizes these results in a more general fashion:

PROPOSITION 6.5   The larger, algebraically, is the degree of cross-country correlation among the real shocks s_i, the more likely is a CMCS to renege on the commitment to price stability.

6.5   Implications for the Desirability of a "Stage Two" in European Monetary Unification

Since an AP system and the CMCS correspond, respectively, to stage two and to the final phase of stage three of the Delors Report, there may be parity adjustments during stage two if this stage is implemented. In particular, if some countries experience substantially larger values of s than others, it is very likely that peg adjustments will occur. The deleterious effect of such developments on the credibility of the process leading toward monetary unification cannot be overemphasized. Since stage two is represented as a move toward more cohesion, realignments during this stage risk being taken, by politicians and the public, as a sign that the movement toward monetary unification is impractical. It actually may undermine the political resolve to move toward stage three. Such a backlash is likely to be more serious the more stage two is construed as a significant move toward monetary unification in comparison to the current EMS. It seems therefore that the benefits of stage two are limited and that the risks it carries are quite substantial.

Frequent realignments during stage two by one or two countries at a time can be highly detrimental. As a matter of fact, even if the probability that $s > S_H$ for a single country is relatively low, the probability that one or two countries in the community will realign their currencies can be quite substantial. To see what is involved, consider the particular case in which

the shocks s have identical and independent (across countries) distributions. Let q be the probability that $s \leq S_H$ in a given country. Hence q is
the probability that a given country maintains the commitment, and $1 - q$
is the probability that it reneges on it.

The probability that at least one country reneges and adjusts its parity
is 1 minus the probability that all twelve countries in the community
experience shocks that are lower than S_H. Hence the probability that at
least one country adjusts its parity is $1 - q^{12}$. Simple combinatorial considerations imply that the probability that at least two countries adjust
their parities is $1 - q^{12} - 12(1 - q) q^{11}$. For $q = 0.9$, the first probability
is almost 0.72, and the probability that at least two countries go through a
realignment is about a third. Such probabilities appear to be dangerously
high for a system that is designed to pave the way toward a common
central bank.

Another drawback of the different currencies management inherent in
stage two is the negative externality due to the common resource problem.
With fixed parities each monetary authority affects the rate of inflation of
the entire community. But national central banks or governments do not
internalize the costs of the inflation they impose on other members of the
community (Aizenman 1989b). On the other hand, the political costs of
changing parities can alleviate this problem by internalizing some of the
externality for countries that are tempted to produce above average monetary growth. However, there is no guarantee that the distribution of those
costs across countries corresponds to the one that would produce the
correct incentive structure.[10] Additional arguments, mostly against stage
two, can be found in either of Cukierman (1991a) or Cukierman (1991b).

6.6   Comparison of Mean Inflation under an AP System and a CMCS

It would seem at first blush that a corollary to proposition 6.4 is that the
expected value of the community average rate of inflation should be lower
under a CMCS than under an AP system. It turns out, however, that this
conjecture is not true in general. The following discussion clarifies the
reasons for the ambiguity and presents conditions under which the conjecture is true. For simplicity, I focus on the case in which the distribution of
s_i is the same across countries.

Let the average rate of inflation in the community under an AP system
be

$$\pi = \sum_{i=1}^{n} f_i \pi_i, \quad \sum_{i=1}^{n} f_i = 1, \tag{6.14}$$

where $f_i (i = 1, \ldots, n)$ is a positive weight that measures the relative size of country i. Let

$$R_{pi} \equiv \{s_i > S_H \text{ in country } i\}. \tag{6.15}$$

R_{pi} is the event; "country i reneges on its commitment." When this occurs, country i inflates at the discretionary rate which is given by equation (6.1). Let $P(R_{pi})$ be the (common across countries) probability of the event R_{pi}. The community expected rate of inflation under an AP system is therefore

$$E\pi_p = \sum_{i=1}^{n} f_i [(1 - P(R_{pi})) \cdot 0 + \alpha A P(R_{pi}) E[s_i | s_i > S_H]]. \tag{6.16}$$

where $E[s_i | s_i > S_H]$ is the expected value of s_i conditional on s_i being larger than S_H. Equation (6.16) can be rewritten as

$$E\pi_p = \alpha A \int_{S_H}^{\infty} s \, dF(s), \tag{6.16a}$$

where $F(s)$ is the (common) cumulative distribution function of s_i.

Consider now the communitywide rate of inflation under a CMCS. The community's central bank reneges only when event R_c in equation (6.13b) occurs and inflates, in this case at rate

$$\alpha A s_m. \tag{6.17}$$

Hence, under a CMCS, the communitywide rate of inflation π_c is either 0 or $\alpha A s_m$. Consequently the expected value of π_c is

$$E\pi_c = [1 - P(R_c)] \cdot 0 + \alpha A \int_{S_H}^{\infty} s_m \, dF_m(s_m), \tag{6.18}$$

where $F_m(s)$ is the distribution function of the median value of the shock across the n countries. Comparison of equations (6.16a) and (6.18) implies that $E\pi_c < E\pi_p$ if and only if

$$\int_{S_H}^{\infty} s \, dF_m(s) < \int_{S_H}^{\infty} s \, dF(s). \tag{6.19}$$

Note that the dummy variable s_m from equation (6.18), has been relabeled s. The inequality in equation (6.19) is not satisfied in general. Whether it holds or not depends on the relative sizes of the probability density of the median of the shocks and of the density of a single shock in the range above S_H.

The reason that the inequality in equation (6.19) may or may not hold in general is due to the fact that there are two opposing effects. On one hand, the requirement that if $s_i > S_H$, there are at least $m - 1$ countries in which $s_i > S_H$ too is more stringent than just requiring $s_i > S_H$. This tends to reduce the density of the median in this range in comparison to the probability density of a single shock in that range. On the other hand, there are many ways in which the shocks of at least m countries can realize in a manner that makes them larger than the threshold S_H. Any group of at least m countries that experience shocks larger than S_H causes the median to fall in that range. This tends to increase the probability that the median will be above S_H in comparison to the probability that the shock realization of a given country will be in that range.[11] An example may help clarify the elements involved. Suppose that all countries have equal voting rights. If the distribution of shocks is independent across countries, it can be shown that the probability density function of the median shock (denoted $f_m(s)$) is given by

$$f_m(s) = n \begin{bmatrix} n-1 \\ \dfrac{n-1}{2} \end{bmatrix} [F(s)]^{(n-1)/2} [1 - F(s)]^{(n-1)/2} f(s) \qquad \text{for } n \text{ odd}, \quad (6.20a)$$

$$f_m(s) = n \begin{bmatrix} n-1 \\ \dfrac{n}{2} - 1 \end{bmatrix} [F(s)]^{n/2-1} [1 - F(s)]^{n/2} f(s) \qquad \text{for } n \text{ even}, \quad (6.20b)$$

where $f(s)$ is the probability density of an individual shock. Details appear in appendix C to this chapter. For n odd $m = [n/2] + 1$. For n even we assume that the CMCS reneges only when there is a strict majority for reneging. Hence $m = n/2$ in this case.[12]

A sufficient, but not necessary, condition for the fulfillment of the inequality in equation (6.19) is

$$f_m(s) < f(s) \qquad \text{for all } s > S_H. \tag{6.21}$$

If $F(s)$ in equations (6.20) is replaced by 1, the resulting expression is not smaller than the expressions in these equations. Hence, for n odd, a sufficient condition for the inequality in equation (6.21) is (using equations 6.20a in 6.21, setting $F(s) = 1$, and rearranging);

$$[1 - F(s)]^{(n-1)/2} < \cfrac{1}{n\left[\cfrac{n-1}{(n-1)/2}\right]} \qquad \text{for all } s > S_H. \qquad (6.22)$$

But since $F(s) \geq F(S_H)$ for all $s > S_H$, a sufficient condition for the last inequality is

$$p^{(n-1)/2} \equiv [1 - F(S_H)^{(n-1)/2} < \cfrac{1}{n\left[\cfrac{n-1}{(n-1)/2}\right]}, \qquad (6.23a)$$

where $p \equiv 1 - F(S_H)$ is the probability that a given country under an AP system reneges. Applying similar considerations to the case of an even n implies that a sufficient condition for the fulfillment of (6.19) in this case is

$$p^{(n-1)/2} < \cfrac{1}{n\left[\cfrac{n-1}{n\over 2} - 1\right]}. \qquad (6.23b)$$

This leads to the following proposition:

PROPOSITION 6.6 Provided the shocks s_i are distributed independently across countries and provided voting rights under a CMCS are shared equally, the expected value of inflation under a CMCS is lower than under an AP system if conditions (6.23a) and (6.23b) are satisfied.

An immediate corollary of the proposition is that if the probability of reneging at the level of an individual country is sufficiently small $E\pi_c$ is smaller than $E\pi_p$. An interesting question, in the context of a possible European Monetary Union, is how small this probability should be in order to deliver the implication that the expected value of the Community inflation rate is lower under a CMCS than under an AP system. To answer this question, we use proposition 6.6 to calculate the upper bound on p, for alternative sizes of the CMCS (alternative values of n), for which $E\pi_c < E\pi_p$. The following table gives these upper bounds for alternative assumptions about the number of countries that will join a European Monetary Union.

n	3	4	5	6	7	8	9	10	11	12
Upper bound	0.166		0.182		0.192		0.199		0.204	
on p		0.289		0.177		0.173		0.174		0.176

The lowest upper bound is 0.166, and it occurs for a union of three countries. Judging by the record of parity adjustments in the European Community during the last decade, it seems not unlikely that the actual probability of reneging at the level of a "representative" country is lower than 0.166. It follows, if one is willing to accept this judgment, that the expected value of the community rate of inflation under a monetary union will be lower than under the EMS. The numbers in the table suggest that this conclusion holds independently of whether all the twelve community countries, or only a subset thereof, join the union.

This comparison holds the level of central bank independence as measured by the coefficient A constant across the two regimes. Obviously recognition of the fact that A is likely to be lower under a CMCS (see section 6.4 and chapter 18 on CB independence) increases the likelihood that mean inflation under this regime is lower.[13] It also holds the level of the political cost of reneging c the same across the two regimes. In practice c is likely to be higher under a monetary union than under the EMS, or under stage two. As a consequence the probability p will be lowered, further making it even more likely that the conditions in equations (6.23) are satisfied and that expected inflation under a EMU will be lower than under the EMS.

6.7 Concluding Remarks

The main results in this chapter can be summarized as follows: (1) A single country under a system of adjustable pegs is more likely to renege on the commitment to price stability than the central bank of a commonly managed currency. (2) The average rate of inflation under a commonly managed currency is not necessarily lower than under a system of adjustable pegs, but it is likely to be lower provided the (common under both systems) cost of reneging is sufficiently large. (3) The central bank of a commonly managed currency system is less likely to renege on the commitment to price stability, the lower (algebraically) is the contemporaneous correlation between the shocks that affect the different countries.

In view of the increased political prospects for achievement of a commonly managed currency in the EEC by the end of this decade comparisons between an adjustable peg system with different currencies and a commonly managed currency system are important for more than one reason: The results of such comparisons could feed back on the political process and affect the attitude of politicians. But even if they do not, a better understanding of the different responses of the two systems would prove useful when a European central bank is ultimately created.[14]

The analysis in this chapter is based on the assumption that policymakers inflate only because of the employment motive. However, a similar analysis can be performed in the presence of systematic or random differences in the potency of the revenue and of the balance-of-payments motives across countries. Cross-country differences in the level of government debt and in the importance of seigniorage revenues will lead to differences in the adherence of different countries to the price stability commitment. Countries that have a relatively high valuation of seignorage revenues ($\delta/\phi_\pi(\cdot)$ in equation 4.7 of chapter 4 is high) and larger debts will normally desire to abandon commitments more frequently than countries with lower valuations. Italy, Spain, Portugal, and Greece are probably in the first group. Analogously, countries that experience larger current account deficits will also desire to abandon commitments more frequently. A comparison of monetary policy outcomes under a CMCS with policy outcomes under an AP system in the presence of those additional motives would proceed along similar lines and is likely to produce similar qualitative conclusions. In particular proposition 6.4 is likely to generalize, implying that the strains on an AP system of the type proposed for stage two in the Delors Report will be more severe the higher and the more divergent the shocks that affect the different countries.

To lay down the groundwork for a systematic comparison of policy outcomes under an AP system with outcomes under a CMCS, this chapter has abstracted from possible systematic differences in the objective functions of different countries and from the stabilizatory function of monetary policy.[15] The model in this chapter can be altered in obvious ways to incorporate these additional elements. For example, to endow monetary policy with stabilizing powers, it is enough to reverse the timing of shocks and of nominal contracts. When contracts are made before the realization of shocks, there is room for stabilization by monetary policy. An example of such a case suggests that the result that a CMCS is less likely to renege on the commitment to price stability than a single country in an AP system extends to the case in which effective stabilization policy is possible (Cukierman 1991c).[16]

The 1990 draft statute for the European System of Central Banks (ESCB) proposes the following structure for the system: The ESCB is to consist of a central body, the European Central Bank (ECB) and the twelve national central banks. The main executive body of the ECB will be the executive board consisting of the president, the vice president, and four other members. They will be appointed for eight-year terms by the European Council. The main decision-making body of the ECB is to be the council, composed of the executive board members and the governors of the twelve national central banks. The council will normally meet monthly, and each member is to essentially have one vote (Goodhart 1991). The framework of this chapter has been applied to examine the effects of the distribution of power between the executive board and the council of the European Central Bank in a monetary union on the likelihood that the commitment to price stability will be maintained. The main result is that a relatively stronger board makes the commitment to price stability more probable and therefore also more credible (Cukierman 1991c).

Appendix A: Proof of Proposition 6.2

Assumption 2 implies that if the central monetary authority reneges, it picks the discretionary rate in equation (6.4) for $s = s_m$. If unions anticipate this behavior,

$$\pi_d(\pi_d, s_m) = \frac{\alpha A}{1 + \alpha^2 A} [s_m + \alpha \pi_d]. \tag{6A.1}$$

This implies that when the community central bank is expected to renege, both actual and expected inflation are $\alpha A s_m$.

Given that $\pi^e = \alpha A s_m$, country m votes to renege if

$$W[\alpha A s_m, \alpha A s_m, s_m] - W[0, \alpha A s_m, s_m] > c \tag{6A.2}$$

which, using (6.2) and rearranging, is equivalent to

$$(\alpha^2 A - 1)s_m^2 + 2s_m^2 > \frac{2c}{(\alpha A)^2} \tag{6A.2a}$$

and to

$$s_m > s_L. \tag{6A.2b}$$

Under the same circumstances country $i \neq m$ also votes to renege if

$$W[\alpha A s_m, \alpha A s_m, s_i] - W[0, \alpha A s_m, s_i] > c. \tag{6A.3}$$

Equation (6A.3) is equivalent to the condition

$$(\alpha^2 A - 1)s_m^2 + 2s_m s_i > \frac{2c}{(\alpha A)^2}. \tag{6A.3a}$$

Comparison of (6A.2a) with (6A.3a) implies that if the median country has a preference for breaking the commitment, so do all the countries with $s_i > s_m$. Hence, when country m prefers to renege, there is a weighted majority in favor of such a move and condition (6.12) in the text is satisfied.

Appendix B: Proof That S_H^2 Is Decreasing in A

Differentiating the expression for S_H^2 in equation (6.5a) with respect to A, we obtain

$$\frac{\partial S_H^2}{\partial A} = -\frac{2c}{A^2} \tag{6A.4}$$

which is unambiguously negative. □

Appendix C: Derivation of the Probability Density of the Median Shock (Equations 6.20)

The sample median is an order statistic. Its density is obtained by deriving the probability density of the kth-order statistic and specializing k to the case of the median. Let $s_1, \ldots, s_n$ be a drawing of size n from the distribution of an identically and independently distributed random variable s. Let $f(s)$ be the probability density of s. Let $s_{(1)}, \ldots, s_{(n)}$ be a rearrangement of the sample $s_1, \ldots, s_n$ such that

$$s_{(1)} < s_{(2)} < \cdots < s_{(k)} < \cdots < s_{(n)}.$$

Then $s_{(k)}$ is known as the kth-order statistic.

The probability that the kth-order statistic falls in the small interval $(s, s + ds)$ is equal to the probability that one of the n sample values of s falls in this range multiplied (by independence) by the probability that exactly $k + 1$ of the remaining sample values are below this interval and exactly $n - k$ are above it. The probability of a particular configuration of sample values that satisfies these requirements is therefore

$$[F(s)]^{k-1}[1 - F(s)]^{n-k}f(s)\,ds, \qquad k = 1, \ldots, n.$$

But there are n ways in which the kth-order statistic can fall in the interval $(s, s + ds)$ since each of s_i, $i = 1, \ldots, n$, can fall in this range. In addition the allocation of the remaining $n - 1$ sample values between those that are above and those that are below the kth-order statistic can occur in $\begin{bmatrix} n - 1 \\ k - 1 \end{bmatrix}$ ways. Hence

$$f_k(s)\,ds = n\begin{bmatrix} n - 1 \\ k - 1 \end{bmatrix}[F(s)]^{k-1}[1 - F(s)]^{n-k}f(s)\,ds, \qquad k = 1, \ldots, n. \quad (6A.5)$$

Equations (6.20) are obtained by eliminating ds from both sides of (6A.5) and by setting $k = (n + 1)/2$ to get the distribution of the median when n is odd and by letting $k = n/2$ to get it when n is even. $\qquad\square$

7 The Financial Stability Motive, Interest Rate Smoothing, and the Theory of Optimal Seigniorage

7.1 Introduction

Central banks of some industrialized countries engage in short-term interest rate smoothing. This policy is particularly evident in the United States where the Federal Reserve normally gears monetary policy to reduce fluctuations in short-term nominal interest rates. Even Paul Volcker's successful monetary experiment, during which wider rates fluctuations were tolerated, did not produce a permanent shift to a nominal stock rule as advocated by monetarists in the United States. This is puzzling for several reasons, not the least of which is the fact that monetarists' prescriptions have proved to be effective in delivering price stability. The tendency to revert to a policy of interest rate smoothing seems to be rather tenacious and as old as the Fed. Thus Miron (1986) and Mankiw, Miron, and Weil (1987) report that there has been a substantial change in the behavior of interest rates after the establishment of the Federal Reserve in 1914. After 1914 interest rates became substantially more persistent. Moreover the Fed was widely expected to dampen fluctuations in interest rates. Goodfriend and King (1988) note that prior to the Fed's creation fluctuations in the monthly average call money rate on short-term broker loans exhibited much wider irregular and seasonal fluctuations. Donaldson (1989) finds that after the foundation of the Fed, violent spikes in interest rates during financial panics virtually disappeared.

This chapter reviews and contrasts two alternative hypotheses about the objectives of monetary policy and their positive implications for the behavior of interest rates. One is that the central bank is concerned about the stability of the financial system. It is willing therefore to compromise on the objective of price stability, particularly when the stability of this system seems to be threatened, in order to reduce the likelihood of instability. In economies with developed financial markets, various intermediaries normally commit to loan contracts that stretch over longer periods than the term for which deposits are committed to them. This makes them vulnerable to surprise increases in market rates, since in the short run such increases affect their cost of funds more quickly than their revenues from loans. When such increases materialize, the central bank injects liquidity into the economy in order to reduce the resulting threat to the stability of the financial system. This moderates temporarily the increase in interest rates. Conversely, when market rates unexpectedly go down, the profits and stability of banks and other intermediaries go up. At such times the central bank mops up some of the liquidity previously injected into the economy because it is also concerned with price stability. These reactions of the central bank to both upward and downward movements in interest rates dampen fluctuations in interest rates. This theory of interest rate smoothing seems to be particularly relevant for the Fed. But it is likely to be relevant also for the central banks of other countries with wide financial markets.

The other hypothesis surveyed, with particular attention to its implications for interest rates, is the *theory of optimal seigniorage*. It states that monetary policy is dominated by optimal public finance considerations in which the revenue motive from chapter 4 plays a central role. Revenues from seigniorage entail, like any other tax, deadweight losses. Hence monetary policy is conducted so as to minimize the discounted present value of deadweight losses from regular taxes and seigniorage subject to the constraint that a certain (fluctuating) level of public expenditures is financed. Provided the marginal social costs of both regular taxes and seigniorage are increasing, this hypothesis implies that seigniorage, and therefore inflation, should be positively related to the relative size of regular taxes. In the long run nominal interest rates and inflation are positively related because of the inflation premium in nominal rates. Hence the optimal seigniorage theory implies that nominal rates should be positively related to the relative size of regular taxes. Mankiw (1987) uses this implication of the theory to test it.[1] Another implication of the theory is that nominal rates and inflation should be positively related to the relative size of government.

Section 7.2 presents an overview of the hypothesis that interest rate smoothing arises as a by-product of the central bank's attempt to optimally trade off the costs of financial instability and the costs of price instability. The argument is developed in more detail in the subsequent two sections. Section 7.5 presents an overview of the optimal seigniorage theory and its implications for the behavior of nominal rates. The two hypotheses are compared and contrasted in section 7.6. This is followed by concluding remarks.

7.2   The Financial Stability Motive as an Explanation for Interest Rate Smoothing[2]

This section presents an overview of a positive explanation for the tendency of some central banks such as the Fed to smooth interest rates. The explanation relies on two presumptions. One is that the central bank (CB) is concerned about the stability of the financial system as well as about price stability. The other is that banks commit to loan contracts that normally stretch over longer periods than the term for which deposits are committed to them. There is little doubt that the Fed is concerned about the stability of the financial system in general and that of the banking system in particular. The Fed has been founded to a large extent in order to avoid financial crises (Mankiw, Miron, and Weil 1987). Its charter makes it responsible for averting such crises and it is widely expected to do so by Congress and the public. The concern of the Fed with financial stability is consistent with general economic welfare; financial crises that are allowed to develop retard capital formation, thereby reducing real output (Bernanke 1983). As a bureaucracy the Fed may reasonably be expected to dislike the risks of banking failures sometimes even more than adverse general economic conditions such as unemployment. After all, the responsibility for the banking system is in the Fed's "own courtyard" while the responsibility for high unemployment is naturally shared by other policymaking institutions such as the fiscal authority. Brimmer (1989) makes a persuasive case that on various occasions the Fed's policy was geared mostly to safeguard the stability of the financial system.

The second presumption relies on the traditional function of banks, which is to transform short-term liabilities into longer-term loan assets. Although some variable rates loans have recently developed, a large fraction of loans in the United States specifies a fixed loan rate and volume in advance for the period of the loan.[3] Many deposits, on the other hand (e.g., demand deposits, short-term money market accounts, and large certificates of deposit), have more flexible terms both with respect to maturity[4] and return. This asymmetry is probably due to the fact that the fundamental service provided by banks on both sides of their balance sheet is liquidity. On the side of assets (loans), liquidity is provided by giving the borrower an advance unconditional assurance for the loan terms. On the side of liabilities (deposits), liquidity is provided by letting customers use their funds on demand. Another possible reason is that loan markets are more influenced by customer-specific considerations than deposit markets.[5] In this chapter we take the asymmetry in the contract provisions of loans and of deposits as given, and explore the implications of its existence for the behavior of the central bank.

The advance commitment of banks to loan terms makes them vulnerable to changes in the conditions of financial markets after they have committed their funds. For example, if after loan contracts have been made, there is an unexpected decrease in the aggregate supply of deposits, banks lose reserves and incur higher marginal costs of illiquidity.[6] To correct this situation, each individual bank tries to regain deposits by raising its deposit rate. Since all banks do that, there is a general increase in the total cost of funds to banks and a decrease in the profits of the banking industry. The squeeze in profits is amplified by the fact that rates rise on the entire stock of deposits after loan rates and quantities have been preset. This in turn increases the likelihood that some relatively weak banks will fail. Since the CB is concerned about the stability of the banking system, it has interest in counteracting the increase in the likelihood of banking failures. Provided the price level is temporarily fixed, the CB can temporarily offset the decrease in banks' profits by stepping up the rate of increase in reserves. This action decreases banks' demand for deposits and dampens some of the increase in the rate of interest paid on deposits, thus offsetting at least some of the increase in the risk of banking failures. However, the higher rate of reserve expansion is also costly from the point of view of the CB, since after a while it leads to a larger rate of inflation. Hence, when the cost of funds to banks unexpectedly goes down, in-creasing bank's profits and decreasing the likelihood of failures, the CB puts more emphasis on the stability of the general price level and decreases the rate of growth of base money. In the short run this action dampens the initial decrease in the cost of funds to the banking industry.

Thus interest rate smoothing by the central bank arises as a by-product of the bank's attempt to minimize some combination of the risks of finan-cial instability and of the costs of inflation. The central bank directs policy mostly to increase the soundness of the banking system when the risks of financial instability are relatively high. It focuses mostly on maintenance of price stability when profits in the banking industry are high and the risks of failure therefore relatively low. Since, owing to the asymmetry in the structure of their contracts, bank's profits are negatively related to the level of interest rates in the short run, the central bank's actions result in interest rate smoothing.

The concern of the Fed and other central banks for the profits of the banking industry may also be due to captive regulator elements. But since the weight given by the central bank to the profits of the banking industry may reflect its concern for financial stability or its concern for banks' profits, or both, the two hypotheses are observationally equivalent. Whatever the motives of the Fed for caring about banks' profits, it is pretty clear that banks dislike large unexpected swings in interest rates, particularly if they are upward. Wooley (1984, p. 228, n. 10) reports, based on the Federal Advisory Council (FAC) minutes, that at the February 1969 FAC meeting the council advised the board that "the principal thesis of the Council's thinking was that bankers would accommodate to almost any policy of restraint when it was applied gradually, but that sudden twists caused serious dislocations."[7] Wooley (p. 72) further notes that during the 1970s many banks became vulnerable to increases in interest rates "because sharp upward movements in interest rates force banks to buy money at rates higher than they have loaned it. Vulnerability of this sort seems, in fact, to be highest for the big multinational banks some observers suspect of being the Federal Reserve's closest friends."

7.3 Central Bank Behavior and the Structure of the Financial Sector

Both by law and custom a self-acknowledged goal of the Federal Reserve is the preservation of the stability of the financial system in general, and that of the banking system in particular (see, e.g., *Federal Reserve Bulletin*, July 1984, p. 548). The financial stability objective is more likely to be attained the higher the profits of the banking system. This statement is particularly relevant if the CB does not know the realizations of idiosyncratic shocks across individual banks. The profits of a single bank can be decomposed into a component that is common to all banks and into a component that is specific to the individual bank. If the common component of profits is large, even banks with particularly adverse realizations of the idiosyncratic shocks will be solvent, but if the common component of profits is small, even banks with moderately adverse idiosyncratic shocks will run into difficulties.[8] Thus the higher the profits of the banking system, the smaller is the probability of a serious financial crisis. If the Fed values financial stability, it should, ceteris paribus, prefer a state of nature with higher profits in the banking industry to a state with lower profits. However, as total profits increase further, the incremental contribution to financial stability most probably diminishes. We will model those features by postulating that one component of the objective function of the central bank is a function $f(\pi)$ that increases in the profits π of the banking industry but at a decreasing rate. In addition, as noted in chapters 3 through 5, the central bank dislikes inflation. Thus the entire objective function of the central bank can be stated as

$$-\tfrac{1}{2}(\ln P_{t+1} - \ln P_t)^2 + gf(\pi_t), f'(\cdot) > 0, f''(\cdot) < 0. \tag{7.1}$$

Here $\ln P_{t+1} - \ln P_t$ is the rate of inflation between period t and period $t + 1$, π_t are the profits of the banking industry in period t, and g is a positive parameter that measures the relative concern of the central bank for financial stability versus price stability. This formulation reflects a basic externality that is internalized by the CB. Each bank cares only about its own profits, but the CB cares about the profits of the entire industry because of the connection between this aggregate and financial stability. To focus on the consequences of the interaction between the central bank and the private banking system in isolation, we abstract from the employment, the revenue and the balance-of-payments motives for inflation.[9]

The CB picks the rate of growth of high-powered money μ_t subject to the structure of the economy so as to maximize the objective function in equation (7.1). To formulate this decision of the CB, it is necessary to specify the structure of the economy. This is our next task. To simply capture the fact that loan contracts are less flexible than the contracts governing banks' deposits, we postulate that each bank determines the quantity of one-period loans and their price at the beginning of each period for the period. This commitment is made before any shocks occur that affect the economy and the banking system during the period. But the volume and cost of deposits are determined within the period after the shocks occur. We refer to the preshocks equilibrium as the *ex-ante equilibrium* and to the equilibrium that determines variables, which are free to adjust after shocks occur, as the *ex-post equilibrium*. The shocks considered affect the supply of deposits to the banking system, the excess demand for bonds, and the demand for loans. These shocks, denoted ε_d, ε_b, and ε_l, respectively, are specified as white noises with zero means.

Suppose that there is an economywide short-term bond market. The (real) bond rate r_b is determined through market clearing after the occurrence of the various shocks that affect the economy. Bonds can be purchased by private banks as well as by the general public. Banks choose their bond portfolios after the occurrence of stochastic shocks within the period. To maintain the complexity of the model at a manageable level, we assume that bonds are traded only once within a period after the shocks occur. Furthermore only one-period bonds that mature just prior to trade in bonds in the next period are considered. This specification abstracts from the function of bonds as secondary liquidity. But it does account for the tendency of banks to reduce their bond portfolios when they lose reserves, thus bringing out part of the function of bonds as secondary reserves[10] as well as the effect of reserve losses on bond market equilibrium.

In addition to the interest it pays on deposits, the individual bank incurs various costs that are associated with illiquidity. Those costs increase at an increasing rate with the degree of the bank's illiquidity, which is measured in turn as the difference between the required reserves of the bank and its actual level of reserves. These costs generally induce banks to demand a positive level of reserves. The supply of reserves is determined by the CB after the occurrence of shocks. It bears repeating that in making this choice, the CB attempts to maximize its objective function in equation (7.1).

Prices of goods and services are relatively more sticky than the prices of highly liquid financial assets (Dornbusch 1976). To capture this element, we assume that the general price level is determined prior to the occurrence of shocks (and the choice of μ by the CB) in a manner that is designed to clear the market for bank reserves in an ex-ante sense.[11]

The ex-post equilibrium determines r_b—the real rate paid on deposits— and the demands for bonds by the banking system and the public as functions of the shocks. The (contractual) variables determined at the beginning of the period in the ex-ante equilibrium are the volume and price of loans and the general price level. Each bank decides how much credit to extend and how much to charge for it so as to maximize expected profits. In doing that, it takes the actions of other banks and its expectation about the upcoming ex-post equilibrium as given. In the ex-post equilibrium each bank chooses the real rate it pays on deposits and the amount of bonds it holds so as to maximize its profits after the occurrence of shocks and after the choice of policy for the period by the CB. In doing that, the individual bank takes the actions of other banks and the market-clearing value of the real bond rate as given.

In summary, the general price level, the price of loans, and the volume of loans are determined in the ex-ante equilibrium by the ex-ante clearing of the market for reserves, the individual bank's first-order condition with respect to the real price of loans, and the demand for loans. The bond rate, the rate paid on deposits, and the volume of deposits are determined in the ex-post equilibrium by the clearing of the bond market, the individual bank's first-order condition with respect to the deposit rate, and the supply of deposits.

Given the number of banks the symmetric Cournot-Nash ex-ante and ex-post equilibria imply that the aggregate profits of the banking system are a decreasing function of the real bond rate r_b. A derivation of this result and related details appear in Cukierman (1990, sec. 3). For our purposes it suffices to present the intuitive reason for this result. An increase in the bond rate induces two opposing effects on the profits of the banking industry. On the one hand, there is an increase in the return on the bond portfolio and a related upward adjustment in the quantity of bonds held by each bank, both of which tend to increase the profits of banks. On the other hand, the more lucrative bond rate causes an intensification of the banks' competition for funds and results in an increase in the deposit rate on the entire stock of deposits. This market effect reduces the profits of the banking industry. If banks had not previously committed a large part of their funds to loans, they would have increased their investment in the bond market by decreasing the amount of loans offered to customers as well as by increasing the loan rate. However, the previously made commitment to a certain level of loans limits the banks' ability to take advantage of the better bond market opportunities. The larger this commitment, the more limited is the ability of banks to increase their bond portfolio because of increasing costs of illiquidity. This limitation is reflected through the fact that the total amount of earning assets of a bank (loans + bonds) is limited by a constant that depends on r_b and on the shock to the demand for deposits. Thus the ability of banks to take advantage of the more lucrative bond rate is limited by past commitments of funds. However, the increase in the deposit rate increases the cost of all funds, including those that are needed to fulfill the obligation to previously contracted loans. As a consequence the negative market-induced effect of an increase in r_b on profits dominates the direct positive effect.

Within the period the CB can temporarily reduce the (real) bond rate by increasing the supply of reserves through open market operations. This ability originates from the fact that the price level has been predetermined by the ex-ante equilibrium.[12] It vanishes once the price level is readjusted at the beginning of the following period. The equilibrium bond rate is also obviously negatively related to the shock ε_b, to the excess demand for bonds. These two facts are summarized in equation (7.2):

$$r_b = r(\varepsilon_b, \mu), \qquad \frac{dr(\cdot)}{d\varepsilon_b} < 0, \frac{dr(\cdot)}{d\mu} < 0. \qquad (7.2)$$

The effects of r_b and of the shock ε_d to the supply of deposits on the profits of the banking industry are summarized in equation (7.3):

$$\pi = \pi(\varepsilon_d, r_b), \qquad \frac{d\pi(\cdot)}{d\varepsilon_d} > 0, \frac{d\pi(\cdot)}{dr_b} < 0. \tag{7.3}$$

The positive effect of ε_d on bank's profits is due to the fact that a rise in the supply of deposits reduces the equilibrium cost of funds to the banking system. The negative effect of r_b on profits has been discussed above.

It is shown in Cukierman (1990) that since the price level is determined at the beginning of each period, the CB problem in equation (7.1) can be reformulated as[13]

$$\max_{\mu_t} \left(-\frac{1}{2}\mu_t^2 + gf[\pi\{\varepsilon_{dt}, r(\varepsilon_{bt}, \mu_t)\}] \right). \tag{7.1a}$$

This restatement emphasizes the basic intraperiod trade-off confronting the central bank. It may, if it wishes, increase the profits of the banking system by stepping up the rate of nominal reserve creation μ_t. Such a policy increases the profits of banks by decreasing the bond rate and decreases the probability of financial failures. This is a benefit for central bank objectives. But an increase in the rate of reserve creation also increases the rate of inflation between the current and the next period, and that is a cost. The choice of μ_t involves weighing the benefits of increased financial stability against the costs of higher inflation. The first-order condition for an internal maximum of (7.1a) is

$$F_\mu \equiv -\mu_t + gf'(\pi_t)\frac{d\pi(\cdot)}{dr_{bt}}\frac{dr(\cdot)}{d\mu_t} = 0. \tag{7.4}$$

Since $d\pi_t(\cdot)/dr_{bt}$ and $dr(\cdot)/d\mu_t$ are negative, the first-order condition in (7.4) implies that the rate of reserve creation by the central bank is positive for every possible realization of the intraperiod shocks. Thus central bank concern for the stability of the banking system creates an inflationary bias similar to the one produced by the employment motive (chapter 3).[14]

7.4   The Trade-off between Financial Stability and Price Stability as an Inducement for Interest Rate Smoothing

We saw in the previous section that an unexpected intraperiod decrease in the demand for deposits, an increase in the bond rate due to an upward shock to the supply of bonds, or a downward shock to the demand for bonds decreases the profits of the banking industry. When profits are lower, bank failures are more likely, and thereby the marginal value to the CB of an incremental increase in the profits of the banking industry is larger. The CB is then more willing to tolerate larger increases in bank reserves, even if they increase the rate of inflation, provided that the decrease in profits is attenuated.

The CB can dampen the short-run decrease in banks' profits by stepping up the rate of reserve creation, which would decrease the bond rate and the deposit rate. The CB's tendency to follow such a policy is stronger when unanticipated shocks to financial markets raise the bond rate and the deposit rate and concurrently decrease profits. In this view the CB has no long-term concern about the *level* of interest rates. However, because of the short-run negative correlation between the bond rate and the profits of the banking industry, the CB at least partially offsets unanticipated increases in interest rates in order to dampen the adverse effect that such increases have on the profits and the stability of the banking system. This implication is consistent with the view expressed by the U.S. Federal Advisory Council regarding what private banks are likely to tolerate (see section 7.2).

Conversely, when unanticipated shocks decrease interest rates and increase the profits of banks, the value to the CB of further increases in profits is diminished. It therefore puts more emphasis on reducing the rate of inflation by lowering the rate of reserve creation below its mean value. As a result the decrease in interest rates is not as large as it would have been without an active policy on the part of the CB.

In effect the central bank smoothes short-run fluctuations in real rates.[15] When shocks push rates unexpectedly above their previously expected level, the bank steps up the rate of reserve creation and dampens the increase in rates. When shocks decrease rates below their previously expected level, the bank slows down the rate of reserve creation and dampens the decrease in rates. Strictly speaking, this smoothing result requires that the number of banks not be too small and/or that the index

$$\theta \equiv \left| \frac{f''(\pi)}{f'(\pi)} \right| \tag{7.5}$$

in the CB objective function be sufficiently large. Readers familiar with the theory of expected utility will recognize that θ is a coefficient of absolute risk aversion. In the present context it measures how quickly the marginal contribution of additional profits to banks' stability diminishes with the level of profits of the banking industry. It can also be interpreted as reflecting how quickly the marginal "utility" of the CB from further increases in banks' stability decreases with additional increases in stability. It obviously may reflect a mixture of both elements. The first element is determined by the structure of the economy, while the second depends on the preferences of the central bank. We refer to θ as the index of aversion to instability remembering that it is in general affected by both the structure of the economy and the preferences of the central bank. The higher the θ, the quicker is the decrease in the marginal utility of profits because of the combined effects of further profits on stability and of more stability on the objectives of the central bank. The following propositions summarize the main qualitative results:

PROPOSITION 7.1   For a sufficiently large number of banks and/or a sufficiently large index of aversion to instability the central bank decreases the rate of growth of reserves when the intraperiod excess demand for bonds ε_b increases.

PROPOSITION 7.2   For a sufficiently large number of banks and/or a sufficiently large index of aversion to instability, the central bank responds to an unanticipated increase in the demand for deposits ε_d by slowing down the rate of reserves' expansion.

The propositions are demonstrated, by means of comparative statics, in Cukierman (1990, sec. 6). They do not state the smoothing result directly. But it nevertheless is a corollary of these propositions. This can be seen by noting that a decrease in ε_b or in ε_d raises the bond rate and reduces the profits of the banking industry. The propositions imply that the central bank reacts to such increases by stepping up the rate of reserves' creation, which pushes the bond rate in the opposite direction.

In general the CB responds to a combination of the shocks ε_b and ε_d. If the realization of shocks changes profits in a given direction, the CB responds by altering the rate of change of reserves so as to move the bond rate in the same direction. Since, in the absence of intervention, profits and the bond rate are negatively correlated, the CB acts on average to dampen fluctuations in r_b. Stated somewhat differently, the effects of ε_b and of ε_d on r_b through the CB response function are opposite in sign to the direct effects of those shocks on r_b.

Since the price level is sticky within a period, the rate of inflation is equal to the rate of increase in high-powered money μ. (Details appear in Cukierman 1990, sec. 5.) It follows from the first-order condition in equation (7.4) that expected inflation is

$$E\mu = gEf'(\cdot)\frac{d\pi(\cdot)}{dr_b}\frac{dr(\cdot)}{d\mu} > 0. \tag{7.6}$$

Since all shocks are transitory, the right-hand side of equation (7.6) is a constant. This reflects the (financial stability–induced) average inflationary bias of the CB. The nominal bond rate in period t is therefore

$$n_{bt} = r_{bt} + E\mu. \tag{7.7}$$

Hence the nominal bond rate is equal to the real bond rate plus a positive constant. It follows that the central bank's response to shocks induces smoothing of short-term nominal as well as of real rates.

To this point the analysis was based on the assumption that the entire volume of loans is predetermined before the realization of shocks during the period of the loan. In practice part of banking credit takes the form of credit lines in which borrowers are free to determine the actual amount borrowed, up to a predetermined ceiling, after the realization of shocks (Brady 1985). To examine the robustness of the smoothing result to the presence of credit lines, consider the other extreme case in which all loans take the form of credit lines. In particular suppose that the loan contract requires banks to passively accommodate any intraperiod changes in the demand for loans at the rate that was preset at the beginning of the period.

The main novelty in this reformulation is that now the profits of the banking industry also depend on the shock ε_l to the demand for loans. An unexpected positive ε_l induces banks to passively substitute loans for bonds in their portfolios, causing an increase in the costs of illiquidity and a rise in the bond rate. If the loan rate is equal to or smaller than the bond rate, the effect on banks' profits is unambiguously negative. If the loan rate is larger than the bond rate, an unexpected increase in the demand for loans generally has an ambiguous effect on the profits of the banking system. On the one hand, profits are squeezed, as in the previous case, because of the increase in the bond rate brought about by the larger demand for loans. On the other hand, since the loan rate is larger than the bond rate, a substitution of loans for bonds increases profits. However, for a sufficiently large number of banks the negative effect on profits is likely to dominate. (Details appear in Cukierman 1990, sec. 8.) Hence in either case an unexpected rise in ε_l increases the bond rate and reduces banks' profits and the stability of the financial system.

The central bank responds to the increased demand for credit by increasing the rate of reserve's creation. It offsets at least partially the upward effect of this increased demand on the bond rate. The bank's attempt to preserve the profits of the banking industry within a "reasonable range" induces it to accommodate changes in credit demand, raising reserves more when demand for credit increases and lowering their rate of expansion when the demand for credit diminishes.

In summary, the major result that the central bank smoothes fluctuations in interest rates extends to the case in which credit is allocated to customers via credit lines. In fact the presence of credit lines enables the bank to smooth fluctuations in interest rates that are due to shocks to the loan market as well as to shocks to the bond and deposit markets. Since shocks to the demand for credit are positively correlated with the cycle, the procyclical response of reserves growth is amplified by the existence of credit lines.

An interesting implication of the theory concerns the effect of an increase in the supply of government bonds on the policy of the CB. The policy response of the CB differs depending on whether the increased supply of bonds has been anticipated at the time loan contracts were made. If it had been anticipated, its consequences would have been built into the price level and loan contracts. In such a case an increase in the supply of bonds by government does not trigger any reaction by the CB. Consider alternatively the case in which the increased supply of bonds has been unexpected at the beginning of the period. Such a change is equivalent to a negative realization of the excess demand for bonds shock ε_b. Since such a shock temporarily reduces banks' profits and their stability, the CB reacts by stepping up the rate of monetary expansion. Hence an unanticipated increase in a bond-financed budgetary deficit triggers increased monetization by the monetary authority. But when the increase is anticipated, the CB does not monetize. Thus the concern of the CB for the stability of the financial system does not imply that budgetary deficits that were widely known in advance will be monetized.

7.5   The Theory of Optimal Seigniorage and Its Implications for the Behavior of Interest Rates

The theory of optimal seigniorage recently reformulated and tested by Mankiw (1987) is an extension of Barro's (1979) tax-smoothing argument. Like regular taxes, seigniorage can be used to finance public expenditures and like them it entails deadweight losses. The optimal allocation of taxes over time, as well as across those two types of taxes within a given period, is obtained therefore by applying the principle that the present discounted value of the social costs of financing public expenditures should be minimized. The minimization is performed subject to the restriction that a certain level of (possibly stochastic) public expenditures is financed in each period.

The principle above implies that the optimal mix of fiscal and monetary policies satisfies three conditions. Two of the conditions ensure the optimal intertemporal allocation of regular taxes and of seigniorage. One equates (as in Barro 1979) the marginal social cost of regular taxes today and in the future. The other similarly equates the marginal social costs of seigniorage today and in the future. The third condition ensures that within each period the total burden of taxation is allocated optimally between regular taxes and seigniorage. It is a static first-order condition that equates contemporaneously the marginal social cost of regular taxes with the marginal social cost of raising revenue through seigniorage.

Conventional wisdom is that the marginal social costs of regular taxes and of seigniorage rise the more intensive is the intraperiod use of each kind of those revenue-raising devices in comparison to the size of the economy. This presumption, in conjunction with the condition for the optimal intraperiod allocation of regular taxes and of seigniorage, implies that seigniorage and regular taxes, both as fractions of output, should rise and fall together.

The intuition underlying this result is compelling. An increase in the amount of public expenditures that have to be financed must lead to an increase in both seigniorage and regular taxes when they are allocated optimally. The reason is that using only (or mostly) one of these revenue sources pushes its marginal social cost above that of the other source, making it worthwhile to increase the other source as well. For the same reason a reduction in the amount of public expenditures leads to a reduction in both regular taxes and seigniorage.

As long as monetary policy is optimal in the sense of this section, seigniorage revenues rise with the rate of inflation.[16] This observation implies that inflation and regular taxes as a fraction of output should be positively related. Furthermore, in the long run, actual inflation pushes up nominal interest rates because of Fisher's premium. This implies that once nominal rates have adjusted to inflation, they should be positively related to the relative size of regular taxes. Mankiw (1987) tests this implication of the theory by regressing the United States Treasury bill rate on federal revenues as a percent of GNP and on a time trend. For the period 1952–85 he finds a positive and significant relationship between the bill rate and the share of federal revenues in GNP. But a more recent test that adjusts for nonstationary disturbances and considers a longer period of time rejects the revenue-smoothing hypothesis for the United States (Trehan and Walsh 1990). The hypothesis also gives mixed results at best for some OECD countries (Poterba and Rotemberg 1990).[17]

Another implication of the theory of optimal seigniorage is that nominal interest rates should be positively related to the relative size of public expenditures. The channels are similar. An exogenous increase in the share of public expenditures requires an increase in seigniorage revenues that is achieved by an increase in the rate of inflation. Higher inflation raises nominal rates, at least in the long run, so ultimately an increase in public expenditures leads to an increase in nominal rates.

As a descriptive, rather than a prescriptive theory, the optimal seigniorage paradigm implies that the CB increases the rate of monetary expansion when the share of public expenditures in GNP rises. Such behavior implies that nominal interest rates should be high when public expenditures are high and should be low when the share of public expenditures is low. It is important to note that, unlike in previous sections, this hypothesis does not lead to interest rate smoothing in the sense that the CB partially offsets autonomous movements in interest rates. As a matter of fact the central bank's policy causes nominal rates to move secularly up and down, together with public spending. Policy is designed to smooth taxes and seigniorage rather than interest rates.

Another implication of the theory of optimal seigniorage is that nominal interest rates should be positively related to the size of budgetary deficits. Because of the efficient allocation of taxes and seigniorage within (as well as across) periods, current seigniorage should be positively related to future taxes and therefore to the size of the deficit. For reasons elaborated earlier in this section, seigniorage and nominal rates are positively related. Hence nominal rates should be positively related to the size of the deficit.

The optimal intertemporal allocation of seigniorage implies that the marginal costs of seigniorage should be equated across periods. Mankiw and Miron (1990) argue that this implies that the nominal rate of interest, which is the opportunity cost of holding money, should be equated across periods. Hence, they argue, it is optimal from a public finance point of view to smooth seasonals in interest rates. Such a policy was actually clearly in evidence after the foundation of the Fed in 1914.

7.6   The Financial Stability Motive versus the Optimal Seigniorage Hypothesis as Positive Theories of Interest Rate Behavior

Previous sections have presented two alternative hypotheses about the objectives of monetary policy and their implications for the behavior of interest rates. In the first hypothesis, interest rate smoothing arises as a by-product of the central bank's attempt to minimize a combination of the costs of financial instability and of price instability. In the second, the behavior of nominal rates is a by-product of a policy attempt to use seigniorage with other taxes in a way that minimizes the present value of the social costs of financing public expenditures. This hypothesis leads to a predicted secular positive relationship between nominal rates, on the one hand, and the relative sizes of taxes, deficits, and total public expenditures, on the other.

This section compares and contrasts these two hypotheses. An important difference concerns the time spans of the two hypotheses. The financial stability hypothesis (FSH) applies within a time span that is sufficiently short to introduce enough stickiness into the price level and loan contracts. Within this run monetary policy is able to affect real as well as nominal interest rates. The optimal seigniorage hypothesis (OSH) applies to a run that is sufficiently long to allow expected inflation to catch up with actual inflation and to have it fully embedded in nominal rates. Hence to a first approximation the OSH implies that monetary policy affects only nominal but not real rates.

The FSH implies that monetary policy accommodates an increase in the budgetary deficit only when this increase is unanticipated. By contrast, the OSH implies that monetary policy accommodates budgetary deficits whether or not they have been previously anticipated by the public.

Which of the two hypotheses is better suited to account for the actual response of policy in various countries? There is no definite answer to this question. But the following instructive observations can be made:

1.   The rate of growth of base money in the United States during the postwar period has been procyclical (Rasche 1988). Does this evidence discriminate between the two hypotheses? The answer is unfortunately no. To understand why, we show that both theories imply that the response of this rate of growth to surprise upturns in the economy is positive. Consider an unanticipated increase in the demand for credit (a decrease in ε_b or/and an increase in ε_l) due to strengthening of the economy. We saw that under the FSH such a change induces the CB to step up the rate of increase of the base (section 7.4). But under reasonable conditions this will also be the policy response for the OSH. A cyclical upturn normally raises the collection of regular taxes by more than it raises output because of the existence of built-in stabilizers. Hence, to maintain the intraperiod efficient allocation of financing across alternative sources of revenues, seigniorage revenues have to be raised as well. To achieve this aim, the CB responds to a cyclical upturn by raising the rate of growth of base money.

2.   The OSH implies that the monetary and the fiscal authorities have to coordinate their actions so as to maintain, within each period, the equality of the marginal social costs of regular taxes with the marginal social costs of seigniorage. This requires a substantial amount of coordination (or alternatively of identity in objectives) between the two authorities. Such level of coordination is achieved perhaps in countries with highly dependent central banks. It is less likely to exist in countries with relatively independent central banks such as the United States.

3.   There is persuasive evidence that there was a substantial change in the behavior of short-term nominal rates after the creation of the Fed in November 1914. Friedman and Schwartz (1963, pp. 292–293) note that the seasonal pattern in call money rates narrowed from that time on. Miron (1986) and Mankiw, Miron, and Weil (1987) find that after the creation of the Fed, short-term nominal rates became nearer to random walks than prior to that. Donaldson (1989) finds that after the foundation of the Fed, violent spikes in interest rates during financial panics virtually disappeared. It is possible to interpret this change in terms of the OSH (in the spirit of Mankiw and Miron 1990) by arguing that equalization of nominal interest rates across seasons was a consequence of the newly created Fed's

attempt to optimally spread the social costs of seigniorage across periods. I doubt that this is a realistic view of the policy motives of the Fed during its early years of operation for several reasons.

To believe that optimal public finance considerations dominated monetary policy in the early years of the Fed, it is necessary to maintain the view that the Fed was created in order to facilitate revenue smoothing. This seems unlikely for more than one reason. First, centralization of both monetary and fiscal policy seems to be the efficient way to conduct revenue-smoothing operations, since monetary policy has to be synchronized with fiscal policy. The creation of an independent monetary authority appears to be pointed in the opposite direction. Second, it is likely that because of the substantially smaller size of the public sector in 1914 (and therefore of fiscal distortions), revenue-smoothing considerations did not occupy a paramount position in the minds of U.S. policymakers.

By contrast the alternative hypothesis—that the Fed engaged in interest rate smoothing because of its concern for financial stability—accounts for the facts and does not raise such problems. Furthermore comparison of the nearness of interest rates to a random walk under the FSH with their nearness to a random walk in the absence of any policy response indicates that nominal rates are nearer to a random walk in the first case.[18] This result is consistent with the change that occurred in the time series properties of short-term interest rates after the creation of the Fed, as reported in Miron (1986), Mankiw, Miron, and Weil (1987), and Donaldson (1989).

More precise tests that would sharply discriminate between the FSH and OSH have yet to be implemented. Two such tests are suggested in what follows. The OSH implies that the CB steps up the rate of growth of base money when the share of regular taxes goes up. The FSH implies that the CB responds in this manner when the aggregate profits of financial intermediaries go down. Which of the two hypotheses is supported by the data can be determined by running a regression of the rate of growth of high-powered money on the share of taxes and on the profits of intermediaries after controlling for other motives for monetary expansion. Obviously the test may reveal that both, only one, or none of the elements stressed by the two theories is operative.

The FSH also implies that the rate of growth of base money should be higher when nominal rates unexpectedly move up. Hence it is possible to discriminate between the two hypotheses by regressing the rate of growth of base money on the share of taxes and on unexpected short-term movements in nominal rates, again controlling for other motives, such as employment, for monetary expansion. A positive and significant coefficient on the share of taxes would be evidence in support of the OSH, and a positive and significant coefficient on unanticipated nominal rates would support the FSH.

7.7 Concluding Remarks

The analytical formulation of the financial stability hypothesis relies on the presumption that the interest rate on all loan contracts is determined prior to the determination of the cost of funds to banks. The assumption that this contractual arrangement applies to all loans is made for simplicity and is not essential. Even if the interest rate on part of bank loans is adjusted simultaneously with changes in the cost of funds, the CB will have an incentive to smooth interest rates, provided that the fraction of loans with predetermined rates is sufficiently large. This observation implies that the incentive of the CB to engage in interest rate smoothing depends on the degree of inflexibility in the terms of banks' loans and on their composition by maturities. In particular when, other things the same, a larger fraction of credit is marketed via variable rates loans, the central banks' tendency to smooth interest rates diminishes. But to the extent that there exists an imperfect correlation between the market rates to which loan rates are indexed and the cost of funds to banks, an incentive to smooth interest rates remains.

A central implication of the FSH is that an accumulation of unexpected losses across wide segments of the financial system induces the central bank to expand high-powered money at a higher rate. This result may have some power in explaining recent monetary accelerations in the United States as being partially due to the arrival of new information about the magnitude of losses in the thrift industry. Most likely this motive was even stronger during the 1960s and the 1970s when regulation Q prevented Savings and Loan Associations (S&Ls) to raise their deposit rates in order to check disintermediation. In fact the financial stability motive may have been particularly potent during the 1960s and the 1970s because a large part of S&Ls' assets took the form of long-term mortgages whose terms were determined long before inflation and interest rates in the United States soared.

II ASYMMETRIC INFORMATION AND CHANGING OBJECTIVES UNDER DISCRETION

8 Overview of Models of Monetary Policy with Private Information

8.1 Introduction

This chapter reviews in an informal manner the different and sometimes subtle ways in which private information on the part of policymakers affects the economy and policy choices. The presence of private information fundamentally alters the effects of monetary policy on the economy. With perfect information its attempt to achieve real objectives such as employment or a balance-of-payments target only leads to an excessively high rate of inflation without having any effect on those variables (see chapters 3 and 5). But in the presence of private information the monetary authority can create inflationary surprises that have temporary effects on real variables such as employment and output. Hence stabilization policy becomes possible. In addition, since the public does not possess all the information used by policymakers and since this information is usually relevant for predicting future inflation rates, the public learns from past inflation about the possible future actions of policymakers.

Since policymakers are aware of this learning process, it affects their current choice of policy. This creates a link between periods. As a result the dynamic objective function of policymakers no longer decomposes into separate one-period problems as in section 3.4 of chapter 3. All the chapters in part II and all but the last chapter of part III plus chapter 18 deal with situations in which policymakers have an information advantage about something that affects their choice of monetary policy.

There are a number of factors that affect policy choices. These factors are at least temporarily known only by the monetary authority. Among them are the current relative importance given by policy to alternative and partially conflicting objectives, shifts in the extent of central bank's (CB) independence, and superior knowledge about some characteristics of the economy such as the demand for money or the natural level of economic activity. Changes in emphasis on alternative policy objectives could be due to changes in the intensity of political pressures emanating from various interest groups. In addition, even if the CB does not possess superior information about the economy, the forecasts it makes are not usually known by the public. Even if these forecasts are poor, they are still relevant for predicting future inflation for they affect the rate of monetary growth chosen by policymakers. The public also does not know with certainty whether policymakers are able to commit.

Existing models of monetary policy in the presence of private information are best characterized by a two-way classification: first, by whether the attribute about which there is private information is fixed or changing over time; second, by the nature of the variable or variables about which policymakers possess private information. Uncertainty about policymakers' ability to commit can be captured by postulating that there are two types of policymakers in the population. One type is able to commit, and the other is not. One of the two types is assumed to be in office for the duration of the analysis, but the public does not know, at least initially, which type is in office. The frameworks in Barro (1986) and Cukierman and Liviatan (1991) belong to this category. A model of this kind is presented in section 16.2 of chapter 16. When there are two possible (time-invariant) types that differ in their relative preference for economic stimulation versus price stability, and the public is uncertain about the identity of the type in office, we obtain the framework proposed by Vickers (1986). Section 16.3 discusses such a framework. As demonstrated by the discussion in section 16.4, policy choices and the behavior of the economy are qualitatively different, depending on whether private information is about the ability to commit or about the relative preference for stimulation versus price stability.

The main advantage of the models in chapter 16 is that they illustrate the effects of two different types of private information in relatively easily analyzable frameworks. But, due to a multitude of factors—such as changing political pressures, changes in the economy and changes in the effective degree of independence of the CB—policymaker types normally change over time.[1] Thus despite the fact that the public learns continually about the changing policymaker type, it never becomes fully informed about the identity of the type in office. The models that belong to this class are more realistic, though somewhat more complex, than those with fixed types in chapter 16. But what is lost in complexity is gained in realism. The added degree of realism makes models with changing types more suitable as frameworks for empirical work. Within this class there are two distinct categories of variables about which there is private information. In the first case the CB has private information about its own objectives, and in the second it has private forecasts about relevant economic variables. In some cases there is private information about both objectives and economic variables.

Chapters 9, 10, 14, and 18 deal with frameworks in which the CB has superior information about the changing objectives of policy. These changes may reflect changing pressures on the executive branch of government as well as changes in the degree of independence of the CB from the executive branch. Chapter 9 presents the minimal private information framework needed to evaluate the effects of changing objectives. The assumption made in that chapter is that two periods after it occurs, a change in objectives becomes public information. Being the first chapter on private information, this chapter is relatively detailed and explicit. It contains (in section 9.1) a discussion whose main objective is to support the view that private information is an important ingredient of actual monetary policy. This chapter is also the first full-fledged analysis of changing policy objectives under private information. It is therefore used as a benchmark for the more general analysis in some of the subsequent chapters. An extended information advantage in which a given change in objectives is never revealed with certainty is considered in chapter 10. Chapter 14 extends this framework to cases in which there are mandatory, but noisy, monetary announcements. To deal with private information about CB independence, the framework from chapter 10 is adapted to handle time variations in independence. This is done in chapter 18, which also analyzes the effect of differences in rates of time preference and in other objectives between the CB and the Treasury.

Chapter 15 explores a framework in which anticyclical monetary policy is possible because the CB has better information than the public about the permanence of real shocks to employment. Chapter 13 combines noisy private information about money demand with private information about the changing objectives of policymakers. Such a framework has been originally suggested by Canzoneri (1985). The basic inference problem faced by the public in this case is that when it observes an upward blip in the rate of inflation, the public is unsure about whether it is due to an error of forecast concerning money demand or to an increased concern for employment. Table 8.1 summarizes the two-way classification of chapters discussed above.

A policymaker's reputation is a prime determinant of the actions taken by him or her and by private individuals. There are two approaches to the modeling of credibility and reputation. One is based on the notion that the public learns from past inflation things about the nature of, or the information available to, policymakers, and this is relevant for predicting future

Table 8.1
Classification of chapters with private information

| Type | Private information about | | |
	Objectives	Ability to commit	The economy
Fixed	16	16	
Changing	9, 10, 11 (partially), 13, 14, 18		13, 15

inflation. The other approach is based on the notion that the public utilizes its inflationary expectation strategically as a device for disciplining policymakers into maintaining low inflation. This approach is an application of trigger strategies from repeated games. These two approaches are compared and contrasted in chapter 11 in a mostly intuitive manner.

Trigger strategies require all individuals in the public to coordinate their expectations on a single strategy profile out of a large number of possible profiles in order to credibly deter policymakers from inflating at the discretionary rate. In reality there seldom is an institution that coordinates the expectations of different individuals. In the absence of such coordination, trigger strategies are not credible and do not therefore deter policymakers from inflating at the discretionary rate. By contrast, the learning approach parametrizes credibility in terms of the degree of cohesion between the actions or announcements of policymakers and the beliefs of the public. Like trigger strategies, learning acts as a deterrent to excessively high inflation. But this occurs as a by-product of the public's attempt to correctly forecast future inflation rather than because of strategic manipulation of expectations by individuals. Because of this and other reasons, which are discussed in chapter 11, this book uses the learning approach to conceptualize credibility and changes in credibility.

The following sections review intuitively the consequences of various types of private information. The materials reviewed are usually arranged in an increasing order of complexity and of realism. There also are sometimes different levels of complexity and of prerequisite materials within the groupings of topics in the following sections. Readers who have no previous familiarity with monetary policy games with private information are advised to follow the same order in reading the chapters and to study initially only the basic framework within each group of subjects. Other readers may follow the natural order of chapters or go directly to chapters in which they are particularly interested. A good number of chapters can be read in separate modules. The following sections describe the breakdown of chapters into such modules and point out cases in which a chapter builds on one or more previous chapters.

8.2   Private Information about the Ability to Commit (Chapter 16, Sections 16.2 and 16.4)

This framework is designed to explore the consequences for policy and for wage contracts of uncertainty, on the part of the public, about policymakers' ability to commit. There are two possible policymaker types with the same objective function that gives a positive weight to employment and a negative weight to inflation. However, one type is able to commit while the other is not. We model this difference by assuming that prior to the formation of expectations the policymaker in office makes an announcement concerning the rate of inflation he or she will choose after contracts have been concluded. Since he or she incurs a cost for not fulfilling his or her promise, the dependable or "strong" policymaker always lives up to his or her announcement. The other type of policymaker, referred to as weak, does not incur such a cost. Hence, after nominal contracts have been concluded, he or she chooses the discretionary rate of inflation. Prior to concluding nominal contracts, the public does not know whether weak or strong types are in office but holds some prior view about the likelihood that either type is in office. Since weak policymakers have an incentive to mimic the announcement of strong policymakers, the public normally gives it some, but not full, credence. As a consequence both types of policymakers can affect expectations by making announcements.

Since announcements are believed only partially, the public's inflationary expectation is a weighted average between the equilibrium announcement and the higher discretionary rate. Hence, when a weak type is in office, unexpected inflation is positive. But when a strong type is in office, unexpected inflation is negative. This lowers employment and deters strong policymakers from delivering the zero rate of inflation that they would have produced if their identity had been known with certainty. The reason is that the potential presence of weak types, by raising expectations, makes it optimal for strong types to partially accommodate those expectations in order to avoid an excessively large reduction in employment.

Thus dependable policymakers partially accommodate inflationary expectations. But they do that by announcing and delivering more modest objectives for stabilization of inflation (in comparison to perfect information) rather than by attempting to surprise the public.

The upshot is that the presence of private information about the ability to commit induces even policymakers who can commit to partially accommodate inflationary expectations.

8.3   Private Information about the Relative Emphasis on Employment versus Price Stability with Fixed Types (Chapter 16, Sections 16.3 and 16.4)

Suppose that among the policymakers neither type is able to commit. Once in office both types are there for the duration of the game, and this is known by the public. The difference between the two types is that one (labeled weak) is more concerned about employment than about price stability in comparison to the other (the strong counterpart). Thus weakness and strength are conceived in terms of the policymakers' relative concern for price stability rather than in terms of their ability to commit.

Under discretion and perfect information the strong policymakers would have inflated at a lower rate than their weak counterparts. This is a direct consequence of the nature of equilibrium under perfect information in conjunction with the fact that the parameter A that measures the relative preference for employment is higher for the weak type (see equation 3.6). But the public is uncertain about the identity of the type in office.

The game considered consists of two periods. In the first the strong policymakers may want to inflate at a rate that is even lower than their full-information discretionary rate in order to separate themselves from their weak counterparts. The decision whether to do that involves weighting the benefits of lower inflationary expectations in the second period against the cost of a lower level of economic activity in the first. If in office the weak policymakers also want to keep inflationary expectations down. To achieve this, they try to behave, during the first period, in the same manner as their strong counterparts. Since the public is aware of these incentives, the strong policymakers, when in office, are forced to reduce the rate of inflation sufficiently to make it unprofitable for their weak counterparts to mimic them. If it pays the strong policymakers to engage in such a course of action, equilibrium is separating and the public starts the second period with precise knowledge of the identity of the policymaker type in office. If it does not pay them to separate, the strong policymakers choose their (relatively low) discretionary rate in the first period and so do their weak counterparts. In this case the public's uncertainty is not resolved in the first period, and a pooling equilibrium emerges. Section 16.13 of chapter 16 focuses mostly on separating equilibria since for the class of models considered they are more likely to arise.

The nature of equilibrium differs fundamentally when the public is uncertain about the commitment ability of policymakers rather than about their relative concern for employment versus price stability. In the first case the strong policymakers partially compromise with the actions expected by the public from their weak counterparts. In the second case the strong policymakers, rather than compromising, inflate at a rate that is even lower than their full-information discretionary rate in order to signal their toughness. Thus, when "strength" is conceived in terms of commitment ability, a strong policymaker type inflates at a higher rate in the presence of private information. When "strength" concerns the relative concern for employment versus price stability, the opposite is true. The intuitive reasons for this basic difference are discussed in section 16.4 of chapter 16.

8.4   Changing Emphasis on Alternative Objectives—A Basic Framework (Chapters 9 and 10)

Although useful as a simplifying pedagogical device, the assumption that the emphasis of policy on alternative objectives is time invariant does not seem very realistic. In most countries CB policy is not totally divorced from the pressures and counterpressures exerted on and by the executive and legislative branches of government. Demands from monetary policy change continually due to shifting alliances, changes in personalities, changes in fiscal policy, changing evaluation by elected officials of the mood of the majority, and of the state of the economy. In countries whose central banks enjoy relatively little independence, these demands are transmitted directly to the CB who translates them into actual policy actions. But even in countries such as the United States where the CB enjoys a substantial degree of statutory independence, some of these shifting demands from monetary policy are translated into actual changes in policy.

Many of the factors that shape the course of monetary policy are initially better known by policymakers within government than by the public at large. The public may have an idea about the type and direction of pressures exerted on policy but is usually not fully informed about the extent and the timing of the policy response. The public may be aware of the cyclical position of the economy but is normally not informed in real time about the forecasts of its future state by policymakers. Since policy is influenced by these forecasts, the public does not possess full knowledge of the information on which current monetary policy decisions are based. The public may learn about changes in the emphasis of policy or about policymakers' forecasts of various economic variables. But this learning process is usually gradual. In the interim monetary policy has real effects since surprises are created. By the time the public learns about factors that have shaped monetary policy in the recent past, new factors become relevant and new surprises are generated. As a result the public's learning process reduces but does not eliminate the public's uncertainty about the course of monetary policy.

A succinct case for this view of the policy process for the United States is made by Havrilesky (1990c) in the context of distributionally driven fiscal and monetary policies. He (p. 53) writes:

> Voters may be forward looking, but they are imperfectly informed about future tax and financial regulatory environments. Therefore, when politicians make redistributive fiscal promises, voters cannot anticipate the timing, magnitude, or location of the subsequent sectoral impacts, nor can they anticipate the timing or magnitude of the related subsequent monetary surprises. Moreover, voters cannot easily filter credible signals for surprises from the often subtle, but continual barrage of political and private pressures on monetary policymakers. Informational asymmetry occurs basically because imperfect private information exists regarding policymakers' responses to these pressures.

Chapters 9, 10, 14, and 18 are all driven by the informational asymmetry regarding the response of the CB (or of the treasury in countries with subservient central banks). The simplest framework is that of chapter 9 in which the information advantage disappears by assumption two periods after an effective change in objectives occurs. Chapter 10 extends the same framework to the case in which new private information is fully assimilated by the public only asymptotically. The formulation in chapter 10 allows a wider range of possible speeds of learning. The discussions in these two chapters thus represent two extreme cases as far as the diffusion of information is concerned. Many of the basic insights can be illustrated in the simpler framework of chapter 9. But the more general form because of its larger degree of flexibility is more appropriate as a framework for empirical work. It also serves as a benchmark for the analysis of the effect of mandatory, but noisy, monetary targets and of the degree of CB independence on expectations and policy choices. The effects of mandatory announcements are discussed in chapter 14 and those of the degree of CB independence in chapter 18.

The basic framework is laid down in chapter 9. The relative preference of policy for price stability versus high economic activity shifts stochastically, though in an autocorrelated manner through time. Those shifts are revealed to policymakers immediately and to the general public with a lag of two periods. In each period policymakers choose planned money growth so as to maximize the expected value of the discounted present value of their objectives. But because of imperfect control over the money supply, actual money growth and inflation can deviate from those that were planned by policymakers.[2] The larger the current preference for high employment, the larger is the rate of monetary expansion planned by policymakers. The public knows that policy objectives are serially correlated over time, so past inflation is relevant for predicting future inflation. As a consequence inflationary expectations rationally adjust up and down to past movements in inflation. But this adjustment is partial, since the public knows that part of the fluctuations in past inflation are due to control errors.

In choosing the current rate of monetary expansion, policymakers weigh the current employment benefits from surprise inflation against the costs of higher current inflation plus the cost of higher future inflationary expectations. This last cost arises because higher inflationary expectations reduce future employment or require a higher rate of inflation to maintain the same level of employment. Policymakers may not take these costs as seriously as they take current costs and benefits. But as long as they do not fully discount the future, the effect of current actions on future expectations moderates their tendency to stimulate current employment through monetary surprises.

Chapter 9 fully characterizes the equilibrium interaction between policymakers and the public as a rational expectations (or Nash) equilibrium in which the public's process of expectation formation is mutually consistent with the decision rule of policymakers. More precisely equilibrium is characterized by the following conditions:

1.   Given its perception of the way expectations are formed, policymakers choose the rate of inflation in each period so as to minimize the conditional expected present value of the combined costs of inflation and of deviations of actual from desired employment.

2.   Given their perception of the policy rule followed by policymakers and the information available to them, individuals form their expectations (and conclude nominal contracts accordingly) so as to minimize the conditional mean forecast error in each period.

3.   The public's perception of the policy rule postulated in condition 2 is identical to the policy rule that emerges as a solution to the problem in condition 1.

4.   Policymakers' perception of the way expectations are formed postulated in condition 1 is identical to the expectations formation process that emerges as a solution to condition 2.

A basic difference between this equilibrium and the one obtained under perfect information is that both positive and negative monetary surprises are now possible, so monetary policy has real effects. Positive surprises occur when the relative concern for employment goes up, and negative surprises occur when it goes down. Credibility is naturally characterized by the difference between policymakers' current policy plans and the public's current perception of these plans. The chapter also investigates the effects of parameters such as the quality of control over the money supply and policymakers' rate of time preference on the distribution of inflation and on credibility.

The main additional contribution of chapter 10 is that it provides a substantially more flexible characterization of the informational advantage of the CB. This formulation leads to a learning process in which all past rates of inflation are relevant for predicting the future. Although more complex, this specification leaves more a priori freedom for empirical implementation. It is also better suited for the investigation of the effects of various parameters on the speed of learning and the determinants of credibility. Because of its wider generality chapter 10 rather than chapter 9 is used as a benchmark for the discussion in chapters 14 and 18, which are reviewed in the following section.

Before closing this section note that (as in Grossman 1990) the positive effect of inflationary surprises on policymakers' objectives need not arise only because of their stimulatory impact on employment. It could also reflect an underlying desire for larger seigniorage revenues, low real costs of servicing the public debt, or a balance-of-payments motive. Since all these motives affect the objectives of policymakers through unexpected inflation, as is the case with the employment motive, practically all the discussion of credibility, learning, and policy under asymmetric information extends naturally to cases in which these other motives operate instead of, or along with, the employment motive.

8.5 Mandatory Announcements and the Interaction of Private Information with Central Bank Independence (Chapters 14 and 18)

The discussion of chapters 14 and 18 is grouped together immediately after that of chapter 10 since both either rely on that chapter or extend it. During the 1970s and 1980s central banks in several developed countries introduced procedures that were designed to partially disclose their policy plans to the public. This was done by issuing monetary targets, official forecasts, or statements of intention. Announcements are (or have been) made in Germany, the United States, Japan, Britain, France, Canada, Switzerland, and Australia. These advance signals are imperfect, but not meaningless, indicators of planned policy actions. Their precision tends to vary across countries. The new (1989) Reserve Bank of New Zealand Act requires the governor of the bank to negotiate a monetary policy agreement with the minister of finance and to make it public. By contrast, under the previous law the governor could be directed to follow a particular policy without that directive being released publicly. The new law is therefore an institutional device that raises the precision of signals about monetary policy plans in comparison to its previous counterpart.

Chapter 14 explicitly recognizes the existence of advance signals about policy plans and analyzes the effects that their precision has on the policy process and on policy outcomes. The analysis takes the framework of chapter 10 as a point of departure. As in that chapter the public utilizes past rates of monetary expansion to forecast future rates. But in addition it has access to noisy signals issued by policymakers about their policy plans. The chapter characterizes policymakers' decision rules and the learning process of the public in the presence of imperfect, but not meaningless, monetary signals and provides answers to such questions as: What determines the credibility of monetary targets, and what is their effect on the distribution of inflation and on monetary uncertainty? In particular the chapter demonstrates that monetary targets, even if imperfect, reduce the public's uncertainty and are likely to reduce the mean level of inflation. The substantial reduction of inflation in New Zealand following its new central bank law is consistent with the last implication. It is also supported by preliminary evidence from part IV which suggests that countries with monetary targets have, ceteris paribus, lower rates of inflation (column 1 of table 20.4).

Advance disclosure of monetary plans usually takes the form of monetary targets or statements of intention. But the discussion in chapter 14 may be viewed more generally as applying to any kind of signal issued by the central bank about its future monetary policy besides past money growth. With this wider interpretation in mind, the chapter implies that the lower the precision of monetary control, the more attention is paid to other signals of planned monetary growth such as public statements, rumors, and personalities. In such circumstances public appearances by high-ranking central bank officials receive wide press coverage. With very precise monetary control, on the other hand, past money growth is a good indicator for future plans and the pronouncements of central bank officials do not draw a lot of attention. Formally chapter 14 is an extension of the model in chapter 10 in which policymakers possess an extended information advantage about their own shifting priorities.

Chapter 18 provides a theoretical framework for the analysis and the subsequent empirical work on the effects of CB independence on the distribution of inflation and other characteristics of the policy process. The degree of CB independence obviously plays a meaningful role only in the presence of differences of emphasis on alternative policy objectives between the political authorities and the CB. The chapter focuses on two main differences. One relates to possible differences between the rate of time preference of political authorities and that of central banks. For various reasons central banks are normally more conservative and tend to take a longer view of the policy process. The other concerns the subjective trade-offs of the CB and of political authorities between price stability and other goals such as high employment, extraction of seigniorage revenues, and balance-of-payments objectives. The presumption is that at least on average, central banks are more conservative also in the sense that they care relatively more than political authorities about price stability. The analysis is conducted within the framework of chapter 10 in which the public is not fully informed about the shifting objectives of the political authorities and in which there is no perfect control of inflation.

In most countries the degree of CB independence is determined by formal institutional characteristics such as the CB charter, which are often mitigated by more fluid and less permanent factors such as personalities and shifting views and alliances within the public sector inclusive of the CB. For example, in the United States, presidents have often tried to pack the Board of Governors of the Federal Reserve System with loyal appointees. Although acquiescence of board members to the shifting desires of administrations is by no means automatic, it does occur. But the degree of acquiescence may vary with professional and other characteristics of board members (Havrilesky 1991b provides interesting evidence). It also may vary with the state of the economy. Since such shifts often occur far from the public eye, there normally is a certain degree of uncertainty about the current level of CB independence. Policymakers within the CB or the Treasury have better information about the current degree of independence than the general public and may use it to further their objectives. Chapter 18 uses the framework of chapter 10 to analyze the effects of this type of uncertainty.

Several general conclusions emerge from the discussion in chapter 18. First a lower degree of CB independence is associated in all cases with more inflation variability as well as with more inflation uncertainty. The intuitive reason is that with less independence a larger fraction of the more volatile shifts in the objectives of the political authorities is injected into the conduct of monetary policy. Second, subject to some reasonable restrictions, a lower degree of CB independence is also associated with a higher mean level of inflation. Third, cross-country variations in CB independence and in the difference between the objectives of political authorities and of the CB tend to produce a positive cross-country correlation between the mean and the variance of inflation. This is a well-documented empirical regularity (Logue and Willet 1976). The hypothesis that it is due to cross-country variations in CB independence is tested in chapter 22. Finally, the lower the degree of CB independence, the lower will be the level of average credibility as measured by the variance of the deviation between actual policy actions and the public's perception of those actions. Since it mostly relies on propositions that are proved in chapter 10, chapter 18 is less technical than chapter 10.

8.6 Private Information about Money Demand and Changing Objectives (Chapter 13)

So far the discussion has abstracted, for simplicity, from shocks to money demand. When the monetary authority has to decide about the rate of monetary expansion prior to observing the current state of money demand, its control over the rate of inflation becomes imperfect even if it has perfect control over the money supply. To see why, note that the money market equilibrium condition implies that the price level is affected by factors on the side of money demand as well as by factors on the side of money supply. If the monetary authority has to choose the latter without perfect knowledge of the former, its control over the price level must in general be imperfect.

Central banks usually have a better feel for the state of money demand than the general public. The staff of the CB has access to indicators for money demand that are not available to the general public. In addition CB research departments are normally in a better position to evaluate the meaning of financial developments for the state of money demand. This does not mean that the CB can perfectly forecast the near-term level of money demand. But it does imply that it possesses private, but not totally accurate, information about the near-term level of money demand. A convenient way to model this information advantage is to assume that policymakers have access to private, but noisy information, on the near-term state of money demand. This way of modeling private information about money demand has been proposed by Canzoneri (1985).

Chapter 13 discusses the consequences of private information about both the changing emphasis of policy on surprise creation versus price stability and the state of money demand. A basic consequence of this conjunction of different types of private information is that past inflation becomes a noisy signal for future inflation even when the monetary authority has perfect control of the money supply. The reason is that actual inflation reflects both the deliberate decisions of policymakers as well as money demand forecast errors on their part. By observing both past money growth and price inflation, the public can deduce what has been the actual value of past shocks to money demand. But this still leaves it in the dark about how much of a given increase in monetary growth was due to a transitory overestimate of money demand by policymakers and how much to a persistent increase in their relative desire for positive monetary surprises. Since only the latter is relevant for forecasting future inflation, the public tries to filter out persistent changes in the emphasis of policy on alternative objectives from forecast errors that were committed by policymakers.

As in chapter 9 policymakers are aware of the public's learning process and take it into consideration when making decisions about current monetary expansion. In particular, when maximizing the present discounted value of their objectives, policymakers take into consideration that an increase in current monetary expansion designed to raise surprise inflation will also raise future inflationary expectations, making it more costly in terms of price stability to achieve the same level of monetary surprise in the future. Factors that enter into this dynamic trade-off are policymakers' rate of time preference and the speed of learning, by the public, about changing policy objectives. This speed of learning, which is a prime determinant of credibility, depends in turn on more basic parameters such as the variability of money demand, the forecasting ability of the monetary authority, and its (politically or bureaucratically determined) rate of time preference.

Chapter 13 characterizes the simultaneous interaction between the choice of policy and the determination of the public's expectations and its choice of nominal contracts. The equilibrium concept is the same as that of chapter 9. It is a Nash (or a rational expectations) equilibrium in which policymakers maximize the expected present value of their objectives, taking the public's learning process as given, and the public picks its inflation forecast so as to minimize the mean square error of forecast. A more precise characterization of the equilibrium concept appears in section 8.4 above.

The chapter analyzes the determinants of reputation, credibility, and the speed of learning. In particular it stresses the effect of learning as a partial deterrent of attempts to push inflation up by policymakers. As a matter of fact the higher the speed of learning, the more potent is the deterring effect of learning.

One of the important aspects of monetary policy is its degree of activism. The framework of chapter 13 makes it possible to determine the degree of activism endogenously and to relate it to more fundamental parameters. The chapter shows that activism is more pronounced, the larger the short-run Phillips trade-off, the larger the (politically determined) rate of time preference of policymakers, and the poorer their ability to forecast changes in the demand for money.

The formal structure of chapter 13 is devised so that it maps into that of chapter 9. This mapping produces a substantial simplification in proofs and algebra, since many of the propositions in chapter 13 can be proved by relying on analogous propositions in chapter 9. This isomorphism between the two chapters is more than coincidental. First, both assume that policymakers possess only a minimal information advantage. At a deeper level the structural analogy between the two chapters reflects the fact that an essential ingredient of both models is policymakers' inability to perfectly control inflation in conjunction with common knowledge of this fact by the public. The reason for imperfect control is different in the two cases. In chapter 9 it is due to imperfect control of the money supply process, and in chapter 13 it is due to imperfect knowledge of the state of money demand. For simplicity of exposition these two types of imperfect control are analyzed separately. It is likely that both operate in reality. But this does not invalidate many of the conclusions in the two chapters, since a good number of them reinforce each other.

8.7   Private Forecasts about the State of the Economy and the Persistence of Inflation (Chapter 15)

An important base for making monetary policy decisions is the forecast by policymakers of the near-term cyclical position of employment and related real variables. Such forecasts require them to evaluate how much of the current deviation of employment from its desired level will persist into the future. Because of their judgmental and complex nature, such forecasts normally are the private information of policymakers. Chapter 15 explores the consequences of this information advantage for the persistence of inflation when the marginal political costs (to policymakers) of deviations from desired employment increase with the size of those deviations.

Policymakers may have some private information about the near-term natural level of employment. But, as is the case with all forecasters, they make errors particularly in forecasting the permanence of employment. Chapter 15 models this state of affairs by assuming that policymakers get information about current employment and its permanence with a small lead relative to the general public. Since the marginal political costs of low employment are increasing with unemployment, policymakers generally tend to inflate at higher rates (in order to create larger surprises) when the natural rate of unemployment is higher. But in doing that, they face an important dynamic trade-off. Since they require larger inflation, larger surprises are not costless. If policymakers forecast that current unemployment, even if high, is lower than future unemployment, they are better off "saving" some of their ability to create surprises for the future. If, on the other hand, they believe that unemployment now is high in comparison to the future, they are better off using their surprise-creating ability already now.

The ability to create surprises rises and falls over time as a function of past rates of inflation. The mechanism responsible for this link is the public's learning process. Being aware of the persistence of natural employment and of government's decision rule, the public interprets recent high inflation as a sign that the former forecasts relatively high unemployment for the near future and that upcoming rates of inflation will therefore be higher. Because of this mechanism government's ability to create future monetary surprises diminishes with current inflation. The higher the current inflation, the higher will be the next period's inflationary expectations, and the costlier it is for government to create a given size inflationary surprise. Because of this effect policymakers try, given their information, to allocate larger surprises to periods with relatively large unemployment and to utilize periods with low natural unemployment to rebuild their credibility. This credibility is then partially used up when natural unemployment rises again.

Chapter 15 utilizes the dynamic interaction between policy and the public's expectations to explain how purely transitory shocks to natural employment contribute to the persistence of inflation. The basic idea is that a purely transitory upward blip in natural employment that leads through the current policy response to higher inflation is partly interpreted by the public as a persistent increase in natural unemployment. As a consequence individuals revise their expectations of near-term inflation upward and adjust nominal contracts accordingly. In the subsequent period policymakers are therefore faced with nominal contracts that are based on the assumption of a higher rate of inflation. Other things the same, these higher nominal settlements tend to reduce employment. Policymakers respond to this adverse effect on employment by inflating at a higher rate. Indeed, in the presence of private forecasts about the phase of the cycle, transitory blips to employment are transformed into a persistent inflationary process.

The analysis in chapter 15 implies that when monetary policy is discretionary, the time series properties of inflation are partially shaped by those of natural employment. Furthermore it implies that the persistence of inflation should be larger under discretion than under rules. One way of testing this implication is to compare the persistence of inflation under fixed exchange rates with its persistence under flexible exchange rates. To the extent that fixed exchange rates function as partial commitment devices, we should expect inflation to be less persistent under fixed than under flexible exchange rates. Evidence presented in Alogoskoufis (1991) supports this implication. Another implication of the chapter is that inflation behaves countercyclically under discretion. This may explain a recent finding by Kydland and Prescott (1990) that the price level in the United States since World War II has been countercyclical.

8.8   Alternative Notions of Credibility and Reputation (Mostly Chapter 11)

In a world of perfect information and no commitments a policy announced today for some future period is either fully credible or not at all. It is fully credible if it is dynamically consistent and not at all credible if it is not dynamically consistent.

Under asymmetric information it is still the case that only dynamically consistent strategies are credible. However, due to the fact that the public is not fully informed about the objectives of policymakers, there may be a divergence between the rate of monetary expansion planned by the central bank and what the public believes about this rate. This divergence occurs because the public is not fully informed about the dynamically consistent or subgame perfect strategy of the central bank for the period. Hence under asymmetric information a natural measure of credibility is the absolute value of the divergence between planned and expected money growth in each period as well as on average. This conception of credibility is particularly appropriate for cases in which the emphasis of policy on alternative objectives changes over time.

Chapter 11 develops and characterizes this notion of credibility and compares it to notions of credibility that are based on trigger strategies. The basic idea underlying the application of such strategies to monetary policy games is that the public uses its inflationary expectation as a device to deter the central bank from producing the excessively high discretionary rate of inflation. The chapter compares and contrasts the learning and the trigger strategy approaches to modeling reputation. It critically discusses the trigger strategy approach and comes strongly in favor of the first approach as more natural and realistic. The fact that private individuals invest resources in activities such as "Fed watching" supports the view that the learning approach is more realistic. Since the chapter is short and largely nontechnical, the reader is referred to it for further details.

What is an appropriate measure of credibility or reputation often depends on the nature of private information. For example, the (lack of) credibility of monetary targets (chapter 14) is naturally measured by the difference between the announced targets and the postannouncement expectation of the public. This is a measure of the average level of credibility. For some purposes it is useful to know by how much a unit change in announced targets changes inflationary expectations. This leads to the concept of a "marginal credibility of announced targets." Chapter 14 presents a formal definition and discusses the basic determinants of marginal credibility.

When, as is the case in chapter 16, the public does not know for sure whether policymakers in office are able to commit, the reputation of policymakers is naturally characterized by the probability assigned by the public to the event that the policymakers in office are able to commit.

8.9   Ambiguity in Monetary Policy (Chapter 12)

Central banks seem to value their private information. Existing evidence does not make it possible to determine whether this is a general feature of central bank policy or a particular characteristic of central banking in some developed countries. But existing evidence makes it clear that the Federal Reserve has an inclination for secrecy. Goodfriend (1986) reports a legal case in which the Federal Open Market Committee (FOMC) was sued under the Freedom of Information Act to make public immediately after each FOMC meeting the policy directives and minutes for the meeting. The Fed vigorously opposed this demand and went to great lengths to preserve its information advantage.

Chapter 12 presents two, not mutually exclusive, explanations for the preference for secrecy and ambiguity. One is based on the notion that a high degree of statutory independence for the central bank in conjunction with some ambiguity enables incumbent politicians to partially influence monetary policy without taking the electoral risks associated with possible adverse effects of the policies they initate.

The other explanation is based on the observation that since only unanticipated inflation affects real variables, ambiguity is needed to enable the monetary authority to influence real variables such as employment and output. In a world with a continually changing emphasis on alternative objectives (as in chapters 9, 10, 13, 14, and 15) there will be both positive and negative monetary surprises. Correspondingly output will sometimes be above its natural level and sometimes below it. On average, over long periods of time, output will be at the natural level since monetary policy is neutral in the long run. But this does not mean that the CB does not value the ability to create surprises. Such ability enables the bank to influence the timing of surprises. This may improve the long-run value of the bank's objectives by allowing it to create positive surprises when they are relatively highly valued and to leave the inevitable negative surprises for periods in which price stability is deemed relatively important. The preservation of this ability requires that the public's perception of the shifting objectives of policy not be totally accurate. This is achieved in turn by choosing money supply control procedures that are not necessarily as accurate as is technically feasible. Chapter 12 uses the analytical framework of chapter 9 to illustrate these ideas more precisely.

8.10   Concluding Reflections

The different models of monetary policy used to illustrate the many aspects of private information can obscure the fact that most of them share common principles. What is really crucial is that policymakers have private information about something. This may involve private information about the current balance of power between different constituencies or policymaking philosophies within government. It may involve the active promotion of particular interests by the central bank in conjunction with changes in its ability to achieve that aim because of changes in CB independence and other changing constraints. In such a case the "changing objectives" in part II and in some of the chapters in part III implicitly reflect changing constraints. The change in the constraints facing policymakers, due to changing economic conditions, can also be modeled explicitly, as is done in chapter 15. For instance, private information may concern a changing evaluation by policymakers of the relative electoral costs of inflation and unemployment.

The common and crucial elements in all cases in which there are changing objectives, changing constraints, or changing forecasts can be summarized as follows.

1.   Policymakers possess a certain amount of temporary private information about one or more shifting variables.

2.   These variables have some persistence, and they influence current policy choices.

3.   The public is not perfectly informed about the persistence of these variables, and current policy choices provide relevant, but noisy, information about their persistence and therefore about future inflation to the public.

These principles transcend the particular stochastic structures used to illustrate the many-faceted aspects of monetary policy under asymmetric information.

9 The Employment Motive in the Presence of a Minimal Information Advantage about Objectives

9.1 Introduction[1]

In most countries the formation of monetary policy is at least partially influenced by political considerations. Even the Fed, which enjoys a high degree of formal independence, is not immune to pressures from the executive and legislative branches of government. There is an increasing body of evidence suggesting that monetary policy in the United States is partly responsive to the desires of the president, Congress, the financial community, and periodically some other less visible institutions or groups. The precise channels through which these responses are elicited are subtle and, at times, elude precise formulation because the president, Congress, and the Federal Reserve all have a common interest in preserving an image of the central bank as an independent, apolitical institution.

Weintraub (1978, p. 356) concludes, after summarizing the history of the postaccord monetary policy, that much of this policy "can be explained just by noting who the president was when the policy under review was in effect." In a study of presidential influence on monetary policy, Beck (1982) concludes that presidential political demands are somehow transmitted to the Fed. Beck notes that the transmission mechanism requires further study but that it seems clear that presidential preferences are an important determinant of Fed policymaking (Beck 1982, p. 443). Woolley (1984) holds a similar view. More precise studies reviewed in chapter 17 find that monetary policy in the United States partially depends on the party affiliation of the president.

Hetzel (1985) argues that current institutional arrangements allow members of Congress to pass on political pressures of various constituent groups to the Fed while avoiding association with the consequences that adversely affect the welfare of other groups. This explains Congress' consistent preference (noted by Woolley, 1984, ch. 7) for attempting to influence monetary policy through a variety of threats to limit the Fed's institutional autonomy rather than through an explicit mandate to guide monetary policy (Hetzel 1985, p. 7). Since the autonomy of the Fed depends on Congress, it must be at least somewhat sensitive to the wishes of Congress provided that the Fed values autonomy. This point of view also explains why, as noted by Beck (1990) and others, Congress has not, to date, attempted to discipline the Fed by exerting budgetary control. A related argument is made by Kane (1980, 1982). He argues that the Federal Reserve performs a scapegoat function for the president and Congress. In return the Fed gets a fair degree of independence, which is necessary in order to credibly perform the scapegoat function. Both Congress and the presidency are institutions largely concerned with various redistributional considerations. As a consequence the Fed is, probably to a lesser degree, also sensitive to redistributional considerations (Havrilesky 1993).

Arthur Burns appears to share the view that the Fed is not a totally free agent. He believes that the Fed can work to achieve price stability only if the policy does not adversely affect production and employment and does not irritate Congress. In Burns' words, the role of the Fed is to continue "probing the limits of its freedom to undernourish ... inflation" (Burns 1979, p. 16). Coming from a former chairman of the Federal Reserve, this statement is particularly revealing. It shows that as chairman of the board, Burns did not view himself as totally free to decide the course of monetary policy on his own. Instead, he viewed the Fed as partially responding to the wishes of other institutions and personalities within the government or, possibly, outside it. Clearly even within a country like the United States, in which the central bank has a high degree of statutory independence, monetary policy is not divorced from the general political process. This is a fortiori true in most other countries whose central banks do not enjoy as high a degree of legal independence as the Federal Reserve.[2]

Politicians and elected officials try to satisfy the conflicting demands of different constituencies. Some groups in society are more adversely affected by low employment than by inflation, and the reverse is true for other groups.[3] These different groups exert conflicting pressures on elected officials. The formation of effective coalitions determined to change the course of monetary policy is subject to stochastic elements about which the concerned officials and the central bank have more timely information than the rest of the public. In terms of the model of chapter 3 this means that the parameter A (which measures the relative aversion of policymakers to employment below the desired level N^* and to inflation) is changing over time. Furthermore the central bank has a temporary information advantage about those changes. Such shifts in emphasis on relative policy objectives may occur almost continuously, though usually in small amounts. Large changes in policy objectives, such as the one that occurred in 1979 under the Volcker chairmanship, occur infrequently. But the probability of such changes is not zero. Since policy objectives usually change by small amounts, there is a fair degree of persistence in the emphasis on various objectives. As a consequence past policy outcomes provide information about the likely state of future objectives and therefore about future inflation.

The view (held by many economists) that monetary policy in the United States does not reflect the optimizing decisions of an apolitical socially motivated monetary authority has recently been eloquently stated by Kane (1990, p. 289):

> Contemporary economists characteristically think of themselves as specialists in positive economics: calculators *extraordinaire* of individual and institutional benefits and costs. To focus on economic problems *per se*, they determinedly strip away normative and political dimensions of policy problems. This predilection undermines the policy relevance of economic research whenever (as in monetary-policy framework decisions) normative and political aspects of the problem fail to be surgically separable issues.

This point of view also clarifies why, despite their evident advantages, many economically sound proposals for monetary reform have not been implemented. More important, it provides documentation for two basic presumptions. One is that the emphasis of policy on alternative objectives shifts continuously over time. The other is that the Fed possesses a temporary information advantage about those shifts. In Kane's (p. 290) words:

> Virtually all reform proposals seek to impose stricter accountability on Fed officials for the monetary policy they choose to follow. If such proposals are to have a substantial chance for success, their sponsors must find a way to undo the political and bureaucratic incentives that make current arrangements so cozy both for incumbent politicians and for the Fed. The Fed minimizes its accountability to the electorate and to politicians in two ways: by accepting contradictory goals and by making discretionary use of a self-selected bevy of intermediate policy targets such as the federal funds rate, nonborrowed reserves, and various monetary growth rates. *The resulting vagueness in the institution's aims and methods lets Fed officials reverse their economic priorities suddenly in response to the ebb and flow of political pressure with minimal embarrassment. FOMC secrecy and the carefully crafted structural ambiguity of Fed decision-making permit Fed officials to fuzz over the important political compromises they effect between goals desired by different political constituencies and let those compromises be made with minimal short-term political stress for elected politicians.* Moreover, the large staff of professional economists whose research on policy issues is directed by the Fed serves the institution's leadership in two ways. *First, staff analysis helps Fed officials to maintain an informational advantage over the other players.* Second, by manipulating the size of

this staff and the activities for which they are rewarded and penalized, Fed officials help to shape the agenda of contemporary economic research on monetary policy. Unless Fed staff members are willing to risk career penalties, they are induced to devote their research to bureaucratically approved issues. Such issues focus on the control subsystem—topics such as the effects of using different arrays of intermediate targets or of moving from contemporary to lagged accounting for reserves and back again—rather than on the broader principal-agent conflicts comprised in the information and incentives subsystems of monetary policymaking. (Italics added for the conception underlying the model of this chapter.)

The existence of an information advantage on the part of the central bank fundamentally alters the nature of the interaction between policymakers and the public. Since policymakers know that current policy outcomes affect future inflationary expectations (which affect in turn their future ability to stimulate employment at any given rate of inflation), their current choice of policy becomes sensitive to reputational considerations even under discretion. The extent to which these considerations deter policymakers from inflating at the one-shot discretionary rate of chapter 3 depends on their degree of time preference and on the speed with which the public detects changes in their objectives. This chapter explores the implications of those new elements for policy outcomes and for expectations formation when the information advantage of the central bank is short lived. The next chapter explores similar issues when the information advantage is larger. In both cases the information advantage about the state of objectives at a particular moment dissipates with the passage of time. But this process is longer and more gradual in the second case. Even in the case of a short-lived information advantage, the public never fully catches up with the current state of objective, since by the time it learns precisely about past changes new changes occur.

Imperfect information is also crucial for understanding the existence of real effects of money on output. Despite the recent upsurge of the real business cycles view in which money growth responds passively to real variables,[4] there are reasons to believe that fluctuations in monetary growth also contribute to real variability.[5] The perfect information framework of chapter 3 does not provide an explanation for the effects of money on economic activity, since it implies that employment is always at the natural rate. By contrast, the asymmetric information framework in this chapter is consistent with some effects of money on output, particularly during periods of change in governmental objectives.

9.2   Shifting Objectives and the Structure of Information

Consider a policymaker whose objective is to maximize the expected value of[6]

$$-\sum_{i=0}^{\infty} \beta^i \left[x_i \phi(N^* - N_i) + \frac{\pi_i^2}{2} \right], \qquad 0 \le \beta \le 1,$$

$$\phi(N^* - N_i) \equiv \begin{cases} N^* - N_i & \text{for } N^* - N_i \ge 0, \\ 0 & \text{otherwise,} \end{cases}$$

(9.1)

subject to a short-run Phillips relation as in equation (3.2) which is reproduced here as equation (9.2).

$$N - N_n = \alpha(\pi - \pi^e), \qquad \alpha > 0. \tag{9.2}$$

As in chapter 3, N, N^*, and N_n are the actual, the desired, and the natural levels of employment; π and π^e are the actual and the expected rates of inflation; β is the politically determined discount factor of the policymaker; x_i measures the aversion of the policymaker to deviations of employment from N^* in comparison to his or her aversion to deviations from price stability.[7] The employment-related term of the objective function implies that the costs of being away from desired employment N^* are positive and increasing in the difference $N^* - N_i$ as long as this difference is positive. But the policymaker does not incur any costs when employment is above the desired level. The short-run Phillips curve in equation (9.2) implies that in the absence of inflationary surprises $N^* - N = N^* - N_n$. Since the desired level of employment is larger than the natural level and inflationary surprises have a mean value of zero, the policymaker normally operates in a range in which $N^* - N > 0$. For simplicity, we will restrict the parameters so that all the realizations of $N^* - N$ occur in the nonnegative range with very high probability. The precise restriction is discussed in appendix C to this chapter. To capture the frequent shifts in relative emphasis on employment and price stability as well as their persistence, we specify x_i as a stochastic variable with the following characteristics:

$$x_i = A + p_i, \qquad A > 0, \tag{9.3a}$$

$$p_i = \rho p_{i-1} + v_i, \qquad 0 < \rho < 1, \tag{9.3b}$$

$$v_i \sim N(0, \sigma_v^2), \tag{9.3c}$$

where A is the mean, publicly known, value of x_i and p_i is the stochastic part of x_i. In period i the realization of A is known by the policymaker but not by the public. The policymaker is as ignorant as the public about future innovations v to his or her objectives. However, the policymaker knows the current value of x (or p) and thus can produce a more precise forecast of future x's than the public. The persistence in the policymaker's objectives is captured by specifying p_i as a first-order Markoff process with a positive autoregressive coefficient as well as through the positive constant A. However, since A is known with certainty by the public while p_i is not, the persistence in these two components of x_i does not affect the equilibrium in identical manners.

The specification of v_i as a standard normal variate implies that there is a large probability that central bank's objectives will change by small amounts and a small (but nonzero) probability that they will change by a large amount. Minor readjustments in policy objectives occur continually but large changes, such as the one that led to Volcker's disinflation in 1979, are rare according to this specification. The recent literature on monetary policy games characterizes policymakers with different relative weights on employment and inflation as having different "types" (Backus and Driffill 1985a, 1985b and Vickers 1986). Here the type is determined by the realization of x_i. However, unlike in that literature, the number of types is not restricted to two and, more important, the type is changing over time. It is those continual changes that give policymakers a permanent information advantage despite the fact that the public continually updates its beliefs.

The public knows the stochastic structure of the political process which leads to changes in x_i. In other words, it knows σ_v^2 and ρ, and it utilizes this knowledge in conjunction with observations on past rates of monetary growth to forecast future inflation.[8] This chapter focuses on the case in which the information advantage of the central bank about any particular x_i is extremely short-lived. In particular it is assumed that individuals obtain, through the media or other sources, a precise observation on p_{i-2} at the beginning of period i prior to the conclusion of nominal wage contracts for that period. (The underlying structure of contracts is identical to the one discussed in chapter 3. Details appear in section 3.6.) This still leaves them in the dark about p_{i-1}. Since p is serially correlated and since inflation in period $i-1$ is, through the central bank's response, influenced by p_{i-1} individuals find it advantageous to use monetary growth in period $i-1$ to sharpen their inflation forecast for period i.

An important consequence of this learning process is that current policy decisions affect next period's inflationary expectations. In particular, if the central bank raises the current rate of monetary expansion, this raises inflationary expectations in the subsequent period. Since (as shown in equation 9.1) the central bank is concerned about the future as well as about the present, it takes into consideration the adverse effect of its current action on next period's objectives. As a result the central bank is at least partly deterred from inflating at the rate it would have inflated at under complete information. Incomplete information about the shifting objectives of policymakers induces policymakers to inflate at a lower rate even under discretion.

Since $A > 0$, the probability that x_i will have a positive realization is larger than the probability it will have a negative realization. Only positive realizations of x_i are consistent with the notion that as long as $N_i < N^*$, policymakers prefer more to less employment given the rate of inflation. By making A sufficiently large in comparison to the variance of x_i, the probability of a negative x_i can be made as small as desired.[9] This chapter maintains the simplification of chapter 3 by assuming that money growth impacts immediately on the rate of inflation.[10] However, policymakers do not have perfect control over the rate of monetary growth and therefore over the rate of inflation. In particular, when the planned rate of monetary growth is m_i^p, the actual rate of monetary inflation is

$$m_i = m_i^p + \psi_i, \tag{9.4}$$

where ψ_i is a random monetary control error that is not known by government when it picks m_i^p. We assume that ψ_i is a standard normal variate with variance σ_ψ^2 and that it is distributed independently of the innovation v to policymakers' objectives.

9.3 Timing of Moves, Public's Beliefs, and the Equilibrium Concept

A "period" is defined by the length of the wage contract. The timing of moves within each period is as follows: First, nominal wage contracts are concluded based on the rate of inflation expected for the period. Then government chooses m_i^p, taking the wage contract and therefore those expectations as given. Then the control error for the period realizes and the rate of inflation for the period is determined by equation (9.4). However, since individuals learn from current inflation about changes in policy-makers' objectives, they take into consideration the effect of their current choices on *future* expectations.

When committing to nominal contracts, individuals in the economy try to forecast as well as possible the rate of inflation for the period of the contract. This forecast depends on what they know about policymakers' objectives and behavior. Policymakers take the public's process of expectations formation as given and pick that part of monetary growth that they control so as to maximize the expected value of the objective function in equation (9.1). This gives rise to a discretionary decision rule in which the actual rate of inflation π depends on the current state of government's objectives and on the current realization of the control error ψ. Individuals know the structure of this decision rule but do not know the current state, p of policymakers' objectives. They utilize this information in an optimal manner to form a minimum variance estimate of the rate of inflation for the period. Thus government's decision rule depends on the process of expectations formation, and this process depends in turn on government's decision rule. In a (Nash) equilibrium the decision rule that emerges, given the process of expectations formation, should be identical to the decision rule individuals posit the government is using when choosing the form of their optimal predictor. This suggests that the process of expectations formation and government's decision rule are determined simultaneously. To find the explicit form of these two processes, we postulate that the public believes that government's decision rule is the following linear function of A and of p_i:[11]

$$m_i^p = B_0 A + B p_i \qquad \text{for all } i, \tag{9.5}$$

where B_0 and B are unknown combinations of parameters to be determined. To establish the consistency of those beliefs, it is necessary to show that given those beliefs, it is indeed optimal for government to behave according to the decision rule in equation (9.5). This is demonstrated in the following section. The remainder of this section derives the form of the optimal predictor of m_i, taking the public's belief in equation (9.5) as given. Readers who are not interested in the details of the derivation and its logic can go directly to the final result in equation (9.12).

The public does not observe m_i^p directly. Instead, it observes (using equations 9.5 in 9.4) the actual rate of monetary inflation

$$m_i = B_0 A + B p_i + \psi_i \tag{9.6}$$

up to and including the previous period. Due to the existence of a control error, m_i is a noisy indicator of m_i^p and p_i. From equation (9.6),

$$E[m_i | I_i] = B_0 A + BE[p_i | I_i], \tag{9.7}$$

where $E[m_i | I_i]$ is the expectation of m_i conditional on the information set I_i that includes past rates of monetary growth up to and including m_{i-1} and the value of p_{i-2}. Equation (9.3b) implies that

$$p_i = \rho^2 p_{i-2} + \rho v_{i-1} + v_i. \tag{9.8}$$

Since p_{i-2} is contained in the information set I_i,

$$E[p_i | I_i] = \rho^2 p_{i-2} + \rho E[v_{i-1} | I_i] + E[v_i | I_i]. \tag{9.9}$$

Furthermore, since I_i does not contain any information about v_i, the last term on the right-hand side of equation (9.9) is equal to zero. Since I_i includes an observation on m_{i-1} which amounts to an observation on[12]

$$B v_{i-1} + \psi_{i-1} \equiv y_{i-1}, \tag{9.10}$$

the middle term in equation (9.9) can be rewritten

$$\rho E[v_{i-1} | y_{i-1}] = \rho \frac{\theta}{B} y_{i-1}, \tag{9.11a}$$

$$\theta \equiv \frac{B^2 \sigma_v^2}{B^2 \sigma_v^2 + \sigma_\psi^2}. \tag{9.11b}$$

Equation (9.11a) is the regression equation of v_{i-1} on y_{i-1} and θ/B is the slope coefficient in this regression.[13] Substituting (9.11a) into (9.9) and inserting the resulting expression into (9.7), we obtain

$$E[m_i | I_i] = B_0 A + B \rho^2 p_{i-2} + \rho \theta y_{i-1}. \tag{9.7a}$$

The intuition underlying this predictor is simple. The public knows that actual inflation for the period is governed by equation (9.6). To forecast m_i, individuals have to forecast, on the basis of I_i, each of the components on the right-hand side of equation (9.6). Knowing the systematic parameters of the economy and of government's objectives, they can use $B_0 A$ as a forecast of itself, which is the first term on the right-hand side of (9.7a). The last two terms represent the forecast of $B p_i$.[14] The first among those terms represents that part of Bp_i that is forecastable on the basis of p_{i-2}. The second term represents the forecast of the part of Bp_i that is related to v_{i-1}—the innovation to government's objectives in period $i-1$. Individuals do not observe this innovation directly but observe y_{i-1}, which is a noisy indicator of that innovation. They therefore use y_{i-1} as a proxy for v_{i-1} but give it less than full weight ($\theta < 1$). Using (9.6), the optimal predictor in (9.7a) can be rewritten in terms of m_{i-1} as

$$E[m_i|I_i] = g(p_{i-2}) + \rho\theta m_{i-1}, \tag{9.12a}$$

$$g(p_{i-2}) \equiv (1 - \rho\theta)B_oA + \rho^2B(1 - \theta)p_{i-2}. \tag{9.12b}$$

Note that given B, a larger σ_ψ^2 implies through (9.11b) that θ is smaller and that the weight given to the last rate of inflation is smaller too. The intuition is that with a larger σ_ψ^2 the signal-to-noise ratio in m_{i-1} is smaller and the weight given to it therefore smaller.[15]

9.4 Derivation of the Policymakers' Decision Rule and Proof of the Rationality of Beliefs

Substituting equation (9.2) into (9.1), using the fact that $N^* - N_i \geq 0$ for all i and rearranging, we can formulate the policymakers' problem as a maximization of the expected value of

$$\sum_{i=0}^{\infty} \beta^i \left[\{\alpha(\pi_i - \pi_i^e) - (N^* - N_n)\}x_i - \frac{\pi_i^2}{2} \right]. \tag{9.1a}$$

The condition ensuring that $N^* - N_i \geq 0$ for all i is derived and discussed in appendix A to this chapter. Since, as in chapter 3, $\pi_i = m_i$ and individuals know this fact, so that $\pi_i^e = E[m_i|I_i]$, equation (9.1a) can be rewritten in terms of actual and expected rates of monetary expansion as

$$\sum_{i=0}^{\infty} \beta^i \left[(m_i - E[m_i|I_i])\alpha x_i - \frac{m_i^2}{2} - (N^* - N_n)x_i \right]. \tag{9.1b}$$

In each period policymakers choose the current planned rate of money growth and the contingent path of future rates so as to maximize the expected value of their objective function in (9.1b), taking the process of expectation formation in (9.12) as given. Using (9.12) and (9.4) in (9.1b), we express the policymakers' objective as

$$\max_{\{m_i^p, i=0,1,\dots\}} E_{G0} \sum_{i=0}^{\infty} \beta^i \Big[\{m_i^p + \psi_i - g(p_{i-2}) - \rho\theta(m_{i-1}^p + \psi_{i-1})\}\alpha x_i$$

$$- \frac{(m_i^p + \psi_i)^2}{2} \Big], \tag{9.13}$$

where E_{G0} stands for the expected value operator conditional on the policymakers' information set in period 0. This set includes the information set I_0 of the public in that period. In addition it includes precise knowledge of x_0 and therefore of p_0 which the public does not have. However, policymakers do not know ψ_i, $i \geq 0$, and x_i, $i \geq 1$, with certainty in period 0. Note that in going from equation (9.1b) to equation (9.13), the term $-\sum_{i=0}^{\infty} \beta^i(N^* - N_n)x_i$ has been dropped. The reason is that this term is not affected by planned monetary growth, which is the instrument at the disposal of policymakers. Hence maximization of the expected value of the expression in equation (9.1b) is equivalent to the problem in equation (9.13).

Since policymakers do not commit in advance to a given path of policy, the problem in equation (9.13) is solved anew in each period. Policymakers can be viewed as choosing the current value of m_0^p and a contingent plan for m_i^p, $i \geq 1$. Recognizing that in each future period policymakers face a problem that has the same structure as the period 0 problem, the stochastic Euler equations necessary for an internal maximum of this problem are[16]

$$\alpha(x_i - \beta\rho\theta E_{Gi}x_{i+1}) - m_i^p = \alpha[x_i - \beta\rho\theta(A + \rho p_i)] - m_i^p = 0, \qquad i \geq 0. \tag{9.14}$$

Rearranging, we obtain

$$m_i^p = \alpha[(1 - \rho\beta\theta)A + (1 - \rho^2\beta\theta)p_i], \tag{9.15}$$

which confirms that the policymakers' decision rule has the form postulated in equation (9.5) with

$$B = \alpha[1 - \rho^2\beta\theta] = \alpha\left[(1 - \rho^2\beta \frac{B^2\sigma_v^2}{B^2\sigma_v^2 + \sigma_\psi^2}\right] \equiv F(B), \tag{9.16a}$$

$$B_0 = \alpha[1 - \rho\beta\theta]. \tag{9.16b}$$

Equation (9.16a) implicitly determines B as a function of the basic parameters α, ρ, β, σ_v^2, and σ_ψ^2. Given those parameters, the solution for B turns

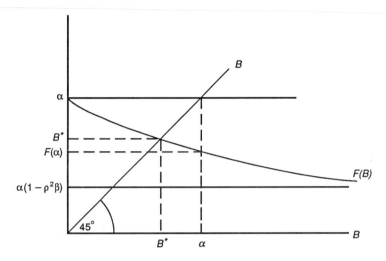

Figure 9.1
Determination of the equilibrium value of B

out to be unique. This can be seen by considering the right-hand side of (9.16a) as a function $F(B)$ of B and by noting that $F(0) = \alpha$ and that $F(B)$ is a monotonically decreasing function of B. The left-hand side of equation (9.16a) is a 45-degree straight line through the origin. The solution for B occurs at the intersection of those two lines. Since $F(B)$ is monotonically decreasing, the solution for B is unique and smaller than α. Figure 9.1 illustrates the argument. B^* in the figure designates the value of the solution.[17] The equilibrium value of θ is determined by substituting B^* into (9.11b). Finally, the equilibrium value of B_0 is determined by substituting the equilibrium value of θ into (9.16b). This completes the solution of the model and the demonstration of the rationality of beliefs.

9.5   A Benchmark—The Policymakers' Strategy under Symmetric Information[18]

The behavior of policymakers under asymmetric information is fundamentally different from their behavior in the presence of symmetric information. To isolate the source of this difference and understand its effects, we first solve for the policymakers' decision strategy under symmetric information as a benchmark. In the context of the model of this chapter, symmetric information means that in each period the public and the central bank possess the same information set. In particular at the beginning of each period, when wage contracts are concluded, the public already knows the realization of x and p for the period.[19] Hence they can calculate precisely (as in chapter 3) the rate of inflation that will be picked up by policymakers after public expectations become embedded in nominal wage contracts.

An important implication of this information structure is that the current policy action does not affect the inflationary expectations of future periods, in particular those held in the subsequent period. Last period's monetary expansion is not used as an indicator for current central bank objectives because those objectives are fully known by the public in the current period. More formally, the partial derivative of $E[m^s_{i+1} | I^s_{i+1}]$ with respect to m^p_i is zero.[20] (By contrast, from equation 9.12a, this partial derivative is equal to $\rho\theta$ under asymmetric information.) As a consequence, with symmetric information, current policy actions do not affect future objectives, and the objective function in equation (9.1b) decomposes into a string of unrelated one-period problems whose typical form is

$$\max_{m^p_i} E_{Gi}\left[(m^p_i + \psi_i - E[m^s_i | I^s_i])\alpha x_i - \frac{(m^p_i + \psi_i)^2}{2} \right], \qquad i \geq 0. \tag{9.17}$$

As in the previous subsection the term $(N^* - N_n)x_i$ has been deleted because it does not depend on the instrument m^p_i. The first-order condition for this problem implies that

$$m^p_i = \alpha x_i = \alpha(A + p_i), \qquad i \geq 0. \tag{9.18}$$

Combining (9.18) and (9.4), we obtain the actual rate of monetary inflation under symmetric information:

$$m^s_i = \alpha(A + p_i) + \psi_i. \tag{9.19}$$

Since the public knows x_i when it commits to nominal contracts,

$$E[m^s_i | I^s_i] = \alpha(A + p_i) \qquad \text{for all } i. \tag{9.20}$$

As was the case in chapter 3, the public's forecast is not affected by current or past actions of policymakers. However, contrary to chapter 3, the public's forecast is not perfect because of the control error ψ. In particular

$$m^s_i - E[m_i | I^s_i] = \psi_i, \tag{9.21}$$

so the variance of the public's forecast error is equal to σ_ψ^2. However, the central bank cannot utilize these surprises to improve its objectives since it is as ignorant of ψ_i (when it picks m_i^p) as the public.

9.6   Comparison of the Distributions of Inflation with and without Asymmetric Information

From (9.4) and (9.15) the rate of monetary expansion under asymmetric information is

$$m_i = \alpha[(1 - \rho\beta\theta)A + (1 - \rho^2\beta\theta)p_i] + \psi_i. \tag{9.22}$$

Comparison of (9.19) with (9.22) suggests that for the same realizations of the shocks p_i and ψ_i, the rate of monetary expansion is always lower with asymmetric information than with symmetric information. The intuitive reason is that under asymmetric information the central bank can lower next period's expected inflation by lowering current inflation, whereas this option does not exist with symmetric information. The fact that its current action affects future expectations checks the tendency of the central bank to inflate, making m_i^s smaller than m_i for all i. Essentially, by giving the central bank the ability to influence future expectations, asymmetric information makes it sensitive to reputational considerations. Such considerations are nonexistent under symmetric information because the central bank does not possess the ability to affect expectations in this case. The preceding discussion is summarized in the following proposition:

PROPOSITION 9.1   For the same realizations of governmental objectives and control error, monetary expansion under asymmetric information is never higher than under symmetric information and almost always strictly lower.

Thus the existence of asymmetric information and learning by the public attenuates the problem of dynamic inconsistency of monetary policy under discretion. However, except under extreme circumstances some of which are discussed below, it does not completely eliminate it.

We turn next to a discussion of the factors that determine the extent to which m_i is lower than m_i^s. Consider first the effect of the signal-to-noise ratio that operates on θ. It is shown in appendix B to this chapter that

$$\frac{d\theta}{d\sigma_\psi^2} < 0. \tag{9.23}$$

Hence, as the level of noise in the control of monetary inflation goes up, θ goes down and inflation under asymmetric information increases. At the limit when σ_ψ^2 tends to infinity, θ tends to zero, and the rate of monetary expansion in equation (9.22) tends toward its symmetric information counterpart. At the other extreme, when σ_ψ^2 tends to zero,

$$\lim_{\sigma_\psi^2 \to 0} m_i = \alpha[(1 - \rho\beta)A + (1 - \rho^2\beta)p_i] + \psi_i.$$

Note that if in addition $\rho = \beta = 1$, reputational considerations are sufficient to induce the central bank to plan a zero rate of inflation.

The intuition underlying the effect of σ_ψ^2 is that with a relatively large noise-to-signal ratio, individuals pay little attention to past inflation in forecasting the upcoming rate of inflation. As a result the effect of current inflation on future expectations is small, making the future cost to the central bank of current inflation small too. Hence the central bank inflates at a rate that is nearer to m_i^s.

It is shown in appendix C to this chapter that

$$\frac{dB}{d\beta} < 0, \qquad \frac{dB_0}{d\beta} < 0, \tag{9.24}$$

so m_i is larger the lower the discount factor β. The less policymakers care about the future, the less meaningful are the future costs of higher expected inflation and the higher therefore their current choice of inflation. At the limit when $\beta = 0$, $m_i = m_i^s$ for all i.

We now turn to a comparison of the levels of monetary uncertainty inflicted on the public with and without asymmetric information. A natural measure of the level of monetary uncertainty is the variance of the forecast error of monetary inflation. From equation (9.21) this variance is simply σ_ψ^2 under symmetric information. Subtracting (9.7a) from (9.22), canceling terms, and calculating the variance of the resulting expression, we obtain the variance of the forecast error under asymmetric information:

$$[1 + (\rho\theta)^2]\sigma_\psi^2 + \alpha^2[1 - \rho^2\beta\theta]^2[1 + \rho^2(1 - \theta)^2]\sigma_v^2 \equiv V. \tag{9.25}$$

This expression is obviously larger than σ_ψ^2. It follows, not too surprisingly, that the public is subjected to more inflation uncertainty in the presence of asymmetric information.

Variability and uncertainty are related but not identical concepts.[21] From (9.19) and (9.22) the variances of inflation in the absence and in the presence of asymmetric information are, respectively,

$$\alpha^2 \sigma_p^2 + \sigma_\psi^2, \tag{9.26a}$$

$$\alpha^2 (1 - \rho^2 \beta \theta)^2 \sigma_p^2 + \sigma_\psi^2, \tag{9.26b}$$

where σ_p^2 is the variance of p. Comparison of those two variances leads to the following proposition:

PROPOSITION 9.2   The variability of inflation under symmetric information is never smaller than its variability under asymmetric information and is almost always strictly larger.

Thus despite the fact that inflation uncertainty is larger under asymmetric information, its variability is smaller in this case. The intuitive reason for this ranking of variabilities is related to the fact that under asymmetric information the central bank's response to changes in its objectives is smaller than under symmetric information. This is the case in turn because under asymmetric information the central bank possesses some control over the speed at which the public learns about its changing objectives. To exercise this control, the central bank's response to changes in objectives has to be weaker than in the symmetric information case. Otherwise, the information advantage is dissipated too quickly.

9.7   A Measure of Credibility under Asymmetric Information

In the presence of perfect information, as in chapter 3, a policy is either fully credible or not credible at all. Thus, as explained there, the socially optimal zero inflation policy is not credible under discretion, since it is dynamically inconsistent.

In the presence of asymmetric information credibility can be measured more continuously. The following definition provides an operational measure of this concept:

DEFINITION 9.1   Credibility is measured as minus the absolute value of the difference between the rate of monetary expansion planned by the central bank and the public's beliefs, at contracting time, about this rate. Formally, credibility in period i is written

$$C_i \equiv -|m_i^p - E[m_i^p | I_i]|. \tag{9.27}$$

When $e_i^p = m_i^p - E[m_i^p | I_i] = 0$, credibility is perfect and it decreases monotonically with the absolute value of e_i^p. The attitude of policymakers toward credibility depends on the direction in which their objectives are changing. If, relative to the past, they become more concerned with price stability, their interest is that the public recognize that swiftly. The reason is that during such episodes e_i^p is typically negative, making employment even lower than the natural rate N_n. At high levels of credibility (large C_i's) the reduction in employment is relatively small, making the output and employment cost of disinflation small. Hence high credibility is useful at such times, as was demonstrated by Volcker's disinflation at the beginning of the 1980s. On the other hand, when policymakers become more concerned with high employment, their interest is that the public be slow in recognizing that. During such periods e_i^p is typically positive, pushing employment above N_n toward the desired level of employment N^*. The lower credibility as measured by C_i, the larger is the temporary employment gains that are realized. This is probably the reason that public concern for lack of credibility is heard only during periods of disinflation. Clearly credibility has important real effects during periods of changes in the policymakers' objectives.

We turn now to a discussion of the determinants of credibility. Recognizing that $E[m_i^p | I_i] = E[m_i | I_i]$ and using (9.7a) and (9.15) in (9.27), we write

$$C_i = - |B[v_i + \rho(1 - \theta)v_{i-1}] - \rho\theta\psi_{i-1}| = - |e_i^p|. \tag{9.27a}$$

Credibility is lower when two neighboring innovations to governmental objectives have the same sign. The reason is that in period i the public is completely ignorant about v_i. It partly recognizes the realization of v_{i-1} through the observation of m_{i-1} but still misses $\rho(1 - \theta)v_{i-1}$ of the realization of v_{i-1}. Hence, if v_i and v_{i-1} have identical signs, the errors cumulate making C_i lower. Given that v_i and v_{i-1} have the same sign, credibility is lower the larger these innovations in absolute value. The more general conclusion from this example is that credibility is lower when there is a bunching of large and identically signed innovations to governmental objectives.[22] The realizations of the control error ψ_{i-1} also affects credibility. Credibility is lower when the sign of ψ_{i-1} is opposite to that of $v_i + \rho(1 - \theta)v_{i-1}$. The reason is that this error is partly interpreted as an innovation to governmental objectives in period $i - 1$ and causes an error in the opposite direction. Hence, if ψ_{i-1} has a sign that is opposite to that of the linear combination of the v_i's, it compounds the error caused by those innovations and reduces credibility even further.

The measure of credibility in equation (9.27) is period and therefore shock specific. To get a more general view of the effect of various parameters on the level of credibility, it is useful to look at some summary statistic of C_i that does not depend on particular shock realizations. Such a measure is the variance of e_i^p whose explicit form is (using equations 9.27a and 9.16a):

$$\alpha^2 [1 - \rho^2 \beta \theta]^2 [1 + \rho^2 (1 - \theta)^2] \sigma_v^2 + (\rho \theta)^2 \sigma_\psi^2 \equiv V^p. \tag{9.28}$$

This variance measures the average divergence between planned monetary growth and the public's beliefs about these plans. The larger it is, the lower will be the mean level of credibility in the economy. The following proposition summarizes the effect of various parameters on V^p.

PROPOSITION 9.3   The mean level of credibility, as measured by V^p, is lower the higher σ_ψ^2, σ_v^2, and α and the lower β.

Proof   See appendix D to this chapter.   □

The intuition underlying proposition 9.3 is straightforward. Credibility is lower, the higher is the level of political uncertainty (the higher σ_v^2) and the worse is the precision in control of the money supply (the higher σ_ψ^2). Larger values of either σ_v^2 or of σ_ψ^2 increase the public's uncertainty and reduce average credibility. A larger value of the trade-off parameter α causes policymakers to be more activist in response to changes in their objectives. This increases the public's uncertainty and reduces credibility too. A corollary is that credibility is lower on average, the more sensitive the demand is for labor to the real wage rate. This follows from the discussion in section 3.6, which implies that α becomes larger as the sensitivity of the demand for labor increases with respect to the real wage rate. Finally, when policymakers care more about the future, their policies are less activist. They respond less strongly to changing political objectives. This reduces uncertainty and increases credibility. A low degree of time preference on the part of policymakers is conducive to higher credibility.

9.8   The Confusion between Persistent Changes in Objectives and Transitory Control Errors

In equilibrium the public optimally utilizes the information at its disposition to forecast the rate of inflation for the period of the contract. But, as we saw, a residual margin of uncertainty remains. This uncertainty is due to several elements. First, at contracting time the public is ignorant about the realizations of the innovation to governmental objectives and of the control error during the period of the contract. This is simply uncertainty about the future. In addition the public does not know last period's innovation to governmental objectives which partly persists into the current one. It does observe last period's inflation which is a noisy indicator of this innovation. But a given value of m_{i-1} may be due to many different combinations of the persistent innovation v_{i-1} and of the transitory control error ψ_{i-1}. Although the information about v_{i-1} is filtered optimally, a residual level of uncertainty about it remains. The public normally confuses between transitory control errors and persistent changes in the objectives of policymakers. We will refer to this confusion as the "persistent-transitory confusion."[23] The filtering of v_{i-1} from m_{i-1} is based on the relative sizes of the average variabilities of v_{i-1} and of ψ_{i-1}. Hence, when only or mainly v_{i-1} is responsible for an increase in m_{i-1}, the public underpredicts it.

This underprediction enables government to utilize its information advantage in order to stimulate output. Similarly positive values of v_i are underpredicted. This too enables government to stimulate output. Since the marginal costs of inflation are increasing, government finds it optimal to spread the stimulus to employment made possible by its information advantage over more than one period. By doing so, government avoids the necessity to inflate at an excessive rate in any given period. This mechanism is responsible for the fact (discussed in section 9.6) that the discretionary rate of inflation is lower in the presence of asymmetric information.

Since we have assumed that p_{i-2} is already known in period i, the persistent-transitory confusion lasts only one period. More generally, when p_{i-2} is not revealed in period i, this confusion lasts longer and may take a long time to be completely resolved. A more general model in which this is the case is presented in chapter 10.

9.9 The Distribution of Monetary Growth under Asymmetric Information

We will characterize the distribution of money growth by the mean and the variance of m_i. From equation (9.22) mean inflation is

$$Em_i = B_0 A = \alpha[1 - \rho\beta\theta]A, \tag{9.29}$$

and the variance of inflation is given by equation (9.25). The following proposition summarizes the effects of various parameters on the mean and on the variance of monetary inflation:

PROPOSITION 9.4

1. Mean inflation is lower the larger σ_v^2 and β and the lower σ_ψ^2.
2. The variance of inflation is lower the larger β and the lower σ_v^2, σ_ψ^2, and α.

Proof See appendix E to this chapter.   □

An intriguing implication of proposition 9.4 is that cross-country variability in the discount factor β and in the imprecision σ_ψ^2 of monetary control combine to produce a positive cross-sectional relationship between the mean and the variance of monetary inflation. A large body of empirical evidence (Okun 1971; Logue and Willet 1976; Jaffe and Kleiman 1977) suggests that the mean level and the variability of inflation are positively related across countries.[24]

Note that when σ_ψ^2 tends to zero (so that the signal-to-noise ratio tends to one) and β and ρ tend to one, mean monetary inflation tends to zero even under discretion. With sufficient persistence, enough concern about the future, and sufficient quick learning by the public the excessive rate of inflation that arose under perfect information (chapter 3), disappears. When $\sigma_\psi^2 \to 0$ and $\theta \to 1$, the public practically has perfect information about last period's innovation to governmental objectives. In view of the fact that under perfect information there is an inflationary bias, it may seem strange that it disappears in this case. The reason for the difference is that in the first case the public knows government's objectives even before it observes last period's monetary expansion. By contrast, in the second case it obtains this information by observing monetary expansion. As a consequence the public expectation is independent of money growth in the first case but dependent on it in the second. This dependence is what deters policymakers from inflating for appropriate values of the parameters.

9.10   Concluding Remarks

Some of the recent literature has interpreted discretion as a situation in which policymakers always pick their one-shot preferred policy without any concern for the future. The discussion of this chapter suggests that this is a narrow view of discretion. The presence of asymmetric information makes policymakers sensitive to the trade-offs between current and future objectives even under discretion. This reduces the inflationary bias of policy under discretion and almost eliminates it completely for some configurations of parameters.

Models of the Lucas (1972, 1973) variety in which money has real effects because of the confusion between aggregate monetary shocks and real relative shocks have been criticized on the ground that this confusion cannot have substantial real effects since figures on the money stock become publicly available fairly quickly. Note that this criticism does not apply to the surprise-generating mechanism of this chapter. Even when they have last period's rate of monetary growth in hand, the public is uncertain about the upcoming rate of inflation because government's objectives change over time. Information about past rates of monetary growth does not resolve the public's confusion between persistent changes in government's objectives and transitory control errors. Because we have assumed that p_{i-2} is perfectly known in period i, this confusion is short-lived. However, when past objectives are not perfectly revealed in a way other than through the observation of past rates of inflation, the confusion may last much longer. The next chapter develops a detailed example of such a case.

Appendix A: Derivation of a Condition for $N^* - N_i \geq 0$ and $x_i \geq 0$ for All i with High Probability

Part a

From (9.2),

$$N^* - N_i = N^* - N_n - \alpha(m_i - E[m_i | I_i]). \tag{9A.1}$$

Subtracting (9.12) from (9.22) and rearranging, we obtain

$$e_i \equiv m_i - E[m_i | I_i] = B[v_i + \rho(1 - \theta)v_{i-1}] + \psi_i - \rho\theta\psi_{i-1}. \tag{9A.2}$$

Substituting (9A.2) into (9A.1) and rearranging, we find that the condition $N^* - N_i \geq 0$ is equivalent to the condition

$$e_i = B[v_i + \rho(1 - \theta)v_{i-1}] + \psi_i - \rho\theta\psi_{i-1} \leq \frac{N^* - N_n}{\alpha} \equiv c. \tag{9A.3}$$

The expression on the left-hand side of (9A.3) is normally distributed. It has a zero expected value and a variance V whose explicit form is given in equation (9.25) in the text. Hence it is possible to use the standard normal distribution to make the probability that condition (9A.3) is violated as small as desired. For instance, when

$$3\sqrt{V} < c, \tag{9A.4}$$

this probability is 0.0013. Using (9.25) and the facts $\rho\theta < 1$, $\rho^2(1-\theta) < 1$, and $B \leq \alpha$, a sufficient condition for the fulfillment of (9A.4) is

$$\sigma_v^2 + \alpha^2\sigma_\psi^2 \leq \frac{(N^* - N_n)^2}{18\alpha^2}. \tag{9A.5}$$

This is a joint restriction on the divergence between the desired and the natural levels of employment, the sensitivity of the demand for labor with respect to the real wage (which determines α), and the variances σ_v^2 and σ_ψ^2.

Part b

To make the probability that the condition $x \geq 0$ is violated no larger than 0.0013, A similarly has to be no smaller than $3\sigma_p^2$. From note 9 this condition is equivalent to

$$\sigma_v^2 \leq (1 - \rho^2)\frac{A^2}{9}. \tag{9A.6}$$

Combining (9A.5) and (9A.6), we obtain

$$\sigma_v^2 \leq \min\left[(1 - \rho^2)\frac{A^2}{9}, \frac{(N^* - N_n)^2}{18\alpha^4} - \frac{\sigma_\psi^2}{\alpha^2}\right]. \tag{9A.7}$$

Appendix B: Demonstration That θ Decreases When σ_ψ^2 Increases

From equation (9.16a) an increase in σ_ψ^2 raises the $F(B)$ curve in figure 9.1 and produces an intersection of $F(B)$ with the 45-degree line at a higher value of B. Hence B increases when σ_ψ^2 goes up. But

$$B = \alpha[1 - \rho^2\beta\theta],$$

which implies that θ decreases. Hence θ is a decreasing function of σ_ψ^2.

Appendix C: Proof That B and B_0 Decrease in β

First, from figure 9.1 and equation (9.16a) an increase in β lowers the curve $F(B)$ and produces a lower equilibrium value of B. Second, since $B = \alpha[1 - \rho^2\beta\theta]$ and since B decreases when β goes up, $\beta\theta$ must increase when β goes up. It follows from (9.16a) that B_0 decreases too when β goes up.

Appendix D: Proof of Proposition 9.3

The conditional expected value in (9.12a) is the point estimate that minimizes the mean square forecast error of m_i given I_i. This mean square forecast error is given by V in equation (9.25). It follows that given the parameters α, β, ρ, σ_v^2, and σ_ψ^2, θ is a minimizer of V. Hence $\partial V/\partial\theta = 0$. Comparison of (9.25) with (9.28) suggests that $V^p = V - \sigma_\psi^2$. Hence θ is a minimizer of V^p as well, and $\partial V^p/\partial\theta = 0$. Let D be a dummy parameter such that $D = \sigma_\psi^2, \sigma_v^2, \alpha, \beta$. Then

$$\frac{dV^p}{dD} = \frac{\partial V^p}{\partial\theta}\frac{d\theta}{dD} + \frac{\partial V^p}{\partial D} = \frac{\partial V^p}{\partial D},$$

since $\partial V^p/\partial\theta = 0$. Hence

$$\frac{dV^p}{d\sigma_\psi^2} = (\rho\theta)^2 > 0,$$

$$\frac{dV^p}{d\sigma_v^2} = \alpha^2[1 - \rho^2\beta\theta]^2[1 + \rho^2(1 - \theta)^2] > 0,$$

$$\frac{dV^p}{d\alpha} = 2\alpha[1 - \rho^2\beta\theta]^2[1 + \rho^2(1 - \theta)^2]\sigma_v^2 > 0,$$

$$\frac{dV^p}{d\beta} = -2(\alpha\rho)^2\theta[1 - \rho^2\beta\theta][1 + \rho^2(1 - \theta)^2]\sigma_v^2 < 0.$$

The signs of the last three expressions are implied by the fact that $\rho^2\beta\theta < 1$.

$\square$

Appendix E: Proof of Proposition 9.4

For part 1, an increase in σ_v^2 lowers the curve $F(B)$ in figure 9.1 and produces a lower value of B, which implies through equation (9.16a) that

θ is higher. A higher θ implies through equation (9.16b) that B_0 is lower. It follows from equation (9.29) that $dEm_i/d\sigma_v^2 < 0$. The result $dEm_i/d\beta < 0$ follows directly from equation (9.29) and the fact, proved in appendix C, that $dB_0/d\beta < 0$.

Finally, from appendix B, $d\theta/d\sigma_\psi^2 < 0$. It follows from equation (9.29) that $dEm_i/d\sigma_\psi^2 > 0$.

For part 2, from (9.25) and the fact that θ is a minimizer of V,

$$\frac{dV}{d\sigma_\psi^2} = \frac{\partial V}{\partial \theta}\frac{d\theta}{d\sigma_\psi^2} + \frac{\partial V}{\partial \sigma_\psi^2} = 1 + (\rho\theta)^2 > 0.$$

The remaining results can be derived by noting that

$$\frac{dV}{dD} = \frac{dV^p}{dD}, \qquad D = \sigma_v^2, \alpha, \beta,$$

and by using the expressions for dV^p/dD in the proof of proposition 9.3.

□

10 An Extended Information Advantage about Central Bank Objectives

10.1 Introduction

For simplicity and focus, the analysis in chapter 9 was conducted under the assumption that any current changes in objectives are revealed to the public with full precision after two periods. But in practice a certain degree of uncertainty about central bank objectives in a given period may remain for a longer time. The relative emphasis on alternative objectives in a given period is not a number that is ultimately published in some statistical bulletin. In some countries the deliberations of monetary policymakers are made public after a certain delay. For example, in the United States the minutes and directive of the Federal Open Market Committee (FOMC) to the New York trading desk are revealed to the public after six weeks. However, as stressed by Meltzer (1990) and others, the directive is usually framed in vague general terms without specific reference to precise rates of monetary growth. As time passes, the public may obtain additional pieces of information that make it possible to make more informed judgments about the policymakers' objectives in that period. But some judgmental process in which currently available information is used to draw inferences about the imperfectly known past (even when it is more distant than two periods away) is normally unavoidable.

This chapter makes an attempt to capture this more realistic information structure by considering a case in which the public never directly obtains information about the past relative emphasis of the central bank on employment and price stability. However, it continuously updates its beliefs about both current and past objectives as new figures about money growth or inflation are published over time. This formulation implies that there always remains, however small, a degree of uncertainty in the public's mind about the central bank objectives in past periods. Besides being more realistic, this formulation is more flexible than that of chapter 9. Depending on the values of the underlying parameters, it can accommodate various speeds of learning by the public about changes in the objectives of policymakers. This added flexibility is important to understand outcomes in periods during which policymakers' objectives undergo large changes that may be characterized as "regime change." During such periods the speed with which the public learns about changes in governmental objectives is an important determinant of the length of a recession following an increased concern for price stability or of the length of an expansion following an increased concern for employment.

10.2   Central Bank Objectives and Its Extended Information Advantage

The deterministic and stochastic structure of policymakers' objective function and of the economy are the same as in chapter 9. The policymakers' objective function is given by equation (9.1) and its stochastic features by equation (9.3). It states that the relative importance assigned to inflation and stimulation shifts in unpredictable ways as individuals within the decision-making body of government change their positions, alliances, and views. In the United States the changing weights may also reflect annual changes in the composition of a committee such as the Federal Open Market Committee or of the Board of Governors as well as unpredictable shifts in the loyalty of individual board members to the president (Havrilesky 1991c). The short-run Phillips relation, which arises because the natural real wage is above its market-clearing level, is given by equation (9.2). As in chapter 9, policymakers do not have perfect control over the money supply. The relation between actual and planned monetary growth is given by equation (9.4).

The timing of moves is identical to that of chapter 9. Within each period wage contracts are concluded first. Then policymakers choose m_i^p, taking the contract nominal wage and the expectations embedded in it as given. Finally, the control error ψ_i realizes, and actual inflation is determined by equation (9.4).

The only difference between the model of this chapter and the previous one is that now individuals have no direct access to p_{i-2} or to any previous realizations of relative central bank preferences. Consequently the information advantage of policymakers lasts longer. But since the information set I_i includes observations about all past rates of monetary expansion up to and including m_{i-1}, the public can make inferences about past values of central bank objectives. In the model of chapter 9 the information about rates of monetary expansion from period $i - 2$ and back, although available, was not used by the public since a direct observation of policymaker type in that period became available in period i. As a result individuals utilized only m_{i-1} to sharpen their inflation forecast for period i. But in the absence of direct observations on past values of p, all past rates of monetary expansion are generally useful for forecasting future inflation. The reason is that now the confusion between transitory control errors and persistent changes in objectives lasts longer. To obtain as precise as possible a forecast of future inflation, the public needs to separate persistent changes in objectives from transitory control errors. To accomplish this task, all past values of inflation are useful, since the persistence (or its lack) of inflation within some range indicates how likely it is that inflation will persist in the same range in the future.

10.3   The Equilibrium Concept

The equilibrium concept is of the Nash variety. Policymakers know the process by which the public forms its perception, $E[m_i | I_i]$, of the current rate of monetary expansion. This process must be consistent with the actual policy strategy followed by government. The government's strategy is derived in turn by solving the maximization problem in equation (9.1) subject to the Phillips relation in (9.2), taking the process for the formation of $E[m_i | I_i]$ as given. In other words, $E[m_i | I_i]$ is a rational expectation of m_i formed by using the public's knowledge about the policymakers' strategy in conjunction with all the relevant information available. As in chapter 9 we proceed in two steps. First we postulate the public's beliefs about the strategy that the government uses to set m^p. Then we show that when government optimizes, given the structure of beliefs, the strategy that emerges is identical to the strategy that the public believes in. The public's beliefs and the consequent form of the optimal predictor $E[m_i | I_i]$ are discussed in section 10.4. The solution of government's optimization and a proof of the rationality of the model are in section 10.5.

10.4   The Public's Beliefs and the Expected Rate of Monetary Expansion

The public believes that the planned rate of monetary expansion is the following linear function of A and of p_i:

$$m_i^p = B_0 A + B p_i \qquad \text{for all } i, \tag{10.1}$$

where B_0 and B are known constants that ultimately depend on the underlying parameters of government's objective function.[1] The public does not observe m_i^p directly. It observes past actual money growth

$$m_j = B_0 A + B p_j + \psi_j, \qquad j \le i - 1, \tag{10.2}$$

which is a noisy indicator of m_j^p because of the existence of a control error. Since p_j displays a certain degree of persistence (as measured by ρ), past values of m are relevant for predicting the current rate of monetary growth. The information set of the public also contains the constants A, B_0, B, ρ, and the variances σ_v^2 and σ_ψ^2. As a consequence from each past observation on m the public can, using (10.2), infer the value of

$$y_j \equiv B p_j + \psi_j. \tag{10.3}$$

In section 10.5 we show that equation (10.2) is implied by policymakers' actions given the public's belief, so this inference is correct for equilibrium positions.

It follows from this remark and equation (10.1) that

$$E[m_i | I_i] = B_0 A + B E[p_i | y_{i-1}, y_{i-2}, \ldots]. \tag{10.4}$$

It is shown in appendix A to this chapter that the conditional expected value on the right-hand side of (10.4) is

$$E[p_i | y_{i-1}, y_{i-2}, \ldots] = \frac{(\rho - \lambda)}{B} \sum_{j=0}^{\infty} \lambda^j y_{i-1-j}, \tag{10.5a}$$

$$\lambda \equiv \frac{1}{2} \left[\frac{1+r}{\rho} + \rho \right] - \sqrt{\frac{1}{4}\left(\frac{1+r}{\rho} + \rho^2\right) - 1}, \tag{10.5b}$$

$$r \equiv B^2 \frac{\sigma_v^2}{\sigma_\psi^2}. \tag{10.5c}$$

Substituting (10.5a) into (10.4), using (10.2) to express y_j in terms of m_j, and rearranging the resulting expression, we obtain

$$E[m_i | I_i] = \sum_{j=0}^{\infty} \lambda^j [(1 - \rho)\bar{m}^p + (\rho - \lambda)m_{i-1-j}], \tag{10.6a}$$

$$\bar{m}^p \equiv B_0 A. \tag{10.6b}$$

Equations (10.1) and (10.6b) show that $\bar{m}^p$ is the mean and median (since m_i^p is normally distributed) value of planned monetary growth. The coefficient λ is bounded between zero and one.[2] The optimal predictor of monetary growth is therefore a geometrically distributed lag, with decreasing weights, of weighted averages of the unconditional mean money growth and actually observed past rates of money growth. In general individuals give some weight to mean governmental planned money growth and assign the rest of the weights to observations on actual past money growth.[3]

It is easily checked that the sum of the weights on the mean and past rates of money growth is one.

The relative weight accorded to $\bar{m}^p$ is a measure of how strongly the public sticks to preconceptions rather than relying on actual developments. At the limit, as ρ tends to 1, the public abandons preconceptions entirely.[4] In this case the governmental preferences tend toward nonstationarity, so the information on the fixed mean $\bar{m}^p$ has less significance. At the other extreme, when ρ tends to zero, there is hardly any persistence in the stochastic component of governmental preferences, so the information on actual past rates of growth becomes less relevant for predicting the future. Hence individuals stick to preconceptions and give negligible weight to actual developments.[5] They rightly interpret any deviation of money growth from its mean value as being largely transitory.

10.5 Derivation of Government's Decision Rule and Proof of the Rationality of Expectations[6]

Policymakers choose the current planned rate of money growth using their objective function and their knowledge of the current value of their objectives, taking as given the public's process of expectations formation in equation (10.6). Retracing the steps that led to equation (10.1b) (see section 10.4) and noting that the term $(N^* - N_n)x_i$ is not influenced by policymakers' decisions, their decision problem may be formulated as

$$\max_{\{m_i^p, i=0,1,\dots\}} E_{G0} \sum_{i=0}^{\infty} \beta^i \left[(m_i - E[m_i \mid I_i])\alpha x_i - \frac{m_i^2}{2} \right]. \tag{10.7}$$

Using (9.4) and (10.6) in this expression and rearranging, the policymakers' decision problem becomes

$$\max_{\{m^p, i=0,1,\dots\}} E_{G0} \sum_{i=0}^{\infty} \beta^i \left[\left\{ m_i^p + \psi_i - \frac{1-\rho}{1-\lambda} B_0 A \right. \right.$$

$$\left. \left. - (\rho - \lambda) \sum_{j=0}^{\infty} \lambda^j (m_{i-1-j}^p + \psi_{i-1-j}) \right\} \alpha x_i - \frac{(m_i^p + \psi_i)^2}{2} \right]. \tag{10.8}$$

Policymakers choose the actual value of m_0^p and a contingency plan for m_i^p, $i \geq 1$. Recognizing that in each period in the future policymakers face a problem that has the same structure as the period zero problem, the stochastic Euler equations necessary for an internal maximum of this problem are (following Sargent 1979, ch. 14)

$$\alpha\{x_i - (\rho - \lambda)\beta E_{Gi}(x_{i+1} + \beta\lambda x_{i+2} + (\beta\lambda)^2 x_{i+3} + \ldots)\} - m_i^p = 0,$$

$$i = 0, 1, \ldots. \qquad (10.9)$$

Equation (10.9) yields the actual choice of m_0^p and the contingency plan for all future rates of money growth for $i \geq 1$.[7]

Although policymakers know x_i in period i (and the public does not), they are uncertain about values of x beyond period i. Based on the information available to them in period i, they compute a conditional expected value for $x_{i+j}, j \geq 1$. In view of (9.3a) and (9.3b), this expected value is

$$E_{Gi}x_{i+j} = A + E_{Gi}p_{i+j} = A + \rho^j p_i = \rho^j x_i + (1 - \rho^j)A, \quad j \geq 0. \qquad (10.10)$$

Substituting (10.10) into (10.9), using (9.3a) and the formulas for infinite geometric progressions, and rearranging, we get

$$m_i^p = \alpha\frac{1 - \beta\rho}{1 - \beta\lambda}A + \alpha\frac{1 - \beta\rho^2}{1 - \beta\rho\lambda}p_i, \qquad (10.11)$$

which confirms the public's beliefs in equation (10.1) with

$$B_0 = \alpha\frac{1 - \beta\rho}{1 - \beta\lambda(B)}, \qquad (10.12a)$$

$$B = \alpha\frac{1 - \beta\rho^2}{1 - \beta\rho\lambda(B)} \equiv F(B). \qquad (10.12b)$$

The dependence of λ on B through equation (10.5) is stressed by writing λ as a function of B. Equation (10.12a) determines B as an implicit function of α, β, ρ, σ_v^2, and σ_ψ^2. A solution for B always exists and is unique. To see this, note that the function $F(B)$ on the right-hand side of equation (10.12a) is monotonically decreasing in B and that $F(0) = \alpha$ and $F(\alpha) \leq \alpha$. (These statements are demonstrated in appendix B to this chapter.) The left-hand side of (10.12a) is a 45-degree straight line through the origin. Since $F(0) = \alpha$ and $F'(B) < 0$, these two functions must intersect at one and only one point. Moreover, since $F(\alpha) < \alpha$ and $F'(B) < 0$, the intersection occurs at a value of B that is never larger than α. Figure 10.1 illustrates the argument graphically. Clearly a solution for B exists and is unique. Given this solution, equation (10.12b) determines a unique solution for B_0.[8]

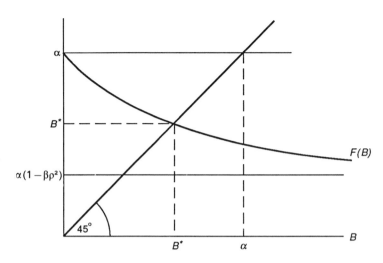

Figure 10.1
Determination of the equilibrium value of B under an extended information advantage

10.6 Speed of Learning, Activism, Credibility, and Their Determinants

Concerns about credibility usually arise during periods of sustained changes in the objectives of the central bank. It is therefore important to determine what are the factors that affect the speed at which the public recognizes sustained changes in policy and objectives. This speed is an important determinant of the length and seriousness of poststabilization recessions and of the length and magnitude of expansions that follow an increased emphasis of policy on the employment objective.

As in chapter 9, the public does not immediately recognize changes in the policymakers' objectives because of its inability to separate persistent changes in objectives from transitory control errors. However, here the public is never fully informed about past objectives. Hence, when sustained changes occur, the confusion between persistent changes in objectives and transitory control errors normally lasts longer than in chapter 9. The parameter λ in equation (10.5b) is a prime determinant of the speed with which the public recognizes sustained changes in objectives. The higher λ, the longer is the "memory" of the public and the less important are recent developments for the formation of current expectations. With a low λ, past policies are quickly forgotten. Proposition 10.1 below demonstrates that λ

is a decreasing function of σ_v^2 and an increasing function of σ_ψ^2; the effects of distant past choices of monetary growth on current expectations are smaller in comparison to more recent choices the larger σ_v^2 and the lower σ_ψ^2. People give less weight to the more distant past the larger the variance of the innovation to governmental objectives and the lower the variance of the control error. The worse the control of the money stock (high σ_ψ^2), the longer will past policies affect future expectations.

Suppose that after remaining above its mean value, m_t^p decreases below the mean and stays there for a while. This more conservative attitude toward inflation takes longer to be recognized by the public the larger the parameter λ. Therefore the worse the control of the money stock, the lower will be the initial credibility of sustained shifts to rates of monetary growth that differ from those previously experienced. λ is therefore a prime determinant of the speed with which changing objectives are detected. The higher the λ, the longer it takes the public to recognize a change in central bank's objectives and the lower therefore the credibility of new central bank objectives.

Since λ is a prime determinant of the speed with which the public detects changes in objectives, we are interested in establishing how it is affected by the more fundamental parameters of the economy and of the policymakers' objective function. The following proposition addresses this issue:

PROPOSITION 10.1   For $\sigma_v^2/\sigma_\psi^2 > 0$, λ is lower and the recognition of sustained changes in objectives faster, the larger σ_v^2 and α and the lower σ_ψ^2 and β.

Proof

1. *Effect of σ_ψ^2 and σ_v^2.* Given B, the definition of $F(B)$ in (10.12a) implies that

$$\frac{\partial F(\cdot)}{\partial a} = \frac{\partial F(\cdot)}{\partial \lambda}\frac{\partial \lambda}{\partial a}, \tag{10.13}$$

where $a \equiv \sigma_v^2/\sigma_\psi^2$. From appendix B, λ is decreasing in r. Since, given B, r is increasing in a, it follows that $\partial \lambda/\partial a < 0$. Together with $\partial F(\cdot)/\partial \lambda > 0$ and (10.13), this implies that when a goes up, the curve $F(B)$ in figure 10.1 shifts downward. As a consequence the equilibrium value of B decreases. Returning to equation (10.12a), this implies that λ must be lower too.

Hence a higher a is associated with a lower λ, implying that λ is increasing in σ_ψ^2 and decreasing in σ_v^2.

2. *Effect of β.* Given B, the definition of $F(\cdot)$ implies that

$$\frac{\partial F(\cdot)}{\partial \beta} = -\frac{\alpha\rho}{(1 - \beta\rho\lambda)^2}(\rho - \lambda), \tag{10.14}$$

which is strictly negative for $\sigma_v^2/\sigma_\psi^2 > 0$. Hence an increase in β lowers the $F(\cdot)$ curve in figure 10.1 and produces a smaller value of B. This implies, via equation (10.5c), that r is lower. But since λ is decreasing in r, λ must be higher. Hence an increase in β raises λ.

3. *Effect of α.* An increase in α raises the $F(B)$ curve in figure 10.1 and produces a larger equilibrium value of B. Since (through equations 10.5b and 10.5c) λ is inversely related to B, it follows that λ goes down. Hence a higher α is associated with a lower λ. $\square$

The intuition underlying the effects of σ_v^2 and of σ_ψ^2 on λ has been discussed above. The intuition underlying the effects of α and of β on λ is the following: A larger value of α is associated with a larger B, which from equation (10.11) implies that policy is more activist; planned money growth responds more vigorously to changes in the objectives of the government. Hence recent changes in the rate of inflation contain more information about current central bank's plans and the upcoming rate of inflation. It is therefore rational for the public to rely a lot on recent developments, which means that λ is low. Exactly the opposite occurs when, other things the same, β is large. A large β leads to less activism. Since the central bank's rate of time preference is low, it reacts relatively little to current changes in objectives. As a consequence recent inflation contains less information about future inflation and it is rational for the public to use it relatively little in forecasting future inflation. As a consequence λ is higher when β is higher, and it therefore takes longer for the public to detect changes in planned monetary growth.

It may seem odd that when policymakers have a long horizon (high β) changes in their policies are less credible in the sense that such changes are detected more slowly. This seeming puzzle is resolved by noting that this is because we are focusing here on credibility *during periods of sustained changes* in objectives. When β is high, the public's learning process is slow. This is rational on the part of the public, for a high β is conducive to less activism by policymakers, and the probability that there will be sustained changes in planned monetary growth is small. But this also means that when relatively infrequent sustained changes do occur, the public is slower in recognizing them. By using a conservative learning process (high λ), the public is nearer to the truth during the more frequent tranquil periods. But it pays a price during the infrequent periods of sustained and large changes in which its forecasts are worse.

A natural question is what is the effect of β and other parameters on credibility and the quality of the public's forecasts, on average, when both periods of little change and large, sustained changes are taken into consideration. This question can be answered by investigating the effects of various parameters on

$$V^p \equiv E[m_i^p - E[m_i^p \,|\, I_i]]^2, \tag{10.15}$$

which, as suggested by the discussion in section 9.7, is a measure of average credibility that appropriately weights tranquil as well as turbulent periods. The following proposition summarizes the effects of various parameters on V^p:

PROPOSITION 10.2 V^p is lower and overall credibility larger the lower σ_ψ^2, σ_v^2 and α and the larger β.

Proof   See appendix C. $\square$

Thus, although a large α and a low β speed up the public's recognition of sustained and large changes in objectives, average credibility is higher when α is small and β large. The intuitive reason is that a low α and a large β reduce the level of activism as measured by the coefficient of p_i in equation (10.11). With a lower level of activism policymakers react less to changes in x_i. This reduces the impact of political uncertainties (as measured by the variability of p_i) on planned monetary growth, reduces the public's uncertainty, and increases average credibility. The effect of σ_v^2 on average credibility is also opposite to its effect on the speed of learning but for a different reason.[9] The reason is simply that any increase in the underlying uncertainty, including in particular political uncertainty, increases the public's uncertainty and reduces credibility. But in the presence of a larger σ_v^2, individuals rationally pay more attention to recent developments. Hence they detect persistent or large changes in objectives more quickly.

10.7   The Distribution of Monetary Inflation and Its Determinants with and without Asymmetric Information

Substituting (10.12) into (10.2), we obtain

$$m_i = \alpha \frac{1 - \beta\rho}{1 - \beta\lambda} A + \alpha \frac{1 - \beta\rho^2}{1 - \beta\rho\lambda} p_i + \psi_i. \tag{10.16}$$

Being a linear combination of normal variates, m_i is normal too. Hence it is fully characterized by the unconditional mean and variance of monetary inflation. From (10.16) and (9.3) the mean and the variance of inflation are given, respectively, by

$$Em_i = \frac{1 - \beta\rho}{1 - \beta\lambda} \alpha A, \tag{10.17}$$

$$V(m_i) = \alpha^2 \left[\frac{1 - \beta\rho^2}{1 - \beta\rho\lambda} \right]^2 \frac{\sigma_v^2}{1 - \rho^2} + \sigma_\psi^2 \equiv B^2 \frac{\sigma_v^2}{1 - \rho^2} + \sigma_\psi^2. \tag{10.18}$$

Since A is positive, $\rho < 1$ and $\lambda \leq \rho$ mean inflation is always strictly positive. Hence average inflation exhibits an inflationary bias similar to the one encountered in chapter 3 under perfect and therefore symmetric information. It is of some interest to compare mean inflation in equation (10.17) to its level under perfect information when the central bank objectives are permanently at their mean level A.[10] In this case the discretionary rate of monetary inflation is αA.[11] Since $\lambda \leq \rho$, it follows that

$$Em_i = \frac{1 - \beta\rho}{1 - \beta\lambda} \alpha A \leq \alpha A, \tag{10.19}$$

which implies that the average inflationary bias under asymmetric information is never larger and almost always strictly smaller than the bias under perfect information. The reason of course is that with asymmetric information the central bank is partially deterred from inflating because of the effect that current inflation has on future expectations and through them on the central bank's future objectives. This suggests that when the rate of time preference under asymmetric information increases, Em_i should approach αA. It is indeed the case that at the limit, when $\beta = 0$, $Em_i = \alpha A$. Thus in this case inflationary biases with and without asymmetric information are equal, since the central bank does not care about the future. At the other extreme, when $\beta = 1$ and the degree of persistence ρ in central bank objectives approaches one, the inflationary bias tends to disappear. In other words, with a sufficiently long horizon and enough persistence in objective, the reputational considerations that operate under asymmetric information practically eliminate the discretionary inflationary bias of chapter 3.

The following proposition summarizes the effects of σ_v^2 and of σ_ψ^2 on mean inflation:[12]

PROPOSITION 10.3   Mean inflation is smaller, the larger the parameter σ_v^2 and the lower σ_ψ^2.

Proof   The proof is immediate from (10.17) and proposition 10.1.   □

The intuition underlying this result is simple. The larger the ratio σ_v^2/σ_ψ^2, the shorter is the learning lag. Hence the effect of current inflation on future expectations is felt more quickly. This increases the deterring impact of reputational considerations thereby reducing mean inflation. Proposition 10.4 summarizes the effects of various parameters on the variance of monetary inflation:

PROPOSITION 10.4   The variability of inflation is lower, the larger the parameter β and the lower σ_v^2 and α.

Proof

1.   *Effect of β.* It is demonstrated in the proof of proposition 10.1 that an increase in β causes a reduction in the activism parameter B. It follows from (10.18) that $V(m_i)$ decreases when β goes up.

2.   *Effect of α.* The activism parameter B is an increasing function of α (see proof of proposition 10.1). Hence, from (10.18), $V(m_i)$ is an increasing function of α.

3.   *Effect of σ_ψ^2.* The direct effect is obviously positive. The indirect effect, through B, is also positive since an increase in σ_ψ^2 raises B (see proof of proposition 10.1). It follows that a larger σ_ψ^2 raises $V(m_i)$ directly, as well as by raising B.   □

A corollary to propositions 10.3 and 10.4 is that cross-sectional variability in σ_ψ^2 produces a positive cross-sectional correlation between the mean and the variance of inflation. This is a generalization of a similar result in chapter 9 and may provide an explanation for this widely documented empirical regularity (for references, see section 9.9).

10.8   Reputation and Its Determinants

The recent literature contains at least two different ways of conceptualizing reputation. Here we use the notion that the reputation of the central bank is better the more it cares about price stability in comparison to employment.[13] This notion has been used by Backus and Driffill (1985a, 1985b), Barro (1986), and Vickers (1986) in the context of only two unchanging possible types of central banks. One type is characterized by a zero value of x and the other by a positive x. Since the first policymaker always plans a zero rate of monetary expansion, he or she is referred to as "tough," whereas the second one who does occasionally inflate is referred to as "weak." Either the tough or the weak policymaker is in office for the duration of the analysis. The public is initially uncertain about which type is in office and updates its probability concerning the type in office using Bayes's rule. Reputation is defined as the probability held by the public that policymakers in office are tough.

Since, in the model presented here, there is an infinite number of possible types, the analogous concept is the probability distribution of x_i conditional on I_i. This probability is normal and has a constant variance. Hence it is uniquely characterized by the conditional mean $E[x_i | I_i]$. But

$$E[x_i | I_i] = A + E[p_i | I_i], \tag{10.20}$$

since A is common knowledge. Hence the lower $E[p_i | I_i]$, the larger is the probability that policymakers care relatively more about price stability. It is therefore a natural measure of reputation. The lower it is, the better the current reputation of the central bank as an inflation fighter.

The explicit expression for $E[p_i | I_i]$ in equation (10.5a) suggests that reputation is built up and depleted gradually. This aspect of reputation makes it similar to a capital good. The speed with which a reputation is built up or destroyed depends on λ. The lower the λ, the faster is the process of reputation building and destruction. Proposition 10.1 implies that the process is faster as σ_v^2 and α become larger and σ_ψ^2 and β lower.

Reputation is a state variable. What are the factors that determine its level in a given time period? The answer to this question can be obtained from equation (10.5a) and by recalling the definition of y_i from equation (10.3). Essentially the reputation of policymakers improves if their relative concern for employment in the past was lower. There is besides an element of luck in the establishment of reputation. Recent large and positive realizations of the control error ψ will diminish current reputation, and more so if λ is smaller. On the other hand, with recent large negative (in absolute value) realizations of ψ, current reputation improves.

Appendix A: Derivation of the Optimal Predictor in Equation (10.5)

Define the dummy stochastic variable $\varepsilon_t \equiv \psi_t/B$. Substituting this relation into equation (10.3)

$$y_t = B(p_t + \varepsilon_t) \equiv By_t^1.$$

Since the public knows the parameter B, an observation on y_t is equivalent to an observation on y_t^1. Hence the expected value of p_t conditioned on past values of y is equal to this expected value conditioned on past values of y^1. We turn now to the calculation of this expected value.

Since p_t and y_t^1 are normally distributed, the expected value of p_t conditioned on y_{t-i}^1, $i \geq 1$, is a linear function with fixed coefficients of the observations on y_{t-i}^1, $i \geq 1$. That is,

$$E[p_t \mid y_{t-1}^1, y_{t-2}^1, \ldots] = \sum_{i=1}^{\infty} a_i y_{t-i}^1. \tag{10A.1}$$

Since this conditional expected value is also the point estimate of p_t which minimizes the mean square error around this estimate, it follows that $\{a_i\}_{i=1}^{\infty}$ are to be chosen so as to minimize

$$Q \equiv E[p_t - \sum_{i=1}^{\infty} a_i y_{t-i}^1]^2. \tag{10A.2}$$

Using the relation between y and y^1 in (10A.2), and the fact that ε and v are mutually independent, and passing the expectation operator through, we can rewrite Q as

$$Q = [1 + (\rho - a_1)^2 + (\rho^2 - \rho a_1 - a_2)^2 + \cdots + (\rho^i - \rho^{i-1}a_1 - \cdots - a_i)^2$$
$$+ \ldots]\sigma_v^2 + \sum_{i=1}^{\infty} a_i^2 \sigma_\varepsilon^2, \tag{10A.3}$$

where $\sigma_\varepsilon^2 = \sigma_\psi^2/B^2$. The necessary first-order conditions for an extremum of Q are

$$\frac{\partial Q}{\partial a_i} = -2[(\rho^i - \rho^{i-1}a_1 - \cdots - a_i) + \rho(\rho^{i+1} - \rho^i a_1 - \cdots - a_{i+1})$$

$$+ \rho^2(\rho^{i+2} - \rho^{i+1}a_1 - \cdots - a_{i+2}) + \ldots] + 2\sigma_\varepsilon^2 a_i = 0, \qquad i \geq 1. \tag{10A.4}$$

Leading (10A.4) by one period, multiplying by ρ, and subtracting (10A.4) from the resulting expression, we have

$$(\rho^i - \rho^{i-1}a_1 - \cdots - a_i)\sigma_v^2 + (\rho a_{i+1} - a_i)\sigma_\varepsilon^2 = 0, \qquad i \geq 1. \tag{10A.5}$$

Then multiplying (10A.5) by ρ, subtracting the resulting expression from (10A.5) led by one period, using the relation $\sigma_\varepsilon^2 = \sigma_\psi^2/B^2$, and rearranging, we obtain

$$a_{i+2} - \left(\frac{1+r}{\rho} + \rho\right)a_{i+1} + a_i = 0, \qquad i \geq 1, \tag{10A.6}$$

where $r = \sigma_v^2/\sigma_\varepsilon^2 = B^2\sigma_v^2/\sigma_\psi^2$. This is a second-order homogeneous difference equation whose general solution is

$$a_i = C\lambda^i, \tag{10A.7}$$

where C is a constant to be determined by initial conditions and λ is the root of the quadratic

$$u^2 - \left(\frac{1+r}{\rho} + \rho\right)u + 1 = 0. \tag{10A.8}$$

The roots of this equation are given by

$$u_{1,2} = \frac{1}{2}\left(\frac{1+r}{\rho} + \rho\right) \pm \sqrt{\left\{\frac{1}{2}\left(\frac{1+r}{\rho} + \rho\right)\right\}^2 - 1}. \tag{10A.9}$$

The positive root in (10A.9) is larger than one and the negative root is bounded between zero and one. Thus a_i does not diverge only if the smaller root is substituted for λ in (10A.7). Since a_i has to yield a minimum for Q, it cannot diverge. Hence

$$\lambda = \frac{1}{2}\left(\frac{1+r}{\rho} + \rho\right) - \sqrt{\left\{\frac{1}{2}\left(\frac{1+r}{\rho} + \rho\right)\right\}^2 - 1}.$$

For $i = 1$, (10A.5) implies that

$$(\rho - a_1)\sigma_v^2 + (\rho a_2 - a_1)\sigma_\varepsilon^2 = 0. \tag{10A.10}$$

Using (10A.7) to express a_1 and a_2 in terms of C and λ, substituting into (10A.10), and rearranging, we obtain

$$C = \frac{\rho \sigma_v^2}{\lambda [\sigma_v^2 + \sigma_\varepsilon^2 - \rho \lambda \sigma_\varepsilon^2]} = \frac{\rho}{\lambda} \frac{r}{1 + r - \rho \lambda}. \tag{10A.11}$$

Since λ is a root of the quadratic in (10A.8), it satisfies

$$\lambda^2 - \left(\frac{1}{\rho} + \rho + \frac{r}{\rho} \right) \lambda + 1 = 0,$$

which implies that

$$r = \rho \lambda + \frac{\rho}{\lambda} - (1 + \rho^2). \tag{10A.12}$$

Substituting (10A.12) into (10A.11) and rearranging, we obtain

$$C = \frac{\rho - \lambda}{\lambda}. \tag{10A.13}$$

Then substituting (10A.13) into (10A.7), substituting the resulting expression into (10A.1), and rearranging, we obtain

$$E[p_t | y_{t-1}^1, y_{t-2}^1, \ldots] = (\rho - \lambda) \sum_{j=0}^{\infty} \lambda^j y_{t-1-j}^1$$

$$= \frac{\rho - \lambda}{B} \sum_{j=0}^{\infty} \lambda^j (B p_{t-1-j} + \psi_{t-1-j}) = \frac{\rho - \lambda}{B} \sum_{j=0}^{\infty} \lambda^j y_{t-1-j}.$$

The optimal predictor in equation (10.5) of the text follows by recalling that past values of y^1 and y carry the same information. Hence

$$E[p_t | y_{t-1}^1, y_{t-2}^1, \ldots] = E[p_t | y_{t-1}, y_{t-2}, \ldots] = \frac{\rho - \lambda}{B} \sum_{j=0}^{\infty} \lambda^j y_{t-1-j},$$

which is equation (10.5a) in text. $\square$

Appendix B: Derivation of the Properties of the Function $F(B)$ in Equation (10.12a)

1. *Demonstration that* $F'(B) < 0$. Let $b \equiv \rho + (1 + r)/\rho$. Then from (10.5b), $\partial \lambda / \partial b = (1/2) \sqrt{b^2/4 - 1} \left(\sqrt{b^2/4 - 1} - b \right)$ which is negative since

$(3/4)b^2 + 1 > 0$. Since b is increasing in r, λ is decreasing in r. From (10.5c), r is increasing in B. Hence λ is decreasing in B. Since, as can be seen from its definition, $F(B)$ is increasing in λ, it follows that $F(B)$ is decreasing in B too.

2. *Demonstration that $F(0) = \alpha$. When $B = 0$,*

$$\lambda = \frac{1}{2}\left[\frac{1}{\rho} + \rho\right] - \sqrt{\frac{1}{4}\left[\frac{1}{\rho} + \rho\right]^2 - 1},$$

which can be shown to be equal to ρ by direct examination. Substitution of $\lambda = \rho$ into the definition of $F(B)$ implies that $F(0) = \alpha$.

3. *Demonstration that $F(\alpha) < \alpha$.* Since $F(0) = \alpha$ and $F'(B) < 0$, $F(\alpha)$ must be smaller than α when $\alpha > 0$. $\square$

Appendix C: Proof of Proposition 10.2

Substituting (10.1) and (10.4) into (10.15) and rearranging, we obtain

$$V^p = B^2 E[p_i - E[p_i|y_{i-1}, y_{i-2}, \dots]]^2. \tag{10A.14}$$

Since $E[p_i|y_{i-1}, y_{i-2}, \dots]$ is a minimum mean square error predictor,

$$E[p_i - E[p_i|y_{i-1}, y_{i-2}, \dots]]] = \min_{\{a_j\}} E[p_i - \sum_{j=1}^{\infty} a_j y_{i-j}]^2. \tag{10A.15}$$

Substituting (10A.15) into (10A.14), passing B to the right of the min operator and redefining variables, we obtain

$$V^p = \min_{\{a_j\}} E[q_i - \sum_{j=1}^{\infty} a_j(q_{i-j} + \psi_{i-j})]^2, \tag{10A.16a}$$

where

$$q_j \equiv Bp_j \quad \text{for all } j. \tag{10A.16b}$$

The definition of q_j in (10A.16b) in conjunction with the fact that $p_i = \rho p_{i-1} + v_i$ implies that

$$Eq = 0, \quad \sigma_q^2 = B^2 \sigma_p^2, \quad Eq_i q_{i-j} = \rho^j \sigma_q^2. \tag{10A.17}$$

Expanding the square term on the right-hand side of (10A.16a), using (10A.17) and the fact that q_j and ψ_j are mutually and serially uncorrelated, we can rewrite equation (10A.16a) as

$$V^p = \min_{\{a_j\}} \left[\sum_{j=1}^{\infty} a_j^2 \sigma_\psi^2 + Q[\{a_j\}] \sigma_q^2 \right], \tag{10A.18}$$

where

$$Q[\{a_j\}] \equiv \left[1 - 2 \sum_{j=1}^{\infty} a_j \rho^j + \sum_{j=1}^{\infty} \sum_{t=1}^{\infty} a_j a_t \rho^{|j-t|} \right]. \tag{10A.19}$$

The difference between the minimization problems in (10A.15) and (10A.16) is only that in the later case the constant B has been absorbed into the minimization problem. Hence the minimizing values of $\{a_i\}$ are identical for the two problems and are (see equation 10.5) given by

$$a_j = (\rho - \lambda)\lambda^{j-1}. \tag{10A.20}$$

Substituting (10A.20) into (10A.19) and rearranging, we obtain

$$Q[\{a_j\}] = \frac{1 - \rho^2}{1 - \lambda^2} > 0. \tag{10A.21}$$

Let D be a dummy variable such that

$$D = \sigma_\psi^2, \quad \sigma_v^2, \quad \alpha, \quad \beta.$$

From (10A.18),

$$\frac{dV^p}{dD} = \sum_{j=1}^{\infty} \frac{\partial V^p}{\partial a_j} \frac{da_j}{dD} + \frac{\partial V^p}{\partial D}. \tag{10A.22}$$

Since the a_j's are chosen so as to minimize the expression in (10A.15), $\partial V^p / \partial a_j = 0$ for all j. It follows that

$$\frac{dV^p}{dD} = \frac{\partial V^p}{\partial D}. \tag{10A.23}$$

Differentiating (10A.18) successively with respect to σ_ψ^2, σ_v^2, and B, and using (10A.21) and (10A.23), we obtain

$$\frac{dV^p}{d\sigma_\psi^2} = \sum_{j=1}^{\infty} a_j^2 > 0, \tag{10A.24a}$$

$$\frac{dV^p}{d\sigma_v^2} = \frac{B^2}{1 - \lambda^2} > 0, \tag{10A.24b}$$

$$\frac{dV^p}{dB} = \frac{2\sigma_v^2}{1 - \lambda^2} B > 0. \tag{10A.24c}$$

Equations (10A.24a) and (10A.24b) establish the result of the proposition for σ_ψ^2 and σ_v^2. The result for β and α follow from (10A.24) in conjunction with the fact (demonstrated in the proof of proposition 10.1) that B is decreasing in β and increasing in α. $\square$

11 Alternative Notions of Credibility and Reputation

11.1 Introduction

Previous chapters in both part I and part II have introduced various characterizations of credibility. The notion that only dynamically consistent policies are credible underlies most of the discussion of central bank behavior under perfect information in part I. However, once an information advantage on the part of the central bank is introduced in part II, additional ways to measure and parameterize credibility arise. The first task of this chapter is to compare and contrast these various notions of credibility and to relate them to popular notions of credibility, on the one hand, and to the game-theoretic notion of subgame perfection in extensive form games, on the other.

The discussion toward the end of the previous chapter introduced the notion of reputation. This notion seems to be inherently linked to the existence of asymmetric information. Nevertheless, part of the recent literature has modeled reputation even in the context of symmetric information environments by using trigger strategies from multiperiods games.[1] Section 11.3 presents the basic logic of this approach. Section 11.4 contains a criticism of trigger strategies as a device to model reputation. Section 11.5 compares and contrasts learning and trigger strategies as models of reputation with particular focus on their descriptive realism.[2]

11.2 Alternative Notions of Credibility

In a world of perfect information and no commitments of the type discussed in part I of the book, a policy announced today for some future period is either fully credible or not credible at all. It is fully credible if it is dynamically consistent and not credible at all if it is not dynamically consistent. The reason is that in each period policymakers reoptimize and choose the policy that is best for them in that period. Since the public is fully informed about the policymakers' objectives and constraints, it can calculate in advance the dynamically consistent policy for the period in question. In the absence of precommitments, any other policy will be disbelieved.

This argument bears a strong similarity to the argument from extensive games that only subgame perfect moves in a game tree are credible. A game tree is a complete description of the timing of moves and of the available strategies at every decision node of each of two or more players. The notion of subgame perfection requires that at each decision node the player, whose turn it is to move, picks the strategy that is best for him or her from that point and on. Hence any strategy that is dominated in the remaining subgame (from the point of view of the player whose turn it is to move) by some other strategy is not credible. Arriving at this point in the game the player will not pick a strategy that is dominated from his or her point of view. Since information is perfect other players can calculate which strategies are subgame perfect for other players and which are not. Hence only subgame perfect strategies are credible. It is easy to see that this concept bears a strong similarity to the concept of dynamic consistency in macro policy games. Both concepts require dynamic individual rationality in the sense that at each stage each player does what is best for him or her from *that point and on*. But there is also a subtle difference between them. Subgame perfection requires that players' beliefs about future moves of other players be based on the notion that at each node, *whether it is on or off the equilibrium path*, the player whose turn it is to move chooses the best course of action for himself or herself from that point and on. Dynamic consistency imposes a similar requirement on beliefs but only along the equilibrium path. In other words, dynamic consistency requires rational behavior from each point in time along the equilibrium path only. Subgame perfection requires such behavior for all subgames. Hence dynamic consistency is weaker than subgame perfection.[3] Most of the models of private information in the book utilize the first, weaker, concept.

Under asymmetric information it is still the case that only dynamically consistent strategies are credible. However, due to the fact that the public is not fully informed about the (moving) objectives of policymakers, there is normally a divergence between the rate of monetary expansion planned by the central bank and what the public believes about this rate. This divergence occurs because the public is not fully informed about the dynamically consistent strategy of the central bank for the period. Hence under asymmetric information a natural measure of credibility is the absolute value of the divergence between planned and expected money growth in each period as well as on average. Sections 9.7 and 10.6 discuss and characterize these measures and their determinants.

The main difference between measure(s) of credibility in the presence and in the absence of asymmetric information is that in the first case credibility is no longer either full or nonexistent. Instead, it is a continuous measure that is inversely related to the absolute value of the divergence between the central bank's plans and public beliefs about those plans.[4] Under asymmetric information imperfect credibility is due to the public's uncertainty concerning the set of dynamically consistent strategies of the central bank. This notion of credibility seems to be closely related to the concept of credibility that policymakers have in mind, particularly during periods of disinflation. In such periods they worry that the public does not believe that planned monetary growth is as low as it really is. The discussion in sections 9.7 and 10.6 indicates that if previous rates of inflation were relatively high, the new lower rate of monetary expansion will indeed have low credibility according to our measure of credibility for asymmetric information environments.

Questions regarding determinants of the speed with which credibility is established are nonexistent in a world of perfect information. But, as suggested by the discussion of the determinants of the speed of learning parameter λ in section 10.6, they hold center stage in the presence of asymmetric information. This parameter is a prime determinant of the speed with which an anti-inflationary reputation is built up or depleted in the presence of asymmetric information.

11.3 Establishing Credibility through Deterrence

The recent literature on monetary policy games has also used trigger strategy mechanisms from multiperiods games to model reputational incentives even in a world of perfect information. The basic idea is that the public uses its inflationary expectation as a device to deter the central bank from producing the one-shot discretionary rate of inflation. This strategy on the part of the public does not necessarily achieve a zero rate of inflation, but it reduces inflation below the one-shot discretionary rate of inflation. Barro and Gordon (1983a) were the first to use trigger strategies to model reputation in the context of monetary policy.[5] This section illustrates the basic logic of this approach by providing a brief description of their model.

Consider the central bank's problem in equation (10.7), when $p_i = \psi_i = 0$ for all i, so that information is perfect and x is permanently fixed at A. This problem is

$$\max \sum_{i=0}^{\infty} \beta^i \left[(m_i^p - m_i^e)\alpha A - \frac{(m_i^p)^2}{2} \right], \tag{11.1}$$

where the less cumbersome symbol m_i^e is used to denote period i's inflationary expectation. We have seen that under discretion and perfect information this problem reduces to a sequence of unrelated, identical, one-period problems whose typical form is

$$\max_{m_i^p} \left\{ (m_i^p - E[m_i|I_i])\alpha A - \frac{(m_i^p)^2}{2} \right\} \qquad \text{for all } i. \qquad (11.2)$$

The corresponding discretionary one-shot rate of inflation is therefore

$$\alpha A. \qquad (11.3)$$

Suppose now that policymakers announce a rate of inflation m^* that is *lower* than αA. The public then sets its inflationary expectation for the current period as follows: If actual inflation in the previous period accords with expectations, the public expects that inflation will continue at m^*. If the previous period's inflation does not accord with expectations, the public expects instead that the monetary authority will inflate at the higher discretionary rate, αA. Thus, whenever the monetary authority inflates at rate αA rather than at its announced rate m^*, the public "punishes" it for one period by believing that it will continue to do so in the next period as well.[6] The monetary authority maximizes its objective function (equation 11.1) subject to the public's behavior. In considering whether to inflate at rate αA today, it compares the difference between the current value of its objectives, when it inflates at rate αA rather than at rate m^* (given that the public expects m^*), with the discounted value of the loss in next period's welfare because the public's inflation expectations increase from m^* to αA.[7] As long as the latter term (which acts as a deterrent) is larger than the former term (which represents the temptation to inflate at rate αA), policymakers pick m^*, the lower inflation rate.

Formally (from equation 11.1) the condition for effective deterrence of the higher inflation αA is

$$\frac{\beta}{2}[(\alpha A)^2 - (m^*)^2] > \alpha A[\alpha A - m^*] + \frac{(m^*)^2 - (\alpha A)^2}{2}. \qquad (11.4)$$

The left-hand term is the discounted value of the loss in the next period's objectives due to the increase in expectations. The right-hand term is the gain in current objectives induced by higher current employment.[8]

The lowest credibly sustainable rate of inflation can be found by equating the two sides of equation (11.4) and by solving for m^*.[9] The solution is shown in equation (11.5):

$$m^* = \frac{1 - \beta}{1 + \beta} \alpha A. \tag{11.5}$$

This rate is higher than the first-best zero inflation but lower than the rate of inflation αA that would occur in the absence of deterrence. Equation (11.5) expresses the best enforceable rule as a function of the discount factor β. The higher the degree of time preference, the higher the minimum sustainable rate of inflation.[10] Once this mechanism is in place, it is self-fulfilling: The public believes that policymakers will inflate at rate m^*, and indeed policymakers do so. Therefore in the absence of commitments a second-best lower rate of inflation can be credibly sustained by an appropriate deterrence mechanism. This mechanism is sometimes referred to as a "reputational mechanism." The notion underlying this terminology is that given the deterrence mechanism used by the public, policymakers stick to the lower rate of inflation m^* because they are concerned with their future reputation.

11.4 A Critical Look at Deterrence via Trigger Strategies as a Model of Reputation

Underlying the deterrence approach as a model of reputation is the notion that the public utilizes its expectations to induce desirable behavior on the part of the central bank. This view raises a number of problems. First, the deterrence equilibrium critically depends on the punishment strategy assumed in the analysis. By the Folk theorem of supergames any rate of inflation below αA, in particular zero inflation, can be sustained by an appropriately chosen trigger strategy. Consequently there is an infinite number of possible reputational (Nash) equilibria with no mechanism for choosing among them.[11] A related aspect of this problem is that any specific link between the current actions of policymakers and the future expectations of the public is strictly arbitrary.

Second, to be credible, a trigger-strategy-based reputational mechanism requires that all individuals coordinate their strategies regarding expectation formation. In reality there is no institution that coordinates the strategies of different individuals on a single unified strategy. In the absence of such coordination the deterrence mechanism is not credible, and the reputational mechanism of section 11.3 breaks down. Note that this problem is negligible in the context of oligopoly theory from which this way of modeling reputation is borrowed. The reason is that in models of oligopoly or cartels there is a small number of big players who can easily coordinate their actions. But when the same technical apparatus is applied to model the interaction between a central bank and a public that is composed of a large number of small players, the coordination problem is quite serious.

Finally, the deterrence strategy may be subject to a free-rider problem. Individuals may simply find that it is not worthwhile to achieve a lower rate of inflation via the deterrence mechanism if the private costs of monitoring policymakers' actions are higher than the marginal private benefit. Although of less importance in oligopoly theory, this problem can be serious if the public is composed of many individuals. If each individual relies on others to deter policymakers from acting in a discretionary manner, the deterrence mechanism that makes the lower inflation policy credible in the first place is eliminated.

Additional objections to trigger strategies as a way to describe the evolution of reputation can be made on grounds of lack of direct realism. Some of these are discussed in the next section, which focuses on a comparison of reputation via deterrence with reputation as a learning process.

11.5   Reputation as Learning versus Reputation as a Deterrence Mechanism[12]

An implication of the trigger strategy model of section 11.3 is that in equilibrium both actual and expected inflation are constant over time. This is obviously contradicted by the data for most countries. By contrast, the reputation as learning approach (described in section 10.8) is consistent with changes in both actual and expected inflation. Furthermore it is consistent with the view that credibility of disinflationary policies is established gradually after policymakers maintain inflation at a lower level for a sufficient length of time. Volcker's disinflation in the United States, the 1985 Israeli stabilization, and the 1989 Mexican stabilization are examples of this general regularity.

There is little doubt that inflationary forecasts change over time (Hardouvelis 1984) and that they are usually influenced by actual inflation and monetary growth. A dramatic example is the decrease in expected inflation between the end of the 1970s and the present in the United States.

Such changes are inconsistent with the trigger strategy approach to reputation but are easily explained within the framework of asymmetric information discussed in chapters 9 and 10.

In both approaches to modeling reputation, the central bank is deterred from inflating too much today because of its concern for its future reputation as an inflation fighter. In both cases the deterring element is the fact that higher current inflation raises future expectations. But in the case of learning this occurs as a by-product of each individual's private attempt to forecast future inflation as precisely as possible. In the case of trigger strategies the same outcome is obtained at the cost of the unrealistic assumption that all individuals agree on an arbitrary trigger strategy and coordinate their actions in order to make it credible.

Casual empiricism suggests that a positive amount of resources is devoted to monitoring the central bank.[13] This makes sense when the central bank has private information that influences its policy. The learning approach to credibility and reputation (chapters 9 and 10) is obviously consistent with this observation. Finally, the learning approach to reputation is more informative since it relates the process of reputation building and destruction to more fundamental characteristics of the economy and of the central bank's objective function.

11.6   Private Information about Revenue and Balance-of-Payments Objectives

The discussion in chapters 9 and 10 as well as in many of the subsequent chapters that deal with private information considers situations in which the public is not perfectly informed about the shifting relative preference of policymakers for economic stimulation and price stability. But these frameworks can be adapted to cases in which private information concerns the shifting relative preference of policymakers for seigniorage revenues or for balance-of-payments objectives versus their preference for price stability. The relative preference for seigniorage versus price stability may change because of unexpected shocks to tax revenues due to inflation and other factors or because of political events. A model in which individuals learn gradually but optimally about the shifting preference of government for seigniorage revenues versus price stability in the context of the post–World War I German hyperinflation appears in Cukierman (1988b). The sluggish adjustment of expectations explains how the German government managed to increase seigniorage revenues by raising the rate of monetary expansion to levels which, by most accounts, should have reduced those revenues had the actual rate of inflation been anticipated.

The relative preference of government for price stability versus current balance-of-payments objectives depends on policymakers' estimates of the economy's future ability to generate foreign exchange reserves through trade or by foreign borrowing. These estimates change continuously as policymakers obtain new private and public information about political and economic developments that affect the competitiveness of the economy and its ability to borrow on international markets or from other governments. The private information element can be modeled relatively easily by assuming that the balance-of-payments target B^* in equation (5.3) depends on the forecasts of policymakers and is therefore their private information. As in the case of private information about the employment motive the public will gradually learn from the rate of devaluations about the changing value of B^* and will adjust its expected rate of devaluation accordingly.

The same concepts of credibility that applied in the case of private information about the employment motive are applicable also in the case of private information about either the revenue or the balance-of-payments objectives. In particular the notion that credibility is larger the smaller the divergence between the central bank's plans and the public beliefs about those plans is independent of whether the primary motive for inflation or devaluation is employment, seigniorage, or the balance of payments.

12 The Politically Optimal Level of Ambiguity

12.1 Introduction

Some central banks have an inclination for secrecy. This inclination has recently been documented for the Federal Reserve by Goodfriend (1986). During the mid-1970s the Federal Open Market Committee (FOMC) was sued under the Freedom of Information Act of 1966 to make public immediately after each FOMC meeting the policy directives and minutes for that meeting. The Federal Reserve resisted and argued the case for secrecy on a number of different grounds. The case went first to a lower court, which ruled in favor of the plaintiff and ordered the FOMC to reveal the minutes of its meeting immediately after each meeting. The Federal Reserve appealed the case to a higher court. In the interim the FOMC stopped taking minutes. After several years of litigation the case ended up at the Supreme Court, which finally ruled in favor of the Fed's position that the minutes should be published only six weeks after each FOMC meeting.

There are at least two explanations for this phenomenon. One is purely politico-bureaucratic. The other combines politically motivated objectives with economic structure. The first explanation relies on the notion that one of the main reasons for the large amount of legal independence conferred on the Fed is to mask some of the redistribution of income effected by fiscal policy (Havrilesky 1990c). More generally it has been argued that the Fed enjoys a large amount of independence because it performs a scapegoat function for incumbent politicians. When things turn right in the monetary area, they can take some of the credit. When things turn sour, they can dissociate themselves from the outcome and blame it on the Fed. The Fed is thus a hedging device for incumbent politicians who are unsure about future developments and public attitudes and who do not wish to take too many chances with voters' perceptions of their performance. Kane has developed this hypothesis in a series of papers. A recent exposition appears in Kane (1990).

If this hedging device is to work in a credible manner the Fed must be endowed with a sufficient amount of independence so that policies enacted in response to the demands of incumbent politicians are not clearly identifiable as such. Otherwise, politicians will not be able to credibly shift the blame to the Fed when electoral and other pressures require it. In this view CB independence and secrecy are indispensible ingredients of the "whipping boy" function performed by Fed officials. These officials take their occasional bashing graciously because they enjoy in return a large degree of financial and other independence.

While this explanation of secrecy probably captures part of reality, it is by no means the only possible reason for making secrecy desirable.[1] If one accepts the widely accepted view that monetary policy has real effects only when it is unanticipated, secrecy and private information become necessary preconditions for monetary policy to have any real effects to start with. Thus a monetary authority that believes in activist monetary policy may value secrecy in order to preserve some ability to influence the real economy. On the other hand, by slowing down the public's learning process, too much secrecy or ambiguity reduces the deterrent effect of learning and raises the average level of inflation under discretion. Thus ambiguity has both desirable and undesirable effects on policy objectives. The remainder of this chapter characterizes the circumstances under which the balance of these two effects tilts toward a positive level of ambiguity. The analysis is anchored on the analytical framework of chapter 9. The following discussion shows that if the central bank can choose the precision of its control over the money supply process, it does not always find it politically optimal to choose the highest degree of precision that is technically feasible. We refer to the politically optimal level of imprecision in monetary control as the "politically optimal level of ambiguity."

The argument in this chapter is the following: Suppose that at some initial point in time the central bank has to make a once-and-for-all choice of the level of imprecision in monetary control.[2] Since this is a once-and-for-all decision, the central bank has to weigh two opposing effects of less precise control on the average value of its objective function. With less precise control the public learns more slowly about changes in central bank's relative emphasis on alternative objectives (see chapters 9 and 10).[3] Slower learning represents an advantage for central bank objectives in periods in which it becomes relatively more concerned with high employment. But it is a disadvantage in periods in which it becomes more concerned with price stability. In such periods the central bank is interested in establishing quick credibility. Hence quick learning and precise monetary control are desirable in such periods. Whatever the precision of monetary control, the effects of monetary policy on employment are nil on average. The reason is that only the inflation that was unexpected by the public at contracting time affects employment. Since unexpected inflation is zero on average, the effect of monetary policy on employment averages out to zero as well. However, there is an important qualitative difference between the case in which the public learns about changes in central bank's objectives with some (short or long) lag and between the case in which it is always precisely informed about the bank's objectives at contracting time. In the latter case monetary policy has no effect on employment not only on average but in each separate period as well (see chapter 3).

In effect, in comparison to perfect information, the existence of imprecise monetary control increases the variability of employment over time without changing its mean. What is the advantage of this increased variability for central bank objectives? The answer is that in the presence of imperfect and gradual learning, the central bank has some control over the distribution of monetary surprises over time. This enables it to allocate the positive, employment-increasing surprises to periods in which its concern for employment is above average and to leave the inevitable negative, employment-reducing surprises for periods in which its concern for price stability is above average. Thus, although the effects of policy on employment average out to zero over time, it is advantageous for the central bank to have some degree of imprecision in monetary control.

Section 12.2 develops this argument precisely for the case of a minimal information advantage of the kind discussed in chapter 9. Section 12.3 discusses the effect of the relative size of common knowledge on the optimal level of ambiguity. Section 12.4 shows that central bank objectives can, at times, attain a higher value in the presence of some information advantage than under a Friedman (1960) rule.

12.2   The Politically Optimal Level of Ambiguity in the Presence of a Minimal Information Advantage

In chapters 9 and 10 we considered the level of noise in the control of money (σ_ψ^2) as a technologically determined parameter. Suppose now that technology only puts a lower bound, $\underline{\sigma}_\psi^2$, on the variance of the control error. Policymakers can choose any $\sigma_\psi^2 \geq \underline{\sigma}_\psi^2$. We assume for simplicity that $\underline{\sigma}_\psi^2 = 0$.

In the case of a minimal information advantage (chapter 9), the optimal policy for policymakers for a *fixed* σ_ψ^2 is given by equation (9.15). Substituting this optimal policy into the policymakers' objective function in equation (9.13), and abstracting from the conditional expected value, we obtain the present value of the central bank's objective function when it follows the optimal policy for a given σ_ψ^2. This is shown as equation (12.1):

$$J[\{\psi_i\}_{-1}^{\infty}, \{p_i\}_{-2}^{\infty}] \equiv \sum_{i=0}^{\infty} \beta^i \left\{ [B_0 A + B p_i + \psi_i - g(p_{i-2}) \right.$$

$$- \rho\theta(B_0 A + B p_{i-1} + \psi_{i-1})]\alpha x_i$$

$$\left. - \frac{(B_0 A + B p_i + \psi_i)^2}{2} \right\}, \tag{12.1}$$

where $\{\psi_i\}_{-1}^{\infty}$ and $\{p_i\}_{-2}^{\infty}$ denote the sequences of ψ and p.

Since policymakers set σ_ψ^2 on the basis of the long-run value of their objective function rather than on the basis of particular recent realizations of x_i, the relevant objective function for the choice of σ_ψ^2 is the unconditional expected value of $J(\cdot)$. Taking the unconditional expected value of equation (12.1), using the stochastic specification of p in equation (9.3), using the fact that $E\psi_i = 0$, and rearranging, we obtain

$$G(\sigma_\psi^2) \equiv EJ[\cdot] = \frac{1}{1-\beta} \left\{ \alpha(1 - \rho^2\beta\theta)[1 + \rho^2(1-\theta)]\sigma_v^2 \right.$$

$$\left. - \frac{1}{2}[\alpha^2(1 - \rho\beta\theta)^2 A^2 + \alpha^2(1 - \rho^2\beta\theta)^2\sigma_p^2 + \sigma_\psi^2] \right\}, \tag{12.2}$$

where (from equations 9.3, 9.11b, and 9.16a)

$$\sigma_p^2 = \frac{\sigma_v^2}{1 - \rho^2}, \tag{12.3a}$$

$$\theta \equiv \frac{B^2\sigma_v^2}{B^2\sigma_v^2 + \sigma_\psi^2}, \tag{12.3b}$$

$$B = \alpha(1 - \rho^2\beta\theta). \tag{12.3c}$$

The first term in brackets on the right-hand side of equation (12.2) represents the mean (positive) contribution of economic stimulation to governmental objectives. The mean value of economic stimulation through surprise creation is zero since negative and positive surprises cancel each other out on average. But the contribution of monetary surprises to governmental objectives is positive on average. The reason is that the rate of money growth is positively related to the marginal benefit of surprise creation to the government. As can be seen from equation (9.15), when the marginal benefit of a surprise is higher than average ($x_i > A \leftrightarrow p_i > 0$), the government chooses a higher-than-average rate of monetary growth, and when the marginal benefit of a surprise is lower than average ($x_i < A \leftrightarrow p_i < 0$), the government chooses a lower-than-average rate of monetary growth. Consequently, when government cares more than on average about economic stimulation, surprises are positive on average, and when it cares less than on average about economic stimulation, surprises are negative on average making the unconditional expected value of the benefits from surprise creation positive. The government derives a positive gain, on average, from the ability to create surprises because it can allocate large positive surprises to periods in which x_i is relatively high and leave the inevitable negative surprises for periods with relatively low values of x_i.

More formally, by using equations (9.3), (9.6), and (9.7a), it can be shown that

$$E \sum_{i=0}^{\infty} \beta^i [m_i - E[m_i | I_i]] \alpha x_i = \frac{\alpha}{1 - \beta} E[m_i - E[m_i | I_i]] x_i$$

$$= \frac{1}{1 - \beta} \alpha (1 - \rho^2 \beta \theta) [1 + \rho^2 (1 - \theta)] \sigma_v^2. \tag{12.4}$$

This expression is identical to the first term on the right-hand side of equation (12.2), which measures the mean positive contribution of economic stimulation to central bank's objectives. The expected value of $m_i - E[m_i | I_i]$ is zero, so the central bank has no effect on output on average. Despite this, equation (12.4) implies that the expected value of the contribution of monetary surprises to central bank objectives is positive. This is due to the fact that the central bank picks the timing of surprises in a manner that creates a positive correlation between surprises and the parameter x_i. By contrast, when the government does not possess an information advantage, $\sigma_v^2 = 0$ and p_i is identically zero. This implies that the expression in equation (12.4) is zero as well. Thus the existence of asymmetric information makes it possible for government to attain a higher value for its objectives through surprise creation in a time-consistent equilibrium.

The negative terms on the right-hand side of equation (12.2) represent the mean negative contribution of inflation to central bank objectives. Since, by proposition 9.4, mean inflation is higher when σ_ψ^2, is higher, this term will tend to discourage the central bank from choosing imprecise control procedures.

It is shown in the appendix to this chapter that the total derivative of $G(\sigma_\psi^2)$ with respect to σ_ψ^2 is

$$G'(\sigma_\psi^2) = \frac{1}{1-\beta}$$

$$\cdot \left\{ \frac{\rho B^2 \sigma_v^2 [\alpha\rho\sigma_v^2 \{\beta[1 + \rho^2(1 - \theta)] + (1 - \rho^2\beta\theta)\} - \beta(1 - \rho\beta\theta)\alpha^2 A^2 - \beta\rho\alpha B\sigma_p^2]}{(B^2\sigma_v^2 + \sigma_\psi^2)^2 + 2\alpha\beta\rho^2 B\sigma_v^2\sigma_\psi^2} - \frac{1}{2} \right\}.$$

(12.5)

If the solution for σ_ψ^2 occurs in the positive range, the condition $G'(\sigma_\psi^2) = 0$ determines the politically optimal level of ambiguity. However, it is a priori possible that the optimal level of σ_ψ^2 is zero. To get a feel for the configurations of parameters for which the optimal level of ambiguity is positive, we evaluate the derivative in equation (12.5) at the point $\sigma_\psi^2 = 0$ and examine under what conditions $G'(\sigma_\psi^2)$ is positive at that point. At $\sigma_\psi^2 = 0$, $\theta = 1$, and $B = \alpha(1 - \rho^2\beta)$. Hence equation (12.5) reduces to

$$G'(0) = \frac{\rho}{\alpha^2(1 - \rho^2\beta)^2\sigma_v^2(1 - \beta)} \{\alpha\rho[1 + \beta(1 - \rho^2)]\sigma_v^2$$

$$- \beta\alpha^2[\rho(1 - \rho^2\beta)\sigma_p^2 + (1 - \rho\beta)A^2]\} - \frac{1}{2}.$$

(12.5a)

If the expression in equation (12.5a) is positive, the optimal level of ambiguity must be positive. Inspection of this equation suggests that this is likely to be the case when the discount factor β is low. Letting $\beta \to 0$, the expression in equation (12.5a) reduces further to

$$\frac{\rho^2}{\alpha} - \frac{1}{2},$$

(12.5b)

which is positive provided that ρ is sufficiently large in comparison to α. This leads to the following proposition:

PROPOSITION 12.1   In the presence of a minimal information advantage of the type discussed in chapter 9,

1.   the set of parameters for which the optimal level of ambiguity is positive is nonempty,

2.   jointly sufficient (but not necessary) conditions for a positive level of ambiguity is a very high degree of time preference ($\beta \to 0$) and $\rho^2/\alpha > 1/2$.

12.3   The Magnitude of Common Knowledge and the Inclination for Ambiguity

From equation (9.3) the distribution of the central bank's relative emphasis on alternative objectives is normal with mean A and variance σ_p^2. A represents the part of central bank objectives that is common knowledge, while deviations of x_i from A represent the part about which the public may be temporarily uncertain. This section discusses the effect of A on the optimal level of ambiguity when this level occurs at a positive value of the noise variance σ_ψ^2.

When this is the case σ_ψ^2 is determined by the condition

$$G'(\sigma_\psi^2) = 0, \tag{12.6}$$

where the explicit form of $G'(\sigma_\psi^2)$ is given in equation (12.5). Performing a comparative statics experiment with respect to σ_ψ^2

$$\frac{d\sigma_\psi^2}{dA} = -\frac{\partial G'(\sigma_\psi^2)/\partial A}{G''(\sigma_\psi^2)} = \frac{2\rho\beta\alpha^2 B^2 \sigma_v^2 (1 - \rho\beta\theta)A}{G''(\sigma_\psi^2)(1 - \beta)\{(B^2\sigma_v^2 + \sigma_\psi^2)^2 + 2\alpha\beta\rho^2 B\sigma_v^2\sigma_\psi^2\}}, \tag{12.7}$$

where $G''(\sigma_\psi^2)$ is the second partial derivative of $G(\sigma_\psi^2)$ with respect to σ_ψ^2 and is negative by the second-order condition for an internal maximum. Since all other terms in equation (12.7) are positive this implies the following:

PROPOSITION 12.2   When the optimal level of ambiguity occurs at a positive value of σ_ψ^2, an increase in A reduces the optimal level of ambiguity.

The intuition underlying this result is that an increase in A raises the average rate of inflation under discretion (see equation 9.29) and moves the economy into a range of higher marginal costs of inflation. Hence at the original value of σ_ψ^2 the cost of inflation outweighs the benefits of ambiguity. Since, given A, a reduction in σ_ψ^2 is associated with a reduction in average inflation (see proposition 9.4), it pays to reduce σ_ψ^2. In conclusion, the optimal level of ambiguity is a nonincreasing function of the common knowledge component in central bank's objectives.

12.4   Friedman's Rule and the Political Value of an Information Advantage

Friedman (1960) has proposed to precommit the central bank to a fixed money growth rule. This obviously would strip the bank of its ability to choose the timing of surprises. On the other hand, it would eliminate the average inflationary bias of monetary policy under discretion. Most central banks, and the Fed in particular, do not follow a Friedman-type rule. The theory developed here may provide a possible explanation for this reluctance to precommit if the average value of central bank's objectives under a Friedman rule is lower than when the bank retains some ability to control the timing of surprises. To examine this possibility, we compare the value of average objectives under a rule that specifies $m_i^p = 0$ for all i with the value of average objectives when the central bank retains some information advantage.

For simplicity we compare the average value of objectives with and without a Friedman rule in the particular case $\sigma_\psi^2 \to 0$. Note that even in this case the central bank retains some information advantage since at the beginning of period i the public is still uninformed about the realization of the innovation v_i (see section 9.3). Under a credible Friedman rule which sets $m_i^p = 0$ for all i, and with $\sigma_\psi^2 \to 0$, actual and expected inflation are both identically zero. Hence the period-by-period, as well as the expected, value of the central bank's objectives under a Friedman rule is zero. Consider now the expected value of the same objective function for the case $\sigma_\psi^2 \to 0$ under discretion. From equation (12.3) when $\sigma_\psi^2 \to 0$, $\theta \to 1$ and $B \to \alpha(1 - \rho^2\beta)$. Substituting those restrictions into equation (12.2) and rearranging, the expected value of objectives under discretion is[4]

$$\frac{\alpha\sigma_p^2}{2}\left\{(1 - \rho^2\beta)[2(1 - \rho^2) - \alpha(1 - \rho^2\beta)] - \alpha(1 - \rho\beta)^2\frac{A^2}{\sigma_p^2}\right\}. \tag{12.8}$$

This expression is larger than zero provided that the expression in brackets is positive. Obviously this will be the case for sufficiently low values of α and/or of A^2/σ_p^2. But it will be recalled from the discussion in chapter 9 that A^2/σ_p^2 cannot be too low. The precise condition (see equation 9A.7 in the appendix to chapter 9) is $A^2/\sigma_p^2 \geq 9$.[5] Substituting this lower bound into equation (12.8) and dropping the positive $\alpha\sigma_p^2/2$ term, a necessary and sufficient condition for discretion with some information advantage to be more desirable than a Friedman rule, from the central bank's point of view, is

$$(1 - \rho^2\beta)[2(1 - \rho^2) - \alpha(1 - \rho^2\beta)] - 9\alpha(1 - \rho\beta)^2 > 0. \tag{12.8a}$$

It can be seen by inspection that the set of parameters for which this condition is satisfied is nonempty. For example, it is satisfied for $\rho = 0.9$,

$\beta \to 0$, and for all α such that $\alpha < 0.038$. Since, for those parameter configurations, condition (12.8a) is satisfied for σ_ψ^2 arbitrarily set at a very small value, it must a fortiori be satisfied when the central bank is allowed to choose σ_ψ^2 optimally. Hence the set of parameters for which a Friedman rule is dominated by discretion is likely to be larger.

To sum up, in the presence of asymmetric information the central bank can actually obtain a better average value for its objectives under discretion than under a commitment to a Friedman rule. It is notable that this happens despite the inflationary bias of monetary policy under discretion.

12.5   Concluding Remarks

The analysis in section 12.2 can be developed also for the case of an extended information advantage of the kind discussed in chapter 10. Within this framework the choice of σ_ψ^2 affects central bank objectives by altering the value of λ and through it the speed with which the public learns about changes in objectives. The general principle of the analysis is similar, but its complexity greater due to the fact that the learning lag is infinite. Cukierman and Meltzer (1986a) characterize the optimal level of ambiguity for this case under the restrictions that m_i^p rather than m_i measures the costs of inflation to the central bank and that $\alpha = 1$. Loosely stated, their analysis implies that σ_ψ^2 is more likely to be positive and larger the higher the rate of time preference of the central bank (low β) and the lower the degree of common knowledge about objectives (low A/σ_p). In particular for internal solutions the politically optimal level of ambiguity is larger the larger is political instability as measured by σ_v^2. Those results are consistent with those obtained in this chapter for the case of a minimal information advantage.

Finally the purely politico-bureaucratic and the politico-economic explanations for secrecy need not be mutually exclusive. To sometimes satisfy the wishes of politicians, the central bank may need to possess the ability to influence the real economy. Since only unanticipated money has real effect, this requires some policy ambiguity. A factor that may reinforce the inclination of the central bank to produce ambiguous policy outcomes is that the choice of noisy control procedures often does not require any active decision. It can often be maintained simply by abstaining from reforming existing institutions.

Appendix: Derivation of Equation (12.5)

Totally differentiating equation (12.2) with respect to σ_ψ^2 and rearranging, we obtain

$$G'(\sigma_\psi^2) = \frac{1}{1 - \beta}\left[\rho(\beta\alpha^2[(1 - \rho\beta\theta)A^2 + \rho(1 - \rho^2\beta\theta)\sigma_p^2]\right.$$

$$\left. - \alpha\rho\sigma_v^2\{\beta[1 + \rho^2(1 - \theta)] + 1 - \rho^2\beta\theta\})\frac{d\theta}{d\sigma_\psi^2} - \frac{1}{2}\right]. \qquad (12A.1)$$

Then differentiating (12.3b) and (12.3c) with respect to σ_ψ^2, we find that

$$\frac{d\theta}{d\sigma_\psi^2} = \frac{B\sigma_v^2}{(B^2\sigma_v^2 + \sigma_\psi^2)^2}\left(2\sigma_\psi^2\frac{dB}{d\sigma_\psi^2} - B\right), \qquad (12A.2a)$$

$$\frac{dB}{d\sigma_\psi^2} = -\alpha\rho^2\beta\frac{d\theta}{d\sigma_\psi^2}. \qquad (12A.2b)$$

Finally we substitute (12A.2b) into (12A.2a) and rearrange to get

$$\frac{d\theta}{d\sigma_\psi^2} = -\frac{B^2\sigma_v^2}{(B^2\sigma_v^2 + \sigma_\psi^2)^2 + 2\alpha\beta\rho^2 B\sigma_v^2\sigma_\psi^2}. \qquad (12A.3)$$

Equation (12.5) is obtained by substituting (12A.3) into (12A.1) and by rearranging.

III VELOCITY SHOCKS, POLITICS, SIGNALING, INFLATION PERSISTENCE, AND ACCOMMODATION

13 Private Information about Money Demand and Credibility

13.1 Introduction

For simplicity we have maintained up to this point that there is no difference between monetary expansion and the rate of inflation in the general level of prices. As is well known, this approximation is nearly correct provided that fluctuations in real money demand are relatively small; it is precisely correct when the real demand for money is fixed. However, when, at a given price level, there are substantial changes in the demand for money, the strict one-to-one relation between monetary growth and inflation is a poorer approximation. At the extreme, when money demand increases at the same rate as money supply does, the rate of inflation is zero despite the fact that monetary growth is positive. The first task of this chapter is to relax the strict one-to-one relationship between monetary growth and inflation by allowing fluctuations in money demand. The second and more basic objective is to analyze the effects of private information about money demand on credibility and the public's speed of learning about changing central bank objectives.

Canzoneri (1985) has pointed out that the central bank's forecast of money demand is private information but that this information generally is not perfect. As a result there generally is a discrepancy between the rate of inflation that the central bank tries to achieve and its realization. Canzoneri superimposes this information structure on a framework in which the public is perfectly informed about the central bank's relative preference for high employment and price stability. We saw in chapter 3 that in such a framework the discretionary rate of inflation is suboptimally high. The central bank may want to claim, prior to the conclusion of wage contracts, that it is committed to the lower, optimal inflation. But the discrepancy between the inflation that is planned by the central bank and actual inflation makes it difficult for the public to judge whether inflation is high because the bank has overestimated money demand or because it deliberately tried to achieve the excessively high, discretionary rate of inflation. Canzoneri handles this problem by hypothesizing that the public uses a trigger strategy of the type discussed in section 11.3 to deter the central bank from inflating at the one-shot discretionary rate. Because it is unsure of whether a given rate of inflation is high because the central bank has reverted to discretion or because it has overestimated money demand, the public uses the following deterrent strategy: It picks a sufficiently high threshold rate of inflation and sets its expectation at the low rate, which corresponds to a precommitment equilibrium as long as actual inflation is below the threshold. But whenever inflation is above the threshold, the public sets its expectation at the one-shot discretionary rate of inflation.

This chapter utilizes Canzoneri's important insight concerning the central bank's information advantage about money demand in a framework in which the public is also uncertain about the (shifting) objectives of the central bank, but in which it optimally learns about those changes. Such a framework has been extensively discussed in chapters 9 and 10. The novelty of this chapter is that it explicitly takes into consideration the effects of private information about money demand on the public's ability to learn about the central bank's objectives. As in Canzoneri (1985), recognition by the central bank that its current actions affect future expectations moderates the range of inflation produced by the bank. But this moderation arises as a by-product of the public's attempt to separate persistent changes in objectives from transitory money demand forecast errors rather than through an exogenously specified trigger strategy.[1] As a consequence it is possible to relate credibility, inflation, and the level of policy activism to some underlying characteristics of the economy and of the central bank, such as the variability of money demand, the precision of central bank forecasts, and its degree of time preference.

A convenient feature of the model in this chapter is that its solution maps directly into the solution of the model in chapter 9, making it possible to directly use some of the results derived there in this chapter.

13.2   Central Bank's Objectives, Instruments, and Information

The structure of the economy and of central bank's objectives is practically identical to that in chapter 9.[2] In particular the (postcontracting) temporary trade-off between employment and unanticipated inflation is given by equation (9.2) and central bank objectives by equations (9.1) and (9.3). For convenience those equations are reproduced here as equations (13.1) and (13.2):

$$-\sum_{i=0}^{\infty} \beta^i \left[x_i |N^* - N_i| + \frac{\pi_i^2}{2} \right], \qquad 0 \leq \beta \leq 1, \tag{13.1a}$$

$$x_i = A + p_i, \tag{13.1b}$$

$$p_i = \rho p_{i-1} + v_i, \tag{13.1c}$$

$$v_i \sim N(0, \sigma_v^2), \tag{13.1d}$$

$$N - N_n = \alpha(\pi - \pi^e). \tag{13.2}$$

Equation (13.1a) is the central bank's objective function. x_i measures the relative concern of the central bank in period i for employment and price stability, and equations (13.1b) through (13.1d) describe the stochastic structure of x_i. N^*, N_n, and N_i are desired, natural, and actual employment, and π and π^e are actual and expected inflation. The rationale for equation (13.1) is discussed in section 9.2. The labor market structure underlying the Phillips relation in equation (9.2) is discussed in section 3.6.

This chapter departs from the framework of chapter 9 in two important respects. First, due to variations in the real demand for money, inflation and monetary growth are not identical. This aspect is captured by assuming that

$$\pi_i = m_i + \delta_i, \tag{13.3}$$

where m_i is money growth during period i and where δ_i is a normal variate (with zero mean and variance σ_δ^2) that is inversely related to period i's rate of increase in the real demand for money.[3] When real money demand is constant, $\delta_i = 0$ and inflation π_i is equal to money growth m_i. When the demand for real money balances shrinks (grows), δ_i is positive (negative) and π_i is larger (smaller) than m_i. Second, the central bank is assumed to possess perfect control of the money supply. Hence, unlike in chapter 9, planned monetary growth is identically equal to actual monetary growth m_i. However, when it decides about m_i, the central bank does not know the realization of the money demand shock δ_i with certainty. Instead, when it picks m_i, the central bank has access to a noisy signal s_i for δ_i. The explicit form of the signal is

$$s_i = \delta_i + \varepsilon_i, \tag{13.4}$$

where ε_i is a white noise, normally distributed process, with variance σ_ε^2. This signal is inside central bank's information and is not observed by the public.

13.3 The Public's Information Set and the Timing of Moves

In each period nominal contracts are concluded at the beginning of the period for the duration of the period. These contracts incorporate the public's expected inflation π_i^e for the period at contracting time. The information available to the public at that time includes all past rates of inflation and past rates of monetary growth up to and including the previous period $(i - 1)$ as well as a direct observation on p_{i-2}. Thus, as in chapter 9, the central bank possesses only a minimal information advantage about the evolution of its own objectives. The relevant part of the information set of the public at the beginning of period i can be formulated as

$$I_i \equiv \{p_{i-2}, \pi_{i-j}, m_{i-j}, j \geq 1\}. \tag{13.5}$$

The sequence of moves and of information revelation within each period is as follows: First, based on I_i, the public forms the expectation π_i^e and commits to nominal contracts. Subsequently the central bank obtains an observation on the signal s_i and chooses the rate of monetary expansion m_i. Finally the actual money demand shock δ_i for the period realizes and, together with the previously chosen value of m_i, determines the rate of inflation π_i via equation (13.3).

13.4   The Equilibrium Concept and the Behavior of the Money Supply

The equilibrium concept is the same as the one used in chapters 9 and 10 and corresponds conceptually to a Nash or a rational expectations equilibrium. More precisely, taking the short-run Phillips curve and the public's expectations formation process as given, the central bank chooses money growth so as to maximize the conditional (on its information) expected value of the objective function in equation (13.1a). This gives rise to a decision rule that maps money growth into the current state of central bank objectives and other information. This decision rule, in conjunction with equation (13.3), determines the behavior of inflation.

Taking the central bank's decision rule and the structural equation for inflation as given, each individual uses his or her information so as to produce an optimal forecast of inflation. This gives rise to an expectations formation process that maps the public's expectation into the public's information set I_i. The requirement of rational expectations imposes the additional consistency requirement that this process be identical with the one taken as given by the central bank when solving its optimization problem. Hence the central bank's decision rule and the public's expectations formation process have to be solved simultaneously. The solution is obtained by applying the method of undetermined coefficients. Since the objective function is quadratic, we postulate the following linear decision rule for the central bank:

$$m_i = B_0 A + B_1 p_{i-2} + B_2 v_{i-1} + B_3 v_i + B_4 s_i, \tag{13.6}$$

where B_i, $i = 0, 1, \ldots, 4$ are coefficients to be determined. A, p_{i-2}, v_{i-1}, and v_i are all components of x_i. They have nevertheless been entered with separate coefficients, since in period i the public is differently informed about these different components.[4] In any case the solution procedure is free to assign the same coefficient to these different components of x_i. In addition m_i has been made a function of the signal s_i to allow for the possibility that the central bank may find it optimal to make the money growth decision contingent on its information about money demand. The implied behavior of inflation may be obtained by substituting (13.6) into (13.3) and using (13.4). This is shown as equation (13.7):

$$\pi_i = B_0 A + B_1 p_{i-2} + B_2 v_{i-1} + B_3 v_i + (1 + B_4)\delta_i + B_4 \varepsilon_i. \tag{13.7}$$

13.5 Derivation of the Public's Expectation and of the Central Bank's Decision Rule

Since the public's information set I_i does not include the signal s_i, nor any other information about δ_i or ε_i, the expected values of δ_i and of ε_i, conditional on I_i, are identical to the unconditional expected values which are zero. Hence

$$\pi_i^e \equiv E[\pi_i | I_i] = E[m_i | I_i]. \tag{13.8}$$

This section derives the explicit solutions for m_i, π_i, and $E[m_i | I_i]$. Readers who are less interested in the technicalities of the solution may go directly to the results stated as equations (13.16) and (13.17) at the beginning of section 13.6.

It is demonstrated in appendix A to this chapter that

$$E[m_i | I_i] = B_0 A + B_1 p_{i-2} + \frac{B_2}{B_3}\theta y_{i-1} = g(p_{i-3}, p_{i-2}, v_{i-2}) + \frac{B_2}{B_3}\theta m_{i-1}, \tag{13.9}$$

where

$$\theta \equiv \frac{B_3^2 \sigma_v^2}{B_3^2 \sigma_v^2 + B_4^2 \sigma_\varepsilon^2},\tag{13.10a}$$

$$y_{i-1} \equiv B_3 v_{i-1} + B_4 \varepsilon_{i-1},\tag{13.10b}$$

$$g(\cdot) \equiv \left(1 - \frac{B_2}{B_3}\theta\right) A + B_1 \left(p_{i-2} - \frac{B_2}{B_3}\theta p_{i-3}\right) - \frac{B_2^2}{B_3}\theta v_{i-2} - \frac{B_2}{B_3}B_4 \theta \delta_{i-1}.$$

$$\tag{13.10c}$$

We turn next to the central bank's optimization problem. Substituting equation (13.2) into (13.1a), noting that the term $\sum_{i=0}^{\infty} \beta^i (N^* - N_n)x_i$ is unaffected by money growth, and using the restriction $N^* - N_i \geq 0$ for all i,[5] the central bank problem can be stated as

$$\max_{\{m_i\}_0^\infty} E_{CBO} \sum_{i=0}^{\infty} \beta^i \left[(\pi_i - E[\pi_i | I_i])\alpha x_i - \frac{\pi_i^2}{2} \right],\tag{13.11}$$

where E_{CBO} designates an expected value conditional on the information available to the central bank in period 0. Using (13.3) and (13.9), we can rewrite this problem as

$$\max_{\{m_i\}_0^\infty} E_{CBO} \sum_{i=0}^{\infty} \beta^i \left[\left\{ m_i + \delta_i - g(\cdot) - \frac{B_2}{B_3}\theta m_{i-1} \right\} \alpha x_i - \frac{(m_i + \delta_i)^2}{2} \right].\tag{13.11a}$$

Recognizing that in each future period policymakers face a problem that has the same structure as period's zero problem, the stochastic euler equations necessary for an internal maximum of this problem are[6]

$$E_{Gi} \left[\alpha x_i - m_i - \delta_i - \beta\alpha \frac{B_2}{B_3}\theta x_{i+1} \right] = 0, \qquad i \geq 0.\tag{13.12}$$

From equation (13.4) the optimal forecast of the money demand shock δ_i by the central bank is

$$E_{Gi}\delta_i = \frac{\sigma_\delta^2}{\sigma_\delta^2 + \sigma_\varepsilon^2} s_i \equiv \lambda s_i.\tag{13.13}$$

We use (13.1) and (13.13) in (13.12) and rearrange to obtain

$$m_i = \alpha\left[1 - \beta\frac{B_2}{B_3}\theta\right] A + \alpha\left[1 - \rho\beta\frac{B_2}{B_3}\theta\right]p_i - \lambda s_i, \qquad i \geq 0.\tag{13.14}$$

Then recalling from (13.1c) that $p_i = \rho^2 p_{i-2} + \rho v_{i-1} + v_i$, we use this identity in (13.14) and equate the coefficients of A, p_{i-2}, $v_{i-1}v_i$, and s_i between the resulting equation and equation (13.6) to obtain

$$B_0 = \alpha(1 - \rho\beta\theta), \tag{13.15a}$$

$$B_1 = B_3\rho^2, \tag{13.15b}$$

$$B_2 = B_3\rho, \tag{13.15c}$$

$$B_3 = \alpha(1 - \rho^2\beta\theta), \tag{13.15d}$$

$$B_4 = -\lambda. \tag{13.15e}$$

13.6 Characterization and Discussion of the Solution and of the Public's Inference Problem

Substituting the explicit form of the coefficients from equations (13.15) into equations (13.6), (13.7), and (13.9), we obtain

$$m_i = \alpha(1 - \rho\beta\theta)A + B_3 p_i - \lambda s_i, \tag{13.16a}$$

$$\pi_i = \alpha(1 - \rho\beta\theta)A + B_3 p_i + (1 - \lambda)\delta_i - \lambda\varepsilon_i, \tag{13.16b}$$

$$\pi_i^e \equiv E[\pi_i | I_i] = E[m_i | I_i]$$

$$= \alpha(1 - \rho\beta\theta)A + \rho^2 B_3 p_{i-2} + \rho\theta(B_3 v_{i-1} - \lambda\varepsilon_{i-1}). \tag{13.16c}$$

Using (13.15e) and (13.13) in (13.10a) and the resulting expression in (13.15d), we obtain

$$B_3 = \alpha[1 - \rho^2\beta\theta] = \alpha\left[1 - \rho^2\beta\frac{B_3^2\sigma_v^2}{B_3^2\sigma_v^2 + \sigma_\delta^4\sigma_\varepsilon^2/(\sigma_\delta^2 + \sigma_\varepsilon^2)^2}\right]. \tag{13.17}$$

The last equation implicitly determines B_3 as a function of the fundamental parameters α, β, ρ, σ_v^2, σ_δ^2, and σ_ε^2. This equation is *identical* to equation (9.16a) with B_3 and $\sigma_\delta^4\sigma_\varepsilon^2/(\sigma_\delta^2 + \sigma_\varepsilon^2)^2$ replaced by B and σ_ψ^2, respectively. Thus the solution for B_3 from equation (13.17) maps into the solution for B from equation (9.16a). Hence the argument developed in section 9.4 implies that a solution for B_3 always exists and that it is unique. Given this solution, the first equality in equation (13.17) determines θ. Once B_3 and θ are determined, the solutions for m_i, π_i, and $E[\pi_i | I_i]$ in equations (13.16) are determined as well.

Since there is persistence in central bank's objectives, last period's state of objectives is relevant for forecasting future inflation. At the beginning of period i the public already knows A and p_{i-2} but does not know period's

$i - 1$ innovation to objectives (v_{i-1}). The observations it has on π_{i-1} and m_{i-1} provide meaningful but noisy information on this innovation (see appendix A to this chapter for details). The reason is that if inflation and money growth turn out to be higher than expected, this could be due to an increased concern for employment $(v_{i-1} > 0)$ or to an overestimate by the central bank of the rate of increase in money demand $(\varepsilon_{i-1} < 0)$. Since the forecast of money demand is private information, the public cannot fully separate the persistent innovation v_{i-1} to central bank objectives from the transitory forecast error ε_{i-1}. This persistent-transitory confusion shows up in equation (13.16c) through the fact that the terms $B_3 v_{i-1}$ and $\lambda \varepsilon_{i-1}$ are multiplied by the same coefficient $\rho\theta$. Had the public been able to separate these two components, it would have given a larger weight to v_{i-1} and a zero weight to ε_{i-1}, since the last period's central bank's forecast error is irrelevant for forecasting future inflation. However, because the public is incapable of separating v_{i-1} and ε_{i-1}, it partly interprets past overestimates of money demand as an increased concern of the central bank for employment. By the same token it partly interprets past underestimates of money demand by the central bank as an increased concern for price stability.

As the variance of the central bank's forecast error diminishes, for given σ_δ^2 and σ_v^2, the signal-to-noise ratio in the public's inference problem increases. At the limit, when the central bank's forecasts of money demand are perfect $(\sigma_\varepsilon^2 = 0)$, the observations on π_{i-1} and m_{i-1} practically reveal v_{i-1} to the public. The general conclusion is that poor forecasting ability by the central bank complicates the inference problem of the public in addition to the obvious direct adverse effect it has on the quality of central bank's forecasts.

13.7   The Value of Private Information to the Central Bank

The central bank has temporary private information about the innovations to its objectives and about innovations to money demand. As we saw in chapters 9, 10, and 12, private information about objectives is sufficient to provide an advantage for the objectives of the central bank.[7] The additional information advantage about money demand does not, as of itself, add any options to fool the public. But the fact that central bank's forecasts are imprecise increases the public's uncertainty about changing objectives (see section 13.11 below) and may increase the opportunities of the bank to gainfully surprise the public.

13.8   Reputation and the Deterring Effect of Learning

The existence of asymmetric information reduces the central bank's temptation to inflate. The reason is that the public learns from past rates of inflation and of monetary expansion about future policies. Since the central bank cares about the future, this learning process acts as a deterrent. By contrast, when the public possesses, to start with, the same information as the central bank its expectation does not depend on the bank's policies and this deterring effect is not operative. This can be seen by comparing the behavior of inflation and of monetary growth with and without asymmetric information.

In the absence of asymmetric information the public knows the central bank's current objectives (x_i) and money demand forecast (λs_i) at contracting time from sources other than past rates of inflation and of monetary expansion. Hence central bank policies have no effect on expectation, and the problem in equation (13.11) reduces to a series of unrelated one-period problems whose typical form is

$$\max_{m_i} E_{\text{CB0}}\left[(m_i + \delta_i - \pi_i^e)\alpha x_i - \frac{(m_i + \delta_i)^2}{2}\right]. \tag{13.18}$$

The solution to this problem is

$$m_i = \alpha(A + p_i) - \lambda s_i, \tag{13.19a}$$

and the associated rate of inflation is

$$\pi_i = \alpha(A + p_i) + (1 - \lambda)\delta_i - \lambda\varepsilon_i. \tag{13.19b}$$

Noting from (13.17) that $B_3 < \alpha$ and that $1 - \rho\beta\theta < 1$, and comparing equations (13.19) with equations (13.16a) and (13.16b), it can be seen that for the same realizations of p_i, δ_i, and ε_i, inflation and monetary growth are lower in the presence of an information advantage. Due to the effect of its current policy on future expectations, the central bank is partly deterred from inflating at the one-shot rate in equation (13.19). However, unlike in Barro and Gordon (1983a) and Canzoneri (1985), the deterring mechanism is a by-product of the public's continuous updating of beliefs about the objectives of the central bank. It bears repeating that this effect operates despite the fact that the policy regime is discretionary. The concern of the central bank about its reputation is the factor that sets off the moderating effect on monetary expansion.

To flesh out some of the factors that determine the magnitude of deterrence, we focus on mean inflation which, using equation (13.16b), is

$$E\pi_i = \alpha(1 - \rho\beta\theta)A. \tag{13.20}$$

The lower the $E\pi_i$, the stronger is the deterring effect of asymmetric information. The following proposition summarizes the effect of various parameters on mean inflation:

PROPOSITION 13.1   Mean inflation is lower and deterrence due to learning stronger the larger σ_v^2 and β and the lower σ_δ^2.

Proof   Except for the fact that σ_ψ^2 is replaced by another term, equation (13.17) is identical to equation (9.16a). Therefore the proof for σ_v^2 and β is identical to the corresponding parts of proposition 9.4.
    To establish the effect of σ_δ^2, let

$$\sigma_\psi^2 \equiv \frac{\sigma_\delta^4 \sigma_\varepsilon^2}{(\sigma_\delta^2 + \sigma_\varepsilon^2)^2}. \tag{13.21}$$

σ_ψ^2 is obviously increasing in σ_δ^2. By proposition 9.4, mean inflation is lower as σ_ψ^2 becomes lower. Hence it is lower as σ_δ^2 becomes lower.   □

Except for the effect of σ_δ^2 which is novel, proposition 13.1 is basically analogous to proposition 9.4. We will therefore discuss only the intuition underlying the positive effect of uncertainty about money demand (as measured by σ_δ^2) on mean inflation. When this uncertainty increases, the signal-to-noise ratio in the public's inference problem goes down. As a result its learning process becomes less vigorous (θ decreases),[8] and next period's increase in expectations following a current increase in monetary growth is smaller. This reduces the deterring effect of learning about changes in objectives and increases the temptation to inflate.

13.9   Determinants of the Degree of Activism

The degree of activism is measured by the size of the central bank's response to a change in the state of its objectives. The stronger this response, as measured by the coefficient B_3 in equation (13.16a), the larger is the degree of activism. The following proposition summarizes the effect of various parameters on the degree of activism:

PROPOSITION 13.2   The degree of activism (as measured by B_3) is larger the larger α and σ_δ^2 and the lower β and σ_v^2.

Proof   The proof utilizes the identical structures of equation (13.17) and of equation (9.16a). Subject to the definition in (13.21), B from the latter equation is equal to B_3 from the first equation. Hence the effects of various parameters on B_3 are identical to the effects of the same parameters on B in equation (9.16a). By referring to figure 9.1 it is easy to see that an increase in α or σ_ψ^2 raises B, and that an increase in either β or σ_v^2 reduces B. The effect of σ_δ^2 on B follows by noting from (13.21) that σ_ψ^2 is increasing in σ_δ^2.   □

The intuition underlying proposition 13.2 is generally similar to the intuition underlying the determinants of activism in the case of an extended information advantage (chapter 10). The larger the effect of surprises on employment (larger α), the larger is the degree of activism, since the effect of surprises on employment is more potent. The larger the σ_δ^2, given σ_ε^2, the better is the central bank's forecasting ability. This implies that given a policy decision, the spread of policy outcomes is smaller and the risk of hitting an undesirably high rate of inflation smaller too. A larger degree of activism is therefore not as risky.

A larger β means that future objectives carry more weight. This moderates the temptation to stimulate employment via monetary expansion, and with it the degree of activism. Finally a higher σ_v^2 implies that the public's learning process is swifter. This raises the effect of current policy on future expectations and deters activism.

The effect of the variance of the central bank's forecast error (σ_ε^2) on activism is generally ambiguous. This can be seen by differentiating equation (13.21) with respect to σ_ε^2 and by noting (from figure 9.1) that an increase in σ_ψ^2 raises activism. The effect of σ_ε^2 on σ_ψ^2 is given (differentiating 13.21) by

$$\frac{d\sigma_\psi^2}{d\sigma_\varepsilon^2} = \frac{\lambda^2}{\sigma_\delta^2 + \sigma_\varepsilon^2}[\sigma_\delta^2 - \sigma_\varepsilon^2]. \qquad (13.22)$$

Hence activism rises or falls with σ_ε^2 depending on whether σ_δ^2 is larger or smaller than σ_ε^2. The source of the ambiguity resides in the fact that an increase in σ_ε^2 reduces the signal-to-noise ratio in the inference problem of the central bank as well as in that of the public. Due to its own diminished forecasting ability, the central bank is more reluctant to be activist. But the fact that the public's ability to detect the central bank's objectives is also reduced slows down the public's learning process and diminishes the deterrent effect of learning. This tends to make policy more activist. When $\sigma_\delta^2 > \sigma_\varepsilon^2$, the second effect dominates. In the opposite case, the first effect dominates.

13.10 Determinants of the Speed of Learning about Large Changes in Objectives

When there is a large change in objectives, the innovation v_{i-1} is likely to be large in comparison to the forecast error ε_{i-1}. Under such circumstances the public is more likely to detect a larger fraction of this change, the larger the learning parameter θ. Hence θ is a measure of the speed of learning when objectives change by large amounts. The following proposition summarizes the effects of various parameters on θ:

PROPOSITION 13.3   The speed of learning about large changes in objectives (θ) is larger the larger σ_v^2 and α and the lower β and σ_δ^2.

Proof   By proposition 13.2, B_3 is larger the larger σ_δ^2 and the lower σ_v^2. It follows from equation (13.7) that θ is negatively related to σ_δ^2 and positively related to σ_v^2.

As in the proof of the previous proposition, we utilize the fact that equation (13.7) maps into equation (9.16a) with $B_3 = B$ and $\sigma_\psi^2 = \sigma_\delta^4 \sigma_\varepsilon^2 /(\sigma_\delta^2 + \sigma_\varepsilon^2)^2$. An increase in β lowers the curve $F(B)$ in figure 9.1 and produces a lower equilibrium value of B. Since

$$\theta \equiv \frac{B^2 \sigma_v^2}{B^2 \sigma_v^2 + \sigma_\psi^2}, \tag{13.23}$$

it is (given σ_v^2 and σ_ψ^2) an increasing function of B. Hence θ is decreasing in β. Similarly an increase in α raises the curve $F(B)$ in figure 9.1 and produces a higher value of B which implies, via equation (13.23), that θ is higher.   □

Note that given the variances σ_v^2, σ_δ^2, and σ_ε^2, the degree of activism and the speed of learning are positively related. Thus an increase in α raises both activism and the speed of learning, and an increase in β reduces both of them. This is intuitively plausible. Given the ratio of signal to noise (determined by the various variances), it is rational for the public to give more weight to recent developments the higher the degree of activism of the central bank.

The intuition underlying the effects of σ_v^2 on the speed of learning is standard. An increase in σ_v^2 raises the signal-to-noise ratio and makes it rational for the public to treat recent developments more seriously. The negative effect of a larger σ_δ^2 on θ can be understood by reference to the last term in equation (13.16c). An increase in σ_δ^2 raises the activism parameter B_3. This induces a larger response of the term $s_{i-1} \equiv B_3 v_{i-1} - \lambda \varepsilon_{i-1}$ to given fluctuations in v_{i-1}. Hence a given fluctuation in s_{i-1} is associated on average with a lower deviation of v_{i-1} from zero. It is therefore rational on the part of the public to attribute less importance to s_{i-1} and recent events when σ_δ^2 is larger.

It is interesting to note that the effect of the degree of imprecision in central bank's forecasts of money demand (σ_ε^2) on the speed of learning is ambiguous in general. This can be seen by differentiating equation (13.23) with respect to σ_ε^2, taking the relationship in (13.22) into consideration. The result is shown in equation (13.24).

$$\frac{d\theta}{d\sigma_\varepsilon^2} = \frac{d\theta}{d\sigma_\psi^2} \frac{\lambda^2}{\sigma_\delta^2 + \sigma_\varepsilon^2} (\sigma_\delta^2 - \sigma_\varepsilon^2). \tag{13.24}$$

Since $d\theta/d\sigma_\psi^2 < 0$ (see equation 9.23), the sign of $d\theta/d\sigma_\varepsilon^2$ is opposite to that of the difference $\sigma_\delta^2 - \sigma_\varepsilon^2$. The source of the ambiguity is the same as that which makes the effect of σ_ε^2 on activism ambiguous (section 13.9). If the degree of activism is increasing in σ_ε^2, the speed of learning is decreasing in it. Conversely, if the degree of activism is decreasing in σ_ε^2, the speed of learning is larger when σ_ε^2 is larger.

13.11 Inflation Uncertainty and Its Determinants

As in section 9.5 of chapter 9, inflation uncertainty can be characterized by the variance of the public's inflation forecast error. From equations (13.16b) and (13.16c) the forecast error is

$$\alpha(1 - \rho^2 \beta \theta)[v_i + \rho(1 - \theta)v_{i-1}] + \rho \theta \lambda \varepsilon_{i-1} + (1 - \lambda)\delta_i - \lambda \varepsilon_i. \tag{13.25}$$

The public's uncertainty has three origins. First, the public is uncertain about the current innovation to central bank objectives, v_i. Second, since the public does not observe v_{i-1} and ε_{i-1} separately, it remains uncertain about the extent to which recent inflation and monetary growth are due to a change in central bank objectives or to an error of forecast on the part of the central bank. The terms in v_{i-1} and ε_{i-1} reflect this second type of uncertainty. Finally, in planning monetary growth for the period, the central bank is uncertain about how much of the signal s_i is due to a change in money demand rather than to forecast error. Since this uncertainty affects policy, it injects an additional element of uncertainty into the public's inflation forecast. The terms in δ_i and ε_i reflect this third reason for the public's uncertainty. From (13.25) the mean square forecast error is

$$V \equiv \alpha^2(1 - \rho^2\beta\theta)^2[1 + \rho^2(1 - \theta)^2]\sigma_v^2 + (\lambda\rho\theta)^2\sigma_\varepsilon^2 + V_{CB}, \qquad (13.26a)$$

where

$$V_{CB} \equiv (1 - \lambda)^2\sigma_\delta^2 + \lambda^2\sigma_\varepsilon^2. \qquad (13.26b)$$

Note that the term V_{CB} that characterizes the uncertainty of the central bank with respect to the position of money demand impacts on a one-to-one basis on the public's uncertainty with respect to inflation. The following proposition characterizes the effects of various parameters on the public's uncertainty as measured by the mean square forecast error in equation (13.26):

PROPOSITION 13.4   The public's uncertainty with respect to inflation is larger the larger are α, σ_v^2, σ_δ^2, and σ_ε^2 and the lower β.

Proof See appendix C to this chapter.   □

The message of the proposition is that central banks with stronger degrees of (political) time preference, larger innovations in objective, and lower forecasting ability inflict larger doses of inflation uncertainty on the public. In addition the more sensitive is labor demand to the real wage and the larger the variance of innovations to money demand, the larger is the public's uncertainty.

13.12   Credibility and Its Determinants

Analogously to section 9.7, we measure credibility as the absolute value of the difference between the rate of inflation *planned* by the central bank and the rate of inflation *expected* by individuals at contracting time. Since the central bank does not know the effect of its policy on inflation with certainty, the rate of inflation that it plans corresponds to the expected value of inflation conditional on the information available to the central bank when it decides on money growth for the period. Denoting this expected value by $E_{CBi}\pi_i$, we can formally define credibility in period i as[9]

$$C_i \equiv -|E_{CBi}\pi_i - E[\pi_i|I_i]| \equiv -|e_i^p|. \qquad (13.27)$$

But from equation (13.3),

$$E_{CBi}\pi_i = E_{CBi}m_i + E_{CBi}\delta_i. \qquad (13.28)$$

The first term on the right-hand side of this equation is given in equation (13.16a) and the second is simply λs_i (the bank's forecast of the shock to money demand). Using these expressions in (13.28) and using the resulting expression in (13.27), we obtain

$$C_i = -|(1 - \rho^2\beta\theta)[v_i + \rho(1 - \theta)v_{i-1}] + \lambda\rho\theta\varepsilon_{i-1}| = -|e_i^p|. \qquad (13.29)$$

Note that the difference between the expression inside the absolute value sign on the right-hand side of (13.29) and the expression in equation (13.25) is the component contributed by the central bank's own uncertainty, $(1 - \lambda)\delta_i - \lambda\varepsilon_i$. This makes sense since now we are comparing the central bank's forecast of inflation rather than actual inflation with the public's expectation. To get an idea about the structural determinants of credibility, we focus on the variance of e_i^p whose explicit form is given in equation (13.30).

$$V^p = \alpha^2(1 - \rho^2\beta\alpha)^2[1 + \rho^2(1 - \theta)^2]\sigma_v^2 + (\lambda\rho\theta)^2\sigma_\varepsilon^2. \qquad (13.30)$$

As explained in chapter 9 (see equation 9.28 in particular), this variance is a measure of average credibility. The following proposition summarizes the effects of various parameters on average credibility:

PROPOSITION 13.5   Average credibility is lower the larger α, σ_v^2, and σ_δ^2 and the lower β and σ_ε^2.

Proof   See appendix D to this chapter.   □

Thus credibility is lower, the more sensitive the labor demand is to the real wage rate and the higher the variances of innovations are to money demand and to the central bank's objectives. It is higher, the lower the degree of central bank's time preference and the less precise the central bank's forecasts of money demand (higher σ_ε^2). The last effect is due to the fact that, when its forecasts are less precise, the central bank is less activist. This moderates the effects of innovations to objectives on monetary policy, thereby increasing average credibility.

Appendix A: Derivation of Equation (13.9)

Since the information set I_i does not contain signals for v_i and s_i and since p_{i-2} is contained in I_i, it follows from (13.6) that

$$E[m_i|I_i] = B_0 A + B_1 p_{i-2} + B_2 E[v_{i-1}|I_i]. \tag{13A.1}$$

Lagging (13.6) by one period and using (13.4),

$$m_{i-1} = B_0 A + B_1 p_{i-3} + B_2 v_{i-2} + B_3 v_{i-1} + B_4(\delta_{i-1} + \varepsilon_{i-1}). \tag{13A.2}$$

We assume there is no forgetfulness. Hence $I_i \supset I_{i-1}$. Since $p_{i-3} \in I_{i-1}$, it must be in I_i as well. Since $p_{i-2} \in I_i$, this implies that $v_{i-2} \in I_i$. In addition, since the public knows π_{i-1}, from (13.3) it can deduce δ_{i-1} so that $\delta_{i-1} \in I_i$. It follows that an observation on m_{i-1} amounts, through (13A.2), to an observation on $y_{i-1} \equiv B_3 v_{i-1} + B_4 \varepsilon_{i-1}$. Hence

$$E[v_{i-1}|I_i] = E[v_{i-1}|(B_3 v_{i-1} + B_4 \varepsilon_{i-1})] = \frac{B_3 \sigma_v^2}{B_3^2 \sigma_v^2 + B_4^2 \sigma_\varepsilon^2} y_{i-1}. \tag{13A.3}$$

The first equality in equation (13.9) follows by substituting (13A.3) into (13A.1), noting the definition of θ in (13.10a) and rearranging. The second equality follows by noting, from (13A.2), that

$$y_{i-1} = m_{i-1} - B_0 A - B_1 p_{i-3} - B_2 v_{i-2} - B_4 \delta_{i-1},$$

by substituting this equation into the middle term in (13.9), and by rearranging.   □

Appendix B: Derivation of a Sufficient Condition for $N^* - N_i \geq 0$, for All i, with High Probability

From equations (13.2) and (13.25) the condition $N^* - N_i \geq 0$ is equivalent to the condition

$$B_3[v_i + \rho(1 - \theta)v_{i-1}] + (1 - \lambda)\delta_i - \lambda\varepsilon_i + \rho\theta\lambda(\delta_{i-1} + \varepsilon_{i-1}) \leq \frac{N^* - N_n}{\alpha} \equiv c. \tag{13A.4}$$

The expression on the left-hand side of (13A.4) is normal with mean zero and a variance V whose explicit form is given in equation (13.26a). Hence, if $3\sqrt{V} < c$, the probability that (13A.4) is satisfied is 0.9987 (see also appendix A to chapter 9). Using the explicit form of V and rearranging this condition is equivalent to

$$\alpha^2(1 - \rho\beta\theta)^2[1 + \rho^2(1 - \theta)^2]\sigma_v^2 + (1 - \lambda)^2\sigma_\delta^2 + \lambda^2[1 + (\rho\theta)^2]\sigma_\varepsilon^2 \leq \frac{c^2}{9}.$$

$$(13A.5)$$

Noting that $1 - \rho\beta\theta < 1$, $\rho^2(1 - \theta)^2 < 1$, $(1 - \lambda)^2 < 1$, and $(\rho\theta)^2 < 1$, a sufficient condition for (13A.5) is

$$2(\alpha^2\sigma_v^2 + \sigma_\varepsilon^2) + \sigma_\delta^2 \leq \frac{c^2}{9}, \tag{13A.6}$$

which is equivalent to the condition

$$\sigma_v^2 \leq \frac{(N^* - N_n)^2}{18\alpha^4} - \frac{\sigma_\delta^2 + 2\sigma_\varepsilon^2}{2\alpha^2}. \tag{13A.7}$$

Since we also require the fulfillment of condition (9A.6), this condition is binding only when the right-hand side of (13A.7) is smaller than $(1 - \rho^2)A/9$.

Appendix C: Proof of Proposition 13.4

Let D be a dummy variable such that $D = \alpha, \beta, \sigma_v^2, \sigma_\delta^2, \sigma_\varepsilon^2$. Totally differentiating equation (13.26a) with respect to D, we obtain

$$\frac{dV}{dD} = \frac{\partial V}{\partial D} + \frac{\partial V}{\partial \theta}\frac{d\theta}{dD}. \tag{13A.8}$$

Given the paramters α, β, σ_v^2, σ_δ^2, and σ_ε^2, the regression coefficient θ is chosen by the public so as to minimize V. Hence $\partial V/\partial\theta = 0$, and

$$\frac{dV}{dD} = \frac{\partial V}{\partial D}. \tag{13A.8a}$$

From equation (13.26) the partial derivatives of V with respect to α, β, and σ_v^2 are

$$\frac{\partial V}{\partial \alpha} = 2\alpha(1 - \rho^2\beta\theta)[1 + \rho^2(1 - \theta)^2]\sigma_v^2, \tag{13A.9a}$$

$$\frac{\partial V}{\partial \beta} = -2(\alpha\rho)^2\theta(1 - \rho^2\beta\theta)[1 + \rho^2(1 - \theta)^2]\sigma_v^2, \tag{13A.9b}$$

$$\frac{\partial V}{\partial \sigma_v^2} = (1 - \rho^2 \beta \theta)^2 [1 + \rho^2 (1 - \theta)^2] \sigma_v^2. \tag{13A.9c}$$

The results of the proposition concerning the effects of α, β, and σ_v^2 on V follow by noting that $\rho^2 \beta \theta < 1$ and by using (13A.8a).

From equation (13.26) the partial derivatives of V with respect to σ_δ^2 and σ_ε^2 are

$$\frac{\partial V}{\partial \sigma_\delta^2} = (1 - \lambda)^2 + 2\lambda(\rho\theta)^2 \sigma_\varepsilon^2 \frac{\partial \lambda}{\partial \sigma_\delta^2} + \frac{\partial V_{CB}}{\partial \sigma_\delta^2}, \tag{13A.10a}$$

$$\frac{\partial V}{\partial \sigma_\varepsilon^2} = (\lambda\rho\theta)^2 + 2\lambda(\rho\theta)^2 \sigma_\varepsilon^2 \frac{\partial \lambda}{\partial \sigma_\varepsilon^2} + \frac{\partial V_{CB}}{\partial \sigma_\varepsilon^2}. \tag{13A.10b}$$

Given σ_δ^2 and σ_ε^2, the central bank chooses λ so as to minimize the variance of its forecast error of δ. The minimized value of this variance is given by V_{CB} (equation 13.26b). It follows that $\partial V/\partial \sigma_\delta^2 = \partial V/\partial \sigma_\varepsilon^2 = 0$. From equation (13.13),

$$\lambda = \frac{\sigma_\delta^2}{\sigma_\delta^2 + \sigma_\varepsilon^2}.$$

Using this relation to calculate the partial derivatives of λ with respect to σ_δ^2 and σ_ε^2 (along with the fact that the partial derivatives of V_{CB} with respect to these variances are zero) in equations (13A.10), we obtain

$$\frac{\partial V}{\partial \sigma_\delta^2} = (1 - \lambda)^2 + 2\lambda[\rho\theta(1 - \lambda)]^2, \tag{13A.11a}$$

$$\frac{\partial V}{\partial \sigma_\varepsilon^2} = \lambda^2 [1 - (\rho\theta)^2 (1 - \lambda)]. \tag{13A.11b}$$

Since $(\rho\theta)^2 (1 - \lambda) < 1$, the effect of both σ_δ^2 and σ_ε^2 on V is positive.   □

Appendix D: Proof of Proposition 13.5

Comparing equations (13.26a) and (13.30), we have

$$V^p = V - V_{CB}. \tag{13A.12}$$

Hence

$$\frac{dV^p}{dD} = \frac{dV}{dD} - \frac{dV_{CB}}{dD},$$

(13A.13)

where the dummy variable D is as defined in appendix C. But

$$\frac{dV^p}{dD} = \frac{dV}{dD} \quad \text{for } D = \alpha, \beta, \sigma_v^2,$$

so that the effects of α, β, and σ_v^2 on V^p are identical to their effects on V. It follows, by proposition 13.4, that V^p is increasing in α and σ_v^2 and decreasing in β.

Using (13A.8a) and (13A.11) in (13A.13) and rearranging, we obtain

$$\frac{dV^p}{d\sigma_\delta^2} = 2\lambda[\rho\theta(1 - \lambda)]^2 > 0,$$

$$\frac{dV^p}{d\sigma_\varepsilon^2} = -(1 - \lambda)(\rho\theta\lambda)^2 < 0. \quad \square$$

14 Partial Disclosure of Policy and Its Effect on Policy Outcomes

14.1 Introduction

During the 1970s and 1980s central banks in several developed countries introduced procedures that were designed to partially disclose their policy plans to the public. The precise methods used to disseminate information about monetary policy plans vary across countries and sometimes over time within a given country. Advance disclosure may take the form of preannounced monetary targets, of official forecasts, or of a weak statement of intention. At times a point target is announced and at others a range. When a range is announced, there is sometimes an attempt to specify the contingencies that will lead to the choice of a particular interval within the target range. But the specification of contingencies is incomplete and leaves a margin of uncertainty. There are also cross-sectional and time variations in the nominal stock used to disclose planned policy actions. Monetary targets or statements of intentions are made in terms of various definitions of money ranging from narrow to broader monetary aggregates.

Monetary targets, official forecasts, or statements of intention are (or have been) made in Germany, the United States, Japan, Britain, France, Canada, Switzerland, and Australia. These advance signals are imperfect but not meaningless indicators of planned policy actions. Their precision varies across countries. Thus monetary announcements of the Bundesbank (the West German central bank) and of the Bank of Japan proved to be more reliable than those of the Federal Reserve and of the Bank of England.

The precision of monetary announcements ultimately depends on how serious is the central bank in its attempt to provide the public with precise information about policy plans. The Bundesbank, which takes its monetary targets very seriously, usually preannounces a range and even loosely specifies the contingencies under which it will aim at the high rather than at the low end of the target range. Actual monetary growth in West Germany has been almost always within the target range.[1] The record of the Federal Reserve, which since the mid-1970s is required, by an act of Congress, to preannounce monetary targets is less precise.

What types of institutional arrangements are conducive to more precise signals about monetary policy? This is largely an open issue. But the following observations can be made: First, the official term used to characterize the signal may give some clue about its precision. It is likely that when signals are described by the central bank as projections or forecasts as is the case in Japan (and used to be the case in Australia until 1985), precision is, ceteris paribus, lower than when the signals are described as statements of intentions as is the case in Britain and France. Moreover the nearer organizationally is the division that is in charge of monetary announcements to the individuals who make the actual daily decisions about monetary policy, the more likely are announcements to be precise. This implies that, ceteris paribus, statements that emanate from a more independent central bank are likely to be more precise. Thus the statements of intentions of the highly independent Bundesbank are likely to be more precise than those of the Bank of England and of the Banque de France. The record of the last twenty years supports this presumption.

Moreover, given the degree of central bank independence, the precision of monetary targets or other statements of intentions by the bank is likely to be higher the more direct is the organizational link between the sender of signals within the central bank and its chief executive officer. In particular, other things the same, precision is likely to be highest when the statements emanate from the governor of the central bank or his or her immediate entourage. Hence a legal framework that compels the governor to state publicly his or her policy objectives is likely to lead to more precise announcements of policy plans than one that leaves this function to lower-level officials within the bank's organizational structure.

The recent (1989) legislation which requires the governor of the Reserve Bank of New Zealand to negotiate a monetary policy agreement with the minister of finance is particularly relevant in this context. The new act requires that the agreement be made public. Although it leaves to the minister of finance the prerogative to override the bank's policy, the act requires that such an action be made public. By contrast under the previous law the governor could be directed to follow a particular policy without that directive being released publicly. The new law can therefore be viewed as an institutional device that raises the precision of signals about monetary policy plans in comparison to its previous counterpart.

This chapter explicitly recognizes the existence of advance signals about policy plans and analyzes the effects that their precision has on the policy process and on policy outcomes. The analysis takes the framework of chapter 10 in which policymakers have an extended information advantage about their shifting objectives as a point of departure. As in that chapter the public utilizes past rates of monetary expansion to forecast future rates. But in addition it has access to noisy signals issued by policymakers about their policy plans. We will also refer to those signals interchangeably as announcements, preannouncements, or monetary targets. This chapter characterizes the policymakers' decision rule and the learning process of the public in the presence of imperfect, but not meaningless, monetary signals and provides answers to questions such as: What determines the credibility of monetary targets, and what is their effect on the distribution of inflation and on monetary uncertainty?

Stein (1989) has recently applied the concept of "cheap talk" proposed by Crawford and Sobel (1982) to announcements about the exchange rate. Unlike signaling, which is a costly activity, cheap talk refers to situations in which some private information can be transmitted at no cost. The main conceptual difference between that framework and the one in this chapter is that here monetary targets convey some information because the central bank must make announcements that are correct on average either because the law requires that or because of some other outside mechanism such as accepted practice that mandates that. In Stein's framework the central bank does not have to preannounce policy. Instead, it chooses to do so because this furthers its objectives. The absence of imposed announcements limits, in this case, the precision of information that can be credibly transmitted to the public.[2] At a more fundamental level Stein focuses on the strategic aspects of cheap talk whereas this chapter stresses the effect of compulsory partial advance disclosure of policy plans on the choice of those plans.

14.2 Monetary Targets, Central Bank Objectives, and the Formation of Expectations

The deterministic and stochastic structure of the policymakers' objective function and of the economy are the same as in chapter 9. The policymakers' objective function is given by equation (9.1) and its stochastic properties by equation (9.3). It states that the relative emphasis of policymakers on price stability and economic stimulation shifts over time and that policymakers have better information about the current state of their objectives than the general public.[3] The short-run Phillips relation is given by equation (9.2). As in chapter 9 policymakers do not have perfect control over the money supply. The relation between actual and expected monetary growth is given by equation (9.4) which is reproduced here as equation (14.1):

$$m_i = m_i^p + \psi_i. \tag{14.1}$$

The basic timing of moves is identical to that of chapters 9 and 10. Within each period expectations, and therefore nominal contracts, are concluded first. Then policymakers choose m_i^p, taking the nominal contract and the expectations embedded in it as given. Finally the control error ψ_i realizes and actual inflation is determined by equation (14.1).

The new element in this chapter is that *prior to the conclusion of nominal contracts and expectations* within each period the monetary authority provides to the public a noisy signal of his or her policy plans for the period. The signal (or monetary target) is

$$m_i^a = m_i^p + \gamma_i, \tag{14.2}$$

where γ_i is a serially uncorrelated normal variate with zero mean, variance σ_γ^2, and is distributed independently of the monetary control error.

Preannouncement of the signal gives the public an additional source of information about future money growth. The public's expectations combine the information that the public gains from the announcement of targets and, as in chapter 10, the information obtained from the history of money growth. Rational policymakers must use the new information structure faced by the public when planning future money growth. To obtain a rational expectations solution for the model in the presence of announcements, we extend the model of chapter 10 to include announcements. As in that chapter we postulate that the public's belief about policymakers' strategy is given by

$$m_i^p = B_0 A + B p_i, \tag{14.3}$$

where B_0 and B are constants to be determined by the requirement of rational expectations.

The public knows the structure of policymakers' decisions regarding m_i^p, given by (14.3), and the relationship between announced and planned monetary growth in (14.2). The public observes only actual and announced monetary growth. At the beginning of period i the public knows the history of past rates of money growth up to and including period $i - 1$ and the history of announced targets up to and including the announcement, m_i^a, made at the beginning of period i. I_i denotes this information set.

Substituting (14.3) into (14.1) and (14.2), we have

$$m_i = B_0 A + B p_i + \psi_i \equiv B_0 A + y_i, \tag{14.4a}$$

$$m_i^a = B_0 A + B p_i + \gamma_i \equiv B_0 A + z_i. \tag{14.4b}$$

Since B_0 and A are known parameters, observations on m_i and m_i^a amount to observations on y_i and z_i, respectively.[4] Note that it pays the public to use announcements to improve its forecast of the stochastic persistent component of policymakers' objectives.

It follows, using (14.4a), that the public's rational expectation of m_i is

$$E[m_i|I_i] = B_0 A + BE[p_i|I_i]$$

$$= B_0 A + BE[p_i|z_i, z_{i-1}, \ldots, y_{i-1}, y_{i-2}, \ldots]. \tag{14.5}$$

Appendix A to this chapter shows that

$$E[p_i|I_i] = \frac{(\rho - \delta)(\sigma_\psi^2 + \sigma_\gamma^2)}{(\rho\sigma_\psi^2 + \delta\sigma_\gamma^2)B} \left\{ \sum_{j=1}^{\infty} \delta^j(\theta y_{i-j} + (1 - \theta)z_{i-j}) + (1 - \theta)z_i \right\}, \tag{14.6a}$$

$$\delta \equiv \frac{1}{2}\left(\frac{1+r}{\rho} + \rho\right) - \sqrt{\frac{1}{4}\left(\frac{1+r}{\rho} + \rho\right)^2 - 1}, \tag{14.6b}$$

$$r \equiv B^2 \frac{\sigma_v^2}{\sigma_\psi^2}\left(1 + \frac{\sigma_\psi^2}{\sigma_\gamma^2}\right) = \left(\frac{\sigma_v^2}{\sigma_\psi^2} + \frac{\sigma_v^2}{\sigma_\gamma^2}\right)B^2, \tag{14.6c}$$

$$\theta \equiv \frac{\sigma_\gamma^2}{\sigma_\psi^2 + \sigma_\gamma^2}. \tag{14.6d}$$

Substituting (14.6a) into (14.5) and using (14.4), we obtain

$$E[m_i|I_i] = \frac{(\rho - \delta)(1 - \theta)}{\delta + (\rho - \delta)(1 - \theta)}m_i^a$$

$$+ \frac{\delta}{\delta + (\rho - \delta)(1 - \theta)} \sum_{j=0}^{\infty} \delta^j[(1 - \rho)\overline{m}^p$$

$$+ (\rho - \delta)(\theta m_{i-1-j} + (1 - \theta)m_{i-1-j}^a)], \tag{14.7}$$

where $\overline{m}^p \equiv B_0 A$ is the mean rate of money growth.

Since δ has the same form in ρ and r as λ in equation (10.5b) of chapter 10, we can apply results from that chapter. (The solution for r differs in the two cases, since implicitly σ_γ^2 is infinity in chapter 10.) It follows that $0 \le \delta \le 1$ and that $\rho - \delta \ge 0$. The optimal predictor is a weighted average of the current announcement and the past history of announcements and monetary growth (including $\overline{m}^p$)—the two terms in (14.7)—with weights that sum to unity. The weight placed on each term depends on σ_γ^2. Imprecise announcements, large σ_γ^2, reduce the usefulness of announcements, so the public pays less attention to them. In the limit as $\sigma_\gamma^2 \to \infty$, $\theta \to 1$; there is no information in the announcements, and they are ignored. (The optimal predictor in equation 14.7 reduces to equation 10.6a in chapter 10.) At the other extreme, $\sigma_\gamma^2 \to 0$,[5] monetary targets are completely accurate statements of planned money growth and the optimal predictor $E[m_i | I_i] = m^a$. The currently announced target is fully credible. This remains true even if σ_ψ^2 is relatively large so that monetary control is relatively poor.

Between the extreme values of σ_γ^2, σ_γ^2, and σ_ψ^2 determine the weights given to past announcements and to the past history of monetary growth. In general the noisier signal gets a smaller weight.[6]

Note that the announcement provides the public with noisy information about the current innovation to policy objectives. By contrast, when, as in chapter 10, there are no announcements, the public has no advance signal about the innovation to current policy objectives and bases its forecast only on the serial correlation between past and current rates of inflation.

14.3 The Policymakers' Decision Rule and Proof of the Rationality of Expectations

Readers who are willing to take the solution on faith may go directly to equations (14.11). The objective function of policymakers is the same as in chapters 9 and 10 and is given by equation (10.7). Policymakers know that the public forms expectations according to (14.7) and use this information when choosing planned monetary growth. Substituting (14.7) into (10.7), using (14.1) and (14.2), and rearranging, we express the maximization problem of the policymakers as

$$
\max_{\{m_i^p, i=0,1,\dots\}} E_{G0} \sum_{i=0}^{\infty} \beta^i \left(\alpha x_i \left(m_i^p + \psi_i - \frac{(1-\rho)\delta}{(1-\delta)(\rho-\delta)(1-\theta)+\delta} B_0 A \right. \right.
$$

$$
- \frac{(\rho-\delta)(1-\theta)}{(\rho-\delta)(1-\theta)+\delta}(m_i^p + \gamma_i) - \frac{\delta(\rho-\delta)}{(\rho-\delta)(1-\theta)+\delta} \sum_{j=0}^{\infty} \delta^j (m_{i-1-j}^p
$$

$$
\left. \left. + \psi_{i-1-j} + \gamma_{i-1-j}\right) \right) - \frac{(m_i^p + \psi_i)^2}{2} \right). \tag{14.8}
$$

The stochastic Euler equations necessary for an internal maximum of this problem are[7]

$$\alpha \left\{ 1 - \frac{(\rho - \delta)(1 - \theta)}{(\rho - \delta)(1 - \theta) + \delta} \right\} x_i - \frac{\alpha\delta(\rho - \delta)}{(\rho - \delta)(1 - \theta) + \delta}$$

$$\times E_{Gi}\{\beta x_{i+1} + \beta^2 \delta x_{i+2} + \cdots\} - m_i^p = 0, \qquad i = 0, 1, \ldots. \qquad (14.9)$$

Using equation (10.10) in (14.9), we reduce this expression after a considerable amount of algebra to the decision rule in equation (14.10). Details appear in appendix B to this chapter:

$$m_i^p = \frac{\alpha\delta(1 - \rho\beta)(1 + \sigma_\psi^2/\sigma_\gamma^2)}{(1 - \delta\beta)[\delta + \rho(\sigma_\psi^2/\sigma_\gamma^2)]} A + \frac{\alpha(1 - \beta\rho^2)\delta(1 + \sigma_\psi^2/\sigma_\gamma^2)}{(1 - \rho\beta\delta)[\delta + \rho(\sigma_\psi^2/\sigma_\gamma^2)]} p_i. \qquad (14.10)$$

Rationality of expectations implies that the coefficients of A and of p_i should be the same across equations (14.3) and (14.10), respectively, so that

$$B_0 = \frac{(1 - \beta\rho)(1 + \sigma_\psi^2/\sigma_\gamma^2)\delta(B)}{[1 - \beta\delta(B)][\delta(B) + \rho\sigma_\psi^2/\sigma_\gamma^2]}, \qquad (14.11a)$$

$$B = \frac{(1 - \beta\rho^2)(1 + \sigma_\psi^2/\sigma_\gamma^2)\delta(B)}{(1 - \beta\rho\delta(B))[\delta(B) + \rho\sigma_\psi^2/\sigma_\gamma^2]} \equiv G[\sigma_\gamma^2, \delta(B)]. \qquad (14.11b)$$

The dependence of δ on B (through equations 14.6) is stressed by writing δ as a function of B. The second equation determines B uniquely as an implicit function of β, ρ, σ_v^2, σ_ψ^2, and σ_γ^2. Uniqueness is demonstrated by noting that the right-hand side of this equation is an increasing function of δ and that δ is a decreasing function of r (see appendix C). Since, from

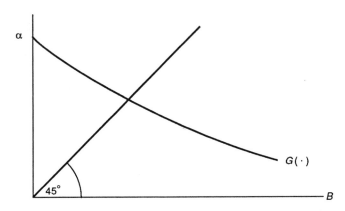

Figure 14.1
Determination of the equilibrium value of B in the presence of monetary targets

(14.6c), r is increasing in B, $G(\cdot)$ is a monotonically decreasing function of B. Since $G[\sigma_\gamma^2, \delta(0)] = \alpha$, this implies that there is a unique positive solution for B. The argument is illustrated graphically in figure 14.1.

When there is no information in the announced targets ($\sigma_\gamma^2 \to \infty$), the decision strategy in (14.10) reduces to the decision strategy in the absence of monetary targets.[8] Hence both the optimal predictor and the policymakers' decision rule in the presence of preannounced targets are generalizations of their respective counterparts in the economy with no announcements. Formally therefore the economy with no announcements can be viewed as a particular case (with $\sigma_\gamma^2 \to \infty$) of the economy with announcements.

14.4   The Effects of the Precision of Disclosure on Activism and the Distribution of Inflation

Advance disclosure of policy plans can be implemented, as we saw, in various ways such as the preannouncement of monetary targets and the issuance of public forecasts. It may also take the form of a publicly announced agreement between the governor of the central bank and the finance minister as in the recent legislation in New Zealand. Depending on the closeness of the disclosing institutions to actual policymakers and other institutional factors the precision of signals about contemplated policy plans may be high or low. The first question we will be interested in answering is: How does the precision of advance signals about policy plans affect the degree of activism of policy when policy is discretionary?

As in chapter 10 the coefficient of p_i in the policymakers' decision rule (equation 14.10) measures the extent of policy activism. The higher it is, the larger will be the response of planned monetary growth to changes in policymakers' objectives. Hence we can determine the effect of the precision of disclosure on the degree of activism by finding the relationship between the coefficient B in equation (14.11b) and the imprecision σ_γ^2 of preannounced signals about monetary policy. It is shown in appendix D that, given B, the derivative of $G(\cdot)$ on the right-hand side of (14.11b) with respect to σ_γ^2 is positive. It follows that the curve $G(\cdot)$ in figure 14.1 shifts upward when σ_γ^2 rises, producing a larger equilibrium value of B. This implies the following proposition:

PROPOSITION 14.1   The more precise the advance disclosure of policy plans, the smaller is the degree of policy activism.

The intuition underlying the proposition is as follows: Policy changes over time because of changes in the relative importance assigned by policymakers to economic stimulation and price stability. When the precision of policy disclosure is high, a given change in the planned rate of monetary expansion has a smaller effect on employment since the public possesses more precise information about current policy plans. Hence, in the presence of relatively precise disclosure of policy plans, a given change in the policymakers' objectives induces a relatively small change in the marginal benefit of economic stimulation. It is therefore optimal in such a case to allow only relatively small variations in the marginal cost of inflation. But in view of the quadratic specification of the costs of inflation, this marginal cost is equal to the rate of monetary expansion. It follows that with a relatively high precision of disclosure monetary policy is less activist.

Proposition 14.1 contains an immediate prediction for the effect of the 1989 legislation on monetary policy activism in New Zealand. Since the new legislation increases the precision of disclosure the implication is that monetary policy in New Zealand will be less activist under the new legislation than prior to it.

We turn next to an investigation of the effects of the precision of disclosure on the distribution of monetary expansion. In the absence of shocks to money demand, from which we abstract in this chapter, the distributions of inflation and of money growth are identical. Hence, if shocks to money demand are relatively small, the following discussion also applies to the relationship between the precision of disclosure and the distribution of inflation. From (14.4a) the unconditional mean and variance of actual money growth are given, respectively, by

$$Em_i = B_0 A, \tag{14.12a}$$

$$V(m_i) = B^2 \frac{\sigma_v^2}{1 - \rho^2} + \sigma_\psi^2 = B^2 \sigma_p^2 + \sigma_\psi^2, \tag{14.12b}$$

where the explicit form of B_0 and B is given in equations (14.11). Since $\beta \leq 1$ and $\rho \leq \delta \leq 1$, B_0 is positive so the average rate of monetary expansion and the average rate of inflation are positive. Not surprisingly, the average rate is an increasing function of A and a decreasing function of the discount factor β.

How does the precision of advance disclosure of policy affect the mean rate of inflation? Intuition suggests that better precision should reduce the average rate of inflation. With higher precision the public gets a pretty accurate picture about current policy plans. This reduces the stimulatory impact of inflation on economic activity and decreases the incentive of policymakers to inflate. This intuition is partially supported by noting that when the precision of disclosure tends to perfection ($\sigma_\gamma^2 \to 0$), mean inflation tends to zero.[9] These remarks raise the possibility that the mean rate of inflation is monotonically decreasing in the precision of disclosure. I have not been able to establish this result in general. However, proposition 14.2 gives an overly strong, sufficient condition for such a monotonous relationship:

PROPOSITION 14.2   If the precision of disclosure is at least twice as large as that of monetary control ($\sigma_\psi^2 > 2\sigma_\gamma^2$), average inflation is monotonically decreasing in the precision of monetary announcements.

Proof   See appendix E to this chapter.   □

As explained in appendix E, this condition is substantially stronger than necessary so that the negative association between mean inflation and the precision of monetary announcements obtains in a wider range than that which is specified in proposition 14.2. Since the absence of monetary announcements is informationally equivalent to an economy with announcements, but with an infinite value of σ_γ^2, a corollary to the proposition is that, ceteris paribus, average inflation is lower with sufficiently precise announcements than without them. Evidence presented in chapter 20 (see table 20.4) supports this implication.

How about the effect of the precision of advance disclosure on the variance of inflation? From equation (14.12b) the variance of inflation is an increasing function of the activism parameter B. But proposition 14.1 implies that B is smaller the larger the precision of disclosure. It follows that

PROPOSITION 14.3   The variability of money growth and of inflation is a decreasing function of the precision of disclosure of policy plans.

As in chapter 10 it can be shown that the variability of inflation is lower the larger the discount factor β (see proposition 10.4). Thus a low time preference is conducive to monetary stability whether or not there is advance disclosure of policy plans. It can also be shown that (as in proposition 13.2) that the level of activism is lower the larger are β and σ_v^2. The intuition underlying this result is similar to that in chapter 13 and is not repeated. The proof of the above statements is left as an exercise to the interested reader.

14.5 The Credibility of Preannounced Policy Plans

In part II credibility has been conceived as a measure of the nearness of beliefs to the actual policy plans of policymakers. In the presence of pre-announced policy plans it is useful to have a measure of the credibility of announcements or of monetary targets taken in isolation. This measure focuses on the nearness between beliefs and announced targets. The nearer beliefs to announced targets the larger the credibility of those targets. Two measures of the credibility of monetary targets suggest themselves. The first—average credibility—measures the overall cohesion between announcements and beliefs. The second—marginal credibility—measures the marginal effect of a change in announced targets on the public's beliefs. The larger this effect, the larger is marginal credibility. This section charac-terizes these two measures and utilizes them to discuss the determinants of the credibility of monetary targets.

Average credibility measures the extent to which the public's expecta-tions of future monetary growth deviate from the current announce-ment. The smaller this deviation, the larger is average credibility. When $m_i^a = E(m_i | I_i)$, average credibility (AC) is perfect.

$$AC \equiv - |m_i^a - E[m_i | I_i]|. \tag{14.13}$$

Substituting (14.7) into (14.13) and rearranging, we obtain

$$AC = \frac{-\delta}{\delta + (\rho - \delta)(1 - \theta)} |m_i^a - m_i^*|, \tag{14.14}$$

where

$$m_i^* \equiv \sum_{j=0}^{\infty} \delta^j [(1 - \rho)\overline{m}^p + (\rho - \delta)(\theta m_{i-1-j} + (1 - \theta)m_{i-1-j}^a)]. \tag{14.15}$$

All the information that individuals have about future money growth before they get the current announcement is summarized in m_i^*. Average credibility is low when the current announcement is far away from m_i^*. The distance between m_i^a and m_i^* rises with the difference between current and past announcements and with the difference between m_i^a and the mean rate of money growth $\bar{m}^p$. Average credibility is reduced both during periods with large changes in announcements and when announcements differ markedly from average experience. Further, for any given divergence between m_i^a and m_i^*, average credibility is lower the larger the coefficient

$$C \equiv \frac{\delta}{\delta + (\rho - \delta)(1 - \theta)}$$

in equation (14.14). This coefficient is, ceteris paribus, an increasing function of δ.[10] Analysis of C leads to the following proposition about average credibility:

PROPOSITION 14.4   For a given divergence between m_i^a and m_i^*, the average credibility of monetary targets is lower,

1.   the lower is the precision of announcements (the larger σ_γ^2),

2.   the lower equiproportionally are the precisions of both announcements and monetary control (the higher are σ_γ^2 and σ_ψ^2 for a given $\sigma_\gamma^2 | \sigma_\psi^2$).

Proof

1.   Increases in σ_γ^2 increase δ and reduce $(1 - \theta)$, so C increases with σ_γ^2.

2.   An equiproportional increase in σ_ψ^2 and σ_γ^2 raises C by increasing δ for a fixed θ.   □

When monetary control is loose and announcements are rather noisy a shift to new rates of monetary growth does not generate immediate credibility. In particular a change in governmental objectives toward less inflation will be recognized only gradually even if government announces the new policy. As a result the period of learning and the consequent lull in economic activity is lengthened; the cost of disinflation increases. A shift to more inflationary objectives also takes more time to be recognized when credibility is low, so the period of economic stimulation increases.

When monetary control is tight and announcements precise, the credibility of new objectives is quickly established. Note that when either monetary control is perfect ($\sigma_\psi^2 = 0$) or announcements fully precise ($\sigma_\gamma^2 = 0$), $\delta = 0$, and average credibility is perfect. Hence perfect credibility can be established either way. However, uncertainty faced by the public is larger when the second method is used.

Average credibility focuses on the difference between the current announced targets and beliefs. One may also be interested in the ability of the current announcement to affect expectations. A useful measure of this ability is marginal credibility (MC):

$$MC = \frac{\partial E[m_i \mid I_i]}{\partial m_i^a} = \frac{(\rho - \delta)(1 - \theta)}{\delta + (\rho - \delta)(1 - \theta)}. \tag{14.16}$$

The second equality in (14.16) follows from equation (14.7).

Considerations similar to those which led to proposition 14.4 show that marginal credibility falls with any increase in σ_γ^2, and with any equiproportional increase in σ_γ^2 and σ_ψ^2. Marginal credibility is perfect when $MC = 1$ and is nonexistent when $MC = 0$. The first limiting case is attained for either $\sigma_\psi^2 \to 0$ or $\sigma_\gamma^2 \to 0$. The second is attained when both σ_ψ^2 and σ_γ^2 tend to infinity.

Before closing this section, note that imperfect credibility of monetary targets arises here without any dynamic inconsistency of the type considered by Kydland and Prescott (1977, p. 475) and in chapter 3. The basis for imperfect credibility here is the policymakers' advantage over the public that is due to their shifting objectives, noisy control, and noisy announcements. Policymakers know their stochastically changing objectives, but the public does not. The best the public can do is to form expectations, allowing for this noise, and use all the information available each period to infer current and future money growth. Announcements are not fully credible, despite the fact that policymakers are known to be following dynamically consistent discretionary policies, because they are not perfectly precise. But the analysis in this section suggests that both the average and the marginal credibility of monetary targets increase with the precision of monetary targets.

14.6   Partial Disclosure, Friedman's Rule, and Monetary Uncertainty

This section compares the monetary uncertainty faced by the public under the following three alternative monetary arrangements: (1) Policy is discretionary, and there are no announcements of target. (2) Policy is discretionary, but policymakers are required to announce a target, as in the United

States since 1975. (3) There is a rule of the type proposed by Friedman (1960) that requires constant planned monetary growth. Uncertainty is measured by the variance of the one-period-ahead error in predicting monetary growth.

We begin by considering the effect of announcements. The variances of the one-period-ahead errors in the presence and in the absence of announced targets are, respectively,

$$V^*(e) \equiv E[m_i - E[m_i|I_i^*]]^2, \tag{14.17a}$$

$$V(e) = E[m_i - E[m_i|I_i]]^2, \tag{14.17b}$$

where I_i^* is the public's information set in the presence of announcements and I_i its information set in the absence of announcements. In this section we will identify parameters and variables in the economy with announcements by a starred superscript. Thus B^* now denotes the coefficient of p_i in equation (14.3), while the symbol B (previously used to denote this coefficient) is reserved for the same coefficient in the absence of announcements. The following discussion establishes that $V^*(e)$ is smaller than $V(e)$. Readers who are not interested in the details of the proof may go directly to proposition 14.5.

The explicit form of $B^*(\cdot)$ is (from equation 14.11b)

$$B^*(\cdot) \equiv \frac{(1 - \beta\rho^2)\delta(1 + \sigma_\psi^2/\sigma_\gamma^2)}{(1 - \rho\beta\delta)(\delta + \rho\sigma_\psi^2/\sigma_\gamma^2)}. \tag{14.18a}$$

The explicit form of $B(\cdot)$ is (from equation 10.12b)

$$B = \frac{1 - \beta\rho^2}{1 - \beta\rho\lambda}, \tag{14.18b}$$

where λ is the value to which δ tends when σ_γ^2 tends to infinity. Using (14.4a) and (14.5) in (14.17a) and using equations (10.2) and (10.4) in (14.17b) and rearranging, we obtain expressions for the variance of unanticipated monetary growth with and without announcements:

$$V^*(e) = E[\psi_i + B^*(p_i - E[p_i|z_i, z_{i-1}, \ldots, y_{i-1}^*, y_{i-2}^*, \ldots])]^2, \tag{14.19a}$$

$$V(e) = E[\psi_i + B(p_i - E[p_i|y_{i-1}, y_{i-2}, \ldots,])]^2, \tag{14.19b}$$

where

$$y_i^* \equiv B^*p_i + \psi_i. \tag{14.20}$$

Noting that ψ_i is distributed independently of its lagged values and of γ_i and using the fact that the conditional expected values of p_i are minimum mean square error estimators of p_i, we can rewrite equations (14.19) as

$$V^*(e) = \sigma_\psi^2 + [B^*(\sigma_\psi^2, \sigma_\gamma^2)]^2 \min_{\{a_j^*, c_j\}} E\left[p_i - \sum_{j=1}^{\infty} a_j^* y_{i-j}^* - \sum_{j=0}^{\infty} c_j z_{i-j}\right]^2,$$

(14.21a)

$$V(e) = \sigma_\psi^2 + [B(\sigma_\psi^2)]^2 \min_{\{a_j\}} E\left[p_i - \sum_{j=1}^{\infty} a_j y_{i-j}\right]^2.$$

(14.21b)

Here a_j^* and c_j are, respectively, the weights of y_{i-j}^* and of z_{i-j} in the expression for the optimal predictor of p_i and a_j is the weight of y_{i-j} when this predictor is based solely on observations of y. The explicit form of those weights is given, respectively, in equation (14.6a) of this chapter and in equation (10.5a) in chapter 10.

Passing $B^*(\cdot)$ and $B(\cdot)$ in equations (14.21) to the right of the min operators, redefining variables, and rearranging, we obtain

$$V^*(e) = \sigma_\psi^2 + \min_{\{a_j^*, c_j\}} E\left[q_i^* - \sum_{j=1}^{\infty} a_j^*(q_{i-j}^* + \psi_{i-j}) - \sum_{j=0}^{\infty} c_j(q_{i-j}^* + \gamma_{i-j})\right]^2,$$

(14.22a)

$$V(e) = \sigma_\psi^2 + \min E\left[q_i - \sum_{j=1}^{\infty} a_j(q_{i-j} + \psi_{i-j})\right]^2.$$

(14.22b)

where

$$q_j^* \equiv B^* p_j, \quad q_j \equiv B p_j, \quad \text{for all } j. \tag{14.23}$$

The definitions in (14.23) in conjunction with (9.3b) imply that

$$Eq = Eq^* = 0, \quad \sigma_q^2 = B^2 \sigma_p^2, \quad \sigma_{q*}^2 = (B^*)^2 \sigma_p^2,$$

(14.24)

$$Eq_i q_{i-j} = \rho^j \sigma_q^2, \quad Eq_i^* q_{i-j}^* = \rho^j \sigma_{q*}^2 \quad \text{for all } i \text{ and } j,$$

where σ_q^2 and σ_{q*}^2 are the variances of q and q^*, respectively.

Expanding the square terms on the right-hand sides of equations (14.22), using (14.24) and the fact that ψ_j^*, ψ_j, and γ_j are all mutually and serially uncorrelated, we rewrite equations (14.22) as

$$V^*(e) = \sigma_\psi^2 + \min_{\{a_j^*, c_j\}} \left\{ \sum_{j=1}^\infty (a_j^*)^2 \sigma_\psi^2 + \sum_{j=0}^\infty c_j^2 \sigma_\gamma^2 + [(1 - c_0)^2 - 2(1 - c_0) \right.$$

$$\left. \times \sum_{j=1}^\infty (a_j^* + c_j)\rho^j + \sum_{j=1}^\infty \sum_{t=1}^\infty (a_j^* + c_t)(a_t^* + c_t)\rho^{|j-t|}]\sigma_{q*}^2 \right\}, \quad (14.25a)$$

$$V(e) = \sigma_\psi^2 + \min_{\{a_j\}} \left\{ \sum_{j=1}^\infty a_j^2 \sigma_\psi^2 + \left[1 - 2 \sum_{j=1}^\infty a_j \rho^j + \sum_{j=1}^\infty \sum_{t=1}^\infty a_j a_t \rho^{|j-t|} \right] \sigma_q^2 \right\}.$$

$$(14.25b)$$

If σ_{q*}^2 and σ_q^2 are equal, the minimum on the right-hand side of (14.25a) is no larger than the minimum on the right-hand side of (14.25b). That is,

$$V^*(e, \sigma_{q*}^2) \le V(e, \sigma_q^2) \equiv V(e). \quad (14.26)$$

The reason is that the value of the minimum in (14.25b) can always be attained in (14.25a) by setting the minimizers in the last equation at the values $a_j^* = a_j, j = 1, 2, \ldots$, and $c_j = 0, j \ge 0$. But in fact

$$\sigma_{q*}^2 \equiv [B^*(\sigma_\psi^2, \sigma_\gamma^2)]^2 \sigma_p^2 < [B(\sigma_\psi^2)]^2 \sigma_p^2 \equiv \sigma_q^2 \quad (14.27)$$

because, by proposition 14.1, $B^*(\cdot) < B(\cdot)$. By the envelope theorem the total effect of a change in σ_{q*}^2 on $V^*(e)$ is equal to the direct effect of σ_{q*}^2 on $V^*(e)$ evaluated at the minimizing values of $\{a_j^*, c_j\}$. This partial derivative is given in turn by the coefficient of σ_{q*}^2 in (14.25a) evaluated at the minimum. For any σ_{q*}^2 and for $\sigma_{q*}^2 = \sigma_q^2$ in particular, this coefficient is positive provided $\rho < 1$.[11] It follows from this observation and (14.27) that

$$V^*(e) \equiv V^*(e, \sigma_{q*}^2) < V^*(e, \sigma_q^2). \quad (14.28)$$

This, together with (14.26), implies that

$$V^*(e) < V(e). \quad (14.29)$$

which leads to the following proposition:

PROPOSITION 14.5.   Monetary uncertainty is lower in the presence of monetary targets containing some information ($\sigma_\gamma^2 < \infty$) than in their absence.

Friedman (1960) proposes a rule requiring a constant growth of money. In our model policymakers cannot control money growth without error. A rule for constant, preannounced money growth sets a constant value of $m_i^p = m_i^a$ but does not make m_i constant because of the control error. The variance of the one-period-ahead forecast error is, in this case, due entirely to imperfect control of the money supply and is given by σ_ψ^2. It follows from this observation in conjunction with (14.22) and (14.29) that

$$\sigma_\psi^2 < V^*(e) < V(e). \tag{14.30}$$

Equation (14.30) is the main result of this section. It states that for an exogenously given variance of the monetary control error, monetary targets reduce uncertainty and that uncertainty can be further reduced if policymakers follow a Friedman-type rule. This result suggests that as long as σ_γ^2 is not infinite, the requirement to preannounce targets is not meaningless. When policymakers behave in a discretionary manner, mandatory announcements of targets reduce uncertainty for the public. Abandoning discretion by adopting Friedman's rule further reduces uncertainty.

In the absence of announcements the level of monetary uncertainty imposed on the public rises with policymakers' time preference.[12] Equations (14.25) also imply that the higher the variance of the monetary control error σ_ψ^2, the higher the level of monetary uncertainty imposed on the public both in the presence and in the absence of preannouncements. The level of uncertainty in the presence of announcements is also larger, the larger the noisiness of those announcements as measured by σ_γ^2. Both results are direct consequences of the envelope theorem and of the fact that the coefficients of σ_ψ^2 and of σ_γ^2 in equations (14.25a) and (14.25b) are positive.

We close the discussion of uncertainty by relating the reduction of uncertainty achieved by Friedman's rule to the credibility problem. The reduced level of uncertainty achieved by a rule requiring a constant planned rate of money growth can be achieved under discretion and announcements if the noise component of those announcements has zero variance (i.e., if $\sigma_\gamma^2 = 0$). We have shown above that in this case (14.7) implies that $E[m_i | i_i^*] = m_i^a$. From (14.2), $m_i^a = m_i^p$. The forecast error is $m_i - E[m_i | I_i^*] = \psi_i$ with variance σ_ψ^2. Hence the level of uncertainty can be reduced to that of Friedman's rule even if planned money growth is not required to be constant provided announcements have perfect credibility. But when $\sigma_\gamma^2 = 0$, the public gets advance perfect information about any changes in the plans of policymakers, and their information advantage disappears. There is no benefit to policymakers from planning any money growth rate other than zero. Perfectly credible announcements induce policymakers to adhere to a Friedman-type rule even when they have the discretion not to do so.

The variability of monetary growth under the three monetary arrangements has the same ordering as uncertainty. Friedman's monetary rule generates the lowest variability; discretionary policy without announcements generates the most. By comparing (10.18) with (14.12b), we obtain

$$V(m_i) = \sigma_\psi^2 + [B(\sigma_\psi^2)]^2 \sigma_p^2, \tag{14.31a}$$

$$V^*(m_i) = \sigma_\psi^2 + [B^*(\sigma_\psi^2, \sigma_\gamma^2)]^2 \sigma_p^2. \tag{14.31b}$$

Under Friedman's rule m_i^p is constant so the variance of monetary growth with such a rule is σ_ψ^2. σ_ψ^2 is lower than the variances in (14.31). Further, for a given variance of the control error, announcements reduce the variance of monetary growth. This is a direct consequence of (14.31) in conjunction with the fact, implied by proposition 14.1, that $B^*(\sigma_\psi^2, \sigma_\gamma^2) < B(\sigma_\psi^2)$.

14.7 Concluding Remarks and Applications

This chapter contains both normative and positive conclusions. Perhaps the main normative conclusion is that monetary targets even if imperfect reduce the public's uncertainty. At the positive level the main conclusion is that even when policy is discretionary and disclosure imperfect, the existence of such disclosure reduces the degree of activism and, for a large range of parameters, both the mean and the variance of monetary growth.

The policy process at the Bundesbank conforms with this prediction. Since the mid-1970s the Bundesbank has published monetary targets and has taken them very seriously. The discussion of this chapter implies that this institutional adherence to precision in announcements exerted a moderating influence on monetary activism, monetary variability, and most likely the average level of inflation. The reader should not conclude that monetary activism and inflation were low in West Germany only because of precise advance disclosure of policy. But monetary targets reinforced and strengthened those tendencies. It is interesting to note that the United States in which less precise announcements have been made, also from the mid-1970s, has experienced a higher and more variable rate of monetary expansion than West Germany. In addition monetary policy in the United States has been relatively more activist.

The average and marginal credibility of monetary announcements made by the monetary authorities of members of the European Monetary System have recently been estimated by Weber (1991).[13] The main result of this study is that the EMS has functioned as a bipolar system in which the announcements of some central banks, such as the Bundesbank, enjoyed a high level of credibility, while those of other banks, such as the Banque de France, did not. A related study by Hutchison and Judd (1991) compares the precision of internal Federal Reserve money projections with publicly announced Bank of Japan projections. Their main finding is that the precision of the internal Federal Reserve forecasts has been higher than that of the public forecasts provided by the Bank of Japan.

Advance disclosure of monetary plans usually takes the form of monetary targets or statements of intention. But the discussion in this chapter may be viewed more generally as applying to any kind of signal issued by the central bank about its future monetary policy besides past money growth. With this wider interpretation in mind, the chapter implies that the lower the precision of monetary control, the more attention will be paid to other signals of planned monetary growth such as public statements, rumors, and personalities. In such circumstances public appearances by high-ranking central bank officials receive wide press coverage. With very precise monetary control, on the other hand, past money growth is a good indicator for future plans and the pronouncements of central bank officials are given relatively less attention.

This wider interpretation of policy disclosure is particularly relevant for the 1989 overhaul of the law that governs the activity of the Reserve Bank of New Zealand. The new law specifies price stability as a major objective of the bank and requires the establishment of inflation objectives. Those objectives are to be set out in a published policy target agreement between the governor of the bank and the minister of finance. The bank is required to publish its intentions with regard to monetary policy at regular six-month intervals and any move away from the published targets is subject to public scrutiny and debate. Finally the governor of the bank is personally accountable for the outcome of monetary policy (Dawe 1990, p. 32).

Clearly the new law creates an institutional environment in which the precision of signals about future policy plans is substantially higher than under the old 1964 Reserve Bank Act. The discussion in this chapter implies that this increase in precision will, ceteris paribus, exert a moderating influence on monetary activism and on monetary variability in New Zealand. It is also likely to exert, as of itself, a moderating influence on the average rate of inflation in addition to the moderating influences of other components of the new law. The behavior of inflation in New Zealand during 1990 and 1991 is consistent with those implications (the new law became effective in 1989).

This chapter has focused on situations in which the monetary authority must make announcements because they are mandated by law or by some other third party. Situations in which the monetary authority is free to decide on whether to make or not to make an announcement are discussed in the first part of chapter 16.

Appendix A: Derivation of Optimal Predictor in Equations (14.6)

Define the stochastic variables $\varepsilon_t \equiv \psi_t/B$ and $\eta_t \equiv \gamma_t/B$. Substituting those relations into equations (14.4a) and (14.4b), we obtain

$$y_t = B(p_t + \varepsilon_t) \equiv By_t^1; \quad z_t = B(p_t + \eta_t) \equiv Bz_t^1. \tag{14A.1}$$

Since the public knows the parameter B, an observation on the pair (y_t, z_t) is equivalent to an observation on the pair (y_t^1, z_t^1). Hence the expected value of p_t conditioned on past values of y and z is equal to this expected value conditioned on past values of y^1 and z^1. In addition from the current announcement the public possesses an observation on z_t^1. We turn next to the calculation of this expected value.

Since p_t, y_t^1, and z_t^1 are all normally distributed, this expected value is a linear function with fixed coefficients of the available observations on y^1 and z^1. That is,

$$E[p_t | I_t^1] = \sum_{i=1}^{\infty} a_i y_{t-1}^1 + \sum_{i=0}^{\infty} c_i z_{t-i}^1, \tag{14A.2}$$

where

$$I_t^1 \equiv \{y_{t-1}^1, y_{t-2}^1, \ldots, z_t^1, z_{t-1}^1, z_{t-2}^1, \ldots\}.$$

Since the conditional expected value in (14A.2) is also the point estimate of p_t which minimizes the mean square error around this estimate, it follows that $\{a_i\}_{i=1}^{\infty}$, $\{c_i\}_{i=0}^{\infty}$ are to be chosen so as to minimize

$$Q \equiv E\left[p_t - \sum_{i=1}^{\infty} a_i y_{t-i}^1 - \sum_{i=0}^{\infty} c_i z_{t-1}^1\right]^2.$$

Using (14A.1) in this expression, using the fact that ε, η, and v are mutually independent, and passing the expectation operator through, we can rewrite Q as

$$Q = \{(1 - c_0)^2 + [(1 - c_0)\rho - (a_1 + c_1)]^2 + [(1 - c_0)\rho^2 - \rho(a_1 + c_1) \\ - (a_2 + c_2)]^2 + \cdots + [(1 - c_0)\rho^i - \rho^{i-1}(a_1 + c_1) - \cdots \\ - (a_i + c_i)]^2 + \ldots\}\sigma_v^2 + \sum_{i=1}^{\infty} a_i^2 \sigma_\varepsilon^2 + \sum_{i=0}^{\infty} c_i^2 \sigma_\eta^2, \tag{14A.3}$$

where $\sigma_\varepsilon^2 = \sigma_\psi^2/B^2$ and $\sigma_\eta^2 = \sigma_\gamma^2/B^2$.

The necessary first-order conditions for a minimum of Q are

$$\frac{\partial Q}{\partial c_0} = -2\{1 - c_0 + \rho[(1 - c_0)\rho - (a_1 + c_1)] + \cdots + \rho^i[(1 - c_0)\rho^i \\ - \rho^{i-1}(a_1 + c_1) - \cdots - (a_i + c_i)] + \cdots\}\sigma_v^2 + 2c_0\sigma_\eta^2 = 0, \tag{14A.4a}$$

$$\frac{\partial Q}{\partial c_i} = -2\{[(1 - c_0)\rho^i - \rho^{i-1}(a_1 + c_1) - \cdots - (a_i + c_i)] + \rho[(1 - c_0)\rho^{i+1} \\ - \rho^i(a_1 + c_1) - \cdots - (a_{i+1} + c_{i+1})] + \cdots\}\sigma_v^2 + 2c_i\sigma_\eta^2 = 0,$$
$$i \geq 1, \tag{14A.4b}$$

$$\frac{\partial Q}{\partial a_i} = -2\{[(1 - c_0)\rho^i - \rho^{i-1}(a_1 + c_1) - \cdots - (a_i + c_i)] + \rho[(1 - c_0) \\ - \rho^{i+1} - \rho^i(a_1 + c_1) - \cdots - (a_{i+1} + c_{i+1})] + \cdots\}\sigma_v^2 + 2a_i\sigma_\varepsilon^2 = 0,$$
$$i \geq 1. \tag{14A.4c}$$

Leading (14A.4b) by one period, multiplying by ρ, and subtracting (14A.4b) from the resulting expression, we obtain

$$[(1 - c_0)\rho^i - \rho^{i-1}(a_1 + c_1) - \cdots - (a_i + c_i)]\sigma_v^2 + (\rho c_{i+1} - c_i)\sigma_\eta^2 = 0,$$
$$i \geq 1. \tag{14A.5}$$

Then multiplying (14A.5) by ρ, subtracting the resulting expression from (14A.5) led by one period, and rearranging, we obtain

$$\rho\sigma_\eta^2 c_{i+2} - [\sigma_v^2 + (1 + \rho^2)\sigma_\eta^2]c_{i+1} - \sigma_v^2 a_{i+1} + \rho\sigma_\eta^2 c_i = 0, \qquad i \geq 1. \tag{14A.6}$$

We rearrange (14A.4b) and (14A.4c), equate their common terms, and rearrange again to get

$$a_i = \frac{\sigma_\eta^2}{\sigma_\varepsilon^2} c_i, \qquad i \geq 1. \tag{14A.7}$$

Now we substitute (14A.7) into (14A.6) and divide the resulting expression by $\rho \sigma_\eta^2$. The result is

$$c_{i+2} - \left\{ \frac{1+r}{\rho} + \rho \right\} c_{i+1} + c_i = 0, \qquad i \geq 1, \tag{14A.8}$$

where

$$r \equiv \frac{\sigma_v^2}{\sigma_\varepsilon^2} \left(1 + \frac{\sigma_\varepsilon^2}{\sigma_\eta^2} \right) = B^2 \frac{\sigma_v^2}{\sigma_\psi^2} \left(1 + \frac{\sigma_\psi^2}{\sigma_\eta^2} \right). \tag{14A.9}$$

Equation (14A.8) is a second-order homogeneous difference equation whose general solution is

$$c_i = K\delta^i, \qquad i \geq 1, \tag{14A.10}$$

where K is a constant to be determined by initial conditions and δ is the root of the quadratic

$$u^2 - \left(\frac{1+r}{\rho} + \rho \right) u + 1 = 0. \tag{14A.11}$$

The roots of this equation are given by

$$u_{1,2} = \frac{1}{2} \left(\frac{1+r}{\rho} + \rho \right) \pm \sqrt{ \left\{ \frac{1}{2} \left(\frac{1+r}{\rho} + \rho \right) \right\}^2 - 1 }. \tag{14A.12}$$

The positive root in (14A.12) is larger than one, and the negative root is bounded between zero and one. Thus c_i does not diverge only if the smaller root is substituted for δ in (14A.10). Since c_i has to yield a minimum for Q, it cannot diverge. Hence

$$\delta = \frac{1}{2} \left(\frac{1+r}{\rho} + \rho \right) - \sqrt{ \left\{ \frac{1}{2} \left(\frac{1+r}{\rho} + \rho \right) \right\}^2 - 1 }. \tag{14A.13}$$

Substituting (14A.10) into (14A.7), we obtain

$$a_i = K \frac{\sigma_\eta^2}{\sigma_\varepsilon^2} \delta^i, \qquad i \geq 1. \tag{14A.14}$$

K is determined from the initial conditions. Substituting (14A.10) and (14A.14) into (14A.5) for the case $i = 1$ and rearranging, we get

$$\rho \sigma_v^2 (1 - c_0) - \sigma_\eta^2 (1 + r) K \delta + \rho \sigma_\eta^2 K \delta^2 = 0. \tag{14A.15}$$

Then specializing (14A.4b) to the case $i = 1$, multiplying by ρ, subtracting (14A.4a) from the resulting expression, and rearranging, we get

$$c_0 = \frac{\sigma_v^2}{\sigma_v^2 + \sigma_\eta^2} + \frac{\sigma_\eta^2}{\sigma_v^2 + \sigma_\eta^2} \rho c_1. \tag{14A.16}$$

We substitute (14A.16) into (14A.15), use (14A.10), and rearrange to get

$$K = \frac{\sigma_v^2}{\sigma_v^2 + \sigma_\eta^2 (1 - \rho \delta)}. \tag{14A.17}$$

Multiplying numerator and denominator of (14A.17) by $(\sigma_\varepsilon^2 + \sigma_\eta^2)/\sigma_\eta^2 \sigma_\varepsilon^2$ and noting the definition of r in (14A.9), we obtain

$$K = \frac{r}{r + 1 - \rho \delta + (\sigma_\eta^2/\sigma_\varepsilon^2)(1 - \rho \delta)}. \tag{14A.17a}$$

Since δ is a root of (14A.11), it satisfies this equation:

$$\delta^2 - \left(\frac{1 + r}{\rho} + \rho \right) \delta + 1 = 0. \tag{14A.18}$$

Solving for r from (14A.18), substituting into (14A.17a), and rearranging, we have

$$K = \frac{\sigma_\varepsilon^2 (\rho - \delta)}{\rho \sigma_\varepsilon^2 + \delta \sigma_\eta^2}. \tag{14A.17b}$$

Substituting K from (14A.17b) into (14A.10) and (14A.14), we get

$$c_i = \frac{(\rho - \delta)(\sigma_\varepsilon^2 + \sigma_\eta^2)}{\rho \sigma_\varepsilon^2 + \delta \sigma_\eta^2} (1 - \theta) \delta^i, \quad a_i = \frac{(\rho - \delta)(\sigma_\varepsilon^2 + \sigma_\eta^2)}{\rho \sigma_\varepsilon^2 + \delta \sigma_\eta^2} \theta \delta^i, \quad i \geq 1, \tag{14A.19}$$

where

$$\theta \equiv \frac{\sigma_\eta^2}{\sigma_\varepsilon^2 + \sigma_\eta^2} = \frac{\sigma_\gamma^2}{\sigma_\psi^2 + \sigma_\gamma^2}.$$

Substituting (14A.17) into (14A.10) specializing to the case $i = 1$, substituting the resulting expression into (14A.16), and rearranging, we obtain

$$c_0 = \frac{\sigma_v^2}{\sigma_v^2 + (1 - \rho\delta)\sigma_\eta^2} = \frac{(\rho - \delta)(\sigma_\varepsilon^2 + \sigma_\eta^2)}{\rho\sigma_\varepsilon^2 + \delta\sigma_\eta^2}(1 - \theta). \tag{14A.20}$$

The second equality in (14A.20) follows by noting that K is given by both (14A.17) and (14A.17b).

The optimal predictor is obtained by inserting equations (14A.19) and (14A.20) into (14A.1) and is given by

$$E[p_t | I_t] \equiv \frac{(\rho - \delta)(\sigma_\varepsilon^2 + \sigma_\eta^2)}{\rho\sigma_\varepsilon^2 + \delta\sigma_\eta^2} \left\{ \sum_{j=1}^{\infty} \delta^j(\theta y_{t-j}^1 + (1 - \theta)z_{t-j}^1) + (1 - \theta)z_t^1 \right\}. \tag{14A.21}$$

Equation (14.6) in the text follows by using (14A.1) and the identities $\sigma_\varepsilon^2 = \sigma_\psi^2/B^2$, $\sigma_\eta^2 = \sigma_\gamma^2/B^2$ in (14A.21).

Appendix B: Derivation of Equation (14.10)

Substituting (9.3a) and (10.10) into (14.9) and rearranging, we obtain

$$m_i^p = \frac{\alpha\delta}{(\rho - \delta)(1 - \theta) + \delta}[A + p_i - (\rho - \delta)\{\rho\beta + (\rho\beta)^2\delta$$

$$+ (\rho\beta)^3\delta^2 + \cdots\}(A + p_i) - (\rho - \delta)\{(\beta + \beta^2\delta + \beta^3\delta^2 + \cdots)$$

$$- (\rho\beta + (\rho\beta)^2\delta + (\rho\beta)^3\delta^2 + \cdots)\}A]. \tag{14A.22}$$

Noting that

$$(\rho - \delta)(1 - \theta) + \delta = \frac{\delta\sigma_\eta^2 + \rho\sigma_\varepsilon^2}{\sigma_\eta^2 + \sigma_\varepsilon^2},$$

summing the geometric progressions in (14A.22), and collecting terms, we obtain

$$m_i^p = \frac{\alpha\delta(\sigma_\eta^2 + \sigma_\varepsilon^2)}{\sigma_\eta^2\delta + \sigma_\varepsilon^2\rho}\left[\left(1 - \frac{(\rho - \delta)\beta}{1 - \beta\delta}\right)A + \left(1 - \frac{(\rho - \delta)\rho\beta}{1 - \rho\beta\delta}\right)p_i\right]. \tag{14A.23}$$

Equation (14A.23) can be rewritten

$$m_i^p = \frac{\alpha\delta(1 - \rho\beta)(\sigma_\eta^2 + \sigma_\varepsilon^2)}{(1 - \delta\beta)(\delta\sigma_\eta^2 + \rho\sigma_\varepsilon^2)}A + \frac{\alpha\delta(1 - \beta\rho^2)(\sigma_\eta^2 + \sigma_\varepsilon^2)}{(1 - \rho\beta\delta)(\delta\sigma_\eta^2 + \rho\sigma_\varepsilon^2)}p_i. \tag{14A.24}$$

Equation (14.10) in the text follows by dividing both numerators and denominators in (14A.24) by σ_η^2 and using the identities in (14A.1).

Appendix C: Proof That δ Is a Decreasing Function of r

Let $b \equiv \rho + (1 + r)/\rho$. It follows from (14.6b) that

$$\delta = \frac{b}{2} - \sqrt{\frac{b^2}{4} - 1}. \tag{14A.25}$$

Hence

$$\frac{\partial \delta}{\partial b} = \frac{1}{2} \sqrt{\frac{b^2}{4} - 1} \left(\sqrt{\frac{b^2}{4} - 1} - b \right),$$

which is always negative since $(3/4)b^2 + 1 > 0$. Hence δ is decreasing in b. Since b is increasing in r, δ is a decreasing function of r. $\square$

Appendix D: Proof That, Given B, $G(\cdot)$ in Equation (14.11b) Is Increasing in σ_γ^2

Partially differentiating $G(\cdot)$ in (14.11b) with respect to σ_γ^2, taking into consideration the dependence of δ on σ_γ^2 and rearranging, we obtain

$$\frac{\partial G(\cdot)}{\partial \sigma_\gamma^2} = \frac{(1 - \beta\rho^2)[\delta(1 - \beta\rho\delta)(\rho - \delta)\sigma_\psi^2 - M(\partial\delta/\partial r)]}{(1 - \beta\rho\delta)^2(\delta + \rho\sigma_\psi^2/\sigma_\gamma^2)\sigma_\gamma^4}, \tag{14A.26}$$

where

$$M \equiv B^2\sigma_v^2 \left(1 + \frac{\sigma_\psi^2}{\sigma_\gamma^2}\right) \left(\beta\delta^2 + \rho\frac{\sigma_\psi^2}{\sigma_\gamma^2}\right). \tag{14A.27}$$

M is obviously positive. Since β, ρ, and δ are all bounded between zero and one and ρ is strictly less than one, $1 - \beta\rho^2$ and $1 - \beta\rho\delta$ are strictly positive. $\rho - \delta$ is always nonnegative. This follows by combining the fact (proved in note 4 of chapter 10) that $\rho - \lambda$ is nonnegative with the fact that δ has the same functional form in r as the functional form of λ from chapter 10 in r. Finally, from appendix C, $\partial\delta/\partial r < 0$. It follows that

$$\frac{\partial G(\cdot)}{\partial \sigma_\gamma^2} > 0. \tag{14A.28}$$

$\square$

Appendix E: Proof of Proposition 14.2

Totally differentiating B_0 from equation (14.11a) with respect to σ_γ^2 and rearranging, we obtain

$$\frac{dB_0}{d\sigma_\gamma^2}$$

$$= \frac{(1 - \beta\rho)\{\delta(1 - \beta\delta)(\rho - \delta)(\sigma_\psi^2/\sigma_\gamma^4) + [1 + (\sigma_\psi^2/\sigma_\gamma^2)][\delta^2\beta + \rho\sigma_\psi^2/\sigma_\gamma^2](d\delta/d\sigma_\gamma^2)\}}{(1 - \beta\delta)^2(\delta + \rho\sigma_\psi^2/\sigma_\gamma^2)^2}.$$

(14A.29)

Since $\rho - \delta \geq 0$, $1 - \beta\rho > 0$, and $1 - \beta\delta > 0$, a sufficient condition for $dB_0/d\sigma_\gamma^2 > 0$ is $d\delta/d\sigma_\gamma^2 > 0$. We therefore look for a sufficient condition for the last inequality.

Given σ_γ^2, δ, and B are determined simultaneously from

$$\delta = F[\sigma_\gamma^2, B], \tag{14A.30a}$$

$$B = G[\sigma_\gamma^2, \delta], \tag{14A.30b}$$

where the explicit form of $F[\cdot]$ is given by equations (14.6b) and (14.6c) and the explicit form of $G[\cdot]$ is given by equation (14.11b). Totally differentiating equations (14A.30) with respect to σ_γ^2 and rearranging, we obtain

$$\frac{d\delta}{d\sigma_\gamma^2} = \frac{F_\gamma + F_B G_\gamma}{1 - F_B G_\delta}. \tag{14A.31}$$

Here F_γ and F_B are the partial derivatives of F with respect to σ_γ^2 and B and G_γ and G_δ are the partial derivatives of G with respect to σ_γ^2 and δ.

From (14.6b) and (14.6c) and the result in appendix C, δ is a decreasing function of B. Hence $F_B < 0$. It can be shown that

$$G_\delta = \frac{(1 - \beta\rho^2)[1 + (\sigma_\psi^2/\sigma_\gamma^2)]\{\rho(1 - \beta\delta)(\sigma_\psi^2/\sigma_\gamma^2) + \beta\delta[\delta + \rho(\sigma_\psi^2/\sigma_\gamma^2)]\}}{(1 - \beta\rho\delta)^2(\delta + \rho\sigma_\psi^2/\sigma_\gamma^2)^2} > 0.$$

(14A.32)

Hence the denominator of (14A.31) is positive so that the sign of $d\delta/d\sigma_\gamma^2$ is determined by the sign of the numerator of (14A.31). From equations (14.6) and (14.11b), we get

$$F_\gamma + F_B G_\gamma = \frac{|\partial\delta/\partial r|\, B^2\sigma_v^2/\sigma_\gamma^4}{\delta + \rho\sigma_\psi^2/\sigma_\gamma^2}\left\{3\delta + \rho\left[\frac{\sigma_\psi^2}{\sigma_\gamma^2} - 2\right]\right\}. \tag{14A.33}$$

Hence a sufficient condition for $d\delta/d\sigma_\gamma^2 > 0$, and therefore for $dB_0/d\sigma_\gamma^2 > 0$, is $\sigma_\psi^2 > 2\sigma_\gamma^2$. It is obviously not necessary since $d\delta/d\sigma_\gamma^2$ may be positive even when this condition is violated. Hence $\sigma_\psi^2 > 2\sigma_\gamma^2$ is overly strong for $d\delta/d\sigma_\gamma^2 > 0$. It is even stronger as a sufficient condition for the positivity of $dB/d\sigma_\gamma^2$ since, from (14A.29), this last term may be positive even when $d\delta/d\sigma_\gamma^2$ is negative. □

Appendix F: Proof That (at the Extremum) the Coefficients of σ_{q*}^2 and σ_q^2 in Equations (14.25) Are Positive

The difference between the minimization problems in (14.21a), and in (14.22a) is only that in the latter equation the constant B^* has been absorbed into the minimization problem. Hence the minimizing values for the problem in (14.22a) are the same as those for the problem in (14.21a) for which the minimizing values of $\{a_j^*\}$ and $\{c_j\}$ have been derived in appendix A and are given by

$$a_j^* = \frac{(\rho - \delta)\theta}{\rho(1 - \theta) + \delta\theta} \delta^j, \quad j = 1, 2, \ldots,$$

$$c_j = \frac{(\rho - \delta)(1 - \theta)}{\rho(1 - \theta) + \delta\theta} \delta^j, \quad j = 0, 1, \ldots.$$

(14A.34)

(Those values of a^* are called a in appendix A. The use of the asterisk is consistent with the notation in section 14.6.)

Substituting (14A.34) into the coefficient of σ_{q*}^2 in (14.25a) and using repeatedly the formula for the summation of infinite geometric progressions, we obtain after a considerable amount of algebra the following expression for the effect of σ_{q*}^2 on $V^*(e)$:

$$\frac{\partial V^*(e)}{\partial \sigma_{q*}^2} = \frac{\delta^2(1 - \rho^2)}{[\rho(1 - \theta) + \delta\theta]^2(1 - \delta^2)}.$$

This expression is unambiguously positive for any $\rho < 1$. Since the proof holds for any positive value of σ_{q*}^2, including in particular all the range between σ_{q*}^2 and σ_q^2, it follows that

$$\frac{\partial V^*(e)}{\partial \sigma_{q*}^2} > 0$$

in all the range $[\sigma_{q*}^2, \sigma_q^2]$. The proof that $\partial V(e)/\partial \sigma_q^2 > 0$ for all $\rho < 1$ proceeds along analogous lines. □

15 Why Does Inflation Persist?—Theories of Monetary Accommodation and of Inflation Cyclicality under Discretion

15.1 Introduction

Inflation is usually a fairly persistent process. This observation seems to fit low- as well as medium- and high-inflation countries. The ranges within which it persists vary across countries as well as across time periods within a given country. But a substantial amount of persistence characterizes most inflations.

Since, in the absence of monetary expansion, inflation cannot persist for sustained periods of time, a full explanation of inflation must incorporate the response of policy to developments in the economy. The type of models analyzed in chapters 9 and 10 take this response into consideration. They imply that (except for a white noise control error) inflation inherits the time series properties and therefore the persistence of shocks to the relative preference of the policymaker for high employment and price stability (e.g., see equation 9.22). But this policy response does not, as of itself, alter the persistence of inflation. This feature of the solution for inflation in chapters 9 and 10 is due to the fact that the marginal political benefit of an increase in employment is independent of the deviation between desired and actual employment or, stated equivalently, to the linearity of the employment term in the policymakers' objective function (see equation 9.1). This linearity was useful because it made it possible to focus on the reputational effects of learning on policy with a minimal amount of complications and to generalize the analysis to an extended information advantage (chapter 10) and to private information about velocity shocks (chapter 13).

However, the linear specification implies that the policy response does not depend on the public's expectations. It therefore leaves little room for partial or full accommodation of expectations by policymakers. By contrast when the marginal political benefits of additional employment rise with the difference between desired and actual employment policy is responsive to expectations under discretion. The quadratic objective function discussed in section 3.2 of chapter 3 has this characteristic. The choice of monetary inflation depends on the public's prior expectation of the policy action (equation 3.4 and figure 3.1). On the other hand, there is no learning and therefore no real dynamics in chapter 3. But the form taken by the policymakers' response function suggests that in the presence of learning past events that get embodied in current expectations will affect current policy. In particular past transitory disturbances that affect current expectations and nominal contracts will have an effect on current inflation through the accommodation of current expectations by policy. This mechanism introduces a novel, policy-induced element of persistence into the inflationary process.

A large part of this chapter is devoted to a discussion of the persistence-creating properties of policy in the presence of learning when, due to decreasing marginal political benefits of employment, the policy process partially accommodates current inflationary expectations. Because of this nonlinearity policymakers behave asymmetrically. They rely more heavily on monetary policy to offset real reductions in unemployment when unemployment is high than when unemployment is low. In contrast to previous chapters which feature private information about policymakers' objectives, this one assumes that these objectives are common knowledge. But, due to their more immediate access to statistics and their professional staff, policymakers (usually but not always the central bank) have a temporary information advantage about shocks to natural employment and their persistence.[1] This enables policymakers to conduct a possibly limited amount of countercyclical monetary policy. An advantage of this specification is that the policymakers' trade-offs between inflation and employment change, not because of changes in their "tastes" but because of changes in the constraints that confront them. Such a formulation is more directly conducive to empirical testing since changes in constraints are more likely to be measurable. As a by-product it anchors the stochastic properties of monetary expansion on the stochastic properties of natural employment. This specification implies that the stochastic properties, and therefore the persistence of inflation, are shaped by the stochastic properties of natural employment and by the structure of policymakers' information advantage.

The assumption that the central bank has better information than the private sector about natural employment and its persistence is reasonable for many developing countries. But it probably is less appropriate for developed economies such as the United States and Britain. For such economies the framework in the following four sections can be reinterpreted in terms of private information about the shifting objectives of policy in the presence of imperfect inflation control (see section 15.7 for details). Such a framework is similar to that of chapter 13. But since objectives now depend nonlinearly on the employment term, unintended upward inflationary bursts translate into a persistently higher inflationary process. The reason is that random upward shocks to inflation raise inflationary expectations which are partially accommodated by policy because of the nonlinearity of objectives in employment. But except for the concluding section the discussion in the sections with private information (15.2–15.5) is conducted in terms of private information about the persistence of employment.

The basic model is presented and solved in section 15.2. Section 15.3 uses the model to investigate the issue of persistence. It is shown first, as a benchmark, that when information about employment and its persistence is symmetric, the rate of inflation inherits the stochastic properties and the persistence of the natural level of employment. The reason essentially is that policymakers are willing to tolerate higher inflation in order to try to stimulate employment when the natural level of employment is lower. Since the public possesses the same information as the policymakers, employment remains at its natural level and the inflationary bias inherits the stochastic properties of employment. In particular transitory blips to the natural level affect inflation only in the period in which they occur. But in the presence of an information advantage current inflation also reacts to past transitory blips to the natural level of employment making the rate of inflation more persistent.

Kydland and Prescott (1990) have recently reported that the price level in the post–World War II U.S. economy behaves countercyclically. One could be led to conclude from this finding that employment-motivated monetary temptations are unimportant. Section 15.4 shows that this is not necessarily the case. The basic idea is that in the presence of partial policy offsets of fluctuations in natural employment, we may observe a negative correlation between employment and inflation precisely because of the existence of such temptations.[2] Section 15.5 briefly discusses some of the determinants of inflation, the speed of learning, and activism in the presence of rising marginal costs of unemployment.

Persistent inflation particularly at moderate rates may arise even in the absence of private information because of the interaction of policy with overlapping contracts or backward-looking indexation. Section 15.6 provides precise examples of those mechanisms. Concluding reflections follow.

15.2 A Minimal Information Advantage about Natural Employment

Central banks normally obtain information about the state of the economy more quickly than most of the public. This is due to the fact that policymakers within the government sector may have access to pertinent statistics before their release. Even when the release time is identical, it is likely that the central bank with its specialized staff is able to absorb and interpret aggregate statistical releases and more detailed information quicker than most of the general public. This information advantage, even if relatively short, enables policymakers to conduct meaningful countercyclical policy in the face of real shocks to the level of employment. In particular, let the level of employment in the absence of inflationary surprises be

$$N_{ni} = \overline{N}_n - p_i - \delta_i. \tag{15.1}$$

Following Milton Friedman, we refer to it as the "natural level of employment." Here i is the period index, and p_i and δ_i are persistent and transitory stochastic variables, respective, and $\overline{N}_n$ is a positive constant. p_i is a first-order Markoff process with a normally distributed innovation v_i, and δ_i is a normally distributed white noise process with variance σ_δ^2. The precise stochastic structure of p_i is given in equation (15.2):

$$p_i = \rho p_{i-1} + v_i, \quad v_i \sim N(0, \sigma_v^2). \tag{15.2}$$

This specification is designed to capture the notion that due to various nonmonetary factors, the natural level of employment undergoes stochastic fluctuations. One can think of this specification as a stylized way to capture the fluctuations in employment that are associated with the real business cycle. Those fluctuations normally contain both persistent and transitory components.[3]

The public discovers actual employment, and the decomposition of its natural part into persistent and transitory components, with a lag of two periods. By contrast policymakers know the *current* state of the natural level of employment as well as its current decomposition into persistent and transitory components.[4] They therefore possess more precise forecasts of current and future natural levels of employment than the public and can use this information advantage to stabilize real fluctuations in employment.

As in chapters 3, 9, and 13 the effect of monetary surprises on employment is summarized by a short-run Phillips curve in which the deviation of actual employment from its natural level is positively related to unexpected inflation. It is given by equation (15.3):

$$N_i - N_{ni} = \alpha(\pi_i - \pi_i^e). \tag{15.3}$$

Here N_i is the actual level of employment, and π_i and π_i^e are actual and expected inflation, respectively. For simplicity we abstract from divergences between planned and actual inflation of the type discussed in chapters 9, 10, and 13 by assuming that the policymaker has perfect control over π_i.

The objective of the central bank is, as in previous chapters, to minimize the present discounted value of the combined costs of low employment and inflation. More precisely the central bank's objective in period 0 is to minimize

$$E_{G0} \sum_{i=0}^{\infty} \beta^i \left[\frac{A}{2}(N^* - N_i)^2 + \frac{\pi_i^2}{2} \right], \qquad 0 \le \beta \le 1, \tag{15.4}$$

where N^* is the preferred level of employment, A is the constant relative importance assigned to employment and price stability objectives, β is the discount factor, and E_{G0} is an expected value conditional on the information available to policymakers in period 0. Since A is common knowledge, policymakers do not possess, as in some previous chapters, an information advantage about their own objectives. Instead, they have more precise information than the public about shifts in the natural level of employment.

Using (15.1) and (15.3) in (15.4) and rearranging, the policymakers' optimization problem can be rewritten as

$$\min E_{G0} \sum_{i=0}^{\infty} \beta^i \left\{ \frac{A}{2}[d_i - \alpha(\pi_i - \pi_i^e)]^2 + \frac{\pi_i^2}{2} \right\}, \tag{15.4a}$$

where

$$d_i \equiv N^* - \overline{N}_n + p_i + \delta_i \equiv D + p_i + \delta_i. \tag{15.5}$$

As in previous chapters we assume that the difference D between the level of employment desired by policymakers and the mean natural level of employment is positive. The more basic reasons underlying this assumption are discussed in chapter 3. Furthermore D is assumed to be sufficiently large in comparison to σ_v^2 and σ_δ^2 to make the divergence between desired and actual employment nonnegative with high probability.[5] The precise condition is presented and developed in appendix D to this chapter.

Analogously to chapters 8 through 14, equilibrium is characterized by the following conditions:

1. Given their perceptions of the way expectations are formed policymakers choose the rate of inflation in each period contingent on the state

of the economy so as to minimize the conditional expected value of the combined costs of inflation and of unemployment in equation (15.4a).

2.   Given the public's perception of the policy rule followed by policymakers and the information available to it, the public forms its expectations (and concludes nominal contracts accordingly) so as to minimize the conditional mean forecast error in each period.

3.   The public's perception of the policy rule postulated in condition 2 is identical to the policy rule that emerges as a solution to the problem in condition 1.

4.   Policymakers' perceptions of the way expectations are formed postulated in condition 1 are identical to the expectations formation process that emerges as a solution to condition 2.

The last two conditions require that the public and policymakers have rational expectations about each other's mode of behavior. The first condition requires that given their objectives, policymakers behave optimally, and the second that the public's inflation forecasts are optimal in the mean square sense. Because of the two-way interaction between the policymakers' decision strategy and the process of expectations formation, it is necessary to characterize their solutions simultaneously. To find the solutions, we apply the method of undetermined coefficients.

Examination of the objective function in (15.4a) reveals that the optimal π depends on the values of d and of π^e in the same period. In addition, to the extent that the current choice of π affects future expectations, the currently expected (by policymakers) future values of d, π^e, and π also affect the current choice of π. But since two periods after its realization the public gets a direct observation on the persistent part of the stochastic component of employment p_i, period's i rate of inflation is needed only for forecasting period's $i + 1$ inflation. Inflationary expectations from period $i + 2$, and on, are not influenced by the choice of π_i, since in those periods p_i is already known in any case by the public. It follows that the optimal value of π_i depends only on d_i, π_i^e, and on the expected values as of period i of d_{i+1}, π_{i+1}^e, and π_{i+1}. Since the objective function is quadratic, we postulate that the decision strategy of policymakers is a linear function of those variables. This function is given by equation (15.6) in which K_i, $i = 1, \ldots, 4$, are coefficients to be determined:[6]

$$\pi_i = K_1 d_i + K_2 \pi_i^e + K_3 E_{Gi} d_{i+1} + K_4 E_{Gi}[\pi_{i+1} - \pi_{i+1}^e]. \tag{15.6}$$

Within each period the timing of moves is as follows: First, inflationary expectations for the period are formed and nominal wage contracts for the period concluded accordingly. Next, policymakers observe current employment and its decomposition into persistent and transitory components and choose current inflation, taking the previously set level of expectations (and of nominal contracts) as given. When they form their expectation π_i^e at the beginning of period i individuals already know p_{i-2} and past rates of inflation up to and including π_{i-1}.[7] But they know past employment levels up to and including period $i - 2$. We denote this information set by I_i. It is shown in appendix A to this chapter that the solution postulated in (15.6) implies that[8]

$$\pi_{i+1}^e = \frac{1}{1 - K_2} \{(K_1 + K_3)D + \rho^2(K_1 + \rho K_3)p_{i-1} + \rho\theta[\pi_i - g(i)]\},$$

(15.7)

where $g(i)$ (whose explicit form appears in the appendix) is a combination of variables that do not depend on the choice of π_i and

$$\theta \equiv \frac{(K_1 + \rho K_3)^2 \sigma_v^2}{(K_1 + \rho K_3)^2 \sigma_v^2 + K_1^2 \sigma_\delta^2}.$$

(15.8)

Equation (15.7) is the public's expectation formation process. It implies that any unit increase in π_i increases inflationary expectations in the next period by

$$\frac{\partial \pi_{i+1}^e}{\partial \pi_i} = \frac{\rho\theta}{1 - K_2}.$$

(15.9)

Differentiating equation (15.4a) with respect to π_0, using (15.9) and the fact that $\partial \pi_{i+j}^e/\partial \pi_i = 0$ for $j \geq 2$, we obtain after some algebra

$$\pi_0 = \frac{\alpha A}{1 + \alpha^2 A} d_0 + \frac{\alpha^2 A}{1 + \alpha^2 A} \pi_0^e - \frac{\rho^2 \beta \alpha A}{1 - K_2} \theta[E_{G0}d_1 - \alpha E_{G0}[\pi_1 - \pi_1^e]].$$

(15.10)

Noting that in each period the structure of the policymakers' problem is the same as in period 0, their decision strategy for any period can be written as

$$\pi_i = \frac{\alpha A}{1 + \alpha^2 A} d_i + \frac{\alpha^2 A}{1 + \alpha^2 A} \pi_i^e - \frac{\rho^2 \beta \alpha A}{1 - K_2} \theta[E_{Gi}d_{i+1} - \alpha E_{Gi}[\pi_{i+1} - \pi_{i+1}^e]].$$

(15.10a)

Since the solutions for π_i in equations (15.6) and (15.10a) have to be identical for all possible realizations of the exogenous variable, the coefficients of d_i, π_i^e, $E_{Gi}d_{i+1}$, and of $E_{Gi}[\pi_{i+1} - \pi_{i+1}^e]$ must be identical, respectively, across these two equations. This leads to the following set of equations for K_i, $i = 1, \ldots, 4$:

$$K_1 = \frac{\alpha A}{1 + \alpha^2 A},$$

$$K_2 = \frac{\alpha^2 A}{1 + \alpha^2 A},$$

$$\text{(15.11)}$$

$$K_3 = -\rho^2 \beta \alpha A (1 + \alpha^2 A) \frac{(\alpha A/(1 + \alpha^2 A) + \rho K_3)^2 \sigma_v^2}{(\alpha A/(1 + \alpha^2 A) + \rho K_3)^2 \sigma_v^2 + (\alpha A/(1 + \alpha^2 A))^2 \sigma_\delta^2}$$

$$\equiv G(K_3), \qquad\qquad\qquad\qquad\qquad\qquad\qquad\qquad\text{(15.12)}$$

$$K_4 = -\alpha K_3. \qquad\qquad\qquad\qquad\qquad\qquad\qquad\qquad\text{(15.13)}$$

Equation (15.11) contains explicit solutions for K_1 and K_2, and equations (15.12) and (15.13) give implicit solutions for K_3 and K_4. In view of equations (15.11)–(15.13) and the fact that $E_{Gi}d_{i+1} = D + \rho p_i$, equation (15.10a) can be rewritten as

$$\pi_i = \frac{\alpha A}{1 + \alpha^2 A}(d_i + \alpha \pi_i^e) - |K_3|[D + \rho p_i - \alpha E_{Gi}(\pi_{i+1} - \pi_{i+1}^e)]. \qquad \text{(15.14)}$$

The first term in parentheses on the right-hand side of equation (15.14) is the deviation between the desired and the actual levels of employment in period i when policymakers set π_i at zero. The term in brackets is the value of the same difference for the following period as expected by policymakers in period i. Equation (15.14) implies that an increase in the first term increases the rate of inflation chosen for period i while an increase in the second term reduces it. The intuition is simple. These two terms in (15.14) are proportional, respectively, to the marginal costs of low employment in the current and in the following period as perceived by policymakers in the current period. An increase in π_i reduces the current marginal costs of low employment and increases next period's marginal costs of low employment by raising expectations in that period. The higher the current marginal costs when $\pi_i = 0$, the stronger the incentive to offset them by raising π_i. The higher the following period marginal costs (given what policymakers expect about their own policy in that period), the stronger the incentive to reduce them by lowering π_i and through it the inflationary expectations of that period. Thus the incentive to raise current inflation in order to stimulate current employment is at least partly checked by the adverse effect that such an action has on employment in the following period.

It is shown in appendix C to this chapter that a solution for K_3 exists and that it is always negative. Furthermore, if the average policy bias is inflationary, the solution is always unique and is bounded between zero, and

$$-\frac{\sigma_v^2}{\sigma_v^2 + \sigma_\delta^2}\alpha A(1 + \alpha^2 A)\rho^2\beta \equiv -\frac{\sigma_v^2}{\sigma_v^2 + \delta_\delta^2}K. \tag{15.15}$$

In this case, which is the most relevant, the current effect of a decrease in employment on inflation dominates the effect of the associated reduction in expected future employment. As a consequence the overall response of current inflation to a current reduction in natural employment is positive. A more detailed discussion appears in section 15.5.

15.3 Persistent Unemployment and Asymmetric Information as Causes for Inflationary Persistence

It is shown in appendix B that the inflationary expectation of period i is given by

$$\pi_i^e = (1 + \alpha^2 A)\left(\frac{\alpha A}{1 + \alpha^2 A} + K_3\right)D + (1 + \alpha^2 A)\left(\frac{\alpha A}{1 + \alpha^2 A} + \rho K_3\right)$$

$$\cdot\left[\rho^2 p_{i-2} + \rho\theta\left(v_{i-1} + \frac{\alpha A}{\alpha A + \rho(1 + \alpha^2 A)K_3}\delta_{i-1}\right)\right]. \tag{15.16}$$

Note that since the public is unable to fully disentangle the previous period innovation to the persistent part of employment (v_{i-1}) from the transitory component of employment in that period (δ_{i-1}), expectations in period i depend on δ_{i-1}. The fact that the public is not as informed as policymakers about the persistence of employment introduces sluggishness into inflationary expectations. In particular past transitory blips to the natural level of employment affect current expectations.

Since policymakers know the decomposition of employment into its persistent and transitory components, they do not react directly to past transitory blips. But, as implied by equation (15.14), they partially accommodate current inflationary expectations.[9] Since these expectations are affected by past transitory blips to employment, so is actual inflation. Thus, through its dependence on expectations, current policy becomes a function of past transitory blips to natural employment. Asymmetric information transforms transitory blips to natural employment into persistent movements in inflation.

To appreciate the persistence-creating properties of asymmetric information, it is instructive to compare the behavior of inflation in the presence of an information advantage with its behavior when the public possesses the same information as policymakers. Suppose in particular that when it forms its expectation in a period, the public possesses the same information as policymakers in that period. In this case past rates of inflation are not required by the public to forecast future inflation, since it knows all the variables that affect the current policy choice in any case. As a consequence the link between current policy choices and future expectations disappears and the policymakers' problem in equation (15.4a) reduces to a series of unrelated one-period problems whose typical form is

$$\min_{\pi_i} E_{Gi} \left\{ \frac{A}{2} [d_i - \alpha(\pi_i - \pi_i^e)]^2 + \frac{\pi_i^2}{2} \right\}. \tag{15.17}$$

Since all the variables in this expression are in the policymakers' information set in period i the expected value operator E_{Gi} can be omitted. The first-order condition for this minimization problem yields

$$\pi_i = \frac{\alpha A}{1 + \alpha^2 A} d_i + \frac{\alpha^2 A}{1 + \alpha^2 A} \pi_i^e. \tag{15.18}$$

This solution is basically identical to equation (3.4). Since the public possesses in each period the same information as policymakers, it can calculate the policymakers' optimal policy without error. Hence

$$\pi_i^e = \pi_i. \tag{15.19}$$

Substituting (15.19) into (15.18) and using (15.2) and (15.5), we obtain

$$\pi_i = \alpha A [D + \rho^2 p_{i-2} + \rho v_{i-1} + v_i + \delta_i] = \alpha A d_i. \tag{15.20}$$

Thus under symmetric information the persistence of inflation is identical to the persistence of the natural level of employment.

It is shown in appendix B that in the presence of asymmetric information of the type discussed in this chapter the behavior of inflation is given by

$$\pi_i = [\alpha A + (1 + \alpha^2 A)K_3]D + [\alpha A + (1 + \alpha^2 A)\rho K_3]\rho^2 p_{i-2}$$

$$+ (1 + \theta\alpha^2 A)\left[\frac{\alpha A}{1 + \alpha^2 A} + \rho K_3\right]\rho v_{i-1}$$

$$+ [1 - \alpha\rho(1 - \theta)K_3]\left[\frac{\alpha A}{1 + \alpha^2 A} + \rho K_3\right]v_i$$

$$+ \frac{1 + \alpha\rho\theta K_3}{1 + \alpha^2 A}\alpha A \delta_i + \left[\frac{\alpha A}{1 + \alpha^2 A} + \rho K_3\right]\frac{\alpha^4 A^2}{\alpha A + \rho(1 + \alpha^2 A)K_3}\rho\theta\delta_{i-1}.$$

$$(15.21)$$

Both equations (15.20) and (15.21) state that the rate of inflation responds to various components of the natural level of employment. In the case of symmetric information this response is simply proportional to the current natural level d_i. This can be seen from the extreme right-hand side of equation (15.20). But under asymmetric information the responses to various constituents of d_i differ depending on how well the public is informed about them in each period. More important perhaps, in the presence of asymmetric information current inflation also responds to the previous period's transitory shock to the natural level of employment, even though this shock no longer affects the current natural level. The reason of course is that this transitory shock influences policy through its effect on current expectations. Since the public is not fully informed about the innovation v_{i-1} to last period's persistent component of the natural level, it utilizes π_{i-1} as a signal for v_{i-1}. But since π_{i-1} also responds to the transitory component δ_{i-1}, the public's current expectation is contaminated by it. Finally, since current inflation responds to expectations, current policy responds to past transitory blips to employment despite policymakers awareness of the fact that they no longer affect the economy.

In effect asymmetric information introduces more persistence into the inflationary process by inducing a nonzero response of current policy to past blips to natural employment. Since for simplicity we have assumed that p_{i-2} is already known by the public in period i, only last period's blip affects expectations and current inflation. Obviously, if the public takes a longer time to become informed about p, current expectations (and therefore current inflation) will be affected also by more distant past values of δ, making the relative persistence of inflation under asymmetric information even greater.

Except for the coefficient of δ_{i-1}, equations (15.20) and (15.21) reveal that if there is a positive inflationary bias on average, all the coefficients are smaller under asymmetric information than their respective counterparts under symmetric information. A demonstration appears in appendix D. The intuition is that the presence of asymmetric information partially deters policymakers from fully responding to their current information because of the dynamic effect of their current action on future expectations. This effect is clearest when the persistent component of unemployment rises unexpectedly by one unit. With symmetric information policy responds by increasing inflation by αA. But under asymmetric information policymakers also take into consideration that the current increase in inflation raises next period's expectations which, ceteris paribus, reduces employment in that period. This deters policymakers from responding by as much under asymmetric as under symmetric information.

The analysis of this section can be summarized as follows: In the absence of asymmetric information the rate of inflation inherits the stochastic properties and therefore the persistence of the natural level of employment. The presence of asymmetric information raises this persistence even more by making inflation responsive to past transitory shocks to the level of employment despite the fact that they do not have any direct effect on current employment.

In addition, if the average positive inflationary bias that exists under symmetric information carries over to the case of asymmetric information, the response of policy to shocks is weaker under asymmetric than under symmetric information. Thus the degree of activism is muted by the existence of asymmetric information. A fuller discussion of the determinants of activism under asymmetric information appears in section 15.5 below.

15.4   Does a Countercyclical Behavior of Inflation Imply That Employment-Motivated Monetary Temptations Are Unimportant?

Between the end of the 1970s and the end of the 1980s professional opinion regarding the importance of real and monetary factors in the generation of business cycles shifted. The current view is that the relative importance of real factors is larger than what had been believed during the 1970s. Some economists even go as far as denying a meaningful quantitative role to money in explaining aggregate fluctuations altogether.[10]

Kydland and Prescott (1990) report that the price level in the United States since World War II has been countercyclical. One may be tempted to conclude from this finding that the employment-motivated inflationary temptations that underlie this and previous chapters are unimportant in practice. The reason of course is that when taken in isolation, the mechanism through which money affects output implies a procyclical behavior of inflation. Although there is an obvious difference between the price level and inflation, it is not unlikely that the countercyclical behavior of the price level detected by Kydland and Prescott also carries over to the rate of inflation. The objective of this section is to show that even if the rate of inflation is also countercyclical, policymakers are not necessarily free from temptations to inflate, nor are they unable to affect output when the structure of information enables them to surprise the public.

The framework developed in the previous sections is well suited to the demonstration of these claims. This framework implies that fluctuations in employment are driven by real factors since the natural level of employment fluctuates exogenously over time. But the monetary policymakers, who are more sensitive to large deviations from their preferred level of employment than to small deviations, react by producing a higher rate of inflation when the natural level is lower. In the absence of private information their attempt to stimulate employment more when the natural level is lower fails, and employment remains at its relatively low natural level. Due to the policymakers' reaction to real fluctuations in employment, inflation behaves countercylically. In the presence of private information policymakers succeed in offsetting some of the real fluctuations in employment. However, to the extent that the offset is partial, total employment and inflation are still negatively correlated.[11] In both cases the countercyclical behavior of inflation arises precisely because of the potential ability of policymakers to stimulate employment through expansionary monetary policy. Since this temptation induces a higher rate of inflation as the natural level of employment drops, the response of policy induces a negative correlation between employment and inflation.

We turn next to a precise description of the workings of this mechanism under symmetric and asymmetric information. With symmetric information the public always forecasts inflation correctly, so employment is always at its natural level. Hence, even if policymakers try to "lean against the wind," the deviation of actual employment from its mean average level $\overline{N}_n$ is due entirely to fluctuations in natural employment. The cyclical deviation of employment from $\overline{N}_n$ is, from equation (15.1), therefore

$$N_i - \overline{N}_n = N_{ni} - \overline{N}_n = -(p_i + \delta_i). \tag{15.22}$$

Equation (15.20) implies that under asymmetric information the policy-makers' response is

$$\pi_i = \alpha A[D + p_i + \delta_i].$$ (15.23)

Obviously $N_i - \overline{N}_n$ and π_i are negatively correlated. The covariance between the cyclical fluctuation in employment and inflation is[12]

$$\text{cov}^s[\pi_i, N_i - \overline{N}_n] = -\alpha A\left[\frac{\sigma_v^2}{1 - \rho^2} + \sigma_\delta^2\right].$$ (15.24)

This covariance is larger in absolute value, the greater the relative concern of policymakers for employment A and the greater the sensitivity α of employment to unanticipated inflation. The coefficient of correlation between π_i and $N_i - \overline{N}_n$ is one. This extreme countercyclical behavior of inflation is a consequence of symmetric information. It vanishes in the case of asymmetric information, to which we turn next.

From (15.1) and (15.3) the cyclical deviation of employment in the presence of asymmetric information is

$$N_i - \overline{N}_n = -(p_i + \delta_i) + \alpha(\pi_i - \pi_i^e).$$ (15.25)

Using (15.16) and (15.21) in (15.25) and using the resulting expression in conjunction with equation (15.21) in order to calculate the (unconditional) covariance between $N_i - \overline{N}_n$ and π_i, we obtain after some algebra

$$\begin{aligned}
\text{cov}[\pi_i, N_i - \overline{N}_n] = &-\left[\frac{\alpha A}{1 - \alpha^2 A} + \rho K_3\right]\left\{\frac{\rho^4(1 + \alpha^2 A)^2}{1 - \rho^2}\right. \\
&+ \rho^2[1 + \theta\alpha^2 A]\left[1 - \alpha\rho(1 - \theta)K_3 - (1 - \theta)\frac{\alpha^2 A}{1 + \alpha^2 A}\right] \\
&+ \frac{1 - \alpha\rho(1 - \theta)K_3}{1 + \alpha^2 A}[1 - \alpha\rho K_3[1 + \theta\alpha^2 A \\
&- \alpha\rho(1 - \theta)(1 + \alpha^2 A)K_3]]\bigg\}\sigma_v^2 \\
&- \left\{\frac{\alpha A}{1 + \alpha^2 A}[1 + \alpha\rho\theta K_3]\left[1 - (1 + \alpha\rho\theta K_3)\frac{\alpha^2 A}{1 + \alpha^2 A}\right]\right. \\
&+ \left(\frac{\alpha A}{1 + \alpha^2 A}\right)^2(\alpha\rho\theta)^2\bigg\}\sigma_\delta^2.
\end{aligned}$$ (15.26)

It is shown in appendix E to this chapter that if there is, on average, a positive inflationary bias,[13]

$$\frac{\alpha A}{1 + \alpha^2 A} + \rho K_3 > 0, \tag{15.27a}$$

$$1 + \alpha \rho \theta K_3 > 0. \tag{15.27b}$$

Those inequalities in conjunction with the fact that $K_3 \leq 0$, $\rho < 1$, $1 > \theta > 0$, and $\alpha^2 A/(1 + \alpha^2 A) < 1$ imply that the right-hand side of equation (15.26) is negative. This leads to the following proposition:

PROPOSITION 15.1   If $D > 0$ and policy has, on average, an inflationary bias, the covariance in equation (15.26) is negative, implying that inflation behaves countercyclically under asymmetric information.

The morale from proposition 15.1 is that a countercyclical behavior of inflation is likely to arise even when, due to asymmetric information, monetary policy has a nonnegligible effect on employment and output. Furthermore such behavior is more likely to arise as the impact of monetary policy on employment becomes more limited in comparison to the magnitude of real cyclical shocks to employment. We have seen earlier that when monetary policy has no real effects in the limit, inflation is perfectly and unconditionally negatively correlated with the phase of the cycle. In the asymmetric information case a similar, but less extreme, pattern emerges. The main difference between the symmetric and the asymmetric information cases is that in the second case policymakers manage to, at least, partially offset real fluctuations in employment. A priori this offset could be partial, full, or even larger. It is shown in appendix E that in the presence of an average inflationary bias the offset is always less than full. The precise statement is summarized in proposition 15.2.

PROPOSITION 15.2   Under the conditions of proposition 15.1 the overall (inclusive of the policy offset) response of employment to various shocks to the natural level of employment is in the same direction as each of the original disturbances to the natural level. This statement holds independently of whether shocks are persistent or transitory and of whether they are private or public information.

Thus in the presence of a positive mean inflationary bias a reduction in any of the stochastic components of the natural level of employment raises inflation (see equation 5.21 and the next section) and reduces employment even after the policy offset. These joint systematic responses of inflation and total employment are responsible for the countercyclical behavior of inflation.

To sum up, a countercyclical behavior of inflation does not imply that monetary temptations are nonexistent nor that monetary policy cannot affect output. Such behavior of inflation is consistent both with the view that the driving and dominant force in the cycle emanates from real factors as well as with the view that monetary policy is being used as a meaningful instrument of countercyclical policy.

15.5   Determinants of Inflation, the Speed of Learning, and Activism

We have seen in section 15.2 that innovations to unemployment[14] trigger two opposing effects on inflation but that there is a presumption that the direct current period effect dominates. This presumption can be defended by noting that factors such as a positive degree of time preference ($\beta < 1$), partial learning ($\theta < 1$), and expected mean reversion of real shocks to employment ($\rho < 1$) combine to make the response of inflation to current considerations stronger than its response to future considerations.

But beyond such intuitive considerations it is possible to show that when, for positive values of D, the mean inflationary bias is positive, the responses of inflation to all shocks (past and present, persistent and transitory) to unemployment are positive as well. This can be seen, by noting from equation (15.21), that the unconditional expected value of inflation is

$$E\pi_i = (1 + \alpha^2 A)\left[\frac{\alpha A}{1 + \alpha^2 A} + K_3\right]D. \tag{15.29}$$

For $D > 0$ this expected value is positive if and only if

$$\frac{\alpha A}{1 + \alpha^2 A} + K_3 > 0. \tag{15.30}$$

It is shown in appendix G that this condition implies that the coefficients of all the shocks in equation (15.21) are positive. This is summarized in proposition 15.3:

PROPOSITION 15.3   Given $D > 0$, the existence of an average positive inflationary bias implies that the policy response of inflation to shocks to unemployment is positive. This is true independently of whether the shock is persistent or transitory and of whether the shock's realization is private or public information.

The remainder of this section summarizes the effect of various parameters on the average inflationary bias, the speed of learning as measured by θ, and some of the coefficients on the right-hand side of equation (15.21) under the presumption that the policy bias is inflationary. The following proposition summarizes some of the determinants of the mean bias:

PROPOSITION 15.4   The mean inflationary bias in equation (15.29) is larger,

1.   the higher the degree of time preference (the lower β),

2.   the higher the variance σ_δ^2 of transitory shocks to employment,

3.   the lower the variance σ_v^2 the persistent innovations to employment.

The proof is given in appendix H. The intuition underlying those effects should be familiar by now. The less policymakers care about the future, the smaller will be the deterring effect of learning on their actions and the higher therefore will be the mean inflationary bias. The effects of σ_δ^2 and of σ_v^2 can be understood by using proposition 15.6 below, which claims that the higher σ_δ^2 and the lower σ_v^2, the lower the speed of learning θ. A lower speed of learning reduces the deterring effect of learning and results in a higher inflationary bias.

As in chapters 9 and 13 the larger the coefficients of various shocks in equation (15.21), the larger will be the degree of policy activism. But unlike in these chapters it is not possible to summarize the degree of activism by one coefficient, since the responses of policy to various constituent shocks to employment differ across those constituents. It is possible to show (details appear in appendix H) that the response of π_i to p_{i-2} is affected by β, σ_δ^2, and σ_v^2 in the same directions as the mean inflationary bias. The next proposition summarizes those effects:

PROPOSITION 15.5   The response of period's i inflation to p_{i-2} is larger,

1.   the lower β,

2.   the higher σ_δ^2,

3.   the lower σ_v^2.

The strong similarity to proposition 15.4 is not surprising in view of the fact that both p_{i-2} and D are public information in period i.

The following proposition, which is proved in appendix H, summarizes some of the determinants of the speed of learning:

PROPOSITION 15.6   The speed of learning θ is lower,

1. the higher β,
2. the higher σ_δ^2,
3. the lower σ_v^2.

Again the intuition underlying these effects is familiar. A higher σ_δ^2 or a low σ_v^2 implies that the natural level of employment is less persistent, and so are as a consequence, policy actions. It is therefore rational, from the public's point of view, to attribute less weight to current policy actions in forecasting future actions. The moderating effect of a higher β on the speed of learning is due to the effect that a higher β has on the relative size of the coefficients of v_i and of δ_i in equation (15.21). As explained in appendixes A and B an observation on π_i amounts, from the public's point of view, to an observation of a linear combination of v_i and of δ_i. When β is higher, the relative size of the coefficient of v_i is probably smaller, making π_i a noisier signal for v_i. As a consequence the current policy action is not as good a signal of the future action, and θ is therefore smaller.

15.6   Inflation Persistence due to Overlapping Wage Contracts under Discretion

Inflation may persist also because of the interaction of overlapping wage contracts with policymakers who try to attain an employment objective. Such a structure may arise when the economy is populated by several unions whose nominal wage contracts stretch over several periods and overlap only partially. The basic idea is that past high inflationary expectation that got embedded in existing nominal contracts induce policymakers to currently inflate at a higher rate. Unions that currently renegotiate their contracts know this fact. They therefore demand and obtain higher wage increases. This reinforces in turn policymakers' tendency to inflate at a higher rate. In summary, high past expectations induce through the policymakers' response a higher current inflation, which then gets embedded in current wage settlements. These settlements in turn affect future monetary expansion. This mechanism creates a positive correlation between past and current expectations and the current rate of monetary expansion. In addition, if the current expectation of next period's inflation is higher, current wage settlements involve a higher rate of increase in nominal wages. This induces a positive current policy response to inflationary expectations concerning next period. In the absence of private information and other types of uncertainty, the hypothesis of rational expectations implies that unions forecast inflation at all leads without errors. Hence actual and expected inflation are equal and the positive response of current policy to past, current, and future expected inflation becomes, in equilibrium, a positive response to past and future values of actual inflation. The remainder of this section illustrates those mechanisms more precisely by means of a stylized overlapping wage contracts model.

The labor market is composed of two segments that may be thought of as unions. Both are characterized by two-period nominal wage contracts. At the beginning of each period, before policymakers choose the rate of inflation for the period, one and only one of the unions commits to a two-period contract. The other union makes a similar two-period commitment at the beginning of the following period. Suppose further that in the absence of inflationary surprises, the level of employment in both unions is below market clearing and below the level desired by policymakers. This implies, as in chapter 3, section 3.6 (since demand in each segment of the labor market is the binding constraint) that inflationary surprises have the potential to stimulate employment and that policymakers have an incentive to try and create such surprises. The short-run trade-offs facing them in period i emanate from the fact that policymakers face fixed nominal contracts, some of which were concluded at the beginning of the previous period and others that were concluded at the beginning of the current period. The nominal wage in the first type of contracts depend on expectations about periods $i - 1$ and i, while the second type depends on inflationary expectations concerning periods i and $i + 1$. Hence the short-run Phillips relations facing policymakers in each segment of the labor market in period i is written

$$N_1^* - N_{1i} = d_1 - \frac{\alpha}{2}\{\pi_i - [\lambda\pi_i^e + (1 - \lambda)\pi_{i-1}^e]\}, \tag{15.31a}$$

$$N_2^* - N_{2i} = d_2 - \frac{\alpha}{2}\{\pi_i - [\lambda\pi_{i+1}^e + (1 - \lambda)\pi_i^e]\}, \tag{15.31b}$$

where N_i^* and N_{ji} ($j = 1, 2$) are desired and actual employment, respectively, $d_j, j = 1, 2$, are positive constants which reflect the presumption that the natural levels of employment are below their respective desired levels and that π and π^e are actual and expected inflation, respectively. α is the slope of the short-run Phillips curve. For simplicity it is assumed to be the same in both segments of the labor market. $1 - \lambda$ is the relative importance given by the union to the first period of the contract. It is always bounded between zero and one and is larger than one-half if unions have positive time preference.[15]

The objective of policymakers is to minimize the present value of the (political) costs of low employment and inflation. It is given by equation (15.32):

$$\sum_{i=0}^{\infty} \beta^i \left\{ \frac{A}{2} [N_1^* + N_2^* - (N_{1i} + N_{2i})]^2 + \frac{\pi_i^2}{2} \right\}, \qquad \beta < 1. \tag{15.32}$$

Using equations (15.31) in equation (15.32), we can rewrite the policymakers' problem as

$$\min_{\{\pi_i\}} \sum_{i=0}^{\infty} \beta^i \left[\frac{A}{2} \left(D - \frac{\alpha}{2} \{ 2\pi_i - [(1 - \lambda)\pi_{i-1}^e + \pi_i^e + \lambda\pi_{i+1}^e] \} \right)^2 + \frac{\pi_i^2}{2} \right], \tag{15.32a}$$

where

$$D \equiv d_1 + d_2 > 0. \tag{15.33}$$

Since there is no private information, current policy actions have no effect on future expectations. As a consequence policymakers take past, current, and future expectations as given when picking the current rate of inflation. This implies that the multiperiod's minimization problem in equation (15.32) decomposes into a series of unrelated one-period problems whose typical form is

$$\min_{\pi_i} \left(\frac{A}{2} \left\{ D - \frac{\alpha}{2} [2\pi_i - [(1 - \lambda)\pi_{i-1}^e + \pi_i^e + \lambda\pi_{i+1}^e] \right\}^2 + \frac{\pi_i^2}{2} \right). \tag{15.32b}$$

The first-order necessary condition for this problem implies that

$$\pi_i = \frac{1}{1 + \alpha^2 A} \left\{ \alpha A D + \frac{\alpha^2 A}{2} [(1 - \lambda)\pi_{i-1}^e + \pi_i^e + \lambda\pi_{i+1}^e] \right\}. \tag{15.34}$$

Thus the rate of inflation chosen by policymakers responds positively to past and current inflationary expectations as well as to the rate of inflation currently expected for the following period.

But in the absence of uncertainty the two unions know exactly the policymakers' response function in equation (15.34) and can use it to perfectly predict the path of inflation. Hence

$$\pi_i^e = \pi_i \quad \text{for all } i. \tag{15.35}$$

Using (15.35) in (15.34) and rearranging, we obtain

$$\frac{\alpha^2 A}{2} \lambda \pi_{i+1} - \left(1 + \frac{\alpha^2 A}{2}\right) \pi_i + \frac{\alpha^2 A}{2}(1 - \lambda)\pi_{i-1} = \alpha AD. \tag{15.36}$$

This is a second-order difference equation in the rate of inflation π. A particular (stationary) solution for it is

$$\pi_i = \alpha AD. \tag{15.37}$$

The general solution for the homogeneous part of (15.36) is

$$\pi_i = K_1 s_1^i + K_2 s_2^i, \tag{15.38}$$

where K_i, $i = 1, 2$, are constants to be determined by initial or end conditions and s_i, $i = 1, 2$, are the roots of the polynomial

$$\frac{\alpha^2 A}{2} \lambda s^2 - \left(1 + \frac{\alpha^2 A}{2}\right) s + \frac{\alpha^2 A}{2}(1 - \lambda) = 0. \tag{15.39}$$

Combining (15.37) and (15.38), the general solution to equation (15.36) is

$$\pi_i = \alpha AD + K_1 s_1^i + K_2 s_2^i. \tag{15.40}$$

It is demonstrated in appendix I that the two roots s_1 and s_2 are real positive and distinct. It follows from equation (15.40) that inflation will exhibit persistent movements over time. If in addition π_i converges to the stationary solution αAD, only the smaller root—denoted s_1—enters with a nonzero coefficient and the solution reduces to[16]

$$\pi_i = \alpha AD + (\pi_0 - \alpha AD)s_1^i. \tag{15.40a}$$

Thus to the extent that $\pi_0 \neq \alpha AD$ the rate of inflation converges gradually to αAD. If $\pi_0 > \alpha AD$, the convergence is from below. But in either case the convergence is gradual, and the rate of inflation is influenced by the initial condition for many periods. The effect of the initial condition lasts longer the nearer is s_1 to one.

Since in the absence of surprises the rate of inflation eventually converges to αAD, one may wonder why π_0 is different from this stationary solution in the first place. One possible answer is that although it is perfectly known almost all the time, D jumps unexpectedly at a particular moment of time and is again expected to remain at its new level forever. After the jump the new value of αAD and of π_0 obviously differ. Such jumps are characteristic of models of money under perfect foresight (e.g., in Sargent and Wallace 1973).

The realization by the public that inflationary policymakers have become more concerned with price stability may also be modeled as a downward one-time jump in D. In such a case $\pi_0 - \alpha AD$ is positive and the rate of inflation converges to its new lower stationary level gradually. Thus, although the new relative emphasis of policy is more conservative, inflation does not immediately jump all the way to its lower stationary level. The reason of course is that the interaction of dynamic inconsistency with overlapping contracts slows down the stabilization of inflation even when policymakers manage to convince the public that they are now, forever, more concerned about inflation than before. A precise example of this mechanism in the context of inflation stabilization is developed in Cukierman (1988a); it is used to demonstrate that a temporary and credible wage-price freeze will speed up the convergence to the lower stationary rate of inflation.

Backward-looking partial or full wage indexation, of the type found in some Latin American countries and Israel, also induces policy to react in a way that creates inflationary persistence. This point is demonstrated in De Gregorio (1990). It can be illustrated by replacing the two segments' short-run Phillips curves in equation (15.31) with one economywide Phillips curve as in equation (15.41):

$$N^* - N_i = D - \alpha\{\pi_i - [(1 - \gamma)\pi_i^e + \gamma\pi_{i-1}]\}, \qquad 0 \le \gamma \le 1. \qquad (15.41)$$

The coefficient γ measures the degree of backward-looking wage indexation. The term $(1 - \gamma)\pi_i^e$ states that to the extent that there is no full indexation, nominal contracts also respond partially to expected inflation. To focus on the persistence-creating properties of backward-looking wage indexation, we replace the previously used overlapping contracts framework by an economy in which all individuals contract simultaneously at the beginning of each period. Except for this change the rest of the model remains the same including in particular the objective function in (15.32) and the absence of any uncertainty. Substituting equation (15.41) into equation (15.32) and noting again that, due to perfect information, the policymakers' problem reduces to a series of unrelated one-period problems, we obtain the following expression for policymakers' decision rule:

$$\pi_i = \frac{1}{1 + \alpha^2 A} \{\alpha AD + \alpha^2 A[(1 - \gamma)\pi_i^e + \gamma\pi_{i-1}]\}. \tag{15.42}$$

Again, since the public fully anticipates the policymakers' actions, expected and actual inflation are equal. Using this perfect foresight constraint in (15.42) and rearranging, we obtain

$$\pi_i = \frac{\alpha A}{1 + \gamma\alpha^2 A} D + \frac{\gamma\alpha^2 A}{1 + \gamma\alpha^2 A} \pi_{i-1}. \tag{15.43}$$

Equation (15.43) is a first-order convergent (since the coefficient of π_{i-1} is smaller than one) difference equation. It converges monotonically to the stationary solution αAD. To the extent that initial inflation is different from αAD, the effect of this initial difference persists for many periods. The intuition is that backward-looking indexation carries some of past inflation into current wage settlements reducing, ceteris paribus, current employment. Policymakers partially offset this effect by inflating at a higher rate. The interaction of these two elements introduces persistence into the inflationary process. Not surprisingly the degree of persistence is larger the higher the level of indexation γ and the larger α and A.

15.7 Concluding Reflections and Some Evidence

A basic message of this chapter is that nonlinearities in the policymakers' concern about employment inject persistence into the inflationary process. This occurs through several, not mutually exclusive, channels. In the presence of asymmetric information about employment and its persistence, this occurs by making current policy responsive to past transitory blips to natural employment. In the absence of private information inflation simply inherits the stochastic properties of natural employment. In the presence of overlapping nominal contracts or backward-looking indexation, persistence is increased because such contracts slow down the (politically) optimal adjustment of policy to changes in expectations.

The persistence-creating properties of private information were illustrated, for simplicity, in a framework without control errors and with a minimal information advantage to policymakers. As a consequence current policy responded to the preceding period transitory shock to natural employment but not to earlier or other transitory shocks. In the presence of control errors or a longer information advantage current policy would have responded to earlier transitory shocks to employment as well as to past control errors at various lags, making inflation even more persistent.

We have assumed that policymakers have more timely information than private forecasters about natural employment and its persistence. In countries such as the United States, private forecasters may have information about the current employment and its persistence that is as precise as that of the monetary authority. But in a world in which neither private forecasters, nor the monetary authority are perfectly informed about the persistence of natural employment, forecasts generally differ across forecasters. The policy decisions of the monetary authority depend on its own forecast, which is private information. As a result the information on which the monetary authority bases its decisions is private and also relevant for predicting the rate of inflation. Private forecasters may sharpen their forecast of money growth by using their knowledge about the persistence of employment in conjunction with the fact that their information is correlated with that of the monetary authority. But when forecasts are noisy, they usually will not be able to replicate the forecasts of the monetary authority precisely. As a consequence monetary policy will have real effects but not always in the direction desired by the monetary authority. Nevertheless, since natural employment and its forecast by the monetary authority are correlated, the result that the time series properties of inflation are shaped by those of natural employment is likely to extend to this alternative framework as well.

In the extreme case in which private forecasters know precisely the forecasts of the monetary authority, inflation inherits, as in section 15.3, the time series properties of natural employment. This result is shown in equation (15.20); it implies that under discretion, inflation gets higher as the natural level of employment rises higher. Provided the coefficients α and A do not differ too much across countries, a direct implication of this result is that inflation and the deviation of natural employment from its desired level should be positively related. Figure 15.1 broadly supports this implication for a group of developed countries during the last twenty years.

It is obviously possible to argue about how much private information the monetary authority has about the future paths of employment and unemployment. It is likely that the importance of private information varies across countries and over time within a given country. But the result that inflation is likely to be more persistent under discretion than under

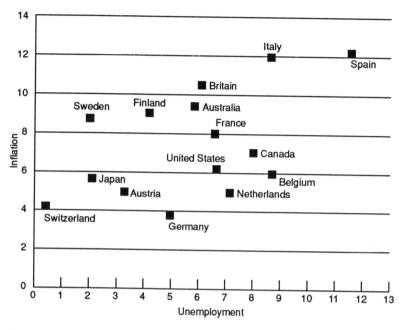

Figure 15.1
Inflation and unemployment, 1971–90: consumer price inflation measured in percent per annum and unemployment rate in percent of the labor force (source: *IMF World Economic Outlook*, May 1991, p. 107)

rules does not depend on the degree of private information. It should therefore be viewed as one of the main results of this chapter. Evidence presented in Alogoskoufis (1991) supports this implication. Alogoskoufis compares the persistence of inflation for twenty-one OECD economies for the period of fixed exchange rates (1952–67) with its persistence during the period of managed float (1972–87). To the extent that under the Bretton-Woods system fixed exchange rates functioned as a partial commitment device that imposed discipline on the discretionary tendencies of national governments, we should expect more inflation persistence in the latter period. This implication is supported by Alogoskoufis's work. He finds the persistence of inflation to be substantially higher in the latter period.

Most of the models that combine a systematic inflationary bias with the possibility of stabilization policy are based on the notion that stabilization is possible because the monetary authority has private information about shocks to money demand (Canzoneri 1985; Flood and Isard 1989; Oh and Garfinkel 1990). In these frameworks the natural level of employment is usually fixed, so stabilization policy attempts to offset only shocks that emanate from the financial sector. As in chapter 13 these shocks are usually conceptualized as shocks to money demand. A recent exception is Lohmann (1992) in which policymakers offset shocks to the natural level of employment. The framework in sections 15.2 through 15.5 shares with Lohmann's framework the feature that the monetary authority tries to stabilize shocks to the real economy. But in addition this chapter features learning by the public about the private forecasts of employment by the monetary authority and therefore about future inflation. Depending on the amount of private information, the attempt to stabilize such shocks may or may not be successful. But in either case the attempt to offset shocks to employment by monetary means contributes to the persistence of inflation.

The private information model presented in section 15.2 is isomorphic to a model in which the public and policymakers are equally informed about natural employment but in which instead policymakers have an information advantage about their shifting employment objective and there is imperfect control of the rate of inflation.[17] For those who would rather base private information on changing objectives, the analysis in this chapter provides the same conclusions but a different interpretation of the sources of asymmetric information. Under either interpretation this model provides a rational explanation for the phenomenon of "Fed watching" in the United States.[18]

Which of the persistence-creating mechanisms presented in this chapter is likely to be more important in practice—the one based on persistence in the natural rate (with or without private information) or the one based on overlapping wage contracts? This is largely an open question. But it is likely (1) that they both are operative in the real world and (2) that in the absence of indexation the relative importance of persistence due to the first mechanism is larger when inflation is higher, since the staggering of nominal contracts is more compressed under high inflation.

Appendix A: Derivation of Equation (15.7)

From equation (15.6) led by one period

$$E[\pi_{i+1}|I_{i+1}] \equiv \pi_{i+1}^e = K_1 E[d_{i+1}|I_{t+1}] + K_2 \pi_{i+1}^e$$

$$+ K_3 E[E_{G,i+1} d_{i+2}|I_{i+1}]$$

$$+ K_4 E[E_{G,i+1}(\pi_{i+2} - \pi_{i+2}^e)|I_{i+1}]. \tag{15A.1}$$

Since the information set of the public in period $i + 1$ is contained in that of policymakers in the same period, it follows from the law of iterated projections[19] that the last two expected values on the right-hand side of (15A.1) are equal, respectively, to

$$E[d_{i+2}|I_{i+1}] = D + \rho^3 p_{i-1} + \rho^2 E[v_i|I_{i+1}], \tag{15A.2a}$$

$$E[E_{G,i+1}(\pi_{i+2} - \pi_{i+2}^e)|I_{i+1}] = 0, \tag{15A.2b}$$

where the equality to zero of the second expression follows from the consideration that given the public's information set in period $i + 1$, the expected value of unexpected inflation in the following period is zero. Otherwise, it could not have been unexpected as of the beginning of period $i + 1$. From (15.6) and (15.2), we get

$$\pi_i - K_1(D + \rho p_{i-1}) - K_2\pi_i^e - K_3(D + \rho^2 p_{i-1}) - K_4 E_{Gi}(\pi_{i+1} - \pi_{i+1}^e)$$

$$= K_1(v_i + \delta_i) + K_3\rho v_1. \tag{15A.3}$$

Except for $E_{Gi}(\pi_{i+1} - \pi_{i+1}^e)$ all the terms on the left-hand side of (15A.3) are known by the public at the beginning of period $i + 1$. We will assume for simplicity that the public assumes that this expression is zero. It will turn out later that under this assumption it is indeed the case that

$$E[E_{Gi}(\pi_{i+1} - \pi_{i+1}^e)|I_{i+1}] = 0. \tag{15A.4}$$

However, $E_{Gi}(\pi_{i+1} - \pi_{i+1}^e)$ is not necessarily zero. Thus by imposing the assumption that it is zero on the public's forecasting procedure, we are limiting somewhat the rationality of that procedure.

An observation on π_i (which belongs to the information set I_{i+1}) is equivalent to an observation on the linear combination of innovations on the right-hand side of (15A.3). Hence

$$E[v_i|I_{i+1}] = \frac{(K_1 + \rho K_3)\sigma_v^2}{(K_1 + \rho K_3)^2\sigma_v^2 + K_1^2\sigma_\delta^2}[\pi_i - g(i)], \tag{15A.5}$$

where

$$g(i) \equiv K_1(D + \rho p_{i-1}) - K_2\pi_i^e - K_3(D + \rho^2 p_{i-1}). \tag{15A.6}$$

Recalling that $d_{i+1} = D + p_{i+1} + \delta_{i+1}$ and using (15.2), we get

$$E[d_{i+1}|I_{i+1}] = D + \rho^2 p_{i-1} + \rho E[v_i|I_{i+1}]. \tag{15A.7}$$

Equation (15.7) in the text is obtained by using equations (15A.2), (15A.5), and (15A.7) in (15A.1) and by rearranging. □

It can be shown that in equilibrium $E_{Gi}(\pi_{i+1} - \pi_{i+1}^e)$ depends on v_i and on δ_i. Hence by postulating that the public assumes that it is zero, we prevent the public from recognizing that the difference $\pi_i - g(i)$ in (15A.3) depends on v_i and δ_i also indirectly through $E_{Gi}(\pi_{i+1} - \pi_{i+1}^e)$. This relatively small degree of bounded rationality significantly reduces the complexity of the solution.

Appendix B: Derivation of Equations (15.16) and (15.21)

Derivation of Equation (15.16)

Equation (15.16) is obtained by noting (from equations 15A.3 and 15A.6) that

$$\pi_i - g(i) = (K_1 + \rho K_3)v_i + K_1\delta_i,$$

and then by using (15.11) in (15.7), rearranging, and by lagging the result by one period.

Derivation of Equation (15.21)

We substitute equations (15.11)–(15.13) into (15.7) and rearrange to get

$$\pi_{i+1}^e = (1 + \alpha^2 A)\left\{\left(\frac{\alpha A}{1 + \alpha^2 A} + K_3\right)D + \left(\frac{\alpha A}{1 + \alpha^2 A} + \rho K_3\right)\rho^2 p_{i-1}\right.$$
$$\left. + \left(\frac{\alpha A}{1 + \alpha^2 A} + \rho K_3\right)\rho\theta\left[v_i + \frac{\alpha A}{\alpha A + \rho(1 + \alpha^2 A)K_3}\delta_i\right]\right\}. \quad (15A.8)$$

Taking the expected value of equation (15.10a) conditional on I_i, subtracting the resulting equation from equation (15.10a), and noting that $E[E_{Gi}(\pi_{i+1} - \pi_{i+1}^e)|I_i] = 0$, we obtain after some rearrangements

$$\pi_i - \pi_i^e = \frac{\alpha A}{1 + \alpha^2 A}[\rho(v_{i-1} - E[v_{i-1}|I_i]) + v_i + \delta_i]$$

$$+ K_3[\rho^2(v_{i-1} - E[v_{i-1}|I_i]) + \rho v_i - \alpha E_{Gi}[\pi_{i+1} - \pi_{i+1}^e]].$$
$$(15A.9)$$

Substituting (15A.3) into (15A.5), using the resulting expression in (15A.9), and leading by one period, we get

$$\pi_{i+1} - \pi_{i+1}^e = \left(\frac{\alpha A}{1 + \alpha^2 A} + \rho K_3\right)\left[\rho(1 - \theta)v_i\right.$$

$$- \rho\theta\frac{\alpha A}{\alpha A + \rho(1 + \alpha^2 A)K_3}\delta_i + v_{i+1}\right]$$

$$+ \frac{\alpha A}{1 + \alpha^2 A}\delta_{i+1} - \alpha K_3 E_{G,i+1}[\pi_{i+2} - \pi_{i+2}^e]. \qquad (15A.10)$$

Note that unexpected inflation in period $i + 1$ depends on realizations of shocks in periods $i, i + 1$, and possibly later periods but not on shocks in earlier periods. It follows that

$$E_{Gi}\{E_{G,i+1}[\pi_{i+2} - \pi_{i+2}^e]\} = E_{Gi}[\pi_{i+2} - \pi_{i+2}^e] = 0. \qquad (15A.11)$$

The first equality in (15A.11) is a consequence of the law of iterated projections, and the second arises from the fact that in period i the policymakers' information set does not include the shocks to be realized from period $i + 1$ on. Taking the expected value of (15A.10) conditional on the policymakers' information in period i and using (15A.11), we obtain

$$E_{Gi}[\pi_{i+1} - \pi_{i+1}^e] = \rho\left[\frac{\alpha A}{1 + \alpha^2 A} + \rho K_3\right](1 - \theta)v_i - \rho\theta\frac{\alpha A}{1 + \alpha^2 A}\delta_i.$$
$$(15A.12)$$

Equation (15.21) is obtained by substituting (15A.8) and (15A.12) into (15.10a), using the fact that $E_{Gi}d_{i+1} = D + \rho p_i$ and by rearranging.

Appendix C: Characterization of Solution for K_3 and Demonstration That It Is Unique Provided There Is, on Average, an Inflationary Bias

Differentiating the function $G(K_3)$ from equation (15.12) with respect to K_3, we get

$$\frac{\partial G(K_3)}{\partial K_3} = -\frac{2\rho^3\beta\alpha A(1 + \alpha^2 A)K_1^2\sigma_v^4\sigma_\delta^2}{[(K_1 + \rho K_3)^2\sigma_v^2 + K_1^2\sigma_\delta^2]^2}\left(\frac{\alpha A}{1 + \alpha^2 A} + \rho K_3\right). \qquad (15A.13a)$$

Hence the sign of this derivative is opposite to that of $K_1 + \rho K_3$. Examination of equation (15.12) in the text reveals that if a solution to K_3 exists, it is nonpositive. Hence only the negative range of K_3 is relevant and $K_1 + \rho K_3$ will be positive, negative, or zero. It follows from (15A.13a) that

$$\frac{\partial G(K_3)}{\partial K_3} = \begin{cases} \text{negative} & K_3 > -\dfrac{1}{\rho}\dfrac{\alpha A}{1 + \alpha^2 A}, \\[2ex] 0 & K_3 = -\dfrac{1}{\rho}\dfrac{\alpha A}{1 + \alpha^2 A}, \\[2ex] \text{positive} & K_3 < -\dfrac{1}{\rho}\dfrac{\alpha A}{1 + \alpha^2 A}. \end{cases} \qquad (15A.13b)$$

Examination of $G(K_3)$ reveals that

$$G(0) = -\frac{\sigma_v^2}{\sigma_v^2 + \sigma_\delta^2}\alpha A(1 + \alpha^2 A)\beta\rho^2 \equiv -\frac{\sigma_v^2}{\sigma_v^2 + \sigma_\delta^2}K, \qquad (15A.14a)$$

$$G\left(-\frac{1}{\rho}\frac{\alpha A}{1 + \alpha^2 A}\right) = 0, \qquad (15A.14b)$$

$$G(-\infty) = -K. \qquad (15A.14c)$$

Thus $G(K_3)$ approaches its minimum at $-K$ when K_3 tends to minus infinity. As K_3 increases from minus infinity $G(K_3)$ increases monotonically, reaching a maximum at

$$K_3 = -\frac{1}{\rho}\frac{\alpha A}{1 + \alpha^2 A} \equiv -\frac{K_1}{\rho}.$$

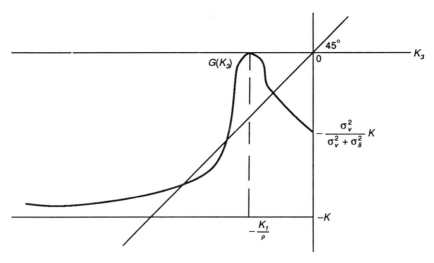

Figure 15.2
Determination of the solution for the equilibrium value of K_3

From that point and on $G(K_3)$ decreases reaching the value in (15.14a) when $K_3 = 0$. The behavior of $G(K_3)$ is summarized in figure 15.2. Depending on the parameter's configuration $G(K_3)$ may or may not intersect the 45-degree line to the left of $-K_1/\rho = 0$. Since $G(-K_1/\rho) = 0$ and since $G(\cdot)$ is decreasing in the range to the right of $-K_1/\rho$, there is one and only one intersection of $G(\cdot)$ with the 45-degree line. Hence in general there may be several equilibrium solutions for K_3 in equation (15.12), but there will always be at least one. When the solution is unique, it is always in the range $(0, -K_1/\rho)$. This can be seen by direct examination of figure 15.2. Moreover the solution in this range is the only one that is consistent with the existence of a positive average inflationary bias. This can be seen by noting that the (unconditional) mean rate of inflation is, from (15.21),

$$E\pi_i = (1 + \alpha^2 A)\left(\frac{\alpha A}{1 + \alpha^2 A} + K_3\right)D.$$

Hence there is an inflationary bias on average if and only if

$$\frac{\alpha A}{1 + \alpha^2 A} + K_3 > 0. \tag{15A.15}$$

Since $\rho \leq 0$ and $K_3 < 0$ condition (15A.15) implies that

$$K_1 + \rho K_3 = \frac{\alpha A}{1 + \alpha^2 A} + \rho K_3 > 0, \tag{15A.16}$$

which implies that the equilibrium value of K_3 must be larger than $-K_1/\rho$. It follows that in the presence of an (average) inflationary bias, the only solution for K_3 is obtained at the intersection of the 45-degree line with the decreasing segment of $G(K_3)$. As we have seen, this solution is bounded between 0 and $-K_1/\rho$ which establishes equation (15.15).

   Condition (15A.16) implies that the coefficients of all shocks in equation (15.21) are positive. Thus in the presence of an average positive inflationary bias the response of inflation to all types of downward shocks to employment in the current and in the previous period is negative.

Appendix D: Proof That, Except for Response to δ_{i-1}, Response of Policy to Shocks Is Weaker under Asymmetric Information

That the coefficients of D, p_{i-2}, v_{i-1}, and δ_i are smaller under asymmetric information can be seen immediately by comparing their coefficients across equations (15.20) and (15.21) and by recalling that K_3 is negative. The proof for the coefficient of v_i follows by noting that

$$\frac{\alpha A}{1 + \alpha^2 A} - \alpha(1 - \theta)(\rho K_3)^2 + \left[1 - \rho(1 - \theta)\frac{\alpha^2 A}{1 + \alpha^2 A}\right]\rho K_3 < \alpha A. \quad \square$$

Appendix E: Derivation of Condition (15.27) and Proof of Proposition 15.2

Derivation of Equation (15.27)

A proof of the fact that the existence of an average inflationary bias implies condition (15.27a) appears in appendix C. But this condition implies that

$$K_3 > -\frac{\alpha A}{\rho(1 + \alpha^2 A)}. \tag{15A.17}$$

It follows from (15A.17) that

$$1 + \alpha\rho\theta K_3 > 1 - \alpha\rho\theta\frac{\alpha A}{\rho(1 + \alpha^2 A)} = 1 - \theta\frac{\alpha^2 A}{1 + \alpha^2 A},$$

which is unambiguously positive since $\theta \leq 1$. This establishes (15.27b).

Proof of Proposition 15.2

Total employment is, from (15.25),

$$N_i = \bar{N}_n - (p_i + \delta_i) + \alpha(\pi_i - \pi_i^e). \tag{15A.18}$$

To get an expression for $\pi_i - \pi_i^e$ only in terms of exogenous shocks, we substitute a led version of (15A.12) into (15A.10) and obtain the desired solution by lagging the result by one period. Substituting this expression into (15A.18) and rearranging, we get

$$N_i = \bar{N}_n - \rho^2 p_{i-2} - \left[1 - (1 - \theta)\frac{\alpha^2 A}{1 + \alpha^2 A} - \alpha\rho(1 - \theta)K_3\right]\rho v_{i-1}$$

$$- \frac{M}{1 + \alpha^2 A}v_i - \left[1 - (1 + \alpha\rho\theta K_3)\frac{\alpha^2 A}{1 + \alpha^2 A}\right]\delta_i - \frac{\alpha^2 A}{1 + \alpha^2 A}\rho\theta\delta_{i-1},$$

$$\tag{15A.19}$$

where

$$M \equiv 1 - \alpha\rho K_3[1 + \theta\alpha^2 A - \alpha\rho K_3(1 - \theta)(1 + \alpha^2 A)]. \tag{15A.20}$$

Since $K_3 < 0$ and $\theta \leq 1$, $M > 0$, so the coefficient of v_i is negative. By a similar reasoning the coefficient of v_{i-1} is negative too. Examination of the remaining coefficients in conjunction with condition (15.27b) and the fact that $\rho < 1$ and $\alpha^2 A/(1 + \alpha^2 A) < 1$ imply that the coefficients of all shocks $(p_{i-2}, v_{i-1}, v_i, \delta_i, \text{ and } \delta_{i-1})$ in (15A.19) are negative. Proposition 15.2 follows by noting that without the monetary policy response the effect of each of those shocks on employment is also negative.

Appendix F: Derivation of a Condition for Nonnegativity of $N^* - N_i$ with High Probability

Using the definition of D in (15.5), we have

$$N^* - N_i = N^* - \overline{N}_n - (N_i - \overline{N}_n) = D - (N_i - \overline{N}_n).$$

Hence $N^* - N_i$ will be nonnegative if and only if

$$D > N_i - \overline{N}_n.$$

But the right-hand side of this inequality is given in terms of the underlying shocks (after slight rearrangement) by (15A.19). Examination of this expression reveals that $N_i - \overline{N}_n$ is a stochastic variable with (unconditional) expected value zero and a variance that can be written as

$$V(N_i - \overline{N}_n) = C_1\sigma_v^2 + C_2\sigma_\delta^2,$$

where C_1 and C_2 are constants that are determined by the coefficients of the various shocks in (15A.19). Since v and δ are distributed normally, so is $N_i - \overline{N}_n$. Hence $N_i - \overline{N}_n$ is nonnegative provided that D is sufficiently large in comparison to the standard deviation of $N_i - N_n$. For example, when

$$D > 2\sqrt{V(N_i - \overline{N}_n)},$$

the probability that $N_i - \overline{N}_n$ is negative is less than 0.03.

Appendix G: Proof of Proposition 15.3

To prove the proposition, we have to show that all the coefficients on the right-hand side of (15.21) are positive. From equations (15.27) and the fact that $\rho < 1$, it follows immediately that the coefficients of all the shocks in equation (15.21) are positive.

Appendix H: Proof of Propositions 15.4, 15.5, and 15.6

From equation (15.12) and figure 15.2 it is clear that an increase in β lowers the function $G(K_3)$. The decreasing segment of $G(K_3)$ shifts downward, producing a lower equilibrium value for K_3. As a result the coefficients of D and of p_{i-2} in equation (15.21) decrease, establishing part 1 of propositions 15.4 and 15.5. Part 1 of proposition 15.6 is demonstrated by noting, from (15.8), that in the presence of an inflationary bias a lower K_3 is associated with a lower θ.

An increase in σ_δ^2 causes an upward shift in the function $G(K_3)$. As a consequence the relevant segment of this function in figure 15.2 shifts upward, producing a larger value of K_3. Hence the coefficients of D and of p_{i-2} in equation (15.21) are larger when σ_δ^2 is larger. This establishes part 2 of propositions 15.4 and 15.5. To establish part 2 of proposition 15.6 note from (15.8) and (15.12) that

$$K_3 = -\rho^2 \beta \alpha A(1 + \alpha^2 A)\theta. \tag{15A.21}$$

Since K_3 is larger when σ_δ^2 is larger, its absolute value must be lower in this case. Examination of (15A.21) reveals that this is possible only if θ is lower. Hence a higher σ_δ^2 is associated with a lower θ.

The proofs of parts 3 of propositions 15.4–15.6 proceed along similar lines. Again we would use figure 15.2 and note that a higher σ_v^2 is associated with a lower equilibrium value of K_3.

Appendix I: Characterization of Dynamic Paths in Equations (15.40) and (15.40a)

The roots of the characteristic equations in (15.39) are

$$s_1 = \frac{1}{\alpha^2 A \lambda}\left(1 + \frac{\alpha^2 A}{2} - \sqrt{M}\right), \tag{15A.22a}$$

$$s_2 = \frac{1}{\alpha^2 A \lambda}\left(1 + \frac{\alpha^2 A}{2} + \sqrt{M}\right), \tag{15A.22b}$$

where

$$M \equiv \left(1 + \frac{\alpha^2 A}{2}\right)^2 - \lambda(1 - \lambda)(\alpha^2 A)^2 = 1 + \alpha^2 A + \left[\frac{1}{4} - \lambda(1 - \lambda)\right](\alpha^2 A)^2.$$

$$\text{(15A.23)}$$

The maximum of $\lambda(1 - \lambda)$ in the range $\lambda \in [0, 1]$ is $1/4$. Hence both roots are real. The middle equality in (15A.23) implies that

$$\sqrt{M} < 1 + \frac{\alpha^2 A}{2}.$$

Hence both roots are positive and distinct.

Examination of (15A.22b) reveals that $s_2 > 1$ is equivalent to the condition

$$\sqrt{M} > -[1 + (\tfrac{1}{2} - \lambda)\alpha^2 A].$$

Since in the presence of positive (or no) time preference $\lambda \leq 1/2$, the condition is always satisfied, implying that the solution in (15.40) diverges unless $K_2 = 0$. Specializing (15.40) to the cases $i = 0$ and $i = 1$ and solving for K_i, $i = 1, 2$, in terms of π_0 and π_1, we obtain

$$K_1 = \frac{1}{s_2 - s_1}[s_2\pi_0 - \pi_1 + (1 - s_2)\alpha AD], \tag{15A.24a}$$

$$K_2 = \frac{1}{s_2 - s_1}[s_1\pi_0 - \pi_1 + (1 - s_1)\alpha AD]. \tag{15A.24b}$$

The constraint $K_2 = 0$ implies that

$$\pi_1 = s_1\pi_0 + (1 - s_1)\alpha AD. \tag{15A.25}$$

As in Sargent and Wallace (1973) the requirement $K_2 = 0$ ensures that inflation jumps to the stable branch of the solution. Equation (15.40a) is obtained by using (15A.25) in (15.40) and by rearranging.

16 Signaling and Private Information about the Ability to Commit and about Objectives with Time-Invariant Types

16.1 Introduction

This chapter considers and compares the consequences of two alternative types of private information about the nature of policymakers. One concerns the ability to commit and the other concerns the relative concern of the policymaker for price stability versus employment.

Unlike in previous chapters, which deal with private or asymmetric information, several simplifications are used. First, only policymakers with finite horizons are considered. Second, it is assumed that the policymaker's type does not change over time and that policy actions are perfectly controllable. Third, only two types—strong and weak—are considered in each case. In one case the strong policymakers possess the ability to commit whereas the weak do not. In the other case the strong types are relatively more concerned about price stability than their weak counterparts. These simplifications permit a sharp comparison between the consequences of asymmetric information about the ability to commit versus asymmetric information about the objectives of policymakers. It also makes it possible to use elements from the theory of signaling (which has been widely applied in modern industrial organization) to characterize equilibrium policy outcomes.

The postulated public's uncertainty about the type of policymakers in office is a proxy for doubts that the public generally has about the commitment of policy to price stability. For example, when central bank or other officials announce monetary targets, the public is generally uncertain about the seriousness of those announcements. By using the "type" device and attaching an a priori probability to the events that weak or strong policymakers are in office, those doubts can be characterized in a precise, quantitative manner.

When policymakers differ in their ability to commit, the public can learn about the commitment ability of policymakers by observing whether there are differences between prior promises and policy outcomes. Strong policymakers (in the commitment sense) always fulfill their prior declarations because their cost of reneging on it is prohibitive. Weak ones renege more easily since their cost of reneging is lower. The cost of reneging is, at least initially, the private information of policymakers. As a consequence preannouncements of policy are not fully believed (since they might have been made by a weak type), but neither are they fully ignored since they also might have been made by strong or dependable policymakers. An example from a different area is President George Bush's preelection statement on television that if elected he will not impose new taxes—the famous "read my lips" statement. The reason this statement was informative is that the public knew that if Bush reneged on the statement, he would incur a cost. Hence the fact that he made that statement conveyed some new information about the likelihood of new taxes to the public. However, in the absence of precise knowledge about the cost of reneging to Bush, the "read my lips" statement, although informative, still left a margin of uncertainty. When policymakers differ in their relative concern for price stability versus other objectives, the strong types (who are relatively more concerned about price stability) can signal their type by picking a sufficiently low rate of inflation.

Both notions of "strength" in the context of asymmetric information have appeared in the literature. "Strength" as an ability to commit has been dealt with in Barro (1986) and Cukierman and Liviatan (1991). "Strength" as a relatively stronger concern for price stability underlies the work of Rogoff (1985), Vickers (1986), and Hoshi (1988). The work of Backus and Driffill (1985a, 1985b) avoids the need to specify the type of "strength" by simply postulating that strong policymakers always pick a zero rate of inflation.[1]

A main message of this chapter is that the kind of strength about which the public is uncertain makes a lot of difference for actual policy outcomes. In particular, when policymaker types differ in their ability to commit, the strong type partially accommodates inflationary expectations by inflating at a higher rate under incomplete than under complete information. By contrast, when policymaker types differ in their relative concern for price stability in comparison to other objectives, the strong policymakers often inflate at a lower rate under incomplete than under complete information.

The consequences of asymmetric information about the ability to commit are illustrated in section 16.2 and those of asymmetric information about objectives in section 16.3. A comparison and an explication of the source of differences in results appears in section 16.4. Extension and related broader issues are discussed in the concluding section.

16.2   Private Information about the Ability to Precommit[2]

This section develops the consequences of private information about the ability to commit within the simplest possible setting. There are two policymaker types with the same objective function that is positively related to surprise inflation and negatively related to actual inflation. This common objective function is given by

$$v(\pi, \pi^e) = A(\pi - \pi^e) - \frac{\pi^2}{2}, \qquad A > 0, \tag{16.1}$$

where π and π^e are actual and expected inflation, respectively. As in chapters 9 through 15, one can think of the positive effect of unexpected inflation on the objectives of policymakers as arising from its expansionary effect on employment in the presence of nominal contracts and market power in the labor market. π^e is a proxy for those contracts. An alternative, not necessarily mutually exclusive, interpretation is that $\pi - \pi^e$ proxies for other objectives such as seigniorage revenues, nondistortionary reductions in the real value of outstanding government debt, or balance-of-payment considerations.[3] This is in the spirit of Grossman's (1990) generic interpretation of objective functions like equation (16.1).

To focus on private information about the ability to commit, we abstract from some of the elements discussed in previous chapters such as imperfect control of inflation and a multiperiod horizon.[4] As in previous chapters, nominal contracts that are proxied by the expectation π^e are determined prior to the actual choice of inflation by the policymakers in office. In the absence of precommitments this timing leads to an inflationary bias that can be eliminated when policymakers are able to commit. However, as will become evident to the reader of this section, such ability does not suffice. To totally eliminate the inflationary bias, the ability to commit must not only be present but must also be recognized beyond any doubts by the public. Otherwise, a possible lower inflationary bias reappears. To illustrate those ideas, we postulate that the only difference between the two types of policymakers is in their ability to commit. The first policymaker type, to which we refer as dependable, or strong, always lives up to his or her declarations. The other policymaker type, to whom we refer as weak, fulfills previously announced plans only if such a course of action is expedient ex post. In the absence of a policy preannouncement, either type of policymaker maximizes $v(\cdot)$ taking π^e as given. This leads to the well-known discretionary equilibrium $\pi = A$. With rational expectation, $\pi^e = A$, so there are no surprises in equilibrium and $v(\cdot) = -A^2/2$. If a preannouncement of policy is made, dependable policymakers always adhere to it, whereas weak policymakers are not bound by the announcement.

The issue of why dependability differs across policymakers and is private information could be approached in two ways. First, the distribution of policymakers by their level of dependability may reflect the general norms of society. The adherence to the norm of dependability varies across individuals in a community and is, at least a priori, the private information of each individual. Since policymakers are drawn from the society in which they live there are similar individual variations in dependability across policymakers. The general public is, at least initially, not fully informed about the dependability of policymakers in office for the same reason that the dependability of a randomly drawn individual is not known with certainty. Given existing norms, each individual is informed a priori about the distribution of the population by dependability but not about the dependability of particular other individuals.

It is also possible to motivate differences in dependability and private information about it through a political economy approach that views policymakers as politicians who seek reelection. As stressed in the political science literature (e.g., see Enelow and Hinich 1984, p. 174), voters view dependability as a desirable attribute. Hence dependability is one of the "electoral assets" that improves the likelihood of reelection. But a candidate for office generally offers an entire package of positions on the issues and various personal characteristics, of which dependability is only one component. Under these circumstances one may reasonably assume that the attitude of each voter toward dependability is private information. This forces each policymaker to estimate the effect of dependability on his or her electoral prospects. This estimate is the private information of the policymaker.[5] In this context a dependable policymaker can be viewed as a policymaker who estimates that the electoral cost of reneging on announcements is larger than the benefits of surprise inflation. The converse holds for a weak policymaker.

The public knows that policymakers may be dependable (type D) or weak (type W), but does not know which types are in office. At the beginning of the period, prior to the choice of π^e, the incumbent policymakers may announce, if they so choose their policy for the period.[6] If they are of type D, and the public is aware of this fact, their statement is fully believed. However, if they are of type W, and this fact is common knowledge, the announcement has no effect on expectations. Under perfect information, where the public knows the policymakers' type, it is easy to see that W's optimal policy is the discretionary solution A. The optimal policy for policymakers D is to announce $\pi = 0$, and since they are bound by their announcement, they will adhere to it. Since the announcements of D are fully credible, the public will set $\pi^e = 0$. This enables D to achieve $v(\cdot) = 0$, which exceeds the discretionary level.

Consider now the imperfect information case. Let α be the prior probability assigned by the public to the event that the policymakers in office are of type D. The policymakers may or may not choose to make an announcement.

The timing of moves is as follows: First, if they choose to, the policymakers in office make an announcement π^a. Then the public forms its expectation π^e. Finally, the policymakers choose actual inflation π. Since the probability that π^a was announced by type D is α, the public's rational inflation expectation after being exposed to the announcement is[7]

$$\pi^e = \alpha\pi^a + (1 - \alpha)A. \tag{16.2}$$

We turn next to a characterization of the optimal announcement for dependable policymakers under the (provisional) assumption that they make an announcement. The optimal announcement can be obtained by maximizing the objective function in (16.1) subject to equation (16.2) and the additional restriction[8]

$$\pi = \pi^a. \tag{16.3}$$

Substituting (16.2) and (16.3) into (16.1) and maximizing with respect to π^a,

$$\pi^a = \pi = (1 - \alpha)A \equiv \pi^*. \tag{16.4}$$

The level of welfare associated with π^* is

$$v(\pi^*, \alpha\pi^* + (1 - \alpha)A) = -(1 - \alpha^2)\frac{A^2}{2}. \tag{16.5}$$

If policymakers D do not preannounce their policy intentions, there is no commitment. Hence the public correctly expects the discretionary rate A, in this case. The corresponding value of welfare is $v(A, A) = -A^2/2$, which is smaller than the level of welfare in (16.5) as long as $\alpha > 0$. Hence, provided that they have some reputation ($\alpha > 0$), policymakers D are better off announcing π^* than remaining silent.

Consider now the behavior of policymakers W. Since they incur cost for reneging on the announcement, they always end up inflating at the discretionary rate A. Given this fact, they have interest to keep themselves indistinguishable, at the announcement stage, from policymakers D, thereby maintaining inflationary expectations below A. The public knows that it is optimal for policymakers D, when they are in office, to announce π^*. Hence, if there is no announcement, or if $\pi^a \neq \pi^*$, the public concludes that policymakers W are in office and sets $\pi^e = A$. Since $\pi^e = A$ is worse for policymakers W than any lower expected rate of inflation, they also announce π^*, thus maintaining the public's expectation at

$$\pi^e = \alpha\pi^* + (1 - \alpha)A = (1 - \alpha^2)A < A \tag{16.6}$$

for all $\alpha > 0$. Hence the announcement of π^* is an equilibrium strategy for both D and W. The subsequent equilibrium actions are π^* for D and A for W.[9]

The main point of this section can now be demonstrated by comparing the behavior of dependable or "strong" policymakers under full and imperfect information. With full information dependable policymakers are believed, and they know that they are believed. Consequently they find it optimal to choose a zero rate of inflation in each period and to preannounce it so as to maintain expectations at this level too. Thus dependable policymakers that are known to be dependable eliminate the inflationary bias of policy.

In the presence of imperfect information strong policymakers inflate at the rate $(1 - \alpha)A$ which is intermediate between zero and the discretionary rate A. The intuitive reason for this compromise is that the public does not give full credence to their announcement because of the possibility that they are weak. Hence, if dependable policymakers announce (and stick to) a zero rate, they create unemployment. At a zero rate of inflation the combined costs of unemployment and inflation can be reduced by announcing and producing a positive rate of inflation. More precisely, surprise inflation when policymakers D are in office is

$$\pi - \pi^e = (1 - \alpha)(\pi - A),$$

where we made use of (16.2). If policymakers D set $\pi = 0$, then surprise inflation is $-(1 - \alpha)A$, which diminishes their utility (e.g., implying a rise in real wages and an increase in unemployment). If, from $\pi = 0$, they raise π by one percentage point, then their utility loss is cut by $(1 - \alpha)A$, while their loss from the increase in inflation is negligible. As π increases, the latter loss becomes significant (i.e., π) until an optimum is struck at $\pi = (1 - \alpha)A$, which yields (16.4).

Essentially the "shadow" of weak policymakers induces strong policymakers to adjust their behavior toward that of weak policymakers. As is clear from equation (16.4), the adjustment is not full. It is stronger, the lower the α—that is, the lower the reputation of policymakers. Thus, if the public has a very pessimistic view about the fraction of dependable policymakers in the population ($\alpha \to 0$), dependable policymakers behave almost as weak ones.

Before continuing, we pause for a methodological remark that highlights the crucial role of the announcement. One could have claimed that the announcement is not necessary by redefining dependable policymakers as those who never cheat on what the public expects from them and by letting them maximize (16.1) subject to (16.2) and (16.3) with π^a reinterpreted as this expectation rather than as an announcement. Since this problem is formally equivalent to the one we have solved, it obviously has the same solution, which is given by equation (16.4). However, this reinterpretation is not possible since it implies that when they choose actual inflation π, after expectations have been set, policymakers can alter those expectations retroactively. This is obviously impossible, since it contradicts the basic timing of moves in the model. By contrast, the announcement (to which strong policymakers always adhere) conveys information to the public before expectations and nominal contracts have been set. Thus, the announcement is crucial in that it conveys some information to the public about the subsequent action of policymakers before the formation of expectations and of nominal contracts.

In conclusion the ability to commit alone does not suffice to eliminate the inflationary bias of policy. To achieve this result, such ability also has to be fully recognized by the public (i.e., $\alpha = 1$). Otherwise, when in office, dependable policymakers announce and produce a positive rate of inflation rather than the zero rate they would have announced and produced under complete information.

Note (from equation 16.4) that the degree of accommodation by dependable policymakers is stronger, the lower their initial reputation α. In particular, when reputation becomes very small, dependable policymakers tend to produce a rate of inflation that is almost as high as the one picked by his weak counterpart.

16.3 Private Information about Objectives—Vickers' Model

Strong and weak policymakers can also be conceived in terms of their attitudes toward price stability compared to other objectives such as employment. In such a framework policymaker types differ in their relative emphasis on price stability and other objectives rather than in their ability to precommit. Since both types are unable to precommit, there is an inflationary bias no matter which type is in office. But the bias is smaller when policymakers who are relatively more concerned about price stability are in office.

This can be illustrated by postulating that both types possess an objective function as in equation (16.1), except for the fact that the parameter A is lower for policymakers who are relatively more concerned about price stability. We refer to them strong or "dry" (D) and to their counterparts who are relatively less concerned about price stability as weak or "wet" (W). Equation (16.7) summarizes the one-period, objective function of the two policymaker types

$$v_i(\pi, \pi^e) \equiv A_i(\pi - \pi^e) - \frac{\pi^2}{2}, \qquad i = \text{D, W}; A_\text{W} > A_\text{D} > 0. \tag{16.7}$$

As in the previous section, expectations π^e are formed first and actual inflation π is chosen subsequently, taking π^e as given, so as to maximize this objective function. In the presence of complete information about the type, we have the familiar discretionary equilibrium

$$\pi = \pi^e = A_i, \qquad i = \text{D, W}. \tag{16.8}$$

Since they are relatively less concerned about employment (and possibly other objectives other than price stability), dry policymakers produce a lower rate of inflation than their weak counterparts even without any commitment ability. This observation led Rogoff (1985) to suggest that one way to alleviate the problems caused by the inflationary bias of policy is to appoint a conservative (or dry in our terminology) central banker.

The nature of the problem changes when the public is uncertain about the type in office. In the presence of a multiperiod horizon over which the type is fixed, weak policymakers would, at least initially, try to emulate their strong counterparts in order to hold down future inflationary expectations. Dry policymakers would try to distinguish themselves from their weak counterparts, and lower future expectations, by producing currently a rate that is sufficiently low to convince the public that only a dry type could have produced it. This would lead to signaling equilibria in which the rate of inflation chosen by policymakers D is, at least for a while, even lower than A_D.

This section characterizes such equilibria within the simplest framework needed for that purpose. The framework involves a two-period horizon and a policymaker type (D or W) who is in office for the duration of the game. Most important, although it is uncertain about the identity of the type in office, the public knows that it does not change between the first and the second periods.[10] This framework is due to Vickers (1986) who is also responsible for the terminology "dry" and "wet" to designate policymakers whose objective functions are as in equation (16.7) with A_D and A_W, respectively.[11] More specifically, let the objective function of the policymaker of type i be

$$V_i(\pi_1^i, \pi_2^i, \pi_1^e, \pi_2^e) \equiv v_i(\pi_1^i, \pi_1^e) + \beta v_i(\pi_2^i, \pi_2^e), \quad 0 \le \beta \le 1, i = D, W. \quad (16.9)$$

Within each period expectations or nominal contracts are formed first, and the actual rates of inflation are chosen subsequently by the policymakers in office. Let $s_i \equiv (\pi_1^i, \pi_2^i)$, $i = D, W$, be a strategy vector for policymakers of type i. Let $e \equiv (\pi_1^e, \pi_2^e)$ be the vector of expectations in the two periods. This framework can be viewed as a game whose equilibrium concept is given in the following definition:

DEFINITION 16.1   An equilibrium is a pair of strategy vectors s_D, s_W and a vector of expectations such that

1.   given e, s_i maximizes $V_i(\cdot)$ for $i = D, W$,
2.   given the strategies s_D and s_W, expectations e are correct.

Equilibrium can be characterized by the method of dynamic programming. In the last period, whatever their identity, policymakers in office take expectation π_2^e as given and solve

$$\max_{\pi_2^i} v_i(\pi_2^i, \pi_2^e), \qquad i = D, W, \quad (16.10)$$

which, in view of (16.7), leads to

$$\pi_2^i = A_i, \qquad i = D, W. \quad (16.11)$$

Due to the linearity of the unexpected inflation term in equation (16.7), the strategies in (16.11) are dominant strategies. They are optimal no matter what the expected rate of inflation is.

The main factor to note with respect to the choice of the first-period strategies is that the public may learn something from this choice about the identity of the policymakers in office and therefore about the second period's rate of inflation. Other things the same, both types of policy-makers prefer lower to higher values of π_2^e. Hence in addition to the effect that the choice of π_1 has on their first-period objectives, the policymakers in office take into consideration the effect that this choice has on their second-period objectives through π_2^e. Since $\pi_2^D < \pi_2^W$ the strong policymakers have an incentive to try to signal their type, perhaps by producing a sufficiently low inflation in the first period. For the same reason weak policymakers have an incentive to try to conceal their identity until the second and last period. Two types of equilibrium are possible: separating equilibria in which the first-period action reveals the policymaker type and pooling equilibria in which it does not. This section focuses on separating equilibria.

A separating equilibrium is possible only if there is a range of π_1 such that, given the effect of π_1 on expectations, it pays policymakers D to pick π_1 in this range and it does not pay policymakers W to pick a π_1 in that range. Under such conditions a value of inflation within the range signals to the public that D is in office and a value outside it signals that W is in office. To find out whether such a range and appropriate expectations exist, it is useful to divide the range of first-period inflation into two non-overlapping ranges. One in which policymakers of type i prefers $\pi_1^i = A_i$, $i = D, W$, over any inflation in that range even if this leads the public to believe that they are weak and consequently that second-period inflation will be A_W rather than A_D. In the other range policymakers prefer any inflation in this range to A_i provided this leads the public to believe that second-period inflation will be A_D rather than A_W.

In the first range policymakers prefer their first-period myopic optimum even if this signals weakness. But in the second range they are willing to abandon their first-period myopic optimum if they can thereby signal that they are strong. We will refer to these ranges as the range of preference for the myopic optimum and the range of preference for signaling strength and denote them by M_i and S_i ($i = D, W$), respectively. The index i that is attached to those sets underscores the fact that they may in general differ across policymakers' types. The set S_D contains all the values of π_1 such that

$$\Delta V_D \equiv V_D(\pi_1, A_D, \pi_1^e, A_D) - V_D(A_D, A_D, \pi_1^e, A_W) > 0 \tag{16.12a}$$

and the set M_D contains all the values of π_1 for which this inequality is reversed. Similarly the set M_W contains all the values of π_1 for which

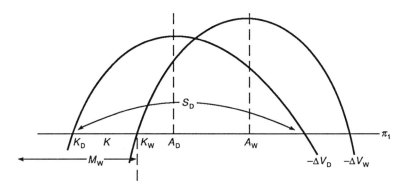

Figure 16.1
The range of preference for signaling of policymakers D and the range of preference for the myopic optimum of policymakers W

$$\Delta V_W \equiv V_W(\pi_1, A_W, \pi_1^e, A_D) - V_W(A_W, A_W, \pi_1^e, A_W) < 0, \qquad (16.12b)$$

and the set S_W contains all the values of π_1 for which this inequality is reversed. It is shown in appendix B to this chapter that the sets S_D and M_W are given by

$$S_D = \{\pi_1 \mid A_D[1 - \sqrt{2\beta(r-1)}] < \pi_1 < A_D[1 + \sqrt{2\beta(r-1)}]\}, \qquad (16.13a)$$

$$M_W = \{\pi_1 \mid \pi_1 < A_W[1 - \sqrt{2\beta(r-1)/r}], \quad \text{and}$$

$$\pi_1 > A_W[1 + \sqrt{2\beta(r-1)/r}]\}, \qquad (16.13b)$$

$$r \equiv \frac{A_W}{A_D} > 1. \qquad (16.13c)$$

It is also shown therein that if

$$r < \left(\frac{2\beta+1}{2\beta-1}\right)^2 \quad \text{and} \quad \beta > \frac{1}{2}, \qquad (16.14)$$

then

$$K_W \equiv A_W[1 - \sqrt{2\beta(r-1)/r}] > A_D[1 - \sqrt{2\beta(r-1)}] \equiv K_D. \qquad (16.15)$$

Abstracting from boundary points such as K_W and K_D, the sets M_D and S_W are the complements of S_D and of M_W, respectively. Figure 16.1 illustrates the relative positions of the various sets. The figure suggests that provided condition (16.14) is satisfied the intersection of the sets S_D and M_W is nonempty.

Consider the following structure of beliefs:

$$\pi_2^e = \begin{cases} A_D & \text{if } \pi_1 \leq K, \\ A_W & \text{if } \pi_1 > K, \end{cases} \tag{16.16}$$

for any arbitrary K in the range (K_D, K_W).

It turns out that, given those beliefs, it pays policymakers D to pick K and it pays policymakers W to pick A_W in the first period. Furthermore these beliefs are correct in equilibrium. The following proposition states this result more precisely:

PROPOSITION 16.1   Suppose that $\beta > 1/2$ and that $r < (2\beta + 1)^2/(2\beta - 1)^2$, in which case $K_W > K_D$. Let K be some number such that $K_D \leq K \leq K_W$. Then there exists a separating equilibrium in which

$$\pi_1^D = K, \quad \pi_2^D = A_D, \quad \pi_1^W = \pi_2^W = A_W \tag{16.17a}$$

(π_2^e is given by equation 16.16) and

$$\pi_1^e = \alpha K + (1 - \alpha)A_W, \tag{16.17b}$$

where α is the prior probability assigned by the public to the event that policymakers in office are of type D.

Proof   Simple algebra establishes that $K_W < A_D$ if and only if $(2\beta - 1)r > -1$. Since $r > 0$ and $\beta > 1/2$, the last inequality is always satisfied. It follows that

$$K_W < A_D. \tag{16.18}$$

From equation (16.9),

$$V_D(\pi_1, A_D, \pi_1^e, A_D) = A_D(\pi_1 - \pi_1^e) - \frac{\pi_1^2}{2} - \beta\frac{A_D^2}{2},$$

from which it follows that

$$\frac{\partial V_D(\pi_1, A_D, \pi_1^e, A_D)}{\partial \pi_1} = A_D - \pi_1. \tag{16.19}$$

In view of the expectations in equation (16.16), policymakers D can signal their type by picking any $\pi_1 \leq K$. But

$$K \leq K_W < A_D, \tag{16.20}$$

where the last inequality follows from (16.18). Together equations (16.19) and (16.20) imply that if policymakers D decide to separate themselves from their weak counterparts their best first-period strategy is K. If they decide not to separate, their best first-period action is A_D, since in the range to the right of K_W the second period's expectation is the same and $\pi_1 = A_D$ maximizes their first-period objectives. To find policymakers D's optimal action given the expectations in (16.16), it suffices to compare the value of their objective function at K with its value at A_D. But the fact that K belongs to S_D (see figure 16.1) implies that D prefers K to A_D in the first period as long as $K > K_D$. To break the tie at $K = K_D$, we make the innocuous assumption that when policymakers D are indifferent between K and A_D, they choose K.

We now turn to policymakers W. Given that they choose $\pi_1 > K$ and that second-period expectations are therefore fixed at A_W, their best first-period strategy is A_W. If they decide to induce the expectation A_D in the second period, their best first-period choice is K, since

$$\frac{\partial V_W(\pi_1, A_W, \pi_1^e, A_D)}{\partial \pi_1} = A_W - \pi_1$$

is positive for all $\pi_1 \leq K$. It suffices therefore to compare the value of their objectives at K with their value at A_W. But the fact that K belongs to M_W (see figure 16.1) implies that W prefers A_W to K as long as $K < K_W$. To break the indifference tie at $K = K_W$, we assume that at this point W still picks A_W. This tie-breaking assumption, together with the previous one, implies that for any K such that

$$K_D \leq K \leq K_W$$

and expectations as specified in (16.16) policymakers D pick K and policymakers W pick A_W in the first period. Hence the expectations in (16.16) are self-fulfilling in equilibrium. □

The proposition implies that there is an infinite number of separating equilibria corresponding to the values of K in the closed range $[K_D, K_W]$. But all of them, except one, can be eliminated by applying the Cho-Kreps (1987) intuitive criterion. Since $K \leq K_W < A_D$, the best set of beliefs from policymakers D's point of view is as specified in equation (16.16) with $K = K_W$. Intuitively the nearer is K to K_W, the smaller will be the sacrifice in terms of their first-period objectives that policymakers D incur in order to achieve separation in the second period. They can induce this set of beliefs by making the following argument to the public:

Any observed value of π_1 that is smaller than K_W should lead you to the conclusion that dry policymakers are in office, for wet policymakers would never pick a rate of inflation in that range even if they would have thereby induced you to believe that they are dry.

Given these beliefs, the best strategy for D is K_W (or a tiny bit below it if we reverse the tie-breaking assumption for W) and the best strategy for W is still A_W. The basic intuition underlying this refinement of the set of possible equilibria is that policymakers D choose the least costly (in terms of first-period objectives) way to signal that they are strong. Hence, given the assumptions on the parameters as specified in proposition 16.1, there is, after application of the refinement, a unique separating equilibrium whose features are summarized in proposition 16.2:

PROPOSITION 16.2   Application of the Cho-Kreps intuitive criterion reduces the set of equilibria in proposition 16.1 to the following unique separating equilibrium:

$$\pi_1^D = K_W, \quad \pi_2^D = A_D,$$

$$\pi_1^W = \pi_2^W = A_W,$$

$$\pi_2^e = \begin{cases} A_D & \text{if } \pi_1 \le K_W, \\ A_W & \text{if } \pi_1 > K_W, \end{cases}$$

$$\pi_1^e = \alpha K_W + (1 - \alpha) A_W.$$

The proposition in conjunction with equation (16.18) implies that strong policymakers undershoot their myopic first-period best strategy A_D in order to signal to the public that they are indeed strong. Stated differently strong policymakers inflate at a rate that is lower than their full-information optimum A_D in order to signal their type to the public.

It is of some interest to establish the effect of the rate of time preference on the equilibrium strategy of strong policymakers. It can be seen from equation (16.15) that as the rate of time preference goes down (β goes up), K_W goes down. It follows from proposition 16.2 that the rate of inflation chosen by D in the first period is lower the lower the rate of time preference. The intuitive reason for this result is that when the rate of time preference is lower, weak policymakers are willing to mimic their strong counterparts within a wider range of low rates of inflation. Since the public is aware of this fact, strong policymakers must undershoot their full-information optimum by more in order to separate themselves from their weak counterparts.

Propositions 16.1 and 16.2 concentrate on parameter ranges in which dry policymakers must undershoot their full-information optimum in order to achieve separation. However, there are also parameter ranges for which D can signal their type even when they pick their full-information optimum in the first period. The following proposition characterizes such equilibria:

PROPOSITION 16.3   Suppose that $\beta < 1/2$ and that $r > (2\beta + 1)^2/(2\beta - 1)^2$ in which case $K_W > K_D$. Then there exists a separating equilibrium in which

$$\pi_1^D = \pi_2^D = A_D,$$

$$\pi_1^W = \pi_2^W = A_W,$$

$$\pi_2^e = \begin{cases} A_D & \text{if } \pi_1^e \leq A_D, \\ A_W & \text{if } \pi_1^e > A_D, \end{cases}$$

and π_1^e is given by equation (16.17c).

Proof   See appendix C to this chapter.   □

The intuition underlying the proposition is simple. If the rate of time preference is sufficiently high and the difference in objectives between the two types sufficiently large, wet policymakers do not mimic dry ones even when the latter chooses their full-information optimum A_D. Due to their high time preference and relatively high A_W, wet policymakers tend to mimic dry ones in a very restricted range. As a consequence policymakers D can signal their type even without deviating from their full-information optimum.

16.4   "Strength" as Commitment Ability versus "Strength" as High Concern about Price Stability

The previous solutions have presented two alternative notions of strength in policymaking. In the first strong policymakers are conceived of as being able to commit and their weak counterparts as being unable to commit. In the second the two policymaker types differ in their relative concern for price stability in comparison to other objectives. In both instances the public is not fully informed about the identity of policymakers in office and may deduce something about their type from their actions or pronouncements. In both cases the choice of policy by incumbents is influenced by their awareness of the fact that their current actions may affect future expectations. As a consequence policy actions under private information differ, in both cases, from actions taken under full information when the public knows the identity of the type in office at the outset.

The two alternative notions of strength lead to qualitatively similar results under complete information. However, under asymmetric information the seemingly modest difference in the notions of strength produces strikingly different results. In the first case (in which strength is equated with commitment ability) strong policymakers inflate at a higher rate under incomplete than under complete information. They do that in order to partially accommodate inflationary expectations which assign a positive probability to the event that a weak type is in office. In the second case, by contrast, strong policymakers inflate at a rate that is not higher, and in many cases strictly lower under incomplete information. They do that in order to signal to the public that they are more concerned about price stability than their weak counterparts.

What is the fundamental reason for this difference in policy outcomes? When policymakers differ in their relative concern for price stability, strong policymakers can signal their type by picking a sufficiently low rate of inflation. The reason is that at sufficiently low rates their weak counterparts do not care to mimic because of their lesser concern for price stability. But when the two policymaker types possess the same objective function and differ only in their commitment ability, the absolute size of the rate of inflation does not discriminate between types. In this case the public can distinguish between types by observing whether or not there is a divergence between promises and deeds.

The reason is that strong policymakers are bound by their prior pronouncements, whereas weak ones abide by them only if it is expedient ex post. Knowing this fact, the public forms its expectation, taking into consideration the possibility that actual inflation will be higher than announced inflation. But since they are bound by their promises, strong policymakers suffer more from the unemployment caused by (a negative) unexpected inflation than their weak counterparts. They therefore commit to and deliver a rate of inflation that is higher than the rate they would have produced under perfect information.

This intuitive argument can be reformulated by defining "perfect credibility" as a situation in which strong policymakers are in office, and the public knows this fact with certainty. When strong policymakers are in office and the public is not sure that this is the case, the potential presence of weak policymakers who may mimic the policy announcement (without being bound by it) makes announced policy targets only partially credible, a fact that has to be taken into account by strong policymakers. Indeed it is the partial credibility of the policy announcement, under imperfect information, that induces strong policymakers to compromise. Thus perfect credibility turns out to be partially self-fulfilling in the sense that strong policymakers do not deliver the zero inflation they would have delivered under perfect credibility. On the other hand, despite their imperfect credibility, strong policymakers are better off announcing (and delivering) a target below the (common) discretionary rate.

The more general lesson from this comparison is that if the major source of uncertainty regarding the nature of policymakers concerns their ability to commit, we should observe some accommodation of inflation by strong policymakers. If the major source of uncertainty is about their (fixed) relative concern for price stability, we should expect strong policymakers to temporarily create strong recessions in order to signal their type. By "biting the bullet" under appropriate circumstances and reducing inflation even below the level that they would have chosen under full information, they can convey their strength to the public.

16.5   Concluding Remarks and Extensions

This chapter has presented the consequences of uncertainty about two alternative notions of strength. An important message of the chapter is that whether strong policymakers undershoot their perfect information strategy in order to separate themselves from their weak counterparts, or compromise upward on it, critically depends on whether policymakers differ in their relative aversion to inflation and unemployment or in their ability to commit. In the first case it is optimal for less inflationary policymakers to signal their type by setting an excessively low inflation so as to make it incompatible with the behavior of the more inflationary type. In the second case strong policymakers do exactly the opposite. They compromise, on their full-information inflation target by partially accommodating inflationary expectations. This difference in results leads to quite different interpretations of frequent failures to stabilize inflation in some Latin American countries. In the first case failure implies that weak policymakers are in office. In the second case failure may be consistent with the view that policymakers who are able to commit, or to stabilize inflation, are in office. But due to their initial low reputation they compromise by announcing and delivering more modest counterinflationary objectives.

In order to demonstrate the main results as directly as possible simple one- and two-period models have been used. But some of the results in this chapter extend to longer finite horizons. In addition, in some cases, there also are pooling equilibria in which the strong policymakers do not, at least initially, separate themselves from their weak counterparts. In particular, Vickers (1986) shows that when policymakers differ in their objectives, there are also pooling equilibria. But Vickers also shows that in the case of no time preference, practically all of those equilibria can be eliminated by using appropriate refinements (which leaves only the separating equilibria discussed in section 16.3 as viable candidates). An intuitive discussion of the criteria used to eliminate the pooling equilibria appears in Persson and Tabellini (1990, ch. 4).

When the model of section 16.2 in which policymakers differ in their commitment ability is extended to two periods and longer horizon, the basic result that strong policymakers partially accommodate inflationary expectations still holds. Details appear in Cukierman and Liviatan (1991) who also show that when the horizon is longer, pooling and mixed strategies, as well as separating equilibria, are possible. For given values of the rate of time preference and of initial reputation, equilibrium is unique. But the type of equilibria may differ depending on the parameters' configuration. Cukierman and Liviatan show that separating equilibria are more likely to occur, the lower the discount factor is, and that pooling equilibria are more likely, the higher it is. The intuition is that weak policymakers with a high rate of time preference prefer to obtain the employment benefits of surprise inflation as soon as possible. As a result their weakness (or the trustworthiness of type D policymakers) gets revealed early on, producing a separating equilibrium. On the other hand, weak policymakers with a low rate of time preference find the current employment benefits smaller than the future costs caused by higher inflationary expectations. Hence they mimic the behavior of type D early on and produce a pooling equilibrium.

Barro (1986) develops a model of policymaking under incomplete information in which the type that can commit is assumed to always commit to zero inflation even if such behavior is not compatible with the maximization of his or her objectives. When this policymaker is allowed to act optimally (as is the case in section 16.2) he or she always sticks to the behavior postulated in Barro's work when reputation is impeccable ($\alpha = 1$). But in all other cases the policymaker partially accommodates the public's expectation by producing positive inflation.

Stein (1989) presents a theory of imprecise policy announcements within a framework in which the policymaker's exchange rate target is private information. The model of section 16.2 shares with his model the feature that announcements convey imperfect but meaningful information to the public, thereby changing the trade-offs facing policymakers. However, unlike in Stein's model the strong policymakers discussed here have no incentive to cheat. They therefore make a fully truthful announcement. But the potential presence of other policymakers who have incentive to cheat renders this announcement imprecise from the public's point of view. Another important difference between his framework and that of section 16.2 concerns the cost of making statements which are not subsequently respected. In Stein's framework talk is cheap, in the sense that policymakers incur no direct cost from announcing targets which they eventually do not deliver. For weak policymakers of section 16.2, talk is cheap in the same sense. But for strong (or dependent) policymakers, talk is not cheap since they incur a cost when their policy deviates from their previously announced policy. In addition the policymakers' objective function postulated by Stein differs from the one used here.

Chapter 14 and section 16.2 have presented two complementary perspectives on the role of policy preannouncements. The model of chapter 14 was more general in that it considers an infinite horizon, the number of types is not restricted to two, and the policymaker type in office can change over time. However, announcements in the model of chapter 14 were compulsory and therefore exogenous. Policymakers were not given the option not to preannounce policy. By contrast, in section 16.2 policymakers have such an option and still choose to issue announcements because it is optimal to do so. In this sense the model of section 16.2 is more general despite other, more restrictive features because it provides a theory of endogenous preannouncements.[12]

Finally, the assumption that policymakers have perfect control of inflation can be relaxed. In such a case separation is replaced, for appropriate configurations of parameters, by a gradual process of Bayesian learning. Such an extension, for a framework in which policymakers differ in their emphasis on alternative objectives, appears in Driffill (1989) and in Cukierman and Liviatan (1992).

Appendix A: Demonstration of the Uniqueness of the Strategy
$\pi^* \equiv (1 - \alpha)A$ for Dependable Policymakers

There may in general exist many self-fulfilling equilibria in which the public's beliefs are

$$\pi^e = \begin{cases} A & \text{for } \pi^a \neq \pi', \\ \alpha\pi^a + (1 - \alpha)A & \text{for } \pi^a = \pi', \end{cases} \tag{16A.1}$$

for some $\pi' \neq \pi^*$. To establish this, it is sufficient to show that (provided both policymakers are aware of the fact that expectations are formed according to equation 16A.1) it is individually rational for both W and D to announce π'. This is obviously the case for W as long as $\pi' < A$ and $\alpha > 0$. To find conditions under which π' is an individually rational policy for D too, we compare the value of policymakers D's objectives when they announce and deliver π' with their value under alternative policies. For any $\pi^a = \pi \neq \pi'$, $\pi^e = A$. Hence the best strategy for D subject to the constraint that $\pi^a \neq \pi'$ can be found by solving

$$\max_{\pi^a} -\frac{1}{2}(\pi^a)^2 + A(\pi^a - A). \tag{16A.2}$$

The solution to this problem is the discretionary rate A, and the associated value of the objective function is

$$-\frac{1}{2}A^2. \tag{16A.3}$$

If, alternatively, policymakers D announce π', the value of their objectives is, in view of (16A.1),

$$-\frac{1}{2}(\pi')^2 + A(1 - \alpha)(\pi' - A). \tag{16A.4}$$

D is better off announcing (and delivering) π' rather than any other rate if and only if the value of objectives in (16A.4) is larger than the value of objectives in (16A.3). Provided $\pi' < A$, this is equivalent to

$\pi' > (1 - 2\alpha)A$.

Hence,

$$E^* \equiv \{\pi' \mid A > \pi' > (1 - 2\alpha)A\} \tag{16A.5}$$

is the entire set of possible self-fulfilling equilibrium announcements. Note in particular that π^* and values of π', in a sufficiently small neighborhood of π^*, are contained in E^*.

Which of these equilibria is best for D? The answer to this question (maximizing (16A.4) with respect to π' subject to $\pi' \in E^*$) is π^*. Thus policymakers D strictly prefer π^* over all other equilibria. Note that all equilibria in the set $E^*(\pi^*$ excepted) can be eliminated by using the Cho-Kreps intuitive criterion. To produce the structure of beliefs in (16A.1), for any arbitrary $\pi' \in E^*$, the policymakers in office could address the public, at the beginning of the game in the following manner: "Your beliefs should be formed as in (16A.1) since, if they are, those beliefs are self-fulfilling." But, as we saw, policymakers D prefer equilibrium π^* over all other equilibria in E^*, and the public knows that. Hence, they can, by using the above argument for $\pi' = \pi^*$, induce the structure of beliefs

$$\pi^e = \begin{cases} A & \text{for } \pi^a \neq \pi^*, \\ \alpha\pi^a + (1 - \alpha)A & \text{for } \pi^a = \pi^*. \end{cases} \tag{16A.6}$$

Policymakers D's argument to the public in this case could be: "We prefer π^* to all other $\pi' \in E^*$, so you should have beliefs as in (16A.6) since (1) this structure of beliefs is best for us, (2) if you believe in it, it is the unique self-fulfilling equilibrium independent of the policymaker type in office."

Finally, note that since the public knows that it is in policymakers D's best interest to make such a statement, policymakers W indeed are compelled to make it too, in order not to be revealed at the outset. It follows that the equilibrium described in the text is unique.

Appendix B: Construction of the Set S_D and M_W and Derivation of Condition (16.14)

Construction of S_D and M_W

Using (16.7) and (16.9) in the inequalities in equations (16.12a) and (16.12b) and rearranging, these inequalities become equivalent to

$$P(\pi_1) \equiv \frac{1}{2}\pi_1^2 - A_D\pi_1 + A_D\left[\left(\frac{1}{2}+\beta\right)A_D - \beta A_W\right] < 0, \qquad (16A.7a)$$

$$Q(\pi_1) \equiv \frac{1}{2}\pi_1^2 - A_W\pi_1 + A_W\left[\left(\frac{1}{2}-\beta\right)A_W + \beta A_D\right] > 0, \qquad (16A.7b)$$

respectively. Since the coefficients of π_1^2 in both polynomials are positive, they both have a minimum and a general form as in figure 16.1. The roots of $P(\pi_1)$ are

$$K_D \equiv A_D[1 - \sqrt{2\beta(r-1)}], \quad A_D[1 + \sqrt{2\beta(r-1)}]. \qquad (16A.8)$$

Since $r > 1$, both roots are real and distinct. Hence the inequality in (16A.7a) is satisfied in the range of π_1 defined by (16.13a) and only in this range. The roots of $Q(\pi_1)$ are

$$K_W \equiv A_W\left[1 - \sqrt{\frac{2\beta(r-1)}{r}}\right], \quad A_D\left[1 + \sqrt{\frac{2\beta(r-1)}{r}}\right]. \qquad (16A.9)$$

Again, since $r > 1$, the roots are real and distinct. Hence the inequality in (16A.7b) is satisfied in the range of π_1 defined by (16.13b) and only in this range.

Derivation of Condition (16.14) for $K_W > K_D$

Rearranging condition (16.15), we obtain that it is equivalent to

$$\sqrt{r-1}(\sqrt{r-1} + \sqrt{2\beta} - \sqrt{2\beta r}) > 0. \qquad (16A.10)$$

Since $r - 1 > 0$, (16A.10) is satisfied if and only if the term in brackets in that equation is positive. Rearranging, we find that term is positive, in turn, if and only if

$$(2\beta - 1)r - 4\beta\sqrt{r} + 1 + 2\beta < 0. \qquad (16A.11)$$

Equation (16A.11) is a polynomial in $\sqrt{r}$. Since $2\beta - 1 > 0$, it has a minimum. Its roots are 1 and $(2\beta + 1)/(2\beta - 1)$. Condition (16A.11) is satisfied for all $\sqrt{r}$ strictly between these two roots. Since $\sqrt{r}$ is larger than one by construction, it follows that a necessary and sufficient condition for (16A.11) is

$$r < \left[\frac{2\beta + 1}{2\beta - 1}\right]^2. \quad \square$$

Appendix C: Proof of Proposition 16.3

When $\beta < 1/2$, the polynomial in (16A.11) has a maximum. This fact, in conjunction with the proposition's hypothesis that

$$r > \left[\frac{2\beta + 1}{2\beta - 1}\right]^2,\tag{16A.12}$$

implies that $K_W > K_D$. The inequality in (16A.12) also implies that $r > 1/(1 - 2\beta)$, which implies in turn that $K_W > A_D$. Figure 16.2 illustrates the position of the curve ΔV_W and its cutoff points in relation to A_D. The main thing to note is that policymakers D first-period myopic optimum A_D is in a range of rates of inflation that policymakers W do not want to mimic even if they can thereby masquerade as a strong type. This observation is essential for the derivation of the equilibrium strategies of the two types to which we turn next.

Given the expectations in proposition 16.3 policymakers must pick π_1 at or below A_D to pass as dry. But any inflation in this range belongs to the set M_W. Hence policymakers W give up the attempt to give the impression that they are D. Given this, their best choice is their first-period optimum. Hence $\pi_1^W = A_W$. Consider now policymakers D first-period strategy. They can prove their identity by picking any π_1 such that $\pi_1 \leq A_D$. But given that they signal their type, the best way to obtain this objective is to pick their first-period optimum. Hence $\pi_1^D = A_D$. Given the

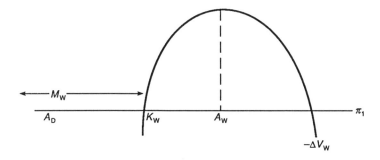

Figure 16.2
The set M_W and the relative positions of A_D and K_W in the case $\beta < 1/2$ and $r > (2\beta + 1)^2/(2\beta - 1)^2$

first-period strategies of W and D, the postulated expectations are correct in equilibrium.

The proof is completed by recalling that in the last period it is always the case that $\pi_2^i = A_i$, $i = D, W$. $\square$

17 Political Parties and Monetary Policy

17.1 Introduction

In most countries monetary policy responds at least partially to electoral and other considerations of the incumbent party. This influence is smaller the more independent is the central bank. But even in a country such as the United States where the CB enjoys a substantial degree of legal independence (chapter 19), there is increasing evidence that political authorities find subtle ways to influence the course of monetary policy. Some of the evidence supporting this view is summarized at the beginning of chapter 9. In particular Beck (1982) concludes that presidential demands from monetary policy are somehow transmitted to the Fed.[1] He notes that presidential preferences are an important determinant of Fed policymaking, but that the mechanism through which this influence is transmitted requires further study.

Recent work by Havrilesky (1988, 1991a, 1991b,) suggests two channels. One is public signaling by the administration to the Federal Reserve. This signaling usually takes the form of a wish list concerning monetary ease or tightness and the discount rate. The other is the appointment of governors whose personal characteristics make them more likely to acquiesce to the wishes of the administration. These two ways are, to some extent, substitutes. A president who managed to pack the Board of Governors with loyal appointees does not need to signal his wishes publicly. All he or she has to do is to convey them privately to the members of the board. Public signaling is needed when, unsure of their loyalty, the president has to exert pressure on board members. This view is supported by the fact that the frequency of public signaling by the administration to the Fed diminishes when the fraction of governors who are loyal appointees is larger (Havrilesky 1991c).[2] Havrilesky also finds that governors who have a background as professional economists are more likely to be loyal than governors who have a background in banking or politics.

This chapter takes the fact that the incumbent administration influences monetary policy as given and focuses on its electorally induced consequences for monetary policy. Electoral influences on monetary policy can be viewed as a segment of the more general area dealing with electoral influences on policy in general, which has become known as the political business cycle (PBC). The segment dealing with such influences only on monetary policy can be referred to as the political monetary cycle (PMC). Two basic approaches have evolved to the PBC in general and to the PMC in particular. One views parties as being only office motivated. The other views them as trying to implement particular ideologically motivated platforms. We refer to these two approaches as the "opportunistic" and the "ideological" or "partisan" views, respectively. In addition voters may be viewed as being either naive or sophisticated. In the first case they evaluate incumbents by examining performance retrospectively. In the second they try to evaluate the future policies of an incumbent if reelected, by using as best as they can the information they have about his or her objectives and ability. We refer to these two hypotheses about voters' behavior as the "naive voter" and the "rational voter" view, respectively.

Early PMC literature combined the opportunistic party and the naive voter view, yielding the implication that all incumbents will stimulate the economy prior to elections and shift the focus back to price stability after elections (Nordhaus 1975; McRae 1977). Another strand combined the ideological party with the naive voter view, yielding the prediction that there should be *persistent* differences in unemployment and inflation between liberal and conservative parties (Hibbs 1977). Both approaches are based on the notion that there exists a permanently exploitable trade-off between inflation and economic activity. This presumption, although currently discredited, was at least internally consistent with the view that voters are naive in the political area, since the existence of such a permanent trade-off requires naiveness in the economic area as well. An extensive survey of this literature appears in Nordhaus (1989).

More recent theoretical and empirical work indicates that a combination of the "partisan party" with the rational voter view is both more plausible and more successful empirically in characterizing the PMC (Alesina 1989). This chapter therefore focuses mainly on partisanship theories of monetary policy in which voters are forward-looking, understand the ideological motives of different parties, but do not always possess perfect information. The basic notion is that although they also try to appeal to voters at large, different parties assign different weights to the welfare of different groups. In particular, left-wing parties are willing to tolerate higher inflation in order to achieve higher levels of economic activity in comparison to right-wing parties. The reason is that the lower middle class, which mostly supports the left, tends to suffer more during recessions than the upper middle class. Thus left- and right-wing parties cater to the distributional desires of different constituencies. With rational voters and perfect information this should lead to a higher inflationary bias under left- than under right-wing governments, but no difference in the behavior of real variables. This is an application of the discussion in chapter 3. However, in the presence of uncertainty about electoral outcomes the monetary policies of different parties have different effects on economic activity even if voters are rational. This idea has been formalized and tested in Alesina and Sachs (1988).

Redistribution of income can obviously be performed by means of policy instruments other than monetary policy. Fiscal policy and regulation are prime examples. Havrilesky (1987, 1990c) proposes the hypothesis that monetary policy is often used to offset the incentive and other politically adverse effects of nonmonetary, distributionally motivated policies. Although it also implies that left-wing parties tend to inflate at higher rates, this point of view provides a somewhat different perspective on the higher degree of monetary permissiveness of leftist parties; since they engage in more redistribution, left-wing parties trigger a larger amount of undesirable side effects that have to be mitigated by higher rates of monetary growth.

The chapter is organized as follows: Section 17.2 presents the Alesina-Sachs rational partisan theory of monetary policy. Section 17.3 discusses and evaluates the partisan, offset theory of monetary policy proposed by Havrilesky. Section 17.4 discusses empirical evidence concerning both views. This is followed by concluding observations.

17.2 The Alesina-Sachs Political Monetary Cycle

Alesina and Sachs (1988) propose a model with two political parties that differ in their relative concern for real output growth and price stability. Policy is discretionary, and individuals are perfectly informed about the policy objectives of the two parties. They can therefore calculate what will be the rate of monetary expansion to be chosen by the party in office after they commit to nominal wage contracts. After elections this leads, as in chapter 3, to a forecast that is not only rational but also perfect. However, prior to elections the public is uncertain about the identity of the party that will be in office and therefore about the postelection rate of inflation. A rational expectation of inflation is, in this case, a weighted average of the discretionary rates to be chosen by the two parties if they get into office. The weights correspond to the probabilities assigned by the public to either of these two events.

The analysis in chapter 3 suggests that, given arbitrary expectations, the discretionary rate of inflation chosen by the party that cares relatively more about price stability (labeled R for "Republicans") is lower than the discretionary rate chosen by the party that cares relatively more about real activity (labeled D for "Democrats"). See equation (3.4) in particular. Prior to elections the inflationary expectation is a weighted average of these two rates. Therefore, if party D is elected, unexpected inflation is positive, and if party R is elected, it is negative. This leads to the empirically testable implication that after the election of a Democratic government, there should be a monetarily induced expansion of output. Similarly, after the election of a Republican government, there should be a monetarily induced contraction in output. In addition the theory implies that rates of monetary expansion should be lower under R than under D administrations. By contrast in the second term of either administration there is no more uncertainty about the identity of the party in office. As a consequence output growth and employment are at their natural levels.

As stressed by Havrilesky (1990c), as well as in chapters 9 and 15, changes in objectives and in economic conditions may impact on monetary policy more continually than just after elections. Here we abstract from these additional sources of uncertainty in order to obtain a sharp focus on the Alesina-Sachs partisan view of monetary policy. Apart from the fact that the two parties have different objective functions, the formal model is similar to that of chapter 3. The objective of party i is to minimize the combined political costs of low growth and inflation, which are given by

$$\frac{A_i}{2}[y^* - y]^2 + \frac{m^2}{2}, \qquad i = \text{D, R}. \tag{17.1}$$

Here y^* and y are the "desired" and the actual rates of output growth, and m is the rate of inflation which, for simplicity, is assumed to be equal to the rate of monetary expansion. The stronger preference of party D for high economic activity is captured by equation (17.2)

$$A_\text{D} > A_\text{R}. \tag{17.2}$$

The effect of unexpected monetary expansion on output growth is given by

$$y - y_n = \gamma(m - m^e), \qquad \gamma > 0, \tag{17.3}$$

where y_n is the natural rate of growth and m^e is the rate of monetary expansion expected by the public at the time nominal wage contracts are made. Equation (17.3) is a variation of the short-run Phillips curve in equation (3.2). It is formulated in terms of the deviation of the real rate of growth from its natural counterpart rather than in terms of the deviation of employment from its natural level. The mechanism underlying it is the same. It is based on nominal wage contracts and some market power in the labor market (details appear in section 3.6.).

Nominal wage contracts that are made just prior to elections incorporate the uncertainty regarding the identity of the party in office. Contracts in other periods are based on a firm knowledge of the identity of the ruling party. There therefore are two types of equilibria depending on whether the identity of the party in office for the duration of the contract period is certain or uncertain. The simplest analytical framework that captures this qualitative difference is the following: A party is elected for two periods. Each period corresponds to the duration of nominal wage contracts. A nominal wage contract is concluded at the end of each period and is in effect during the subsequent period. Money growth for the period is chosen after the conclusion of contracts. Elections are held at the beginning of the first period. Since the wage rate for the first period is agreed upon prior to elections, it is based on expectations that incorporate the uncertainty about the identity of the party in office. Hence the discretionary equilibrium rate of inflation in the second period is the same as the one derived in section 3.2 and is given by

$$m_{i2} = \gamma A_i(y^* - y_n), \qquad i = D, R. \tag{17.4}$$

It is obtained by minimizing equation (17.1) with respect to money growth, taking expectations as given, and imposing rational expectations—which in the absence of uncertainty—reduce to perfect foresight expectations. Since $A_D > A_R$, the rate of inflation in the second period of a D administration is larger than the rate of inflation in the second period of an R administration.

What type of equilibrium emerges in the first period? After elections the party in office takes the wage contract, or the expectation on which it is based, as given and chooses money growth so as to minimize the expression in equation (17.1). This yields the expression in equation (17.5), where m_{e1} denotes expected inflation just prior to elections and m_{i1} stands for the rate of monetary expansion chosen by party i during its first period in office:

$$m_{i1} = \frac{\gamma A_i}{1 + \gamma^2 A_i}(y^* - y_n) + \frac{\gamma^2 A_i}{1 + \gamma^2 A_i}m_{e1}, \qquad i = D, R. \tag{17.5}$$

It is easily checked that the coefficients of $y^* - y_n$ and of m_{e1} are both increasing in A_i. It follows that the rate of inflation chosen by a D administration in the first period after elections is larger than the rate of inflation chosen by an R administration during the first period after elections. This leads to the first testable implication of the theory which is summarized in proposition 17.1.

PROPOSITION 17.1 For the same natural rate of real output growth, the rate of monetary expansion under a D administration is larger than under an R administration.

We turn next to the formation of the expectation m_{e1}. Let p be the probability assigned by the public, prior to elections, to the event that party D will be elected. Since the public knows the postelection discretionary rates of both parties in equation (17.5), its expectation is

$$m_{e1} = \gamma \left[\frac{pA_D}{1 + \gamma^2 A_D} + \frac{(1-p)A_R}{1 + \gamma^2 A_R} \right] (y^* - y_n)$$

$$+ \gamma^2 \left[\frac{pA_D}{1 + \gamma^2 A_D} + \frac{(1-p)A_R}{1 + \gamma^2 A_R} \right] m_{e1}. \tag{17.6}$$

Solving for m_{e1}, we obtain

$$m_{e1} = \frac{\gamma}{H} [(1 + \gamma^2 A_D)A_R + p(A_D - A_R)](y^* - y_n), \tag{17.7}$$

where

$$H \equiv 1 + \gamma^2 A_R + \gamma^2 (1 - p)(A_D - A_R) > 0. \tag{17.8}$$

Note that m_{e1} is larger, the larger the probability p that party D wins and the larger the (positive) discrepancy $A_D - A_R$ between the objectives of the two parties. We substitute (17.7) into (17.5) and rearrange to get

$$m_{i1} = \frac{1}{H} [\gamma^3 A_D A_R + \gamma A_i](y^* - y_n), \qquad i = D, R, \tag{17.9}$$

which confirms that $m_{D1} > m_{R1}$. Note that if $A_R = 0$, $m_{R1} = 0$. This occurs despite the fact that m_{e1} is still positive, because party R does not care at all about real growth in this case. It therefore picks zero inflation at every level of inflationary expectations. Subtracting (17.9) from (17.4) and rearranging, we observe that

$$m_{D2} - m_{D1} = \frac{\gamma^3(A_D - A_R)}{H}(1 - p)A_D(y^* - y_n), \tag{17.10a}$$

$$m_{R2} - m_{R1} = \frac{\gamma^3(A_D - A_R)}{H}pA_R(y^* - y_n). \tag{17.10b}$$

Equations (17.10) imply that the time paths of inflation under different administrations differ. The rate of inflation in the second half of the term in office of a D administration is higher than inflation during the first half. The converse holds for the R party. This and related implications are summarized in the following proposition:

PROPOSITION 17.2   For a fixed value of y_n,

1. the rate of monetary expansion in the second half of a D administration is larger than this rate during the first half term of such an administration.

2. the rate of monetary expansion under an R administration is lower during the second half of its term in office than during the first half of the term.

3. the difference between m_{D2} and m_{D1} is larger, the more of a surprise is the election of party D (the lower p) and the larger $A_D - A_R$.

4. the difference between m_{R2} and m_{R1} is larger in absolute value, the more of a surprise is the election of party R (the larger p) and the larger $A_D - A_R$.

All parts of the proposition follow from equations (17.10) and the definition of H in equation (17.8). The intuition underlying the proposition is simple. Except for the extreme case $A_R = 0$, both parties partially accommodate inflationary expectations. Thus, other things the same, the rates of inflation are higher, the higher the inflationary expectations (see equation (17.5). Under a Democratic administration expectations are lower during the first part of the term because, prior to elections, there was a positive probability that the less inflationary Republican party would be elected. As a consequence accommodation is stronger in the second period of a D administration, when its identity is common knowledge, than in the first period of such an administration. The intuition is similar but operates in the opposite direction when the R party is voted into office. Wage contracts in the first period of such an administration are based on the presumption that there is a positive probability that the more inflationary D party will be elected. By contrast, in the second period the fact that R is in office is already common knowledge. As a consequence inflationary expectations and accommodation go down between the first and the second halves of the term in office of an R administration.

The intuition underlying the last two parts of proposition 17.2 is also simple. The larger the surprise associated with the election of any given part, the larger will be the absolute value of the change in expectations and therefore in accommodation. In addition the change in expectations, and therefore accommodation, is larger, the larger the difference in the relative emphasis of the two parties on alternative objectives (the larger $A_D - A_R$).

We turn next to the implications for the deviation of real growth from its natural path. Since there are no surprises in nonelection periods, this deviation is zero. During election periods this deviation can be calculated by using (17.7) and (17.9) in equation (17.3). The result is

$$y_D - y_n = \frac{\gamma^2(A_D - A_R)}{H}(1 - p)(y^* - y_n), \tag{17.11a}$$

$$y_R = y_n = -\frac{\gamma^2(A_D - A_R)}{H}p(y^* - y_n), \tag{17.11b}$$

where y_D and y_R designate the real rates of growth in the postelection period of a D and of an R administration, respectively. Provided that $y^* - y_n$ is positive, equations (17.11) imply that the real rate of growth is above its natural rate in the first half of a D administration and below its natural rate in the first half of an R administration. This and related implications are summarized in the following proposition:

PROPOSITION 17.3

1. For the same natural real rate of growth, the deviation of actual growth from its natural rate during the first period after elections is positive under a D administration and negative under an R administration.

2. These deviations are larger in absolute value, the more surprising is the access of a given party to power and the larger the discrepancy between the relative emphasis of the two parties on real growth and price stability.

The second part of the proposition can be demonstrated by differentiating equations (17.11) successively with respect to p and with respect to $A_D - A_R$ and by evaluating the signs of the resulting partial derivatives. The intuition underlying proposition 17.3 is straightforward. Since wage contracts are based on an expectation that is a weighted average between the rates produced by an R and by a D party, the election of R creates a negative surprise and therefore a recession. The election of D leads to a rate of monetary expansion above the one that had been expected at contracting time and therefore to an expansion. Both effects are compounded, the more unexpected the election of a given party into office and the larger the difference in objectives between the two parties.

17.3   The Havrilesky Partisan "Offset" Theory of Monetary Policy

Havrilesky (1987) proposes a theory of differential (across parties) monetary policy which, like the Alesina-Sachs framework is motivated by the U.S. political institutions. The basic idea is that the main difference between Democrats and Republicans in the United States is in their redistributive platforms. Havrilesky sets up a model in which the (fiscally implemented) redistributive platform of Democrats has more negative disincentive effects than that of Republicans. Since they operate through the effect of redistribution on interest rates, effective tax rates, employment, and output, these burdens trigger adverse electoral consequences that are stronger when liberal redistributive platforms are implemented (see also Havrilesky 1990c). These adverse effects can be alleviated, at least temporarily, by more expansionary monetary policy. As a consequence the incentive of Democrats to expand the money supply is stronger than that of Republicans.

This implication of the theory is similar to that of Alesina-Sachs (1988). However, it occurs for a different reason. In the Alesina-Sachs framework Democrats inflate at a higher rate than Republicans because they are relatively more concerned about employment. In the Havrilesky framework Democrats inflate at a higher rate because of the larger adverse effects of their redistributive programs which require stronger corrective doses of unexpected inflation. But the two theories do not yield identical implications on all dimensions. For example, Havrilesky's view implies that monetary growth should be higher the larger is the size of fiscal redistributive programs. By contrast, the Alesina-Sachs framework does not imply such a relationship, since the difference between the parties arises only because of differences in their (exogenously specified) relative concerns for employment. In terms of the model of the previous section Havrilesky's view implies that monetary policy differs because y_n is different between the two administrations due to different incentives rather than because of the difference between A_D and A_R.

Havrilesky (1990a, 1990b, 1990c) presents a suggestive descriptive analysis of American monetary policy under successive administrations to back up the view that monetary policy is driven mainly by the need to offset adverse consequences of fiscal, regulatory, and other policies. For example, under President Lyndon Johnson the Fed's policy was often geared to keep interest rates sufficiently low to prevent disintermediation in the Saving and Loans sector and the associated negative impact on the housing market. Such a policy was needed, in the first place, because of the existence of ceilings on depository rates at mortgage-providing financial institutions. This policy had originally been enacted in order to achieve certain distributional objectives.

Although plausible, this view of monetary policy in the United States raises the following question: Why do politicians prefer to offset the adverse consequences of fiscal and regulatory policies by means of monetary policy instead of partial or full elimination of the policies that created the adverse effects in the first place? There are two possible types of answers. One relies on the notion that it is easier to camouflage the redistributional consequences of monetary than of fiscal or regulatory policies. Hence, if an administration finds it expedient to partially back off from its redistributive platform, it is more expedient to do so indirectly by means of monetary policy rather than by an explicit reversal of the original policies. In the process the administration may even succeed in convincing voters that it is more efficient than it really is (Rogoff and Sibert 1988; Rogoff 1990). This tendency is stronger, the larger the fraction of voters that has relatively little or no understanding of the intricacies of financial and money markets. Such voters may also find it difficult to decipher the sometimes subtle signals sent by the administration to the Fed (Havrilesky 1988). This makes it politically easier for an administration to offset the adverse effects of other policies by monetary means rather than by a rolling back of these policies.[3]

However, there is an additional reason that operates even if all individuals fully understand the redistributive effects of monetary policy and the role of the administration in influencing it. In comparison to fiscal and regulatory policies, which usually require a lengthy legislative process and whose full effect becomes operational in the longer run, monetary policy can be adjusted *swiftly* and its real effects are *transitory*. Hence monetary policy is an ideal instrument when quick but temporary measures are needed. As a consequence policymakers tend to rely more heavily on monetary policy to offset the adverse effects of policies in other areas when they are unsure about the permanence of those effects or when a lengthy legislative process slows down the rolling back of fiscal and other policies that have proved too disruptive. In other words, monetary policy is used as a shock absorber for the unanticipated (by policymakers) adverse effects of slower and more permanent policies. The abandonment of tight money in 1985–86 under President Ronald Reagan can be viewed in this light as a reaction to mounting sectoral protests associated with the trade deficit, the Farm Aid, and the protectionist movements (Havrilesky 1990b).

17.4   Empirical Evidence on Partisanship Effects in Monetary Policy

Alesina and Sachs (1988) present evidence from the United States between 1949 and 1984 that is reasonably supportive of their partisan theory of monetary policy. The evidence is based on simple econometric tests of the propositions in section 17.2 under the maintained assumption that the R and D administrations of these propositions can be identified with Republican and Democratic administrations in the United States.

Proposition 17.1 implies that the rate of monetary growth should be lower on average under Republican than under Democratic administrations. This is tested by regressing money growth on a time trend and a dummy variable that assumes a value of 1 under Republican administrations and 0 otherwise. The dummy turns out negative as expected and significant at the 5 percent level. Proposition 17.2 implies that the rate of monetary growth during the second halves of Democratic administrations should be higher than during the first halves and that the converse should hold for Republican administrations. A regression of money growth on dummy variables D2, R1, and R2 (where D2 assumes a value of 1 in the second half of Democratic administrations, and 0 otherwise, and R1 and R2 assume a value of 1 only during the first and second halves of Republican administrations) is not inconsistent with proposition 17.2. The effect of D2 is positive, and the effects of R1 and of R2 are negative as expected. However, none of these coefficients is significant at usual levels of significance. Part of this low significance is due to monetary policy patterns that run counter to the implications of the theory during the Kennedy and the

Nixon administrations. When these two episodes are controlled for, the significance of the various dummies increases but remains on the low side.

Proposition 17.3 implies that there should be an expansion of output growth above its natural rate following the election of a Democratic government and a contraction below the natural rate following the election of a Republican government. This is tested by regressing output growth on a time trend, a dummy to control for the effects of the oil shocks and the dummies R1, R2 (defined above), and D1 which assumes a value of one during the first halves of Democratic administrations and zero otherwise. The signs of D1 and R1 are positive and negative, respectively, as expected. In addition the (negative) coefficient of R1 is relatively large in absolute value and strongly significant. Alesina and Sachs also present a structural estimation of their model that utilizes nonlinear least squares. The most striking implication of this exercise is that A_D is significantly larger than A_R, which in turn is not significantly different from zero.

Some of the above results are also consistent with the theory proposed by Havrilesky (1987) that monetary expansion is higher under Democratic administrations because of the need to offset the adverse effects of larger redistributive programs. Havrilesky tests this implication by introducing a change in government variable into a first-order autoregressive specification of money growth. His main finding is that money growth is significantly lower when a conservative government replaces a liberal government. Moreover this effect persists even after allowance is made for fluctuations in projected values of inflation and unemployment. Obviously this result is also consistent with the Alesina-Sachs framework. A test that could potentially discriminate between the two theories involves relating monetary growth directly to the relative size of fiscal redistribution. Havrilesky (1987) tests this implication by adding to the money growth equation an index of "social expenditures"[4] measured as a fraction of aggregate income. The effect of this variable on money growth is positive and significant, yielding support to the view that larger social programs tend to raise money growth. The same regression also includes a change in government variable that is marginally significant and that indicates that money growth is lower, ceteris paribus, when there is a change from a liberal to a conservative administration. These results support the view that independently of the identity of the party in office, larger social expenditures are associated with higher rates of monetary expansion. This is an implication that obtains only in Havrilesky's framework. But since the money growth equation also features a marginally significant "change of party" effect, it is likely that there are additional party effects on money growth as in Alesina-Sachs. The evidence therefore points to the view that a hybrid model may be the "right" one. But more definite conclusions will have to await further work.

17.5   Concluding Observations

Although recent evidence seems to favor the partisan party–rational voter view of monetary policy, the issue is by no means closed. For example, Grier (1987, 1989) finds evidence that is consistent with the older opportunistic party-naive voter PMC hypothesis, for the United States. Mild support for this hypothesis also appears periodically in other developed countries (Alesina, Cohen, and Roubini 1992). Perhaps these results suggest that from time to time circumstances and voters change sufficiently to provide enough room for periodic new surprises.

As a matter of fact Havrilesky's "offset" theory relies, at least implicitly, on imperfect information by policymakers about the economy and voters and by the public about the current effective objectives of policymakers. As stressed by him, this is consistent with forward-looking and rational voters who are imperfectly informed about future tax and financial regulatory environments. In his words, "when politicians make redistributive fiscal promises, voters cannot anticipate the timing, magnitude, or location of the subsequent sectoral impacts, nor can they anticipate the timing or magnitude of the related subsequent monetary surprises" (Havrilesky 1990c, p. 53). This point of view implies that objectives change more continually than just after elections and suggests the usefulness of models in which policymakers have a temporary information advantage about objectives or projected economic conditions. Models with private and continually changing information about objectives are discussed at length in part II. Models with temporary private information about the projected position of economic variables are discussed in chapters 13 and 15.

Imperfect information about the economy on the part of policymakers also complicates the task of testing alternative theories of monetary policy. Errors of forecast on their part make it difficult to detect their behavioral rules from the data. This problem is likely to become more acute when the real economy produces large uncertainties or when discrimination between closely related hypotheses about monetary policy is sought. But if the errors committed by policymakers are not systematic while their behavior is, it is still possible to extract useful information from the data provided the sample is sufficiently large.

Future tests of partisan or other theories of monetary policy should probably pay more attention to, and control for, the state of the economy. An important lesson from chapter 15 is that any administration, whether liberal or conservative, will raise the rate of monetary expansion when it expects real activity to be relatively low. In the absence of variables that proxy for the state of the economy the estimated policy mode may be biased.

The early partisan theory of monetary policy (Hibbs 1977) which is based on a permanently exploitable trade-off between inflation and economic activity implies that differences in real economic outcomes between liberal and conservative governments should be marked and persistent. But the evidence is not as clear-cut (Alesina 1989; Alesina, Cohen, and Roubini 1992). This evidence appears to be broadly consistent with the type of models discussed in this and previous chapters. The distinguishing features of these models are that they do not have a permanently exploitable trade-off and that policy objectives may change even during the term of office of the same party.

More sophisticated versions of the "opportunistic" preelectoral cycle have appeared in the recent literature. In these versions parties are only office motivated, and voters are forward-looking but imperfectly informed about the relative competence of the parties. Since a more competent party provides a higher level of welfare, voters try to identify which of the competing parties is abler in providing employment opportunities. This may lead to equilibria in which the less able party pumps up the money supply prior to elections in order to mimic its competent counterpart. An example of such a model appears in Persson and Tabellini (1990, ch. 5).

IV CENTRAL BANK INDEPENDENCE AND POLICY OUTCOMES: THEORY AND EVIDENCE

18 Aspects of Central Bank Independence and Their Impact on Policy Outcomes and the Distribution of Inflation

18.1 Introduction

There is a widespread feeling among economists and other observers of monetary policy that the degree of independence of a nation's central bank (CB) is an important determinant of policy actions and therefore of inflation. There exists a growing body of relatively informal literature that tries to characterize and quantify CB independence.[1] The basic objective difficulty in characterizing and measuring CB independence is that it is determined by a multitude of legal, institutional, cultural, and personal factors, many of which are difficult to quantify and some of which are unobservable to the general public. Most central bank observers would agree that the Bundesbank (the German CB) enjoys a high degree of independence, while the Banco Central de la Republica Argentina (the Argentinian CB) is extremely dependent on the political authorities in practice. The ranking of central banks by their degree of independence in the intermediate range, however, is much murkier. Some of the work listed in the first note to chapter 19 provides partial rankings, but the basic measurements are rudimentary as well as restricted in scope.

This chapter provides a theoretical framework for the analysis of the effects of CB independence on the distribution of inflation and other characteristics of the policy process such as inflation uncertainty and average credibility. The following chapter provides various indicators of CB independence. These indicators are used in subsequent chapters to find the effect of independence on policy outcomes. Obviously the degree of CB independence plays a meaningful role only in the presence of differences of emphasis on alternative policy objectives between the political authorities and the CB. The chapter focuses on two main differences. One relates to possible differences between the rate of time preference of political authorities and that of central banks. For various reasons central banks are normally more conservative and tend to take a longer view of the policy process. The other concerns the subjective trade-offs of the CB and of political authorities between price stability and other goals such as high employment, extraction of seigniorage revenues, and balance-of-payments objectives. The presumption is that at least on average, central banks are more conservative also in the sense that they care relatively more than political authorities about price stability. The analysis is conducted within the framework of chapter 10 in which the public is not fully informed about the shifting objectives of the political authorities and in which there is no perfect control of inflation.[2]

The conveyance of authority to the CB by political authorities can be viewed as an act of partial commitment. By delegating some of their authority to a relatively apolitical institution, politicians accept certain restrictions on their future freedom of action. The main motive for such delegation is usually the preservation of price stability. This objective competes with a number of other objectives such as high economic activity, financing of the budget, and the other objectives discussed in part I. By delegating some of their authority to the CB, political authorities try to reduce the set of circumstances under which price stability is sacrificed in order to achieve other objectives. The higher the independence of the CB, the stronger will be the commitment.[3]

In most countries the degree of CB independence is determined by formal institutional characteristics such as the CB charter as well as by more fluid and less permanent factors such as personalities and shifting views and alliances within the public sector inclusive of the CB. Since such shifts often occur far from the public eye, there normally is a certain degree of uncertainty about the current level of CB independence. Policymakers within the CB or the Treasury have better information about the current degree of CB independence than the general public and may use it to further some combination of their objectives. The chapter also analyzes the effects of this type of uncertainty when the CB is more concerned about price stability than the political authorities. Some of the implications of the theoretical analysis in this chapter are confronted with the facts in chapters 20 through 23.

To preserve clarity, each type of difference in objectives or in sources of private information is dealt with separately. Section 18.2 discusses the consequences of differences in rates of time preference between the political authorities and the CB, while section 18.3 focuses on differences in their relative preference for surprise creation. The consequences of private information about a shifting degree of CB independence are discussed in section 18.4.

Despite this multitude of formulations several general conclusions emerge. First, a lower degree of CB independence is associated in all cases with more inflation variability as well as with more inflation uncertainty. Second, subject to some reasonable restrictions, a lower degree of CB independence is also associated in all cases with a higher mean level of inflation. Third, cross-country variations in CB independence and in the difference between the objectives of political authorities and of the CB tend to produce a positive cross-country correlation between the mean and the variance of inflation. This is a well-documented empirical regularity (Logue and Willet 1976). Chapter 22 below evaluates empirically how much of this regularity is due to the common association of inflation and its variability with CB independence. Finally, the lower the degree of CB independence, the lower will be the level of average credibility as measured by the variance of the deviation between actual policy actions and the public's perception of those actions.

18.2   Central Bank Independence, Political Time Preference, and Policy Outcomes

This section focuses on the case in which the CB and the political authorities (to which we sometimes refer to as the Treasury for brevity) possess identical objective functions except for the fact that the rate of time preference of the former is lower. Several considerations suggest that such a difference in rates of time preference may be realistic. First, because of the inflationary bias of policy it is generally felt that the appointment of a central banker who is more conservative than the population average is a good strategy.[4] Conservatives usually take a longer view. Hence to the extent that there is a tendency to appoint relatively conservative individuals to high office in the central bank, the bank's rate of time is likely to be lower than that of the political authorities. The fact that in many countries high CB officials are drawn from banking or academic circles is consistent with this view. Second, due to the pervasiveness of distributional conflicts there is usually a positive probability that the government in office will be replaced by a government with a different emphasis on alternative objectives. This tends to shorten the effective planning horizon of political authorities and the more so the higher the level of political instability.[5]

The framework of chapter 10 in which policymakers have an extended information advantage about their changing preference for price stability versus employment is used here to investigate the interaction between CB independence and differences in time preference on policy outcomes. Let the objective functions of the political authorities (or Treasury) and of the CB be, respectively, to maximize

$$E_{G0} \sum_{i=0}^{\infty} \beta_T^i \left[(m_i - E[m_i | I_i]) x_i - \frac{m_i^2}{2} \right],$$ (18.1a)

$$E_{G0} \sum_{i=0}^{\infty} \beta_{CB}^i \left[(m_i - E[m_i | I_i]) x_i - \frac{m_i^2}{2} \right],$$ (18.1b)

where

$$\beta_T < \beta_{CB}.$$ (18.2)

The objective functions in equations (18.1) are essentially identical to the objective function in equation (10.7) with the following modifications: First, for simplicity and without loss of generality, α has been set equal to one. Second, it is assumed that the information sets of the CB and of the Treasury (T) are identical. Both possess the same information advantage in comparison to the public. This assumption is reflected in the notation through the fact that the index G (for government sector) attached to the conditional expected values in equations (18.1) appears in the objective function of the Treasury as well as in that of the CB. Last, but not least, although the objective functions of the T and of the CB within each period are the same, the former has a stronger preference for earlier achievements.

Actual policy outcomes will normally be influenced by both the objectives of the CB as well as by those of the T. The higher the CB independence, the larger will be the impact of the CB's lower degree of time preference in actual policy. The degree of CB independence is introduced here by postulating that there exists a nonnegative fraction $1 - \delta$ that measures the impact of the CB on actual policy choices. The lower the δ, the higher will be CB independence and the impact of the CB on policy outcomes. In particular we assume that actual policy choices can be represented as outcomes of the following problem:

$$\max_{\{m_i^p, i=0, 1, \ldots\}} E_{G0} \sum_{i=0}^{\infty} \beta^i \left[(m_i - E[m_i | I_i]) x_i - \frac{m_i^2}{2} \right],$$ (18.3)

where

$$\beta \equiv \delta \beta_T + (1 - \delta) \beta_{CB}, \qquad 0 \leq \delta \leq 1,$$ (18.4)

and where, as in chapter 10, m_i^p is the rate of inflation planned for period i and $m_i = m_i^p + \psi_i$. At the extremes when $\delta = 1$, the Treasury dictates policy, and when $\delta = 0$, the central bank dictates policy. For intermediate values of δ actual policy is nearer to the desires of the political authorities the larger is δ.

Obviously the objective functions of the CB and of the T may differ in dimensions other than the discount factor. In this section we abstract from possible other differences in order to highlight the effect of varying degrees of CB independence in the presence of systematic differences in time preference between central banks and political authorities. The consequences of some other differences in objectives are discussed in the remaining sections of this chapter.

In line with the discussion in chapters 3, 9, and 10 the unexpected inflation term in equation (18.3) is a proxy for employment. But, as stressed in Grossman (1990), the policymaker's preference for positive unexpected inflation may also reflect an underlying desire for low real costs of servicing nominally denominated debt or high revenue from seigniorage (chapter 4). It may also arise as a consequence of the balance-of-payments motive (chapter 5). Hence the unexpected inflation term in equation (18.3) may be interpreted more broadly as a proxy for a number of more basic motives for the creation of inflationary surprises. Such a "generic" interpretation (à la Grossman 1990) is less explicit than the narrower interpretation in terms of the employment motive alone. But it possesses the virtue of making it possible to aggregate in a simple manner all the motives which are served by unexpected inflation.

Since the information structure and the problem in equation (18.3) are formally identical to their respective counterparts in chapter 10, they have the same formal solutions. In particular equations (10.16) and (10.17) imply that the mean and the variance of inflation are given, respectively, by

$$Em_i = \frac{1 - \beta\rho}{1 - \beta\lambda(B)} A, \tag{18.5a}$$

$$V(m_i) = B^2 \frac{\sigma_v^2}{1 - \rho^2} + \sigma_\psi^2, \tag{18.5b}$$

where (from 10.12b)

$$B = \frac{1 - \beta\rho^2}{1 - \beta\rho\lambda(B)} \tag{18.6}$$

and where $\lambda(B)$ is given by equations (10.5). We turn next to an investigation of the effect of CB independence, as measured by $1 - \delta$, on the mean level and on the variance of inflation. Equations (18.4) and (18.2) imply that β from chapter 10 is equal to $\delta\beta_T + (1 - \delta)\beta_{CB}$ and therefore that

$$\frac{\partial \beta}{\partial \delta} = \beta_T - \beta_{CB} < 0. \tag{18.7}$$

Thus, ceteris paribus, a reduction in CB independence is equivalent to a reduction in the combined discount factor β. Hence under the conditions of this section, comparative statics with respect to β can be used to determine the effect of CB independence on the mean and on the variance of inflation. The effect of β on mean inflation Em_i seems to be ambiguous because it also affects the equilibrium value of B and through it the equilibrium value of $\lambda(B)$. However, it is shown in appendix A that even after account is taken of this channel

$$\frac{\partial Em_i}{\partial \beta} < 0. \tag{18.8}$$

This leads to the following proposition:

PROPOSITION 18.1   The mean rate of inflation in a country is higher, the lower the independence of its CB (the higher δ).[6]

Proposition 10.4, in conjunction with the result in equation (18.7), implies that

PROPOSITION 18.2   The variance of inflation in a country is higher, the lower the independence of its CB (the higher δ).

Propositions 18.1 and 18.2 imply that countries with lesser degrees of central bank independence should exhibit higher mean levels of inflation as well as larger inflation variabilities. This is summarized in proposition 18.3:

PROPOSITION 18.3   Other things the same, cross-country differences in CB independence induce a positive cross-country correlation between the mean and the variance of inflation.

The degree of CB independence also affects the public's speed of learning, the average credibility of policy plans and the level of inflation uncertainty. Proposition 18.4 summarizes these effects:

PROPOSITION 18.4   The lower the degree of CB independence, the higher is the public's speed of learning about changing objectives, the lower is average credibility, and the higher is the level of inflation uncertainty.

Proof The first two parts of the proposition are direct consequences of propositions 10.1 and 10.2 in conjunction with equation (18.7). The last result follows by noting that

$$E[m_i - E[m_i|I_i]] = E\{m_i^p - E[m_i^p|I_i]\} + \sigma_\psi^2 \equiv V^p + \sigma_\psi^2$$

and by recalling that V^p is increasing in δ by part two of the proposition. □

The intuition underlying these results is similar to the intuition that underlies similar results in chapter 10. Lower CB independence means that policy is characterized by a stronger degree of time preference. This increases the degree of activism of policy which speeds in turn the public's learning process. However, a higher level of activism also increases the expected value of the squared difference between planned and expected inflation. This means that average credibility is lower and that the level of inflation uncertainty inflicted on the public is higher.

An obvious consequence of proposition 18.4 is that the level of inflation uncertainty in a country such as Germany, which has a highly independent CB, is relatively low. By the same token a unit change in the rate of inflation in such a country has a relatively strong impact on output, since the public is relatively slow in detecting changes in policy trends. During the second half of the 1980s France reduced its rate of inflation to the German level. However, because the Banque de France is less independent than the Bundesbank, the level of inflation uncertainty in France did not fully converge to the German level.

18.3 Central Bank Independence in the Presence of Differences in Emphasis on Alternative Objectives

In many cases central banks are more conservative than political authorities also in the sense that they attribute relatively more importance to the goal of price stability. This higher concern may take two forms. First, the mean value of the coefficient of unexpected inflation in the CB objective function is lower than the mean value of this coefficient in the objective function of the political authorities. Second, central banks are less affected by political developments and pressures than Treasury departments. Hence, provided that they are sufficiently independent, central banks tend to stick more consistently to some basic objectives. This means that the relative preference of the Treasury for surprise inflation undergoes wider and more uncertain fluctuations than its counterpart in the objective function of the CB.

We approximate this state of affairs here by postulating that the relative preference of the CB for price stability is constant over time while that of the Treasury is subject to random but persistent political shocks. The objective functions of the Treasury and of the Central Bank in equations (18.9) as well as equations (18.10) and (18.11) reflect these hypotheses:

$$E_{GO} \sum_{i=0}^{\infty} \beta^i \left[(m_i - E[m_i|I_i])(A_T + u_i) - \frac{m_i^2}{2} \right], \qquad (18.9a)$$

$$E_{GO} \sum_{i=0}^{\infty} \beta^i \left[(m_i - E[m_i|I_i])A_{CB} - \frac{m_i^2}{2} \right], \qquad (18.9b)$$

where

$$u_i = \rho u_{i-1} + \tilde{v}_i, \qquad 0 < \rho < 1, \qquad (18.10a)$$

$$\tilde{v}_i \sim N(0, \sigma_{\tilde{v}}^2), \qquad (18.10b)$$

$$A_T > A_{CB} \geq 0. \qquad (18.11)$$

The objective functions of the Treasury (T) and of the CB differ only in two elements. The Treasury's relative preference for surprises is larger on average and is also more variable than that of the CB. To focus on those differences in isolation, the formulation abstracts from CB − T differentials in rates of time preference of the type discussed in the previous section. But in several other dimensions it is similar. The information structure is the same. The CB and the T are equally informed about shocks to the relative objectives of the T. These shocks exhibit a certain degree of persistence whose precise structure is given by equations (18.10). The public sector (T and CB) knows the current and past values of u_i, while individuals can only make inferences about them from past inflation. But since policymakers do not have perfect control over the money supply, these inferences are subject to error and the public's learning process takes time as in chapter 10. The precise manner in which the public's learning process and the governmental (T and CB) policymaking process interact is discussed below. Note that as in the previous section the benefits from surprises may be interpreted as arising from the effect of surprises on employment or more generally in terms of several additional objectives such as the revenue and the balance-of-payments motives, all of which produce a preference for positive surprises.

Let δ be a parameter between zero and one that measures the extent to which the CB depends on political authorities. In particular suppose that given δ, the actual choice of policy can be represented as arising from the maximization of a weighted average of the objective functions in (18.9a) and (18.9b) with weights δ and $1 - \delta$, respectively. This intermediate objective function, which reflects the relative influence of the CB on the choice of policy instruments, is given in equation (18.12):

$$\max_{\{m_i^p, i=0,1,\ldots\}} E_{G0} \sum_{i=0}^{\infty} \beta^i \left[(m_i - E[m_i|I_i])x_i - \frac{m_i^2}{2} \right], \tag{18.12}$$

where

$$x_i \equiv (1 - \delta)A_{CB} + \delta A_T + \delta u_i. \tag{18.13}$$

As in chapter 10,

$$m_i = m_i^p + \psi_i, \tag{18.14}$$

where m_i^p is the planned rate of monetary expansion and ψ_i is a control error with mean zero and variance σ_ψ^2. Examination of equations (18.12) and (18.13) reveals that the maximization problem in the first equation is formally identical to the problem in equation (10.7), with A and p_i from chapters 9 and 10 replaced now by $(1 - \delta)A_{CB} + \delta A_T$ and δu_i, respectively. Defining $p_i \equiv \delta u_i$ and $v_i \equiv \delta \tilde{v}_i$ and using (18.10a), we obtain

$$p_i = \delta[\rho u_{i-1} + \tilde{v}_i] = \rho p_{i-1} + v_i, \tag{18.15}$$

which is formally identical to the stochastic component of the policy-maker's objectives in equation (9.3b). Since the stochastic and information structure presented here is identical to that of chapter 10, all the results from that chapter carry over to this section with

$$A = (1 - \delta)A_{CB} + \delta A_T = A_{CB} + \delta(A_T - A_{CB}), \tag{18.16a}$$

$$p_i = \delta u_i. \tag{18.16b}$$

In particular equation (18.16a) implies that the mean relative preference of policy for surprise creation A is larger, the lower the degree of CB independence (higher δ) and the larger, ceteris paribus, the average difference $A_T - A_{CB}$ between the relative objectives of the Treasury and those of the

CB. From (18.15) and (18.16b), we note that

$$\sigma_p^2 = \delta^2 \sigma_u^2 = \frac{\delta^2 \sigma_{\bar{v}}^2}{1 - \rho^2}. \tag{18.17}$$

Thus a lower degree of CB independence (a higher δ) is also associated with a higher variability in the relative preference of the actual policy process for price stability versus surprise creation. Essentially with a lesser degree of CB independence a larger portion of the uncertainties confronting political authorities is injected into the policy process. Equation (18.17) implies that $\delta^2 \sigma_{\bar{v}}^2$ plays the same role as σ_v^2 in chapter 10. It follows from proposition 8.4 that the variability of inflation is larger the larger is δ. This is summarized in the following proposition:

PROPOSITION 18.5   In the presence of differences in objectives between the CB and the political authorities of the type summarized in equations (18.9)–(18.11), inflation variability and CB independence are negatively related.

The larger the mean difference $A_T - A_{CB}$ between the objectives of the Treasury and those of the CB, the larger is A and the larger is (from equation 18.5a) the mean level of inflation. It would seem at first blush that in view of the relation in (18.16a), an increase in δ affects mean inflation in the same direction as an increase in $A_T - A_{CB}$. However, the matter is more involved since, given $\sigma_{\bar{v}}^2$, a change in δ also changes σ_v^2, λ, and B. This can be seen more clearly by noting, from (18.6a) and (18.5), that

$$Em_i = \frac{1 - \beta \rho}{1 - \beta \lambda} [A_{CB} + \delta(A_T - A_{CB})]. \tag{18.18}$$

Since $A_T - A_{CB}$ is positive, the direct effect of an increase in δ on Em_i is positive. But, by raising $\delta^2 \sigma_{\bar{v}}^2$, an increase in δ also reduces λ, and this affects Em_i in the opposite direction. However, if A_{CB} is sufficiently small or the difference between A_T and A_{CB} sufficiently large, the first effect dominates. This is summarized in proposition 18.6:

PROPOSITION 18.6   If the CB relative concern for price stability is large in comparison to the average difference in objectives between the CB and the T (A_{CB} is small in comparison to $A_T - A_{CB}$), lower CB independence is associated with higher mean inflation.

The proof of the proposition and a precise statement of the condition appear in appendix B. Note that the condition in proposition 8.6 is sufficient but not necessary so that CB independence and mean inflation may be negatively related even when the condition is not satisfied.[7] Combining propositions 18.5 and 18.6 we obtain the following:

PROPOSITION 18.7   Under the conditions of propositions 18.5 and 18.6 a larger degree of CB independence (a lower δ) is associated with a higher mean level of inflation as well as with more inflation variability.

An important corollary of proposition 18.7 is that, other things the same, cross-country variations in CB independence induce a positive cross-country correlation between the mean and the variance of inflation.

The effects of CB independence on credibility, inflation uncertainty, and the speed of learning can be established by recalling that σ_v^2 from chapter 10 is replaced here by $\delta^2 \sigma_{\tilde{v}}^2$ and by using some of the results in chapter 10. The following proposition summarizes these effects:

PROPOSITION 18.8   In the presence of differences in objectives between CB and T of the type summarized in equations (18.9)–(18.11), a lower degree of CB independence is associated with a faster speed of learning, a lower level of average credibility, and a higher level of inflation uncertainty.

Proof   Letting

$$\sigma_v^2 = \delta^2 \sigma_{\tilde{v}}^2$$

it can be seen that a reduction in independence (an increase in δ) is equivalent to an increase in σ_v^2 in the model of chapter 10. But the effects of σ_v^2 on the speed of learning and on average credibility are given by propositions 10.1 and 10.2. This establishes the first two parts of the proposition. The third part follows by noting (as in the proof of proposition 18.4) that inflation uncertainty is equal to average credibility plus a constant which does not depend on σ_v^2. $\square$

18.4   Private Information about Central Bank Independence

The degree of CB independence is determined by the nature of political and legal institutions as well as by less formal and more fluid factors such as accepted practice, culture, and personalities. At the legal level the degree of CB independence is determined by the charter of the CB. Charters normally specify CB objectives, procedures for appointment, and periods of tenure of high CB officials, monetary instruments under the control of the bank, and at times procedures for the resolution of policy conflicts between the CB and the political authorities.[8]

But the actual, as opposed to the legislated, degree of CB independence also depends on many other less formal factors. This occurs for several reasons. First, the law covers only a small subset of the contingencies that arise in practice. Second, even when the law specifies explicitly what should be done, actual practice may deviate from the letter of the law.[9] Last, but not least, actual independence depends on a multitude of informal factors like personalities and internal developments within the bank, the Treasury, and other concerned institutions within the public sector. The less explicit the CB charter the larger the relative importance of such more fluid factors in shaping the actual degree of CB independence. Such factors tend to change over time, and the noninitiated public normally realizes their full impact with a lag, mostly through their effect on policy outcomes.

This section discusses the effects of private information about a changing degree of CB independence on policy outcomes and the distribution of inflation. The setup is similar to that of the previous section. In particular the relative preference of the Treasury for surprise creation is larger on average than that of the CB. To focus on the effects of private information about CB independence in isolation, we abstract from variations in the Treasury's relative preference for inflationary surprises. More precisely the Treasury's objective function is given by equation (18.9a) with u_i identically equal to zero, that of the CB is given by equation (18.9b), and equation (18.11) specifies the relative sizes of A_T and A_{CB}. Actual policy is determined so as to maximize a weighted average of those two objective functions with weights δ_i and $1 - \delta_i$, respectively, where the mean of δ_i is $\bar{\delta}$ and

$$\delta_i - \bar{\delta} = \rho(\delta_{i-1} - \bar{\delta}) + \tilde{v}_i, \qquad 0 < \rho < 1, \tag{18.19a}$$

$$\tilde{v}_i \sim N(0, \sigma_v^2). \tag{18.19b}$$

In these equations δ is obviously bounded between zero and one and is publicly known. However, the fluctuations of actual independence, δ_i, around $\bar{\delta}$ are the private information of the public sector which as in the previous sections includes both the Treasury and the CB. The mean level of independence $\bar{\delta}$ captures that part of independence that is firmly grounded in the charter and other institutions of the country, while deviations from the mean, $\delta_i - \bar{\delta}$, stand for the more fluid determinants of independence such as personal relationships between CB and Treasury officials. The specification in equation (18.19) postulates that, although temporary in nature, fluctuations in CB independence possess a certain degree of persistence whose magnitude is characterized by the positive coefficient ρ. This specification is designed to capture the fact that if, for example, due to his or her personality, the governor currently has more influence on the policy process than what his or her formal powers grant, this state of affairs is likely to persist for some time.

The larger δ_i the lower the actual current degree of CB independence in period i. As in previous sections the nature of the discussion requires that δ_i be bounded between 0 and 1 which is obviously in contradiction with the normal specification adopted for $\tilde{v}_i$ in equation (18.19). But, if the variance $\sigma_{\tilde{v}}^2$ is sufficiently small, the probability that δ_i will be outside the range $[0, 1]$ can be made as small as desired. The precise condition is stated and developed in appendix C. The remainder of the discussion in this section is based on the presumption that such a condition is satisfied so that δ_i is almost always in the range $[0, 1]$.

Forming a weighted average, with weights δ_i and $1 - \delta_i$, of the objective functions of the T and of the CB the choice of planned inflation can be derived from the maximization problem in equation (18.12) where, however, equation (18.13) is replaced with

$$x_i = (1 - \delta_i)A_{CB} + \delta_i A_T = A_{CB} + (A_T - A_{CB})\delta_i. \tag{18.20}$$

The fluctuating degree of CB independence δ_i affects x_i and, through it, the choice of planned monetary growth. The public observes past rates of monetary inflation and learns from it about fluctuations in the degree of CB independence. Since shocks to CB independence exhibit positive serial correlation, past rates of inflation are relevant for predicting future levels of CB independence and of inflation. However, these predictions, as well as inferences about past levels of independence, are subject to error because of the existence of monetary control errors.

At the formal level the framework of this section is identical to that of chapter 10 with

$$Ex_i = A_{CB} + (A_T - A_{CB})\bar{\delta} \equiv A, \tag{18.21a}$$

$$x_i - A = (A_T - A_{CB})(\delta_i - \bar{\delta}) \equiv D(\delta_i - \bar{\delta}). \tag{18.21b}$$

Note that the expression in equation (18.21a) plays the role of A from chapter 10 and that, in view of equations (18.19) and (18.21b),

$$x_i - A = D(\delta_i - \bar{\delta}) = \rho D(\delta_{i-1} - \bar{\delta}) + D\tilde{v}_i. \tag{18.22a}$$

Letting $D(\delta_i - \bar{\delta})$ be equal to p_i from chapter 10, this equation can be rewritten as

$$p_i = \rho p_{i-1} + D\tilde{v}_i \equiv \rho p_{i-1} + v_i. \tag{18.22b}$$

It follows that $D(\delta_i - \bar{\delta})$ has the same stochastic structure as p_i in chapter 10, with

$$\sigma_v^2 = D^2 \sigma_{\tilde{v}}^2 \quad \text{and} \quad \sigma_p^2 = \frac{D^2 \sigma_{\tilde{v}}^2}{1 - \rho^2} = \frac{\sigma_v^2}{1 - \rho^2}. \tag{18.23}$$

Thus, subject to the correspondence between the two models as given by equations (18.21)–(18.23), we can use results from chapter 10 in order to characterize the effects of CB independence and its distribution on the distribution of inflation and on related matters. Using equations (18.21a) and (18.23) in equations (10.17) and (10.18), we obtain that the mean and the variance of inflation are, respectively,[10]

$$Em_i = \frac{1 - \beta\rho}{1 - \beta\lambda}[A_{CB} + D\bar{\delta}], \tag{18.24a}$$

$$V(m_i) = \left[\frac{1 - \beta\rho^2}{1 - \beta\rho\lambda}\right]^2 \frac{D^2 \sigma_{\tilde{v}}^2}{1 - \rho^2} + \sigma_\psi^2. \tag{18.24b}$$

Since $D \equiv A_T - A_{CB} > 0$, a reduction in the mean level of CB independence (an increase in $\bar{\delta}$) obviously raises average inflation. Interestingly the size of the difference between the relative preference of the T and of the CB for surprise creation affects both the mean and the variance of inflation. The following proposition summarizes the effects:

PROPOSITION 18.9   In the presence of private information about CB independence larger values of D are associated, ceteris paribus, with

1.   more inflation variability,

2. a larger mean level of inflation provided that D is sufficiently large in comparison to A_{CB} or provided that β is sufficiently small.

Proof   Part 1 is a direct consequence of proposition 10.4 in conjunction with equation (18.23). The proof of part 2, as well as a more precise statement of the conditions, is in appendix D. $\square$

As in the previous section the effect of D on mean inflation is not unconditionally positive because, besides its obvious and direct positive effect, D also affects σ_v^2 and λ which operates in the opposite direction. But, under the sufficient, but not necessary, conditions stated in the proposition, the positive effect dominates.

The positive effect of D on inflation variability can be understood intuitively by noting that changes in the degree of CB independence induce larger changes in actual policy the larger the difference in objectives between T and CB as measured by $D \equiv A_T - A_{CB}$. In the limit when those two institutions have identical objectives changes in CB, independence has no effect on policy plans (in this case σ_v^2 in equation 18.23 is equal to zero).

The following proposition summarizes the effect of the size of the divergence $A_T - A_{CB}$ between the objectives of the Treasury and those of the CB on the speed of learning, average credibility, and inflation uncertainty.

PROPOSITION 18.11   In the presence of private information about CB independence, a larger divergence $D \equiv A_T - A_{CB}$ between the objectives of the Treasury and those of the CB is associated with a faster speed of learning, a lower level of average credibility, and a higher level of inflation uncertainty.

Proof   After noting from equation (18.23) that σ_v^2 is an increasing function of D, the proof is identical to that of proposition 18.8. $\square$

Essentially a larger divergence in objectives implies that changes in the degree of CB independence have a stronger impact on the actual choice of policy. In terms of the model of chapter 10 this is equivalent to an increase in the variance σ_v^2 of the innovations to the objectives of the consolidated government sector. The results in proposition 18.11 then follow directly from the propositions in chapter 10 dealing with the effects of a change in σ_v^2.

The variance $\sigma_{\bar{v}}^2$ of innovations to CB independence measures the extent to which the law leaves the CB at the discretion of the political authorities. The less specific is the law about the responsibilities and authority of the CB the larger the potential impact of political authorities on CB independence. This does not necessarily mean that central banks with less explicit charters are less independent on average although this is likely to be the case. But it most certainly means that the range of possible variations in CB independence in such countries is larger. The consequences of this observation are summarized in proposition 18.12:

PROPOSITION 18.12   In the presence of private information about CB independence a lower degree of formal independence, which takes the form of a higher $\sigma_{\bar{v}}^2$, is associated with a faster speed of learning, a higher level of inflation uncertainty, and a lower level of average credibility.

Proof   After noting that σ_v^2 and $\sigma_{\bar{v}}^2$ are positively related, the proof is identical to that of proposition 18.11.   □

18.5   Concluding Remarks

This chapter has discussed the effects of CB independence on the distribution of inflation and related issues under the hypotheses that central banks are usually more conservative than political authorities, in the sense that they take a longer view of policy objectives and are more concerned about price stability than the political authorities. Several broad conclusions emerge from the analysis. In particular it is found that lower levels of CB independence are associated with more inflation variability and, under some plausible restrictions, also with higher mean levels of inflation. These and other results of the analysis are used as an organizing framework for some of the empirical chapters that follow.

Appendix A: Derivation of Equation (18.8)

Differentiating equation (18.5a) totally with respect to β,

$$\frac{dEm_i}{d\beta} = \frac{\alpha A}{(1 - \beta\lambda)^2}\left[-(\rho - \lambda) + \beta(1 - \rho\beta)\frac{d\lambda}{d\beta}\right]. \tag{18A.1}$$

From equations (10.5) and (10.12b) specialized to the case $\alpha = 1$, we obtain

$$\frac{d\lambda}{d\beta} = \frac{\partial\lambda}{\partial r}\frac{\partial r}{\partial B}\frac{dB}{d\beta}, \tag{18A.2}$$

$$\frac{dB}{d\beta} = \frac{\rho(1 - \beta\rho^2)[\lambda + \beta(d\lambda/d\beta)] - \rho^2(1 - \beta\rho\lambda)}{(1 - \beta\rho\lambda)^2}. \tag{18A.3}$$

Using (10.5b) and (10.5c) to calculate $\partial\lambda/\partial r$ and $\partial r/\partial\beta$, substituting the resulting expressions and (18A.3) in (18A.2), we obtain after some rearrangement

$$\frac{d\lambda}{d\beta} = \frac{(\rho - \lambda)\lambda r}{(1 - \beta\rho^2)\{(1 - \beta\rho\lambda)\sqrt{b} + \beta\lambda r\}}, \tag{18A.4}$$

where r is given by equation (10.5c) and

$$b \equiv \frac{1}{4}\left(\frac{1 + r}{\rho} + \rho\right)^2 - 1 > 0. \tag{18A.5}$$

Substituting (18A.4) into (18A.1) and rearranging, we get

$$\frac{dEm_i}{d\beta} = -\frac{A(\rho - \lambda)[\rho\beta^2\lambda r(1 - \rho) + (1 - \beta\rho^2)(1 - \beta\rho\lambda)\sqrt{b}]}{(1 - \beta\lambda)^2(1 - \beta\rho^2)[(1 - \beta\rho\lambda)\sqrt{b} + \beta\lambda r]}. \tag{18A.6}$$

Since (except for the case $\sigma_v^2/\sigma_\psi^2 \to 0$) $\rho - \lambda > 0$ and since β, λ, and ρ are all bounded between zero and one, the expression in (18A.6) is negative. □

Appendix B: Proof and Precise Statement of Proposition 18.2

Differentiating equation (18.5a) totally with respect to δ

$$\frac{dEm_i}{d\delta} = \frac{1 - \beta\rho}{(1 - \beta\lambda)^2}\left[(1 - \beta\lambda)(A_T - A_{CB}) + \beta(\delta A_T + (1 - \delta)A_{CB})\frac{d\lambda}{d\delta}\right]. \tag{18A.7}$$

Since

$$\sigma_v^2 = \delta^2\sigma_{\tilde{v}}^2, \tag{18A.8}$$

$$\frac{d\lambda}{d\delta} = \frac{d\lambda}{d\sigma_v^2}\frac{\partial\sigma_v^2}{\partial\delta} = 2\delta\sigma_{\tilde{v}}^2\frac{d\lambda}{d\sigma_v^2}. \tag{18A.9}$$

From equations (10.5b) and (10.5c),

$$\frac{d\lambda}{d\sigma_v^2} = \frac{\partial\lambda}{\partial r}\frac{dr}{d\sigma_v^2} = \frac{\partial\lambda}{\partial r}\frac{1}{\sigma_\psi^2}\left[2\sigma_v^2 B\frac{dB}{d\sigma_v^2} + B^2\right]. \tag{18A.10}$$

From equation (10.12b),

$$\frac{dB}{d\sigma_v^2} = \frac{\beta\rho B}{1 - \beta\rho\lambda} \frac{d\lambda}{d\sigma_v^2}.$$ (18A.11)

Using (18A.11) in (18A.10), rearranging, and using (10.5b) to calculate $\partial\lambda/\partial r$, we obtain

$$\frac{d\lambda}{d\sigma_v^2} = -\frac{(1 - \beta\rho\lambda)\lambda B^2}{2\rho[\beta\sigma_v^2\lambda B^2 + (1 - \beta\rho\lambda)\sigma_\psi^2\sqrt{b}]},$$ (18A.12)

where b is given by (18A.5). Substituting (18A.12) into (18A.9), inserting the resulting expression in (18A.7), and rearranging, we obtain

$$\frac{dEm_i}{d\delta} = \frac{1 - \beta\rho}{(1 - \beta\lambda)^2}$$

$$\cdot\frac{\delta\{\rho(1 - \beta\rho\lambda)(1 - \beta\lambda)\sqrt{b} - (1 - \rho)\lambda\beta r\}(A_T - A_{CB}) - (1 - \beta\rho\lambda)\lambda\beta r A_{CB}}{\rho\delta[\beta\lambda r + (1 - \beta\rho\lambda)\sqrt{b}]}$$ (18A.13)

The denominator of (18A.13) is unambiguously positive and so are $(1 - \beta\rho)$ and $(1 - \beta\rho\lambda)$.

A necessary and sufficient condition for the coefficient of $A_T - A_{CB}$ to be positive is

$$b > \left[\frac{\lambda\beta(1 - \rho)}{\rho(1 - \beta\rho\lambda)(1 - \beta\lambda)}r\right]^2.$$ (18A.14)

In view of (18A.5), this condition is equivalent to

$$\left(\frac{1}{\rho} + \rho\right) - 4 + 2\left(\frac{1}{\rho} + \rho\right)r + \left\{1 - 4\left[\frac{\lambda(1 - \rho)\beta}{\rho(1 - \beta\lambda)(1 - \rho\lambda\beta)}\right]^2\right\}r^2 > 0.$$ (18A.15)

Since $(1/\rho + \rho)^2$ is always larger than or equal to 4 in the range $0 \le \rho \le 1$, the first two terms in (18A.15) are unambiguously positive. The last term is also positive if and only if

$$T(\lambda) \equiv \frac{\lambda(1 - \rho)\beta}{\rho(1 - \beta\lambda)(1 - \rho\beta\lambda)} < \frac{1}{2}.$$ (18A.16)

But, since $\rho \ge \lambda$,

$$T(\lambda) \le T(\rho) = \frac{(1 - \rho)\beta}{(1 - \beta\rho)(1 - \beta\rho^2)}.$$

It follows from the last two equations that

$$T(\rho) < \tfrac{1}{2} \qquad\qquad\qquad\qquad\qquad\qquad\qquad (18A.17)$$

is sufficient for the condition in (18A.16). Rearranging condition (18A.17) it is equivalent to

$$P(\beta) \equiv \rho^3\beta^2 - [2 - \rho(1 - \rho)]\beta + 1 > 0. \qquad\qquad (18A.18)$$

This is a polynomial in β whose minimum value is $1 - \rho^3\beta^2$, which is nonnegative since both β and ρ are bounded from above by one. Hence $P(\beta) > 0$ for all values of β and ρ in the relevant range. Hence the coefficient of r^2 in (18A.15) is also nonnegative, and the coefficient of $A_T - A_{CB}$ in (18A.13) is therefore unambiguously positive.

Since the coefficient of A_{CB} in (18A.13) is negative the sign of $dEm_i/d\delta$ may in general be either positive or negative. However, if A_{CB} is sufficiently small in comparison to $A_T - A_{CB}$, the positive effect dominates.

Examination of (18A.13) also reveals that for any values of A_T and of A_{CB} such that $A_T - A_{CB} > 0$, the positive effect dominates provided that β is sufficiently small. $\square$

Appendix C: A Condition for δ_i to Be Bounded between Zero and One with High Probability

From equations (18.19), we have

$$\delta_i - \bar{\delta} \sim N\left[0, \frac{\sigma_{\tilde{v}}^2}{1 - \rho^2}\right].$$

δ_i is bounded between zero and one if and only if $\delta_i - \bar{\delta}$ is bounded between $-\bar{\delta}$ and $1 - \bar{\delta}$. To make the probability of a realization of δ_i outside the range $[0, 1]$ lower than some preassigned level, we require that

$$K\frac{\sigma_{\tilde{v}}}{\sqrt{1 - \rho^2}} \le \max[\bar{\delta}, 1 - \bar{\delta}], \qquad\qquad\qquad (18A.19)$$

where K is a constant which depends on that probability. Rearranging equation (18A.19), we obtain

$$\sigma_{\tilde{v}} \leq \frac{\sqrt{1 - \rho^2}}{K} \max[\bar{\delta}, 1 - \bar{\delta}].$$ (18A.20)

When condition (18A.20) is satisfied for $K \geq 2.6$, δ_i falls in the range $[0, 1]$ with a probability that is at least 0.99.

Appendix D: Proof of Part 2 in Proposition 18.8

Differentiating (18.24a) totally with respect to D and using (18.23), we have

$$\frac{dEm_i}{dD} = \frac{1 - \beta\rho}{(1 - \beta\lambda)^2} \left[(1 - \beta\lambda)\bar{\delta} + 2\beta D\sigma_{\tilde{v}}^2 (A_{CB} + D\bar{\delta}) \frac{d\lambda}{d\sigma_v^2} \right].$$ (18A.21)

Then substituting (18A.12) into (18A.21) and rearranging, we get

$$\frac{dEm_i}{dD} = \frac{1 - \beta\rho}{(1 - \beta\lambda)^2} \times \frac{K_1 \bar{\delta}(A_T - A_{CB}) - K_2 A_{CB}}{\rho D[\beta\lambda r + (1 - \beta\rho\lambda)\sqrt{b}]},$$ (18A.22)

where

$$K_1 \equiv \rho(1 - \beta\rho\lambda)(1 - \beta\lambda)\sqrt{b} - (1 - \rho)\lambda\beta r,$$ (18A.23a)

$$K_2 \equiv (1 - \beta\rho\lambda)\lambda\beta r.$$ (18A.23b)

Since ρ, λ, and β are all bounded between zero and one, all the terms in (18A.22) (except possibly K_1) are positive. However, K_1 is also the coefficient of $A_T - A_{CB}$ in equation (18A.13). It was shown in appendix B that this coefficient is positive too. Hence all terms in (18A.22) including K_1 and K_2 are positive. It follows that dEm_i/dD is positive if

$$A_T - A_{CB} > \frac{K_2}{\bar{\delta}K_1} A_{CB}.$$

Alternatively, it can be seen from equations (18A.23) that dEm_i/dD is positive provided that β is sufficiently small. $\square$

19 The Measurement of Central Bank Independence

19.1 Introduction

Economists and practitioners in the area of monetary policy generally believe that the degree of CB independence from other parts of government affects the rates of expansion of money and credit and through them important macroeconomic variables such as inflation and the size of the budget deficit. In particular it is generally felt that a high level of CB independence coupled with an explicit mandate for the bank to focus on the price stability objective are important institutional devices for the assurance of price stability.

This belief has eluded comprehensive verification because of the obvious difficulties in objectively measuring the degree of independence of various central banks. Actual, as opposed to formal, CB independence depends on the degree of independence conferred on the bank by law but also on a myriad of other less structured factors such as informal arrangements between the bank and other parts of government, the quality of the bank's research department, and the personalities of key individuals in the bank and other economic policymaking organs like the Treasury. It is obviously hard to quantify such features in an impartial manner. As a consequence existing efforts to develop indices of CB independence have focused mostly on legal independence and only for the developed countries at that.[1] Additional indicators of CB independence are therefore called upon. Such indicators would usefully complement those that are based only on the law for at least two reasons. First, CB laws are usually incomplete in the sense that they do not specify explicitly the limits of authority between the CB and the political authorities under all contingencies. These voids are filled by informal practices, tradition, and the like. Second, even when the law is quite explicit, actual practice may deviate from it.

This chapter presents three different sets of indicators for CB independence. The first set includes various proxies of legal independence. The other two indicators are designed to proxy for deviations of actual from legal independence. One is the actual turnover of CB governors or, in some cases, the ratio of the actual to the legal term of office of the governor. These proxies are motivated by the notion that above some threshold, turnover and actual CB independence are negatively related, and by the observation that in many countries there are substantial discrepancies between the actual and the legal terms of office of the CB governor. For example, in Argentina the legal term of office is four years. However, the actual average term in office of Argentinian CB governors has been less than a year over the 1980s. The last set of indicators (which, unlike the previous two, refers only to the 1980s and to a subset of twenty-four countries) is based on the responses of specialists on monetary policy in the respective countries to a questionnaire designed to identify factors that may induce divergences between the CB charter and actual practice.

The concept of independence that this chapter attempts to measure is not the independence to do anything that the CB pleases. It is rather the ability of the bank to stick to the price stability objective even at the cost of other short-term real objectives. This point of view implies that tighter limitations on borrowing by government from the CB make the bank more independent. It also implies that, ceteris paribus, a bank whose charter specifies explicitly that the bank's first priority should be price stability is more independent than a bank whose charter mentions price stability along with several other objectives without specifying which objective is more important.

The use of many different proxies to characterize independence is based on the notion that each proxy is a noisy indicator that captures a somewhat different aspect of CB independence. Using them all to characterize independence is therefore desirable, first because they partly complement each other and second because this reduces the noisiness of the overall measure. This idea is implemented in several steps. In the first stage CBs are ranked by combining information only within each set of indicators. This produces three alternative rankings of CBs by their degree of independence: one by legal independence, the other by CB governors' turnover rates, and the third by an aggregate of coded responses to the questionnaire on CB independence. In the second stage the first two sets of indicators are combined by using their relative impacts on inflation to produce an overall ranking. The first and second stages are discussed in this and the next chapters respectively.

This chapter extends existing measures of CB independence along several dimensions. First, the set of countries is wider. Second, additional new proxies for CB independence are used in addition to the legal proxies. The sample considered is composed of up to seventy countries including all the developed (or industrial) countries (DC) as well as up to forty-nine less developed or developing countries (LDC). The wider sample makes it possible to rank central banks by their independence over a more heterogeneous group of countries and to examine whether there are systematic differences in CB independence between the two groups. Finally, the legal proxies for independence are constructed in a uniform manner for the entire sample.

The following two chapters utilize the indices of independence presented here in order to test some of the implications developed in chapter 18 as well as less structured, but wider related hypotheses. This chapter is organized as follows: Measures of legal independence are presented in section 19.2 and used, in section 19.3, to rank central banks by overall legal independence. Data on CB governors' turnover rates is presented and discussed in section 19.4. Questionnaire-based indices of independence are described in section 19.5. The interrelationships between the various proxies of independence are examined in section 19.6. Additional dimensions of CB independence are discussed in section 19.7.

19.2 Measures of Legal Central Bank Independence and Their Coding

Besides being an essential component of actual independence, legal independence is of independent interest for several reasons. First, it suggests what is the degree of independence that legislators *meant to confer* on the CB. Second, practically all existing attempts at the systematic characterization of CB independence rely solely on legal aspects of independence (Bade and Parkin 1980; Banaian, Laney, and Willet 1983; Skanland 1984; Parkin 1987; Alesina 1988; Masciandaro and Tabellini 1988; Grilli, Masciandaro, and Tabellini 1991). Availability of an index of legal independence is therefore needed for the purpose of establishing comparability with previous studies.

There generally are substantial differences in the focus, scope, and degree of detail of various CB laws. Many of the provisions in CB charters have no direct bearing on the issue of CB independence. At times the spirit of the law and its application in practice are more important than the letter of the law. Ranking of CB charters by their degree of legal independence is therefore a difficult task involving an inescapable amount of subjective judgment.

The indices of legal aspects of CB independence presented below are constructed in the following manner: First, they are based on a limited number of narrow but relatively precise legal characteristics. Second, a code of independence is assigned to each central bank for each characteristic. In doing that, only the written information from the charters is used.

Additional information on how the law is applied is deliberately left out because it is reflected through separate indices that are discussed in sections 19.4 and 19.5. These principles make it possible to rank central banks by their degree of independence on various legal dimensions with a relatively small amount of subjective judgment and to focus on concrete details of the law rather than on a broader but more impressionistic view of it.

The legal characteristics or "variables" which are coded can be divided into four groups: (1) variables concerning the appointment, dismissal, and term of office of the chief executive officer of the bank (usually the governor); (2) variables concerning the resolution of conflicts between the executive branch and the CB and the degree of participation of the CB in the formulation of monetary policy and in the budgetary process; (3) final objectives of the CB as stated in its charter; and (4) legal restrictions on the ability of the public sector to borrow from the CB. Such restrictions take the form of various limitations on the volume, maturity, rates, and width of direct advances and of securitized lending from the CB to the public sector. These four groups of legal provisions are classified under the four following headings:

Chief executive officer: CEO

Policy formulation: PF

Final objectives: OBJ

Limitations on lending: LL

The detailed classification and codings appear in table 19.1. In coding various central banks by the degree of independence within each group of characteristics, the following criteria are used: Central banks in which the legal term of office of the CEO is longer and in which the executive branch has little legal authority in the appointment or dismissal of the governor are classified as more independent on the CEO dimension. By the same logic, central banks with wider authority to formulate monetary policy and to resist the executive branch in cases of conflict are classified as more independent on the PF dimension.

Central banks in which the only or main objective of policy (as specified in the charter) is price stability are classified as being more independent on this dimension than central banks with a number of objectives in addition to price stability. These banks are in turn classified as being more independent than banks with a large number of objectives or banks in whose

Table 19.1
Legal variables and their codings

Group	Definition of variable	Variable	Levels of independence and their meanings	Numerical codings
CEO	Term of office of CEO in years	*too*	1. *too* ≥ 8	1
			2. $8 > too \geq 6$	0.75
			3. *too* = 5	0.50
			4. *too* = 4	0.25
			5. *too* < 4	0
	Who appoints the CEO?	*app*	1. CEO appointed by CB board	1
			2. CEO appointed by council composed of members from executive and legislative branches as well as from CB board	0.75
			3. CEO appointed by legislative branch (Congress, king)	0.50
			4. CEO appointed by executive branch (council of ministers)	0.25
			5. CEO appointed through decision of one or two members of executive branch (e.g., prime minister or minister of finance)	0
	Provisions for dismissal of CEO	*diss*	1. No provision for dismissal	1
			2. Dismissal possible only for nonpolicy reasons (e.g., incapability or violation of law)	0.83
			3. Dismissal possible and at discretion of CB board	0.67
			4. Dismissal for policy reasons at legislative branch's discretion	0.50
			5. Unconditional dismissal possible at legislative branch's discretion	0.33
			6. Dismissal for policy reasons at executive branch's discretion	0.17
			7. Unconditional dismissal possible at executive branch's discretion	0
	Is CEO allowed to hold another office?	*off*	1. CEO prohibited by law from holding any other office in government	1
			2. CEO not allowed to hold any other office in government unless authorized by executive branch	0.5
			3. Law does not prohibit CEO from holding another office	0

Table 19.1 (continued)

Group	Definition of variable	Variable	Levels of independence and their meanings	Numerical codings
Policy formulations	Who formulates monetary policy?	*monpol*	1. CB alone has authority to formulate monetary policy	1
			2. CB participates in formulation of monetary policy together with government	0.66
			3. CB participates in formulation of monetary policy in an advisory capacity	0.33
			4. Government alone formulates monetary policy	0
	Government directives and resolution of conflict	*conf*	1. CB given final authority over issues clearly defined in the law as CB objectives	1
			2. Government has final authority only over policy issues that have not been clearly defined as CB goals or in case of conflict within CB	0.8
			3. In case of conflict final decision up to a council whose members are from CB, legislative branch, and executive branch	0.6
			4. Legislative branch has final authority on policy issues	0.4
			5. Executive branch has final authority on policy issues, but subject to due process and possible protest by CB	0.2
			6. Executive branch has unconditional authority over policy	0
	Is CB given an active role in the formulation of government's budget?	*adv*	1. Yes	1
			2. No	0
CB objectives		*obj*	1. Price stability mentioned as the only or major goal, and in case of conflict with government CB has final authority to pursue policies aimed at achieving this goal	1
			2. Price stability mentioned as the only goal	0.8
			3. Price stability mentioned along with other objectives that do not seem to conflict with price stability (e.g., stable banking)	0.6
			4. Price stability mentioned with a number of potentially conflicting goals (e.g., full employment)	0.4

Limitations on lending			
Limitations on advances	*lla*	5. CB charter does not contain any objectives for CB	0.2
		6. Some goals appear in the charter, but price stability not one of them	0
		1. Advances to government prohibited	1
		2. Advances permitted but subject to limits in terms of absolute cash amounts or to other types of relatively strict limits (e.g, up to 15% of government revenues)	0.66
		3. Advances subject to relatively accommodative limits (e.g., advances can exceed 15% of government revenues or are specified as fractions of government expenditures)	0.33
		4. No legal limits on advances; their quantity subject to periodic negotiations between government and CB	0
Limitations on securitized lending	*lls*	Specification of levels identical to those for advances	
Who decides control of terms of lending?[a]	*ldec*	1. CB controls terms and conditions of government borrowing from it	1
		2. Terms of CB lending specified in the law, or CB given legal authority to set these terms	0.66
		3. Law leaves the decision about the terms of CB lending to government to negotiations between CB and executive branch	0.33
		4. Executive branch alone decides the terms of CB lending to government and imposes them on CB	0
How wide is the circle of potential borrowers from CB?	*lwidth*	1. Only central government can borrow from CB	1
		2. Central and state governments as well as all political subdivisions can borrow from CB	0.66
		3. In addition to the institutions mentioned under 2 public enterprises can borrow from CB	0.33
		4. CB can lend to all of the above as well as to the private sector	0

Table 19.1 (continued)

Group	Definition of variable	Variable	Levels of independence and their meanings	Numerical codings
	Type of limit when such limit exists	ltype	1. Limit specified as an absolute cash amount	1
			2. Limit specified as a percentage of CB capital or other liabilities	0.66
			3. Limit specified as a percentage of government revenues	0.33
			4. Limit specified as a percentage of government expenditures	0
	Maturity of loans	lmat	1. Maturity of CB loans limited to a maximum of 6 months	1
			2. Maturity of CB loans limited to a maximum of one year	0.66
			3. Maturity of CB loans limited to a maximum of more than one year	0.33
			4. No legal upper bounds on the maturity of CB loans	0
	Restrictions on interest rates[b]	lint	1. Interest rate on CB loans must be at market rate	1
			2. Interest rate on CB loans to government cannot be lower than a certain floor	0.75
			3. Interest rate on CB loans cannot exceed a certain ceiling	0.50
			4. No explicit legal provisions regarding the interest rate on CB loans	0.25
			5. Law stipulates no interest rate charge on government's borrowing from the CB	0
	Prohibition on lending in primary market	lprm	1. CB prohibited from buying government securities in primary market	1
			2. CB not prohibited from buying government securities in primary market	0

Sources: (1) Computerized legal data files on CB charters from the Central Banking Department at the IMF, (2) Aufricht (1961, 1967), (3) Eight European central banks (1963), and (4) Effros (1982). These sources were supplemented by updates of various laws from the IMF legal library files.
a. Terms of lending concern maturity, interest, and amount of loans subject to the relevant legal limits.
b. The rationale for the classification of this variable is that minimum rates are likely to have been devised in order to discourage borrowing at the CB while maximum rates are probably meant to facilitate borrowing at the CB. But the requirement of a minimum rate is classified below "market rates," since minimum rates, when they exist, are usually lower than market rates.

charter price stability is not mentioned as an objective at all. This classification of the "objectives" variable is designed to capture the legal mandate of the bank to single-mindedly pursue the objective of price stability. (One of the few central banks in which such an unequivocal legal mandate exists is the Bundesbank.) It does not therefore reflect (as the previous two groups of variables) the general level of independence from government. It proxies instead the legal independence of the CB to elevate the target of price stability above other objectives. In Rogoff's (1985) terminology, it measures how strong is the "conservative bias" of the CB as embodied in the law.

Similarly we classify banks in which the limitations on lending from the CB to the public sector are stricter as more independent to pursue the objective of price stability. These limitations encompass a number of more detailed variables such as separate limitations on advances and securitized lending and restrictions on maturities and on interest rates. Generally the stricter the limitation, the higher is the independence coding given to the bank on that dimension. The comparability of various types of limitations is complicated by the fact that limitations are specified in terms of different reference amounts in different countries. In a small number of countries limitations on lending are specified in absolute cash amounts and in others as a percentage of CB liabilities. The most prevalent type of limitation is formulated as a percentage of government's revenues from taxes and in a minority of cases as a percentage of government's expenditures.[2] The "bite" of these limitations obviously depends on the magnitudes of the reference variables. However, other things the same, absolute cash limits are more binding than limits in terms of CB liabilities which in turn seem more binding than limits in terms of government's revenues. The most accommodative limits are those specified in terms of government's expenditures. These considerations are embodied in a "type of limit" variable (*ltype*) and also influence the classification of the variables *lla* (limitation on lending—advances) and *lls* (limitations on lending—securities). Details appear in table 19.1 in the group of variables under the heading "limitations on lending."

Limitations on lending are classified as stricter, the nearer the rates paid by government to market rates and the shorter the maturities of the loans from the CB to the public sector. They are also stricter, the narrower the circle of institutions that are allowed to borrow from the CB (the variable *lwidth* in table 19.1) and the smaller the discretion of the executive branch in deciding to whom and how much the CB will lend (the variable *ldec* in table 19.1). In addition central bank laws that prohibit the CB from buying government securities on the primary market are considered, ceteris paribus, stricter than laws that do not contain such a prohibition (the variable *lprm* in table 19.1).

Altogether sixteen different legal variables are coded using a uniform scale ranging between 0 (smallest level of independence) to 1 (highest level of independence). The number of independence levels generally varies across legal variables depending on the fineness of data on alternative legal characteristics. Let n_j be the number of independence levels of legal variable j. The range $[0, 1]$ is divided into $n_j - 1$ equal intervals yielding n_j numerical codings that correspond to the n_j levels of independence of that legal variable. Thus for $n_j = 4$, for example, the numerical codings are 0, 0.33, 0.66, and 1. In the data n_j varies from a minimum of 2 to a maximum of 7.

Table 19.1 summarizes the sixteen legal variables and the meaning of their codings. The time period considered covers the four decades, starting in 1950 and ending in 1989. It is divided into four subperiods: 1950–59, 1960–71, 1972–79, and 1980–89. They correspond to the dollar standard period, the period of convertibility with the dollar, the period of the two oil shocks, and the period of disinflation and the debt crisis. We will refer to them as subperiods 1 through 4. Legal variables are coded separately for each subperiod. Since central bank legislation changes relatively slowly the codes are, in many cases, identical across subperiods. Nevertheless, this procedure captures important legislative changes for some countries.[3] Whenever the charter of a CB does not contain enough information to reliably code a particular legal variable, a NA (no account) entry is entered. The basic codings of the sixteen legal variables described in table 19.1 are summarized in appendix A to this chapter.

19.3   Aggregation of Legal Variables and Ranking of Central Banks by Legal Independence

Some of the legal variables whose codings appear in table 19.1 are defined quite narrowly. The advantage of narrowness in the definition of legal variables is that it makes it easier to objectively code them. But narrowness has its drawbacks too. First, the narrower the definition of variables, the more likely it is that there is a substantial degree of multicollinearity among them. This makes it difficult to pinpoint the partial contribution of each legal variable to policy outcomes such as inflation or inflation variance with reasonable precision. Second, not all the laws contain information about all the legal variables. As a consequence when the legal variables appear at a high level of disaggregation any missing observation on at least one of them precludes the use of the legal variables that are available for that country and time period.

To alleviate these problems the sixteen legal variables described in table 19.1 are aggregated into eight legal variables by applying the following procedure: The four variables concerning matters such as the appointment and term of office of the governor of the CB are aggregated into a single variable *ceo* by calculating the unweighted mean of the codings of those variables. The three variables under "policy formulations" are aggregated into a new variable *pf* by computing a weighted mean of the variables in that group.[4] The weights are 0.5 for *conf* and 0.25 for each of *monpol* and *adv*. Finally, the last four variables in the group of "limitations on lending" are aggregated into the single variable *lm* by calculating an unweighted average of those variables. This aggregation procedure produces one summary legal variable for each of the first three groups in table 19.1 and five legal variables for the "limitations on lending" group. When there is an NA entry for one or more variables within a subgroup only, the variables with meaningful entries are aggregated. In such cases the weights of the missing variables are allocated proportionally to the remaining variables within the subgroup.

To assess the overall legal independence of a CB, it is also useful to go to a second level of aggregation whose ultimate product is a *single* index of *legal independence* per country and subperiod. Two alternative indices of this type are computed. An unweighted index, calculated as a simple average of the codings of the eight variables obtained in the first round of aggregation, and a weighted index. The (subjective) weights assigned to each of the eight variables in the second case are displayed in table 19.2. We refer to the resulting overall indices of independence as *LVAU* and *LVAW*, respectively. As in the first round of aggregation the weights of legal variables with an NA entry are allocated proportionally to the legal variables with meaningful information. This procedure is applied only when the sum of the weights of the legal variables for which information is available is larger than some minimal level (0.6 for *LVAU* and 0.7 for *LVAW*). Otherwise, an NA entry is entered.

Table 19.2
Weights used in the construction of the index $LVAW$ of legal CB independence

Legal variable		Weight
ceo	(chief executive officer)	0.20
pf	(policy formulations)	0.15
obj	(objectives)	0.15
lla	(limitations on lending—advances)	0.15
lls	(limitations on lending—securitized)	0.10
ldec	(limitations on lending—who decides)	0.10
lwidth	(limitations on lending—width)	0.05
lm	(limitations on lending—miscellaneous)	0.10
		1.00

The variables $LVAU$ and $LVAW$ are summary measures of the degree of legal independence of different central banks. Table 19.3 presents a ranking of countries during the last subperiod (1980–89) by the overall level of legal independence of their central banks as measured by $LVAU$. Table 19.4 presents similar rankings only for the subset of developed countries. Both tables also present the (geometric) average yearly rate of inflation in each country during the same period. The rankings in table 19.3 range from a maximum of 0.68 for Switzerland to a minimum of 0.10 for Poland. Among the seven countries with the highest rank, four are developed; among the seven countries with the lowest rank, six are less developed countries (LDC). Nevertheless, the median level of legal independence for the entire sample of countries, which is 0.33, is very close to the median level within the group of developed countries in table 19.4. This level is 0.31. But there is a higher concentration of developed countries at the top 10 percent and a higher concentration of developing countries at the bottom 10 percent of the distribution. The ranking by $LVAW$ produces a broadly similar picture. In the overall sample the rank coefficient of correlation between $LVAU$ and $LVAW$ is 0.91. Table 19.4 also shows the index $LVAU$ in the group of developed countries during the 1980s. The rank coefficient of correlation during that period alone is 0.90.

There are no hyperinflations among developed countries during the 1980s. The highest average rate of inflation in this group is 38 percent for Iceland followed quite distantly by New Zealand with 12 percent. But some of the countries with the highest average rates of inflation such

Table 19.3
Ranking of central banks by overall legal independence (as measured by $LVAU$) during the 1980s

Country	$LVAU^a$	Average yearly inflation[b]	Country	$LVAU^a$	Average yearly inflation[b]
Switzerland	0.68	3	India	0.33	9
West Germany	0.66	3	Indonesia	0.32	10
Austria	0.58	4	Britain	0.31	7
Egypt	0.53	17	Zambia	0.31	28
Greece	0.51	19	Australia	0.31	8
United States	0.51	5	South Africa	0.30	15
Chile	0.49	21	China	0.29	8
Tanzania	0.48	31	Romania	0.29	4
Ethiopia	0.47	4	Ghana	0.28	44
Denmark	0.47	7	France	0.28	7
Canada	0.46	6	Western Samoa	0.28	8
Bahamas	0.45	6	Sweden	0.27	8
Malta	0.45	3	Singapore	0.27	3
Kenya	0.44	11	Finland	0.27	7
Argentina	0.44	319	New Zealand	0.27	12
Turkey	0.44	50	Thailand	0.26	6
Peru	0.43	194	Brazil	0.26	230
Israel	0.42	105	Nepal	0.25	11
Costa Rica	0.42	25	Bolivia	0.25	230
Netherlands	0.42	3	Hungary	0.24	9
Philippines	0.42	14	Zimbabwe	0.23	13
Nicaragua	0.42	258	South Korea	0.23	8
Honduras	0.41	7	Italy	0.22	11
Zaire	0.41	58	Uruguay	0.22	56
Barbados	0.40	7	Spain	0.21	10
Ireland	0.39	9	Pakistan	0.19	7
Venezuela	0.37	21	Belgium	0.19	5
Uganda	0.37	105	Qatar	0.18	4
Luxembourg	0.37	5	Morocco	0.16	8
Botswana	0.36	11	Japan	0.16	3
Iceland	0.36	38	Panama	0.16	3
Mexico	0.36	65	Norway	0.14	8
Malaysia	0.34	4	Yugoslavia	0.13	108
Nigeria	0.33	19	Poland	0.10	43

a. The range of $LVAU$ is from zero (minimal independence) to one (maximum independence).
b. Inflation is measured as the yearly geometric average during the 1980s and is rounded to nearest full percentage.

Table 19.4
Ranking of central banks by average legal independence (as measured by $LVAU$) during
the 1980s in developed countries

Country	$LVAU$[a]	Average yearly inflation[b]
Switzerland	0.68	3
West Germany	0.66	3
Austria	0.58	4
United States	0.51	5
Denmark	0.47	7
Canada	0.46	6
Netherlands	0.42	3
Ireland	0.39	9
Luxembourg	0.37	5
Iceland	0.36	38
Britain	0.31	7
Australia	0.31	8
France	0.28	7
Sweden	0.27	8
Finland	0.27	7
New Zealand	0.27	12
Italy	0.22	11
Spain	0.21	10
Belgium	0.19	5
Japan	0.16	3
Norway	0.14	8

a. The range of $LVAU$ is from zero (minimal independence) to one (maximum independence).
b. Inflation is measured as the yearly geometric average during the 1980s and is rounded to
the nearest full percentage.

as Argentina, Peru, and Nicaragua have rankings of legal independence
above the median. On the other hand, countries such as Panama, Japan,
and Belgium, with very low rates of inflation, are ranked in the lowest
quartile of legal CB independence. These preliminary, somewhat impressionistic observations suggest that legal CB independence may be neither
necessary nor sufficient for low inflation. This, however, is not inconsistent
with the view that, other things the same, a higher degree of legal independence is conducive to lower inflation. These issues are investigated more
precisely in chapter 20.

19.4 The Turnover Rate of Central Bank Governors as a Proxy for Actual Independence

As most practioners in the area of monetary policymaking are well aware, the legal status of a central bank is only one of several elements that determines its actual independence. Although there are important variations in the degree of completeness of different CB laws, many are highly incomplete and leave a lot of room for interpretation. As a result factors such as tradition or the personalities of the governor and other high officials of the bank at least partially shape the actual level of CB independence. Even when the law is quite explicit, it may not be operational if there is a tradition or an understanding within government that things should be done in a different way. A striking example is Argentina in which the legal term of office of the governor is four years. But there is also an informal tradition that the governor of the CB is supposed to offer his resignation to the executive whenever there is a change of government or even of the finance minister. Argentinian governors invariably adhered to this tradition. As a consequence the average actual term of office of the governor in Argentina during the 1980s was about ten months. Obviously the actual degree of independence of the Argentinian CB is substantially lower than the one implied by our measures of legal independence including, in particular, the four years legal term of office.

There are no obvious indicators of actual, as opposed to legal, CB independence. This is not because the matter is not important, but because it is hard to find systematic indicators of actual independence when it diverges from legal independence. This chapter does not fully resolve this measurement issue. However, it presents two direct indicators of actual CB independence, one of which is based on the actual average term of office of CB governors in different countries. This indicator is based on the presumption that at least above some threshold, a larger turnover of CB governors indicates a lower level of CB independence.

The other indicator, or rather group of indicators, is based on responses to a questionnaire on CB independence that was sent to specialists on monetary policy and institutions in various central banks. These indices are discussed in the next section.

Table 19.5 presents the average turnover rate of Central Bank governors for over fifty countries during the forty years ending in 1989. These rates are presented separately for developing and developed countries. Within

Table 19.5
CB governors' turnover rates 1950–89 (average number of changes per annum)

Developed countries		Developing countries	
Country	Turnover rate	Country	Turnover rate
Iceland	0.03	Malaysia	0.13
Netherlands	0.05	Honduras	0.13
Denmark	0.05	Zimbabwe	0.15
Luxembourg	0.08	Barbados	0.11
Norway	0.08	Philippines	0.13
Italy	0.08	Tanzania	0.13
Britain	0.10	Israel	0.14
Canada	0.10	Nigeria	0.19
West Germany	0.10	Kenya	0.17
United States	0.13	Greece	0.18
Finland	0.13	South Africa	0.10
Belgium	0.13	Hungary	0.18
Switzerland	0.13	Lebanon	0.19
Sweden	0.15	Bahamas	0.19
Ireland	0.15	Mexico	0.15
France	0.15	Romania	0.20
New Zealand	0.15	Colombia	0.20
Japan	0.20	Thailand	0.20
Spain	0.20	Zaire	0.23
		Yugoslavia	0.23
		Panama	0.24
		Ghana	0.28
		Malta	0.28
		Venezuela	0.30
		Egypt	0.31
		India	0.33
		Peru	0.33
		Uganda	0.34
		Zambia	0.38
		Singapore	0.37
		Ethiopia	0.20
		Chile	0.45
		Botswana	0.41
		China	0.34
		Turkey	0.40
		South Korea	0.43
		Uruguay	0.48
		Costa Rica	0.58
		Argentina	0.93

each group countries are ranked from the lowest to the highest turnover rate. Turnover rates range from a minimum of 0.03 (average tenure of 33 years) in Iceland to a maximum of 0.93 (average tenure of about thirteen months) in Argentina. It is apparent that turnover rates in LDCs tend to spread into a range that has not been experienced in the developed countries (DC). The highest turnover among the DC is 0.2 (average tenure of five years) for Spain and Japan. More than half of the LDCs have turnover rates exceeding this maximum.

It may be argued that low turnover does not necessarily imply a high level of CB independence on the grounds that a relatively subservient governor will tend to stay in office longer than a governor who stands up to the executive branch. This may be true for countries with exceptionally low turnover rates such as Iceland, Denmark, and Britain.[5] On the other hand, it is very likely that above some critical turnover rate CB independence is lower the higher the turnover rate of CB governors. One reason is that for sufficiently high turnover rates the tenure of the CB governor is shorter than that of the executive branch. This makes the governor more susceptible to influence by the executive branch and discourages him or her from trying to implement longer-term policies the lower the expected tenure. Since in most countries the electoral cycle is at least four years, it is likely that the threshold turnover is somewhere between 0.2 and 0.25 (average tenure of four to five years). In addition, for very short terms of office such as three years or less (turnover rates of 0.33 or larger), it is generally more difficult to implement long-term policies for any electoral cycle. In any case the threshold turnover will be determined (in chapter 20) by using a goodness-of-fit criterion.

Since all DCs have turnover rates below 0.2, it is not very likely that these rates are effective proxies for independence in that group of countries. On the other hand, since a majority of LDCs in the sample is characterized by turnover rates above 0.2, it is likely that governors' turnover is a meaningful proxy for independence among the LDCs.

An interesting side issue is whether actual turnover is affected by the legal term of office of the governor as stipulated in the law. To answer this question, actual turnover rates in the four subperiods were regressed on the legal terms of office and on subperiod dummies to control for possible period-specific effects on turnover. The coefficient of the term of office variable as stipulated in the law was negative and significant indicating that it has an effect on actual turnover. But the goodness of fit was low indicating that actual turnover is affected by many other factors besides the legal term of office.

19.5   Characterization of Central Bank Independence by Answers to a Questionnaire

Responses to a questionnaire containing questions on various aspects of CB independence were secured from qualified individuals in various central banks. The questionnaire contains questions on the following five groups of issues: (1) legal aspects of CB independence, (2) actual practice when it differs from the stipulation of the law, (3) monetary policy instruments and the agencies controlling them, (4) intermediate targets and indicators, and (5) final objectives of monetary policy and their relative importance. Responses to the questionnaire were obtained for twenty-four countries. Since policymakers' thinking is usually dominated by the present and the recent past, these responses are taken to refer to the last subperiod (1980–89). An obvious drawback of the questionnaire method is that it is, to some extent, based on the subjective judgment of qualified but different individuals at various central banks. On the other hand, it is an efficient method for discovering serious divergences between actual and legal independence.

Answers to the questionnaire were used in order to code the nine questionnaire variables described in table 19.6. Only a subset of the answers was used for the codings. This was done to minimize the impact of variations in the quality of responses across questions and also because some answers are more easily translated into precise codings than others. Appendix B to this chapter reports the questions whose answers were used for the coding of variables in table 19.6. The codings appear in appendix C. Variable 1 is designed to capture the extent to which the terms of office of the governor and of the board of directors are likely to be independent from government. If their legal terms are longer than that of government, the bank is considered, ceteris paribus, to be more independent and the more so the larger the difference between the terms of office of the bank's officials and the term of office of general government. Banks for which the reverse is true, or for which there is evidence that some high CB officials are terminated when there is a change in government, are classified in the lowest category of independence. Variable 2 is self-explanatory. The actual coding is done by applying criteria similar to those used to classify the legal

Table 19.6
Questionnaire variables and their codings

Definition of variable	Variable name	Numerical codings
1. Tenure overlap with political authorities	*qto*	
Little overlap		1
Some overlap		0.5
Substantial overlap		0
2. Limitations on lending in practice	*qll*	
This scale measures the tightness of limitations on lending and how they have been adhered to in practice as evaluated by the respondent to the questionnaire. The scale has four points: 1, 0.66, 0.33, and 0, where 1 stands for the most binding limitations		
3. Resolution of conflict	*qrc*	
In some cases clear evidence of resolution in favor of CB		1
Everything except what is covered under the first and last items		0.5
Clear evidence of resolution in favor of government in all cases		0
4. Who determines the budget of CB?	*qbcb*	
Mostly CB		1
Mixture of CB and executive or legislative branches		0.5
Mostly executive or legislative branches		0
5. Who determines the salaries of high CB officials and the allocation of CB profits?	*qsp*	
Mostly CB or law		1
Mixture of CB and executive or legislative branches		0.5
Mostly executive or legislative branches		0
Whenever the decision about salaries and the allocation of profits is not done by the same institution, the answer is coded according to the identity of the institution determining salaries		
6. Are there quantitative monetary stock targets?	*qst*	
Such targets exist and are well adhered to		1
Such targets exist and there is mixed adherence		0.66
Such targets exist and are poorly adhered to		0.33
There are no stock targets		0
7. Are there formal or informal interest rate targets?	*qirt*	
No		1
Yes		0

Table 19.6 (continued)

Definition of variable	Variable name	Numerical codings
8. What is the actual priority assigned to price stability?	*qpps*	
First priority assigned to price stability		1
First priority assigned to a fixed exchange rate		0.66
Price or exchange rate stability are among the objectives of monetary policy, but neither has first priority		0.33
No mention of price or exchange rate stability as objectives at any priority level		0
9. Does CB function as a development bank that grants credits at subsidy rates?	*qsc*	
No		1
To some extent		0.66
Yes		0.33
CB is heavily involved in granting subsidized credits to the private and public sectors		0

limitations on lending in the previous section. The lowest level of independence is assigned mostly to cases in which there are no limitations on lending and/or there is evidence that government can adjust the limits very easily in practice.

The remaining variables are self-explanatory, except perhaps for the sixth and seventh variables which focus on the existence of intermediate targets and on how they operate. The existence of stock targets is taken to indicate that the CB is freer to focus mostly on price stability and the more so the better its performance in attaining the targets. The existence of interest rate targets indicates that the CB has less freedom to focus on price stability. The codings of those variables reflect these presumptions. Variable 9 on the existence of subsidized credits from the central bank is important in some LDCs with limited private supplies of savings. In such countries the ability of the central bank to pursue price stability may be severely restricted by the fact that it has to function as a development bank. The detailed codings of individual questionnaire variables appear in the appendix to this chapter.

The questionnaire variables reflect the judgment of specialists on monetary policy. This judgment is based on legal as well as on other pertinent information. As a consequence these variables may at times overlap with some of the legal variables. But they also reflect information about actual practice and independence that is not captured by the legal variables. For example, the legal limitations on lending may be tight but easy to adjust, or to evade, in practice. Questionnaire variable 2 is likely to detect such discrepancies.

As in the case of the legal variables, two rounds of aggregation are applied to the questionnaire variables. In the first round the fourth and the fifth variables are aggregated, with equal weights, into a single financial independence variable qfi. Also the sixth and seventh variables are replaced by a single unweighted average qit for intermediate targets. This first round of aggregation reduces the number of variables from nine to seven. In the second round of aggregation these seven variables are aggregated into two alternative overall indices of independence as reflected by the responses to the questionnaire: $QVAU$ is an unweighted average of the codings of the seven variables resulting from the first round of aggregation. $QVAW$ is obtained by calculating a weighted average of the same variables. The weights reflect a subjective evaluation of the relative importance of each variable's contribution to the CB ability to focus on the goal of price stability. They are summarized in table 19.7. The aggregate indices $QVAU$ and $QVAW$ reflect both the law and the ways it is applied in practice. Being based on subjective evaluations, they probably contain more noise than the aggregate indices $LVAU$ and $LVAW$ of legal CB independence. However, they are also likely to contain additional pertinent information about actual independence. Hence, as far as overall actual independence is concerned, the signal-to-noise ratio in $QVAU$ and $QVAW$ is not necessarily larger than this ratio for $LVAU$ and $LVAW$. In

Table 19.7
Weights used in the construction of the questionnaire-based index $QVAW$ of CB independence

Questionnaire variable	Weight
qto (tenure overlap)	0.10
qll (limitations on lending)	0.20
qrc (resolution of conflict)	0.10
qfi (financial independence)	0.10
qit (intermediate targets)	0.15
$qpps$ (priority to price stability)	0.15
qsc (subsidized credits)	0.20
	1.00

Table 19.8
Ranking of central banks by aggregate indices of independence derived from questionnaires

	Ranked by $QVAU$			Ranked by $QVAW$	
Country	$QVAU$	Average yearly inflation 1980–89[a]	Country	$QVAW$	Average yearly inflation 1980–89[a]
West Germany	1.00	3	West Germany	1.00	3
Costa Rica	0.79	25	Costa Rica	0.81	25
Italy	0.76	11	Finland	0.78	7
Finland	0.75	7	Australia	0.76	8
Australia	0.73	8	Italy	0.73	11
Denmark	0.70	7	Denmark	0.73	7
Bahamas	0.69	6	Bahamas	0.71	6
Luxembourg	0.67	5	Luxembourg	0.66	5
France	0.65	7	France	0.65	7
Zaire	0.64	58	Britain	0.64	7
South Africa	0.61	15	South Africa	0.64	15
Lebanon	0.60		Zaire	0.61	58
Britain	0.60	7	Lebanon	0.59	
Uganda	0.57	105	Ireland	0.57	9
Belgium	0.53	5	Barbados	0.54	7
Barbados	0.51	7	Uganda	0.53	105
Ireland	0.51	9	Uruguay	0.49	56
Uruguay	0.49	56	Belgium	0.47	5
Turkey	0.48	50	Turkey	0.44	50
Tanzania	0.40	31	Tanzania	0.38	31
Nepal	0.30	11	Peru	0.22	194
Peru	0.23	194	Yugoslavia	0.17	108
Yugoslavia	0.18	108	Ethiopia	0.13	4
Ethiopia	0.12	4			

a. Inflation is measured as a geometric yearly average and is rounded to the nearest full percentage.

any case there is no need to choose either the legal or the questionnaire variables. To the extent that each group proxies for somewhat different dimensions of independence, both types of variables (when available) can be used to measure independence.

Table 19.8 presents a ranking of the countries for which questionnaire responses are available, using alternatively $QVAU$ and $QVAW$. The indices are calculated only for countries in which there are responses for questions whose sum of weights exceeds a certain minimal percentage (70 percent for $QVAW$ and 60 percent for $QVAU$). It is apparent that under both rankings Germany is at the top and Ethiopia at the bottom and that for the countries for which enough responses are available, the two rankings are very similar. As a matter of fact the rank coefficient of correlation between $QVAU$ and $QVAW$ is 0.99.

The median of $QVAU$ occurs at 0.6 for Britain and Lebanon. The median of $QVAU$ within the group of LDCs is 0.49 (for Uruguay). Thus the median level of CB independence (as measured by $QVAU$) in the group of LDCs appears to be significantly lower than this median within the group of DCs. This contrasts with the finding for legal independence. It will be recalled from tables 19.3 and 19.4 that the medians of $LVAU$ in the overall sample and in the group of DCs are very close to each other.

19.6   Interrelationships between Alternative Indices of Central Bank Independence

To this point three groups of measures of CB independence have been introduced. Legal independence, CB governors' turnover rates, and independence as coded from responses to a questionnaire on CB independence.[6] The first source reflects only the letter of the law. The second, by contrast, is based on actual developments. The third source combines both legal and actual information on CB independence but is more judgmental than the first two.

It is of some interest to examine the comovements between these groups of variables for at least two reasons. First, since they are all devised to bring out various dimensions of CB independence, a high degree of correlation among them would imply that any one group may suffice as an overall index of CB independence. If, on the other hand, the correlation is not high, there is room for usefully combining them in order to obtain better measures of overall CB independence. The second reason is related to the

Table 19.9
Correlations between legal and questionnaire-based measures of CB independence

Correlation between	All countries	Developed countries	Less developed countries
Rank coefficients of correlation			
$LVAU$ and $QVAU$	0.01	0.01	0.00
$LVAW$ and $QVAW$	0.04	0.33	0.06
Simple coefficients of correlation			
qll and ll	0.19		
qll and all the legal "limitations on lending" variables from table 19.2	0.46		

discussion in chapter 20 in which inflation is related to CB independence. If the various groups of indices are highly collinear, it will be difficult to identify the separate contribution of each to inflation. If they are not, however, there is hope for identifying the separate effect of each on inflation.

We focus first on the correlation between legal independence and overall independence as reflected in responses to the questionnaire. The rank coefficients of correlation between the summary measures of independence in the two groups are summarized in table 19.9. The table shows that the correlation between these two measures of independence for the entire group of (up to) twenty-six countries is modest. But this hides somewhat different types of correlations for developed and less developed countries. The correlation between legal provisions and questionnaire-based measures of independence is somewhat higher for the subset of DC than for the LDCs in the sample.[7] It appears therefore that although far from being identical, legal and actual independence are more closely related in DCs than in LDCs.

The other relationship explored is between governors' turnover and legal independence. This is done by regressing average turnover in each country and subperiod alternatively on $LVAU$ and $LVAW$ and on subperiods' dummies to control for period-specific effects. Again this is done for all countries (over fifty of them) as well as for DCs and LDCs separately. In all regressions the coefficient of the aggregate legal variable is not significant at usual significance levels indicating that the turnover variable and the legal variables are likely to be proxying for rather different dimensions of CB independence.

The questionnaire variable *qll* incorporates information about legal limitations on lending as well as on how they are implemented in practice. The last two entries in table 19.9 show the coefficients of correlation between *qll* and between the variables that measure the tightness of legal limitations on lending. The variable *ll* is an aggregate of the last five legal variables in table 19.2 with weights that are proportional to their weights in the table. Even when the legal limitations variables are entered in disaggregated form, they contribute only 46 percent to the explanation of the variation in *qll*. This indicates that the answers to questions concerning limitations on lending generally include information beyond the information contained in legal limitations on lending alone.

Questionnaire variable *qpps* measures the relative importance given to price stability in practice as evaluated by respondents to the questionnaire. Legal variable *obj* measures the same concept as specified in the law. The correlation between these two variables is therefore a measure of the extent to which the actual and the legally specified emphasis on price stability are related to each other. A regression of *qpps* on *obj* yields a significant (at the 0.04 level) and positive coefficient.[8] But the squared coefficient of correlation between the two variables is only 0.14. These results suggest that although the actual emphasis on price stability (as evaluated by respondents to the questionnaire) depends on the emphasis given to this objective by the law, there are substantial divergences between these two measures. It follows that *qpps* contains information beyond that contained in the definition of objectives as specified in the CB charter.

19.7 Additional Dimensions of Central Bank Independence[9]

Although the indices of CB independence presented in this chapter are probably the most comprehensive that exist on a unified basis, they do not quantify all the aspects of independence. This section discusses informally some additional dimensions. A potentially important component of independence is the quality of the bank's research department and its standing in comparison to other economic research institutions within the public sector. A governor who is backed by an absolutely and relatively strong research department carries more weight vis-à-vis the Treasury and other branches of government. The reason is probably that the governor is perceived as a relatively impartial provider of reliable information about the economy. A possible indicator of the quality of a bank's research department is the quality of the annual report it produces.

Other things the same, independence is probably higher in countries with broad and well-developed financial markets. The reason is that the prudential supervision of financial institutions and related intricacies are almost always under the authority of the CB. The larger the financial sector, the wider is the span of authority of the CB and the areas in which it is the main or even sole representative of the public sector. This raises its power and prestige vis-à-vis the treasury and other political authorities. For example, the Bank of England probably carries more weight than what might appear from its moderate degree of legal independence (see table 19.4) because it is the main representative of government in the wide British financial sector.

In some countries such as Israel one of the official duties of the governor of the bank is to function as the economic advisor to government. This function allows the governor to periodically address parliament or the cabinet on matters like fiscal and labor market policies. Although unable to vote on these policies, the governor's official capacity as advisor may give him or her some influence in areas outside the realm of monetary policy.

In countries with fixed exchange rates that are allowed to fluctuate within a prespecified band, the width of the band affects the span of authority of the CB. The reason is that the decision about the center rate is usually made by political authorities, while the daily interventions are often left to the discretion of the bank.[10] A widening of the band therefore raises the span of authority of the CB.

Provisions concerning the appointment procedures of the CB board members also affect the degree of independence from government. In general the smaller the involvement of the executive or the legislative branch in such appointments, and the longer the term in office of board members, the higher is the level of independence. In the United States, for example, the president appoints all seven members of the Board of Governors. Each governor is appointed for fourteen years, and the terms in office are staggered. Havrilesky and Gildea (1990, 1991) and Havrilesky and Schweitzer (1990) argue that the president can influence monetary policy by appointing loyal Governors to the Board. However, the staggering of board member terms (one governor terminates his or her term every two years) substantially reduces the president's ability to pack the board (Keech and Morris 1991). In addition not all appointees are continually loyal to the president's wishes.

Independence also depends on the ability of the CB to maintain a sufficiently large volume of open market operations when needed. In general the larger the relative size of government obligations that are nonmarketable, the more restricted is the ability of the CB to conduct meaningful open market operations. For example, the ability of the Bank of Israel to conduct open market operations is seriously restricted despite the fact that it holds a large amount of government securities. The reason is that these securities are not tradable and the Israeli Treasury has consistently refused to make them tradable. The effective degree of independence is also likely to be smaller, the larger the relative size of government as a borrower on capital markets. In extreme cases such as Belgium in which government is the main borrower on the capital market actual CB independence is likely to be lower than legal independence.[11]

Appendix A: Codings of Basic Legal Variables

	Term of office, *too*				Who appoints CEO, *app*			
	1950–59	1960–71	1972–79	1980–89	1950–59	1960–71	1972–79	1980–89
Argentina	NA	NA	0.25	0.25	NA	NA	0.25	0.25
Australia	NA	0.75	0.75	0.75	NA	0.00	0.00	0.00
Austria	0.50	0.50	0.50	0.50	0.00	0.00	0.00	0.00
Belgium	0.50	0.50	0.50	0.50	0.00	0.00	0.00	0.00
Bahamas	NA	NA	0.50	0.50	NA	NA	0.00	0.00
Bolivia	0.00	0.00	0.00	0.00	0.00	0.00	0.00	0.00
Brazil	NA	0.00	0.00	0.00	NA	0.50	0.50	0.50
Barbados	NA	NA	0.50	0.50	NA	NA	0.00	0.00
Botswana	NA	NA	0.50	0.50	NA	NA	0.00	0.00
Canada	0.75	0.75	0.75	0.75	0.75	0.75	0.75	0.75
Switzerland	0.75	0.75	0.75	0.75	0.25	0.25	0.25	0.25
Chile	0.00	0.00	0.50	0.50	1.00	1.00	0.00	0.00
China	0.50	0.50	0.50	0.50	NA	NA	NA	NA
Colombia	NA	0.00	0.00	0.00	NA	0.75	0.75	0.75
Costa Rica	NA	NA	NA	NA	NA	1.00	1.00	1.00
West Germany	1.00	1.00	1.00	1.00	0.75	0.75	0.75	0.75
Denmark	0.00	0.00	0.00	0.00	0.00	0.00	0.00	0.00
Egypt	0.50	0.50	0.50	0.50	0.50	0.50	0.50	0.50
Spain	0.00	0.00	0.00	0.25	0.25	0.25	0.25	0.00
Ethiopia	NA	0.50	0.00	0.00	NA	0.25	0.25	0.25
Finland	1.00	1.00	1.00	1.00	0.00	0.00	0.00	0.00
France	0.00	0.00	0.00	0.00	0.25	0.25	0.25	0.25
Britain	0.50	0.50	0.50	0.50	0.00	0.00	0.00	0.00
Ghana	0.50	0.50	0.50	0.50	0.00	0.00	0.00	0.00
Greece	0.25	0.25	0.25	0.25	0.75	0.75	0.75	0.75
Honduras	0.75	0.75	0.75	0.75	0.00	0.00	0.00	0.00
Hungary	0.50	0.50	0.50	0.50	0.25	0.25	0.25	0.25
Indonesia	0.50	0.50	0.50	0.50	0.25	0.25	0.25	0.25
India	0.50	0.50	0.50	0.50	0.25	0.25	0.25	0.25
Ireland	0.75	0.75	0.75	0.75	0.50	0.50	0.50	0.50
Iceland	1.00	1.00	1.00	1.00	NA	0.75	0.75	0.75
Israel	0.50	0.50	0.50	0.50	0.50	0.50	0.50	0.50
Italy	0.00	0.00	0.00	0.00	0.75	0.75	0.75	0.75
Japan	0.50	0.50	0.50	0.50	0.25	0.25	0.25	0.25
Kenya	NA	0.25	0.25	0.25	NA	0.00	0.00	0.00

	Term of office, *too*				Who appoints CEO, *app*			
	1950–59	1960–71	1972–79	1980–89	1950–59	1960–71	1972–79	1980–89
South Korea	0.25	0.25	0.25	0.25	0.25	0.25	0.25	0.25
Lebanon	0.75	0.75	0.75	0.75	0.25	0.25	0.25	0.25
Luxembourg	NA	NA	NA	0.75	NA	NA	NA	0.25
Morocco	NA	NA	NA	NA	NA	0.25	0.25	0.25
Mexico	NA	NA	NA	NA	0.00	1.00	1.00	1.00
Malta	NA	0.50	0.50	0.50	NA	0.50	0.50	0.50
Malaysia	NA	0.50	0.50	0.50	NA	0.00	0.00	0.00
Nigeria	NA	0.50	0.50	0.50	NA	0.00	0.00	0.00
Nicaragua	NA	0.00	0.00	0.00	NA	0.00	0.00	0.00
Netherlands	0.75	0.75	0.75	0.75	0.00	0.00	0.00	0.00
Norway	0.75	0.75	0.75	0.75	0.00	0.00	0.00	0.00
Nepal	0.50	0.50	0.50	0.50	0.25	0.25	0.25	0.25
New Zealand	0.50	0.50	0.50	0.50	0.00	0.00	0.00	0.00
Pakistan	0.50	0.50	0.50	0.50	0.25	0.25	0.25	0.25
Panama	NA	NA	NA	NA	0.25	0.25	0.25	0.25
Peru	NA	0.00	0.00	0.00	NA	1.00	1.00	1.00
Philippines	0.75	0.75	0.75	0.75	0.00	0.00	0.00	0.00
Poland	0.50	0.50	0.50	0.50	0.25	0.25	0.25	0.25
Qatar	NA	NA	0.50	0.50	NA	NA	0.25	0.25
Romania	0.50	0.50	NA	NA	0.25	0.25	0.25	0.25
Singapore	NA	NA	0.25	0.25	NA	NA	0.00	0.00
Sweden	0.00	0.00	0.00	0.00	1.00	1.00	1.00	1.00
Thailand	0.25	0.25	0.25	0.25	0.50	0.50	0.50	0.50
Turkey	0.50	0.50	0.50	0.50	0.75	0.75	0.75	0.75
Tanzania	NA	0.25	0.25	0.25	NA	0.00	0.00	0.00
Uganda	NA	0.50	0.50	0.50	NA	0.50	0.50	0.50
Uruguay	0.25	0.25	0.25	0.25	0.00	0.00	0.25	0.25
United States	0.25	0.25	0.25	0.25	0.50	0.50	0.50	0.50
Venezuela	0.50	0.50	0.50	0.50	0.00	0.00	0.00	0.00
Western Samoa	NA	NA	NA	0.25	NA	NA	NA	0.25
Yugoslavia	NA	0.25	0.25	0.25	NA	0.25	0.25	0.25
South Africa	0.50	0.50	0.50	0.50	0.00	0.00	0.00	0.00
Zaire	NA	NA	0.50	0.50	NA	NA	0.00	0.00
Zambia	NA	0.50	0.50	0.50	NA	0.25	0.25	0.25
Zimbabwe	0.75	0.75	0.75	0.75	0.00	0.00	0.00	0.00

Note: Codes range from 0 (minimal independence) to a maximum of 1.

	Provision for dismissal, *diss*				Another office held, *off*			
	1950–59	1960–71	1972–79	1980–89	1950–59	1960–71	1972–79	1980–89
Argentina	NA	NA	0.83	0.83	NA	NA	1.00	1.00
Australia	NA	0.83	0.83	0.83	NA	1.00	1.00	1.00
Austria	0.83	0.83	0.83	0.83	1.00	1.00	1.00	1.00
Belgium	0.00	0.00	0.00	0.00	0.50	0.50	0.50	0.50
Bahamas	NA	NA	0.83	0.83	NA	NA	0.50	0.50
Bolivia	0.83	0.83	0.83	0.83	1.00	1.00	1.00	1.00
Brazil	NA	0.00	0.00	0.00	NA	0.00	0.00	0.00
Barbados	NA	NA	0.83	0.83	NA	NA	0.00	0.00
Botswana	NA	NA	0.83	0.83	NA	NA	0.50	0.50
Canada	0.83	0.83	0.83	0.83	1.00	1.00	1.00	1.00
Switzerland	NA	NA	NA	NA	1.00	1.00	1.00	1.00
Chile	1.00	1.00	0.83	0.83	0.50	0.50	0.50	0.50
China	NA	NA	NA	NA	0.00	0.00	0.00	0.00
Colombia	NA	0.83	0.83	0.83	NA	0.00	0.00	0.00
Costa Rica	NA	0.67	0.67	0.67	NA	1.00	1.00	1.00
West Germany	1.00	1.00	1.00	1.00	0.00	0.00	0.00	0.00
Denmark	0.33	0.33	0.33	0.33	0.00	0.00	0.00	0.00
Egypt	1.00	1.00	1.00	1.00	1.00	1.00	0.00	0.00
Spain	0.00	0.00	0.00	0.00	0.50	0.00	0.00	1.00
Ethiopia	NA	0.00	0.00	0.00	NA	0,00	0.00	0,00
Finland	NA	NA	NA	NA	0.00	0.00	0.00	0.00
France	1.00	1.00	1.00	1.00	0.50	0.50	0.50	0.50
Britain	0.83	0.83	0.83	0.83	1.00	1.00	1.00	1.00
Ghana	0.83	0.83	0.83	0.83	0.50	0.50	0.50	0.50
Greece	0.67	0.67	0.67	0.67	0.50	0.50	0.50	0.50
Honduras	0.83	0.83	0.83	0.83	1.00	1.00	1.00	1.00
Hungary	1.00	1.00	1.00	1.00	0.00	0.00	0.00	0.00
Indonesia	0.00	0.00	0.00	0,00	0.50	0.50	0.50	0.50
India	0.83	0.83	0.83	0.83	0.50	0.50	0.50	0.50
Ireland	0.83	0.83	0.83	0.83	1.00	1.00	1.00	1.00
Iceland	NA	0.83	0.83	0.83	NA	0.50	0.50	0.50
Israel	0.50	0.50	0.50	0.50	0.50	0.50	0.50	0.50
Italy	0.67	0.67	0.67	0.67	1.00	1.00	1.00	1.00
Japan	0.83	0.83	0.83	0.83	0.50	0.50	0.50	0.50
Kenya	NA	0.83	0.83	0.83	NA	0.50	0.50	0.50

	Provision for dismissal, *diss*				Another office held, *off*			
	1950–59	1960–71	1972–79	1980–89	1950–59	1960–71	1972–79	1980–89
South Korea	0.83	0.83	0.83	0.83	0.00	0.00	0.50	0.50
Lebanon	0.83	0.83	0.83	0.83	1.00	1.00	1.00	1.00
Luxembourg	NA	NA	NA	0.83	NA	NA	NA	0.00
Morocco	NA	0.00	0.00	0.00	NA	0.00	0.00	0.00
Mexico	0.83	0.83	0.83	0.83	1.00	1.00	1.00	1.00
Malta	NA	0.83	0.83	0.83	NA	1.00	1.00	1.00
Malaysia	NA	0.83	0.83	0.83	NA	0.00	0.00	0.00
Nigeria	NA	0.83	0.83	0.83	NA	0.50	0.50	0.50
Nicaragua	NA	0.83	0.83	0.83	NA	1.00	1.00	1.00
Netherlands	0.17	0.17	0.17	0.17	1.00	1.00	1.00	1.00
Norway	0.33	0.33	0.33	0.33	1.00	1.00	1.00	1.00
Nepal	0.00	0.00	0.00	0.00	0.00	0.00	0.00	0.00
New Zealand	0.83	0.83	0.83	0.83	0.00	1.00	1.00	1.00
Pakistan	0.83	0.83	0.83	0.83	0.50	0.50	0.50	0.50
Panama	0.83	0.83	0.83	0.83	1.00	1.00	1.00	1.00
Peru	NA	0.83	0.83	0.83	NA	1.00	1.00	1.00
Philippines	0.83	0.83	0.83	0.83	0.50	0.50	0.50	0.50
Poland	0.00	0.00	0.00	0.00	0.50	0.50	0.00	0.00
Qatar	NA	NA	0.83	0.83	NA	NA	0.50	0.50
Romania	1.00	1.00	NA	NA	1.00	1.00	0.00	0.00
Singapore	NA	NA	0.83	0.83	NA	NA	0.00	0.00
Sweden	NA	NA	NA	NA	0.50	0.50	0.50	0.50
Thailand	0.00	0.00	0.00	0.00	0.00	0.00	0.00	0.00
Turkey	1.00	1.00	0.83	0.83	1.00	1.00	0.00	0.00
Tanzania	NA	0.83	0.83	0.83	NA	0.50	0.50	0.50
Uganda	NA	0.83	0.83	0.83	NA	0.50	0.50	0.50
Uruguay	NA	NA	0.83	0.83	0.50	0.50	0.00	0.00
United States	0.00	0.00	0.00	0.00	1.00	1.00	1.00	1.00
Venezuela	NA	NA	0.83	0.83	0.00	0.00	0.50	0.50
Western Samoa	NA	NA	NA	0.83	NA	NA	NA	0.00
Yugoslavia	NA	0.83	0.83	0.83	NA	0.00	0.00	0.00
South Africa	0.83	0.83	0.83	0.83	0.50	0.50	0.50	0.50
Zaire	NA	NA	1.00	1.00	NA	NA	0.00	1.00
Zambia	NA	0.83	0.83	0.83	NA	1.00	1.00	0.50
Zimbabwe	0.00	0.00	0.00	0.00	1.00	0.50	0.50	0.50

	Monetary policy formulation, monpol				Conflict resolution, conf			
	1950–59	1960–71	1972–79	1980–89	1950–59	1960–71	1972–79	1980–89
Argentina	NA	NA	0.33	0.33	NA	NA	0.00	0.00
Australia	NA	0.33	0.33	0.33	NA	0.20	0.20	0.20
Austria	0.67	0.67	1.00	1.00	0.60	0.60	0.60	0.60
Belgium	0.00	0.00	0.00	0.00	0.00	0.00	0.20	0.20
Bahamas	NA	NA	0.33	0.33	NA	NA	NA	NA
Bolivia	0.67	0.67	0.67	0.67	0.20	0.20	0.20	0.20
Brazil	NA	0.33	0.33	0.33	NA	NA	NA	NA
Barbados	NA	NA	0.33	0.33	NA	NA	0.20	0.20
Botswana	NA	NA	NA	NA	NA	NA	0.00	0.00
Canada	0.33	0.33	0.33	0.33	0.20	0.20	0.20	0.20
Switzerland	NA	NA	NA	NA	1.00	1.00	1.00	1.00
Chile	0.67	0.67	0.67	0.67	0.00	0.00	0.20	0.20
China	NA	NA	NA	NA	0.80	0.80	0.80	0.80
Colombia	NA	0.00	0.00	0.00	NA	0.20	0.20	0.20
Costa Rica	NA	NA	NA	NA	NA	NA	NA	NA
West Germany	0.67	0.67	0.67	0.67	1.00	1.00	1.00	1.00
Denmark	NA	NA	NA	NA	1.00	1.00	1.00	1.00
Egypt	0.33	0.33	0.33	0.33	0.00	0.00	0.00	0.00
Spain	0.33	0.33	0.33	0.33	0.00	0.00	0.00	0.00
Ethiopia	NA	NA	NA	NA	NA	NA	1.00	1.00
Finland	NA	NA	NA	NA	0.00	0.00	0.00	0.00
France	0.33	0.33	0.67	0.67	0.60	0.60	0.60	0.60
Britain	0.00	0.00	0.00	0.00	0.00	0.00	0.00	0.00
Ghana	0.33	0.33	0.33	0.33	0.00	0.00	0.00	0.00
Greece	0.33	0.33	0.33	0.33	0.60	0.60	0.60	0.60
Honduras	0.33	0.33	0.33	0.33	1.00	1.00	1.00	1.00
Hungary	0.33	0.33	0.33	0.33	0.00	0.00	0.00	0.00
Indonesia	0.67	0.67	0.67	0.67	0.00	0.00	0.20	0.20
India	NA	NA	NA	NA	0.00	0.00	0.00	0.00
Ireland	NA	NA	NA	NA	NA	NA	NA	NA
Iceland	NA	0.33	0.33	0.33	NA	0.20	0.20	0.20
Israel	0.67	0.67	0.67	0.67	0.20	0.20	0.20	0.20
Italy	NA	NA	NA	NA	NA	NA	NA	NA
Japan	0.67	0.67	0.67	0.67	0.00	0.00	0.00	0.00
Kenya	NA	NA	NA	NA	NA	0.20	0.20	0.20

	Monetary policy formulation, *monpol*				Conflict resolution, *conf*			
	1950–59	1960–71	1972–79	1980–89	1950–59	1960–71	1972–79	1980–89
South Korea	0.33	0.33	0.33	0.33	NA	NA	NA	NA
Lebanon	0.67	0.67	0.67	0.67	NA	NA	NA	NA
Luxembourg	NA	NA	NA	0.33	NA	NA	NA	NA
Morocco	NA	NA	NA	NA	NA	NA	NA	NA
Mexico	0.00	0.67	0.67	0.67	0.20	0.20	0.20	0.20
Malta	NA	0.00	0.00	0.00	NA	0.20	0.20	0.20
Malaysia	NA	0.00	0.00	0.00	NA	0.20	0.20	0.20
Nigeria	NA	0.33	0.33	0.33	NA	0.20	0.20	0.20
Nicaragua	NA	1.00	1.00	1.00	NA	NA	NA	NA
Netherlands	0.33	0.33	0.33	0.33	0.20	0.20	0.20	0.20
Norway	0.00	0.00	0.33	0.33	0.20	0.20	0.20	0.20
Nepal	NA	NA	NA	NA	0.00	0.00	0.00	0.00
New Zealand	0.00	0.00	0.00	0.00	0.00	0.00	0.00	0.00
Pakistan	0.00	0.00	0.00	0.00	0.00	0.00	0.00	0.00
Panama	0.33	0.33	0.33	0.33	0.00	0.00	0.00	0.00
Peru	NA	0.67	0.67	0.67	NA	0.20	0.20	0.20
Philippines	0.67	0.67	0.67	0.67	0.20	0.20	0.20	0.20
Poland	0.33	0.33	0.67	0.67	0.00	0.00	0.00	0.00
Qatar	NA	NA	0.33	0.33	NA	NA	0.00	0.00
Romania	0.67	0.67	1.00	1.00	0.60	0.60	0.80	0.80
Singapore	NA	NA	NA	NA	NA	NA	NA	NA
Sweden	NA	NA	NA	NA	NA	NA	NA	NA
Thailand	0.00	0.00	0.00	0.00	0.20	0.20	0.20	0.20
Turkey	0.67	0.67	0.33	0.33	0.20	0.20	0.80	0.80
Tanzania	NA	0.67	0.67	0.67	NA	0.20	0.20	0.20
Uganda	NA	0.00	0.00	0.00	NA	0.20	0.20	0.20
Uruguay	0.67	0.67	0.67	0.67	0.00	0.00	0.20	0.20
United States	NA	NA	NA	NA	0.20	0.20	0.20	0.20
Venezuela	0.00	0.00	0.33	0.33	NA	NA	1.00	1.00
Western Samoa	NA	NA	NA	0.00	NA	NA	NA	0.20
Yugoslavia	NA	0.00	0.00	0.00	NA	0.20	0.20	0.20
South Africa	NA	NA	NA	NA	NA	NA	NA	NA
Zaire	NA	NA	0.67	0.67	NA	NA	0.20	0.60
Zambia	NA	0.00	0.00	0.33	NA	0.20	0.20	0.20
Zimbabwe	0.00	0.00	0.00	0.00	0.00	0.00	0.00	0.00

	Active role in budget, *adv*				CB's objectives, *obj*			
	1950–59	1960–71	1972–79	1980–89	1950–59	1960–71	1972–79	1980–89
Argentina	NA	NA	0.00	0.00	NA	NA	0.40	0.40
Australia	NA	0.00	0.00	0.00	NA	0.40	0.40	0.40
Austria	0.00	0.00	0.00	0.00	0.60	0.60	0.60	0.60
Belgium	0.00	0.00	0.00	0.00	0.00	0.00	0.00	0.00
Bahamas	NA	NA	0.00	0.00	NA	NA	0.60	0.60
Bolivia	0.00	0.00	0.00	0.00	0.60	0.60	0.60	0.60
Brazil	NA	0.00	0.00	0.00	NA	0.00	0.00	0.00
Barbados	NA	NA	0.00	0.00	NA	NA	0.80	0.80
Botswana	NA	NA	0.00	0.00	NA	NA	0.20	0.20
Canada	0.00	0.00	0.00	0.00	0.20	0.20	0.20	0.20
Switzerland	0.00	0.00	0.00	0.00	0.00	0.00	0.00	0.00
Chile	0.00	0.00	0.00	0.00	0.20	0.20	0.80	0.80
China	0.00	0.00	0.00	0.00	0.20	0.20	0.20	0.20
Colombia	NA	0.00	0.00	0.00	NA	0.00	0.00	0.00
Costa Rica	NA	0.00	0.00	0.00	NA	0.60	0.60	0.60
West Germany	0.00	0.00	0.00	0.00	1.00	1.00	1.00	1.00
Denmark	0.00	0.00	0.00	0.00	0.60	0.60	0.60	0.60
Egypt	0.00	0.00	0.00	0.00	0.60	0.60	0.60	0.60
Spain	0.00	0.00	0.00	0.00	0.00	0.00	0.00	0.60
Ethiopia	NA	0.00	1.00	1.00	NA	0.60	0.00	0.00
Finland	0.00	0.00	0.00	0.00	0.80	0.80	0.80	0.80
France	0.00	0.00	0.00	0.00	0.20	0.20	0.00	0.00
Britain	0.00	0.00	0.00	0.00	0.20	0.20	0.20	0.20
Ghana	0.00	0.00	0.00	0.00	0.60	0.60	0.60	0.60
Greece	0.00	0.00	0.00	0.00	0.80	0.80	0.80	0.80
Honduras	0.00	0.00	0.00	0.00	0.00	0.00	0.00	0.00
Hungary	0.00	0.00	0.00	0.00	0.40	0.40	0.40	0.40
Indonesia	0.00	0.00	0.00	0.00	0.00	0.40	0.40	0.40
India	0.00	0.00	0.00	0.00	0.40	0.40	0.40	0.40
Ireland	0.00	0.00	0.00	0.00	0.80	0.80	0.80	0.80
Iceland	NA	0.00	0.00	0.00	NA	0.40	0.40	0.40
Israel	0.00	0.00	0.00	0.00	0.40	0.40	0.40	0.40
Italy	0.00	0.00	0.00	0.00	0.20	0.20	0.20	0.20
Japan	0.00	0.00	0.00	0.00	0.00	0.00	0.00	0.00
Kenya	NA	0.00	0.00	0.00	NA	0.40	0.40	0.40

	Active role in budget, *adv*				CB's objectives, *obj*			
	1950–59	1960–71	1972–79	1980–89	1950–59	1960–71	1972–79	1980–89
South Korea	0.00	0.00	0.00	0.00	0.60	0.60	0.60	0.60
Lebanon	0.00	0.00	0.00	0.00	0.00	0.00	0.00	0.00
Luxembourg	NA	NA	NA	0.00	NA	NA	NA	0.60
Morocco	NA	0.00	0.00	0.00	NA	0.20	0.20	0.20
Mexico	0.00	0.00	0.00	0.00	0.00	0.00	0.00	0.00
Malta	NA	0.00	0.00	0.00	NA	0.40	0.40	0.40
Malaysia	NA	0.00	0.00	0.00	NA	0.60	0.60	0.60
Nigeria	NA	0.00	0.00	0.00	NA	0.60	0.60	0.60
Nicaragua	NA	0.00	0.00	0.00	NA	0.00	0.00	0.00
Netherlands	0.00	0.00	0.00	0.00	0.80	0.80	0.80	0.80
Norway	0.00	0.00	0.00	0.00	0.00	0.00	0.00	0.00
Nepal	0.00	0.00	0.00	0.00	0.20	0.20	0.20	0.20
New Zealand	0.00	0.00	0.00	0.00	0.00	0.40	0.40	0.40
Pakistan	0.00	0.00	0.00	0.00	0.40	0.40	0.40	0.40
Panama	0.00	0.00	0.00	0.00	0.40	0.40	0.40	0.40
Peru	NA	0.00	0.00	0.00	NA	0.40	0.40	0.40
Philippines	0.00	0.00	0.00	0.00	1.00	1.00	1.00	1.00
Poland	0.00	0.00	0.00	0.00	0.00	0.00	0.00	0.00
Qatar	NA	NA	0.00	0.00	NA	NA	0.40	0.40
Romania	0.00	0.00	0.00	0.00	0.60	0.60	0.20	0.20
Singapore	NA	NA	0.00	0.00	NA	NA	0.60	0.60
Sweden	0.00	0.00	0.00	0.00	0.20	0.20	0.20	0.20
Thailand	0.00	0.00	0.00	0.00	0.60	0.60	0.60	0.60
Turkey	0.00	0.00	0.00	0.00	0.40	0.40	0.60	0.60
Tanzania	NA	0.00	0.00	0.00	NA	0.40	0.40	0.40
Uganda	NA	0.00	0.00	0.00	NA	0.40	0.40	0.40
Uruguay	0.00	0.00	0.00	0.00	0.20	0.20	0.40	0.40
United States	0.00	0.00	0.00	0.00	0.40	0.40	0.40	0.40
Venezuela	0.00	0.00	0.00	0.00	0.20	0.20	0.40	0.40
Western Samoa	NA	NA	NA	0.00	NA	NA	NA	0.40
Yugoslavia	NA	0.00	0.00	0.00	NA	0.40	0.40	0.40
South Africa	0.00	0.00	0.00	0.00	0.20	0.20	0.20	0.20
Zaire	NA	NA	0.00	0.00	NA	NA	0.60	0.40
Zambia	NA	0.00	0.00	0.00	NA	0.80	0.80	0.40
Zimbabwe	0.00	0.00	0.00	0.00	0.00	0.00	0.00	0.00

	Limit on advances, *lla*				Limit on securitized lending, *lls*			
	1950–59	1960–71	1972–79	1980–89	1950–59	1960–71	1972–79	1980–89
Argentina	NA	NA	0.33	0.33	NA	NA	0.33	0.33
Australia	NA	0.33	0.33	0.33	NA	0.00	0.00	0.00
Austria	1.00	1.00	1.00	1.00	0.67	0.67	0.67	0.67
Belgium	0.00	0.00	0.00	0.00	0.00	0.00	0.00	0.00
Bahamas	NA	NA	0.33	0.33	NA	NA	0.33	0.33
Bolivia	0.33	0.33	0.33	0.33	0.00	0.00	0.00	0.00
Brazil	NA	0.67	0.67	0.67	NA	0.00	0.00	0.00
Barbados	NA	NA	0.33	0.33	NA	NA	0.33	0.33
Botswana	NA	NA	0.33	0.33	NA	NA	0.67	0.67
Canada	0.33	0.33	0.33	0.33	0.33	0.33	0.33	0.33
Switzerland	0.67	0.67	0.67	1.00	0.33	0.33	0.33	NA
Chile	0.00	0.00	0.33	0.33	0.00	0.00	0.33	0.33
China	NA	NA	NA	NA	0.33	0.33	0.33	0.33
Colombia	NA	0.67	0.67	0.67	NA	0.00	0.00	0.00
Costa Rica	NA	0.67	0.67	0.67	NA	0.33	0.33	0.33
West Germany	0.67	0.67	0.67	0.67	0.67	0.67	0.67	0.67
Denmark	1.00	1.00	1.00	1.00	0.33	0.33	0.33	0.33
Egypt	0.67	0.67	0.67	0.67	0.67	0.67	0.67	0.67
Spain	0.33	0.33	0.33	0.33	0.00	0.00	0.00	0.00
Ethiopia	NA	NA	0.33	0.33	NA	NA	0.33	0.33
Finland	0.00	0.00	0.00	0.00	0.00	0.00	0.00	0.00
France	0.33	0.33	0.00	0.00	0.00	0.00	0.00	0.00
Britain	0.00	0.67	0.00	0.00	0.00	0.67	0.00	0.00
Ghana	0.67	0.00	0.00	0.00	0.67	0.33	0.33	0.33
Greece	0.67	0.33	0.67	0.67	0.67	0.67	0.67	0.67
Honduras	NA	NA	NA	NA	0.33	0.33	0.33	0.33
Hungary	0.00	0.00	0.00	0.00	0.00	0.00	0.00	0.00
Indonesia	0.33	0.33	0.00	0.00	0.33	0.33	0.00	0.00
India	0.00	0.33	0.33	0.33	0.00	0.00	0.00	0.00
Ireland	NA	NA	NA	NA	0.00	0.00	0.00	0.00
Iceland	NA	0.00	0.00	0.00	NA	0.00	0.00	0.00
Israel	0.33	0.33	0.33	0.33	0.00	0.00	0.00	0.00
Italy	0.33	0.33	0.33	0.33	0.00	0.00	0.00	0.00
Japan	0.00	0.00	0.00	0.00	0.00	0.00	0.00	0.00
Kenya	NA	0.67	0.67	0.67	NA	0.67	0.67	0.67

	Limit on advances, *lla*				Limit on securitized lending, *lls*			
	1950–59	1960–71	1972–79	1980–89	1950–59	1960–71	1972–79	1980–89
South Korea	0.33	0.33	0.33	0.00	0.00	0.00	0.00	0.00
Lebanon	0.67	0.67	0.67	0.67	0.00	0.00	0.00	0.00
Luxembourg	NA	NA	NA	0.00	NA	NA	NA	0.00
Morocco	NA	0.33	0.33	0.33	NA	0.00	0.00	0.00
Mexico	0.00	0.00	0.00	0.00	0.00	0.00	0.00	0.00
Malta	NA	0.67	0.67	0.67	NA	0.00	0.00	0.00
Malaysia	NA	0.33	0.33	0.33	NA	NA	NA	NA
Nigeria	NA	0.33	0.33	0.33	NA	0.33	0.33	0.33
Nicaragua	NA	1.00	1.00	1.00	NA	0.33	0.33	0.33
Netherlands	0.67	0.67	0.67	0.67	0.00	0.00	0.00	0.00
Norway	NA	0.00	0.00	0.00	NA	0.00	0.00	0.00
Nepal	0.00	0.00	0.00	0.00	0.00	0.00	0.00	0.00
New Zealand	NA	0.00	0.00	0.00	NA	0.00	0.00	0.00
Pakistan	0.00	0.00	0.00	0.00	0.00	0.00	0.00	0.00
Panama	0.00	0.00	0.00	0.00	0.00	0.00	0.00	0.00
Peru	NA	0.00	0.00	0.00	NA	0.67	0.67	0.67
Philippines	0.33	0.33	0.33	0.33	0.00	0.00	0.00	0.00
Poland	0.00	0.00	0.00	0.00	0.00	0.00	0.00	0.00
Qatar	NA	NA	0.00	0.00	NA	NA	0.00	0.00
Romania	0.67	0.67	NA	NA	0.33	0.33	NA	NA
Singapore	NA	NA	NA	NA	NA	NA	NA	NA
Sweden	0.33	0.33	0.33	0.33	0.00	0.00	0.00	0.00
Thailand	0.33	0.33	0.33	0.33	0.00	0.00	0.00	0.00
Turkey	0.33	0.33	0.33	0.33	0.00	0.00	0.67	0.67
Tanzania	NA	0.67	0.67	0.67	NA	0.33	0.33	0.33
Uganda	NA	0.33	0.33	0.33	NA	NA	NA	NA
Uruguay	NA	NA	0.00	0.00	NA	NA	0.00	0.00
United States	1.00	1.00	1.00	1.00	0.33	0.33	0.33	0.33
Venezuela	NA	NA	0.67	0.67	NA	NA	0.00	0.00
Western Samoa	NA	NA	NA	0.33	NA	NA	NA	0.33
Yugoslavia	NA	0.00	0.00	0.00	NA	NA	NA	NA
South Africa	0.00	0.00	0.00	0.00	0.00	0.00	0.00	0.00
Zaire	NA	NA	NA	0.33	NA	NA	0.00	0.33
Zambia	NA	0.33	0.33	0.33	NA	0.33	0.33	0.33
Zimbabwe	0.33	0.33	0.33	0.33	0.33	0.33	0.33	0.33

	Who decides on lending terms, *ldec*				Width of circle of borrowers, *lwidth*			
	1950–59	1960–71	1972–79	1980–89	1950–59	1960–71	1972–79	1980–89
Argentina	NA	NA	0.33	0.33	NA	NA	1.00	1.00
Australia	NA	0.33	0.33	0.33	NA	0.00	0.00	0.00
Austria	0.33	0.33	0.33	0.33	1.00	1.00	0.33	0.33
Belgium	0.33	0.33	0.33	0.33	0.33	0.33	0.33	0.33
Bahamas	NA	NA	0.33	0.33	NA	NA	1.00	1.00
Bolivia	0.00	0.00	0.00	0.00	0.00	0.00	0.00	0.00
Brazil	NA	0.00	0.00	0.00	NA	1.00	1.00	1.00
Barbados	NA	NA	0.33	0.33	NA	NA	0.67	0.67
Botswana	NA	NA	0.33	0.33	NA	NA	0.67	0.67
Canada	0.67	0.67	0.67	0.67	0.67	0.67	0.67	0.67
Switzerland	0.67	0.67	0.67	1.00	1.00	1.00	1.00	1.00
Chile	0.67	0.67	0.67	0.67	0.00	0.00	1.00	1.00
China	0.00	0.00	0.00	0.00	NA	NA	NA	NA
Colombia	NA	0.33	0.33	0.33	NA	0.00	0.00	0.00
Costa Rica	NA	0.33	0.33	0.33	NA	0.33	0.33	0.33
West Germany	0.67	0.67	0.67	0.67	0.33	0.33	0.33	0.33
Denmark	0.67	0.67	0.67	0.67	0.00	0.00	0.00	0.00
Egypt	0.33	0.33	0.33	0.33	1.00	1.00	1.00	1.00
Spain	0.33	0.00	0.00	0.00	0.00	0.33	0.33	0.33
Ethiopia	NA	NA	0.67	0.67	NA	NA	1.00	1.00
Finland	0.67	0.67	0.67	0.67	NA	NA	NA	NA
France	0.33	0.33	0.33	0.33	0.00	1.00	1.00	1.00
Britain	0.00	0.00	0.00	0.00	1.00	1.00	1.00	1.00
Ghana	0.33	0.33	0.33	0.33	1.00	0.00	0.00	0.00
Greece	0.33	0.33	0.33	0.33	0.33	0.33	0.00	0.00
Honduras	0.67	0.67	0.67	0.67	0.33	0.33	0.33	0.33
Hungary	0.00	0.00	0.00	0.00	0.33	0.33	0.33	0.33
Indonesia	0.00	0.33	0.33	0.33	1.00	1.00	1.00	1.00
India	0.33	0.67	0.67	0.67	0.33	0.33	0.33	0.33
Ireland	0.33	0.33	0.33	0.33	0.33	0.33	0.33	0.33
Iceland	NA	0.33	0.33	0.33	NA	1.00	1.00	1.00
Israel	0.67	0.67	0.67	0.67	1.00	1.00	1.00	1.00
Italy	0.33	0.33	0.33	0.33	NA	NA	NA	NA
Japan	0.33	0.33	0.33	0.33	NA	NA	NA	NA
Kenya	NA	0.33	0.33	0.33	NA	0.33	0.33	0.33

	Who decides on lending terms, *ldec*				Width of circle of borrowers, *lwidth*			
	1950–59	1960–71	1972–79	1980–89	1950–59	1960–71	1972–79	1980–89
South Korea	0.33	0.33	0.33	0.33	0.00	0.00	0.00	0.00
Lebanon	0.33	0.33	0.33	0.33	0.33	0.33	0.33	0.33
Luxembourg	NA	NA	NA	0.33	NA	NA	NA	1.00
Morocco	NA	0.00	0.00	0.00	NA	0.33	0.33	0.33
Mexico	0.33	0.33	0.33	0.33	1.00	1.00	1.00	1.00
Malta	NA	0.33	0.33	0.33	NA	1.00	1.00	1.00
Malaysia	NA	0.67	0.67	0.67	NA	0.00	0.00	0.00
Nigeria	NA	0.33	0.33	0.33	NA	0.00	0.00	0.00
Nicaragua	NA	0.67	0.67	0.67	NA	0.00	0.00	0.00
Netherlands	0.00	0.00	0.00	0.00	1.00	1.00	1.00	1.00
Norway	0.00	0.00	0.00	0.00	0.00	0.00	0.00	0.00
Nepal	0.33	0.33	0.33	0.33	1.00	1.00	1.00	1.00
New Zealand	0.00	0.00	0.00	0.00	0.33	1.00	1.00	1.00
Pakistan	0.00	0.00	0.00	0.00	0.33	0.33	0.33	0.33
Panama	0.00	0.00	0.00	0.00	0.33	0.33	0.00	0.00
Peru	NA	0.67	0.67	0.67	NA	0.33	0.33	0.33
Philippines	0.33	0.33	0.33	0.33	0.67	0.67	0.67	0.67
Poland	0.33	0.33	0.33	0.33	0.00	0.00	0.00	0.00
Qatar	NA	NA	0.00	0.00	NA	NA	0.33	0.33
Romania	0.67	0.67	0.67	0.67	0.00	0.00	0.00	0.00
Singapore	NA	NA	0.33	0.33	NA	NA	0.00	0.00
Sweden	0.67	0.67	0.67	0.67	0.00	0.00	0.00	0.00
Thailand	0.33	0.33	0.33	0.33	0.33	0.33	0.33	0.33
Turkey	0.33	0.33	0.33	0.33	0.00	0.00	0.33	0.33
Tanzania	NA	0.33	0.33	0.33	NA	1.00	1.00	1.00
Uganda	NA	0.33	0.33	0.33	NA	0.33	0.33	0.33
Uruguay	0.33	0.33	0.67	0.67	0.33	0.33	0.00	0.00
United States	0.33	0.33	0.33	0.33	1.00	1.00	1.00	1.00
Venezuela	0.67	0.67	0.67	0.67	1.00	1.00	0.00	0.00
Western Samoa	NA	NA	NA	0.33	NA	NA	NA	0.00
Yugoslavia	NA	0.00	0.00	0.00	NA	0.00	0.00	0.00
South Africa	0.33	0.33	0.33	0.33	1.00	1.00	1.00	1.00
Zaire	NA	NA	0.33	0.33	NA	NA	0.33	0.33
Zambia	NA	0.00	0.00	0.00	NA	0.33	0.33	0.33
Zimbabwe	0.00	0.00	0.00	0.00	0.67	0.67	0.67	0.67

	Type of limit, *ltype*				Maturity of loans, *lmat*			
	1950–59	1960–71	1972–79	1980–89	1950–59	1960–71	1972–79	1980–89
Argentina	NA	NA	0.33	0.33	NA	NA	1.00	1.00
Australia	NA	NA	NA	NA	NA	0.67	0.67	0.67
Austria	1.00	1.00	0.33	0.33	1.00	1.00	1.00	1.00
Belgium	NA	NA	NA	NA	1.00	1.00	1.00	1.00
Bahamas	NA	NA	0.33	0.33	NA	NA	1.00	1.00
Bolivia	0.00	0.00	0.00	0.00	1.00	1.00	1.00	1.00
Brazil	NA	NA	NA	NA	NA	0.00	0.00	0.00
Barbados	NA	NA	NA	NA	NA	NA	0.33	0.33
Botswana	NA	NA	0.33	0.33	NA	NA	0.33	0.33
Canada	0.33	0.33	0.33	0.33	0.67	0.67	0.67	0.67
Switzerland	NA	NA	NA	NA	1.00	1.00	1.00	1.00
Chile	NA	NA	NA	NA	0.00	0.00	0.00	0.00
China	NA	NA	NA	NA	0.00	0.00	0.00	0.00
Colombia	NA	0.67	0.67	0.67	NA	0.67	0.67	0.67
Costa Rica	NA	0.00	0.00	0.00	NA	0.67	0.67	0.67
West Germany	1.00	1.00	1.00	1.00	1.00	1.00	1.00	1.00
Denmark	NA	NA	NA	NA	1.00	1.00	1.00	1.00
Egypt	0.33	0.33	0.67	0.67	0.00	0.00	0.67	0.67
Spain	0.00	0.00	0.00	0.00	0.00	0.00	0.00	0.00
Ethiopia	NA	NA	0.33	0.33	NA	0.00	0.67	0.67
Finland	NA	NA	NA	NA	0.00	0.00	0.00	0.00
France	1.00	1.00	NA	NA	0.00	1.00	NA	NA
Britain	NA	1.00	1.00	1.00	0.00	1.00	1.00	1.00
Ghana	0.33	0.33	0.33	0.33	0.67	1.00	1.00	1.00
Greece	1.00	1.00	1.00	1.00	0.67	0.67	1.00	1.00
Honduras	0.33	0.33	0.33	0.33	0.67	0.67	0.67	0.67
Hungary	1.00	1.00	1.00	1.00	0.67	0.67	0.67	0.67
Indonesia	0.33	0.33	0.33	0.33	0.00	0.00	0.33	0.33
India	1.00	1.00	1.00	1.00	0.33	0.33	0.33	0.33
Ireland	NA	NA	NA	NA	0.67	0.67	0.67	0.67
Iceland	NA	NA	NA	NA	NA	0.33	0.33	0.33
Israel	0.00	0.00	0.00	0.00	0.67	0.67	0.67	0.67
Italy	0.00	0.00	0.00	0.00	0.00	0.00	0.00	0.00
Japan	NA	NA	NA	NA	0.00	0.00	0.00	0.00
Kenya	NA	1.00	1.00	1.00	NA	0.67	0.67	0.67

	Type of limit, *ltype*				Maturity of loans, *lmat*			
	1950–59	1960–71	1972–79	1980–89	1950–59	1960–71	1972–79	1980–89
South Korea	NA	NA	NA	NA	0.67	0.67	0.67	0.67
Lebanon	0.33	0.33	0.33	0.33	1.00	1.00	1.00	1.00
Luxembourg	NA	NA	NA	NA	NA	NA	NA	1.00
Morocco	NA	0.33	0.33	0.33	NA	0.67	0.67	0.67
Mexico	NA	NA	NA	NA	0.67	0.67	0.67	0.67
Malta	NA	0.33	0.33	0.33	NA	1.00	1.00	1.00
Malaysia	NA	0.33	0.33	0.33	NA	0.67	0.67	0.67
Nigeria	NA	0.33	0.33	0.33	NA	0.67	0.67	0.67
Nicaragua	NA	0.33	0.33	0.33	NA	0.67	0.67	0.67
Netherlands	1.00	1.00	1.00	1.00	0.00	0.00	0.00	0.00
Norway	NA	NA	NA	NA	0.67	0.67	0.67	0.67
Nepal	NA	NA	NA	NA	0.67	0.67	0.67	0.67
New Zealand	0.33	NA	NA	NA	1.00	0.00	0.00	0.00
Pakistan	NA	NA	NA	NA	0.67	0.67	0.67	0.67
Panama	NA	NA	NA	NA	0.00	0.00	0.00	0.00
Peru	NA	0.33	0.33	0.33	NA	1.00	1.00	1.00
Philippines	0.33	0.33	0.33	0.33	0.33	0.33	0.33	0.33
Poland	NA	NA	NA	NA	0.67	0.67	0.00	0.00
Qatar	NA	NA	NA	NA	NA	NA	0.00	0.00
Romania	0.67	0.67	NA	NA	0.67	0.67	0.00	0.00
Singapore	NA	NA	NA	NA	NA	NA	1.00	1.00
Sweden	1.00	1.00	1.00	1.00	0.67	0.67	0.67	0.67
Thailand	0.00	0.00	0.00	0.00	0.67	0.67	0.67	0.67
Turkey	0.67	0.67	0.00	0.00	1.00	1.00	0.67	0.67
Tanzania	NA	0.33	0.33	0.33	NA	0.67	0.67	0.67
Uganda	NA	0.33	0.33	0.33	NA	1.00	1.00	1.00
Uruguay	NA	NA	NA	NA	0.00	0.00	0.00	0.00
United States	NA	NA	NA	NA	1.00	1.00	1.00	1.00
Venezuela	NA	NA	0.33	0.33	0.67	0.67	0.00	0.00
Western Samoa	NA	NA	NA	0.33	NA	NA	NA	1.00
Yugoslavia	NA	NA	NA	NA	NA	0.00	0.00	0.00
South Africa	NA	NA	NA	NA	1.00	1.00	1.00	1.00
Zaire	NA	NA	0.33	0.33	NA	NA	0.67	0.67
Zambia	NA	0.33	0.33	0.33	NA	0.33	0.33	0.33
Zimbabwe	0.33	0.33	0.33	0.33	0.33	0.33	0.33	0.33

	Limit on interest rate, *lint*				Lending in primary market, *lprim*			
	1950–59	1960–71	1972–79	1980–89	1950–59	1960–71	1972–79	1980–89
Argentina	NA	NA	0.50	0.50	NA	NA	0.00	0.00
Australia	NA	1.00	1.00	1.00	NA	0.00	0.00	0.00
Austria	1.00	1.00	1.00	1.00	0.00	0.00	0.00	0.00
Belgium	0.50	0.50	0.50	0.50	0.00	0.00	0.00	0.00
Bahamas	NA	NA	0.25	0.25	NA	NA	0.00	0.00
Bolivia	0.25	0.25	0.25	0.25	0.00	0.00	0.00	0.00
Brazil	NA	0.25	0.25	0.25	NA	0.00	0.00	0.00
Barbados	NA	NA	0.25	0.25	NA	NA	0.00	0.00
Botswana	NA	NA	0.25	0.25	NA	NA	0.00	0.00
Canada	0.75	0.75	0.75	0.75	0.00	0.00	0.00	0.00
Switzerland	0.25	0.25	0.25	0.25	0.00	0.00	0.00	0.00
Chile	0.25	0.25	0.25	0.25	0.00	0.00	0.00	0.00
China	0.25	0.25	0.25	0.25	1.00	1.00	1.00	1.00
Colombia	NA	0.25	0.25	0.25	0.00	0.00	0.00	0.00
Costa Rica	NA	0.25	0.25	0.25	NA	0.00	0.00	0.00
West Germany	0.25	0.25	0.25	0.25	0.00	0.00	0.00	0.00
Denmark	0.25	0.25	0.25	0.25	0.00	0.00	0.00	0.00
Egypt	0.25	0.25	0.25	0.25	0.00	0.00	0.00	0.00
Spain	0.00	0.00	0.00	0.00	0.00	0.00	0.00	0.00
Ethiopia	NA	0.25	0.50	0.50	NA	0.00	0.00	0.00
Finland	0.25	0.25	0.25	0.25	0.00	0.00	0.00	0.00
France	0.00	0.00	NA	NA	0.00	0.00	0.00	0.00
Britain	0.25	0.75	0.75	0.75	0.00	0.00	0.00	0.00
Ghana	0.75	0.50	0.50	0.50	0.00	0.00	0.00	0.00
Greece	0.75	0.75	0.75	0.75	0.00	0.00	0.00	0.00
Honduras	0.25	0.25	0.25	0.25	0.00	0.00	0.00	0.00
Hungary	1.00	1.00	1.00	1.00	0.00	0.00	0.00	0.00
Indonesia	0.25	0.25	0.25	0.25	0.00	0.00	0.00	0.00
India	0.25	0.25	0.25	0.25	0.00	0.00	0.00	0.00
Ireland	0.75	0.75	0.75	0.75	0.00	0.00	0.00	0.00
Iceland	NA	0.25	0.25	0.25	NA	0.00	0.00	0.00
Israel	0.25	0.25	0.25	0.25	0.00	0.00	0.00	0.00
Italy	0.25	0.25	0.25	0.25	0.00	0.00	0.00	0.00
Japan	0.25	0.25	0.25	0.25	0.00	0.00	0.00	0.00
Kenya	NA	0.75	0.75	0.75	NA	0.00	0.00	0.00

	Limit on interest rate, *lint*				Lending in primary market, *lprim*			
	1950–59	1960–71	1972–79	1980–89	1950–59	1960–71	1972–79	1980–89
South Korea	0.25	0.25	0.25	0.25	0.00	0.00	0.00	0.00
Lebanon	1.00	1.00	1.00	1.00	0.00	0.00	0.00	0.00
Luxembourg	NA	NA	NA	0.25	NA	NA	NA	0.00
Morocco	NA	0.25	0.25	0.25	NA	0.00	0.00	0.00
Mexico	0.25	0.25	0.25	0.25	0.00	0.00	0.00	0.00
Malta	NA	0.25	0.25	0.25	NA	0.00	0.00	0.00
Malaysia	NA	0.25	0.25	0.25	NA	0.00	0.00	0.00
Nigeria	NA	0.75	0.75	0.75	NA	0.00	0.00	0.00
Nicaragua	NA	0.50	0.50	0.50	NA	0.00	0.00	0.00
Netherlands	0.00	0.00	0.00	0.00	0.00	0.00	0.00	0.00
Norway	0.25	0.25	0.50	0.50	0.00	0.00	0.00	0.00
Nepal	0.25	0.25	0.25	0.25	0.00	0.00	0.00	0.00
New Zealand	0.75	0.50	0.50	0.50	0.00	0.00	0.00	0.00
Pakistan	0.25	0.25	0.25	0.25	0.00	0.00	0.00	0.00
Panama	0.25	0.25	0.25	0.25	0.00	0.00	0.00	0.00
Peru	NA	0.25	0.25	0.25	NA	0.00	0.00	0.00
Philippines	0.25	0.25	0.25	0.25	0.00	0.00	0.00	0.00
Poland	0.25	0.25	0.25	0.25	0.00	0.00	0.00	0.00
Qatar	NA	NA	0.25	0.25	NA	NA	0.00	0.00
Romania	0.00	0.00	0.25	0.25	0.00	0.00	0.00	0.00
Singapore	NA	NA	0.25	0.25	NA	NA	0.00	0.00
Sweden	0.25	0.25	0.25	0.25	0.00	0.00	0.00	0.00
Thailand	0.25	0.25	0.25	0.25	0.00	0.00	0.00	0.00
Turkey	0.25	0.25	0.25	0.25	0.00	0.00	0.00	0.00
Tanzania	NA	0.75	0.75	0.75	NA	0.00	0.00	0.00
Uganda	NA	0.75	0.75	0.75	NA	0.00	0.00	0.00
Uruguay	0.25	0.25	0.25	0.25	0.00	0.00	0.00	0.00
United States	0.25	0.25	0.25	0.25	0.00	0.00	0.00	0.00
Venezuela	0.25	0.25	0.50	0.50	0.00	0.00	0.00	0.00
Western Samoa	NA	NA	NA	0.25	NA	NA	NA	0.00
Yugoslavia	NA	0.25	0.25	0.25	NA	0.00	0.00	0.00
South Africa	0.25	0.25	0.25	0.25	0.00	0.00	0.00	0.00
Zaire	NA	NA	0.75	0.75	NA	NA	0.00	0.00
Zambia	NA	0.75	0.75	0.75	NA	0.00	0.00	0.00
Zimbabwe	0.25	0.25	0.25	0.25	0.00	0.00	0.00	0.00

**Appendix B: Relevant Parts of the Questionnaire on
Central Bank Independence**

This part of the appendix presents the introduction to the questionnaire
and only the questions that have been used for the coding of questionnaire
variables. As in the full questionnaire these questions are classified by
areas. The symbol appearing to the right of a question indicates what is
the questionnaire variable (in table 19.6) for which the answer to that
question provides the material for coding that questionnaire variable.
Questions are numbered as in the full questionnaire.

The purpose of this questionnaire is to provide guidance in identifying
various parameters of central bank independence and the main objectives
of monetary policy. The questionnaire refers to the following areas: (I)
formal independence as expressed in the central bank's charter and/or
other laws and ordinances, (II) the actual practice whenever it differs from
the stipulation of the law, (III) identification of monetary policy instruments and of the governmental agency that controls them, (IV) identification of intermediate targets and indicators of monetary policy, (V) identification of final objectives, and (VI) background questions on the financial
structure.

In case a particular question is not relevant to your country please
explain why. In case there are issues concerning central bank independence
and monetary policy that have not been addressed in the questionnaire
please flush them out.

I.   *Legal aspects of central bank independence.*

2.   Are the terms of office of the high officials of the CB independent from
the term of office of the central government?—*qto*

3.   Is the Treasury or the central government allowed to borrow directly
from the CB?—*qll*

4.   Is there a legal limit on the nominal amount of government borrowings from CB?—*qll*

6.   Are there provisions in the law for the resolution of policy conflicts
between the CB and the executive branch?—*qrc*

7.   Who determines the budget of the CB?—*qbcb*

8.   Who determines the salaries of high officials of the bank and the
allocation of its profits?—*qsp*

II. *Actual practice when it differs from the stipulation of the law.*

3. Is the resolution of policy conflicts between the CB and the executive branch usually done informally or by appealing to the law? Please elaborate.—*qrc*

III. *Monetary policy instrument and the agencies controlling them.–qsc*

Consider the following list of instruments: open market operations, the discount rate, reserve requirements, credit ceilings, selective direct or indirect credits from the CB at subsidy rates, interest rate ceilings, exchange rate policy, quantitative restrictions on capital flows, surcharges on capital flows, and other instruments if relevant. In each case state whether the instrument exists and if it does identify the agency controlling it. A ranking of the instruments by the frequency of their use would be helpful.

IV. *Intermediate targets and indicators.*

1. Are there quantitative monetary stock targets?—*qst*

6. Are there formal or informal interest rate targets?—*qirt*

V. *Final objectives of monetary Policy.–qpps*

Please rank the following objectives according to their importance in determining the course of monetary policy (if you believe that the ranking was different in different subperiods, give the ranking for each subperiod): price stability, a high level of employment, extraction of revenue from seigniorage, strong export markets, equilibrium in the current account of the balance of payments, maintenance of a sufficient level of foreign exchange reserves, anticyclical policy, low real rates of interest, low nominal rates of interest, low variability of real or nominal rates, maintenance of a fixed parity with other currencies.

If you feel that this framework is too simplistic to characterize the final objectives of policy in your country please elaborate. References on basic sources concerning the final objectives in your country would be helpful.

Appendix C: Codings of Basic Questionnaire Variables

	qto	qll	qrc	qbcb	qsp	qst	qirt	qpps	qsc
Australia	1.00	0.67	0.00	1.00	0.50	0.33	1.00	1.00	1.00
Belgium	1.00	0.00	0.00	1.00	1.00	0.00	1.00	0.67	NA
Bahamas	0.50	0.67	0.50	1.00	1.00	0.00	1.00	0.67	1.00
Barbados	0.50	0.67	0.00	1.00	0.50	0.00	0.00	1.00	0.67
Chile	NA	NA	NA	NA	NA	NA	NA	1.00	NA
Costa Rica	0.50	0.67	0.50	1.00	1.00	0.67	1.00	1.00	1.00
West Germany	1.00	1.00	1.00	1.00	1.00	1.00	1.00	1.00	1.00
Denmark	1.00	1.00	0.50	0.50	1.00	0.00	0.00	0.67	1.00
Ethiopia	0.00	0.00	0.00	0.00	0.00	0.00	1.00	0.33	0.00
Finland	1.00	1.00	1.00	0.50	0.00	0.00	NA	1.00	1.00
France	0.50	0.33	0.50	0.50	1.00	0.67	1.00	1.00	0.67
Britain	0.50	0.33	0.00	0.50	NA	0.67	1.00	1.00	1.00
Ireland	0.50	0.33	0.00	0.50	0.00	0.00	1.00	1.00	1.00
Italy	1.00	0.00	0.50	1.00	1.00	0.67	1.00	1.00	1.00
Lebanon	0.50	0.33	0.50	1.00	1.00	0.00	1.00	0.33	1.00
Luxembourg	0.50	0.33	NA	1.00	1.00	0.00	1.00	0.67	1.00
Nepal	0.00	0.00	0.50	1.00	1.00	0.00	NA	NA	NA
New Zealand	NA	0.00	NA	NA	NA	0.00	NA	NA	1.00
Peru	0.00	0.00	0.00	1.00	0.50	0.33	0.00	0.33	0.33
Turkey	0.50	0.00	0.00	1.00	1.00	0.00	1.00	1.00	0.33
Tanzania	0.50	0.33	0.50	1.00	0.00	0.33	1.00	0.00	0.33
Uganda	0.50	0.33	0.50	1.00	1.00	0.33	NA	1.00	0.33
Uruguay	0.50	0.33	0.50	1.00	0.50	0.00	NA	0.33	1.00
Yugoslavia	NA	0.00	0.00	0.50	0.00	0.33	1.00	NA	0.00
South Africa	0.50	0.33	0.50	1.00	0.00	0.67	1.00	NA	1.00
Zaire	0.50	0.33	0.50	1.00	1.00	0.67	1.00	1.00	0.33

Note: Definitions of variables appear in table 19.6. Codes range from 0 (minimal independence) to a maximum of 1.

20 Inflation and Central Bank Independence

20.1 Introduction

This chapter presents various tests of the hypothesis that countries with more independent central banks have more stable currencies or lower rates of inflation. The tests are based on regressions of the rate of depreciation in the value of money d as the rate of inflation π on the various indices of CB independence presented in chapter 19. Since the legal and questionnaire variables are all coded in a way that assigns a higher numerical code to a variable the higher the level of independence, the hypothesis implies that the effect of each of these variables on inflation should be negative. But the effect of central banks governors' turnover, at least above some threshold, is predicted to be positive.

The hypothesis that inflation should be negatively related to the level of CB independence has been developed in chapter 18. It is a consequence of either (or both) of the two following underlying elements: a stronger degree of time preference on the part of political authorities in comparison to that of the CB, and/or relatively higher concern of the CB for price stability against the background of private information about its independence. In addition there also are cross-country variations in the extent to which the CB is given an explicit mandate to pursue price stability at the expense of other objectives. The variable *obj* is meant to capture the extent to which such a mandate is made explicit in the legal structure underlying the activity of the CB. For a given level of independence from the political authorities as measured by the other variables, a more focused legal mandate to pursue price stability is expected to result in a lower rate of inflation. But this is not because the CB is independent to do what it pleases. Rather, it is because the CB is directed by law to focus on price stability more than on other objectives, and vice versa. Thus the variable *obj* is a measure of the relative importance assigned by the CB to price stability. In terms of the model in section 18.3 the higher the *obj*, the lower is the relative focus of actual policy on objectives other than price stability and the lower therefore is the rate of inflation under discretion even for a given level of independence.[1]

The importance assigned to price stability in practice may obviously deviate from its specification in the law. Questionnaire variable *qpps*, which measures the actual as opposed to legal priority, assigned to price stability is designed to detect such cases. This variable becomes more important, the larger the divergence between the priority assigned to price stability in the CB charter and the priority assigned to it in practice. The expected sign of both *obj* and of *qpps* is therefore negative. It is worth noting, however, that unlike the variable *obj*, the variable *qpps* also reflects the relative preference of the political establishment for price stability. In terms of the model in section 18.3 *obj* can be viewed as a proxy for A_{CB}, while *qpps* can be thought of as a rough measure of A that aggregates the objectives of the CB with those of the political authorities along the lines of equation (18.16a).

The chapter is organized as follows: Section 20.2 relates the rate of depreciation in the real value of money to the legal variables after a first round of aggregation and to governors' turnover. This is done separately for developed and less developed countries as well as for their union. The following section repeats these experiments with aggregate rather than disaggregate measures of legal independence. Both sections reveal differences in the impact of legal independence and of turnover on inflation in developed and in less developed countries. Section 20.3 discusses possible reasons for these differences. A comparison to previous work on CB independence for the common subset of countries appears in section 20.4. The relation between inflation and CB independence as proxied by questionnaire variables is discussed in section 20.5. The results of an instrumental variables estimation of the relation between inflation and governors' turnover rates are reported in section 20.6. The direction of Granger causality between inflation and CB independence as proxied by turnover is discussed in section 20.7. This is followed by concluding reflections.

20.2   Inflation and Disaggregated Measures of Central Bank Independence

Table 20.1 presents regressions of the rate of depreciation in the real value of money d on disaggregated indices of legal CB independence with and without the governors' turnover variable for all countries as well as for developed and less developed countries separately. As explained in chapter 19, the period between 1950 and 1989 is broken down into four subperiods, and an observation on d, each of the legal variables and turnover is constructed for each country in each time period. Since some observations are missing, and the number of countries in the sample is 70, this produces at most 280 observations each one of which is drawn from the cartesian product of 70 countries and 4 broad time periods. The rate of depreciation

Table 20.1
The depreciation in the real value of money versus legal proxies of independence and the turnover of central bank governors (dependent variable: rate of depreciation in the real value of money d)

Explanatory variable	All countries			Developed countries	Less developed countries
	(1)	(2)	(3)	(4)	(5)
Intercept	0.21	0.11	0.12	0.09	0.13
	(5.2)	(2.5)	(2.6)	(3.3)	(1.7)
obj	−0.04	0.04	0.03	0.01	0.07
	(−0.9)	(−0.9)	(−0.9)	(0.4)	(−1.2)
ceo	0.03	−0.01	−0.01	0.02	−0.00
	(0.5)	(−0.2)	(−0.2)	(0.5)	(−0.0)
pf	0.03	0.01	0.10	−0.01	0.09
	(0.4)	(1.0)	(1.0)	(−0.4)	(0.9)
ldec	0.03	0.04	0.05	0.01	0.06
	(0.6)	(1.0)	(1.0)	(0.5)	(0.8)
lwidth	−0.01	0.02	0.03	0.00	0.02
	(−0.3)	(1.0)	(1.1)	(0.3)	(0.7)
lm	−0.18	−0.09	−0.07	−0.05	−0.10
	(−2.7)	(1.4)	(1.1)	(−1.6)	(−0.9)
lla	−0.02	−0.05	−0.05	−0.02	−0.06
	(−0.5)	(−1.4)	(−1.4)	(−0.8)	(−1.0)
lls	0.07	0.05	0.05	−0.01	0.07
	(1.4)	(1.0)	(0.9)	(−0.3)	(1.0)
tor		0.29		−0.06	0.28
		(5.5)		(−0.9)	(3.7)
torl			0.12		
			(0.7)		
torh			0.27		
			(4.8)		
Dummy, 50–59	−0.11	−0.09	−0.10	−0.03	−0.11
	(−3.3)	(−2.9)	(−3.1)	(−2.0)	(−2.1)
Dummy, 60–71	−0.11	−0.10	−0.10	−0.02	−0.12
	(−3.9)	(−3.9)	(−4.0)	(−1.3)	(−3.2)
Dummy, 72–79	−0.04	−0.03	−0.04	0.03	−0.04
	(−1.6)	(−1.3)	(−1.5)	(1.9)	(−1.2)
$\bar{R}^2$	0.11	0.28	0.28	0.25	0.22
Number of observations	175	161	161	60	101

Note: t statistics are in parentheses under the coefficients. The coefficients are rounded to the nearest second digit after the decimal point. The construction and definitions of the legal variables appear in sections 19.2 and 19.3 (see tables 19.1 and 19.2 in particular). tor is the average number of CB governors' changes per annum in a country/subperiod. torh is identical to tor whenever $tor > 0.25$ and is equal to zero otherwise. torl is equal to tor whenever $tor \leq 0.25$ and is equal to zero otherwise. The period dummies are equal to one in the period under consideration and zero otherwise. The number of observations differs across regressions because the number of missing observations depends on the identity of the regressors used.

in the real value of money in year t is defined as

$$d_t \equiv 1 - \frac{1}{1 + \pi_t} = \frac{\pi_t}{1 + \pi_t}, \tag{20.1}$$

where π_t is the rate of inflation in year t. The observation on d is calculated as the geometric yearly average of the d_t's within each country/subperiod. The turnover variable (denoted tor) is calculated as the average number of changes in CB governors per annum within each subperiod/country.

In most of the regressions presented in table 20.1, d rather than π is the dependent variable. This choice of dependent variable is dictated by two considerations. First, the real losses on holding of money balances are more accurately represented by d than by π. Second, the use of d rather than of π moderates the effects of outliers such as Argentina or Bolivia during the hyperinflation on the regression results. To account for possible period-specific effects, period dummies are used in most regressions.

The first three regressions in table 20.1 refer to all countries and always include all the legal variables after a first level of aggregation. The first regression does not include the governors' turnover variable. This variable is added in the second regression and decomposed into high and low turnover ranges in the third regression. The general picture that emerges with respect to the effect of the legal variables in the overall sample is the following. The overall contribution of the legal variables alone to the rate of depreciation in the real value of money in the entire sample of countries is not significant. This is true independently of whether the turnover variable is included (column 1) or excluded (columns 2 and 3) in the regression.

The individual contribution of each legal variable is usually not significant. The addition of the governors' turnover variable increases the adjusted multiple coefficient of correlation from 0.11 to 0.28 (compare columns 1 and 2). This, together with the fact that the t statistic of this variable is highly significant, suggests that the turnover variable captures important elements of actual independence over and above those contained in the legal variables. The third regression decomposes the turnover variable into high and low turnover ranges. The cutoff (0.25 turnovers per annum or an average tenure of four years) is chosen by using goodness of fit as a criterion. This threshold is also in a range that seems reasonable a priori in view of the average length of the electoral cycle. Regression number 3 suggests that the significance of the turnover variable originates from the high turnover range—the variable $torl$ being insignificant and the variable *torh* being significant at conventional levels of significance. This result is consistent with the view that turnover is negatively associated with actual CB independence only in the high turnover range.

As far as individual legal variables are concerned, it is noteworthy that in all the regressions limitations on advances have the expected negative effect on *d*. Although more significant in the presence of turnover than in its absence, this effect is not significant at usual levels. The variable *lm*, which aggregates various other aspects of restrictions on government's borrowing at the CB such as restrictions on interest rates and maturity structure, is also negative but not always significant.

Regressions 4 and 5 are replications of regression 2 for the groups of developed and less developed countries separately. Again the contribution of individual legal variables is in most cases not significant. Their overall contribution to explaining the variation in *d* is significant at the 0.22 level in the group of developed countries and insignificant in the group of developing countries. The turnover variable is insignificant and negative for the developed countries, but it remains significant and positive for the group of developing countries. This suggests that turnover is a better measure of actual independence in developing than in developed countries. Such a conclusion is consistent with the observation that turnover is likely to be a good proxy for independence only above a certain threshold and the fact (documented in table 19.5) that, at least on average, more than half of the developing countries have higher turnover rates than the highest rate within the group of developed countries.

20.3 Inflation, Aggregate Measures of Legal Independence, Compliance, and Turnover

It is likely that the insignificant performance of most legal variables at the individual level is due to multicollinearity. A way of overcoming this problem is to use only one aggregate measure of legal independence. A beneficial by-product of aggregation is that it increases the number of utilizable observations by reducing the number of missing observations needed for a regression. Table 20.2 presents regressions in which *LVAW* is used as the aggregate measure of legal independence. Details on the construction of this proxy appear in table 19.2.

It may be argued that it is not the actual value of governors' turnover that matters but rather the relative magnitudes of actual to legal terms of

Table 20.2
Depreciation in the real value of money versus a weighted average of legal variables, compliance, and turnover (dependent variable: rate of depreciation in the real value of money d)

Explanatory variable	All countries	Developed countries	Less developed countries	Developed countries	Less developed countries
Intercept	0.22	0.81	0.24	0.08	0.11
	(6.2)	(6.4)	(4.0)	(6.5)	(2.1)
$LVAW$	−0.02	−0.05	0.02		
	(−0.3)	(−2.0)	(0.2)		
comp	−0.04	−0.00	−0.04	0.01	0.02
	(−2.7)	−0.3	(−1.7)	(−0.5)	(0.6)
tor				−0.12	0.26
				(−2.0)	(3.6)
Dummy, 50–59	−0.11	−0.03	−0.14	−0.03	−0.13
	(−3.6)	(−2.1)	(−2.5)	(−2.6)	(−2.9)
Dummy, 60–71	−0.09	−0.02	−0.12	−0.02	−0.14
	(−3.9)	(−1.7)	(−3.4)	(−2.1)	(−4.0)
Dummy, 72–79	−0.03	0.03	−0.05	0.03	−0.04
	(−1.2)	(2.4)	(−1.4)	(2.5)	(1.3)
$\bar{R}^2$	0.13	0.28	0.10	0.29	0.20
Number of observations	188	69	116	73	122

Note: t statistics are in parentheses under the coefficients. The coefficients are rounded to the nearest second digit after the decimal point.

office. On this view deviations of actual from legal independence can be proxied by the ratio of the actual average term in office in a country/ subperiod to the legal term of office in that country and subperiod. Such a compliance variable, which is an index of the degree of compliance to the law, is denoted *comp*. The a priori hypothesis is that d is negatively related to compliance, since the lower actual tenure in comparison to that which is stipulated in the law, the lower is the actual independence of the CB and the larger therefore is the rate of depreciation in the real value of money. It is interesting to note that actual average terms in office are usually shorter than legal terms in most countries and subperiods.

The first three columns in table 20.2 are regressions of d on $LVAW$ and *comp* for all countries as well as for the separate groups of developed and less developed countries. As in table 20.1 period dummies are used in all regressions to control for period-specific effects. Both $LVAW$ and *comp* have the expected negative signs in the overall regression, but only *comp* is

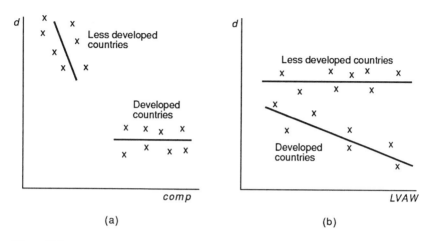

Figure 20.1
Partial relations between d, $LVAW$, and *comp* in developed and less developed countries

statistically significant. A broadly similar picture emerges for the subset of less developed countries. The compliance variable has a negative and significant effect, and the aggregate legal variable is now positive but still insignificant. The converse happens for developed countries. The effect of the compliance variable is practically zero while the aggregate legal variable is negative and significantly different from zero at the 3 percent level.

These results suggest that legal independence is a reasonably good proxy for actual CB independence in developed but not in developing countries. In the latter group the divergence between the actual and the legal terms of office of the chief executive officer of the bank is a better proxy. This result also indicates that the divergence between the letter of the law and actual practice is subtantially higher in developing than in developed countries. This may be due to a general norm of more adherence to the law in developed countries. Further discussion of this issue appears in chapter 23, section 23.6.

On this interpretation the significance of *comp* in the overall sample is caused by its effect only within the group of developing countries. It is therefore puzzling that the t statistic of *comp* in the overall regression indicates a higher level of significance than the t statistic of that variable in the regression for the LDCs alone. This apparent puzzle as well as the insignificance of $LVAW$ in the overall regression can be understood by reference to figure 20.1. Panels a and b of the figure illustrate hypothetical partial relations between d and *comp* and d and *LVAW* for developed and less developed countries. The horizontal line in panel a reflects the fact that *comp* does not affect d in developed countries, and the horizontal line in panel b reflects the fact that *LVAW* does not affect d in LDCs. The downward-sloping line in panel a reflects the fact that *comp* negatively affects d in LDCs, as well as the fact that *comp* is generally lower and d generally higher in LDCs than in developed countries. Finally the downward-sloping line in panel b reflects the fact that *LVAW* negatively affects d in developed countries.

The curves in panel a can be used to clarify why the coefficient of *comp* is more significant in the overall regression than in that for LDCs only. The reason is that the overall regression also captures, through *comp*, differences in the general location of d and of *comp* between developed and less developed countries. The insignificance of *LVAW* in the overall regression, despite its significance in that for developed countries alone, can be understood by reference to panel b of the figure. The combination of the two samples masks the partial effect of *LVAW* on d in developing countries, since the inclusion of the developing countries raises the average level of d without inducing much change in the spread of *LVAW*. This masking effect is reinforced by the lack of a systematic relationship between d and *LVAW* within the group of LDCs.

There is no a priori theoretical presumption as to whether actual independence should be proxied by the compliance or the turnover variable. It is even possible that both variables are significantly related to the inflationary performance of a country. To examine these issues, we regressed d on both *tor* and *comp* in both the developed and the less developed countries. The results are reported in the last two columns of table 20.2. It is apparent that in the LDCs, in which a turnover proxy is needed the most, *comp* loses all significance in the presence of *tor* whose effect remains positive and significant. The compliance variable is also insignificant within the group of developed countries.[2] In view of these results, whenever a turnover-based variable (*tor* or *comp*) is utilized below, it is mostly *tor* rather than *comp*.

20.4 Comparison with Previous Evidence

Existing work on inflation and CB independence is scant. The little that exists is based only on legal data and refers to a subset of the developed countries. Alesina (1988, table 9) combines several previous sources on legal aspects of CB independence for a group of sixteen developed countries and uses this data to classify their banks into four different levels of independence.[3] He then shows informally that countries with higher degrees of CB independence tend to have lower average rates of inflation. More recently Grilli, Masciandaro, and Tabellini (1991) construct more detailed and homogeneous indices of legal independence for a group of European countries plus the United States, Canada, Japan, Australia, and New Zealand. They find a significant negative relationship between some of their indices and average inflation in some periods. Since the indices of legal independence used here do not fully conform with those used in these studies, it is interesting to examine whether their qualitative conclusions can be replicated with the set of legal variables used here. For that purpose some of the regressions from previous tables are reproduced for the union of countries used in the above-mentioned studies but excluding Portugal.[4] Those countries are referred to as the Alesina–Grilli-Masciandaro-Tabellini countries, or the ATC for briefness. They are Australia, Austria, Belgium, Canada, Denmark, Finland, France, Germany, Greece, Iceland, Ireland, Italy, Japan, Luxembourg, the Netherlands, New Zealand, Spain, Switzerland, Britain, and the United States. The difference between our group of developed countries (DC) and the ATC is that Norway and Sweden appear in the first group and not in the second, while Greece appears in the second and not in the first.

Table 20.3 reports several regressions of d on legal proxies of CB independence at various levels of aggregation without and with the turnover variable. Regression 1 includes all the basic legal variables and does not include turnover whereas regression 2 is identical to regression 1 with the turnover variable added in. These two regressions are identical, respectively, to regressions 1 and 2 in table 20.1, except that they refer to the ATC rather than to the entire sample of countries.

A comparison of these equations across tables reveals that the goodness of fit in the ATC is substantially higher ($\overline{R}^2$ of 0.49 for legal variables and time dummies alone in the ATC versus an $\overline{R}^2$ of only 0.11 for the same regression in the entire sample of countries). Moreover almost all the coefficients of the legal variables in regressions 1 and 2 of the ATC have the expected negative sign, and in the presence of turnover some such as *ldec* and *lwidth* are even significant at conventional levels of significance. In addition the joint contribution of all the legal variables to the variation

Table 20.3
Inflation, legal independence, and turnover in the Alesina–Grilli-Masciandaro-Tabellini
countries (dependent variable: rate of depreciation in the real value of money d)

Explanatory variable	(1)	(2)	(3)
Intercept	0.09	0.07	0.06
	(7.6)	(5.3)	(6.7)
obj	−0.01	0.00	0.02
	(−0.1)	0.00	(2.0)
ceo	−0.02	−0.01	−0.02
	(−0.9)	(−0.4)	(−1.4)
pf	−0.02	−0.01	−0.02
	(−1.0)	(−0.4)	(−1.5)
ldec	−0.03	−0.03	
	(−1.7)	(−2.2)	
lwidth	−0.02	−0.02	
	(−1.9)	(−2.1)	
lm	−0.01	−0.00	
	(−0.5)	(−0.1)	
lla	−0.01	−0.00	
	(−0.6)	(−0.3)	
lls	0.03	0.01	
	(1.4)	(0.6)	
ll			−0.03
			(−1.5)
tor		0.09	0.07
		(2.7)	(2.4)
Dummy, 50–59	−0.02	−0.02	−0.02
	(−2.9)	(−2.6)	(−3.1)
Dummy, 60–71	−0.02	−0.02	−0.02
	(−3.0)	(−3.0)	(−3.1)
Dummy, 72–70	0.02	0.02	0.02
	(2.9)	(2.4)	(3.6)
$\bar{R}^2$	0.49	0.55	0.55
Number of observations	60	60	75

Note: t statistics are in parentheses under the coefficients. The coefficients are rounded to the nearest second digit after the decimal point.

in d is significant at the 0.07 and 0.09 levels in equations 1 and 2, respectively. Thus legal variables and time dummies alone perform relatively well in accounting for the variability of d within the group of ATC. The addition of turnover in regression 2 improves the $\bar{R}^2$ even more (to 0.55) and yields a positive and significant effect of governors' turnover on the rate of depreciation in the real value of money.[5] We conclude that for the ATC both legal proxies as well as the turnover variable are instrumental in capturing the degree of CB independence.

Regression 3 is identical to regression 2, except for the fact that all the five legal variables that concern limitations on lending are aggregated into one variable ll. The weights used in the aggregation sum to one and are proportional to the weights of those five variables in table 19.2. The coefficient of ll has the expected negative sign but is not quite significant. Surprisingly the coefficient of obj, which was negative and insignificant prior to the aggregation, becomes positive and significant. The coefficient of turnover remains positive and significant, and the goodness of fit deteriorates a bit. But the joint contribution of the legal variables is now significant even at the 0.01 level.

The general conclusion from this subsection is that despite some differences in the precise proxies of legal independence, the results presented here and those obtained in previous work are qualitatively similar when applied to the same subset of countries. It is therefore likely that any divergences in results between our full sample and that of the ATC is due to differences in institutional features across the samples of countries rather than to differences in the legal proxies of CB independence. In addition, although the legal variables perform relatively well for the ATC, the addition of the governors' turnover variable improves matters even more.

20.5 Inflation and Central Bank Independence as Proxied by Questionnaire Variables during the 1980s

This section presents preliminary evidence on inflation and CB independence as measured by the coded responses to the questionnaire on CB independence. Details on the questionnaire and the coding procedure appear in chapter 19, section 19.5. Responses to the questionnaire combine information on legal as well as on actual independence. We therefore initially relate d to the questionnaire variables alone and only then add turnover and an aggregate legal variable to assess their additional contributions. One can therefore view the main question that is asked in this subsection to be: How much of the cross-sectional variability in d and in inflation during the 1980s can be explained by the questionnaire variables alone? Two subsidiary questions are: (1) Does the governors' turnover variable add anything to the explanation of the remaining unexplained variability? (2) A similar question with respect to the legal variables.

To answer the first question, we regress d on the questionnaire variables in table 19.7. The first subsidiary question is handled by regressing d on the aggregate index of questionnaire-based proxies for CB independence—$QVAW$ (details regarding the construction of this index appear in section 19.5) and on the governors' turnover variable. The second subsidiary question is handled by using $LVAW$ and all the questionnaire variables to explain d. Results appear in table 20.4. Since meaningful individual questionnaire responses were obtained only for a subset of the twenty-six questionnaire countries, the sample is smaller when individual responses are used as regressors. (The full list of countries appears in the first panel of table 19.8.) The first regression, which uses only questionnaire variables, produces a reasonably high goodness of fit—$\bar{R}^2$ is equal to 0.42. Most of the questionnaire variables have the expected negative signs.[6] Those that are significant or nearest to being significant are the intermediate targets and the limitations on lending variables. The overall contribution of the questionnaire variables to the explanation of the variation in d is significant at the 0.07 level.

The second regression in table 20.4 examines the marginal contribution of tor in the presence of an aggregate of the questionnaire variables. The coefficient of $QVAW$ has the expected negative sign and is significant at the 0.05 level. The coefficient of turnover has the expected positive sign and is significant at the 0.025 level. The third regression in table 20.4 shows that the aggregate of legal variables $LVAW$ does not add much to the explanation of the variation in d in the presence of the questionnaire variables. The joint contribution of these variables is still significant (at the 0.10 level).

We conclude that when questionnaire variables are used to explain variations in d, there is not much additional information in legal variables, but there is additional information in CB governors' turnover rates. At least for the 1980s and for the sample of countries for which responses to the questionnaire were obtained, all the available information (as far as

Table 20.4
Depreciation in the real value of money and questionnaire-based indices of central bank independence (questionnaire countries 1980–89; dependent variable: rate of depreciation in the real value of money d)

Explanatory	(1)	(2)	(3)
Intercept	0.28	0.32	0.23
	(2.7)	(3.1)	(1.2)
qto	−0.18		−0.17
	(−1.0)		(−0.9)
qll	−0.19		−0.25
	(−1.2)		(−1.2)
qrc	0.12		0.14
	(0.9)		(0.9)
qfi	0.30		0.28
	(2.5)		(2.1)
qit	−0.21		−0.23
	(−1.9)		(−1.8)
qpps	−0.03		−0.01
	(−0.2)		(−0.1)
qsc	−0.10		−0.06
	(−0.7)		(−0.4)
QVAW		−0.43	
		(−3.0)	
tor		0.55	
		(2.2)	
LVAW			0.20
			(0.5)
$\bar{R}^2$	0.42	0.39	0.37
Number of observations	18	22	18

Note: t statistics appear in parentheses under the coefficients. The coefficients are rounded to the nearest second digit after the decimal point.

explaining d) is contained in the coded questionnaire responses and in turnover. Examination of the generality of this conclusion will have to wait for the availability of more evidence.

20.6 Instrumental Variables Estimation and the Issue of Two-Way Causality between Inflation and Central Bank Independence

It is conceivable that there is a two-way causality between inflation and the actual degree of CB independence. On the one hand, a lower level of independence is conducive to a higher level of inflation. This is the relation investigated in previous sections. On the other hand, a high rate of inflation is likely to result, at least after a while, in a lower level of independence for the CB. High inflation encourages processes that make it easier for the executive to influence monetary policy even if the CB charter does not change. Most CB laws are highly incomplete contracts that do not fully delimit the areas of responsibility of the CB and of the executive branch. In times of high inflation it is harder for the bank to closely control the money supply. In addition high inflation is partly blamed on the bank which tarnishes the bank's public image and reduces its authority vis-à-vis the Treasury, even if this contradicts the charter. Argentina is a dramatic example. Thus even if the degree of independence conferred on the bank by law does not change, actual independence may be affected by the rate of inflation. If that is the case, we should expect the rate of turnover in CB governors to be affected by inflation. It is therefore possible that at least part of the positive relation found between inflation and turnover in the previous sections is due to the effect of inflation on the independence of central banks, and therefore on the turnover rate of their chief executive officers.

The possibility of a two-way relation between inflation and governors' turnover raises two issues. One is related to the possibility that the regressions of d or π on turnover and other variables are affected by a simultaneity bias. The other concerns the direction of Granger causality between inflation and actual CB independence as proxied by governors' turnover. The first issue is discussed in this section and the second in the following one.

To examine the possibility that the significance of the turnover variable in some of the equations for d is due to a simultaneity bias a regression of d on $LVAW$, turnover, and subperiod dummies is estimated with the instrumental variables method. The instruments used are d and tor in the previous subperiod,[7] $LVAW$, the (coded) legal term of office, and the subperiods' dummies. For comparison purposes we also estimate the same equation by ordinary least squares (OLS). The only variables that are significant in the OLS regression are turnover and two of the subperiod dummies. The coefficient of $LVAW$ has the expected negative sign but is not significant. When reestimated using the instrumental variables method, the goodness of fit deteriorates a bit, but the general picture remains the same. In particular the coefficient of turnover remains highly significant. Other experiments with π instead of d as the dependent variable yield qualitatively similar results. Qualitatively similar results are also obtained when the instrumental variables procedure is applied only to the group of LDCs.

In conclusion, it is unlikely that the turnover variable's significant positive effect on d is due only to causality stemming from inflation to turnover. At least within broad subperiods the evidence is consistent with the view that there is a contemporaneous significant effect of actual CB independence as proxied by turnover on d and the rate of inflation.

20.7 Granger Causality between Inflation and Central Bank Independence as Proxied by Turnover

To determine the direction of Granger causality between inflation and CB governors' turnover, bivariate autoregressive processes for inflation and turnover are estimated. The periods are taken to be the four basic subperiods, each one of which is about one decade.[8] The long time periods seem appropriate for slow-moving processes such as the erosion or the buildup of CB independence and its interaction with inflation. The estimated processes for inflation and turnover are given in equations (20.2) and (20.3) with t statistics in parentheses under the coefficients. The coefficient of lagged turnover in the inflation equation is

$$\pi = -1.01 + 0.93\pi_{-1} + 54.77tor_{-1} \qquad \frac{\overline{R}^2}{0.30}, \tag{20.2}$$
$$(-0.2) \quad (5.6) \qquad (3.3)$$

$$tor = 0.10 + 0.002\pi_{-1} + 0.43tor_{-1} \qquad 0.31, \tag{20.3}$$
$$(5.2) \quad (3.1) \qquad (5.2)$$

significant at the 0.001 level, and the coefficient of lagged inflation in the turnover equation is significant at the 0.002 level. A similar picture emerges when d is substituted for π.

This evidence supports the view that there is a two-way Granger causality between inflation and CB independence as proxied by governors' turnover. Lagged turnover positively affects current inflation, and a higher lagged inflation is associated with a current higher turnover of CB governors. Recalling that a higher turnover is associated with lower CB independence, this conclusion also implies that there is a vicious circle between inflation and low levels of independence. When sufficiently sustained, inflation erodes CB independence after a while. But low, sustained levels of independence breed higher inflation after a while. Thus, as hypothesized at the beginning of the previous section, low CB independence and inflation reinforce each other.

20.8 Concluding Reflections

The evidence presented in this chapter is consistent with the view that CB independence affects the rate of inflation in the expected direction but that there are other factors as well. An important conclusion is that discrepancies between actual and legal independence are larger in developing than in developed countries. As a consequence legal measures of CB independence that have been applied with some success in the past to a subset of developed countries perform relatively poorly in less developed countries. On the other hand, the turnover rate of CB governors appears to capture significant variations in independence within the second group of countries.

Individual legal or questionnaire variables are for the most part insignificant, but their joint contribution to the explanation of inflation is often significant. In particular the variables *obj* and *qpps*, which are supposed to measure the relative preference of the CB and of the entire public sector for price stability, respectively, do not have significant effects on inflation. But both usually have the expected negative effect on d. This indicates that the emphasis of policy on price stability as estimated by specialists on monetary policy is likely to be nearer to the actual emphasis of policy than the one derived from the objectives of the CB as specified in the law.

The coding, classification, and weighting of legal information and of responses to questionnaires involves a number of subjective judgments. But any systematic attempt at the measurement of CB independence and of its impact on inflation will have to make some judgments. There obviously is room for sensitivity analysis. The results in this chapter and the previous one should therefore be viewed as a systematic step toward the measurement of CB independence and of its impact on inflation within a wide group of countries rather than a final verdict on the issue.

In particular there is room for the systematization of some of the additional dimensions of CB independence which are discussed in section 19.7. It is likely that when some of these additional elements are quantified more precisely, the goodness of fit between CB independence and inflation will increase. But since independence is also affected by factors that are difficult to quantify, such as personalities, it is likely that the unexplained fraction of the cross-country variation in inflation will remain nonnegligible. In addition different shocks elicit different policy responses even at the same level of independence. A partial attempt to control for differences in world-wide shocks across periods was made in the chapter by introducing sub-period dummies. But there is room for additional refinements.

This chapter has focused on the effects of CB independence on inflation, but not on real variables. An important question is whether the degree of independence affects the long-run rate of growth of the economy. Preliminary evidence for a group of developed economies suggests that it does not (Alesina and Summers 1990).

21 Ranking of Central Banks by an Overall Index of Inflation-Based Central Bank Independence

21.1 Introduction

Alternative indices of CB independence, one based on legal independence and another on CB governors' turnover rates, have been presented in chapter 19. Both indices were combined in chapter 20 in order to explain variations in the rate of depreciation in the value of the currency d. Each group of indices captures a somewhat different dimension of independence. It is therefore natural to combine them with a weighting scheme in order to obtain an overall measure of CB independence. Such weighting is perforce arbitrary. But it is possible to reduce arbitrariness by setting the weights equal to the coefficients of those proxies from the regressions in which they are used to explain the variation in d. This procedure assigns weights to various proxies for independence in proportion to their contribution in explaining variations in d. We therefore refer to the resulting index of overall independence as "inflation based."

The discussion in chapter 20 showed substantial differences in the impact of different proxies for CB independence between the group of developed and the group of developing countries. Different regressions are therefore used to generate the measure of overall CB independence for each of the two groups. For the developed countries (DCs) we use a version of equation 4 in table 20.1 in which the coefficient of *tor* is constrained to zero. This seems reasonable in view of the fact that *tor* is insignificantly different from zero in that equation and since turnover in most DCs is below the relevant threshold. For less developed countries (LDCs) we use a version of equation 5 from table 20.1.[1] The ranking of central banks by overall independence generally changes across subperiods since both turnover and (to a lesser extent) various aspects of the CB charter change over time. Hence the ranking of central banks by overall independence generally differs across subperiods.

21.2 Ranking by Overall Independence

Table 21.1 presents a ranking of countries by the level of overall CB independence during the 1980s. The first column, labeled $\hat{d}$, presents the overall index of independence used for the ranking. It is obtained by calculating the predicted values of d for the decade of the 1980s.[2] The actual values of d are also presented for comparison purposes and in order to identify countries in which the overall index of independence is not a

Table 21.1
Ranking of central banks by an overall index of CB independence during the 1980s

Country[a]	$\hat{d}$[b]	d[c]	$LVAU$[d]	tor[e]	Country[a]	$\hat{d}$[b]	d[c]	$LVAU$[d]	tor[e]
Denmark	0.04	0.05	0.47		Bahamas	0.16	0.05	0.45	0.20
West Germany	0.05	0.02	0.66		India	0.17	0.07	0.33	0.30
United States	0.06	0.04	0.38		Zimbabwe	0.18	0.11	0.23	0.10
Canada	0.06	0.05	0.46		Egypt	0.18	0.13	0.53	0.30
Norway	0.06	0.07	0.14		Israel	0.20	0.47	0.42	0.20
Sweden	0.07	0.06	0.27		Zaire	0.20	0.34	0.41	0.20
Britain	0.07	0.05	0.31		South Africa	0.20	0.12	0.30	0.20
Australia	0.08	0.07	0.31		Indonesia	0.21	0.07	0.32	0.20
France	0.09	0.06	0.28		Costa Rica	0.23	0.19	0.42	0.40
Hungary	0.09	0.07	0.24		Nicaragua	0.25	0.67	0.42	0.40
Spain	0.10	0.08	0.21	0.10	South Korea	0.25	0.05	0.23	0.50
New Zealand	0.10	0.08	0.27		Uruguay	0.26	0.33	0.22	0.30
Iceland	0.11	0.24	0.36		Western Samoa	0.26	0.05	0.28	0.56
Greece	0.11	0.14	0.51	0.20	Zambia	0.26	0.25	0.31	0.50
Thailand	0.11	0.04	0.26	0.10	Ethiopia	0.27	0.04	0.47	0.10
Nigeria	0.12	0.16	0.33	0.10	Peru	0.27	0.64	0.43	0.30
Tanzania	0.13	0.2	0.48	0.10	Mexico	0.28	0.38	0.36	0.30
Malta	0.13	0.02	0.45	0.20	Venezuela	0.28	0.04	0.37	0.50
Kenya	0.13	0.09	0.44	0.20	Turkey	0.29	0.28	0.44	0.40
Philippines	0.14	0.11	0.42	0.20	Botswana	0.30	0.09	0.36	0.40
Barbados	0.14	0.05	0.40	0.10	Chile	0.35	0.15	0.49	0.80
Nepal	0.16	0.08	0.25	0.10	Brazil	0.36	0.68	0.26	0.80
Ghana	0.16	0.28	0.28	0.20	Argentina	0.39	0.74	0.44	1.00

a. The countries in the table are ranked from high to low overall independence by the size of $\hat{d}$. Lower values of $\hat{d}$ indicate higher overall independence.
b. $\hat{d}$ is the predicted value of d using equation 5 in table 20.1 for LDCs and a version of equation (4) without tor for DC.
c. d is the yearly (geometric) average rate of depreciation in the real value of money during the 1980s.
d. $LVAU$ is reproduced from table 19.3.
e. tor is shown only when it is used to calculate $\hat{d}$.

good predictor of inflation. The idea is that such an analysis of outliers helps to identify factors other than CB independence (as characterized here) that are conducive to price stability. Finally an average measure of legal independence and the governors' turnover variable (in cases in which it was used to calculate overall independence) are also presented in order to get a feel for the broad constituents of $\hat{d}$ in particular cases. The table summarizes and aggregates a good deal of information. The main lessons from the table are summarized in what follows:

1.   The overall index usually classifies extreme cases in the expected ranges. Thus Germany and the United States are classified not far from the top, and Mexico, Brazil, and Argentina toward the bottom.

2.   The overall index significantly alters the ranking that is based on legal independence alone. Thus Argentina and Egypt would have been ranked as fifteenth and fourth from the top in terms of $LVAU$ alone, instead of last and twenty-eighth in terms of the overall index of independence. The reason for this drastic change of rankings is not hard to see. Egypt has a moderately high rate of CB governors' turnover as well as a moderately high inflation. Argentina has very high rates of both inflation and governors' turnover. Thus the turnover variable picks up, for these countries, some of the variation in actual independence that is not picked up by the slow-moving legal variables. Actual independence changes more frequently and with a larger amplitude than legal independence. The governors' turnover variable picks some of this differential variation producing a better proxy for overall independence in the process. A similar phenomenon occurs for Turkey, Mexico, Venezuela, Costa Rica, Ethiopia, Uruguay, and several others countries.

3.   For sixteen out of the forty-seven countries in the table the difference between the actual rate of depreciation in the value of money and the predicted rate ($|d - \hat{d}|$) is less than or equal to 0.03. Most of these countries are at the top in terms of their overall level of CB independence.

4.   Ghana, with a value of 0.16 for $\hat{d}$, is located at the median of the distribution of central banks by overall independence. The table suggests that most of the developed countries are above the median of overall independence and most of the LDCs are below it. Within the group of countries with overall independence above the median, only three (Iceland, Nigeria, and Tanzania) have actual d values above 0.15. However, the number of countries with $d < 0.15$ within the group of countries with lower

than median overall CB independence is larger. This indicates that a reasonably high level of overall independence is highly likely to prevent high inflation where high is taken to be $d > 0.15$. But lower than median levels of overall CB independence are not necessarily associated with high inflation. As a matter of fact eleven countries within this subgroup have d values below 0.15. Still all the countries with exceptionally high inflation ($d > 0.3$) have lower than median overall levels of CB independence.

These findings are consistent with the view that below-median independence by itself does not necessarily result in high inflation. However, in the presence of appropriate shocks, countries with independence levels within the low range are more likely to develop high and even exceptionally high rates of inflation than countries with overall levels of independence above the median level.

21.3 Outliers and Rule Countries

Cases in which the index of overall CB independence grossly fails in ranking countries by their rates of inflation include Iceland, Zaire, Israel, the Bahamas, Ethiopia, and Korea. In the first three cases the index of overall independence substantially underpredicts inflation, and in the last three it substantially overpredicts it. A more detailed scrutiny of the institutional structure and of the shocks that affected these countries is called upon. For example, a possible reason for the substantial underprediction of inflation in Israel and Iceland is the widespread utilization of indexed contracts in these countries. The existence of indexation reduces the aversion of policymakers to inflation and increases their tendency to emphasize alternative objectives such as employment. In terms of the model of chapter 3 this implies that indexation raises the parameter A that measures the relative importance given by policymakers to employment in comparison to price stability. It is easily seen from equation (3.6) that when A is larger, the equilibrium rate of inflation under discretion is higher.

More generally, when A or α (the short-run Phillips trade-off coefficient) are higher, no matter for what reason, inflation is predicted to be higher. The economic philosophy and education of policymakers is a factor that may influence the size of α. For example, if policymakers have a Keynesian orientation, they are likely to believe that α is higher than if they have a monetarist orientation. This observation, in conjunction with equation

(3.6) implies that, given CB independence, inflation will be higher under Keynesian policymakers.[3] The general public's aversion to inflation is also a factor that affects the size of A. The low value of this parameter in Germany is most likely related to the collective traumatic memories of two hyperinflations during this century. It is likely that in their absence the Bundesbank would not have been able to maintain its tough anti-inflationary stance for as long as it did.

Chile is classified as the country with one of the lowest levels of overall independence in spite of the fact that it did not have an extremely high inflation during the 1980s. At the mechanical level this largely reflects the high rate of CB governors' turnover in Chile. At a more fundamental level this classification suggests that our measure misses the strong resolve that developed to maintain price stability in Chile after several painful rounds of inflation and stabilization during the 1970s and early 1980s. The same resolve is probably responsible for the recent new CB law in Chile.

Countries such as Austria, Belgium, Luxembourg, the Netherlands, Ireland, and Panama have been excluded altogether from table 21.1 since monetary policy in these countries is dominated by a policy rule of one kind or another. Austria, the Netherlands, and, to a lesser extent, Belgium and Luxembourg, have subjugated their monetary policies to the objective of maintaining a fixed parity with the German mark. In Panama the U.S. dollar functions as legal tender. During the 1980s Ireland followed an exchange rate rule. It therefore is to be expected that these countries enjoy rather low rates of inflation irrespectively of the independence levels of their central banks. This indeed is the case. The average values of d in these countries during the 1980s range between 0.03 and 0.05. Moreover, since they achieved price stability by means other than CB independence, we should expect to find that $d \leq \hat{d}$ in these countries. Incorporation of these countries into the rankings in table 21.1 supports this hypothesis.

The experience of these "rule" countries suggests that high levels of legal or overall CB independence are not necessary for price stability. Egypt, with its relatively high degree of legal independence and moderately high inflation, demonstrates that legal independence alone is also insufficient.

Another reason for outliers is that different countries experience different real shocks. Since, for a given level of CB independence, policy responses to shocks depend on the magnitude and the type of shocks, it is possible that some of the outliers can be explained by obvious differences in the realizations of real shocks. Monetary policy is generally sensitive to shocks to government revenues and expenditures, employment, and the balance of payments. Shocks to these areas are therefore potential candidates for understanding the behavior of some of the outliers.

22 The Mean and the Variance of Inflation, Central Bank Credit, and Central Bank Independence

22.1 Introduction

This chapter presents tests of two separate issues. One is an evaluation of the hypothesis (developed in chapter 18) that the strong positive association between the mean and the standard deviation of inflation is due to their common relation with CB independence. The other is a test of the hypothesis that CB credit to the public sector and seigniorage are negatively related to its legal independence and, in particular, to the tightness of legal limitations on lending.

It is well known that the mean and the variance of inflation are positively correlated across countries. Logue and Willet (1976) and others have documented this relationship in the mid-1970s for a cross section of countries. This result appears to be quite robust. The mean and the standard deviation of yearly inflation calculated for each of 117 countries over the 1950–89 period produce two rankings of countries—one by mean inflation and the other by its standard deviation—which are almost identical. As a matter of fact the simple cross-countries coefficient of correlation between the means and the standard deviations of inflation is 0.98. When similar coefficients of correlation are calculated separately for high-, intermediates and low-inflation countries, the correlation remains 0.98. Propositions 18.3 and 18.7 imply that this positive association is due to the common negative association of both the mean and the variance of inflation with the level of CB independence. This implication of the theory is evaluated in section 22.2.

CB policy affects the price level through the monetary base and the money supply. An important determinant of the monetary base is CB credit to the public sector. Section 22.3 investigates empirically whether CB credit to the public sector is negatively related to legal proxies of CB independence. In particular the effectiveness of legal limitations on lending is examined by investigating the relationship between the growth of CB credit to the public sector and seigniorage, on the one hand, and the tightness of those limitations, on the other. The effect of actual independence on seigniorage, as proxied by CB governors' turnover, is also examined.

22.2 The Cross-sectional and Cross Period Distribution of Inflation and of Its Variance and Their Relation to Central Bank Independence

This subsection reports the results of various experiments designed to determine how much of the very high covariation between the means and the standard deviations of inflation is due to their common link to CB independence. The basic test is implemented by regressing both the mean and the standard deviation of inflation on various proxies for CB independence and on subperiod dummies and by examining how much of the total correlation between them is due to their common association with our proxies of CB independence. The experiments differ in the variables used to proxy CB independence and in the groups of countries and subperiods used. As a consequence they also differ in the number of observations used.

In the first experiment both the means and the standard deviations of inflation within each country/subperiod are regressed on all legal variables, governors' turnover rates, and period dummies. Fitted values of both the means and the standard deviations of inflation that are based *only on the variation in indices of CB independence* are then calculated. Finally the ratio of the covariance between those fitted values and the covariance between the actual values of the means and the standard deviations of inflation are obtained. The higher this ratio, the larger is the fraction of the covariability between the means and the standard deviations of inflation that is due to variations in our measures of CB independence. Based on 161 country/subperiod observations during the period between 1950 and 1989, this ratio is 0.14. The same ratios calculated separately for the groups of developed and less developed countries are 0.19 and 0.14, respectively. (The corresponding numbers of observations are 60 for DCs and 101 for LDCs.)

Hence, for all subperiods taken together, between 14 to 19 percent of the large positive covariance between the means and the standards deviations of inflation is accounted for solely by variations in legal variables and CB governors' turnover rates.

A similar experiment is repeated only for the 1980s with the seven questionnaire variables[1] and turnover as proxies for CB independence. Since the number of countries with responses to the questionnaire is smaller than the number of countries in the full sample, the number of observations is reduced to 18. But the fraction of the covariance between the mean and the variance of inflation that is due to variations in our measures of CB independence rises to 0.49. The same experiment is also repeated with aggregates of the legal and of the questionnaire variables and turnover as proxies for independence. For the unweighted versions of these groups of variables ($LVAU$ and $QVAU$), the fraction of the correlation between means and variances that is due to variations in $LVAU$,

$QVAU$, and turnover is 0.30. (The number of observations in this case is 14.) The increase in this fraction in comparison to the full sample of countries and subperiods is partly due to the reduction in the number of observations. Nevertheless, it is likely that some part of the increase in it is due to the additional information contained in responses to the questionnaire about CB independence.

In conclusion the results of this section suggest that at least a seventh of the positive covariability between the mean and the standard deviation of inflation is due to their common relation with the various indices of CB independence developed in chapter 19.

22.3   Central Bank Credit to the Public Sector and Central Bank Independence

This section reports preliminary evidence on the relationship between the measures of CB independence developed in chapter 19 and the yearly average rate of growth (per subperiod) in CB credit to the public sector (gcr).[2] It also reports the effect of those provisions on seigniorage. Of particular interest in this context is the effect of legal provisions that are specifically designed to discourage or limit the ability of government to borrow from the CB. These provisions are quantified by lla, lls, $ldec$, $lwidth$, and lm. We therefore enter these variables both in a disaggregated manner as well as in the form of the subaggregate ll which combines all the legal variables that concern legal limitations on lending.[3] Sizable and significant coefficients for these variables would indicate good compliance of actual practice with legal limitations. Lack of significance would indicate poor adherence to the legal limitations on lending.

Table 22.1 reports two regressions. In the first one the rate of growth of CB credit is regressed on the limitations on lending subaggregate, the remaining legal variables, and subperiods' dummies. In the second regression each of the eight legal variables is entered separately. Finally, to account for the possibility that central banks increase credit in a manner that at least partly accommodates inflation, we also include the rate of depreciation in the value of money d as an explanatory variable and exclude the subperiods' dummies.[4] Both regressions suggest that the relationship between the rate of growth of credit and legal independence is tenuous at best. Most of the coefficients of the legal variables are insignificant. In particular the coefficient of the limitations on lending subaggre-

Table 22.1
The rate of growth of CB credit to the public sector, limitations on lending, and CB independence (dependent variable: rate of growth of CB credit to the public sector gcr)

Explanatory variable	(1)	(2)
Intercept	−0.35	−0.05
	(3.8)	(0.1)
obj	0.01	0.13
	(0.1)	(1.6)
ceo	0.07	−0.01
	(0.5)	(−0.1)
pf	0.09	−0.07
	(0.6)	(−0.7)
ll	−0.20	
	(−1.0)	
$ldec$		0.04
		(0.5)
$lwidth$		0.01
		(2.0)
lm		−0.11
		(−0.8)
lla		−0.01
		(−0.1)
lls		−0.07
		(−0.7)
d		2.33
		(15.5)
$\bar{R}^2$	0.04	0.64
Number of observations	168	146

Note: t statistics appear in parentheses under the coefficients. The coefficients are rounded to the nearest second digit after the decimal point. The first regression includes subperiods' dummies whose coefficients are not shown in the table.

gate in the first equation has the expected negative sign but is insignificant. When these variables are entered in a disaggregated form (in the second equation), they are all still insignificant.

By contrast, the coefficient of d is large and highly significant. This finding is probably due to the fact that CB credit behaves in an accommodative manner.

In conclusion the evidence is consistent with the view that the compliance to legal limitations on lending is rather poor on average and that there may be a substantial degree of accommodation of inflation in the behavior of CB credit. The first conclusion is consistent with findings obtained by Leone (1991). The qualification regarding the second conclusion is needed because of the possibility that the coefficient of d also reflects a more conventional inverse causality in which the growth of credit causes inflation. The separation of this effect from accommodation is left for future work.

Additional regressions (not shown) of the rate of growth of CB credit and of the ratio between this credit and GDP on proxies of legal limitations on lending for DC and LDC separately show that compliance to the limitations, although low in both groups, is worse in LDCs. Furthermore, other things the same, the rate of growth of CB credit responds more strongly to inflation in LDCs than in DCs. In other words, for the same level of legal limitations on lending, CB credit to the public sector is more accommodative in LDCs than in DCs.

Another way of evaluating the effectiveness of legal limitations on lending and of actual CB independence is to relate seigniorage to those limitations and to CB governors' turnover rate as a proxy for actual independence.[5] This has been done for a sample of thirty-three countries during the 1970s. Figures on seigniorage are taken from table 4.1 in which seigniorage is measured as the increase in base money as a percentage of total government revenues inclusive of the increase in base money. The results (not reported) confirm the view that legal limitations on lending are poorly adhered to. But a higher level of actual CB independence, as proxied by turnover, exerts a significant negative effect on the fraction of governmental revenues that are obtained via the creation of base money.

23 The Determinants of Central Bank Independence

23.1 Introduction

Previous chapters provided measures of CB independence and used them to examine some of the effects of differing degrees of CB independence. This chapter focuses on the factors that influence the level of independence conferred on the CB by political authorities. These include political instability, past inflation, the size of the financial sector, and other structural and economic factors. Part of the material in the chapter is based on systematic empirical evidence, while the other part is more impressionistic but also wider in scope.

The chapter is organized as follows: Section 23.2 discusses the effect of political instability on the legal independence of the CB and presents preliminary evidence on the issue. The effect of inflation on CB independence is discussed and documented in the subsequent section. Other determinants of independence are discussed in section 23.4. This section also discusses possible structural reasons for the fact that some countries try to ensure real stability by indexation while many other countries try to achieve it by nominal stability.

Price stability may be achieved either by granting sufficient independence to the CB or by adhering to a rule. Section 23.5 compares and contrasts the experiences of countries that chose the first method with that of rule countries. The difference in the meaning of legal independence between developed and less developed countries and possible reasons for this difference are discussed in section 23.6. The last section discusses a number of cases in which the successful stabilization of inflation was followed by an increase in the degree of CB independence and speculates about possible reasons for this development.

23.2 Political Instability and Legal Central Bank Independence[1]

This section presents preliminary evidence on the effect of various dimensions of political instability on the legal independence of the CB. The degree of legal independence conferred on the CB ultimately depends on the decisions of political authorities as expressed through the legislative process. The effect of political instability on the size of the public debt and on seigniorage has recently been stressed in a series of papers (Alesina and Tabellini 1990; Persson and Svensson 1989; Tabellini and Alesina 1990;

Cukierman, Edwards, and Tabellini 1992). The effects of political instability on seigniorage are discussed in chapter 4. Political instability probably also influences the degree of legal independence conferred on the CB by political authorities.

It is not obvious whether greater political instability leads to less or more independence for the CB. It could be argued, on the one hand, that when the ruling party faces a greater probability that it will be removed from office, it has a stronger interest in developing an apolitical institution that will restrict the range of actions of the opposition if and when the latter comes to office. On the other hand, such an attitude requires a certain minimal level of concensus about the rules of the game. When the degree of polarization is above this threshold, the incumbent's desire to use all available institutions to fortify its hold on power would tend to reduce CB independence the less stable the regime.

It therefore would seem at first that there is no clear-cut relationship between political instability and CB independence. But there is really no contradiction between the two hypotheses. It is possible to combine them into one single, internally consistent, hypothesis as follows: In countries with a sufficient degree of internal cohesion, more political instability should be associated with a higher degree of CB independence, whereas the reverse should be true in countries with relatively low levels of national concensus.

To secure preliminary evidence on this hypothesis, we use two indices of political instability constructed by Haggard, Kaufman, Shariff, and Webb (1991) for a group of fourteen middle income countries for the seventies and eighties. The first index, *pip* (for party political instability), is a measure of political instability within a given regime. It is designed to capture the frequency and extent of change on the left–right dimension, in the identity of ruling governments within a given regime.[2] The other index, *pir* (for regime political instability), is a count of the number of changes in the type of regime (from authoritarian to democratic, and vice versa) per subperiod. We consider the first index as a measure of political instability in cases in which the degree of national concensus is above the threshold discussed earlier. The second index is taken to be a measure of political instability when the degree of national concensus is below the threshold. The aggregate indices of legal independence, *LVAW* and *LVAU*, are used as measures of legal CB independence. Details on their construction appear in chapter 19, section 19.3.

Table 23.1
Legal central bank independence, party instability, and regime instability (dependent
variable: $LVAW$)

Explanatory variable	(1)	(2)	(3)
Intercept	0.36	0.4	0.38
	(15.7)	(17.9)	(16.7)
pip	0.01		0.03
	(1.1)		(2.2)
pir		−0.02	−0.04
		(−1.4)	(−2.3)
$\bar{R}^2$	0.01	0.03	0.15
Number of observations	28	28	28

Note: t statistics are in parentheses under the coefficients. The coefficients are rounded to the
nearest second digit after the decimal point. The regressions are based on data from the
subperiods 1972–79 and 1980–89 in the following countries: Argentina, Bolivia, Chile, Costa
Rica, Egypt, Indonesia, Korea, Mexico, Peru, Philippines, Thailand, Turkey, Uruguay, and
Venezuela. As in the three previous chapters a data point refers to observations on the
relevant variables in a given country within one of the subperiods.

Table 23.1 reports three regressions in which $LVAW$ is the dependent
variable. In the first regression the only regressor is pip, and in the second
the only regressor is pir. The third equation combines both measures of
political instability into one regression. When each of pip and pir appears
as the only explanatory variable (equations 1 and 2, respectively), pip has
the expected positive sign and pir has the expected negative sign. However,
neither of them is significant at conventional levels. Also the fractions of
variation in $LVAW$ explained by regressions 1 and 2 are very low. When
the two measures of political instability are combined into one regression
(equation 3), the signs remain as before, but the coefficients of both variables increase in absolute value. More important, both coefficients are now
significantly different from zero at the 0.02 level, and $\bar{R}^2$ is substantially
higher. The same regressions (not shown) with $LVAU$ instead of $LVAW$
as dependent variable yield basically similar results. The fact that $\bar{R}^2$ is
only 0.15 suggests that there are other important factors that affect the
level of legal CB independence. Nevertheless, the fact that both pip and pir
are significant in conjunction with the fact that their joint inclusion dramatically improves the goodness of fit support the basic hypothesis of this
section.

This preliminary and partial evidence is sufficiently intriguing to justify
a more thorough investigation of the hypothesis in this section. Such an

investigation would have to control for more variables and include a wider sample of countries.

23.3 The Effect of Inflation on Central Bank Independence

Once it has been allowed to run its course for a sufficiently long period of time, inflation tends to erode the independence of the CB even without any change in legal independence. This conclusion is supported both by evidence presented in previous chapters as well as by episodic experiences of individual countries. In particular higher past inflation reduces the current level of CB independence as proxied by the turnover of CB governors (details appear in chapter 20, section 20.7). There is also evidence that for a given level of legal independence, the rate of growth of CB credit to the public sector is larger with higher inflation (details appear in chapter 22, section 22.3). This finding indicates that the ability of central banks to resist pressures to increase credit according to the "needs of trade" diminishes with the rate of inflation even if there is no change in legal independence.

Sufficiently high and sustained inflation leads to the evolution of automatic or semiautomatic accommodative mechanisms. One of the most powerful of these mechanisms is indexation of contracts in the labor and capital markets to the general price level or to the price of foreign exchange. Countries such as Brazil, Israel, and Argentina have had elaborate indexation schemes for many years. But even countries with relatively mild inflationary experiences such as the United States, France, and Britain experienced an increase in the proportion of indexed contracts following the inflationary experience of the 1970s. The evolution of indexation, particularly in the capital market, gives rise to monetary conventions that encourage the CB to accommodate inflation. Such conventions are most likely behind the finding (in table 22.1) that the rate of growth of CB credit responds positively to inflation even at a given level of legal independence.

A dramatic example of accommodation by the CB because of indexation in the capital market are the *Patam* accounts in Israel between 1979 and 1985. These are local residents' deposits with the banking system that are indexed to the exchange rate. Since banks were required to hold a very high liquidity ratio against those deposits with the CB, they effectively were deposits of the public with the CB. As a consequence of this arrangement the (indirect) nominal obligations of the CB to the public increased automatically whenever there was a devaluation. During the high inflation years in Israel (1979–85) this mechanism contributed about 50 percent of the total change in M3 (Cukierman and Sokoler 1989).

When inflation reaches hyperinflationary dimensions, the granting of formal independence to the CB without complementary measures is usually not sufficient for the restoration of price stability. A dramatic illustration is the privatization of the Reichsbank during the post–World War I German hyperinflation. In May 1922, at the insistence of the Allies, the president of the Reichsbank was made accountable to an independent board of directors rather than to the German chancellor. The hope was that this institutional change would decrease the discounting of government bills at the CB. Instead the CB continued to discount government bills at a high pace and, in addition, started to discount bills of private industrialists and bankers who, after the change, had better representation on the board of the Reichsbank (Holtfrerich 1986, p. 168). Rather than use its newly acquired independence for stabilizing monetary growth, the new board continued to accommodate the budgetary deficit while simultaneously allowing particular groups to get a share of revenues from seigniorage.

It seems therefore that CB independence is more effective as a preventive than as a remedial device. Once a fast inflationary process is underway, its eradication cannot be left to the CB alone. It requires the active participation of the central government as well as of other institutions and the simultaneous deployment of policy measures from several areas. The 1985 successful Israeli stabilization is consistent with this view (Cukierman 1988a). But once price stability has been restored and expectations calmed down, the efficiency of CB independence as a safeguard is restored. The post–World War II record of the Bundesbank supports this view.

23.4 Other Determinants of Central Bank Independence

This section briefly discusses additional structural and historical reasons for cross-country (and sometimes cross period) differences in the degree of CB independence.

1. Countries with broad financial markets and a substantial amount of financial intermediation are more likely to grant high levels of independence to their central banks. The reason is that the disruptions that infla-

tion and inflation uncertainty inflict on the process of intermediation between savings and investment are proportional to the size of the financial sector. As a result price stability is more valuable in countries with relatively large and well-developed capital markets. Since more independence to the CB is conducive to less inflation, this implies that countries with large financial markets are more likely to have more independent banks than countries with narrow financial markets. The ranking of central banks by overall independence (table 21.1) broadly supports this view. There is a large concentration of countries with sizable financial markets such as the United States, Germany, Britain, and France well above the median level of overall independence. On the other hand, most of the countries that are well below the median level of independence have relatively narrow internal financial markets or rely extensively on capital market indexation.

This conjecture is also consistent with the fact that the central banks of centrally planned economies (which do not rely much on financial intermediation to allocate savings) such as Poland, Yugoslavia, and Hungary have low levels of legal independence (table 19.3).

2.   Governments facing relatively inelastic (with respect to the real rate of interest) supplies of funds tend to rely, ceteris paribus, more heavily on seigniorage revenues to bridge temporary discrepancies between expenditures and tax revenues. They prefer therefore relatively dependent central banks. This preference is reinforced by the fact that such governments are usually found in developing countries characterized by narrow financial markets in which the inflation-induced distortions of financial markets are relatively less important. A factor that reinforces this preference is the desire of developing countries for fast growth and low interest rates (Chandler 1962). This induces the central banks of such countries to act as development banks, thus limiting their independence to pursue price stability.

3.   A large outstanding internal debt reduces the attractiveness of CB independence to the political authorities. This occurs for two reasons. First, as shown in chapter 4, section 4.4 the incentive to partially default on the public debt through inflation is stronger the larger the public debt. Second, if (as is most likely the case) the elasticity of demand for government bonds is smaller the larger the debt/GDP ratio, government does not lose much if due to default its future access to the loan market is temporar-

ily shut off. Both elements reduce the attractiveness of CB independence to government and the political authorities.

4.   Ceteris paribus, governments of countries in which the size of shocks to government expenditures and revenues is larger are more likely to value the option to have recourse to seigniorage. Such government prefers relatively less independent central banks.

5.   Governments of countries with relatively large flexibility of wages and therefore little sensitivity of employment and output to nominal shocks are more likely to tolerate more independent central banks. Thus to the extent that Weitzman's (1985) claim that the Japanese bonus system makes the levels of employment and output in Japan less sensitive to nominal shocks than their U.S. counterparts,[3] we should expect the Bank of Japan to be more independent than the Federal Reserve. Judging by the charter of the two banks, the Fed is substantially more independent (see table 19.3). However, during most of the 1980s Japan had a consistently lower inflation than the United States. Since the operating procedures of the Fed and of the Bank of Japan are similar (Dotsey 1986), it is likely that this difference in outcomes is deliberate. This suggests that, given the degree of independence, differences in the structure of the economy may influence monetary policy.[4]

6.   Indexation, by partially maintaining the real value of key economic variables in the face of inflation, reduces the costs of inflation. This reduces the relative importance of price stability and therefore of CB independence. It would seem therefore that in countries with a long history of indexation political authorities would be less inclined to delegate authority to the CB. The recent history of some Latin American countries and of Israel until the 1985 stabilization is consistent with this view. Israel, for example, had widespread indexation in both the labor and the financial markets long before inflation penetrated the three-digit level at the end of the 1970s. This supports the view that the existence of indexation contributed to the limited degree of independence of the Bank of Israel. This bank's rank in terms of overall independence is twenty-ninth out of forty-seven central banks (table 21.1).

Behind these observations lurks a wider question: Why is real stability achieved by indexation in some countries and by nominal stability in others? Historical accident is, no doubt, a component of the answer. For

example, the strong aversion of the Bundesbank to inflation is related
to the trauma that the German people experienced during two hyperinflations. But there also are more systematic long-run forces at work. The
breadth of the internal capital market and its importance in the process of
allocating funds from surplus to deficit units seems to be a basic determinant of the ways countries choose to ensure real stability. The wider these
markets are in terms of both flows and stocks, the more likely it is that real
stability will be ensured by nominal stability. The United States, Britain,
Japan, Canada, and several other developed countries in which there are
widespread financial markets in conjunction with a relatively strong emphasis on price stability yield support to this view.

Although suggestive, the discussion in this section is not definitive. It
could perhaps be viewed as a summary of reasonable conjectures awaiting
more systematic testing in the future.

23.5 Rules versus Central Bank Independence as Alternative Methods for the Achievement of Price Stability

CB independence is generally not a necessary condition for price stability.
The discussion in section 21.3 suggests that price stability can also be
achieved by rigid rules. This is the case in Austria, Belgium, Luxembourg,
the Netherlands, and Panama. These countries either peg their currency to
a very stable currency such as the German Mark or do not issue their own
currency.

The establishment of the European Monetary System (EMS) in 1978
restricted the independence of the non-German central banks by forcing
them to pay more attention to the maintenance of a fixed parity with the
German Mark. But, due to the high independence and aggressive anti-
inflationary stance of the Bundesbank, this reduction in independence
resulted in more, rather than less stable prices (Giavazzi and Giovannini
1989). A variation on this theme is Canada whose main trading partner on
both the current and the capital accounts is the United States. The Bank
of Canada's primary objective during the eighties may be described as an
attempt to minimize a weighted average of fluctuations in the rate of
exchange with respect to the U.S. dollar and of the interest rate differential
with the United States (Howitt 1986; and Beaudry and Fortin 1987). Thus
the Bank of Canada followed a policy similar to that followed by some

EMS countries without any formal currency agreement. By following those objectives, the Bank of Canada imported the U.S. disinflation without large capital flows.

These examples suggest that a rigidly adhered to exchange rate rule or dollarization (as in Panama) can ensure price stability even in the absence of CB independence provided that the peg is to the currency of a relatively independent CB. In other words, the subjugation of monetary policy to the objective of maintaining a fixed peg is a way of benefiting from the credibility of a more independent CB without having to change the level of independence of the domestic CB.

On the other hand, a high degree of legal independence does not fully insulate the CB from political pressure. For example, the Fed, which enjoys a relatively large degree of formal independence, responds (as do many other bureaucracies) to political pressures (Friedman 1982; Toma 1982; Alesina and Sachs 1988; Kane 1990). In this respect the Fed seems to be in a unique position among central banks in the world. As a bureaucracy it prizes its high level of independence and tries not to strongly alienate other governmental institutions like Congress and the executive branch that can infringe on this independence. This makes it partially receptive to such pressures. But since it is supposed to be independent it cannot acknowledge such responses. This may provide another explanation for the Fed's well-documented preference for noisy operating procedures (e.g., Brunner and Meltzer 1964; Friedman 1982) as well as its penchant for secrecy (Goodfriend 1986).[5] This point of view also implies that the Fed may not accommodate some pressures and only partially accommodate other pressures. By contrast, central banks that are not supposed to be as independent from other branches of government are more at ease to acknowledge their cooperation with them. This implies that central banks with lower degrees of legal independence such as the Bank of England (see tables 19.3 and 19.4) should not be as secretive as the Fed.[6]

23.6   The Different Meanings of Legal Independence in Developed and in Developing Countries

Many features of CB laws in developing countries have been copied from the CB charters of developed countries. However, due to different degrees of compliance with the law between the two groups of countries legal independence is not as effective in ensuring price stability in developing countries as it is in developed countries. Details appear in chapter 20 (see sections 20.3 and 20.4 in particular).

Several reasons contribute to this state of affairs. First, the norm of general adherance to the law is probably more deeply rooted in developed Western democracies than in absolute regimes or newer democracies. Second, due to the limited stage of development of their financial systems, governments of developing countries are particularly concerned with the deepening of the financial structure and the mobilization of savings for investment purposes (Bhatt 1980). As a consequence they often tend to operate their central banks as development banks in order to overcome the scarcity of domestic savings. This restricts the ability of their central banks to focus on the price stability objective. In the absence of adverse shocks this central banking structure does not necessarily lead to inflation. But it is much more vulnerable to adverse real shocks than a structure in which the CB does not assume the functions of a development bank. Third, many developing countries have totalitarian regimes that do not respect the division of authority between different branches of government character-istic of Western democracies. This attitude tends to relegate the CB to the status of one more department of the central government even if the CB charter grants it a substantial amount of independence. Examples are Argentina, Peru, Uganda, and Venezuela (see table 19.3). This argument implies that the legal independence of a CB should be evaluated against the background of the regime of the country in which it resides.

23.7   The Effect of Successful Stabilizations on Central Bank Independence

Economic crises that are accompanied by large inflation but that are ultimately successfully stabilized often lead after stabilization to a more independent CB. The periods following the stabilization of the classic German hyperinflation (Holtfrerich 1986) and the recent Israeli stabiliza-tion (Cukierman and Sokoler 1989) are examples. The new (1989) CB law in Chile, which grants a wide degree of legal independence to the bank, is to a large extent a reaction to the severe real disruptions this country suffered during several stabilization attempts. Similar tendencies are likely to develop in the aftermath of the successful 1987–88 Mexican stabilization (a description of the Mexican program and its effects appears in Ortiz 1991).

A common feature of these episodes is that successful stabilizations were implemented only when the absence of stabilization became sufficiently unbearable. A recent explanation for this phenomenon relies on the supposition that stabilizations are delayed because they require sacrifices from different interest groups and because these groups are, at least initially, not fully informed about each other's propensity to bear the costs of stabilization. In this view, a successful stabilization takes place when enough time has elapsed to reveal each group's type to the other group. When this occurs, the weaker group, whose weakness is now common knowledge, concedes immediately and stabilization takes place (Alesina and Drazen 1992; Drazen and Grilli 1991).

This mechanism explains why stabilizations are delayed and also shows that a crisis, by speeding reforms, can be beneficial for economic welfare. But it does not explain the tendency of central banks to become more independent after the implementation of successful stabilizations. A likely explanation is that once they have experienced the disruptions associated with high inflation and its stabilization, competing interest groups become more acutely aware of the benefits of avoiding those painful cycles altogether.[7] In particular they learn that it is much easier to prevent high inflation than to cure it and turn to enhanced CB independence as a preventive device. However, only societies that first manage to agree on the allocation of the costs of stabilization reach this stage. Enhancement of CB independence is a sign that there is enough concensus and perhaps mutual information to largely give up monetary expansion as a policy instrument. Countries such as Argentina and Brazil that have not reached this threshold level of concensus are also unlikely to raise the independence of their central banks. In such countries the vicious circle between low independence and high inflation is likely to continue until inflation becomes sufficiently unbearable to mobilize the concensus needed for a serious stabilization. When this occurs there may be a discrete upward jump in CB independence through a reform or a change in the CB charter. But until this happens low CB independence and inflation tend to continually reinforce each other. These conclusions are consistent with the empirical evidence presented in sections 23.2 and 20.7.

Notes

Chapter 1

1. This statement refers to the twentieth century and abstracts from the Great Depression. In previous centuries commodity money standards, when they existed, prevented sustained inflation. But such standards virtually disappeared during this century.

2. A policy is dynamically consistent if the plan made for future periods in the present is not revised as time goes by.

3. But for the sake of completeness one chapter (16) is devoted to a review of policy choices under private information with fixed policymaker types.

Chapter 2

1. Some of the factors and institutions that affect the form of this objective function are discussed in part IV. The consequences of political parties with differing objectives are discussed in chapter 17.

2. The natural rate is the level of employment that would obtain in the absence of monetary surprises.

3. Barro and Gordon (1983b) have argued that this conflict arises because of distortionary labor taxes. Chapter 3, section 3.5, shows that if nominal contracts are set so as to clear the labor market in an ex ante sense, an inflationary bias arises only by postulating a counterintuitive and undocumented form for labor contracts. Section 3.6 provides alternative foundations for the employment-motivated bias that rely on minimum wage legislation or union power in part of the labor market.

4. This statement presumes that seigniorage revenues are increasing in rates of monetary expansion. Except for periods of extremely high inflation this is generally the case.

5. The Delors Report (named after the president of the EEC) was issued in 1989. It contains a plan for moving from the EMS to full monetary unification in three stages. Stage two would involve a system such as the EMS with the additional proviso that parities will be adjusted only under exceptional circumstances.

Chapter 3

1. This is strictly true under full certainty. In the presence of asymmetric information the central bank has some effect on employment.

2. The natural level is the one that obtains in the absence of monetary surprises.

3. Some of those assumptions are relaxed in later chapters.

4. The "setting" of expectations is really a proxy for irreversible actions taken by the public prior to the realization of inflation. More explicit formulations of these actions are discussed in section 3.6.

5. This example first appeared in the pioneering work of Kydland and Prescott (1977) and was developed further by Barro and Gordon (1983b).

6. A further discussion of this concept and of the closely related concept of subgame perfection appears in chapter 11, section 11.2.

7. These expressions are obtained by alternatively inserting equation (3.6) and $m = 0$ into the objective function in equation (3.1).

8. We assume for simplicity that the target rate of employment and the natural rate do not change over time. Some of these assumptions are relaxed later.

9. When $m^e > A\alpha(N^* - N_n)$, policymakers settle for an employment level even below N_n in order to refrain from producing inflation at the high expected rate. There are no equilibria in this range precisely because $m \neq m^e$.

10. This argument is not quite identical to the Cho-Kreps intuitive criterion which was developed for situations of private information. There is no private information here, but due to the multiplicity of possible equilibria, there is strategic uncertainty. The argument in the text is an extension of the intuitive criterion to the case in which there is strategic uncertainty but no private information.

11. I am indebted to Nissan Liviatan for raising questions that led to the framework in this section.

12. We consider later the case in which nominal contracts also characterize the competitive segment of the labor market.

13. If union and nonunion labor are complementary factors of production, dN/dw_u is even more likely to be negative since in this case $D_u^u + D_u^c$ is unambiguously negative.

14. The chapters in part IV on the degree of central bank independence in various countries contain a more detailed discussion.

15. Those problems arise even if we abstract from the questions raised in section 3.5 about the structure of contracts underlying the inflationary bias result.

16. For example, when there is too much of the public good in the no-intervention equilibrium, the central bank has a deflationary bias provided that labor demand is sufficiently elastic.

Chapter 4

1. Those sections draw freely on Cukierman, Edwards, and Tabellini (1992).

2. Evidence for Israel appears in Ben-Bassat and Marom (1988), Leiderman and Marom (1988), and Melnick (1988). Evidence for Argentina and several other Latin American countries appears in Piterman (1988). Those articles all appear in *The Economic Review* of the Bank of Israel and are summarized in Offenbacher (1988).

3. This effect was first discovered by Bresciani-Turroni (1937) in the context of the German hyperinflation. It is also known as the Olivera-Tanzi effect.

4. Money market equilibrium implies $M/P = L(\pi^e)$. Since, once expectations have been set, the right-hand side is given, any increase in money supply must be matched one to one by an increase in the price level.

5. In deriving this expression, we have used the equalities $\pi^e = \pi = \mu$ which result from the following considerations: Government announces a rate of inflation π. Since government's commitment is credible, $\pi^e = \pi$ and real money balances chosen by the public at the beginning of the period are determined at $L(\pi)$. Once money demand is determined, government has to raise money supply at rate $\mu = \pi$ in order to make good on its promise that inflation will be π.

6. The structural approach to the efficiency of the tax system is discussed in Hinrich (1966), Musgrave (1969), and Aizenman (1987). For a survey of the more recent literature, see Goode (1984).

7. But the empirical tests in section 4.7 control for the effects of structural factors on seigniorage.

8. All the results go through if the political process is modeled as in Alesina and Tabellini (1990), where rational voters elect the policymaker type at the beginning of each period.

9. Because of the concavity of $U(\cdot)$ and the convexity of $\delta(\cdot)$, and $\gamma(\cdot)$, the second-order conditions are always satisfied.

10. Because the $H^i(\cdot)$ function is linear, all the income effects of a more inefficient tax system fall on public consumption. If $H^i(\cdot)$ was concave, this would no longer be true, and we would need additional conditions to sign $C'(\theta)$ and $T'(\theta)$.

11. Recall that $1 - \theta_t$ is the efficiency of the tax system in period $t + 1$. But it is chosen in period t.

12. This basic result extends, under mild restrictions, to more general forms of the utility from the two public goods.

13. The variable P is a generated regressor. As such, the estimates of the standard errors may be biased in general. However, this problem does not invalidate the t statistics for the null hypothesis that the estimated coefficient of P is zero, since under the null the standard errors are unbiased (Pagan 1984). This is precisely the hypothesis that is being tested, so there is no need to try a correction. However, this may be a problem in interpreting the t statistics of the remaining variables.

14. Doing so results in a positive and barely significant coefficient in most regressions.

15. As an alternative way of capturing the role of polarization Cukierman, Edwards, and Tabellini (1992) use an index of income distribution. To the extent that societies with more unequal income distribution are more polarized, this variable should have a positive effect on seigniorage. Since data on income distribution are limited, an index of income distribution was available only for thirty-seven countries. As expected, for this limited sample the coefficient of income inequality turned out to be positive although not significant at conventional levels.

16. This point of view is stressed, for instance, in Berg and Sachs (1988) and Huntington (1968).

17. For example, during the last year of the German hyperinflation, which was characterized by astronomical rates of monetary expansion, seigniorage collected was higher than in its first year (1921) during which inflation was "only" 142 percent (Cukierman 1988b, table 2).

18. Olivera (1967) and Tanzi (1977).

Chapter 5

The model of this chapter has been adapted from Cukierman and Liviatan (1990).

1. The precise transmission mechanism is discussed in chapter 3, section 3.6.

2. This statement is based on the presumption that due to bequest or liquidity constraints the neo-Recardian proposition does not hold. In the presence of idiosyncratic differences across individuals, this is a natural presumption (Cukierman and Meltzer 1989; Aiyagari 1989).

3. A more detailed account appears in Cukierman (1988a) and Liviatan (1987).

4. Models of policymaking in the presence of centralized wage setting have been developed by Horn and Persson (1988) and Tabellini (1988). The basic conclusions of this chapter remain unaltered in the presence of partial unionization of the labor force provided that the conditions in section 3.6 are satisfied. An elaboration of this statement appears in section 5.6.

5. The desired exchange rate is attained by the appropriate choice of the quantity of money by the central bank. Since, given the quantity of money in the rest of the world, there is a one-to-one relation between the exchange rate and the domestic quantity of money, we view the central bank (or whoever else decides on e) as directly choosing the exchange rate.

6. Such a specification is general enough to include as particular cases many of the current hypotheses about the objectives of unions as summarized in Oswald's (1985) survey. In particular it includes as a particular case the objective of maximizing the union's total wage bill.

7. Obviously, when $B - B^* \geq 0$, the rate of devaluation chosen is zero. In that case policy-makers are concerned only with inflation (see equation 5.3).

8. The precise condition is $F_{NNN}F_N/F_{NN}^2 < 2$, where F_N, F_{NN}, and F_{NNN} are the first, second, and third derivatives of the production function F with respect to labor input N, respectively. This condition is always satisfied when F_{NNN} is negative. When it is positive, the condition is satisfied provided that F_{NNN} is not too large. This condition requires that if the rate of decrease in marginal productivity levels off at higher quantities of labor, it does not do that at a rate that is too high. The ambiguity arises because the marginal effectiveness of decreases in the real wage in affecting the current account can decrease with the level of employment.

9. The balance of payments was also helped by the fact that the nominal magnitudes at which the exchange rate and wages were frozen resulted in a substantial reduction of the real wage rate. More details about the Israeli stabilization appear in Bruno (1986) and Cukierman (1988a).

10. An interesting political economy question concerns the factors that induce such a change in regime. A discussion of mechanisms that leads to the replacement of short-sighted discretion with a certain level of commitment appears in Alesina and Drazen (1992), Grilli and Drazen (1991), and Cukierman (1988b, sec. 5).

11. A related phenomenon is the almost complete destruction in the real value of Mark-denominated assets held by foreigners. Holtfrerich (1986) calculates that by the end of the hyperinflation in 1924 the resulting transfer of purchasing power from foreigners to Germany was roughly of the same order of magnitude as all the reparation Germany had paid till that time.

Chapter 6

This chapter draws on and extends the framework in Cukierman (1991a).

1. Because of the stronger aversion of the Bundesbank to inflation, this results in other community members emulating German monetary policy (Giavazzi and Giovannini 1989). In this range of shocks the Bundesbank provides an externality to other EEC countries by playing the role of Rogoff's (1985) conservative central banker. Rogoff has suggested that a way to handle the inflationary bias of monetary policy (see chapter 3) is to appoint as central banker an individual who is more concerned about price stability than society on average.

2. A framework in which the cost c is derived endogenously from principal-agent considerations appears in Flood and Isard (1989). See also Lohmann (1990). Lohmann (1992) uses a similar idea to investigate the normative trade-off between commitment and flexibility.

3. I do not identify who, within the public sector, makes this decision. To underscore this deliberate vagueness, the terms "policymaker," "government," and "central bank" are used interchangeably.

4. Strictly speaking, the intuitive criterion has been developed for games with private information about the type of some players rather than for games of complete information in which there is strategic uncertainty because of multiplicity of equilibria, as is the case here. But there is no compelling reason to prevent the application of the same refinement criterion in the second case as well. In both cases the recipient of the message has no reason to doubt that the sender of the message will indeed fulfill his or her promise if the recipient acts on the assumption that the sender will.

5. This equilibrium can be thought of as a time-consistent commitment to a state-contingent policy.

6. In the presence of asymmetric information and gradual learning by the public about government's perception of s the policymaker can temporarily reduce the divergence between natural and desired employment. Chapter 15 in part III deals with such a situation.

7. In the particular case $\sum_{i=1}^{m} \lambda_i = 1/2$, m is exactly at the weighted median of votes. When $\sum_{i=1}^{m} \lambda_i > 1/2$, the median country and all countries below it form a strict majority.

8. The argument in note 4 obviously applies to this case too.

9. A fuller discussion of the impact of central bank independence on A and other parameters appears in chapter 18.

10. A detailed analysis of one difficulty in achieving the correct incentive structure appears in Obstfeld (1990).

11. Note that the probability that a particular country reneges is not identical to the probability that at least one country in the community reneges. The second probability is always larger.

12. $[n/2]$ stands for the largest integer contained in $n/2$. If, for example, $n = 3$, the CMCS reneges if and only if at least two of the country shocks are above S_H. If $n = 4$, the CMCS reneges if and only if at least three of the country shocks are above S_H.

13. Since S_H is higher, p is lower.

14. Various other aspects of a prospective monetary unification in Europe are discussed in De Cecco and Giovannini (1989).

15. Analyses of monetary policy in the presence of such a function within a single country appear in Canzoneri (1985), Rogoff (1985), Flood and Isard (1989), Lohman (1992), and in chapter 15.

16. But a more general formulation may have multiple equilibria. Obstfeld (1991) shows that there generically are multiple equilibria in AP systems in which stabilization policy is possible. This suggests that refinements will generally have to be used to narrow down the range of equilibria.

Chapter 7

1. The notion that inflation should be determined by public finance considerations goes back to Phelps (1973). Mankiw presents a model in which such considerations lead to an optimal composition of taxes within each time period as well as to an optimal intertemporal allocation of taxes as in Barro (1979). Phelps's idea is prescriptive. But both Barro and Mankiw use the theory of optimal taxation descriptively.

2. This and the following two sections draw on Cukierman (1990).

3. The fraction of credit marketed through such contracts was even larger prior to the acceleration of inflation in the 1970s.

4. The maturity of demand deposits and of money market accounts is obviously at the continuous discretion of depositors.

5. A bank normally has to invest some resources in gathering information about a borrower before granting a loan. No similar investment is necessary in order to accept a deposit.

6. This rise in costs partially reflects the increasing difficulties of borrowing successively larger amounts at the discount window.

7. The footnote continues with the following revealing paragraph:

An example of financial sector anger over unpredictable Federal Reserve action can be found in the period October–November 1977. The Federal Reserve abruptly raised the federal funds rate in the middle of a Treasury financing operation—traditionally an "even keel" period for monetary policy. Many cries of confusion were reported in the financial press, and the event seemed almost to precipitate a minor crisis between the board and the Carter administration over the direction of monetary policy. See, for example, *New York Times* articles of November 1, 1977, p. 53; November 2, 1977, pp. A1, A56; November 3, 1977, p. 52; and November 7, 1977, p. 55. Also see "The Bond Market Falls into a Fed Trap," *Business Week*, November 14, 1977, pp. 187, 190. There, an "exasperated banker" is quoted as saying, "Our industry spends millions of dollars on brains to follow what the Fed is doing. If it's going to be capricious and irrational, then our ability to assume risk as government bond dealers is diminished. What is especially irritating here is their timing."

8. Incomplete information by the central bank about the realizations of the specific shocks and of profits across individual banks makes it difficult to apply bank-specific measures, and it increases the reliance of the central bank on industrywide measures to preserve profits. Even if the realizations of the specific shocks were known to the central bank, the latter may find it preferable and more in the spirit of free markets to use industrywide instruments rather than bank-specific interventions.

9. These motives are discussed in chapters 3, 4, and 5, respectively.

10. Treasury bills and other good quality short-term paper are the most frequently used real life counterparts of the "bonds" in the model (Tobin 1982).

11. This specification abstracts from the existence of cash.

12. Shiller (1980) presents evidence which supports the view that the Fed has some temporary influence on short-term real rates.

13. Banks' profits are not affected by the shock ε_l to the demand for loans because the quantity of loans is determined before the realization of shocks. In the presence of credit lines, which are discussed later, ε_l affects profits.

14. But in contrast to the employment motive that only gives rise to an inflation bias but does not affect real variables, the financial stability motive induces both an inflationary bias and an expansion in the real quantity of loans. Details appear in Cukierman (1990, sec. 5).

15. It is argued at the end of this section that this translates into the smoothing of nominal rates as well.

16. It is well known from the work of Cagan (1956) and others that during some hyper-inflationary episodes, seigniorage revenue could have been increased by reducing the rate of inflation. (An illustration appears in chapter 4.) Since such behavior is ruled out by its optimality concept, the theory of optimal seigniorage relies on the presumption that seigniorage revenues rise with monetary expansion and inflation.

17. A test of the hypothesis in high inflation countries (that unlike many other tests starts from an explicit formulation of the private sector's utility function) also produces mixed results (Calvo and Leiderman 1990).

18. Details appear in Cukierman (1990, sec. 7).

Chapter 8

1. A difference in types may also reflect differences in information about the economy across types.

2. No distinction is drawn in this chapter between money growth and inflation. The implications of such a distinction are discussed in chapter 13.

Chapter 9

1. The introduction to this chapter draws on Cukierman (1986).

2. In a sample of seventy countries the United States is always in the top decile of legal CB independence. See table 19.3, for example.

3. The discussion of asymmetric information here is conducted within the context of the employment motive. An analysis of the effects of asymmetric information in the context of the revenue motive appears in Cukierman (1988b). Remarks about the effects of asymmetric information in the presence of a balance-of-payments motive appear in chapter 11, section 11.6.

4. An eloquent case for this position appears in Plosser (1990).

5. The most striking example of causality from money growth to employment occurred during the Great Depression (Friedman and Schwartz 1963). Recent evidence provided in Romer and Romer (1989) suggests that many postwar recessions were preceded by decceler-ations in monetary growth. There is also recent evidence supporting the view that the liquidity effect of money on interest rates is nonnegligible (Christiano and Eichenbaum 1992).

6. Here the convention that $\lim_{\beta \to 0} \beta^0 = 1$ is adopted. Hence, for $\beta = 0$, equation (9.1) reduces to $x_0(N^* - N_0) + \pi_0^2/2$.

7. The quadratic on $N^* - N_i$, which was present in chapter 3 (equation 3.1), is omitted for reasons of tractability. This formulation abstracts from possible increasing political costs of successively lower levels of employment. But the intraperiod objective function remains con-vex because of the quadratic on π. A framework that combines a quadratic on $N^* - N_i$ with asymmetric information appears in chapter 15.

8. The change in x_i may be a policy response to economic or political events that the public is aware of. But as long as the public is not totally certain about the magnitude or the timing of this response, a margin of uncertainty remains, and it pays to utilize it past inflation to sharpen its forecast of future inflation.

9. The distributional assumptions on v imply that $x - N(A, \sigma_p^2)$, where $\sigma_p^2 \equiv \sigma_v^2/(1 - \rho^2)$. Thus, for example, the probability of a negative x_i is less than 0.03 when $A = 2\sigma_p^2$ and 0.0013 for $A = 3\sigma_p^2$. See also appendix A to this chapter.

10. As a consequence there is no difference between the rate of inflation π and the rate of monetary growth m. This restriction is released in chapter 13.

11. Since A is known by the public whereas p_i is not, it is reasonable to conjecture that B_0 and B will generally be different. In any case the solution procedure is a priori free to assign identical values to B_0 and to B.

12. From (9.6) and (9.3b),

$$m_{i-1} = B_0 A + B(\rho p_{i-2} + v_{i-1}) + \psi_i.$$

Since p_{i-2} is contained in I_i, an observation on m_{i-1} is equivalent to an observation on the linear combination y_i.

13. θ/B is obtained by calculating the simple regression coefficient

$$\frac{Ev_{i-1}(Bv_{i-1} + \psi_{i-1})}{E[Bv_{i-1} + \psi_{i-1}]^2}.$$

14. Recall that $E[\psi_i | I_i] = 0$.

15. In fact B changes too when σ_ψ^2 changes. But as shown in appendix B, the combined effect of an increase in σ_ψ^2 on θ is still negative so that this intuition is correct.

16. The Euler equations are basically first-order conditions in a maximization problem with an infinite number of instruments. The transversality condition

$$\lim_{i \to \infty} \beta^i E_{G0}[\alpha x_i - \alpha\beta\rho\theta E_{Gi}x_{i+1} - m_i^p] = 0$$

is satisfied for any $\beta < 1$ since $E_{G0}[\cdot]$ is finite. This condition is sufficient for an internal maximum. More mathematical details appear in Sargent (1979, ch. 14).

17. Note that the solution always exists and is bounded between α and $\alpha[1 - \rho^2\beta\sigma_v^2/(\sigma_v^2 + \sigma_\psi^2)]$. The reason is that $\alpha > \alpha[1 - \rho^2\beta\sigma_v^2/(\sigma_v^2 + \sigma_\psi^2)] = F(\alpha)$.

18. This section and the next one were stimulated by a discussion with Larry Ball.

19. This implies that when they set contracts for period i individuals know the innovations v_{i-1} and v_i. However, policymakers and the public are ignorant of the current and future realizations of the control error as well as of future innovations to the central bank's objective function.

20. The superscript s on m_{i+1}^s and I_{i+1}^s designates that those magnitudes refer to a perfect information environment.

21. An elaboration appears in Cukierman (1984, ch. 4).

22. This conclusion generalizes to the case in which the public's learning process is more stretched out. Details appear in chapter 10.

23. Additional implications of this confusion and the closely related "permanent-transitory confusion," in which the permanent component is a random walk, are discussed in Brunner, Cukierman, and Meltzer (1980) and in Cukierman and Meltzer (1982).

24. But cross-sectional variation in σ_v^2 produces, ceteris paribus, a negative cross-sectional correlation between V and Em_i. Hence this theory fits the facts provided the effects of the variation in β and σ_ψ^2 on the sign of the correlation between V and Em_i dominate the effect of the variation in σ_v^2 on the sign of this correlation. A related and more general explanation is presented in chapter 18 and tested in chapter 22.

Chapter 10

This chapter draws on Cukierman and Meltzer (1986a).

1. Although the same symbols as in chapter 9 are used to denote the coefficients of A and of p_i, they turn out to be different combinations of the underlying parameters of the model because of the different information structure.

2. As a matter of fact, $\lambda \leq \rho$, which is strictly smaller than 1. A proof appears in the next note.

3. Note that λ is always smaller than or equal to ρ so that the weight $\rho - \lambda$ is always nonnegative. This can be seen by noting from (10.5b) that the condition $\rho - \lambda \geq 0$ is implied by the condition $r \equiv [B\sigma_v/\sigma_\psi]^2 \geq 0$, which is always satisfied.

4. Formally, when $\rho = 1$, p becomes a random walk and the predictor reduces to Muth's (1960) predictor. However, we exclude this case by requiring $\rho < 1$.

5. At the limit when $\rho \to 0$, $\lambda \to 0$, and the predictor tends to $\bar{m}^p$.

6. Readers who are willing to take the results of this section on faith may go to the next one.

7. Note that the transversality condition

$$\lim_{i \to \infty} \beta^i E_{G0}\left[\alpha\left\{x_i - (\rho - \lambda)\beta E_{Gi}\sum_{j=0}^{\infty}(\beta\lambda)^j x_{i+j+1}\right\} - m_i^p\right] = 0$$

is satisfied for any $\beta < 1$, since the term inside the brackets following E_{G0} is finite. This condition is sufficient for an internal maximum.

8. Strictly speaking, we have demonstrated that this solution is unique within the class of decision rules in which government's action depends only on the current realization of p_i. But as long as the equilibrium optimal predictor of money growth is linear in the information set of the public, the solution in the text is also unique within the wider class of solutions, which a priori allows m_i^p to depend on the current as well as on the past history of p_i. This can be demonstrated by writing the optimal predictor as a general linear function of all past rates of money growth and by allowing m_i^p to be a general function

$$m_i^p = F(p_i, p_{i-1}, p_{i-2}, \ldots)$$

of the entire history of governmental objectives. This formulation is similar to that of Green and Porter (1984) in which the current action of a representative firm depends on the entire history of the industry price.

The proof of uniqueness proceeds by substituting the general linear predictor into government's objective function in (10.7), deriving the Euler equations and showing that they imply the function F above to be a linear function of p_i only, as postulated in equation (10.1).

9. Note that with a higher σ_v^2, λ is lower and the activism parameter B is actually lower.

10. I am indebted to Larry Ball for raising this question.

11. Under perfect information the central bank loses the ability to influence expectations, so the problem in equation (10.7) reduces (as in chapter 9, section 9.5) to a series of unrelated identical one-period problems of the form

$$\max_{m_i^p} \left[(m_i^p - A)\alpha A - \frac{(m_i^p)^2}{2} \right].$$

The first-order condition for this problem implies that $m_i^p = \alpha A$ for all i, so αA is trivially also mean inflation.

12. The effect of β on Em_i seems to be generally ambiguous due to the fact that the sign of its direct effect on Em_i is negative whereas the sign of its effect through λ is positive.

13. The other notion, which utilizes trigger strategies, is discussed in the next chapter, section 11.3.

Chapter 11

1. An early example of this approach is in Barro and Gordon (1983a). Surveys of literature using trigger strategies in the context of monetary policy games appear in Rogoff (1987, 1989).

2. A related discussion appears in Persson and Tabellini (1990, ch. 4).

3. Despite their strong similarity the terms used to describe these two concepts are very different. This is due to the fact that when they were developed, in the mid-1970s, the interchange between macroeconomics and game theory was almost nonexistent. A fuller discussion of the differences and similarities between them appears in Fershtman (1989).

4. In the absence of asymmetric information, this measure is zero for dynamically consistent plans, thus indicating full credibility.

5. This device has been used extensively in industrial organization to model the repeated interaction between oligopolists. See, for example, Friedman (1971, 1977).

6. Despite its popularity this term does not quite catch the function of this strategy. The idea is not to punish the monetary authority but rather to deter it from inflating at the discretionary rate αA.

7. The calculation of this loss is based on the understanding that the monetary authority chooses αA also in the next period. The reason is that this choice yields a better value to its objective function than the choice m^*. Given that in the next period expectations are at αA, inflation at αA yields $-(\alpha A)^2/2$, whereas inflation at m^* yields $\alpha A(m^* - \alpha A) - (m^*)^2/2$, which is smaller for any $m^* \neq \alpha A$.

8. Note that the ideal inflation expectation, $m^* = 0$, cannot be sustained if there is positive time preference. It would require the inequality

$$\beta \frac{(\alpha A)^2}{2} > \frac{(\alpha A)^2}{2}.$$

to hold; however, this condition cannot be satisfied when $\beta < 1$. But a somewhat higher rate of inflation can be sustained by this mechanism even for $\beta < 1$.

9. Since this is a quadratic equation, there are two roots, the smallest of which corresponds to the minimum credibly sustainable inflation.

10. Obviously other deterrence mechanisms will yield different sustainable ranges for the rate of inflation.

11. This point is raised in Backus and Driffill (1985a) and Rogoff (1987).

12. A related discussion appears in Blackburn and Christensen (1989, sec. IIIB).

13. In the United States, this activity is sometimes called "Fed watching." See Bull (1982) for some evidence and Jones (1986) for practical advice on how to watch the Fed.

Chapter 12

The analytical material in this chapter is a simplified version of the discussion in Cukierman and Meltzer (1986a, sec. 6).

1. Moreover it seems to be applicable mostly to the United States. Political authorities in most other countries are more open about CB independence or its lack. The collective schizophrenia in which Congress confers a large degree of legal independence on the Fed only to continually attempt to influence its policy by threatening to revoke this independence seems very much a U.S. phenomenon.

2. Altering the precision of monetary control normally requires a reform in monetary institutions and practices. The once-and-for-all restriction is meant to capture, in a stylized manner, the fact that institutional reform is attempted rather infrequently.

3. In chapter 9, slower learning takes the form of a lower θ, which implies that the public pays less attention to the information contained in last period's rate of inflation (see equation 9.7a). As a consequence the process of learning about recent changes in x is slower.

4. It is important that σ_ψ^2 does not quite reach zero for equation (12.2) to hold. But σ_ψ^2 can be made as close to zero as desired.

5. It is implicitly assumed here that in equation (9A.7) the requirement $\sigma_v^2 \leq (1 - \rho^2)A^2/9$ is the binding constraint. This will be the case for sufficiently low values of $(N^* - N_n)^2$.

Chapter 13

1. The descriptive realism of trigger strategies in the context of the interaction between the central bank and a large number of uncoordinated individuals is very limited. A fuller discussion appears in section 11.4.

2. The only (very minor) difference is that the formulation used here implies that the policy-maker dislikes any deviation of actual employment from its desired level irrespective of its sign. But since we later impose the restriction that the probability that $N^* - N_i < 0$ is very small, the two formulations are practically equivalent. See section 13.5 and appendix B to this chapter.

3. δ_i can reflect changes in money demand due to various causes like changes in the structure of financial markets, deregulation, and other innovations to the demand for liquidity. However, since δ_i does not depend on the interperiod's change in inflationary expectations, this specification abstracts from changes in money demand that are due to changes in expectation. In general δ_i may have some persistence over time from which we abstract too. Explicit introduction of persistence into the specification of δ_i complicates the algebra but does not alter the basic qualitative conclusions of this chapter.

4. An additional reason that will become apparent later is that the central bank knows A with certainty but has to forecast p_{i+1} in period i.

5. A sufficient condition for this to be the case is derived and discussed in appendix B to this chapter. It essentially puts a bound on some linear combination of the variances σ_v^2, σ_ε^2, and σ_δ^2.

6. The transversality condition

$$\lim \beta^i E_{\text{CB0}} \left[\alpha \left(x_i - \beta \frac{B_2}{B_3} \theta x_{i+1} \right) - m_i - \delta_i \right] = 0$$

is satisfied for any $\beta < 1$ as long as $E_{\text{CB0}}[\cdot]$ is finite. $E_{\text{CB0}}[\cdot]$ is finite in turn provided that B_2/B_3 is finite. This is demonstrated at the end of this section.

7. As explained in chapter 12, this is due to the fact that private information enables the bank to exert some control over the timing of surprises.

8. This is demonstrated in section 13.10.

9. Compare to equation (9.27).

Chapter 14

The analytical structure of this chapter draws on Cukierman and Meltzer (1986b). I am indebted to Mark Swinburne for introducing me to the new central bank legislation in New Zealand.

1. Documentation and further details appear in section 4.2 of *The Deutsche Bundesbank* (1982).

2. A related discussion of those issues appears in chapter 16, in the second half of section 16.5.

3. The current state of objectives may reflect a shifting compromise between the objectives of the executive branch and those of the central bank when the degree of independence of the latter is subject to stochastic shocks due to idiosyncratic factors. Such a model is discussed in chapter 18.

4. Formally y_i and z_i are combinations of exogenous stochastic processes. But their particular form is a consequence of the fact (demonstrated later) that in equilibrium the planned rate of monetary expansion is given by equation (14.3).

5. As $\sigma_\gamma^2 \to 0$, $\theta \to 0$, $r \to \infty$, and $\delta \to 0$.

6. The sign of the partial derivative of the coefficient of m_i^a with respect to σ_γ^2 is opposite to that of $\partial \delta / \partial \sigma_\gamma^2 + \delta \partial \theta / \partial \sigma_\gamma^2$. Since both δ and θ are increasing in σ_γ^2, the weight given to the current announcement is monotonically decreasing in σ_γ^2.

7. Since all the terms in (14.9) are finite, the transversality condition is satisfied for any $\beta < 1$.

8. As $\sigma_\gamma^2 \to \infty$, δ tends to λ in chapter 10, B_0 and B become identical to B_0 and B in chapter 10, and the decision strategy in (14.10) reduces to that in equation (10.11). In addition the optimal predictor in (14.7) reduces to equation (10.6a) which describes the optimal predictor in the absence of announcements.

9. When $\sigma_\gamma^2 \to 0$, $r \to \infty$. Since B is bounded, $\delta \to 0$ and $B_0 \to 0$. Hence mean inflation tends to zero when disclosure tends to perfection.

10. The sign of its partial derivative with respect to δ is the same as the sign of $\rho(1 - \theta) > 0$.

11. The proof of this statement appears in appendix F to this chapter.

12. This is an immediate consequence of proposition 10.2.

13. See also Weber (1990).

Chapter 15

1. The natural level of employment is the level that is generated by various real shocks in the absence of monetary surprises.

2. Inflation and the price level are obviously not identical. But to the extent that they are positively correlated, the argument carries over to the price level as well.

3. Kydland and Prescott (1982) have stressed time to build as a reason for persistence in aggregate fluctuations.

4. This specification is adopted for simplicity. The qualitative nature of the results remains the same if instead policymakers get private noisy signals about these variables.

5. It is shown in appendix F to this chapter that if D is sufficiently large in comparison to σ_v^2 and σ_δ^2, the difference $N^* - N_i$ in (15.4) is almost always nonnegative. As a consequence only the nonnegative range of $N^* - N_i$ is relevant for the analysis.

6. π_{i+1} and π_{i+1}^e have been entered in a difference form because they enter the objective function of policymakers in this way.

7. As explained previously, only π_{i-1} contains information beyond the information contained in p_{i-2}. Hence although all the history of past inflation is available to it, the public utilizes only π_{i-1} in forming π_i^e.

8. This predictor is based on a certain degree of bounded rationality whose precise nature is discussed in appendix A to this chapter.

9. The accommodation is partial since the coefficient of π_i^e in equation (15.14) is smaller than one.

10. An example is Plosser (1990).

11. Note that a partial offset is consistent with the view that real factors dominate the cycle.

12. The superscript s denotes that this is the covariance under symmetric information.

13. Further discussion of the conditions in equations (15.27) appears in the next section.

14. Recall that "unemployment" is defined by reference to policymakers' employment objective N^*. Hence the precise measure of unemployment used here is $N^* - N_i$. It obviously need not coincide with the rate of unemployment published by various statistical agencies.

15. If unions have no time preference $1 - \lambda = 1/2$.

16. Details appear in appendix I to this chapter.

17. This can be achieved by making the natural level of employment in (15.1) equal to the constant $\overline{N}_n$, respecifying the desired level as $N_i^* = N^* + p_i$, and respecifying actual inflation as $\pi_i = \pi_i^p - \delta_i/\alpha$. Here π_i^p is the planned rate of inflation, δ_i/α is reinterpreted as a disturbance arising from imperfect control of inflation by policymakers, and p_i is reinterpreted as a persistent shock to desired employment.

18. Jones (1986) provides an extensive practical discussion of this activity.

19. See, for example, Sargent (1979, p. 208).

Chapter 16

1. Some of these papers draw on analogous problems in industrial organization and in particular on the work of Kreps and Wilson (1982) and Milgrom and Roberts (1982), which is also the source of the terminology "weak" and "strong" to designate the policymakers' type.

2. This section draws on Cukierman and Liviatan (1991).

3. Detailed discussions of these other objectives appear in chapters 4 and 5.

4. The consequences of the relaxation of the latter assumption are discussed later in this chapter.

5. Moreover even the elections outcome is not sufficient to enable policymakers to evaluate the contribution of this component alone to the outcome with full precision, since each candidate offers an entire package of characteristics.

6. This differs from the framework of chapter 14 in which announcements are mandated by an outside authority.

7. By choosing π^a, dependable policymakers signal to the public which equilibrium within the set of potential equilibria they aim at. A precise game-theoretic characterization of this set appears in appendix A to this chapter.

8. Note that even if we had assumed that the public identifies policymakers as weak *only* if they inflate at a rate that is *higher* than their prior announcement, this restriction is always satisfied in equilibrium. Whatever the actual value of π that they plan, it never pays D to announce a higher rate of inflation in this case. The reason is that by lowering π^a to the level of π, policymakers reduce inflationary expectations without changing anything else. In view of the objective function in equation (16.1) this raises the value of their objectives. Hence, in equilibrium, D equates actual and announced inflation also in the case in which policymakers lose credibility only when π^a is lower than π.

9. There could a priori be other self-fulfilling equilibria of this type. However, all but the equilibrium described in the text can be eliminated by appealing to the Cho-Kreps (1987) intuitive criterion. Details appear in appendix A to this chapter.

10. This contrasts with the framework used in part II and other chapters of part III in which the type may change from period to period and in which the number of possible types is infinite.

11. The framework here is slightly more general than that of Vickers in that it allows for positive time preference on the part of policymakers. Formally Vickers' framework can be obtained from that in the text by setting β in equation (16.8) at one.

12. The two frameworks also differ in that the "types" in chapter 14 differ in their emphasis on alternative objectives, whereas in section 16.2 they differ in their ability to commit.

Chapter 17

1. Many papers in Mayer (1990) reach a similar conclusion.

2. Obviously in countries with more legally dependent central banks such as France, the channels of influence are more direct to start with.

3. This is yet another manifestation of the "politics of ambiguity" according to which it may pay policymakers to equivocate on their choices of policies (Alesina and Cukierman 1990). In this view, an independent Fed is needed partly in order to mask the actual choice of policies by the political authorities.

4. These expenditures are composed of outlays on income security, veterans benefits, health, and education.

Chapter 18

1. A list of references appears in note 1 to chapter 19.

2. An alternative formulation in which the interaction between the CB and the political authorities is formulated as a game appears in Alesina and Tabellini (1987).

3. However, as pointed out in chapters 22 and 23, CB independence is not the only mechanism for preventing politicians from sacrificing price stability in favor of other objectives.

4. Rogoff (1985) develops this argument in detail.

5. Section 4.5 develops this relationship explicitly in the context of seigniorage and shows that the effective rate of time preference of an incumbent government is larger the higher the political instability.

6. Strictly speaking, this proposition as well as other propositions in this chapter should be interpreted in the context of the model of chapter 10 in which inflation and monetary expansion are identical but in which there is imperfect control of the money supply. It is likely, however, that qualitatively similar propositions hold also when, as in chapter 13, inflation and monetary expansion differ.

7. For example, even when the condition is not satisfied, the proposition holds provided that β is sufficiently low. Details appear in appendix B to this chapter.

8. A fuller discussion of CB charters appears in chapter 19.

9. A striking example is Argentina in which the legislated term of office of the governor is four years but in which the actual average term in office during the 1980s nevertheless was about ten months. A fuller discussion appears in chapter 19, section 19.4.

10. We continue to use the innocuous simplification $\alpha = 1$.

Chapter 19

This and the following two chapters draw freely on Cukierman, Webb, and Neyapti (1991).

1. The most notable among those are Bade and Parkin (1980), Banaian, Laney, and Willet (1983), Skanland (1984), Parkin (1987), Alesina (1988), Masciandaro and Tabellini (1988), and Grilli, Masciandaro, and Tabellini (1991). There are also several internal studies of the IMF Central Banking Department along related lines such as Swinburne and Castello-Branco (1991), Bodart (1990), and Leone (1991). The last study is a comprehensive comparison of limitations on lending across countries rather than a comparison of independence. The distinguishing feature of all these papers is that they attempt to rank various central banks by their independence levels. The ranking is obtained by focusing on a limited, but usually uniform, number of legal features of the charters of the central banks involved.

There also is a wider and more voluminous literature that does not try to rank many banks by legal independence but that focuses instead on more broadly based discussions of one or several central banks. A noncomprehensive list of references within this group includes Mittra (1977), Schokker (1980), Eizenga (1983), Kearney (1984), Dotsey (1986), Epstein and Schor (1986), Bordes and Strauss-Kahn (1987), Bordo and Redish (1987), Eizenga (1987), Keenan and Mayes (1987), Suzuki (1987), Goodhart (1988), Toniolo (1988), Holtfrerich (1988), Willet (1988), Fazio (1991), Cargill and Hutchison (1990), Mayer (1990), Meltzer (1991), and Volcker, Mancera, and Godeaux (1991).

2. A detailed classification of limitations on lending by types appears in Leone (1991).

3. Only one code per subperiod was assigned in each country for each legal variable. Whenever a change occurred within a subperiod, the classification was done in line with the legislation that was in effect during at least 50 percent of the time in that subperiod. When a CB was founded within a subperiod, its legal variables were coded only if it existed for at least three years during the subperiod. Otherwise, an NA entry was entered. Since the sample includes 70 countries and 4 subperiods, there are at most 280 observations on each legal variable.

4. "A weighted mean of the variables" is obviously a shorter expression for the more precise but also more cumbersome term "a weighted mean of the codings of the variables."

5. It is interesting in this context that Norway, which has a rather low rank on legal independence, also has a rather low turnover rate.

6. This last source of information is available only for a subset of countries and only for the decade of the 1980s.

7. Except for the correlation between $LVAW$ and $QVAW$ in DCs, none of the correlations are significant.

8. This regression is based on a sample of twenty-two countries.

9. This section was stimulated by a discussion with Michael Bruno.

10. One exception is the United States in which both the Treasury and the CB have the means to intervene in foreign exchange markets. Another striking exception is Argentina in which Congress is in charge of exchange rate policy since March 1991.

11. This is perhaps the reason that Belgium has chosen to safeguard price stability by means of an exchange rate rule. See also in chapter 23, section 23.5.

Chapter 20

1. This can be seen from equation (18.16a). The lower the parameter A_{CB}, the lower is A, even for a given δ.

2. The significantly negative sign of tor in the group of developed countries is surprising. It may be due to the omission of the legal variables from the regression.

3. The sources are Fair (1980), Bade and Parkin (1985), Hansson (1987), and Masciandaro and Tabellini (1988).

4. Portugal is included in the study of Grilli, Masciandaro, and Tabellini (1991).

5. This contrasts with the negative and insignificant coefficient for tor in our group of developed countries (see column 4 in table 20.1). The difference is probably due to the somewhat different coverage of countries in the two groups. In particular the fact that Greece is included in the ATC and not in our group of DC could explain the positive and significant effect of turnover in the ATC. Greece has some of the highest turnover and inflation rates within the group of ATC.

6. The fact that the coefficient of financial independence as reported by questionnaire respondents is positive and significant is puzzling. It may be related to the fact that in some countries such as Britain and Belgium, price stability was achieved during the 1980s despite lack of financial independence.

7. Since subperiods are of the order of magnitude of decades, the center of the "previous subperiod" is about ten years away from the center of the current one. The use of lagged values of d and tor as instruments cuts the number of observations used in the equation by about a quarter to 198.

8. As a consequence the number of country/periods observations is reduced to 150.

Chapter 21

1. The difference between the regressions in table 20.1 and those used to generate the overall measure of CB independence concerns the sample of countries. In the second case countries that had a monetary rule during the 1980s (see section 21.3 below) were excluded.

2. All the variables besides the subperiod's dummy are proxies for independence, so the inclusion of this dummy in the generation of the predicted values is innocuous because it does not affect the ranking within a subperiod.

3. The public's sophistication in economic matters may also be a factor that affects the level of A in a democracy. If, for example, a large fraction of voters is sensitive to high nominal rather than to high real rates, so will be their elected representatives. There is evidence that the number of interest-rate-related hearings (and other hearings on reforming monetary policy and the Fed) conducted by the U.S. Congress is more strongly related to high nominal than to high real rates (Orszag 1991). This evidence is not inconsistent with the view that money illusion in part of the American public is transformed through the pressures of Congress and various "low interest" lobbies into a demand for lower nominal rates. The fact that lower interest rates can be attained by unanticipated monetary shocks implies that money illusion by part of the public induces a higher value of A.

Chapter 22

1. A description of these variables appears in table 19.7.

2. For the purposes of this measure the public sector includes the central government, local governments, and, when appropriate credit data is available, public enterprises.

3. It will be recalled that the weights in this subaggregate sum to one and that they are proportional to the weights of the component of the "limitations on lending" variables in table 19.2.

4. In the presence of imperfect credibility there are powerful incentives to accommodate (see chapter 16, section 16.2). The subperiods' dummies have been excluded in this regression, since their effect is at least partly proxied by d.

5. Although related, seigniorage and CB credit to the public sector are not identical.

Chapter 23

1. This section draws on Cukierman, Webb, and Neyapti (1991).

2. The index pip is a weighted count of the number of changes in the identity of the ruling party per subperiod within a given regime. The weight associated with a given change in the identity of the government in office is an increasing function of the distance of the new government from the previous government on the left–right dimension. To implement this weighting scheme, governments in each country have been classified into four ideological groups labeled 1, 2, 3, 4, ranging from extreme left to extreme right. The weight associated with a given change in the identity of the government in office was taken to equal the absolute value of the ideological distance between the new and the old government.

3. Gordon (1982) finds that wage flexibility in Japan is substantially higher than in the United States.

4. A discussion along these lines appears in Cargill and Hutchinson (1990).

5. An additional and more articulate explanation for secrecy appears in chapter 12.

6. A normative discussion of the case for and against disclosing monetary policy is in Mayer (1987).

7. A documentation of these cycles in Argentina and Brazil appears in Kiguel and Liviatan (1991).

References

Agenor, Pièrre-Richard. 1991. Credibility and exchange rate management in developing countries. IMF Working Paper 91-87.

Aiyagari, Rao S. 1989. Equilibrium existence in an overlapping generations model with altruistic preferences. *Journal of Economic Theory* 47: 130–152.

Aizenman, Joshua. 1987. Inflation, tariffs and tax enforcement costs. *Journal of International Economic Integration* 2: 12–28.

Aizenman, Joshua. 1989. Competitive externalities and the optimal seigniorage. NBER Working Paper 2937.

Alesina, Alberto. 1988. Macroeconomics and politics. In Stanley Fischer (ed.), *NBER Macroeconomics Annual*. Cambridge: MIT Press.

Alesina, Alberto. 1989. Politics and business cycles in industrial democracies. *Economic Policy* 89, 8: 57–98.

Alesina, Alberto, Gerald D. Cohen, and Nouriel Roubini. 1992. Macroeconomic policy and elections in OECD democracies. In Alex Cukierman, Zvi Hercowitz, and Leonardo Leiderman (eds.), *Political Economy, Growth and Business Cycles*. Cambridge: MIT Press.

Alesina, Alberto, and Alex Cukierman. 1990. The politics of ambiguity. *The Quarterly Journal of Economics* 105: 829–850.

Alesina, Alberto, and Allan Drazen. 1992. Why are stabilizations delayed? *American Economic Review*, forthcoming.

Alesina, Alberto, and Jeffrey Sachs. 1988. Political parties and the business cycle in the U.S., 1948–1984. *Journal of Money, Credit and Banking* 20: 63–82.

Alesina, Alberto, and Lawrence H. Summers. 1990. Central bank independence and macroeconomic performance: Some comparative evidence. Unpublished manuscript. Harvard University.

Alesina, Alberto, and Guido Tabellini. 1987. Rules and discretion with non-coordinated monetary and fiscal policies. *Economic Inquiry* 25: 619–630.

Alesina, Alberto, and Guido Tabellini. 1990. A political theory of fiscal deficits and government debt in a democracy. *The Review of Economic Studies* 57: 403–414.

Alogoskoufis, George. 1991. Monetary accommodation, exchange rate regimes and inflation persistence. CEPR Discussion Paper 503.

Aufricht, Hans. 1961. *Central Bank Legislation*. Washington: IMF.

Aufricht, Hans. 1967. *Central Bank Legislation*. Vol. 2: *Europe*. Washington: IMF.

Backus, David, and John Driffill. 1985a. Inflation and reputation. *American Economic Review* 75: 530–538.

Backus, David, and John Driffill. 1985b. Rational expectations and policy credibility following a change in regime. *Review of Economic Studies* 52: 211–221.

Bade, Robin, and Michael Parkin. 1980, 1985. Central bank laws and monetary policy. Unpublished manuscript. Department of Economics, University of Western Ontario.

Bailey, Martin, J. 1956. The welfare cost of inflationary finance. *Journal of Political Economy* 64: 93–110.

Banaian, King, Leroy Laney, and Thomas Willett. 1983. Central bank independence: An international comparison. *Economic Review*, Federal Reserve Bank of Dallas (March): 1–13.

Banks, Arthur F., and William Overstreet (eds.). *Political Handbook of the World*. New York: McGraw-Hill. Various issues.

Barro, Robert J. 1979. On the determination of the public debt. *Journal of Political Economy* 87: 940–971.

Barro, Robert. 1983. Inflationary finance under discretion and rules. *Canadian Journal of Economics* 16: 3–16.

Barro, Robert. 1986. Reputation in a model of monetary policy with incomplete information. *Journal of Monetary Economics* 17: 3–20.

Barro, Robert, and David Gordon. 1983a. Rules, discretion and reputation in a model of monetary policy. *Journal of Monetary Economics* 12: 101–122.

Barro, Robert, and David Gordon. 1983b. A positive theory of monetary policy in a natural rate model. *Journal of Political Economy* 91: 589–610.

Beaudry, P., and Pierre Fortin 1987. The central bank, the market and the joint determination of the interest rate and the exchange rate in Canada. Paper presented at the meeting of the Canadian Economic Association, Hamilton, June 1987.

Beck, Nathaniel. 1982. Presidential influence on the Federal Reserve in the 1970's. *American Journal of Politcal Science* (August): 415–445.

Beck, Nathaniel. 1990. Congress and the Fed: Why the dog doesn't bark in the night. In Thomas Mayer (ed.), *The Political Economy of American Monetary Policy*. Cambridge: Cambridge University Press.

Ben Bassat, Avraham, and Arie Marom. 1988. Is the demand for money in Israel stable? (1965–1983). *Economic Review*, Bank of Israel, 60: 52–71.

Berg, Andrew, and Jeffrey Sachs. 1988. The debt crisis: Structural explanations of country performance. NBER Working Paper 2607.

Bernanke, Ben. 1983. Nonmonetary effects of the financial crisis in the propagation of the Great Depression. *American Economic Review* 73: 257–276.

Bhatt, V. V. 1980. Some aspects of financial policies and central banking in developing countries. In W. L. Coats, Jr., and D. R. Khatkhate (eds.), *Money and Monetary Policy in Less Developed Countries*. Oxford: Pergamon Press.

BIS (Bank for International Settlements). 1963. *Eight European Central Banks*. London: Praeger.

Blackburn, Keith, and Michael Christensen. 1989. Monetary policy and policy credibility. *The Journal of Economic Literature* 27: 1–45.

Bodart, Vincent. 1990. Central bank independence and the effectiveness of monetary policy: A comparative analysis. Unpublished manuscript. IMF Central Banking Department, Washington.

Bohn, Henning. 1991. Time consistency of monetary policy in the open economy. *Journal of International Economics* 30: 249–266.

Bordes, C., and Marc Olivier Strauss-Kahn. 1987. 1977–1986: Dix ans de politique d'objectifs en France ou le "targeting" à la française. SUERF papers on Monetary Policy and Financial Systems, No. 4, Tilburg.

Bordo, Michael, and Angela Redish. 1987. Why did the Bank of Canada emerge in 1935? *Journal of Economic History* 47: 405–417.

Brady, Thomas F. 1985. Changes in loan pricing and business lending at commercial banks. *Federal Reserve Bulletin* 71: 1–3.

Bresciani-Turroni, Constantino. 1937. *The Economics of Inflation—A Study of Currency Depreciation in Post War Germany*. London: George Allen and Unwin Ltd.

Brimmer, Andrew F. 1989. Distinguished lecture on economics in government: Central banking and systemic risks in capital markets. *Journal of Economic Perspectives* 3: 3–16.

Bronfenbrenner, Martin, and Franklyn D. Holzman. 1963. Survey of inflation theory. *American Economic Review* 53: 593–661.

Brunner, Karl, Alex Cukierman, and Allan H. Meltzer. 1980. Stagflation, persistent unemployment and the permanence of economic shocks. *Journal of Monetary Economics* 6: 467–492.

Brunner, Karl, and Allan H. Meltzer. 1964. The Federal Reserve's attachment to the free reserve concept. Washington: House Committee on Banking and Currency. Reprinted in K. Brunner and A. H. Meltzer (eds.). 1989. *Monetary Economics*. Oxford: Basil Blackwell.

Bruno, Michael. 1986. Sharp disinflation strategy: Israel 1985. *Economic Policy* 2: 379–407.

Bruno, Michael, Guido Di Tella, Rudiger Dornbusch, and Stanley Fischer (eds.). 1988. *Inflation Stabilization: The Experience of Israel, Argentina, Brazil, Bolivia, and Mexico.* Cambridge: MIT Press.

Bull, Clive. 1982. Rational expectations, monetary data and central bank watching. *Giornale degli Economisti e Annali di Economia* (January–February): 31–40.

Burns, Arthur F. 1979. *The Anguish of Central Banking.* Belgrade, Yugoslavia: Per Jacobsson Foundation.

Cagan, Phillip. 1956. The monetary dynamics of hyperinflation. In Milton Friedman (ed.), *Studies in the Quantity Theory of Money.* Chicago: University of Chicago Press.

Calvo, Guillermo. 1978. On the time consistency of optimal policy in a monetary economy. *Econometrica* 46: 1411–1428.

Calvo, Guillermo, and Leonardo Leiderman. 1990. Optimal inflation tax under precommitment. Unpublished manuscript. IMF, Washington, and Tel-Aviv University.

Canzoneri, M. 1985. Monetary policy games and the role of private information. *American Economic Review* 75: 1056–1070.

Cargill, Thomas F., and Michael M. Hutchison. 1990. Monetary policy and political economy: The Federal Reserve and the Bank of Japan. In Thomas Mayer (ed.), *The Political Economy of Monetary Policy.* Cambridge: Cambridge University Press.

Chandler, Lester V. 1962. *Central Banking and Economic Development.* University of Bombay Series in Monetary and International Economics, No. 3.

Cho, In-Koo, and David Kreps. 1987. Signaling games and stable equilibria. *Quarterly Journal of Economics* 102: 179–221.

Christiano, Lawrence J. 1987. Cagan's model of hyperinflation under rational expectations. *International Economic Review* 28: 33–49.

Christiano, Lawrence, and Martin Eichenbaum. 1992. Identification and liquidity effect of a monetary policy shock. In Alex Cukierman, Zvi Hercowitz, and Leonardo Leiderman (eds.), *Political Economy, Growth and Business Cycles.* Cambridge: MIT Press.

Cukierman, Alex. 1984. *Inflation, Stagflation, Relative Prices, and Imperfect Information.* Cambridge: Cambridge University Press.

Cukierman, Alex. 1986. Central bank behavior and credibility: Some recent theoretical developments. *Federal Reserve Bank of St. Louis Review* 68: 5–17.

Cukierman, Alex. 1988a. The end of the high Israeli inflation—An experiment in heterodox stabilization. In Michael Bruno, Guido Di Tella, Rudiger Dornbusch, and Stanley Fisher (eds.), *Inflation Stabilization: The Experience of Israel, Argentina, Brazil, Bolivia, and Mexico.* Cambridge: MIT Press, pp. 48–94.

Cukierman, Alex. 1988b. Rapid inflation—Deliberate policy or miscalculation? *Carnegie-Rochester Conference Series on Public Policy* 29 (*Money, Cycles and Exchange Rates: Essays in Honor of A. H. Meltzer*): 11–75.

Cukierman, Alex. 1990. Why does the Fed smooth interest rates? In Michael Belongia (ed.), *Monetary Policy on the Fed's 75th Anniversary.* Proceedings of the 14th Annual Economic

Policy Conference of the Federal Reserve Bank of St. Louis. Norwell, MA: Kluwer Academic Publishers.

Cukierman, Alex. 1991a. Discretion, precommitments and the prospects for a European central bank—Fixed parities versus a commonly managed currency. In Zvi Eckstein (ed.), *Aspects of Central Bank Policy Making*. Berlin: Springer-Verlag.

Cukierman, Alex. 1991b. Fixed parities versus a commonly managed currency and the case against "stage two." Paper presented at the international colloquium on Toward Economic and Monetary Union in Europe, Paris, June 21, 1990.

Cukierman, Alex. 1991c. Extensions to policy outcomes in stage two and in the EMS versus outcomes in a monetary union. Paper presented at the conference on Monetary Policy in Stage Two of EMU, Universita Bocconi, Milano, September 27–28, 1991.

Cukierman, Alex, and Allan Drazen. 1987. Do distortionary taxes induce policies biased towards inflation? A microeconomic analysis. Unpublished manuscript. Tel-Aviv University.

Cukierman, Alex, Sebastian Edwards, and Guido Tabellini. 1992. Seignorage and political instability. *American Economic Review* 82, forthcoming.

Cukierman, Alex, and Nissan Liviatan. 1990. Rules, discretion, credibility and reputation. *Economic Review, Bank of Israel*, No. 65: 3–25 (Hebrew).

Cukierman, Alex, and Nissan Liviatan. 1991. Optimal accommodation by strong policy-makers under incomplete information. *Journal of Monetary Economics* 27: 99–127.

Cukierman, Alex, and Nissan Liviatan. 1992. The dynamics of optimal gradual stabilizations. *World Bank Economic Review*, forthcoming.

Cukierman, Alex, and Allan H. Meltzer. 1982. What do tests of market efficiency in the presence of the permanent-transitory confusion show? Unpublished manuscript. Tel-Aviv University.

Cukierman, Alex, and Allan H. Meltzer. 1986a. A theory of ambiguity, credibility, and inflation under discretion and asymmetric information. *Econometrica* 54: 1099–1128.

Cukierman, Alex, and Allan H. Meltzer. 1986b. The credibility of monetary announcements. In M. J. M. Neumann (ed.), *Monetary Policy and Uncertainty*. Baden-Baden: Nomos Verlagsgesellschaft, pp. 39–68.

Cukierman, Alex, and Allan H. Meltzer. 1989. A political theory of government debt and deficits in a neo-Ricardian framework. *American Economic Review* 79: 713–732.

Cukierman, Alex, and Meir Sokoler. 1989. Monetary policy and institutions in Israel, past, present and future. *Economic Quarterly* 139: 371–426 (Hebrew).

Cukierman, Alex, Steven Webb, and Bilin Neyapti. 1991. The measurement of central bank independence and its effect on policy outcomes. Paper presented at the NBER Conference on Political Economics, Cambridge, MA, November 15–16, 1991.

De Cecco, Marcello, and Alberto Giovannini (eds.). 1989. *A European Central Bank? Perspectives on Monetary Unification after Ten Years of the EMS*. Cambridge: Cambridge University Press.

Delors, Jacques. 1989. Report on economic and monetary union in the European communities. In *Report on Economic and Monetary Union in the European Community and Collection of Papers*. Luxembourg: Office for Official Publications of the European Communities.

Donaldson, Glen R. 1989. Sources of panics: Evidence from the weekly data. Discussion Paper 149. Woodrow Wilson School, Princeton University.

Dornbusch, Rudiger. 1976. Expectations and exchange rate dynamics. *Journal of Political Economy* 84: 1161–1176.

Drazen, Allan, and Vittorio Grilli. 1991. The benefits of crises for economic reforms. Working Paper 27–91. Foerder Institute for Economic Research, Tel-Aviv University.

Dotsey, Michael. 1986. Japanese monetary policy, a comparative analysis. *Economic Review*, Federal Reserve Bank of Richmond, 72, 6: 12–24.

Driffill, John. 1989. Macroeconomic policy games with incomplete information: Some extensions. In F. van de Ploeg and A. J. de Zeeuw (eds.), *Dynamic Policy Games in Economics*. Amsterdam: Elsevier Science Publishers B.V. (North-Holland), pp. 289–322.

Edwards, Sebastian, and Guido Tabellini. 1991. Political instability, political weakness and the inflation tax. NBER Working Paper No. 3721.

Effros, Robert (ed). 1982. *Emerging Financial Centers—Legal and Institutional Framework*. Washington: IMF.

Eizenga, Weitze. 1983. The independence of the Federal Reserve System and of the Netherlands Bank. SUERF Series, Tilburg.

Eizenga, Weitze. 1987. The independence of the Deutsche Bundesbank and the Nederlansche Bank with regard to monetary policy: A comparative study. SUERF papers on Monetary Policy and Financial Systems, No. 2, Tilburg.

Enelow, James, and Melvin Hinich. 1984. *The Spatial Theory of Voting: An Introduction*. Cambridge: Cambridge University Press.

Epstein, Gerald, and Juliet Schor. 1986. The divorce of the Banca d'Italia and the Italian Treasury: A case study of central bank independence. Harvard Institute of Economic Research, No. 1269.

Fair, Don. 1980. Relationships between central banks and governments in the determination of monetary policy. SUERF Working Paper, Tilburg.

Fazio, Antonio. 1991. Role and independence of central banks. In P. Downes and R. Vaez-Zadeh (eds.), *The Evolving Role of Central Bank*. Washington: IMF, pp. 121–139.

The Federal Reserve position on restructuring of financial regulation responsibilities. 1984. *Federal Reserve Bulletin* 70: 547–557.

Fershtman, Chaim. 1989. Fixed rules and decision rules. *Economics Letters* 30: 191–194.

Fischer, Stanley. 1977. Long term contracts, rational expectations and the optimal money supply rule. *Journal of Political Economy* (April): 191–206.

Flood, Robert P., and Peter Isard. 1989. Monetary policy strategies. *IMF Staff Papers* 36: 612–632.

Friedman, James. 1971. A noncooperative equilibrium for supergames. *Review of Economic Studies* (January): 861–874.

Friedman, James. 1977 *Oligopoly and the Theory of Games*. Amsterdam: North-Holland.

Friedman, Milton. 1960. *A Program for Monetary Stability*. New York: Fordham University Press.

Friedman, Milton. 1982. Monetary policy—Theory and practice. *Journal of Money, Credit and Banking* 14: 98–118.

Friedman, Milton, and Anna J. Schwartz. 1963. *A Monetary History of the United States: 1867–1960*. Princeton: Princeton University Press.

Giavazzi, Francesco, and Alberto Giovannini. 1989. *Limiting Exchange Rate Flexibility: The European Monetary System*. Cambridge: MIT Press.

Goode, Richard. 1984. *Government Finance in Developing Countries*. Washington: Brookings Institution.

Goodfriend, Marvin. 1986. Monetary mystique: Secrecy and central banking. *Journal of Monetary Economics* 17: 63–92.

Goodfriend, Marvin. 1987. Interest rate smoothing and price level trend—Stationarity. *Journal of Monetary Economics* 19: 335–348.

Goodfriend, Marvin, and Robert G. King. 1988. Financial deregulation, monetary policy and central banking. *Federal Reserve Bank of Richmond Economic Review* 74, 5: 3–22.

Goodhart, Charles. 1988. *The Evolution of Central Banks*. Cambridge: MIT Press.

Goodhart, Charles. 1991. The draft statute of the European system of central banks: A commentary. Paper presented at the conference on Monetary Policy in State Two of EMU, Milano, September 27–28, 1991.

Gordon, Robert J. 1982. Why U.S. wage and employment behavior differs from that in Britain and Japan. *Economic Journal* 92: 13–44.

Green, Edward J., and Robert H. Porter. 1984. Noncooperative collusion under imperfect price information. *Econometrica* 52: 87–100.

Grier, Kevin B. 1987. Presidential elections and Federal Reserve policy: An empirical test. *Southern Economic Journal* 54: 475–486.

Grier, Kevin B. 1989. On the existence of a political monetary cycle. *American Journal of Political Science* 33: 376–389.

Grilli, Vittorio, Donato Masciandaro, and Guido Tabellini. 1991. Political and monetary institutions and public financial policies in the industrial countries. *Economic Policy* 13: 341–392.

Grossman, Herschel I. 1990. Inflation and reputation with generic policy preferences. *Journal of Money, Credit and Banking* 22: 165–177.

Haggard, Stephen, Robert Kaufman, Karim Shariff, and Steven Webb. 1991. Politics, inflation and government deficits in middle-income countries. Unpublished manuscript. World Bank.

Hansson, A. 1987. Politics, institutions and cross-country inflation differentials. Unpublished manuscript.

Hardouvelis, Gikas. 1984. Market perceptions of Federal Reserve policy and the weekly monetary announcements. *Journal of Monetary Economics* 14: 225–240.

Havrilesky, Thomas M. 1987. A partisanship theory of fiscal and monetary regimes. *Journal of Money, Credit and Banking* 19: 308–325.

Havrilesky, Thomas. 1988. Monetary policy signaling from the administration to the Federal Reserve. *Journal of Money, Credit and Banking* 20: 83–101.

Havrilesky, Thomas M. 1990a. A public choice perspective on the cycle in monetary policy. *The Cato Journal* 9: 709–718.

Havrilesky, Thomas M. 1990b. The new political economy of monetary policy. *Public Budgeting and Financial Management* 2: 431–451.

Havrilesky, Thomas M. 1990c. Distributive conflict and monetary policy. *Contemporary Policy Issues* 8: 50–61.

Havrilesky, Thomas M. 1991a. Screening FOMC members for their biases and dependability. *Economics and Politics* 3: 139–149.

Havrilesky, Thomas M. 1991b. The frequency of monetary policy signalling from the administration to the Federal Reserve. *Journal of Money, Credit and Banking* 23: 423–428.

Havrilesky, Thomas M. 1993. *The Pressures on Monetary Policy*. Norwell, MA: Kluwer Academic Publishers, forthcoming.

Havrilesky, Thomas M., and John A. Gildea. 1990. Packing the Board of Governors. *Challenge* (March–April): 52–55.

Havrilesky, Thomas M., and John A. Gildea. 1991. The policy preferences of FOMC members as revealed by dissenting votes. *Journal of Money, Credit and Banking* 23: 130–138.

Havrilesky, Thomas M., and Robert Schweitzer. 1990. A theory of FOMC dissent voting with evidence from the time series. In Thomas Mayer (ed.), *The Political Economy of American Monetary Policy*. Cambridge: Cambridge University Press.

Hetzel, Robert L. 1985. The formulation of monetary policy. Unpublished manuscript. Federal Reserve Bank of Richmond.

Hetzel, Robert L. 1990. The political economy of monetary policy. In Thomas Mayer (ed.), *The Political Economy of American Monetary Policy*. Cambridge: Cambridge University Press.

Hibbs, Douglas A. 1977. Political parties and macroeconomic policy. *American Political Science Review* 71: 1467–1487.

Hinrichs, Harley. 1966. *A general theory of tax structure change during economic development.* Unpublished manuscript. Harvard University Law School.

Holtfrerich, Carl-Ludwig. 1986. *The German Inflation 1914–1923*. Berlin: Walter de Gruyter.

Horn, Henrick, and Torsten Persson. 1988. Exchange rate policy, wage formation and credibility. *European Economic Review* 32: 1621–1636.

Hoshi, Takeo. 1988. Government Reputation and Monetary Policy. Ph.D. dissertation. Massachusetts Institute of Technology.

Howitt, Peter. 1986. Monetary policy in transition—A study of Bank of Canada policy 1982–85. Policy Study No. 1. C. D. Howe Institute, Toronto.

Huntington, Samuel. 1968. *Political Order in Changing Societies*. New Haven: Yale University Press.

Hutchison, Michael, and John P. Judd. 1992. Central bank secrecy and money surprises: International evidence. *The Review of Economics and Statistics*, forthcoming.

Jaffe, Dwight M., and Ephraim Kleiman. 1977. The welfare implications of uneven inflation. In Eric Lundberg (ed.), *Inflation Theory and Anti-Inflation Policy*. London: Macmillan.

Jones, David M. 1986. *Fed Watching and Interest Rate Projections*. New York: New York Institute of Finance.

Kane, Edward J. 1980. Politics and Fed policymaking: The more things change the more they remain the same. *Journal of Monetary Economics* (April): 199–212.

Kane, Edward J. 1982. External pressure and the operation of the Fed. In R. E. Lombra and W. E. Witte (eds.), *Political Economy of International and Domestic Monetary Relations*, Ames: Iowa State University Press, pp. 211–232.

Kane, Edward J. 1990. Bureaucratic self interest as an obstacle to monetary reform. In Thomas Mayer (ed.), *The Political Economy of American Monetary Policy*. Cambridge: Cambridge University Press.

Kearney, Colm. 1984. The British anti-inflation strategy: Implementing monetarism or turning to Radcliffe? SUERF Series 44A, Tilburg.

Keech, William R., and Irwin L. Morris. 1991. Institutional limitations on presidential influence over the Federal Reserve. Working Paper 2, Institute for Research in Social Science, Department of Political Science, University of North Carolina, Chapel Hill.

Keenan, Peter, and David Mayes. 1987. Monetary targets and monetary management: The New Zealand experience. SUERF Papers on Monetary Policy and Financial Systems, No. 3, Tilburg.

Kiguel, Miguel, and Nissan Liviatan. 1991. The inflation-stabilization cycles in Argentina and Brazil. In Michael Bruno et al. (eds.), *Lessons of Economic Stabilization and Its Aftermath*. Cambridge: MIT Press.

Kreps, David M., and Robert Wilson. 1982. Reputation and Imperfect Information. *Journal of Economic Theory* 27: 253–279.

Kydland, Finn E., and Edward C. Prescott. 1977. Rules rather than discretion: The inconsistency of optimal plans. *Journal of Political Economy* 85: 473–492.

Kydland, Finn E., and Edward C. Prescott. 1982. Time to build and aggregate fluctuations. *Econometrica* 50: 1345–1370.

Kydland, Finn E., and Edward C. Prescott. 1990. Business cycles: Real facts and a monetary myth. *Federal Reserve Bank of Minneapolis Review* 14: 1–18.

Leiderman, Leonardo, and Arie Marom. 1988. New estimates of the demand for money in Israel. *Economic Review*, Bank of Israel, No. 60: 19–35.

Leone, Alfredo. 1991. Effectiveness and implications of limits on central bank credit to the government. In P. Downes and R. Vaez-Zadeh (eds.), *The Evolving Role of Central Banks*. Washington: IMF, 363–413.

Liviatan, Nissan. 1987. The evolution of disinflationary policies in Israel: 1980–1986. *Economic Quarterly* 131: 902–913 (Hebrew).

Logue, Dennis E., and Thomas D. Willet. 1976. A note on the relation between the rate and the variability of inflation. *Economica* 43: 151–158.

Lohmann, Susanne. 1990. Monetary policy strategies—A correction. *IMF Staff Papers* 37: 440–448.

Lohmann, Susanne. 1992. Optimal commitment in monetary policy: Credibility versus flexibility. *American Economic Review* 82, forthcoming.

Lucas, Robert E., Jr. 1972. Expectations and the neutrality of money. *Journal of Economic Theory* 4: 103–124.

Lucas, Robert E., Jr. 1973. Some international evidence on output–inflation tradeoffs. *American Economic Review* (June): 326–335.

McRae, Duncan. 1977. A political model of the business cycle. *Journal of Political Economy* 85: 239–263.

Mankiw, Gregory N. 1987. The optimal collection of seigniorage, theory and evidence. *Journal of Monetary Economics* 20: 327–341.

Mankiw, Gregory N., and Jeffrey A. Miron. 1991. Should the Fed smooth interest rates? The case of seasonal monetary policy. *Carnegie–Rochester Conference Series on Public Policy*, No. 34.

Mankiw, Gregory N., Jeffrey A. Miron, and David N. Weil. 1987. The adjustment of expectations to a change in regime: A study of the founding of the Federal Reserve. *American Economic Review* 77: 358–374.

Masciandaro, Donato, and Guido Tabellini. 1988. Monetary regimes and fiscal deficits: A comparative analysis. In H. S. Cheng (ed.), *Monetary Policy in Pacific Basin Countries*, Norwell, MA: Kluwer Academic Publishers.

Mayer, Thomas. 1987. *Disclosing Monetary Policy*. Monograph Series in Finance and Economics, Monograph 1987-1. New York University: Solomon Brothers Center for the Study of Financial Institutions.

Mayer, Thomas (ed.). 1990. *The Political Economy of American Monetary Policy*. Cambridge: Cambridge University Press.

Melnick, Rafi. 1988. Two Aspects of the Demand for Money in Israel, 1970–1981. *Economic Review*, Bank of Israel, no. 60: 36–51.

Meltzer, Allan H. 1990. The Federal Reserve at seventy-five. In *Monetary Policy on the Fed's 75th Anniversary*. Proceedings of the 14th Annual Economic Policy Conference of the Federal Reserve Bank of St. Louis, Michael Belongia (ed.). Norwell, MA: Kluwer Academic Publishers.

Meltzer, Allan H. 1991. U.S. policy in the Bretton Woods era. The 1991 Homer Jones Lecture, St. Louis, April 8.

Milgrom, Paul, and John Roberts. 1982. Predation, reputation and entry deterrence. *Journal of Economic Theory* 27: 280–312.

Miron, Jeffrey A. 1986. Financial panics, the seasonality of the nominal interest rate, and the founding of the Fed. *American Economic Review* 76: 125–140.

Mittra, Sid. 1977. *Central Bank versus Treasury: An International Study*. Lanham, MD: University Press of America.

Musgrave, Richard. 1969. *Fiscal Systems*. New Haven: Yale University Press.

Muth, John. 1960. Optimal properties of exponentially weighted forecasts. *Journal of the American Statistical Association* 55: 299–306.

Nordhaus, William D. 1975. The political business cycle. *Review of Economic Studies* 42: 169–190.

Nordhaus, William D. 1979. Alternative approaches to the political business cycle. *Brookings Papers on Economic Activity* 2: 1–68.

Obstfeld, Maurice. 1991. Destabilizing effects of exchange-rate escape clauses. Paper presented at the *Conference on Monetary Policy in Stage Two of EMU*, Milan, September 27–28, 1991.

Offenbacher, Edward K. (Akiva). 1988. Empirical studies of the demand for money in Israel: Introduction. *Economic Review*, Bank of Israel, 60: 1–18.

Oh, Seonghwan, and Michelle R. Garfinkel. 1990. Strategic considerations in monetary policy with private information: Can secrecy be avoided? *The Federal Reserve Bank of St. Louis Review* 72: 3–16.

Okun, Arthur M. 1971. The mirage of steady anticipated inflation. *Brookings Papers on Economic Activity* 2: 485–498.

Olivera J. 1967. Money, prices and fiscal lags: A note on the dynamics of inflation. *Banca Nazionale del Lavoro Quarterly Review* 20: 258–267.

Orszag, Peter. 1991. Congressional oversight of the Federal Reserve: Empirical and theoretical perspectives. Senior thesis. Department of Economics, Princeton University.

Ortiz, Guillermo. 1991. Mexico beyond the debt crisis: Toward sustainable growth with price stability. In Michael Bruno et al. (eds.), *Lessons of Economic Stabilization and Its Aftermath*. Cambridge: MIT Press.

Oswald, Andrew J. 1985. The economic theory of trade unions: An introductory survey. *Scandinavian Journal of Economics* 87: 160–193.

Pagan, Adrian. 1984. Econometric issues in the analysis of regressions with generated regressors. *International Economic Review* 25: 221–247.

Parkin, Michael. 1987. Domestic monetary institutions and deficits. In James M. Buchanan et al. (eds.), *Deficits*. Oxford: Basil Blackwell, 310–337.

Persson, Torsten, and Lars Svensson. 1988. Checks and balances on the government budget. In Elhanan Helpman, Assaf Razin, and Efraim Sadka (eds.), *Economic Effects of the Government Budget*. Cambridge: MIT Press.

Persson, Torsten, and Lars Svensson. 1989. Why a stubborn conservative would run a deficit? Policy with time consistent preferences. *Quarterly Journal of Economics* 104: 325–345.

Persson, Torsten, and Guido Tabellini. 1990. *Macroeconomic Policy, Credibility and Politics*. London: Harwood Publishers.

Phelps, Edmund S. 1973. Inflation in the theory of public finance. *Swedish Journal of Economics* 75: 67–82.

Piterman, Sylvia. 1988. The irreversibility of the relationship between inflation and real balances. *Economic Review*, Bank of Israel, 60: 72–83.

Plosser, Charles I. 1990. Money and business cycles: A real cycle interpretation. In *Monetary Policy on the Fed's 75th Anniversary.* Proceedings of the 14th Annual Economic Policy Conference of the Federal Reserve Bank of St. Louis, Michael Belongia (ed.). Norwell, MA: Kluwer Academic Publishers.

Poterba, James M., and Julio J. Rotemberg. 1990. Inflation and taxation with optimizing governments. *Journal of Money, Credit and Banking* 22: 1–18.

Rasche, Robert. 1988. Demand functions for U.S. money and credit measures. Econometrics and Economic Theory Paper 8718, Department of Economics, Michigan State University.

Rogoff, Kenneth. 1985. The optimal degree of commitment to an intermediate monetary target. *Quarterly Journal of Economics* 100: 1169–1190.

Rogoff, Kenneth. 1987. Reputational constraints on monetary policy. *Carnegie–Rochester Conference on Public Policy* 26: 141–182.

Rogoff, Kenneth. 1989. Reputation, coordination and monetary policy. In Robert Barro (ed.), *Modern Business Cycle Theory.* Cambridge: Harvard University Press.

Rogoff, Kenneth. 1990. Equilibrium political budget cycles. *American Economic Review* 80: 21–36.

Rogoff, Kenneth, and Anne Sibert. 1988. Elections and macroeconomic policy cycles. *Review of Economic Studies* 55: 1–16.

Romer, Christina D., and David H. Romer. 1989. Does monetary policy matter? A new test in the spirit of Friedman and Schwartz. *NBER Macroeconomic Annual* 4: 121–170.

Sanguinetti, Pablo. 1990. Federalism, political instability and inflation. Working Paper. Department of Economics, University of California, Los Angeles.

Sargent, Thomas J. 1977. The demand for money during hyperinflations under rational expectations: I. *International Economic Review* 18: 59–82.

Sargent, Thomas J. 1979. *Macroeconomic Theory.* New York: Academic Press.

Sargent, Thomas J., and Neil Wallace. 1973. The stability of models of money and growth with perfect foresight. *Econometrica* 41: 1043–1048.

Schokker, E. 1980. The central bank and the state in the light of European integration. SUERF Series 34A Tilburg.

Shiller, Robert J. 1980. Can the Fed control real interest rates? In Stanley Fischer (ed.), *Rational Expectations and Economic Policy.* Chicago: University of Chicago Press.

Skanland, Hermod. 1984. *The Central Bank and Political Authorities in Some Industrial Countries.* Oslo: Norges Bank.

Stein, Jeremy. 1989. Cheap talk and the Fed: A theory of imprecise policy announcements. *American Economic Review* 79: 32–42.

Summers, Robert, and Alan Heston. 1987. A new set of international comparisons of real product and price level estimates for 130 countries, 1950–1985. *Review of Income and Wealth* 25: 1–25.

Suzuki, Yoshio. 1987. *The Japanese Financial System.* Oxford: Clarendon Press.

Swinburne, Mark, and Marta Castello-Branco. 1991. Central bank independence and central bank functions. In P. Downes and R. Vaez-Zadeh (eds.), *The Evolving Role of Central Banks.* Washington: IMF, pp. 414–444.

Swoboda, Alexander K. 1991. The road to European monetary union: Lessons from the Bretton Woods regime. Per Jacobsson Lecture, Basle, Switzerland, June 9, 1991.

Tabellini, Guido. 1988. Centralized wage setting and monetary policy in a reputational equilibrium. *Journal of Money, Credit and Banking* 20: 102–118.

Tabellini, Guido, and Alberto Alesina. 1990. Voting on the budget deficit. *American Economic Review* 80: 37–49.

Tanzi, Vito. 1977. Inflation, lags in collection and the real value of tax revenues. *IMF Staff Papers* 24: 154–167.

Taylor, Charles L., and David Jodice. 1983. *World Handbook of Social and Political Indicators*. New Haven: Yale University Press.

Taylor, John B. 1980. Aggregate dynamics and staggered contracts. *Journal of Political Economy* 88: 1–23.

Tobin, James. 1982. The commercial banking firm: A simple model. *Scandinavian Journal of Economics* 84: 495–530.

Toma, Mark. 1982. Inflationary bias of the Federal Reserve system: A bureaucratic perspective. *Journal of Monetary Economics* 10: 163–190.

Toniolo, Gianni (ed.). 1988. *Central Banks' Independence in Historical Perspective*. Berlin: Walter de Gruyter.

Trehen, Bharat, and Carl E. Walsh. 1990. Seigniorage and tax smoothing in the U.S. 1914–1986. *Journal of Monetary Economics* 25: 97–112.

Usher, Daniel. 1981. *The Economic Prerequisite to Democracy*. New York: Columbia University Press.

Vickers, John. 1986. Signalling in a model of monetary policy with incomplete information. *Oxford Economic Papers* 38: 443–455.

Volcker, Paul, Miguel Mancera, and Jean Godeaux. 1991. *Perspectives on the Role of a Central Bank*. People's Bank of China, U.N. Development Program. Washington: IMF.

Weber, Axel A. 1990. The credibility of monetary target announcements: An empirical evaluation. Discussion Paper 9031. Center for Economic Research. UCLA.

Weber, Axel. 1991. EMS credibility. *Economic Policy* (April): 58–102.

Weintraub, Robert E. 1978. Congressional supervision of monetary policy. *Journal of Monetary Economics* 4: 341–362.

Weitzman, Martin L. 1985. Profit sharing as macroeconomic policy. *American Economic Review, Papers and Proceedings* 75: 41–45.

Willet, Thomas (ed.). 1988. *Political Business Cycles—The Political Economy of Money, Inflation and Unemployment*. Durham, NC: Duke University Press.

Woolley, John T. 1984. *Monetary Politics—The Federal Reserve and the Politics of Monetary Policy*. Cambridge: Cambridge University Press.

Index